MACROMEDIA® DREAMWEAVER® MX
DESIGN PROFESSIONAL

Sherry Bishop, Marjorie Hunt, and Piyush Patel

D1305105

THOMSON
COURSE TECHNOLOGY

Macromedia® Dreamweaver® MX—Design Professional

Sherry Bishop, Marjorie Hunt, and Piyush Patel

Executive Editor:
Nicole Jones Pinard

Product Managers:
Rebecca Berardy
Jane Hosie-Bounar

Associate Product Managers:
Elizabeth Harris
Christina Kling Garrett

Production Editor:
Christine Gatliffe

Composition House:
GEX Publishing Services

QA Manuscript Reviewers:
Ashlee Welz, Matt Degraff, Harris
Bierhoff, Susan Whalen, and
Christian Kunciw

Text Designer:
Ann Small

Illustrator:
Philip Brooker

Cover Design:
Philip Brooker

Design Professional Series Vision

The Design Professional Series is your guide to today's hottest multimedia applications. These comprehensive books teach the skills behind the application, showing you how to apply smart design principles to multimedia products, such as dynamic graphics, animation, Web sites, software authoring tools, and video.

A team of design professionals including multimedia instructors, students, authors, and editors worked together to create this series. We recognized the unique learning environment of the digital media or multimedia classroom and have created a series that:

- Gives you comprehensive step-by-step instructions
- Offers in-depth explanation of the "why" behind a skill
- Includes creative projects for additional practice
- Explains concepts clearly using full-color visuals

It was our goal to create a book that speaks directly to the multimedia and design community—one of the most rapidly growing computer fields today.

This series was designed to appeal to the creative spirit. We would like to thank Philip Brooker for developing the inspirational artwork found on each unit opener and book cover. We would also like to give special thanks to Ann Small of A Small Design Studio for developing a sophisticated and instructive book design.

—The Design Professional Series

Author Vision

What a delight it was to work with not one, but two great teams on this project. The Course Technology Design Professional team is creative and energetic. The Macromedia team is an inspiration. We'd like to thank Robert DeKoch, Julie Hallstrom, and Bentley Wolfe for providing exceptional feedback in their reviews of each unit, and Alisse Berger for coordinating their efforts. Macromedia products make the Web sing. It is a joy to teach such exciting and creative software. Dreamweaver is appropriately named.

We would also like to thank the reviewers—Michael Hanna, Colorado State University, Deborah Stockbridge, Quincy College, David Rhugnanan, Miami Dade Community College, James Kelley, Wor-Wic Community College, and Anita Philipp, Oklahoma City Community College—for their critiques and extremely helpful suggestions.
—The authors

Thank you to Nicole Pinard and Rebecca Berardy, who have supported this project from the beginning. Without them, there would be no Design Professional Series. Jane Hosie-Bounar joined the team in the middle of the project and saw it skillfully to its completion. Ann Fisher and Marjorie Hunt caught the vision immediately with this new series and wove the new format into the best of both worlds: a clear, concise reference book and an easy-to-use textbook.

Thank you to my family for their support, especially my husband Don. His fictitious role as a travel agent in the TripSmart Web site is symbolic of one of his roles in my life. May we have many, many more adventures together.
—Sherry Bishop

I would first like to thank Nicole Pinard for inviting me aboard this project. Thanks also to Rebecca Berardy, whose guidance, support, and enthusiasm for this book kept me on track. I would also like to recognize and thank Jane Hosie-Bounar for her support and good humor in seeing this through to a bound book, and Christine Gatliffe for her excellent production management. Most of all, I'd like to thank my husband Cecil and our sons Trey and Stephen for their constant love and support, which make anything possible.
—Marjorie Hunt

I would like to dedicate this book to the memory of Tom Tucker. Your spirit will always be with my family. I would like to thank my son Nicholas and my wife Lisa for being the driving force in my life. Heartfelt thanks to my parents Nirmala and Ramesh as well as my MMDC family—Brad, Kyle, and especially Tanya—for helping me find creative solutions, new projects, and the general push to learn new things.
—Piyush Patel

Introduction

Welcome to *Macromedia® Dreamweaver® MX—Design Professional*. This book offers creative projects, concise instructions, and complete coverage of basic to intermediate Dreamweaver MX skills, helping you to create and publish Dreamweaver Web sites. Use this book both in the classroom and as your own reference guide.

This text is organized into fourteen units. In these units, you will learn many skills you need to create dynamic Dreamweaver Web sites.

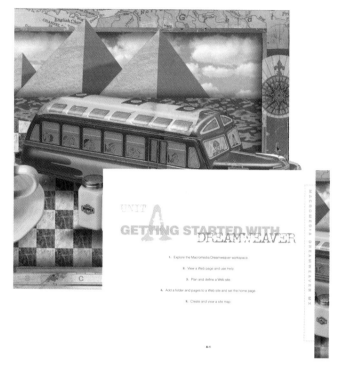

LESSON 4

ADD A FOLDER AND PAGES
AND SET THE HOME PAGE

What You'll Do

In this lesson, you will use the Site panel to set the home page. You'll also create a new folder and new pages for the Web site.

Adding a Folder to a Web Site
After defining a Web site, you need to create folders to organize the files that will make up the Web site. Creating a folder called assets is a good beginning. You can use the assets folder to store all non-HTML files, such as pictures or sound files. After you create the assets folder, it is a good idea to set it as the default location to store the Web site images. This saves a step when you import new images into the Web site.

Creating an effective navigation structure
When you create a Web site, it's important to consider how your viewers will navigate from page to page within the site. A navigation bar is a critical tool for moving around a Web site, so it's important that all text, buttons, and icons used in a navigation bar have a consistent look across all pages. If a complex navigation bar is used, such as one that incorporates JavaScript, it's a good idea to include plain text links in another location on the page for accessibility. Otherwise, viewers might become confused or lost within the site. A navigation structure can include more links than those included in a navigation bar, however. For instance, it can contain other sets of links that relate to the content of a specific page and which are placed at the bottom or sides of a page in a different format. No matter what navigation structure you use, make sure that every page includes a link back to the home page. Don't make viewers rely on the Back button on the browser toolbar to find their way back to the home page. It's possible that the viewer's current page might have opened as a result of a

MACROMEDIA DREAMWE...   ...rted with Dreamweaver

What You'll Do

A What You'll Do figure begins every lesson. This figure gives you an at-a-glance look at the skills covered in the unit and shows you the completed data file for that lesson. Before you start the lesson, you will know—both on a technical and artistic level—what you will be creating.

Comprehensive Conceptual Lessons

Before jumping into instructions, in-depth conceptual information tells you "why" skills are applied. This book provides the "how" and "why" through the use of professional examples. Also included in the text are tips and sidebars to help you work more efficiently and creatively, or to teach you a bit about the history behind the skill you are using.

Step-by-Step Instructions

This book combines in-depth conceptual information with concise steps to help you learn Dreamweaver MX. Each set of steps guides you through a lesson where you will apply tasks to a Dreamweaver MX data file. Step references to large colorful images and quick step summaries round out the lessons.

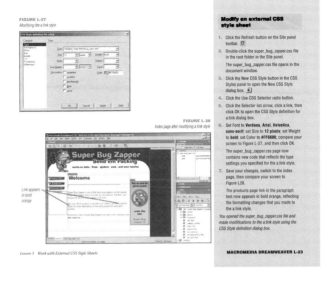

FIGURE L-27
Modifying the a:link style

FIGURE L-28
Index page after modifying a link style

Link appears in bold orange

Lesson 3   Work with External CSS Style Sheets

Modify an external CSS style sheet

1. Click the Refresh button on the Site panel toolbar.

2. Double-click the super_bug_zapper.css file in the root folder in the Site panel.

   The super_bug_zapper.css file opens in the document window.

3. Click the New CSS Style button in the CSS Styles panel to open the New CSS Style dialog box.

4. Click the Use CSS Selector radio button.

5. Click the Selector list arrow, click a:link, then click OK to open the CSS Style definition for a:link dialog box.

6. Set Font to **Verdana, Arial, Helvetica, sans-serif**; set Size to **12 pixels**; set Weight to **bold**; set Color to **#FF6600**; compare your screen to Figure L-27, and then click OK.

   The super_bug_zapper.css page now contains new code that reflects the type settings you specified for the a:link style.

7. Save your changes, switch to the index page, then compare your screen to Figure L-28.

   The products page link in the paragraph text now appears in bold orange, reflecting the formatting changes that you made to the a:link style.

You opened the super_bug_zapper.css file and made modifications to the a:link style using the CSS Style definition dialog box.

MACROMEDIA DREAMWEAVER L-23

PROJECT BUILDER 2

In this Project Builder, you will continue your work on the Jacob's Web site that you started in Project Builder 2 in Unit A. Chef Jacob wants to ensure that certain text elements and text links in the Web site are formatted consistently. He has provided you with instructions for how he would like the links to be formatted. He has also asked you to add code to the style sheet that will make the scrollbar appear in colors that match the Web site when viewed in a browser.

1. Open the Jacob's Web site that you created in Units A through K. (If you did not create this site in Units A through K, contact your instructor for assistance.)

2. Open the menus template, then attach the jacobs.css style sheet that you created in Unit C to this file.

3. Add a new CSS style to the jacobs.css style sheet. Use the CSS Selector to choose a:link, then set Font to **Arial, Helvetica, sans-serif**; Size to **14 pixels**; Weight to **bolder**, and Color to dark purple (**#660033**).

4. Add another new CSS style to the jacobs.css style sheet. Use the CSS Selector to choose a:hover, then set Font to **Arial, Helvetica, sans-serif**; Size to **14 pixels**; Weight to **bolder**, and Color to dark blue (**#000099**).

5. Add a new style to the jacobs.css style sheet that redefines the body tag. Set Font to **Arial, Helvetica, sans-serif**; Size to **16 pixels**; Style to **normal**, and Color to black (**#000000**).

6. Add the following line of code to the end of the body tag in the jacobs.css style sheet file: **scrollbar-track-color:#660033;**.

7. Add the following line of code below the code you just typed: **scrollbar-face-color:#FFCC99;**.

8. Save your changes, then close the jacobs.css style sheet.

9. Preview the menus template in a browser, position the mouse pointer over one of the text links, then compare your screen to Figure L-39.

10. Close your browser, save the menus template, update all pages in the site, then close the menus template.

FIGURE L-39
Completed Project Builder 2

Using Styles and Style Sheets

MACROMEDIA DREAMWEAVER L-31

Projects

This book contains a variety of end-of-unit materials for additional practice and reinforcement. The Skills Review contains hands-on practice exercises that mirror the progressive nature of the lesson material. The unit concludes with four projects: two Project Builders, one Design Project, and one Group Project. The Project Builders require you to apply the skills you've learned in the unit to create powerful Web sites. Design Projects explore design principles by sending you to the Web to view Dreamweaver in action. Group Projects encourage group activity as students use the resources of a team to create a Web site.

What Instructor Resources Are Available with This Book?

The Instructor Resources CD-ROM is Course Technology's way of putting the resources and information needed to teach and learn effectively into your hands. All the resources are available for both Macintosh and Windows operating systems, and many of the resources can be downloaded from *www.course.com*.

Instructor's Manual

Available as an electronic file, the Instructor's Manual is quality-assurance tested and includes unit overviews and detailed lecture topics for each unit, with teaching tips. The Instructor's Manual is available on the Instructor Resources CD-ROM, or you can download it from *www.course.com*.

Syllabus

Prepare and customize your course easily using this sample course outline (available on the Instructor Resources CD-ROM).

PowerPoint Presentations

Each unit has a corresponding PowerPoint presentation that you can use in lectures, distribute to your students, or customize to suit your course.

Figure Files

Figure Files contain all the figures from the book in bitmap format. Use the figure files to create transparency masters or use them in a PowerPoint presentation.

Data Files for Students

To complete most of the units in this book, your students will need Data Files. Put them on a file server for students to copy. The Data Files are available on the Instructor Resources CD-ROM, the Review Pack, and can also be downloaded from *www.course.com*. Instruct students to use the Data Files List at the end of this book. This list gives instructions on copying and organizing files.

Solutions to Exercises

Solution Files are Data Files completed with comprehensive sample answers. Use these files to evaluate your students' work. Or, distribute them electronically or in hard copy so students can verify their work. Sample solutions to all lessons and end-of-unit material are provided.

Test Bank and Test Engine

ExamView is a powerful testing software package that allows instructors to create and administer printed, computer (LAN-based), and Internet exams. ExamView includes hundreds of questions that correspond to the topics covered in this text, enabling students to generate detailed study guides that include page references for further review. The computer-based and Internet testing components allow students to take exams at their computers, and also save the instructor time by grading each exam automatically.

Additional Activities for Students

We have included **Macromedia Fundamentals** interactive training tutorials to help students learn the basics of each of the applications in Macromedia Studio MX.

Series & Author Vision iii

Preface iv

Instructor's Resources vi

Read This Before You Begin xx

Unit A   Getting Started with Dreamweaver

Lesson 1   Explore the Dreamweaver Workspace A-4

2   View a Web Page and Use Help A-10

3   Plan and Define a Web Site A-14

4   Add a Folder and Pages and Set the Home Page A-22

5   Create and View a Site Map A-30

Unit B   Developing a Web Page

Lesson 1   Create Head Content and Set Page Properties B-4

2   Create, Import, and Format Text B-10

3   Add Links to Web Pages B-18

4   Use the History Panel and Use the Code Inspector B-24

5   Modify and Test Web Pages B-30

Unit C   Working with Text and Graphics

Lesson 1   Create Unordered and Ordered Lists C-4

2   Create, Apply, and Edit Cascading Style Sheets C-10

3   Insert and Align Graphics C-16

4   Enhance an Image and Use Alternate Text C-22

5   Insert a Background Image and Perform Site Maintenance C-28

Unit D   Working with Links

Lesson 1   Create External and Internal Links D-4

2   Create Internal Links to Named Anchors D-10

3   Insert Flash Text D-16

4   Create and Modify a Navigation Bar D-20

5   Manage Web Site Links D-28

Unit E   Working with Tables

Lesson 1   Create a Table E-4

2   Resize, Split, and Merge Cells E-10

3   Insert and Align Graphics in Table Cells E-16

4   Insert Text and Format Cell Content E-20

5   Perform Web Site Maintenance E-26

Unit F   Collecting Data with Forms

Lesson 1   Plan and Create a Form F-4

2   Format a Form F-14

3   Work with Form Objects F-20

4   Create a Jump Menu F-32

Unit G   Positioning Objects with Layers

Lesson 1   Create a Layer G-4

2   Set the Position and Size of a Layer G-12

3   Use the Layers Panel G-16

4   Configure Layer Preferences G-20

5   Convert Layers to Tables and Tables to Layers G-24

Unit H   Using Frames for Page Layout

Lesson 1   Insert a Frame H-4

2   Configure Frames H-8

3   Add Content to Frames H-14

4   Create NoFrames Content H-18

Unit I   Adding Multimedia Elements

Lesson 1   Add Macromedia Flash Objects I-4

2   Add Rollover Images I-10

3   Add Sounds and Popup Messages I-14

Unit J   Creating Interactions Using Behaviors and Timelines

Lesson 1   Animate Layers Using Timelines J-4

2   Change Text Using Behaviors J-14

3   Swap Images and Create Pop-Up Windows and Menus J-20

Unit K   Creating and Using Templates

Lesson 1   Create Templates with Editable and Optional Regions K-4

2   Enhance and Nest Templates K-10

3   Use Templates to Create Pages K-20

4   Use Templates to Update a Site K-30

Unit L   Using Styles and Style Sheets

Lesson 1   Create and Use HTML Styles L-4

2   Create and Use Inline Styles L-10

3   Work with External CSS Style Sheets L-20

Unit M   Working with Library Items and Snippets

Lesson 1   Create and Modify Library Items M-4

2   Add Library Items to Pages M-12

3   Add and Modify Snippets M-18

Unit N   Managing a Web Server and Files

Lesson 1   Publish a Web Site and Transfer Files N-4

2   Check Files Out and In N-12

3   Cloak Files N-16

4   Import and Export a Site Definition N-20

Data Files List 1

Glossary 13

Index 22

BRIEF CONTENTS

INTRODUCTION
Using Dreamweaver Tools   A-2

LESSON 1
Explore the Dreamweaver Workspace   A-4
Examining the Dreamweaver Workspace   A-4
Working with Dreamweaver Views   A-5
Tasks   Start Dreamweaver (Windows)   A-6
        Start Dreamweaver (Macintosh)   A-7
        Change views and view panels   A-8

LESSON 2
View a Web Page and Use Help   A-10
Opening a Web page   A-10
Viewing basic Web page elements   A-10
Getting Help   A-11
Tasks   Open a Web page and view basic page
        elements   A-12
        Use Dreamweaver Help   A-13

LESSON 3
Plan and Define a Web Site   A-14
Understanding the Web Site Creation
Process   A-14
Planning a Web Site   A-14
Setting up the Basic Structure   A-15
Creating the Web Pages and Collecting the
Page Content   A-17
Testing the Pages   A-17

Modifying the Pages   A-17
Publishing the Site   A-17
Tasks   Create a root folder (Windows)   A-18
        Create a root folder (Macintosh)   A-19
        Define a Web site   A-20
        Set up Web server access   A-21

LESSON 4
**Add a Folder and Pages and Set the
Home Page**   A-22
Adding a Folder to a Web Site   A-22
Setting the Home Page   A-23
Adding Pages to a Web Site   A-23
Tasks   Add a folder to a Web site (Windows)   A-24
        Add a folder to a Web site (Macintosh)   A-24
        Set the default images folder   A-25
        Set the home page   A-26
        Copy a graphic in an imported file and
        paste it to the assets folder   A-27
        Add pages to a Web site (Windows)   A-28
        Add pages to a Web site (Macintosh)   A-29

LESSON 5
Create and View a Site Map   A-30
Creating a Site Map   A-30
Viewing a Site Map   A-30
Using Site Map Images in Web Pages   A-31
Tasks   Select site map options   A-32
        View a site map   A-33

CONTENTS

CONTENTS

INTRODUCTION
Understanding Page Layout   B-2

LESSON 1
Create Head Content and Set Page Properties   B-4
Creating the Head Content   B-4
Setting Web Page Properties   B-5
Tasks   Edit a page title   B-6
    Enter keywords   B-7
    Enter a description   B-8
    Set the page background color   B-9

LESSON 2
Create, Import, and Format Text   B-10
Creating and Importing Text   B-10
Formatting Text Using the Property Inspector   B-11
Changing Fonts   B-11
Changing Font Sizes   B-11
Formatting Paragraphs   B-11
Tasks   Enter text   B-12
    Format text   B-13
    Save graphics in the assets folder   B-14
    Import text   B-15
    Set text properties   B-16

LESSON 3
Add Links to Web Pages   B-18
Adding Links to Web Pages   B-18
Using Navigation Bars   B-19
Tasks   Create a navigation bar   B-20
    Format a navigation bar   B-20
    Add links to Web pages   B-21
    Create an e-mail link   B-22
    View the linked pages in the site map   B-23

LESSON 4
Use the History Panel and Use the Code Inspector   B-24
Using the History Panel   B-24
Viewing HTML Code in the Code Inspector   B-25
Tasks   Use the History panel   B-26
    Use the Code Inspector   B-27
    Use the Reference panel   B-28
    Insert a date object   B-29

LESSON 5
Modify and Test Web Pages   B-30
Testing and Modifying Web Pages   B-30
Testing a Web Page Using Different Browsers   B-31
Tasks   Modify a Web page   B-32
    Test Web pages by viewing them in a browser   B-33

UNIT C — WORKING WITH TEXT AND GRAPHICS

INTRODUCTION

Formatting Text as Lists   C-2
Using Cascading Style Sheets   C-2
Using Graphics to Enhance Web Pages   C-2

LESSON 1

Create Unordered and Ordered Lists   C-4
Creating Unordered Lists   C-4
Formatting Unordered Lists   C-4
Creating Ordered Lists   C-4
Formatting Ordered Lists   C-5
Creating Definition Lists   C-5
Tasks   Create an unordered list   C-6
         Format an unordered list   C-7
         Create an ordered list   C-8
         Format an ordered list   C-9

LESSON 2

Create, Apply, and Edit Cascading Style Sheets   C-10
Using Cascading Style Sheets   C-10
Understanding CSS Style Sheet Settings   C-11
Tasks   Create a Cascading Style Sheet and
         a style   C-12
         Apply a Cascading Style Sheet   C-13
         Edit a Cascading Style Sheet   C-14
         Add a style to a Cascading Style Sheet   C-15

LESSON 3

Insert and Align Graphics   C-16
Understanding Graphic File Formats   C-16
Understanding the Assets Panel   C-16
Aligning Images   C-17
Tasks   Insert a graphic   C-18
         Align a graphic   C-20

LESSON 4

Enhance an Image and Use Alternate Text   C-22
Enhancing an Image   C-22
Using Alternate Text   C-23
Tasks   Add a border   C-24
         Add horizontal space   C-24
         Resize graphics   C-25
         Use alternate text   C-26
         Set the alternate text accessibility
         option   C-27

LESSON 5

Insert a Background Image and Perform Site Maintenance   C-28
Inserting a Background Image   C-28
Managing Graphics   C-28
Removing Colors from a Web Site   C-29
Tasks   Insert a background image   C-30
         Remove a background image from
         a page   C-31
         Delete files from a Web site   C-32
         Remove non-Web-safe colors from a
         Web site   C-33

UNIT D   **WORKING WITH LINKS**

INTRODUCTION
Understanding Internal and External Links   D-2

LESSON 1
Create External and Internal Links   D-4
Creating External Links   D-4
Creating Internal Links   D-5
Tasks   Create an external link   D-6
        View external links in the site map   D-7
        Create an internal link   D-8
        View internal links in the site map   D-9

LESSON 2
Create Internal Links to Named Anchors   D-10
Inserting Named Anchors   D-10
Creating Internal Links to Named
Anchors   D-11
Tasks   Insert a named anchor   D-12
        Create an internal link to a named
        anchor   D-14

LESSON 3
Insert Flash Text   D-16
Understanding Flash Text   D-16
Inserting Flash Text on a Web Page   D-16
Tasks   Create Flash text   D-18
        Change the alignment of Flash text   D-19

LESSON 4
Create and Modify a Navigation Bar   D-20
Creating a Navigation Bar Using Images   D-20
Copying and Modifying a Navigation Bar   D-20
Tasks   Create a navigation bar using images   D-22
        Add elements to a navigation bar   D-24
        Copy and paste a navigation bar   D-26
        Customize a navigation bar   D-26

LESSON 5
Manage Web Site Links   D-28
Managing Web Site Links   D-28
Task   Manage Web site links   D-29

INTRODUCTION

Inserting Graphics and Text in Tables E-2
Maintaining a Web Site E-2

LESSON 1

Create a Table E-4
Understanding Table Views E-4
Creating a Table in Standard View E-4
Setting Table Accessibility Preferences
for Tables E-5
Drawing a Table in Layout View E-5
Planning a Table E-5
Tasks Set table accessibility preferences E-6
       Create a table E-6
       Set table properties E-8
       View the table in Layout View E-9

LESSON 2

Resize, Split, and Merge Cells E-10
Resizing Table Elements E-10
Splitting and Merging Cells E-11
Tasks Resize columns E-12
       Resize rows E-13
       Split cells E-14
       Merge cells E-15

LESSON 3

Insert and Align Graphics in Table Cells E-16
Inserting Graphics in Table Cells E-16
Aligning Graphics in Table Cells E-17

Tasks Insert graphics in table cells E-18
       Align graphics in table cells E-19

LESSON 4

Insert Text and Format Cell Content E-20
Inserting Text in a Table E-20
Formatting Cell Content E-20
Formatting cells E-21
Tasks Insert text E-22
       Format cell content E-23
       Format cells E-24
       Modify cell content E-25

LESSON 5

Perform Web Site Maintenance E-26
Maintaining a Web Site E-26
Checking Links Sitewide E-26
Using the Assets Panel E-26
Using Site Reports E-26
Using the Site Map E-27
Testing Pages E-27
Tasks Check for broken links E-28
       Check for orphaned files E-29
       Remove orphaned files E-30
       Verify that all colors are Web-safe E-32
       Check for untitled documents E-32
       Check for missing alternate text E-33

UNIT F — COLLECTING DATA WITH FORMS

INTRODUCTION
Using Forms to Collect Information   F-2

LESSON 1
Plan and Create a Form   F-4
Planning a Form   F-4
Creating Forms   F-4
Setting Form Properties   F-6
Understanding CGI Scripts   F-7
Tasks   Create the Northwest Warehouse Web
site (Win)   F-8
Create the Northwest Warehouse Web
site (Mac)   F-10
Insert a form   F-12
Set form properties   F-13

LESSON 2
Format a Form   F-14
Using Tables to Lay Out a Form   F-14
Using Fieldsets to Group Form Objects   F-14
Adding Labels to Form Objects   F-15
Tasks   Create fieldsets   F-16
Add a table to a fieldset   F-17
Add form labels to table cells   F-18
Add form labels using the Label button   F-19

LESSON 3
Work with Form Objects   F-20
Understanding Form Objects   F-20
Tasks   Insert single-line text fields   F-23
Insert a multiple-line text field   F-24
Insert a checkbox   F-24
Add radio groups to a form   F-26

Add an image field   F-27
Add a menu   F-28
Add a file field   F-29
Insert hidden fields   F-30
Add Submit and Reset buttons   F-31

LESSON 4
Create a Jump Menu   F-32
Understanding Jump Menus   F-32
Updating Jump Menus   F-33
Testing Jump Menus   F-33
Tasks   Insert a jump menu   F-34
Modify a jump menu   F-35

UNIT G — POSITIONING OBJECTS WITH LAYERS

INTRODUCTION
Using Layers versus Tables for
Page Layout   G-2

LESSON 1
Create a Layer   G-4
Understanding Layers   G-4
Using HTML Tags to Create Layers   G-4
Understanding Layer Content   G-5
Using Advanced Layer Formatting   G-5
Tasks   Draw a layer   G-6
Define a layer   G-7
Set a background image   G-8
Set a background color   G-9
Add text to a layer   G-10
Add an image to a layer   G-11

LESSON 2
Set the Position and Size of a Layer   G-12
Understanding Absolute Positioning   G-12
Setting Positioning Attributes   G-12
Tasks   Set the left and top position of a layer   G-14
Set layer height and width   G-14
Set a layer's z-index value   G-15

LESSON 3
Use the Layers Panel   G-16
Controlling Layers   G-16
Tasks   Change the name of a layer   G-17
Control layer visibility   G-18
Work with nested layers   G-19

LESSON 4

Configure Layer Preferences G-20
Setting Layer Preferences G-20
Fixing the Netscape Resize Problem G-20
Tasks Control the appearance of a layer G-22
          Adjust for Netscape resize problems G-23

LESSON 5

**Convert Layers to Tables and Tables
to Layers** G-24
Using Layers and Tables for Page Layout G-24
Converting Layers to Tables G-24
Converting Tables to Layers G-25
Tasks Convert layers to a table G-26
          Convert a table to layers G-27

UNIT H   USING FRAMES FOR PAGE LAYOUT

INTRODUCTION
Using Frames for Page Layout H-2

LESSON 1

Insert a Frame H-4
Understanding Frames and Framesets H-4
Choosing a Predefined Frameset H-4
Adding Content to Frames H-5
Saving a Frameset and Frames H-5
Tasks Create a frameset H-7
          Save a frameset H-7

LESSON 2

Configure Frames H-8
Understanding Frames Configuration H-8
Selecting Frames H-8
Naming Frames H-8

Setting Frame Size H-8
Controlling Frame Borders and Scroll Bars H-9
Tasks Set frame names H-10
          Control frame sizes H-11
          Set frame borders and border colors H-12
          Configure frame scrollbars H-13
          Control page margins H-13

LESSON 3

Add Content to Frames H-14
Understanding How to Add Content to
a Frame H-14
Loading Existing Pages in a Frame H-14
Creating Content from Scratch H-15
Tasks Specify a source file to display in
          a frame H-16
          Add content to a frame H-17

LESSON 4
Create Noframes Content H-18
Understanding NoFrames Content H-18
Adding NoFrames Content H-18
Task Add NoFrames content to a Web page H-20

UNIT I ADDING MULTIMEDIA ELEMENTS

INTRODUCTION
Understanding Multimedia I-2

LESSON 1
Add Macromedia Flash Objects I-4
Understanding Macromedia Flash I-4
Inserting Flash Buttons and Movies I-5
Tasks Insert Flash buttons I-6
Insert Flash movies I-8
Play a Flash movie in Dreamweaver and in
a browser I-9

LESSON 2
Add Rollover Images I-10
Understanding Rollover Images I-10
Adding Rollover Images I-11
Task Add a rollover image I-12

LESSON 3
Add Sounds and Popup Messages I-14
Adding Interactive Elements I-14
Using the Behaviors Panel I-14
Inserting Sound Effects I-14
Inserting Popup Messages and
Alert Boxes I-15
Tasks Add sound effects I-16
Add a popup message I-17

CONTENTS

UNIT J — CREATING INTERACTIONS USING BEHAVIORS AND TIMELINES

INTRODUCTION
Using Animations and Interactive Elements
Effectively   J-2

LESSON 1
Animate Layers Using Timelines   J-4
Animating Layers   J-4
Using the Timelines Panel   J-4
Using Behaviors to Animate a Layer   J-5
Adding Keyframes   J-5
Previewing Animations Using the
Timelines Panel   J-5
Creating Draggable Layers   J-6
Tasks   Create the Super Bug Zapper Web
        site (Win)   J-7
        Create the Super Bug Zapper Web
        site (Mac)   J-8
        Add layers to a timeline   J-9
        Add start and stop frames to a timeline   J-10
        Add a keyframe to a timeline   J-11
        Preview an animation in Dreamweaver and
        your browser   J-12
        Create a draggable layer   J-13

LESSON 2
Change Text Using Behaviors   J-14
Using Behaviors to Change Text   J-14
Changing Text in a Layer   J-14
Changing the Text of the Status Bar   J-14
Displaying Text in a Form Field   J-15
Tasks   Change text in a layer   J-16
        Add text to the status bar   J-17
        Change the text of a text field in a form   J-18

LESSON 3
**Swap Images and Create Pop-Up Windows
and Menus**   J-20
Creating Interactive Elements Using
Behaviors   J-20
Swapping Images   J-20
Creating Pop-Up Windows   J-20
Creating Pop-Up Menus   J-21
Tasks   Swap images   J-22
        Create a pop-up window   J-23
        Create a pop-up menu   J-24
        Format a pop-up menu   J-25

CONTENTS

xvii

UNIT K   CREATING AND USING TEMPLATES

INTRODUCTION
Understanding How to Use Templates   K-2

LESSON 1
Create Templates with Editable and Optional Regions   K-4
Creating a Template from an Existing Page   K-4
Defining Editable Regions   K-4
Defining Optional Regions   K-4
Defining Editable Optional Regions   K-5
Tasks   Create a template from an
     existing page   K-6
     Create an editable region   K-7
     Create an optional region   K-8
     Create an editable optional region   K-9

LESSON 2
Enhance and Nest Templates   K-10
Setting Parameters for Optional Regions   K-10
Nesting Templates   K-10
Creating Repeating Regions and
Repeating Tables   K-11
Creating Editable Attributes   K-12
Tasks   Adjust advanced settings   K-13
     Nest a template in another template   K-14
     Insert a repeating table   K-14
     Modify a template   K-16
     Create editable attributes for color   K-17
     Create editable attributes for a URL   K-18
     Save a template and update nested
     templates   K-19

LESSON 3
Use Templates to Create Pages   K-20
Creating Pages with Templates   K-20
Modifying Editable Regions   K-20
Modifying Object Attributes   K-21
Using Repeating Tables   K-21
Creating Links in Template-Based Pages   K-21
Attaching a Template to an Existing Page   K-22

Tasks   Create a new page based on a template   K-23
     Modify editable regions in a template   K-24
     Modify object attributes   K-25
     Add links to template-based pages   K-26
     Use repeating tables   K-27
     Attach a template to an existing page   K-28

LESSON 4
Use Templates to Update a Site   K-30
Making Changes to a Template   K-30
Updating All Pages Based on a Template   K-31
Tasks   Make changes to a template   K-32
     Update all template-based pages
     in a site   K-33

UNIT L   USING STYLES AND STYLE SHEETS

INTRODUCTION

LESSON 1
Create and Use HTML Styles   L-4
Understanding HTML Styles   L-4
Using the HTML Styles Panel   L-4
Creating and Editing HTML Styles   L-4
Understanding Benefits and Disadvantages of
HTML Styles   L-5
Tasks   Create an HTML style   L-6
     Apply an HTML style   L-7
     Clear an HTML style   L-8
     Modify an HTML style   L-9

LESSON 2
Create and Use Inline Styles   L-10
Understanding Inline Styles   L-10
Creating, Applying, and Modifying a
Custom Style   L-10
Redefining HTML Tags   L-11
Tasks   Create a custom style   L-13
     Apply a custom style   L-14

     Modify a custom style   L-15
     Redefine an HTML tag   L-16
     Edit an inline style   L-18
     Delete an inline style   L-19

LESSON 3
Work with External CSS Style Sheets   L-20
Using External CSS Style Sheets   L-20
Attaching an External CSS Style Sheet to a
Page or Template   L-20
Adding Hyperlink Styles to a CSS
Style Sheet   L-21
Adding Custom Code to a CSS
Style Sheet   L-21
Tasks   Attach a style sheet to an existing page   L-22
     Modify an external CSS style sheet   L-23
     Add hyperlink styles   L-24
     Add custom code to a style sheet   L-25
     Use a style sheet with a template   L-26
     Delete external styles from a Web page   L-27

UNIT M — WORKING WITH LIBRARY ITEMS AND SNIPPETS

INTRODUCTION
Understanding Library Items   M-2
Understanding Snippets   M-2

LESSON 1
Create and Modify Library Items   M-4
Understanding the Benefits of
Library Items   M-4
Viewing and Creating Library Items   M-4
Modifying Library Items   M-5
Tasks   Create a text-based library item   M-6
Create an image-based library item   M-7
Edit an image-based library item   M-8
Update library items   M-10
Edit a text-based library item   M-11

LESSON 2
Add Library Items to Pages   M-12
Adding Library Items to a Page   M-12
Making Library Items Editable on a Page   M-12
Deleting and Recreating Library Items   M-13
Tasks   Add a library item to a page   M-14
Make a library item editable on a page   M-15
Delete a library item   M-16
Recreate a library item   M-17

LESSON 3
Add and Modify Snippets   M-18
Using the Snippets Panel   M-18
Inserting and Modifying Snippets   M-18
Creating New Snippets   M-19
Tasks   Add a predefined snippet to a page   M-20
Modify snippet text   M-21
Modify snippet links   M-22
Create a new snippet   M-23

UNIT N — MANAGING A WEB SERVER AND FILES

INTRODUCTION
Preparing to Publish a Site   N-2

LESSON 1
Publish a Web Site and Transfer Files   N-4
Defining a Remote Site   N-4
Viewing a Remote Site   N-4
Transferring Files to and from a
Remote Site   N-5
Synchronizing Files   N-6
Tasks   Set up Web server access on an
FTP site   N-7
Set up Web server access on a local or
network folder   N-8
View a Web site on a remote server   N-9
Upload files to a remote server   N-10
Synchronize files   N-11

LESSON 2
Check Files Out and In   N-12
Managing a Web Site with a Team   N-12
Checking Out and Checking In Files   N-12
Enabling the Check In/Check Out Feature   N-13
Tasks   Enable the Check In/Check Out feature   N-14
Check out a file   N-14
Check in a file   N-15

LESSON 3
Cloak Files   N-16
Understanding Cloaking Files   N-16
Cloaking a Folder   N-16
Cloaking Selected File Types   N-17
Tasks   Cloak and uncloak a folder   N-18
Cloak selected file types   N-19

LESSON 4
Import and Export a Site Definition   N-20
Exporting a Site Definition   N-20
Importing a Site Definition   N-20
Tasks   Export a site definition   N-22
Import a site definition   N-22

Data Files List   1
Glossary   13
Index   22

Intended audience

This text is designed for the beginner or intermediate student who wants to learn how to use Dreamweaver MX. The book is designed to provide basic and in-depth material that not only educates, but also encourages the student to explore the nuances of this exciting program.

Approach

The text allows you to work at your own pace through step-by-step tutorials. A concept is presented and the process is explained, followed by the actual steps. To learn the most from the use of the text, you should adopt the following habits:

- Proceed slowly: Accuracy and comprehension is more important than speed.
- Understand what is happening with each step before you continue to the next step.
- After finishing a skill, ask yourself if you could do it on your own, without referring to the steps. If the answer is no, review the steps.

Icons, buttons, and pointers

Symbols for icons, buttons, and pointers are shown in the step each time they are used.

Fonts

Data and Solution Files contain a variety of commonly used fonts, but there is no guarantee that these fonts will be available on your computer. In a few cases, fonts other than those common to a PC or a Macintosh are used. If any of the fonts in use is not available on your computer, you can make a substitution, realizing that the results may vary from those in the book.

Creating a portfolio

Students can create a portfolio of Design Projects and Group Projects in which they can store their original work.

Windows and Macintosh

Macromedia Dreamweaver MX works virtually the same on Windows and Macintosh operating systems. In those cases where there is a significant difference, the abbreviations (Win) and (Mac) are used.

Dreamweaver MX Workspace

If you are running Dreamweaver with a Windows operating system, you have the choice of using two different workspaces. One is based on the Dreamweaver 4 Workspace that uses floating windows. The document window and the site window are not displayed at the same time on the screen and the various documents, panels, and inspectors can float on the screen. You can easily reposition, open, or close them to tailor your workspace.

The second layout option is the Dreamweaver MX Workspace, which is an integrated workspace. You can display the document window and the site window simultaneously, along with the panels and inspectors. The figures used in this text are captured using the integrated workspace layout. It is easy to change the workspace layout by using the General dialog box option from the Preferences command on the Edit menu.

Macintosh users do not have the option of changing the workspace layout. Macintosh users must use the floating workspace layout.

Building Web sites

You will create and develop three different Web sites in the lesson material in this book. In Units A through E, you will create and develop the TripSmart Web site. In Units F through I you will develop the Northwest Warehouse Web site. Finally, in Units J through N, you will work on the Super Bug Zapper Web site. Additionally, you will create four Web sites in the end-of-unit material, all of which build on each other from unit to unit. Because each unit builds off of the previous unit, it is recommended that you work through the units in consecutive order. However, if you choose to complete the units in a different sequence, or if you make mistakes and would like to start one of the Web sites with fresh files, contact your instructor for assistance.

Creating Dreamweaver Web sites that have not been built through previous consecutive units (Windows)

If you begin an assignment that requires a Web site that you did not create or maintain before a unit, you will need to perform the following steps:

1. Copy the solution files folder from the preceding unit for the Web site you wish to create onto the hard drive, Zip drive, or a high-density floppy disk. For example, if you are working on Unit E, you will need the solution files folder from Unit D. Your instructor will furnish this folder to you.

2. Start Dreamweaver.

3. Click Site on either menu bar, then click Edit Sites.

4. Click New to display the Site Definition for Unnamed Site 1 dialog box.

5. Type the name you want to use for your Web site in the Site Name text box. Spaces and uppercase letters are allowed in the Site name.

6. Click the Browse for File icon (folder) next to the Local Root Folder text box.

7. Click the drive and folder where your solution files folder is placed to locate the local root folder. The local root folder contains the name of the Web site you are working on. For example, the local root folder for the TripSmart Web site is called tripsmart.

8. Double-click the local root folder, click Select, then click OK to close the Site Definition for Unnamed Site 1 dialog box.

9. A dialog box appears stating that the "Initial site cache will now be created. This scans the files in your site and starts tracking links as you change them." Click OK to accept this message.

10. Click Done to close the Edit Sites dialog box.

11. Click index.htm in the Local View list of the Site window to select it.

12. Click Site on the menu bar, then click Set as Home Page.

Creating Dreamweaver Web sites that have not been built through previous consecutive units (Macintosh)

If you begin an assignment that requires a Web site that you did not create or maintain before a unit, you will need to perform the following steps:

1. Copy the solution files folder from the preceding unit for the Web site you wish to create onto the hard drive, Zip drive, or a high-density floppy disk. For example, if you are working on Unit E, you will need the solution files folder from Unit D. Your instructor will furnish this folder to you.

2. Start Dreamweaver and show the Site window by clicking Window on the menu bar and choosing Site.

3. Click Site on the menu bar, then click New Sites.

4. Type the name you want to use for your Web site in the Site Name text box. Spaces and uppercase letters are allowed in the Site name.

5. Click Browse for File icon (folder) next to the Local Root Folder text box.

6. Click the drive and folder where your solution files folder is stored to locate the local root folder. The local root folder contains the name of the Web site you are working on. For example, the local root folder for the TripSmart Web site is called tripsmart.

7. Click the local root folder, click Choose, then click OK to close the Site Definition for Unnamed Site 1 dialog box.

8. A dialog box appears stating that the "Initial site cache will now be created. This scans the files in your site and starts tracking links as you change them." Click OK to accept this message.

9. Click Done to close the Edit Sites dialog box.

10. Click index.htm in the Local Folder list of the Site window to select it.

11. Click Site on the menu bar, point to Site Map View, then click Set as Home Page.

Data Files

To complete the lessons and end-of-unit material in this book, you need to obtain the necessary Data Files. Please refer to the directions on the inside back cover for various methods to obtain these files. Once obtained, select where to store the files, such as the hard drive, a network server, or a Zip drive. The instructions in the lessons will refer to "the drive and folder where your Data Files are stored" when referring to the Data Files for the book.

When opening a file from the Data Files folder to import into a Web site, it is necessary to check all internal links, including those to images, and remove all absolute path references. For example, if a page with the TripSmart banner is opened and saved in the TripSmart Web site:

1. Click the image on the page to select it.

2. Use the Property inspector to check the Src text box.

3. The Src text box should read assets/tripsmart.jpg

4. If the Src text box has a longer path, the extra characters should be removed. Example: file:/d:/data_files/unit_h/assets/tripsmart.jpg should be changed to assets/tripsmart.jpg.

5. Save the file with the same name, over-writing the original file.

UNIT A

GETTING STARTED WITH DREAMWEAVER

1. Explore the Macromedia Dreamweaver workspace.

2. View a Web page and use Help.

3. Plan and define a Web site.

4. Add a folder and pages to a Web site and set the home page.

5. Create and view a site map.

UNIT A

GETTING STARTED WITH DREAMWEAVER

Introduction

Macromedia Dreamweaver MX is **Web design software** that lets you create dynamic, interactive Web pages containing text, images, hyperlinks, animation, sounds, video, and other elements. You can use Dreamweaver to create an individual Web page or a complex Web site consisting of many Web pages. A **Web site** is a group of related Web pages that are linked together and share a common interface and design. You can use Dreamweaver to create some Web page elements such as text, tables, and interactive buttons, or you can import elements from other software programs. You can save Dreamweaver files in many different file formats including HTML, JavaScript, or XML to name a few. **HTML** is the acronym for Hypertext Markup Language, the language used to create Web pages.

QUICKTIP

You use a browser to view your Web pages on the Internet. A **browser** is a program, such as Microsoft Internet Explorer or Netscape Communicator, that lets you display HTML-developed Web pages.

Using Dreamweaver Tools

Creating a good Web site is a complex task. Fortunately, Dreamweaver has an impressive number of tools that can help. Using Dreamweaver design tools, you can create dynamic and interactive Web pages without writing a word of HTML code. However, if you prefer to write code, Dreamweaver makes it easy to enter and edit the code directly and see the visual results of the code instantly. Dreamweaver also contains organizational tools that help you work with a team of people to create a Web site. You can also use Dreamweaver management tools to help you manage a Web site. For instance, you can use the **Site panel** to create folders to organize and store the various files for your Web site. You also use the Site panel to add pages to your Web site, and to set the **home page** in Dreamweaver, the first page that viewers will see when they visit the site. You can also use the **site map**, a graphical representation of how the pages within a Web site relate to each other, to view and edit the navigation structure of your Web site. The **navigation structure** is the way viewers navigate from page to page in your Web site.

Tools You'll Use

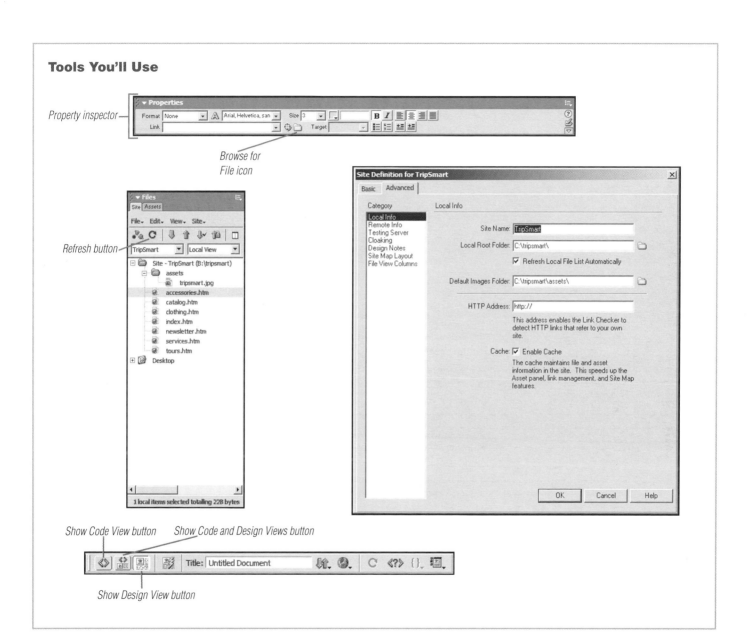

Property inspector

Browse for
File icon

Refresh button

Show Code View button

Show Code and Design Views button

Show Design View button

EXPLORE THE DREAMWEAVER WORKSPACE

What You'll Do

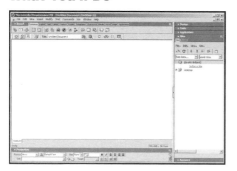

 In this lesson, you will start Dreamweaver, examine the components that make up the Dreamweaver workspace, and change views.

Examining the Dreamweaver Workspace

The **Dreamweaver workspace** is designed to provide you with easy access to all the tools you need to create Web pages. Refer to Figure A-1 as you locate the components described below.

The **document window** is the large white area in the Dreamweaver program window where you create and edit Web pages. The **menu bar**, located at the top of the document window, includes menu names, each of which contains Dreamweaver commands. To choose a menu command, click the menu name to open the menu, then click the menu command. The **Insert bar** contains buttons you can click to insert objects, such as images, tables, and horizontal rules.

The **Document toolbar** contains buttons you can use to change the current work mode, preview Web pages, debug Web pages, and view file-management options. The **Standard toolbar** contains buttons you can use to execute frequently used commands also available on the File and Edit menus. The Standard toolbar is not part of the default workspace setup and might not be showing on your screen.

QUICKTIP

To hide or display the Standard or Document toolbars, click View on the menu bar, point to Toolbars, then click Document or Standard.

The **Property inspector**, located at the bottom of the Dreamweaver window, lets you view and change the properties of a selected object. The **Status bar** is located below the document window. The left end of the status bar displays the **tag selector**, which shows the HTML tags used at the insertion point location. The right side displays the window size and estimated download time for the current page.

A **panel** is a window that displays information on a particular topic or contains related commands. **Panel groups** are sets of related panels that are grouped together. To view the contents of a panel in a panel group, click the panel tab you want. Panel groups can be collapsed and docked on the right side of the screen, or undocked by dragging the **gripper** on the left side of the panel group title bar. To collapse or expand a panel group, click the **expander arrow** ▽ on the left side of the panel group title bar, as shown in Figure A-2. When you use Dreamweaver for the first time, the Design, Code, Application, Files, and Answers panel groups are open by default.

Working with Dreamweaver Views

You view a Web page in the document window using one of three different views. A **view** is a particular way of displaying page content. **Design view** shows the page as it would appear in a browser, and is primarily used for designing and creating a Web page. **Code view** shows the underlying HTML code for the page; use this view to read or edit the underlying code. **Code and Design view** is a combination of Code view and Design view. Code and Design view is the best view for **debugging** or correcting errors because you can see immediately how code modifications will change the appearance of the page. The view buttons are located on the Document toolbar.

FIGURE A-1
The Dreamweaver MX workspace

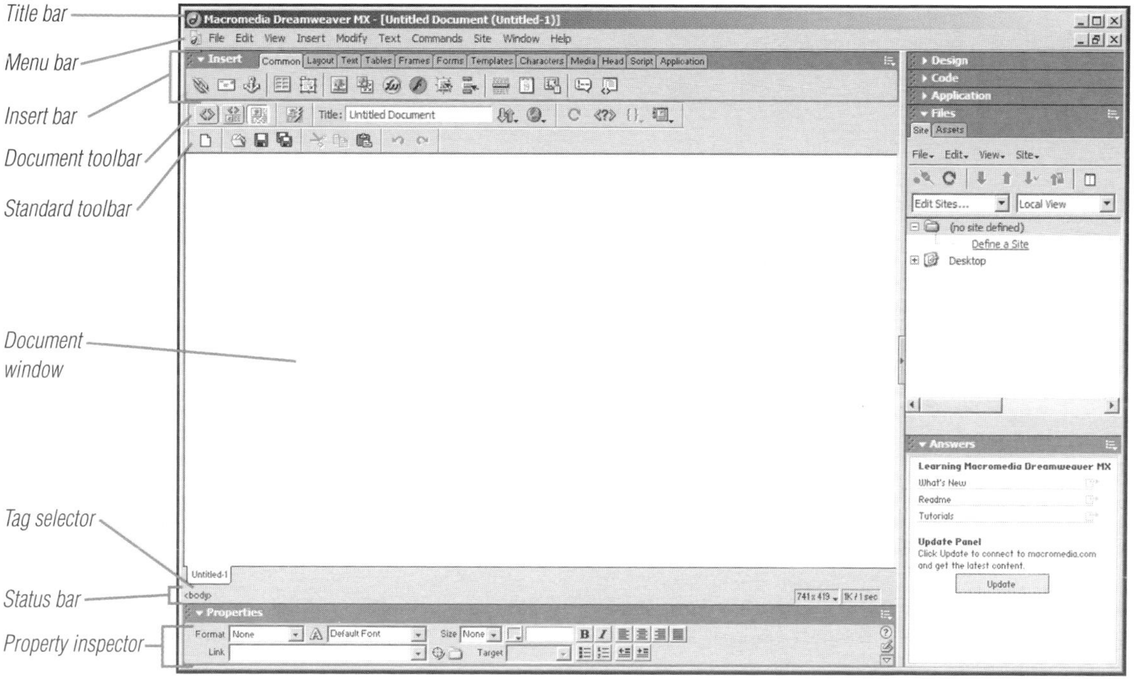

Title bar
Menu bar
Insert bar
Document toolbar
Standard toolbar

Document window

Tag selector
Status bar
Property inspector

FIGURE A-2
Panels in Design panel group

Expander arrow

Active panel tab

Start Dreamweaver (Windows)

1. Click the Start button on the taskbar.

   Start

2. Point to Programs or All Programs, point to Macromedia, then click Macromedia Dreamweaver MX, as shown in Figure A-3.

You started Dreamweaver MX for Windows.

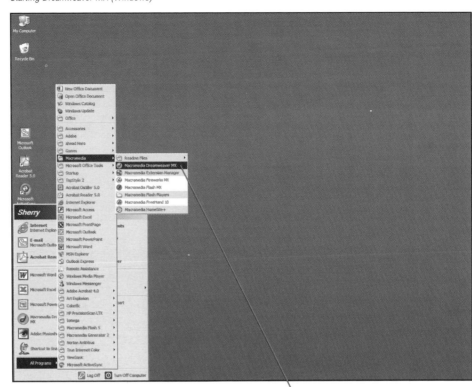

Click Macromedia Dreamweaver MX

Choosing a workspace layout (Windows)

If you are starting Dreamweaver MX for Windows for the first time after installing it, you will see the Workspace Setup dialog box, which asks you to choose between the Dreamweaver MX workspace layout and the Dreamweaver 4 workspace layout. The Dreamweaver MX workspace layout is an integrated workspace where the Dreamweaver windows and tools are positioned within one large application Window. The Dreamweaver 4 workspace is based on the Dreamweaver 4 interface and is composed of separate floating windows. Macintosh users must use the floating workspace. Most figures in this book show the Dreamweaver MX workspace. Ask your instructor which workspace layout option you should choose.

FIGURE A-4

Starting Dreamweaver MX (Macintosh)

Double-click the
hard drive icon

1. Double-click the hard drive icon, as shown in Figure A-4.

   The hard drive icon is usually in the upper-right corner of the desktop.

2. Double-click the Macromedia Dreamweaver MX folder.

   > **TIP** Your Macromedia Dreamweaver folder might be in another folder called Applications. See your instructor or technical support person if you have trouble locating Dreamweaver.

3. Double-click the Macromedia Dreamweaver MX program icon.

You started Dreamweaver MX for Macintosh.

Change views and view panels

1. Click the Show Code View button on the Document toolbar as shown in Figure A-5. ◇〉

   The HTML code for an untitled, blank document appears in the document window.

2. Click the Show Code and Design Views button on the Document toolbar. ◇▤

3. Click the Show Design View button on the Document toolbar. ▤◇

(continued)

FIGURE A-5
Code view for blank document

Show Code
View button

Show Code
and Design
Views button

Show Design
View button

Collapsed
panel groups

Expanded
panel group

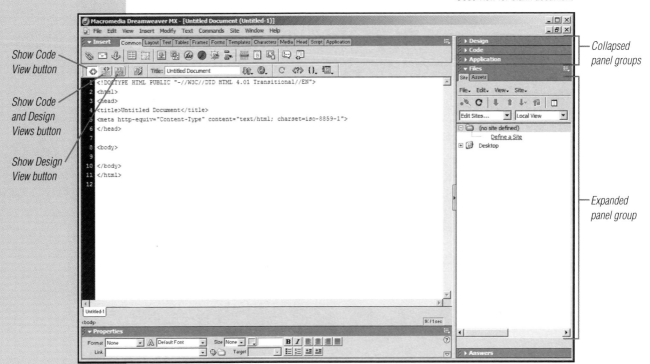

Displaying a panel group

Expander arrow

Drag to undock or "float" panel group

Code panel group

Panel tabs

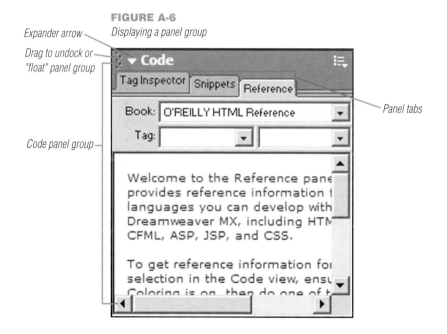

4. Click the expander arrow on the Code panel group title bar, then compare your screen to Figure A-6. ▷

   TIP If the Code Panel group is not displayed, click Window on the menu bar, then click Snippets.

5. Click each panel tab to display the contents of each panel.

6. Click the expander arrow on the Code panel group title bar to collapse the Code panel group. ▽

7. Repeat Steps 4 through 6 to expand the Design, Application, Files, and Answers panel groups and view the contents of each panel.

   TIP If you are a Mac user, you first need to open the panel groups. To open each panel group, click Window on the menu bar, then click Snippets (for the Code panel group), or Bindings (for the Application group) or Assets (for the Files panel group).

You viewed a blank Web page using three views, opened each panel group and displayed the contents of each panel, and closed each panel group.

VIEW A WEB PAGE AND USE HELP

What You'll Do

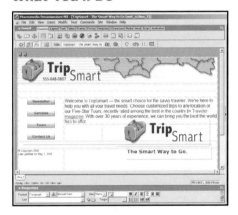

 In this lesson, you will open a Web page, view several page elements, and access the Help system.

Opening a Web page

After starting Dreamweaver, you can create a new Web site, create a new Web page, or open an existing Web site or Web page. The first Web page that appears when viewers go to a Web site is called the home page. The home page sets the look and feel of the Web site and directs viewers to the rest of the pages in the Web site.

Viewing basic Web page elements

There are many elements that make up Web pages. Web pages can be very simple, and designed primarily with text, or they can be media-rich with text, graphics, sound, and movies. Figure A-7 is an example of a Web page with several different page elements that work together to create a simple and attractive page.

Most information on a Web page is presented in the form of text. You can type text directly onto a Web page in Dreamweaver or import text created in other programs. You can then use the Property inspector to format text so that it is attractive and easy to read. Text should be short and to the point to prevent viewers from losing interest and leaving your site.

Hyperlinks, also known as links, are graphic or text elements on a Web page that users click to display another location on the page, another Web page on the same Web site, or a Web page on a different Web site.

Graphics add visual interest to a Web page. The saying that "less is more" is certainly true with graphics, though. Too many graphics will cause the page to load too slowly and discourage viewers from waiting for the page to download. Many pages today have banners, which are graphics displayed across the top of the screen that can incorporate a company's logo, contact information, and links to the other pages in the site.

Navigation bars are bars that contain multiple links that are usually organized in rows or columns. Sometimes, navigation bars are used with an image map. An image map is a graphic that has been divided into sections, each of which contains a link.

Flash button objects are objects created in Macromedia Flash that can serve as links to other files or Web pages. You can insert them onto a Web page without requiring the Macromedia Flash program to be installed. They add "pizzazz" to a Web page.

Getting Help

Dreamweaver has an excellent Help feature that is both comprehensive and easy to use. When questions or problems arise, you can use the commands on the Help menu to find the answers you need. Clicking the Using Dreamweaver command on a Windows computer opens the Using Dreamweaver MX window that contains four tabs you can use to search for answers in different ways. The Contents tab lists Dreamweaver Help topics by category. The Index tab lets you view topics in alphabetical order, and the Search tab lets you enter a keyword to search for a specific topic. You can use the Favorites tab to bookmark topics that you might want to view later. On a Macintosh you can choose between Index or Table of Contents view and the Search field is always present at the top of the window. You can also use the Tutorials command on the Help menu to get step-by-step instructions on how to complete various tasks, and the What's New command to learn about the new features of Dreamweaver MX.

FIGURE A-7
Common Web page elements

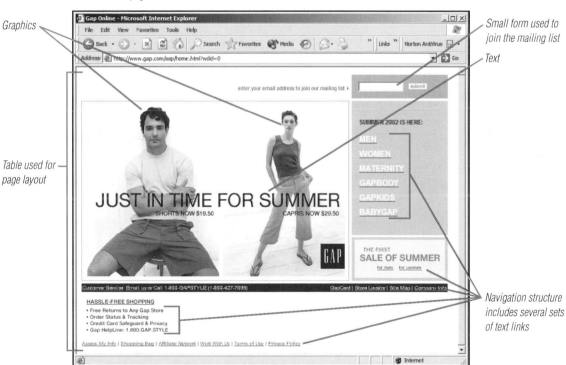

Graphics

Small form used to join the mailing list

Text

Table used for page layout

Navigation structure includes several sets of text links

Open a Web page and view basic page elements

1. Click File on the menu bar, then click Open.

2. Click the Look in list arrow (Win), or From list arrow (Mac), locate the drive and folder where your data files are stored, then double-click the unit_a folder (Win), or click the Unit_a folder (Mac).

3. Click dwa_1.htm, then click Open.

4. Locate each of the Web page elements shown in Figure A-8.

5. Click the Show Code View button to view the code for the page.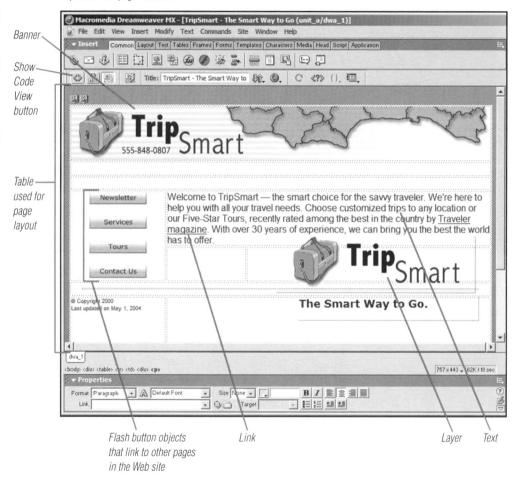

6. Scroll down to view all the code, then click the Show Design View button to return to Design view.

   TIP To view the code for a particular page element, select the page element in Design view, then click the Show Code View button.

7. Click File, then click Close to close the page without saving it.

You opened a Web page, located several page elements, viewed the code for the page, then closed the Web page without saving it.

FIGURE A-8
TripSmart Web page elements

Banner

Show Code View button

Table used for page layout

Flash button objects that link to other pages in the Web site

Link

Layer Text

FIGURE A-9
Using Dreamweaver Help

Click to see topics

Keywords

Topics found with keywords

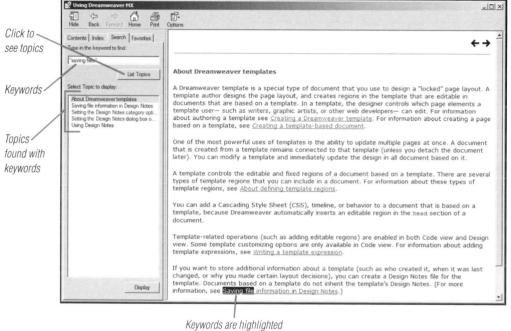

Keywords are highlighted in the text

Use Dreamweaver Help

1. Click Help on the menu bar, then click Using Dreamweaver.

2. Click the Search tab (Win).

3. Type **saving** in the Type in the keyword to find text box (Win) or type **saving** in the text box at the top of the Help window (Mac).

4. Click List Topics (Win), or Ask (Mac), then scroll down to view the topics.

5. Select saving in the keyword to find text box, type **"saving files"**, (be sure to type the quotation marks), then press [Enter] (Win) or [return] (Mac).

   Because you placed the keywords in quotation marks, Dreamweaver shows only the topics that contain the exact phrase "saving files." Topics that contain the individual words "saving" or "files" are not listed.

6. Double-click About Dreamweaver templates in the topic list.

   Information on Dreamweaver templates appears in the right frame, as shown in Figure A-9.

   TIP If you don't see the topic About Dreamweaver templates, double-click a different topic (Mac).

7. Scroll down and scan the text.

   The search words you used are highlighted in the Help text. Help will find both the exact words you enter and the derivatives of the words you enter.

8. Click Close (Win) or Quit (Mac).

You used the Dreamweaver Help files to read information about Dreamweaver templates.

PLAN AND DEFINE A WEB SITE

What You'll Do

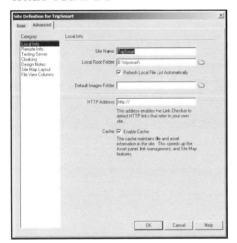

In this lesson, you will review a Web site plan for TripSmart, a full-service travel outfitter. You will also create a root folder for the TripSmart Web site, and then define the Web site.

Understanding the Web Site Creation Process

Creating a Web site is a complex process. It can often involve a large team of people working in various roles to ensure that the Web site contains accurate information, looks good, and works smoothly. Figure A-10 illustrates the steps involved in creating a Web site.

Planning a Web Site

Planning is probably the most important part of any successful project. Planning is an *essential* part of creating a Web site, and is a continuous process that overlaps the subsequent phases. To start planning your Web site, you need to create a checklist of questions and answers about the site. For example, what are your goals for

Understanding IP addresses and domain names

To be accessible over the Internet, a Web site must be published to a Web server with a permanent IP address. An **IP address** is an assigned series of numbers, separated by periods, that designate an address on the Internet. To access a Web page, you can enter either an IP address or a domain name in the address text box of your browser window. A **domain name** is a Web address that is expressed in letters instead of numbers, and usually reflects the name of the business represented by the Web site. For example, the domain name of the Macromedia Web site is *www.macromedia.com*, but the IP address would read something like 123.456.789.123. Because domain names use descriptive text instead of numbers, they are much easier to remember. Compare an IP address to your Social Security number and a domain name to your name. Both your Social Security number and your name are used to refer to you as a person, but your name is much easier for your friends and family to use than your Social Security number. You can type the IP address or the domain name in the address text box of the browser window to access a Web site.

Getting Started with Dreamweaver

the Web site? Who is the audience you want to target? Teenagers? Senior Citizens? How can you design the site to appeal to the target audience? The more questions you can answer about the site, the more prepared you will be when you begin the developmental phase. Because of the public demand for "instant" information, your plan should include not just how to get the site up and running, but how to keep it current. Table A-1 lists some of the basic questions you need to answer during the planning phase for almost any type of Web site. In addition to a checklist, you should also create a timeline and a budget for the Web site.

Setting up the Basic Structure

Once you complete the planning phase, you need to set up the structure of the site by creating a storyboard. A **storyboard** is a small sketch that represents every page in a Web site. Like a flowchart, a storyboard shows the relationship of each page in the Web site to all the other pages. Storyboards

FIGURE A-10

Steps in creating a Web site

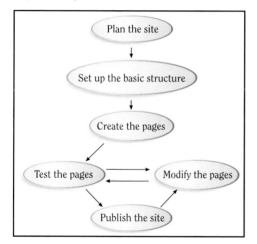

TABLE A-1: Web Site Planning Checklist

question	examples
1. Who is the target audience?	Seniors, teens, children
2. How can I tailor the Web site to reach that audience?	Specify an appropriate reading level, decide the optimal amount of multimedia content, use formal or casual language
3. What are the goals for the site?	Sell a product, provide information
4. How will I gather the information?	Recruit other company employees, write it myself, use content from in-house documents
5. What are my sources for multimedia content?	Internal production department, outside production company, my own photographs
6. What is my budget?	Very limited, well financed
7. How long do I have to complete the project?	Two weeks, 1 month, 6 months
8. Who is on my project team?	Just me, a complete staff of designers
9. How often should the site be updated?	Every 10 minutes, once a month
10.Who is responsible for updating the site?	Me, other team members

are very helpful when planning a Web site, because they allow you to visualize how each page in the site is linked to others. You can sketch a storyboard using a pencil and paper or using a graphics program on a computer. The storyboard shown in Figure A-11 shows all the pages that will be contained in the TripSmart Web site that you will create in this book. Notice that the home page appears at the top of the storyboard, and has four pages linked to it. The home page is called the **parent page**, because it is at a higher level in the Web hierarchy and has pages linked to it. The pages linked to it below are called **child pages**. The Catalog page, which is a child page to the home page, is also a parent page to the Accessories and Clothing pages. You can refer to this storyboard as you create the actual links in Dreamweaver.

QUICKTIP

You can create a storyboard on a computer using a software program such as Word, Paint, Paintshop Pro, or Macromedia Freehand. You might find it easier to make changes to a computer-generated storyboard than to one created on paper.

In addition to creating a storyboard for your site, you should also create a folder hierarchy for all of the files that will be used in the Web site. Start by creating a folder for the Web site with a descriptive name, such as the name of the company. This folder, known as the **root folder**, will store all the Web pages or HTML files for the site. Then create a subfolder called **assets** in which you store all of the files that are not Web pages, such as images and video clips. You should avoid using spaces, special characters, or uppercase characters in your folder names.

FIGURE A-11
TripSmart Web site storyboard

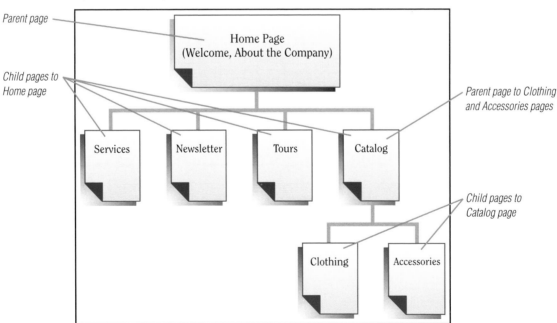

After you create the root folder, you need to define your Web site. When you **define** a Web site, the root folder and any folders and files it contains appears in the **Site panel**, the panel you use to manage your Web site's files and folders. Using the Site panel to manage your files ensures that the site links work correctly when the Web site is published. You also use the Site panel to add or delete pages.

Creating the Web Pages and Collecting the Page Content

This is the fun part! After you create your storyboard, you need to gather the files that will be used to create the pages, including text, graphics, buttons, video, and animation. Some of these files will come from other software programs, and some will be created in Dreamweaver. For example, you can create text in a word-processing program and insert it into Dreamweaver or you can create and format text in Dreamweaver. Graphics, tables, colors, and horizontal rules all contribute to making a page attractive and interesting. In choosing your elements, however, you should always carefully consider the file size of each page. A page with too many graphical elements might take a long time to load, which could cause visitors to leave your Web site. Before you actually add content to each

page, however, you need to use the Site panel to add all the pages to the site according to the structure you specified in your storyboard. Once all the blank pages are in place, you can add the content you collected.

Testing the Pages

Once all your pages are completed, you need to test the site to make sure all the links work and that everything looks good. It is important to test your Web pages using different browser software. The two most common browsers are Microsoft Internet Explorer and Netscape Navigator. You should also test your Web site using different versions of each browser. Older versions of Internet Explorer and Netscape Navigator do not support the latest Web technology. You should also test your Web site using a variety of screen sizes. Some viewers may have small monitors, while others may have large, high-resolution monitors. You should also consider modem speed. Although more people use cable modems or DSL (Digital Subscriber Line) these days, some still use slower dial-up modems. Testing is a continuous process, for which you should allocate plenty of time.

Modifying the Pages

After you create a Web site, you'll probably find that you need to keep making changes

to it, especially when information on the site needs to be updated. Each time you make a change, such as adding a new button or graphic to a page, you should test the site again. Modifying and testing pages in a Web site is an ongoing process.

Publishing the Site

Publishing a Web site means that you transfer all the files for the site to a **Web server**, a computer that is connected to the Internet with an IP (Internet Protocol) address, so that it is available for viewing on the Internet. A Web site must be published or users of the World Wide Web cannot view it. There are several options for publishing a Web site. For instance, many Internet Service Providers (ISPs) provide space on their servers for customers to publish Web sites and some commercial Web sites provide limited free space for their viewers. Although publishing happens at the end of the process, it's a good idea to set up Web server access in the planning phase. You use the Site panel to transfer your files using the FTP (**File Transfer Protocol**) capability. FTP is the process of uploading and downloading files to and from a remote site.

Create a root folder (Windows)

1. Click the Start button on the taskbar, point to Programs, point to Accessories, then click Windows Explorer. *Start*

2. Navigate to the drive and folder where you will create a folder to store your files for the TripSmart Web site.

3. Click File on the menu bar, point to New, then click Folder.

4. Type **tripsmart** to rename the folder, then press [Enter] as shown in Figure A-12.

   > TIP Your desktop will look different than Figure A-12 if you are not using Windows XP.

5. Close Windows Explorer.

You created a new folder to serve as the root folder for the TripSmart Web site.

FIGURE A-12

Creating a root folder using Windows Explorer

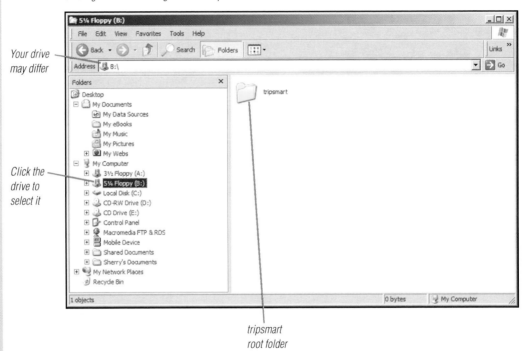

Your drive may differ

Click the drive to select it

tripsmart root folder

FIGURE A-13

Creating a root folder using a Macintosh

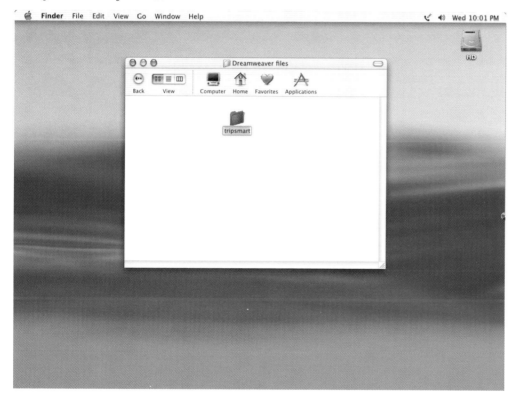

1. Double-click the Macintosh hard drive, then double-click the folder where you will create a folder to store your data files to open it.

2. Click File on the menu bar, then click New Folder.

3. Type **tripsmart** to rename the folder, as shown in Figure A-13.

   TIP   If you cannot type a new folder name, click the current folder name once to highlight it, then type a new folder name.

You created a new folder to serve as the root folder for the TripSmart Web site.

Define a Web site

1. Return to Dreamweaver, click Site on the menu bar, then click New Site.

2. Click the Advanced tab if necessary, then type **TripSmart** in the Site Name text box.

   | TIP   It is acceptable to use uppercase letters in the site name because it is not the name of a folder or a file.

3. Click the Browse for File icon next to the Local Root Folder text box, click the Select list arrow (Win) or click the From list arrow (Mac) in the Choose Local Folder dialog box, click the drive and folder where your data files are stored, then click the tripsmart folder. 📁

4. Click Open (Win) or Choose (Mac), then click Select.

5. Verify that the Refresh Local File List Automatically and the Enable Cache check boxes are both checked, as shown in Figure A-14, then click OK.

   Clicking Enable Cache tells Dreamweaver to use your computer's temporary memory, or **cache**, while you work. The Refresh Local File List Automatically tells Dreamweaver to automatically display changes you make in your file lists, which eliminates the need to use the Refresh command.

You created a Web site and defined it with the name TripSmart. You verified that both the Refresh Local Files List Automatically and the Enable Cache options were enabled in the Site Definition dialog box.

FIGURE A-14
Site Definition dialog box

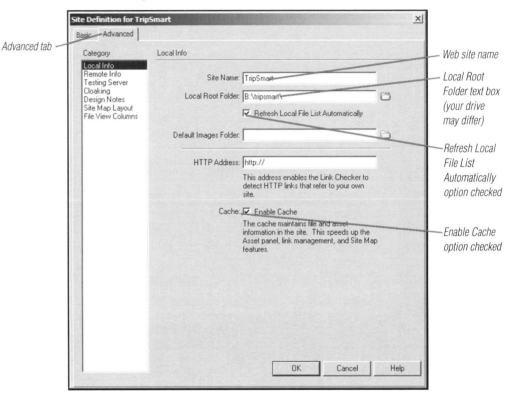

Advanced tab

Web site name

Local Root Folder text box (your drive may differ)

Refresh Local File List Automatically option checked

Enable Cache option checked

FIGURE A-15

Setting up remote access for the TripSmart Web site

Remote Info

Your instructor will provide you with this information

Access list arrow

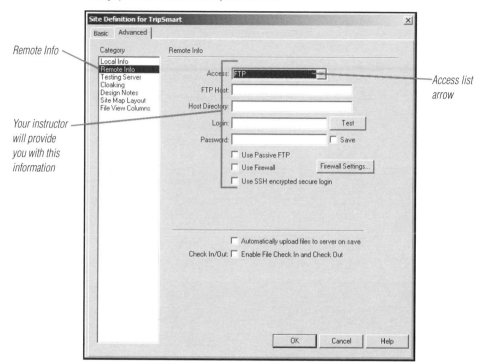

Set up Web server access

1. Click Site on the menu bar, then click Edit Sites.

2. Click TripSmart in the Edit Sites dialog box (if necessary), then click Edit.

3. Click the Advanced tab (if necessary), click Remote Info in the Category list, click the Access list arrow, then choose the method you will use to publish your Web site.

   > TIP Your instructor will provide you with this information. If you do not have the information to publish your Web site, choose None in the Site Definition dialog box. You can specify this information later.

4. Enter the necessary information in the Site Definition dialog box shown in Figure A-15, filling in the blanks with information from your instructor, click OK, then click Done.

You set up the remote access information to prepare you for publishing your Web site.

Understanding the process of publishing a Web site

Before publishing a Web site so that viewers of the Web can access it, you should first create a local root folder, called the **local site**, to house all the files for your Web site. Next, you need to gain access to a remote server. A **remote server** is a Web server that hosts Web sites and is not directly connected to the computer housing the local site. Many Internet Services Providers, or ISPs, provide space for publishing Web pages on their servers. Once you have access to a remote server, you can then use the Site Definition Remote Info dialog box to enter information such as the FTP host, host directory, login, and password. After entering this information, you can then use the Put File(s) icon in the Site panel to transfer the files to the designated remote server. Once the site is published to a remote server, it is called a **remote site**.

ADD A FOLDER AND PAGES
AND SET THE HOME PAGE

What You'll Do

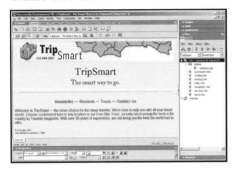

 In this lesson, you will use the Site panel to set the home page. You'll also create a new folder and new pages for the Web site.

Adding a Folder to a Web Site

After defining a Web site, you need to create folders to organize the files that will make up the Web site. Creating a folder called **assets** is a good beginning. You can use the assets folder to store all non-HTML files, such as pictures or sound files. After you create the assets folder, it is a good idea to set it as the default location to store the Web site images. This saves a step when you import new images into the Web site.

Creating an effective navigation structure

When you create a Web site, it's important to consider how your viewers will navigate from page to page within the site. A navigation bar is a critical tool for moving around a Web site, so it's important that all text, buttons, and icons used in a navigation bar have a consistent look across all pages. If a complex navigation bar is used, such as one that incorporates JavaScript, it's a good idea to include plain text links in another location on the page for accessibility. Otherwise, viewers might become confused or lost within the site. A navigation structure can include more links than those included in a navigation bar, however. For instance, it can contain other sets of links that relate to the content of a specific page and which are placed at the bottom or sides of a page in a different format. No matter what navigation structure you use, make sure that every page includes a link back to the home page. Don't make viewers rely on the Back button on the browser toolbar to find their way back to the home page. It's possible that the viewer's current page might have opened as a result of a search and clicking the Back button will take the viewer out of the Web site.

Setting the Home Page

The home page of a Web site is the first page that viewers see when they visit your Web site. Most Web sites contain many other pages that all connect back to the home page. Dreamweaver uses the home page that you have designated as a starting point for creating a site map, a graphical representation of the Web pages in a Web site. When you set the home page, you tell Dreamweaver which page you have designated to be your home page. You set the home page in the Define Sites dialog box. The home page filename usually has the name index.htm.

Adding Pages to a Web Site

Web sites might be as simple as one page or might contain hundreds of pages. When you create a Web site, you need to add all the pages and specify where they should be placed in the Web site folder structure in the root folder. Once you add and name all the pages in the Web site, you can then add the content, such as text and graphics, to each page. It is better to add as many "empty" pages as you think you will need in the beginning, rather than adding them one at a time with all the content in place. This will enable you to set up the navigation structure of the Web site at the beginning of the development process, and view how each page is linked to others. When you are satisfied with the overall structure, you can then add the content to each page.

Using the Site panel for file management

You can use the Site panel to add, delete, move, or rename files and folders in a Web site. It is very important that you perform these file maintenance tasks in the Site panel rather than in Windows Explorer (Windows) or in the Finder (Mac). Dreamweaver will not recognize any changes you make to the Web site folder structure outside the Site panel. You use Windows Explorer (Win) or the Finder (Mac) only to create the root folder or to move or copy the root folder of a Web site to another location. If you move or copy the root folder to a new location, you will have to define the Web site again in the Site panel, as you did in Lesson 3 of this unit.

Add a folder to a Web site (Windows)

1. Click File on the Site panel menu bar, then click New Folder.

2. Type **assets** in the folder text box, then press [Enter].

3. Compare your screen with Figure A-16.

You used the Site panel to create a new folder in the tripsmart folder, and named it assets.

Add a folder to a Web site (Macintosh)

1. Click Window on the menu bar, click Site to open the Site panel (if necessary), press and hold [Ctrl], click the tripsmart folder, and then click New Folder.

2. Click the triangle to the left of the tripsmart folder to open it (if necessary), then click untitled on the new folder, type **assets** as the folder name, then press [return].

   TIP You will not see the new folder until you expand the tripsmart folder by clicking the triangle to the left of the tripsmart folder (Mac).

3. Compare your screen with Figure A-17.

You used the Site panel, to create a new folder under the tripsmart folder, and named it assets.

FIGURE A-16

TripSmart site in Site panel with assets folder created (Windows)

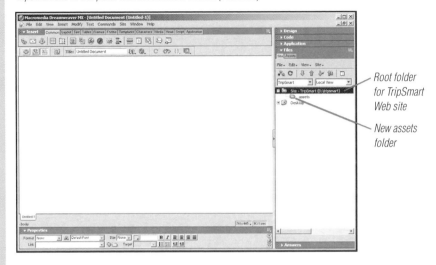

Root folder for TripSmart Web site

New assets folder

FIGURE A-17

TripSmart site in Site panel with assets folder created (Macintosh)

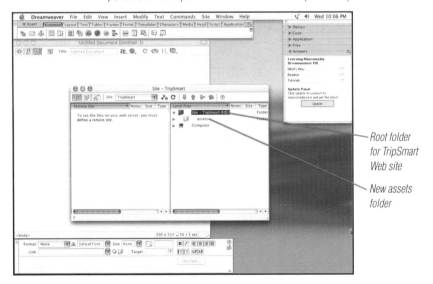

Root folder for TripSmart Web site

New assets folder

FIGURE A-18

Site Definition for TripSmart with assets folder set as the default images folder

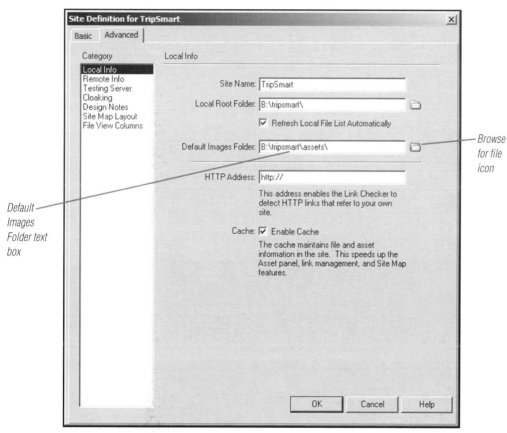

Default Images Folder text box

Browse for file icon

Set the default images folder

1. Click Site on the menu bar, click Edit Sites, select TripSmart if necessary, then click Edit.

2. Click the Browse for File icon next to the Default Images Folder text box.

3. Navigate to the folder where your Web site files are stored, double-click the tripsmart folder (Win), or click the tripsmart folder (Mac), double-click the assets folder (Win), or click the assets folder (Mac), then click Select (Win) or Choose (Mac).

   Compare your screen to Figure A-18.

4. Click OK, then click Done.

You set the assets folder as the default images folder so that imported images will be automatically saved in it.

Set the home page

1. Open the file dwa_2.htm from the unit_a folder where your data files are stored.

2. Click File on the menu bar, click Save As, click the Save in list arrow (Win) or the Where list arrow (Mac), navigate to the tripsmart folder, type **index.htm** in the File name text box (Win), or Save As text box (Mac), then click Save.

   See Figure A-19. The title bar now displays the page title, TripSmart - The Smart Way to Go, followed by the root folder (tripsmart) and the name of the page (index.htm) in parentheses. The information within the parentheses is called the **path**, or location of the open file in relation to other folders in the Web site.

3. Click index.htm in the Site panel to select it, click Site on the Site panel menu bar, then click Set as Home Page (Win), or click Site on the menu bar, point to Site Map View, then click Set as Home Page (Mac).

   TIP If you want your screen to match the figures in this book, make sure the document window is maximized.

You opened a file, saved it with the filename index.htm, and set it as the home page.

index.htm placed in the tripsmart root folder

Page title and path for file

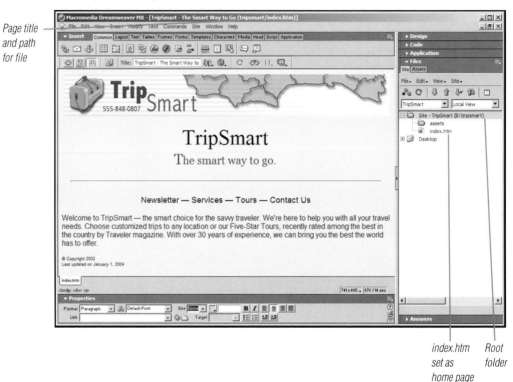

index.htm set as home page   Root folder

FIGURE A-20

Property inspector showing properties of the TripSmart banner

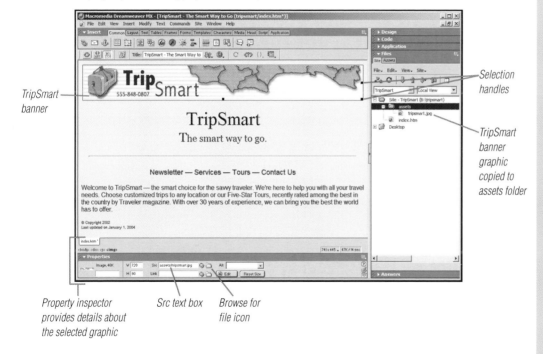

TripSmart banner

Selection handles

TripSmart banner graphic copied to assets folder

Property inspector provides details about the selected graphic

Src text box

Browse for file icon

1. Click the TripSmart banner to select it.

   The Src text box in the Property inspector displays the current location of the selected banner.

2. Click the Browse for File icon next to the Src text box in the Property inspector, click the Look in list arrow (Win) or From list arrow (Mac), navigate to the unit_a assets folder, click tripsmart.jpg, then click OK (Win), or Choose (Mac).

   The TripSmart banner is automatically copied to the assets folder of the TripSmart Web site, the folder that you designated as the default images folder. The Src text box now shows the path of the banner to the assets folder in the Web site.

3. Compare your screen to Figure A-20.

   > TIP If you see a small gold icon next to the banner, click View on the menu bar, point to Visual Aids, then click Invisible Elements.

   Until you copy a graphic from an outside folder to your Web site, the graphic is not part of the Web site and the image will appear as a broken link on the page when the Web site is copied to a remote site.

You copied the TripSmart banner to the assets folder.

Add pages to a Web site (Windows)

1. Click the plus sign to the left of the assets folder (if necessary) to open the folder and view its contents, tripsmart.jpg.

   TIP If you do not see any contents in the assets folder, click View on the Site panel menu bar, then click Refresh.

2. Click the tripsmart root folder to select it, click File on the Site panel menu bar, click New File, type **catalog.htm** to replace untitled.htm, then press [Enter].

   TIP If you create a new file in the Site panel, you must type the filename extension (.htm or .html) manually.

3. Repeat Step 2 to add five more blank pages to the TripSmart Web site, and name the new files services.htm, tours.htm, newsletter.htm, clothing.htm, and accessories.htm.

   TIP Make sure to add the new files to the root folder, not the assets folder. If you accidentally add them to the assets folder, just drag them to the root folder.

4. Click the Refresh button on the Site panel, then compare your screen to Figure A-21. C

You added the following six pages to the TripSmart Web site: catalog, services, tours, newsletter, clothing, and accessories.

FIGURE A-21

New pages added to the TripSmart Web site (Windows)

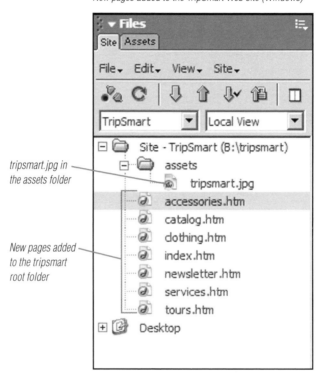

tripsmart.jpg in the assets folder

New pages added to the tripsmart root folder

FIGURE A-22

New pages added to the TripSmart Web site

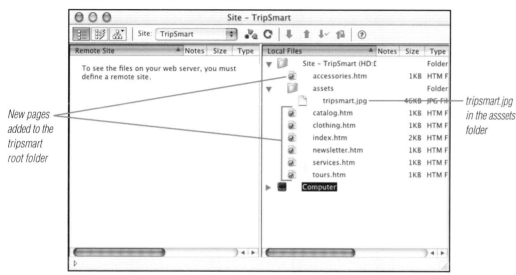

New pages added to the tripsmart root folder

tripsmart.jpg in the asssets folder

1. Click Site on the menu bar, then click Open Site to open the site panel.

2. Click the triangle to the left of the assets folder to open the folder and view its contents.

    TIP If you do not see any contents in the assets folder, click Site on the menu bar, then click Refresh.

3. Click the tripsmart root folder to select it.

4. Click Site on the menu bar, point to Site Files View, click New File, type **catalog.htm** to replace untitled.html, then press [return].

    TIP If you create a new file in the Site panel, you must type the filename extension (.htm or .html) manually.

5. Repeat Step 4 to add five more blank pages to the TripSmart Web site, and name the new files **services.htm**, **tours.htm**, **newsletter.htm**, **clothing.htm**, and **accessories.htm**.

6. Click Site on the menu bar, click Refresh to list the files alphabetically, then compare your screen to Figure A-22.

You added six pages to the TripSmart Web site: catalog, services, tours, newsletter, clothing, and accessories.

CREATE AND VIEW A SITE MAP

What You'll Do

In this lesson, you will create and view a site map for the TripSmart Web site.

Creating a Site Map

As you add new Web pages to a Web site, it is easy to lose track of how they all link together. You can use the site map feature to help you keep track of the relationships between pages in a Web site. A **site map** is a graphical representation of the pages in the Web site and shows the folder structure for the Web site. You can find out details about each page by viewing the visual clues in the site map. For example, the site map uses icons to indicate pages with broken links, e-mail links, and links to external Web sites. It also indicates which pages are currently **checked out**, or being used by other team members.

Viewing a Site Map

You can view a site map using the Site Map command, or the Map View command. You can expand the Site panel to display both the site map and the Web site file list. You can specify that the site map show a filename or a page title for each page. You can also edit page titles in the site map. Figure A-23 shows the site map and file list for the TripSmart Web site. Only the home page and pages that are linked to the home page will display in the site map. As more child pages are added, the site map will display them using a

Verifying page titles

When you view a Web page in a browser, its page title is displayed in the browser window title bar. The page title should reflect the page content and set the tone for the page. It is especially important to use words in your page title that are likely to match keywords viewers may enter when using a search engine. Search engines compare the text in page titles to the keywords typed into the search engine. When a title bar displays "Untitled Document," the designer has neglected to give the page a title. This is like giving up free "billboard space," and looks very unprofessional.

tree structure, or a diagram that visually represents the way the pages are linked to each other.

Using Site Map Images in Web Pages

It is very helpful to include a graphic of the site map in a Web site to help viewers understand the navigation structure of the site. Using Dreamweaver, you have the options of saving a site map for printing purposes or for displaying a site map on a page in a Web site. Windows users can save site maps as either a BMP (bitmapped) file or as a PNG (Portable Network Graphics) file. The BMP format is the best format to use for printing the site map or inserting it into a page layout program or slide show. The PNG format is best for inserting the site map on a Web page. Macintosh users can save site maps as PICT or JPEG file. The PICT format is the best format for printing the site map and inserting it into a page layout program or a slide show. The JPEG format is best for inserting the site map on a Web page. Though gaining in popularity, PNG files are not available on the Macintosh platform and are not supported by older versions of browsers. However, they are capable of showing millions of colors, are small in size, and compress well without losing image quality.

FIGURE A-23
The TripSmart site map

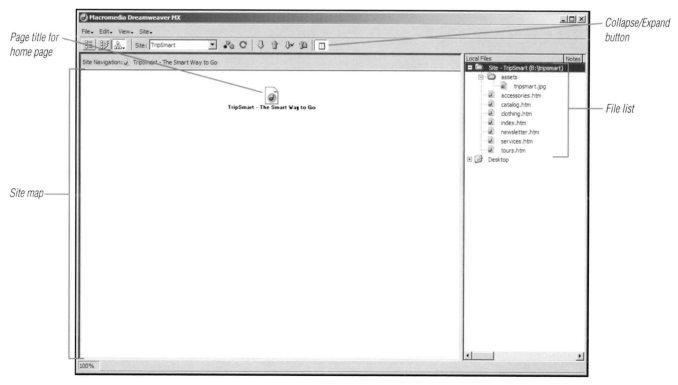

Select site map options

1. Click the Site list arrow in the Site panel, click Edit Sites, click TripSmart (if necessary), then click Edit to open the Site Definition dialog box.

2. Click Site Map Layout in the Category list.

3. Verify that index.htm is specified as the home page in the Home Page text box, as shown in Figure A-24.

   TIP   If the index.htm file is not specified as your home page, click the Browse for File icon next to the Home Page text box, then locate and double-click index.htm.

4. Click the Page Titles option button to select it (if necessary).

5. Click OK, then click Done.

You designated index.htm as the home page for the TripSmart Web site to create the site map. You also specified that page titles instead of filenames display in the site map.

FIGURE A-24
Options for the site map layout

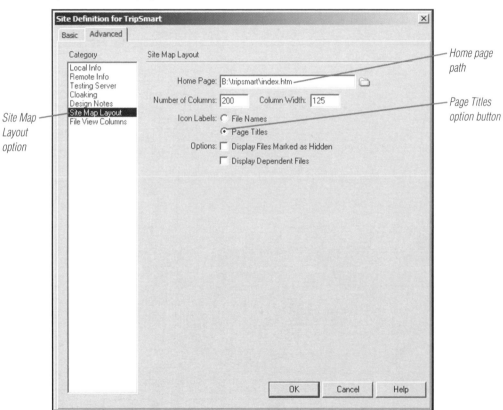

Site Map Layout option

Home page path

Page Titles option button

FIGURE A-25

Expanding the site map

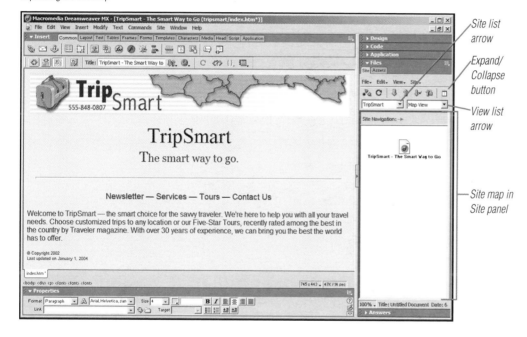

Site list arrow

Expand/ Collapse button

View list arrow

Site map in Site panel

1. Click the View list arrow on the Site panel, then click Map View (Win), or click the Site Map button (Mac).

2. Click the Expand/Collapse button on the Site panel toolbar, as shown in Figure A-25, to display the site map in the document window (Win). ▣

   The site map shows the home page and pages that are linked to it. Because there are no pages linked to the home page, the site map shows only the home page.

   > TIP You can drag the border between the two panes on the screen to resize them.

3. Click the Expand/Collapse button on the toolbar to collapse the site map. ▣

4. Click the View list arrow, then click Local View (Win). ▣

   The file list appears again in the Site panel.

You opened and closed the TripSmart site map in the Site panel.

Explore the Dreamweaver workspace.

1. Start Dreamweaver.
2. Change the view to Code view.
3. Change the view to Code and Design views.
4. Change the view to Design view.
5. Expand the Code panel group.
6. View each panel in the Code panel group.
7. Collapse the Code panel group.

View a Web page and use Help.

1. Open the file dwa_3.htm from the folder where your data files are stored.
2. Locate the following page elements: a table, a banner, a graphic, and some formatted text.
3. Change the view to Code view.
4. Change the view to Design view.
5. Use the Dreamweaver Help feature to search for information on panel groups.
6. Display and read one of the topics you find.
7. Close the Help window.
8. Close the page without saving it.

Plan and define a Web site.

1. Select the drive and folder where you will store your Web site files using Windows Explorer or Macintosh Finder.

2. Create a new root folder called **blooms**.
3. Close Explorer or Finder and activate the Dreamweaver window.
4. Create a new site called Blooms & Bulbs.
5. Specify the blooms folder as the Local Root folder.
6. Verify that the Refresh Local File List Automatically option and the Enable Cache option are both selected.
7. Use the Remote Info category in the Site Definition dialog box to set up Web server access by entering the information supplied to you by your instructor. (Specify None if you do not have the necessary information to set up Web server access.)
8. Close the Site Definition dialog box.

Add a folder and pages to a Web site and set the home page.

1. Create a new folder in the blooms root folder called **assets**.
2. Edit the site to set the assets folder as the default location for the Web site graphics.
3. Open the file dwa_4.htm from the folder where your data files are stored, then save this file in the blooms root folder as **index.htm**.

4. Set index.htm as the home page.
5. Select the banner on the page.
6. Use the Property inspector to browse for the file blooms.gif, and then save it in the assets folder of the Blooms & Bulbs Web site.
7. Create three new pages in the Site panel and name them: plants.htm, workshops.htm, and tips.htm.
8. Refresh the view to list the new files alphabetically.

Create and view a site map.

1. Use the Site Map Layout dialog box to verify that the index.htm file is shown as the home page.
2. Show the page titles.
3. View the expanded site map for the Web site and compare your screen to Figure A-26.
4. Save your work.

FIGURE A-26

Completed Skills Review

You have been hired to create a Web site for a river expedition company named Rapids Transit, located on the Buffalo River in Arkansas. In addition to renting canoes, kayaks, and rafts, they have a country store and a snack bar. If requested, river guides are available to accompany clients on float trips. The clients range from high school and college students to families to vacationing professionals. The owner, Mike Andrew, has requested a dynamic Web site that conveys the beauty of the Ozark Mountains and the Buffalo River.

1. Using the information in the paragraph above, create a storyboard for this Web site, using either a pencil and paper or a software program such as Microsoft Word. Include the home page with links to three child pages named guides.htm, rentals.htm, and store.htm.

2. Create a folder named **rapids** in the drive and folder where you store your Web site files.

3. Start Dreamweaver and define the Web site with the name **Rapids Transit**.

4. Create an assets folder and set it as the default location for images.

5. Open dwa_5.htm from the location where your data files are stored, then save it in the rapids root folder as index.htm.

6. Save the rapids.jpg file in the assets folder.

7. Set index.htm as the home page.

8. Create three additional pages for the site, and name them as follows: **guides.htm**, **rentals.htm**, and **store.htm**. Use your storyboard and Figure A-27 as a guide.

9. Refresh the Site panel.

10. Create a site map for the Web site, then save your work.

FIGURE A-27
Completed Project Builder 1

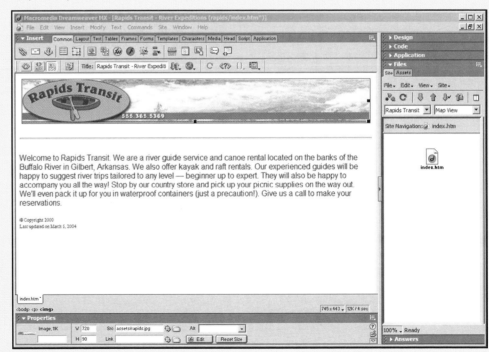

Your company has been selected to design a Web site for Jacob's, a new upscale restaurant in London that caters to business executives and theatre patrons. Jacob's has an extensive menu featuring French cuisine that includes set dinners and pre- and post-theatre dinner specials. They also like to feature some of their more popular recipes on their Web site. The chef, Jacob Richard, is famous in London for his creative cuisine and innovative culinary events.

1. Create a storyboard for this Web site that includes a home page and child pages called directions.htm, menus.htm, and recipes.htm.
2. Create a folder for the Web site in the drive and folder where you save your Web site files and name it **jacobs**.
3. Define the Web site with the name **Jacob's**.
4. Create an assets folder for the Web site and set the assets folder as the default location for images.
5. Open the file dwa_6.htm from the folder where your data files are stored, then save it as **index.htm** in the jacobs folder.
6. Save the jacobs.jpg file in the assets folder.
7. Set index.htm as the home page.
8. Using Figure A-28 and your storyboard as guides, create the additional pages shown for the Web site.
9. Create a site map that displays page titles, then save your work.

FIGURE A-28
Completed Project Builder 2

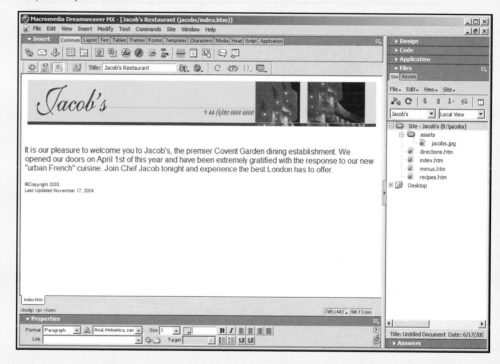

Figure A-29 shows the Audi Web site, a past selection for the Macromedia Site of the Day. To visit the current Audi Web site connect to the Internet, go to *www.course.com*, navigate to the page for this book, click the Student Online Companion link, then click the link for this unit. The current page might differ from the figure since dynamic Web sites are updated frequently to reflect current information. If you are viewing the Web page on a screen whose resolution is set to 800 × 600, you will see that the design fits very well. The main navigation structure is accessed through the images along the right side of the page. You can also click images in the center of the page to open new pages. You'll notice that as you place the pointer over an image, a tooltip appears with a description of the page that will open if the image is clicked. The page title is Audi World Site.

Go to the Macromedia Web site at *www.macromedia.com*, click the Visit Showcase link, then click the current Site of the Day. Explore the site and answer the following questions:

1. Do you see page titles for each page you visit?
2. Do the page titles accurately reflect the page content?

3. View the pages using more than one screen resolution, if possible. For which resolution does the site appear to be designed?
4. Is the navigation structure clear?

5. How is the navigation structure organized?
6. Why do you think this site was chosen as a Site of the Day?

FIGURE A-29
Design Project

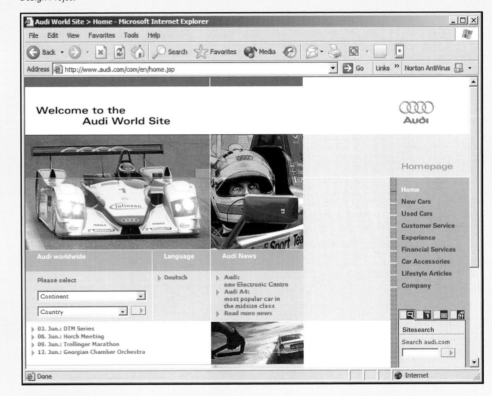

Work with a group to come up with a plan for a Web site that the group will create entirely on its own, without any data files. The focus of the Web site can be on any topic, organization, sports team, club, or company that you would like. Depending on the size of your group, you can assign individual elements of the project to group members, or work collectively to create the finished product. You will build on this Web site from unit to unit, so you must do each Group Project assignment in each unit to complete your Web site.

1. Decide among your members what type of Web site you would like to create. It can be a personal Web site about your class or school, a business Web site that promotes a fictitious or real company, or an informational Web site that provides information about a topic, cause, or organization. Your instructor may direct your choices for this assignment.

2. With the whole group participating, write a list of questions and answers about the Web site you have decided to create. Assign team members questions and have them report back to the group with answers.

3. Brainstorm as a group to construct a storyboard for your Web site to include at least four pages. The storyboard should include the home page with at least three child pages under it. Assign a team member the task of creating the storyboard.

4. Assign a team member the task of creating a root folder and an assets folder to house the Web site assets and set it as the default location for images.

5. Create a blank page named index.htm as a placeholder for the home page and set it as the home page.

6. Assign team members to collect content, such as pictures or text to use in your Web site. You can use a digital camera to take photos, scan pictures, or create your own graphics using a program such as Macromedia Fireworks. Gather the content in a central location that is accessible to the team as you develop your site.

UNIT B

DEVELOPING A WEB PAGE

1. Create head content and set page properties.

2. Create, import, and format text.

3. Add links to Web pages.

4. Use the History panel and Code Inspector.

5. Modify and test Web pages.

UNIT B
DEVELOPING A WEB PAGE

Introduction

The process of developing a Web page requires several steps. If the page is a home page, you need to decide on the head content. The head content contains information used by search engines to help viewers find your Web site. You also need to choose the colors for the page background as well as the links. You then need to add the page content and format it attractively, and add links to other pages in the Web site or to other Web sites. To ensure that all links work correctly and are current, you need to test them regularly.

Understanding Page Layout

Before you add content to a page, consider the following guidelines for laying out pages:

Use White Space Effectively. A living room crammed with too much furniture makes it difficult to appreciate the individual pieces. The same is true of a Web page. Too many text blocks, links, and images can be distracting. Consider leaving some white space on each page. White space, which is not necessarily white, is the area on a Web page that contains no text or graphics.

Limit Multimedia Elements. Too many multimedia elements, such as graphics, video clips, or sounds, may result in a page that takes too much time to load. Viewers may leave your Web site before the entire page finishes loading. Use multimedia elements only if you have a good reason.

Keep it Simple. Often the simplest Web sites are the most appealing and are also the easiest to create and maintain. A simple Web site that works well is far superior to a complex one that contains errors.

Use an Intuitive Navigation Structure. Make sure the navigation structure is easy to use. Viewers should always know where they are in the site and be able to find their way back to the home page. If viewers get lost, they may leave the site rather than struggle to find their way around.

Apply a Consistent Theme. To help give pages in your Web site a consistent appearance, consider designing your pages using elements that relate to a common theme.

Tools You'll Use

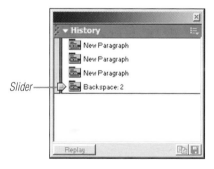

Slider

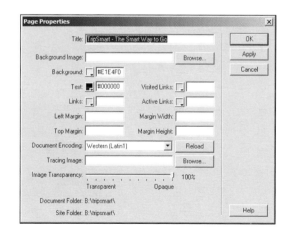

CREATE HEAD CONTENT AND SET PAGE PROPERTIES

What You'll Do

 In this lesson, you will learn how to enter titles, keywords, and descriptions in the head content section of a Web page. You will also change the background color for a Web page.

Creating the Head Content

A Web page is composed of two distinct sections: the head content and the body. The **head content** includes the page title that is displayed in the title bar of the browser and some important page elements, called meta tags, that are not visible in the browser. **Meta tags** are HTML codes that include information about the page, such as keywords and descriptions.

Keywords are words that relate to the content of the Web site. A **description** is a short paragraph that describes the content and features of the Web site. For instance, "travel" and "tours" would be appropriate keywords for the TripSmart Web site. It is important to include concise, useful information in the head content, because search engines find Web pages by matching the title, description, and keywords in

Using Web-Safe Colors

Before 1994, colors appeared differently on different types of computers. For instance, if a designer chose a particular shade of red in a document created on a Windows computer, he or she could not be certain that the same shade of red would appear on a Macintosh computer. In 1994, Netscape developed the first **Web-safe color palette**, a set of colors that appears consistently in all browsers and on Macintosh, Windows, and Unix platforms. If you want your Web pages to be viewed across a wide variety of computer platforms, make sure you choose Web-safe colors for all your page elements. Dreamweaver has two Web-safe color palettes, Color Cubes and Continuous Tones, each of which contains 216 Web-safe colors. Color Cubes is the default color palette. To choose a different color palette, click Modify on the menu bar, click Page Properties, click the Background, Text, or Links color box to open the color picker, click the Color Palette list arrow, then click the color palette you want.

the head content of Web pages with keywords that viewers enter in search engine text boxes. The **body** is the part of the page that appears in a browser window. It contains all the page content that is visible to viewers, such as text, graphics, and links.

Setting Web Page Properties

When you create a Web page, one of the first design decisions that you should make is choosing the **background color**, or the color that fills the entire Web page. The background color should complement the colors used for text, links, and graphics that are placed on the page. A strong

contrast between the text color and the background color makes it easier for viewers to read the text on your Web page. You can choose a light background color and a dark text color, or a dark background color and a light text color. A white background with dark text, though not terribly exciting, provides good contrast and is the easiest to read for most viewers. The next important design decision you need to make is to choose the **default font** and **default link colors**, which are the colors used by the browser to display text, links, and visited links. The default color for **unvisited links**, or links that the viewer has not clicked yet,

is blue. In Dreamweaver, unvisited links are simply called **links**. The default color for **visited links**, or links that have been previously clicked, is purple. You change the background color, text, and link colors using the color picker in the Page Properties dialog box. You can choose colors from one of the five Dreamweaver color palettes, as shown in Figure B-1.

QUICK**TIP**

Not all browsers recognize link color settings.

FIGURE B-1
Color picker showing color palettes

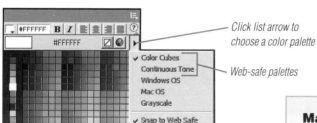

Click list arrow to
choose a color palette

Web-safe palettes

Making pages accessible to viewers of all abilities

Never assume that all your viewers have perfect vision and hearing or full use of both hands. There are several techniques you can use to ensure that your Web site is accessible to individuals with disabilities. These techniques include using alternate text with graphic images, avoiding certain colors on Web pages, and supplying text as an alternate source for information that is presented in an audio file. You can test your Web site for accessibility before publishing it by submitting it to be tested by Bobby, a free service provided by CAST, the Center for Applied Special Technology. The Web site address for information about Bobby is *www.cast.org/bobby/*. Macromedia also provides a vehicle for testing Web site compliance with Section 508 accessibility guidelines. For more information, visit the Macromedia Web site at http://*www.macromedia.com/macromedia/accessibility/*.

Edit a page title

1. Click the Site pop-up menu on the Site panel, then click TripSmart (if necessary).

   If you do not have the completed TripSmart site from Unit A, contact your instructor.

2. Double-click index.htm in the Site panel to open the TripSmart home page, click View on the menu bar, then click Head Content.

   The Title icon and Meta icon are now visible in the head content section, as shown in Figure B-2.

3. Click the Title icon in the head content section.

   The page title TripSmart - The Smart Way To Go appears in the Title text box in the Property inspector.

4. Select TripSmart - The Smart Way To Go in the Title text box in the Property inspector, type **TripSmart - Serving All Your Travel Needs**, then press [Enter] (Win) or [return] (Mac).

   Compare your screen with Figure B-3. The new title is better, because it incorporates the word "travel," a word that potential customers might use as a keyword when using a search engine.

   TIP You can also change the page title using the Title text box on the Document toolbar.

5. Click File on the menu bar, then click Save to save your work.

You opened the TripSmart Web site, opened the home page in Design view, opened the head content section, changed the page title, and saved your work.

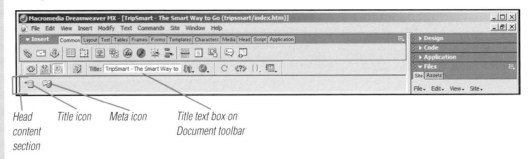

Head content section   Title icon   Meta icon   Title text box on Document toolbar

FIGURE B-3
Property inspector displaying new page title

Planning the page layout

When you begin developing the content for your Web site, you need to decide what content to include and how to arrange each element on each page. You must design the content with the audience in mind. What is the age group of your audience? What reading level is appropriate? Should you use a formal or informal tone? Should the pages be simple, containing mostly text, or rich with images and multimedia files? Usually the first page that your audience will see when they visit your Web site is the home page. The home page should be designed so that viewers will feel "at home," and comfortable finding their way around the pages in your site. To ensure that viewers do not get lost in your Web site, make sure you design all the pages with a consistent look and feel. You can use templates to maintain a common look for each page. **Templates** are Web pages that contain the basic layout for each page in the site, including the location of a company logo or a menu of buttons.

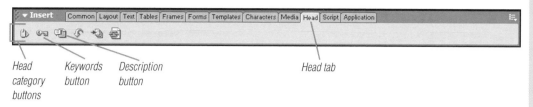

Head category buttons   *Keywords button*   *Description button*   *Head tab*

Enter keywords

1. Click the Head tab on the Insert bar, then click the Keywords button on the Insert bar as shown in Figure B-4.

2. Type **travel**, **traveling**, **supplies**, **trips**, **vacations** in the Keywords text box, as shown in Figure B-5, then click OK.

3. Save your work.

You added keywords relating to travel to the head content of the TripSmart home page.

FIGURE B-5
Keywords dialog box

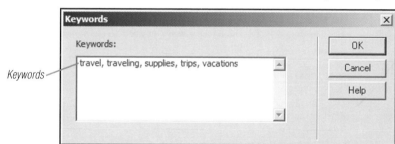

Keywords

Entering keywords and descriptions

Search engines use keywords, descriptions, and titles to find pages after a user enters search terms. Therefore, it is very important to anticipate the search terms your potential customers would use and include these words in the keywords, description, or title. Many search engines display page titles and descriptions in their search results. Some search engines limit the number of keywords that they will index, so make sure you list the most important keywords first. Keep your keywords and description concise to ensure that all search engines will include your site.

Enter a description

1. Click the Description button on the Insert bar.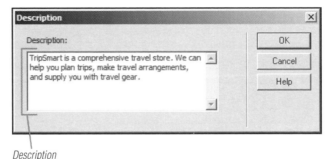

2. Type **TripSmart is a comprehensive travel store. We can help you plan trips, make travel arrangements, and supply you with travel gear.**

   Compare your screen with Figure B-6.

3. Click OK.

4. Click the Show Code View button on the Document toolbar.

   Notice the title, keywords, and description appear in the HTML code in the document window, as shown in Figure B-7.

5. Click the Show Design View button to return to Design view.

6. Click View on the menu bar, then click Head Content to close the Head Content section.

7. Save your work.

You added a description of the TripSmart company to the head content of the home page. You then viewed the home page in Code view and examined the HTML code for the head content.

FIGURE B-6
Description dialog box

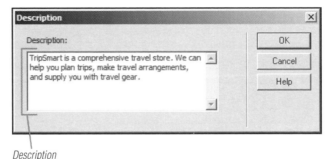

Description

FIGURE B-7
Head Content displayed in Code view

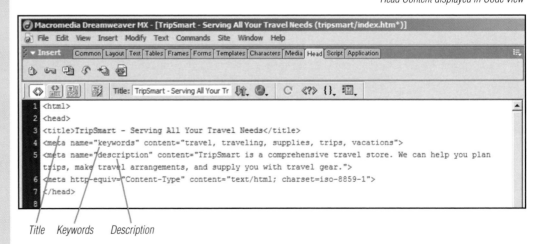

Title   Keywords   Description

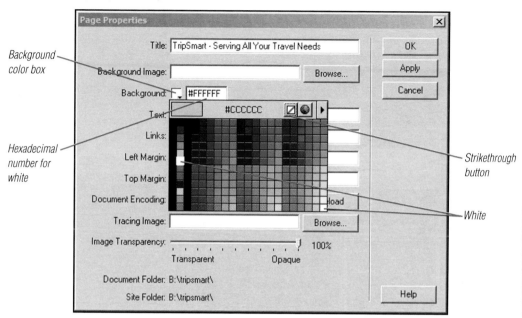

Background color box

Hexadecimal number for white

Strikethrough button

White

1. Click Modify on the menu bar, then click Page Properties to open the Page Properties dialog box.

2. Click the Background color box to open the color picker, as shown in Figure B-8.

3. Click the last color in the bottom row (white).

4. Click Apply, then click OK.

   Clicking Apply lets you see the changes you made to the Web page without closing the Page Properties dialog box. Clicking OK makes the changes you specified, then closes the dialog box.

   > TIP If you don't like the color you chose, click the Strikethrough button in the Page to switch back to the default color.

5. Save your work.

   The background color of the Web page is now white. The black text against the white background provides a nice contrast and makes the text easy to read.

   You used the Page Properties dialog box to change the background color to white.

Understanding hexadecimal values

Each color is assigned a **hexadecimal value**, a value that represents the amount of red, green, and blue present in the color. For example, white, which is made of equal parts of red, green, and blue, has a hexadecimal value of FFFFFF. Each pair of characters in the hexadecimal value represents the red, green, and blue values. The hexadecimal number system is based on 16, rather than 10 in the decimal number system. Since the hexadecimal number system includes only numbers up to 9, values after 9 use the letters of the alphabet. A represents the number 10 in the hexadecimal number system. F represents the number 15.

CREATE, IMPORT AND FORMAT TEXT

What You'll Do

 In this lesson, you will apply heading styles and text styles to text on the TripSmart home page. You will also create a new page and import an HTML file created in Microsoft Word into it. Last, you will set text properties for the text on the new page.

Creating and Importing Text

Most information in Web pages is presented in the form of text. You can type text directly in Dreamweaver or copy and paste it from another software program. To import text from a Microsoft Word file, you use the Import Word HTML command, which deletes all extraneous HTML tags from a file and then shows the results of the cleanup in the Clean Up Word HTML Results window. You can then copy and paste the text from this window to another Dreamweaver page. When you import text, it is important to keep in mind that visitors to your site must have the same fonts installed on their computers as the fonts applied to the imported text. Otherwise, the text may appear incorrectly. Some software programs, such as Adobe Photoshop and Adobe Illustrator

Using keyboard shortcuts

When working with text, the standard Windows keyboard shortcuts for the Cut, Copy, and Paste commands are very useful. These are [Control] [X] for Cut, [Control] [C] for Copy, and [Control] [V] for Paste. You can view all Dreamweaver keyboard shortcuts using the Keyboard Shortcuts dialog box, which lets you view existing shortcuts for menu commands, tools, or miscellaneous functions, such as copying HTML or inserting an image. You can also create your own shortcuts or assign shortcuts from other applications, such as Macromedia FreeHand or Adobe Illustrator and Photoshop. To view or modify keyboard shortcuts, click the Keyboard Shortcuts command on the Edit menu, then select the shortcut key set you want. The Keyboard Shortcuts feature is also available in Macromedia Fireworks and Flash. A printable version of all Dreamweaver keyboard shortcuts can be downloaded from the Dreamweaver Support Center at *http://www.macromedia.com/support/dreamweaver/documentation/dwmx_shortcuts/.*

can convert text into graphics so that the text retains the same appearance no matter what fonts are installed. However, text converted into graphics is no longer editable.

Formatting Text Using the Property Inspector

Because text is more difficult and tiring to read on a computer screen than on a printed page, you should make the text in your Web site attractive and easy to read. You can format text in Dreamweaver by changing its font, size, and color, just as you would in other software programs. To apply formatting to text, you first select the text you want to enhance, and then use the Property inspector to apply formatting attributes, such as font type, size, color, alignment, and indents.

Changing Fonts

You can format your text with different fonts by choosing a font combination from the Font list in the Property inspector. A **font combination** is a set of three fonts that specify which fonts a browser should use to display the text of your Web page. Font combinations are used so that if one font is not available, the browser will use the next one specified in the font combination. For example, if text is formatted with the font combination Arial, Helvetica, sans serif, the browser will first look on the viewer's system for Arial. If Arial is not available then it will look for Helvetica. If Helvetica is not available, then it will look for a sans-serif font to apply to the text. Using fonts within the default settings is wise, as fonts set outside the default settings may not be available on all viewers' computers.

Changing Font Sizes

There are two ways to change the size of text using the Property inspector. You can select a font size between 1 and 7, (where 1 is the smallest and 7 is the largest), or you can change the font size relative to the default base font. The **default base font** is size 3. For example, choosing +1 in the Size list increases the font size from 3 to 4. Choosing –1 decreases the font size from 3 to 2. Font sizes on Windows and Macintosh computers may differ slightly, so it's important to view your page on both platforms, if possible.

Formatting Paragraphs

You can format blocks of text as paragraphs or as different sized headings. To format a paragraph as a heading, click anywhere in the paragraph, then select the heading size you want from the Format list in the Property inspector. The Format list contains six different heading styles. Heading 1 is the largest size, and Heading 6 is the smallest size. Browsers display text formatted as headings in bold, setting them off from paragraphs of text.

QUICKTIP

Avoid mixing too many different fonts and formatting attributes on a Web page. This can result in pages that are visually confusing and that may be difficult to read.

Enter text

1. Position the insertion point directly after the text the "best the world has to offer" at the end of the paragraph, press [Enter] (Win) or [return] (Mac), then type **TripSmart**.

   Pressing [Enter] (Win) or [return] (Mac) creates a new paragraph that is two lines down from the previous paragraph.

2. Press and hold [Shift], press [Enter] (Win) or [return] (Mac), then type **1106 Beechwood**.

   Pressing and holding [Shift] while you press [Enter] (Win) or [return] (Mac) is called adding a soft return. A **line break** places a new line of text on the next line down without creating a new paragraph. Line breaks are useful when you want to add a new line of text directly below the current line of text.

3. Add the following text below the 1106 Beechwood text, using soft returns after each line:

   Fayetteville, AR 72704

   (555) 848-0807

4. Compare your screen with Figure B-9, then save your work.

You entered text for the address and telephone number on the home page.

Entering the address and telephone number on the TripSmart home page

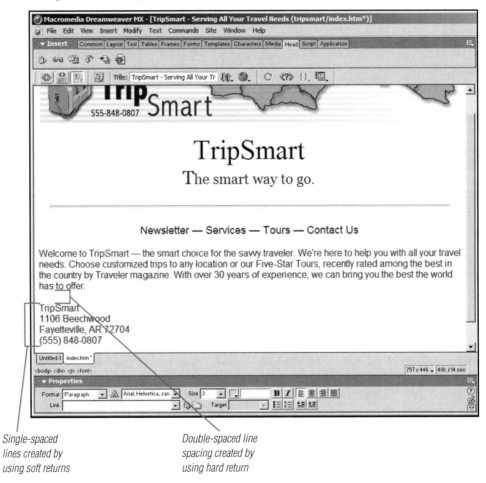

Single-spaced lines created by using soft returns

Double-spaced line spacing created by using hard return

Developing a Web Page

Formatting the address on the TripSmart home page

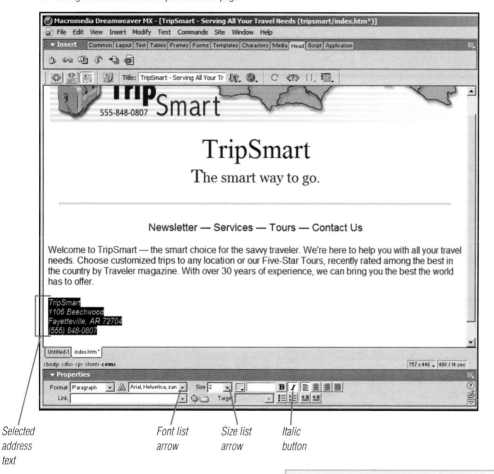

Selected
address
text

Font list
arrow

Size list
arrow

Italic
button

Format text

1. Select the address lines and telephone number, then click the Italic button in the Property inspector to italicize the text. *I*

2. With the text still selected, click the Size list arrow, click 2, then compare your screen to Figure B-10.

3. Save your work and close the file.

You formatted the address and phone number for TripSmart by changing the font style to italic and changing the size to 2.

Preventing data loss

When you are ready to stop working with a file in Dreamweaver, it is a good idea to save your changes, close the page or pages on which you are working, and exit Dreamweaver. Doing this will prevent the loss of data if power is interrupted. In some cases, loss of power can corrupt an open file and render it unusable.

Save graphics in the assets folder

1. Open dwb_1.htm from the unit_b data files folder, then save it as newsletter.htm in the tripsmart folder, overwriting the existing file.

2. Select the TripSmart banner.

   The Src box in the Property inspector shows the path as the unit_b assets folder. You need to change the path to the tripsmart.jpg file in the TripSmart assets folder.

3. Click the Browse for File icon next to the Src text box in the Property inspector, navigate to the tripsmart root folder, double-click the assets folder, click tripsmart.jpg, then click OK.

4. Click Travel Tidbits to select it, click the Browse for File icon next to the Src text box in the Property inspector, navigate to the unit_b assets folder, click tidbits.jpg, then click OK (Win) or Choose (Mac).

   Using the Browse for File icon to select the source of the original graphic file causes the file to be copied automatically to the assets folder of the Web site.

5. Click the Refresh button on the Site panel toolbar, then click the plus sign (Win) or expander arrow (Mac) next to the assets folder in the Site panel, if necessary.

   A copy of the tidbits.jpg file is now in the assets folder, as shown in Figure B-11.

6. Save your work.

You opened a new file and saved it as the new newsletter page. You changed the path of the two graphics to the TripSmart assets folder.

FIGURE B-11

Graphic file added to TripSmart assets folder

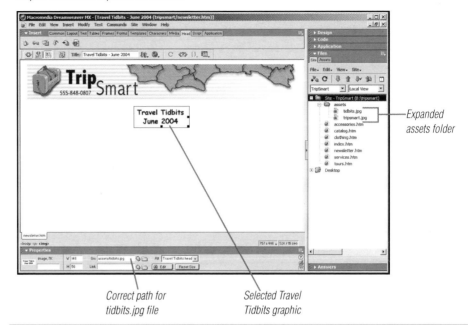

Expanded assets folder

Correct path for tidbits.jpg file

Selected Travel Tidbits graphic

Choosing filenames for Web pages

When you choose a name for a Web page, you should use a descriptive name that reflects the contents of the page. For example, if the page is about your company's products, you could name it products.htm. You should also follow some general rules for naming Web pages. For example, you should name the home page **index.htm**. Most file servers look for the file named index.htm to use as the initial page for a Web site. Do not use spaces, special characters, or punctuation in Web page filenames or the names of any graphics that will be inserted in your Web site. Spaces in filenames can cause errors when a browser attempts to read a file, and may cause your graphics to load incorrectly. You should also never use a number for the first character of a filename. To ensure that everything will load properly on all platforms, including UNIX, assume the filenames are case-sensitive and use lowercase characters. Files are saved with the .htm or .html file extension. While either file extension is appropriate, the default file extension is .htm for Windows platforms, and .html for Mac/UNIX platforms.

FIGURE B-12

Clean Up Word HTML dialog box

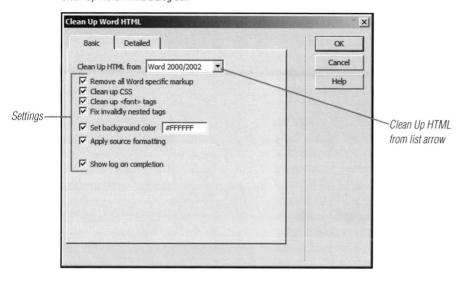

Settings

Clean Up HTML
from list arrow

1. Click File on the menu bar, point to Import, click Word HTML, navigate to the drive and folder where your data files are stored, double-click the unit_b folder (Win) or click the unit_b folder (Mac), then double-click packing_essentials.htm.

   TIP To specify a different version of Microsoft Word for the clean up, you can click the Clean Up HTML from list arrow, then click the appropriate version of Microsoft Word.

2. Make sure each check box in the Clean Up Word HTML dialog box is checked, as shown in Figure B-12, click OK, then click OK again to close the Clean Up Word HTML Results window.

3. Click Edit on the menu bar, click Select All, click Edit on the menu bar, click Copy, then close the file without saving changes.

4. Click to the right of the Travel Tidbits graphic on the newsletter.htm page, click Edit on the menu bar, then click Paste.

   TIP If the newsletter.htm page is not currently showing in the document window, click the newsletter.htm tab on the status bar.

5. Save your work.

You imported a Word HTML file and copied the text onto the newsletter page.

Saving a Word file as HTML

When you create text in Microsoft Word that you know will eventually be used on a Web page, you should not format the text. You should format the text after you import it into Dreamweaver. Formatting the text in Microsoft Word will create unnecessary HTML code that will be automatically removed when the file is imported into Dreamweaver. This practice will save time and avoid unnecessary frustration.

Set text properties

1. Click the Common tab on the Insert bar, then place the insertion point anywhere within the words Packing Essentials.

2. Click the Format list arrow in the Property inspector, then click Heading 3.

   The Heading 3 style is applied to the entire line of text. When you apply a heading, the entire paragraph in which the insertion point is placed becomes a heading and the appearance of the entire paragraph changes.

3. Click the Align Center button in the Property inspector to center the heading.

4. Select the words Packing Essentials, click the Font list arrow, then click Arial, Helvetica, sans-serif.

   Because setting a font is a character command, you must select all the characters you want to format before applying a font.

   TIP   You can modify the font combinations in the Font list by clicking Text on the menu bar, pointing to Font, then clicking Edit Font List.

5. With the heading still selected, click the Text Color button in the Property inspector to open the color picker, then click the dark blue color in the third row of the first column (#000066).

   TIP   You can also type #000066 in the color text box in the Property inspector to select the color in Step 5.

(continued)

FIGURE B-13

Properties of Packing Essentials text

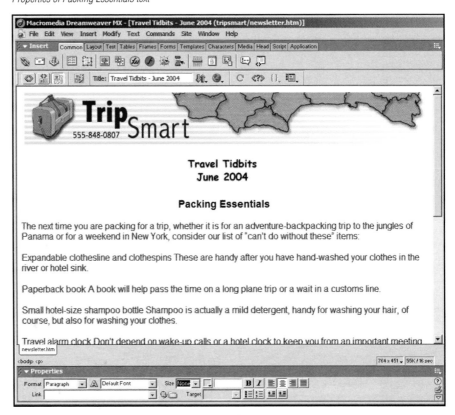

6. Click to the left of the T in The next time you are packing, press and hold [Shift], scroll to the end of the text, click to place the insertion point after the end of the last sentence, then release [Shift].

7. Click the Font list arrow in the Property inspector, click Arial, Helvetica, sans-serif, click the Size list arrow in the Property inspector, then click 3.

   TIP   To change the size of selected text, use either the Format list arrow or the Size list arrow, but not both.

8. Click anywhere on the page to deselect the text, save your work, then compare your screen to Figure B-13.

You formatted the Packing Essentials text using the Heading 3 style and the Arial, Helvetica, sans-serif font combination. Next, you centered the heading on the page and changed the text color to a dark blue. You then selected the rest of the text on the page and changed it to the Arial, Helvetica, sans-serif font combination with a text size of 3.

Choosing fonts

There are two classifications of fonts: sans serif and serif. **Sans-serif fonts** are block-style characters that are often used for headings and subheadings. The headings in this book use a sans-serif font. Examples of sans-serif fonts include Arial, Verdana, and Helvetica. **Serif fonts** are more ornate, and contain small extra strokes at the beginning and end of the characters. Some people consider serif fonts easier to read in printed material, because the extra strokes lead your eye from one character to the next. This paragraph you are reading uses a serif font. Examples of serif fonts include Times New Roman, Times, and Georgia. Many designers feel that a sans-serif font is preferable when the content of a Web site is primarily intended to be read on the screen, but that a serif font is preferable if the content will be printed. When you choose fonts, you need to keep in mind the amount of text each page will contain and whether most viewers will read the text on-screen or print it out. A good rule of thumb is to limit each Web site to no more than three font variations. Using more than three may make your Web site look unprofessional and suggest the "ransom note effect." The phrase **ransom note effect** implies that fonts have been randomly used in a document without regard to style, similar to a ransom note made up of words cut from various sources and pasted onto a page.

ADD LINKS TO WEB PAGES

What You'll Do

 In this lesson, you will open the home page and add links to the navigation bar that link to the Catalog, Services, Tours, and Newsletter pages. You will then insert an e-mail link at the bottom of the page and create page titles for the untitled pages in the site map.

Adding Links to Web Pages

Links provide the real strength for Web pages. Links make it possible for viewers to navigate through all the pages in a Web site and to connect to other pages you choose anywhere on the Web. Viewers are more likely to return to Web sites that have a user-friendly navigation structure. Viewers also enjoy Web sites that have interesting links to other Web pages or other Web sites.

To add links to a Web page, you first select the text or graphic that you want to serve as a link, then you specify a path to the page to which you want to link in the Link text box in the Property inspector. After you add all your links, you can open the site map to see a diagram of how the linked pages relate to each other.

When you create links on a Web page, it is important to avoid **broken links,** or links that cannot find their intended destinations. You can accidentally cause a broken link by typing the incorrect address for the link in the Link text box. Broken links are often caused by companies merging, going out of business, or simply moving their Web site addresses.

In addition to adding links to your pages, you should also provide a **point of contact**, or a place on a Web page that provides viewers with a means of contacting the company. A common point of contact is a **mailto: link,** which is an e-mail address that viewers with questions or problems can use to contact someone at the company's headquarters.

Using Navigation Bars

A navigation bar is an area on a Web page that contains links to the main pages of a Web site. Navigation bars are usually located at the top or side of the main pages of a Web site and can be created with text, graphics, or a combination of the two. To make navigating through a Web site as easy as possible, you should place navigation bars in the same position on each Web page. Navigation bars are the backbone of a Web site's navigation structure, which includes all navigation aids for moving around a Web site. You can, however, include additional links to the main pages of the Web site elsewhere on the page. The Web page in Figure B-14 shows an example of a navigation bar that contains both text and graphic links within a Flash movie. Notice that when the mouse is placed on the Features item at the top of the navigation bar, a menu appears.

Navigation bars can also be simple and contain only text-based links to the pages in the site. You can create a simple navigation bar by typing the names of your Web site's pages at the top of your Web page, formatting the text, and then adding links to each page name.

FIGURE B-14
Coca-Cola Web site

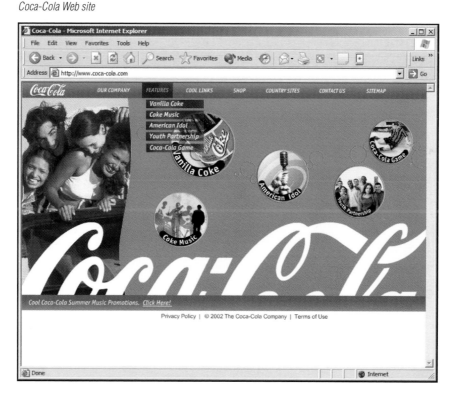

Create a navigation bar

1. Close the newsletter page, then open the home page.

2. Position the insertion point to the left of N in Newsletter, then drag to select Newsletter — Services — Tours — Contact Us, as shown in in Figure B-15.

3. Type **Home - Catalog - Services - Tours - Newsletter**.

   These five text labels will serve as a navigation bar. You will add the links later.

4. Save your work.

You created a new navigation bar using text, replacing the original navigation bar.

Format a navigation bar

1. Select Home - Catalog - Services - Tours - Newsletter, click the Size list arrow in the Property inspector, then click None.

   None is equal to size 3, the default text size. The None setting also eliminates any prior size formatting that was applied to the text.

   > TIP   If your Property inspector is not displayed, click Window on the Document menu bar, then click Properties to open it.

2. Click the Format list arrow in the Property inspector, then click Heading 4.

3. Click the Font list arrow in the Property inspector, click Arial, Helvetica, sans-serif (if necessary), then compare your screen to Figure B-16.

4. Save your work.

You formatted the new navigation bar, using a heading and a font combination.

FIGURE B-15

Selecting the current navigation bar

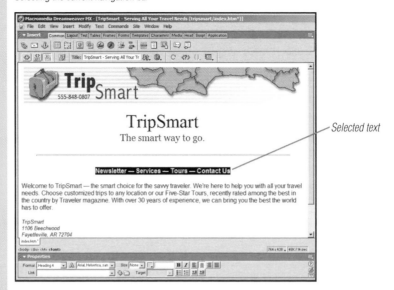

Selected text

FIGURE B-16

Formatting the navigation bar

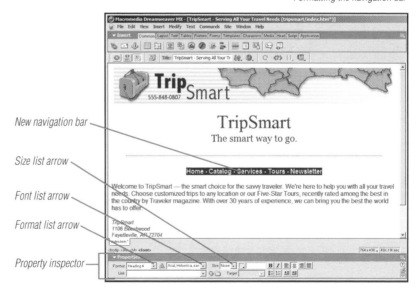

New navigation bar

Size list arrow

Font list arrow

Format list arrow

Property inspector

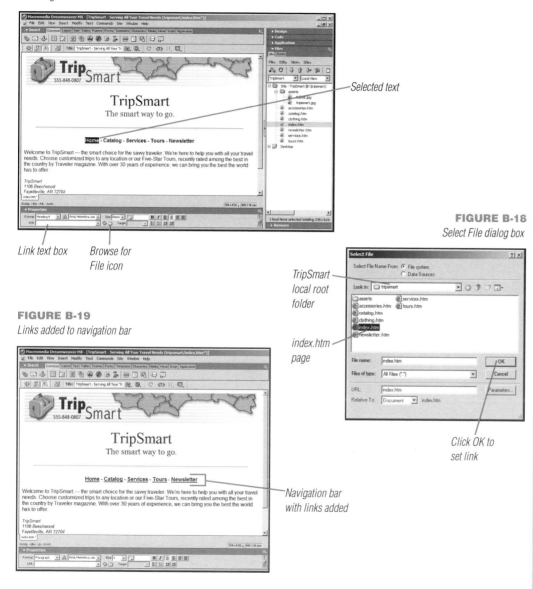

Selected text

Link text box *Browse for File icon*

Navigation bar with links added

TripSmart local root folder

index.htm page

Click OK to set link

Add links to Web pages

1. Double-click Home to select it, as shown in Figure B-17.

2. Click the Browse for File icon next to the Link text box in the Property inspector, then navigate to the tripsmart root folder (if necessary). 🗁

3. Click index.htm as shown in Figure B-18, click OK (Win) or Choose (Mac), then click anywhere on the page to deselect Home.

   Home now appears in blue with an underline, indicating it is a link. In fact, clicking Home will not open a new page because the link is to the home page. It might seem odd to create a link to the same page on which the link appears, but this will be helpful when you copy the navigation bar to other pages in the site.

4. Repeat Steps 1–4 to create links for Catalog, Services, Tours, and Newsletter to their corresponding pages in the tripsmart root folder.

   When you finish adding the links to the other four pages, compare your screen to Figure B-19.

5. Save your work.

You created a link for each of the five navigation bar elements to their respective Web pages in the TripSmart Web site.

Create an e-mail link

1. Place the insertion point after the last digit in the telephone number, then insert a soft return.

2. Click the Common tab on the Insert bar (if necessary), then click the Email Link button on the Insert bar to insert an e-mail link.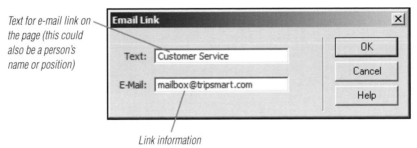

3. Type **Customer Service** in the Text text box, and **mailbox@tripsmart.com** in the E-Mail text box, as shown in Figure B-20, then click OK to close the Email Link dialog box.

   TIP   You must enter the correct e-mail address in the E-Mail text box for the link to work. However, you can enter any descriptive name, such as customer service or Bob Smith in the Text text box.

4. Save your work.

   TIP   An asterisk after the filename in the title bar indicates that you have altered the page since you last saved it. After you save your work, the asterisk will disappear.

You inserted a mailto: link to serve as a point of contact for TripSmart.

FIGURE B-20
Email Link dialog box

Text for e-mail link on the page (this could also be a person's name or position)

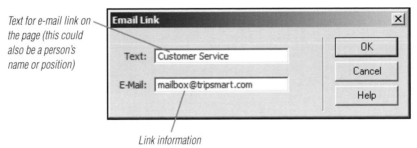

Link information

FIGURE B-21

TripSmart site map

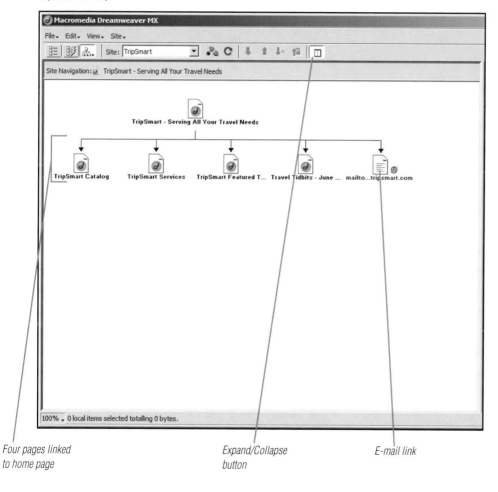

Four pages linked
to home page

Expand/Collapse
button

E-mail link

1. Click the View list arrow on the Site panel, then click Map View to view the site map **(Win)** or click Site on the menu bar, click Open Site, click TripSmart to open the Site panel, click the Site Map button to change to Map view, then click Map only (Mac).

2. Click the Expand/Collapse button on the Site panel to expand the site map (Win). ▢

   The site map shows the home page, the four pages that are linked to it, and the e-mail link on the home page.

3. Click View on the Site panel menu bar, then click Show Page Titles (Win), or click Site on the menu bar, point to Site Map View, then click Show Page Titles (Mac) to select it (if necessary.)

4. Select the first Untitled Document page in the site map, click the words Untitled Document, click again, type **TripSmart Catalog,** then press [Enter] (Win) or [return] (Mac).

5. Repeat Step 4 for the other two Untitled Document pages, naming them **TripSmart Services** and **TripSmart Featured Tours**, as shown in Figure B-21.

6. Click the Expand/Collapse button on the toolbar to collapse the site map (Win) or click the Site Files button on the Site panel to change to Local view (Mac). ▢

7. Click the View list arrow on the Site panel, then click Local View (Win).

You viewed the site map and added page titles to the untitled pages.

USE THE HISTORY PANEL AND USE THE CODE INSPECTOR

What You'll Do

 In this lesson, you will use the History panel to undo formatting changes you make to a horizontal rule. You will then use the Code Inspector to view the HTML code for the horizontal rule. You will also insert a date object and then view its code in the Code Inspector.

Using the History Panel

Throughout the process of creating a Web page, it's likely that you will make mistakes along the way. Fortunately, you can use the History panel to undo your mistakes. The **History panel** records each editing and formatting task you perform and displays each one in a list in the order in which you completed them. Each task listed in the History panel is called a **step**. You can drag the **slider** on the left side of the History panel to undo or redo steps, as shown in Figure B-22. By default, the History panel records 50 steps. You can increase the number of steps the History panel records by adjusting the settings in the General category of the Preferences dialog box. However, keep in mind that setting this number too high might require additional memory and could hinder the way Dreamweaver operates.

Understanding other History panel features

Dragging the slider up and down in the History panel is a quick way to undo or redo steps. However, the History panel offers much more. It has the capability to "memorize" certain tasks and consolidate them into one command. This is a useful feature for steps that are executed repetitively on Web pages. Some Dreamweaver features, such as drag and drop, cannot be recorded in the History panel and have a red x placed next to them. The History panel also does not show steps performed in the Site panel.

Viewing HTML Code in the Code Inspector

If you enjoy writing code, you occasionally might want to make changes to Web pages by entering HTML code rather than using the panels and tools in Design view. You can view HTML code in Dreamweaver using Code view, Code and Design views, or the Code inspector. The **Code inspector,** shown in Figure B-23, is a separate floating window that displays the current page in Code view. The advantage of using the Code inspector is that you can see a full-screen view of your page in Design view while viewing the underlying code in a floating window that you can resize and position wherever you want.

You can add advanced features, such as JavaScript functions, to Web pages by copying and pasting code from one page to another in the Code inspector. A **JavaScript** function is a block of code that adds dynamic content such as rollovers or interactive forms to a Web page. A **rollover** is a special effect that changes the appearance of an object when the mouse "rolls over" it.

QUICKTIP

If you are new to HTML, you can use the Reference panel to find answers to your HTML questions. The Reference panel is part of the Code panel group and contains many resources besides HTML help, such as JavaScript help.

FIGURE B-22
History panel with Options menu open

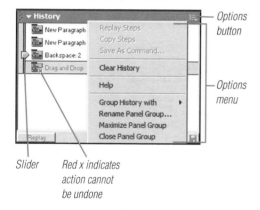

Options button

Options menu

Slider   Red x indicates action cannot be undone

FIGURE B-23
Code inspector

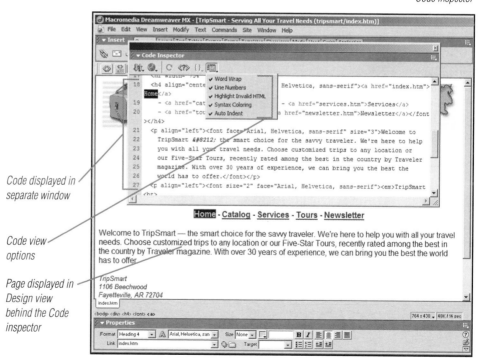

Code displayed in separate window

Code view options

Page displayed in Design view behind the Code inspector

Use the History panel

1. Click Window on the menu bar, point to Others, then click History.

   The History panel opens and displays steps you have recently performed.

2. Click the Options button on the History panel group title bar to open the Options menu, click Clear History, as shown in Figure B-24, then click Yes to close the warning box (if necessary).

3. Select the Horizontal Rule on the home page.

   A **horizontal rule** is a line used to separate page elements or to organize information on a page.

4. Select the number in the W text box, type **90**, click the list arrow next to the W text box, click %, press [Tab], then compare your screen to Figure B-25.

5. Using the Property inspector, change the width of the horizontal rule to 80%, then set the Align text box to Left.

6. Drag the slider on the History panel up to Set Width: 90%, as shown in Figure B-26.

   The bottom two steps in the History panel appear gray, indicating that these steps have been undone.

7. Save your work, click the Options button on the History panel group menu bar, then click Close panel group to close the History panel.

You formatted the horizontal rule, made changes to it, then used the History panel to undo the changes.

FIGURE B-24
Clearing the History panel

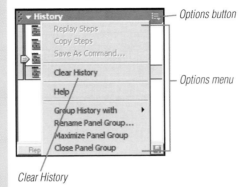

— Options button

— Options menu

Clear History

FIGURE B-25
Property inspector settings for horizontal rule

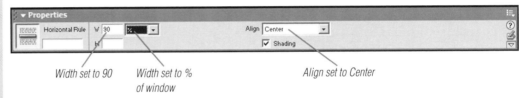

Width set to 90   *Width set to % of window*   *Align set to Center*

FIGURE B-26
Undoing steps using the History panel

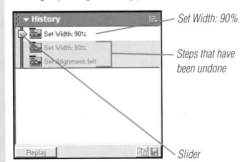

Set Width: 90%

Steps that have been undone

Slider

Use the Code Inspector

1. Click the horizontal rule to select it (if necessary), then click Window on the menu bar, point to Others, then click Code Inspector.

   The Code Inspector highlights the code for the horizontal rule.

   | TIP You can also press [F10] to open the Code Inspector.

2. Click the View Options button on the Code Inspector toolbar to open the View Options menu, then click Word Wrap (if necessary), to activate Word Wrap. 🔲

   Word Wrap forces the text to stay within the window, allowing you to read without scrolling sideways.

3. Click the View Options button to open the View Options menu, then verify that Highlight Invalid HTML and Syntax Coloring are checked, as shown in Figure B-27. 🔲

You viewed the underlying HTML code for the horizontal rule using the Code Inspector.

FIGURE B-27

Code Inspector View Options menu

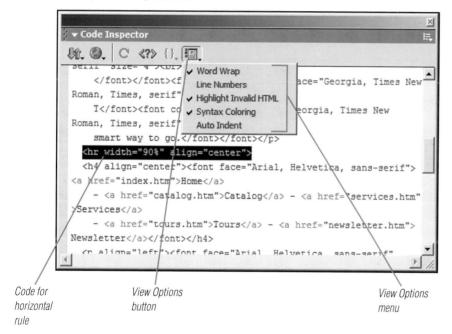

Code for horizontal rule

View Options button

View Options menu

Use the Reference panel

1. Click the Reference button on the Code Inspector toolbar, as shown in Figure B-28, to open the Code panel group with the Reference panel displayed. <?>

2. Read the information about horizontal rules in the Reference panel, as shown in Figure B-29, then click the expander arrow on the Code panel group title bar to collapse the Code panel group.

3. Click the Code Inspector Close button to close the Code Inspector.

You viewed the underlying HTML code for the horizontal rule using the Code Inspector and read information about horizontal rule settings in the Reference panel.

FIGURE B-28
Reference button on the Code Inspector toolbar

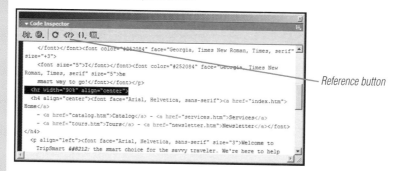

Reference button

FIGURE B-29
Viewing the Reference panel

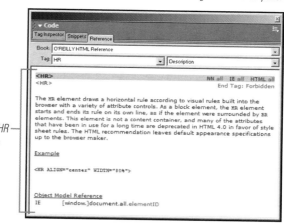

Information on the HR (horizontal rule) tag

Inserting comments

A handy Dreamweaver feature is the ability to insert comments into HTML code. Comments can provide helpful information describing portions of the code, such as a JavaScript function. You can create comments in any Dreamweaver view, but you must turn on Invisible Elements to see them in Design view. To create a comment, click the Common tab on the Insert bar, click the Comment button 🖫, type a comment in the Comment dialog box, then click OK. Comments are not visible in browser windows.

Developing a Web Page

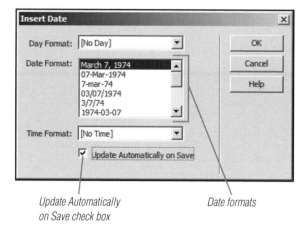

*Update Automatically
on Save check box*   *Date formats*

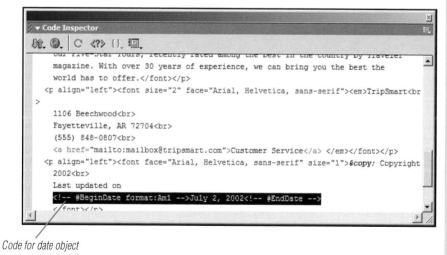

Code for date object

Insert a date object

1. Select January 1, 2004, then press [Delete] (Win) or [delete] (Mac) on your keyboard.

2. Click the Date button on the Insert bar, then click March 7, 1974 in the Date Format text box. 🗐

3. Click the Update Automatically on Save check box, as shown in Figure B-30, then click OK.

4. Open the Code Inspector.

   Notice that the code in the Code Inspector has changed to reflect the date object, as shown in Figure B-31.

5. Close the Code Inspector.

6. Save your work.

You inserted a date object that will be updated automatically when you open and save the home page.

MODIFY AND TEST WEB PAGES

What You'll Do

 In this lesson, you will preview the home page in the browser to check for typographical errors, grammatical errors, broken links, and overall appearance. After previewing, you will make slight formatting adjustments to the page to improve its appearance.

Testing and Modifying Web Pages

Testing Web pages is a continuous process. You never really finish a Web site, as there are always additions and corrections to make. As you add and modify pages, you must test each page as part of the development process. The best way to test a Web page is to preview it in a browser window to make sure that all text and graphic elements appear the way you expect them to. You should also test your links to make sure they work properly. You also need to proofread your text to make sure it contains all the necessary information for the page and no typographical or grammatical errors. Designers typically view a page in a browser, return to Design view to make necessary changes, then view the page in a browser again. This process may be repeated many times before the page is ready for publishing. In fact, it is sometimes difficult to stop making improvements to a page and move on to another project. You need to strike a balance between quality, creativity, and productivity.

Using "Under Construction" pages

Many people are tempted to insert an unfinished page as a placeholder for a page that will be finished later. Rather than have real content, these pages usually contain text or a graphic that indicates the page is not finished, or "under construction". You should not publish a Web page that has a link to an unfinished page. It is frustrating to click a link for a page you want to open only to find an "under construction" note or graphic displayed. You want to make the best possible impression on your viewing audience. If you cannot complete a page before publishing it, at least provide enough information on it to make it "worth the trip."

Testing a Web Page Using Different Browsers

Because users access the Internet using a wide variety of computer systems, it is important to design your pages so that all browsers and screen sizes can display them well. You should test your pages using different browsers and a wide variety of screen sizes and resolutions to ensure the best view of your page by all types of computer equipment. Although the most common screen size that designers use today is 800 × 600, many viewers view at 1024 × 768. A page that is designed for a screen resolution of 800 × 600 will look much better at that setting than at a higher one. Many designers place a statement such as "this Web site is best viewed at 800 × 600" on the home page. To view your page using different screen sizes, click the Window Size pop-up menu in the middle of the status bar (Win) or at the bottom of the document window (Mac), then choose the setting you want to use. Table B-1 lists the default Dreamweaver window screen sizes.

TABLE B-1: Dreamweaver Default Window Screen Sizes

window size (inside dimensions of the browser window without borders)	monitor size
592W	
536 × 196	640 × 480, default
600 × 300	640 × 480, maximized
760 × 420	800 × 600, maximized
795 × 470	832 × 624, maximized
955 × 600	1024 × 768, maximized
544 × 378	Web TV

Modify a Web page

1. Click the Restore down button on the index.htm title bar to decrease the size of the home page window.

2. Click the Window Size list arrow on the status bar, as shown in Figure B-32, click 600 × 300 (640 × 480, Maximized).

   A viewer using this setting will be forced to use the horizontal scroll bar to view the entire page. This should be avoided, but very few people view at this resolution anymore.

   > TIP   You cannot use the Window Size options if your document window is maximized.

3. Click the Window Size list arrow, click 760 × 420 (800 × 600, Maximized).

4. Replace the period after The smart way to go with an exclamation point.

5. Shorten the horizontal rule to 75%.

6. Select the text "The Smart way to go!" then change the text size to 5.

7. Click the Maximize button on the index.htm title bar to maximize the home page window.

8. Save your work.

You viewed the home page using two different window sizes and you made simple formatting changes to the page.

FIGURE B-32
Window screen sizes

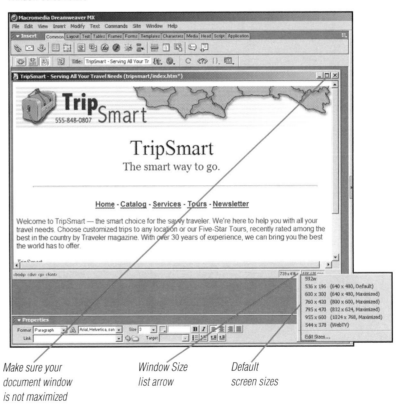

Make sure your document window is not maximized

Window Size list arrow

Default screen sizes

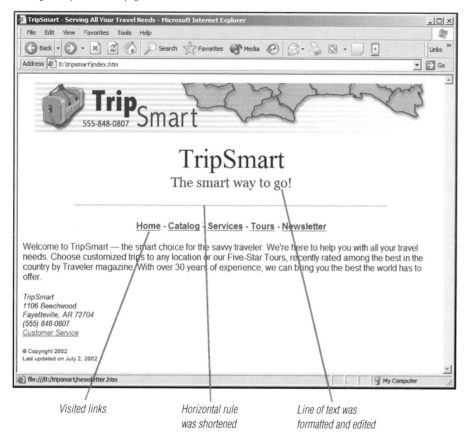

Visited links   Horizontal rule   Line of text was
                     was shortened   formatted and edited

Test Web pages by viewing them in a browser

1. Click the Preview/Debug in Browser button on the Document toolbar, then choose your browser from the menu that opens. 🌐

   The TripSmart home page opens in your default browser.

   > TIP If you do not see a browser listed after clicking Preview/Debug in Browser, contact your instructor for assistance.

2. Click all the links on the navigation bar, then use the Back button on the browser toolbar to return to the home page.

   Pages with no content at this point will appear as blank pages. Compare your screen to Figure B-33.

3. Close your browser window.

You viewed the TripSmart home page in your browser and tested each link on the navigation bar.

Choosing a window size

The 640 × 480 window size is not used by many viewers today, but you should still keep this size in mind when designing your Web pages. The 800 × 600 window setting is used on 15-inch monitors and some 17-inch monitors. Most consumers have at least a 15-inch monitor at their homes or offices, making this window size a good choice for a Web page.

Create head content and set Web page properties.

1. Open the Blooms & Bulbs Web site. (If you did not create this Web site in Unit A, contact your instructor for assistance.)
2. Open the home page and view the head content.
3. Change the page title to **Blooms & Bulbs - Your Complete Garden Center**.
4. Insert the following keywords: **garden**, **plants**, **water**, **nursery**, **flowers**, **supplies**, **landscape**, **annuals**, **perennials**, and **greenhouse**.
5. Insert the following description: **Blooms & Bulbs is a premier supplier of garden plants for both professional and home gardeners.**
6. Switch to Code view to view the HTML code for the head content, then switch back to Design view.
7. Open the Page Properties dialog box and view the current page properties.
8. Change the background color to a color of your choice.
9. Change the background color to white again, then save your work.

Create, import, and format text.

1. Select the current navigation bar and replace it with **Home**, **Featured Plants**, **Gardening Tips**, and **Workshops**. Use the [Spacebar] key and a hyphen to separate the items.
2. Using the Property inspector, apply the Heading 4 style to the navigation bar.

3. Create a hard return after the paragraph of text and type the following text, inserting a soft return after each line.
   Blooms & Bulbs
   Highway 7 North
   Alvin, TX 77511
   (555) 248-0806
4. Italicize the address and phone number lines and change them to a size 2.
5. Change the copyright and last updated statements to a size 2.
6. Save your work and close the home page.
7. Open dwb_2.htm and save it as **tips.htm** in the Blooms and Bulbs Web site, overwriting the existing file.
8. Set the banner path to the assets folder of the Blooms & Bulbs Web site and save the planting_tips.jpg in the assets folder of the Blooms & Bulbs Web site.
9. Import the gardening_tips.htm file from the drive and folder where your unit_b data files are stored, using the Import Word HTML command.
10. Copy the imported text and close the gardening_tips.htm file without saving the file.
11. Paste the text onto the tips.htm page below the navigation bar and left align the imported text (if necessary).
12. Format all the text on the page with the Arial, Helvetica, sans-serif font combination.
13. Select the Seasonal gardening checklist heading and use the Property inspector to center the text.

14. Use the Property inspector to format the selected text with a Heading 3 style, then save your work.
15. Apply the color #006633 (the third color in the second row) to the text.
16. Select the rest of the text on the page except for the Seasonal gardening checklist heading, then set the font to size 3.
17. Select the Basic Gardening Tips heading, then format this text in bold, with the color #006633 and a size of 3.
18. Save your work and close the tips page.

Add links to Web pages.

1. Open the home page (if necessary) and use the Property inspector to link Home on the navigation bar to the index.htm page.
2. Link Featured Plants on the navigation bar to the plants.htm page.
3. Link Gardening Tips on the navigation bar to the tips.htm page.
4. Link Workshops on the navigation bar to the workshops.htm page.
5. Using the Insert bar, create a mailto: link under the telephone number.
6. Type **Customer Service** in the Text text box and **mailbox@blooms.com** in the E-Mail text boxes.
7. Title the plants.htm page **Our Featured Plants**.
8. Title the workshops.htm page **Scheduled workshops**, then save your work.

Use the History Panel and Code Inspector.

1. Open the home page.
2. Open the History panel, then clear its contents.
3. Delete the current date in the Last updated statement and replace it with a date that will update automatically when the file is saved.
4. Change the font for the last updated statement.
5. Change the last updated statement to boldface.
6. Use the History panel to go back to the original font and style settings for the last updated statement.
7. Close the History panel.
8. Using the Code Inspector, examine the code for the last updated statement.
9. Close the Code Inspector.
10. Save your work.

Modify and test Web pages.

1. Using the Window Size pop-up menu, view the home page at 640 × 480 and at 800 × 600, then maximize the document window.
2. View the page in your browser.
3. Verify that all links work correctly.
4. Change the text Stop by and see us soon! to **We ship anywhere!**
5. Save your work, then view the pages in your browser, comparing your screens to Figure B-34 and Figure B-35.
6. Close your browser.
7. Adjust the spacing (if necessary), then save your work and preview the home page in the browser again.
8. Close the browser, save your work, then close all open pages.

FIGURE B-34
Completed Skills Review home page

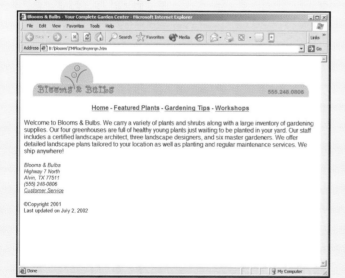

FIGURE B-35
Completed Skills Review tips page

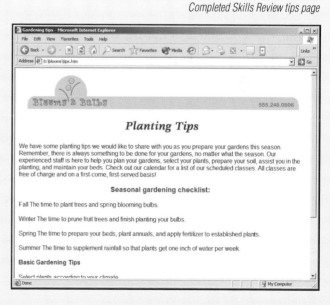

Developing a Web Page

You have been hired to create a Web site for a river expedition company named Rapids Transit, located on the Buffalo River in Arkansas. You have created the basic framework for the Web site and are now ready to format and edit the home page to improve the content and appearance.

1. Open the Rapids Transit Web site, then open the home page. If you did not create this Web site in Unit A, contact your instructor.

2. Enter the following keywords: **river**, **rafting**, **Buffalo**, **Arkansas**, **Gilbert**, **kayak**, **canoe**, and **float**.

3. Enter the following description: **Rapids Transit is a river expedition company located on the Buffalo River in Gilbert, Arkansas.**

4. Change the page title to **Rapids Transit - Buffalo River Expeditions**.

5. Create a centered navigation bar below the Rapids Transit logo with the following text links: **Home**, **Our Guides**, **Equipment Rentals**, and **Country Store**. Place hyphens between each text link.

6. Apply the Heading 4 style to the text links and apply the Arial, Helvetica, sans-serif font combination.

7. Type the following address two lines below the paragraph about the company, using soft returns after each line:
   Rapids Transit
   Hwy 65

Gilbert, AR
(555) 365-5369

8. Insert an e-mail link in the line below the telephone number, using **Mike Andrew** for the Text text box and **mailbox@rapidstransit.com** for the E-mail text box in the Email Link dialog box.

9. Italicize the address, phone number, and e-mail link and format it to size 2, Arial, Helvetica, sans-serif.

10. Link the navigation bar entries to index.htm, guides.htm, rentals.htm, and store.htm.

11. Delete the horizontal rule.

12. View the HTML code for the page.

13. View the page using two different window sizes, then test the links in your browser window.

14. View the site map.

15. Create the following page titles:
    guides.htm = **Meet Our Guides**
    rentals.htm = **Equipment Rentals**
    store.htm = **Shop At Our Country Store**

16. Verify that all the page titles are entered correctly.

17. Preview the page in your browser and test all the links.

18. Compare your page to Figure B-36, close the browser, save your work, then close all open pages.

FIGURE B-36
Completed Project Builder 1

Your company has been selected to design a Web site for Jacob's, a new upscale restaurant in London catering to business executives and theatre patrons. You are now ready to add content to the home page and apply formatting options to improve the page appearance, using Figure B-37 as a guide.

1. Open the Jacob's Web site, then open the home page. If you did not create this Web site in Unit A, contact your instructor.

2. Add the following sentence to the end of the paragraph: **Dinner is served from 5:00 p.m. until 11:00 p.m. with our signature desserts and bar service until 2:00 a.m. Tuesday through Saturday.**

3. Add a navigation bar under the banner and above the paragraph that contains the following entries: **Home - Menus - Favorite Recipes - Directions and Hours**.

4. Center the navigation bar and apply a Heading 5 style.

5. Add the following 3 lines of text below the paragraph about the restaurant, using soft returns after each line:
   **For reservations: please call
   +44 (0)20 0000 0000
   or e-mail reservations.**

6. Delete the word reservations, then use the Email Link dialog box to insert an e-mail link using mailbox@jacobs.com for the e-mail address and reservations as the text.

7. Right-align the three lines of text that contain the reservation information.

8. Apply the Arial, Helvetica, sans-serif font to all text on the page.

9. Format the reservation information to size 2.

10. Create links from each navigation bar element to its corresponding Web page.

11. Replace the date that follows the text Last updated with a date object, then save your work.

12. View the completed page in your default browser and test each link.

13. Close your browser.

14. View the site map and rename any untitled pages with appropriate titles.

15. Save your work and close all pages.

FIGURE B-37
Completed Project Builder 2

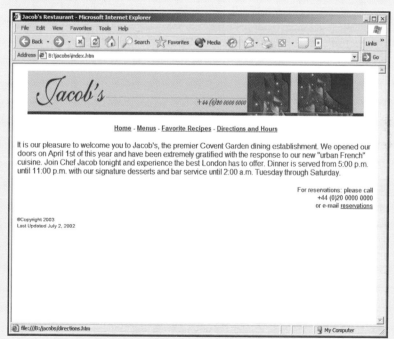

Angela Lou is a freelance photographer. She is searching the Internet looking for a particular type of paper to use in processing her prints. She knows that Web sites use keywords and descriptions in order to receive "hits" with search engines. She is curious about how they work. Follow the steps below and write your answers to the questions.

1. Connect to the Internet, go to *www.course.com*, navigate to the page for this book, click the Student Online Companion link, then click the link for this unit to see the Kodak Web site's home page. See Figure B-38.

2. View the page source by clicking View on the menu bar, then clicking Source (Internet Explorer) or Page Source (Netscape Navigator or Communicator).

3. Can you locate a description and keywords? If so, what are they?

4. How many keywords do you find?

5. Is the description appropriate for the Web site? Why or why not?

6. Look at the numbers of keywords and words in the description. Is there an appropriate number? Or are there too many or not enough?

7. Use a search engine such as Google at *www.google.com* and search for "photography" and "paper" in the Search text box.

FIGURE B-38
Source for Design Project

8. Click the first link in the list of results and view the source code for that page. Do you see keywords and a description? Do any of them match the words you used in the search?

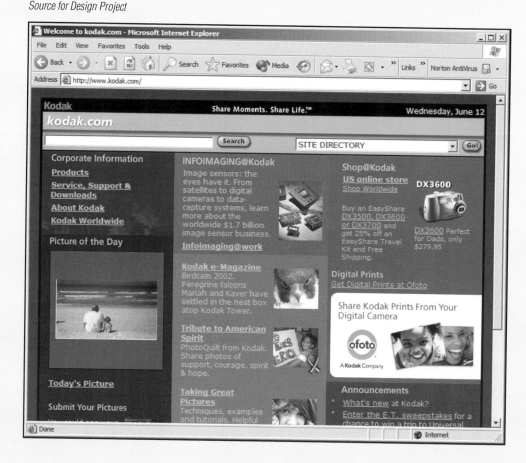

Depending on the size of your group, you can assign individual elements of the project to group members, or work collectively to create the finished product.

In this assignment, you will continue to work on the Web site your group defined in Unit A. In Unit A, you created a storyboard for your Web site with at least four pages. You also created a local root folder for your Web site and an assets folder to store the Web site asset files. You set the assets folder as the default storage location for your images. You began to collect information and resources for your Web site and started working on the home page.

1. Brainstorm as a group and come up with a title and several appropriate keywords for your site. Work together to write a description for the site.
2. Add the title, keywords, and description to the head content for the home page.
3. Assign a team member the task of creating the main page content for the home page and formatting it attractively.
4. Assign a team member the task of adding the address and other contact information to the home page, including an e-mail address.
5. Consult your storyboard and assign a team member the task of designing the navigation bar and linking it to the appropriate pages.

6. Add a last updated statement to the home page with a date that will automatically update when the page is saved.
7. Edit and format the page content until the group is satisfied with the results.
8. Verify that each page has a page title by viewing the site map.
9. Verify that all links, including the e-mail link, work correctly.
10. When you are satisfied with the home page, review the check list questions shown in Figure B-39, then make any necessary changes.
11. Save your work.

FIGURE B-39
Group Project check list

Web Site Check List

1. Do all pages have a page title?
2. Does the home page have a description and keywords?
3. Does the home page contain contact information, including an e-mail address?
4. Do all completed pages in the Web site have consistent navigation links?
5. Does the home page have a last updated statement that will automatically update when the page is saved?
6. Do all pages have attractively formatted text?
7. Do all paths for links and images work correctly?
8. Does the home page view well using at least two different screen resolutions?

UNIT C

WORKING WITH TEXT AND GRAPHICS

1. Create unordered and ordered lists.

2. Create, apply, and edit Cascading Style Sheets.

3. Insert and align graphics.

4. Enhance an image and use alternate text.

5. Insert a background image and perform site maintenance.

UNIT C
WORKING WITH TEXT AND GRAPHICS

Introduction

Most Web pages contain a combination of text and graphics. Dreamweaver provides many tools for working with text and graphics that you can use to make your Web pages attractive and easy to use. Dreamweaver also has tools that help you format text quickly and ensure a consistent appearance of text elements across all your Web pages.

Formatting Text as Lists

If a Web page contains a large amount of text, it can be difficult for viewers to digest it all. You can break up the monotony of large blocks of text by creating lists. You can create three types of lists in Dreamweaver: unordered lists, ordered lists, and definition lists.

Using Cascading Style Sheets

You can save time and ensure that all your page elements have a consistent appearance by using Cascading Style Sheets (CSS). You can use Cascading Style Sheets to define formatting attributes for page elements such as text and tables. You can then apply the formatting attributes you define to any element in a single document or to all of the pages in a Web site.

Using Graphics to Enhance Web Pages

Graphics make Web pages visually stimulating and more exciting than pages that contain only text. However, you should use graphics sparingly. If you think of text as the meat and potatoes of a Web site, the graphics would be the seasoning. You should add graphics to a page just as you would add seasoning to food. A little seasoning enhances the flavor and brings out the quality of the dish. Too much seasoning overwhelms the dish and masks the flavor of the main ingredients. Too little seasoning results in a bland dish. There are many ways to work with graphics so that they complement the content of pages in a Web site. There are specific file formats that should be used to save graphics for Web sites to ensure maximum quality with minimum file size. You should store graphics in a Web site's assets folder in an organized fashion.

Tools You'll Use

Apply Styles option

Edit Styles option

New CSS Style button

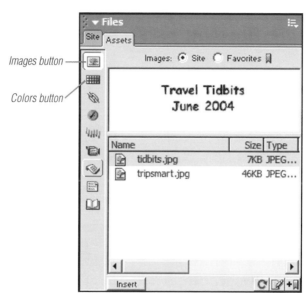

Images button

Colors button

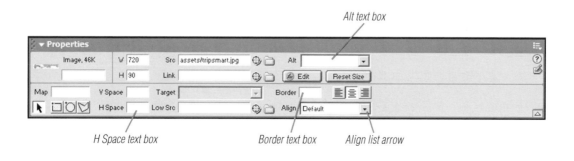

Alt text box

H Space text box

Border text box

Align list arrow

CREATE UNORDERED AND ORDERED LISTS

What You'll Do

 In this lesson, you will create an unordered list of essential items to pack on the TripSmart newsletter page. You will also import text describing the steps for packing a suitcase, place a copy of the imported text on the newsletter page, and format it as an ordered list.

Creating Unordered Lists

Unordered lists are lists of items that do not need to be placed in a specific order. A grocery list that lists items in a random order is a good example of an unordered list. Items in unordered lists are usually preceded by a **bullet**, or a small raised dot or similar icon. Unordered lists that contain bullets are sometimes called **bulleted lists**. Though you can use paragraph indentations to create an unordered list, bullets can often make lists easier to read. To create an unordered list, you first select the text you want to format as an unordered list, then you use the Unordered List button in the Property inspector to insert bullets at the beginning of each paragraph of the selected text.

Formatting Unordered Lists

In Dreamweaver, the default bullet style is a round dot. To change the bullet style to square, you need to expand the Property inspector to its full size as shown in Figure C-1, click List Item in the Property inspector to open the List Properties dialog box, then set the style for bulleted lists to square. Be aware, however, that not all browsers display square bullets correctly, in which case the bullets will appear as round dots.

Creating Ordered Lists

Ordered lists, which are sometimes called **numbered lists**, are lists of items that are presented in a specific order and that are preceded by numbers or letters in sequence.

An ordered list is appropriate for a list in which each item must be executed according to its specified order. A list that provides numbered directions for driving from Point A to Point B or a list that provides instructions for assembling a bicycle are both examples of ordered lists.

Formatting Ordered Lists

You can format an ordered list to show different styles of numbers or letters using the List Properties dialog box, as shown in Figure C-2. You can apply numbers, Roman numerals, lowercase letters, or capital letters to an ordered list.

Creating Definition Lists

You can also use Dreamweaver to create definition lists. A **definition list** consists of a list of terms, where each term is followed by an indented paragraph. Definitions in a dictionary or topics in a book index are both examples of definition lists.

FIGURE C-1
Expanded Property inspector

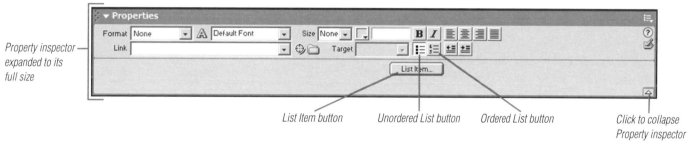

Property inspector expanded to its full size

List Item button   Unordered List button   Ordered List button   Click to collapse Property inspector

FIGURE C-2
Choosing a numbered list style in the List Properties dialog box

List Type list arrow

Numbered List styles

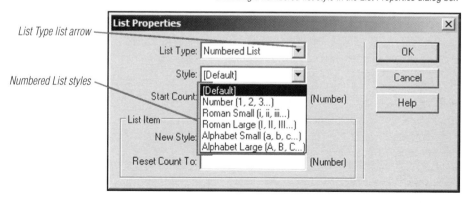

Create an unordered list

1. Open the newsletter page in the TripSmart Web site. (If you do not have the completed TripSmart Web site from Unit B, contact your instructor for assistance.)

2. Position the insertion point to the left of Expandable clothesline and clothespins in the second paragraph, scroll to the end of the page, press and hold [Shift], click to the right of the last sentence on the page, then release [Shift].

3. Click the Unordered List button in the Property inspector to format the selected text as an unordered list, click anywhere to deselect the text, then compare your screen to Figure C-3. ▤

4. Click the insertion point after the last sentence on the page, then press [Enter] (Win) or [return] (Mac) twice to end the unordered list.

   | TIP Pressing [Enter] (Win) or [return] (Mac) once at the end of an unordered list creates another bulleted item. To end an unordered list, press [Enter] (Win) or [return] (Mac) twice.

5. Save your work.

You opened the newsletter page in Design view and formatted the list of essential items to pack as an unordered list.

FIGURE C-3
Creating an unordered list

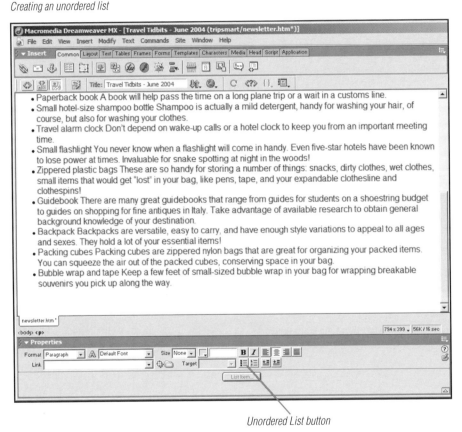

Unordered List button

Working with Text and Graphics

FIGURE C-4
List Properties dialog box

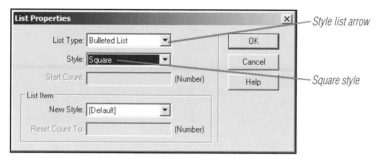

Style list arrow

Square style

1. Click any of the items in the unordered list to place the insertion point in the list.

2. Expand the Property inspector (if necessary), click the List Item button in the Property inspector to open the List Properties dialog box, click the Style list arrow, click Square, as shown in Figure C-4, then click OK.

   [List Item...]

   The bullets in the unordered list now have a square shape.

3. Position the insertion point to the left of the first item in the unordered list, then click the Show Code View button on the toolbar to view the code for the unordered list, as shown in Figure C-5.

   Notice that there is a pair of HTML codes, or tags, surrounding each type of element on the page. The first tag in each pair begins the code for a particular element, and the last tag ends the code for the element. For instance, the tags <ul></ul> surround the unordered list. The tags <li> and </li> surround each item in the list.

4. Click the Show Design View button on the toolbar, then save your work.

You used the List Properties dialog box to apply the square bullet style to the unordered list. You then viewed the HTML code for the unordered list in Code view.

FIGURE C-5
HTML tags in Code view for unordered list

Beginning tag for unordered list

First pair of tags for the first item in the list

Click to open List Properties dialog box

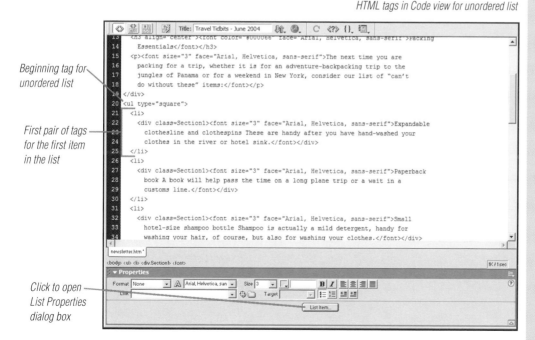

Create an ordered list

1. Use the Import Word HTML command to import the data file how_to_pack.htm from the unit_c folder where your data files are stored, copy all the text in the how_to_pack.htm file, then close the file without saving it.

2. Paste the copied text just below the last unordered list item on the newsletter page.

3. Place the insertion point to the left of Avoiding Wrinkle Woes, then click the Horizontal Rule button on the Insert bar.

   A horizontal rule appears and helps to separate the unordered list from the text you just pasted.

4. Select the text beginning with Decide what items to take and ending with the last sentence on the page.

5. Click the Ordered List button in the Property inspector to format the selected text as an ordered list.

6. Deselect the text, compare your screen to Figure C-6, then save your work.

You imported text, copied it, and then pasted it on the newsletter page. You also added a horizontal rule to help organize the page. Finally, you formatted selected text as an ordered list.

FIGURE C-6
Creating an ordered list

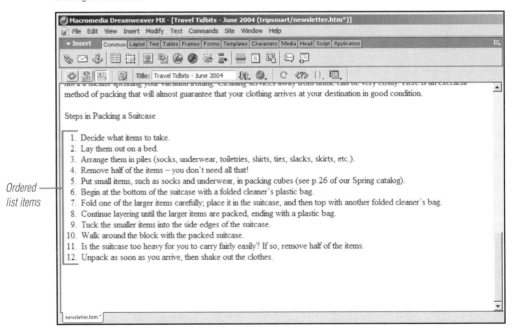

Ordered list items

Working with Text and Graphics

FIGURE C-7
Newsletter page with ordered list

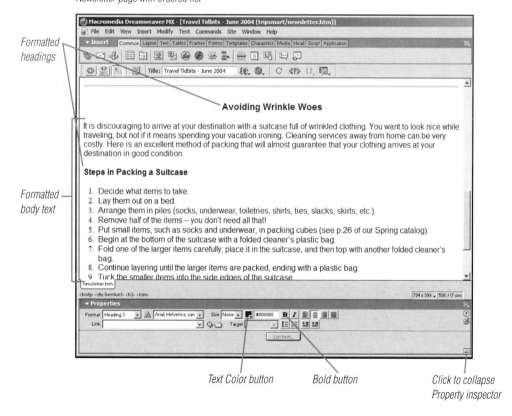

Formatted headings

Formatted body text

Text Color button   Bold button   Click to collapse Property inspector

1. Select all the text below the horizontal rule, then change the font to Arial, Helvetica, sans-serif, size 3.

2. Select the heading Steps in Packing a Suitcase, then click the Bold button in the Property inspector. **B**

3. Click the Text Color button in the Property inspector to open the color picker, then click the first square in the third row, color #000066.

4. Format the Avoiding Wrinkle Woes heading to match the Packing Essentials heading.

5. Compare your screen to Figure C-7, then save your work.

> TIP If you want to see more of your Web page in the document window, you can collapse the Property inspector.

You applied a new font and font size to the ordered list. You also formatted the Avoiding Wrinkle Woes heading to match the Packing Essentials heading.

CREATE, APPLY AND EDIT CASCADING STYLE SHEETS

What You'll Do

 In this lesson, you will create a Cascading Style Sheet file for the TripSmart Web site. You also will create styles called bullets and heading and apply them to the newsletter page.

Using Cascading Style Sheets

When you want to apply the same formatting attributes to page elements such as text, objects, and tables, you can save a significant amount of time by using Cascading Style Sheets. A **Cascading Style Sheet** (CSS) is a made up of sets of formatting attributes that are either saved with a descriptive name or that redefine the appearance of an HTML tag. CSS style sheets are saved as individual files with the .css extension and stored in the directory structure of a Web site, as shown in Figure C-8. CSS style sheets contain **styles**, which are formatting attributes that can be applied to page elements.

You use the buttons on the CSS Styles panel to create, edit, and apply styles. To add a style, you use the New CSS Style dialog box to name the style and specify whether to add it to a new or existing style sheet. You then use the CSS Style Definition dialog box to set the formatting attributes for the style. Once you add a new style to a style sheet, it appears in a list in the CSS Styles panel. To apply a

style, you select the text to which you want to apply the style, then you click the style name in the CSS Styles panel. You can apply CSS styles to any element on a Web page or to all of the pages in a Web site. When you make a change to a style, all page elements formatted with that style are automatically updated. Once you create a CSS style sheet you can attach it to other pages in your Web site.

You can use CSS Styles to save an enormous amount of time. Being able to define a style and then apply it to page elements on all the pages of your Web site means that you can make hundreds of formatting changes in a few minutes. Be aware, however, that not all browsers can read CSS Styles. Versions of Internet Explorer that are 4.0 or lower do not support CSS styles. Only Netscape Navigator version 6.0 or higher supports CSS styles.

QUICKTIP

You can also use CSS styles to format other page content such as backgrounds, borders, lists, and boxes.

Understanding CSS Style Sheet Settings

If you open a style sheet file, you will see the coding for the CSS styles. A CSS style consists of two parts: the selector and the declaration. The **selector** is the name or the tag to which the style declarations have been assigned. The **declaration** consists of the property and the value. For example, Figure C-9 shows the code for the tripsmart.css style sheet. In this example, the first property listed for the bullets style is font-family. The value for this property is Arial, Helvetica, sans-serif.

FIGURE C-8
Cascading Style Sheet file listed in tripsmart root folder

FIGURE C-9
tripsmart.css style file

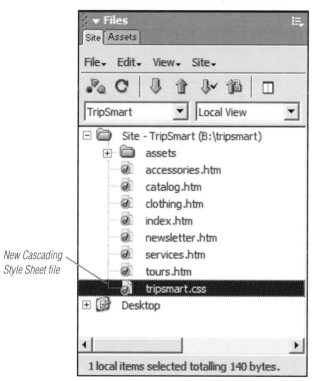

New Cascading Style Sheet file

```
1   .bullets {
2       font-family: Arial, Helvetica, sans-serif;
3       font-size: 16px;
4       font-style: normal;
5       font-weight: bold;
6       color: #000066;
7   }
8   .heading {
9       font-family: Arial, Helvetica, sans-serif;
10      font-size: 16px;
11      font-style: normal;
12      font-weight: bold;
13      color: #000066;
14      text-align: center;
15  }
16
```

Create a Cascading Style Sheet and a style

1. Click Window on the menu bar, then click CSS Styles to open the CSS Styles panel (if necessary).

2. Click the New CSS Style button at the bottom of the CSS Styles panel to open the New CSS Style dialog box, verify that the Make Custom Style (class) option button is selected, then type **bullets** in the Name text box.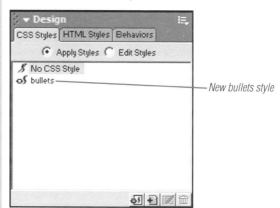

   > TIP Class names are preceded by a period. If you don't enter a period when you type the name, Dreamweaver will add the period for you.

3. Click the Define in list arrow, click New Style Sheet File, compare your screen with Figure C-10, then click OK.

   The Save Style Sheet File As dialog box opens.

4. Type **tripsmart** in the File name text box (Win) or the Save As text box (Mac), then click Save to open the CSS Style Definition for .bullets in tripsmart.css dialog box.

   The bullets style will be stored within the tripsmart.css file.

5. Verify that Type is selected in the Category list, set the Font to Arial, Helvetica, sans-serif, set the Size at 12 pixels, set the Weight to bold, set the Color to #000066, set the Style to normal, compare your screen to Figure C-11, then click OK.

   The CSS style named bullets appears in the CSS Styles panel, as shown in Figure C-12.

6. Save your work.

You created a Cascading Style Sheet file named tripsmart.css and a style called .bullets.

FIGURE C-10
New CSS Style dialog box

New style name

FIGURE C-11
CSS Style Definition for .bullets in tripsmart.css dialog box

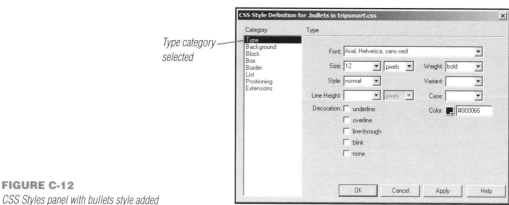

Type category selected

FIGURE C-12
CSS Styles panel with bullets style added

New bullets style

Working with Text and Graphics

FIGURE C-13

Applying a CSS style to selected text

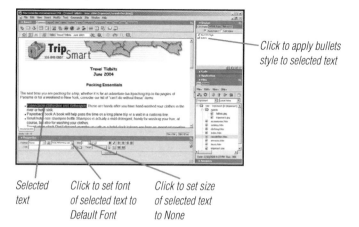

Click to apply bullets
style to selected text

Selected
text

Click to set font
of selected text to
Default Font

Click to set size
of selected text
to None

FIGURE C-14

Unordered list with bullets style applied

bullets style
applied to each
item in list

1. Verify that the Apply Styles option is selected in the CSS Styles panel, select the text Expandable clothesline and clothespins, as shown in Figure C-13, then use the Property inspector to set the Format to Default Font and the Size to none.

   > **TIP** Before you apply a style to selected text you need to remove all formatting attributes such as font and color from it, or the style will not be applied correctly.

2. Click bullets in the CSS Styles panel to apply the bullets style to the selected text.

3. Repeat Steps 1 and 2 to apply the bullets style to each of the nine remaining items in the unordered list.

4. Compare your screen to Figure C-14, then save your work.

You applied the bullets style to each item in the Packing Essentials list.

Attaching a style sheet file to another document

When you have several pages in a Web site, you will probably want to use the same CSS style sheet for each page to ensure that all your elements have a consistent appearance. To attach a style sheet to another document, click the Attach Style Sheet button 🔳 on the CSS Styles panel to open the Link External Style Sheet dialog box, make sure the Add as Link option is selected, browse to locate the file you want to attach, then click OK. The styles contained in the attached style sheet will appear in the CSS Styles panel in the Edit Styles mode, and you can use them to apply styles to any text on the page.

Edit a Cascading Style Sheet

1. Click the Edit Styles option at the top of the CSS Styles panel, click bullets in the CSS Styles panel, then click the Edit Style Sheet button at the bottom of the CSS Styles panel to open the CSS Style Definition for .bullets in tripsmart.css dialog box. 📝

   TIP You can also double-click a style in the CSS Styles panel to open the CSS Style Definition dialog box.

2. Click the Size list arrow, click 16, compare your screen to Figure C-15, click OK, then compare your screen to Figure C-16.

   The bullet text is now much bigger than before, reflecting the changes you made to the bullets style.

   TIP If you position the insertion point in text that has a CSS style applied to it, that style is highlighted in the CSS Styles panel.

3. Save your work.

You edited the bullet style to change the font size to 16 pixels. You then viewed the results of the edited style in the unordered list.

FIGURE C-15
Editing a CSS Style

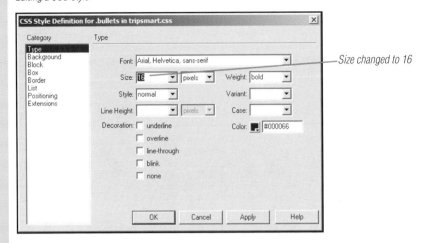

Size changed to 16

FIGURE C-16
Unordered list with edited bullets style applied

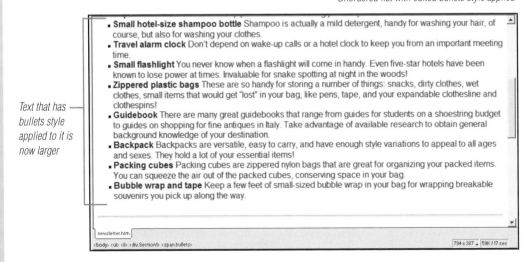

Text that has bullets style applied to it is now larger

Working with Text and Graphics

FIGURE C-17
Adding a style to a CSS style sheet

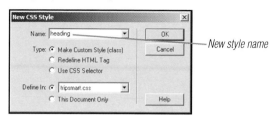

— *New style name*

FIGURE C-18
Formatting options for heading style

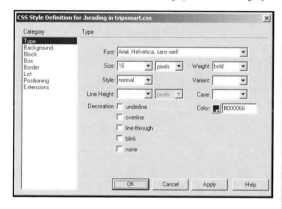

FIGURE C-19
Setting text alignment for headings style

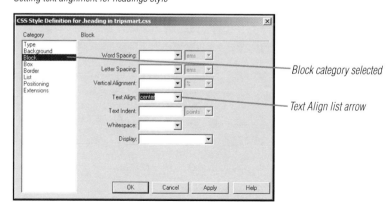

— *Block category selected*

— *Text Align list arrow*

Lesson 2   Create, Apply, and Edit Cascading Style Sheets

Add a style to a Cascading Style Sheet

1. Click the New CSS Style button at the bottom of the CSS Styles Panel. ⊞

2. Type **heading** in the Name Text box, as shown in Figure C-17, then click OK.

3. Set the Font to Arial, Helvetica, sans-serif, set the Size to 16, set the Style to normal, set the Weight to bold, set the Color to #000066, then compare your screen to Figure C-18.

4. Click the Block category in the New CSS Style Definition for .heading in tripsmart.css dialog box, click the Text Align list arrow, click center, as shown in Figure C-19, then click OK.

5. Select the heading Packing Essentials, use the Property inspector to set the Format to Paragraph and the Font to Default Font then click the Align Center button to remove the alignment setting.

6. With the heading still selected, click the Text Color button to open the color picker, then click the Strikethrough button. ☐ ☑

7. Click the heading style in the CSS Styles panel to apply the heading style to the Packing Essentials heading.

8. Repeat Steps 5 through 7 to apply the heading style to the text Avoiding Wrinkle Woes, collapse the Design panel group, then save your work.

> TIP   Be careful not to click a style name with the insertion point in text unless you intend to apply that style to that text.

You added a new style called heading to the tripsmart .CSS file. You then applied the heading style to selected text.

INSERT AND ALIGN GRAPHICS

What You'll Do

In this lesson, you will insert three graphics on the tours page in the TripSmart Web site. You will then stagger the alignment of the images on the page to make the page more visually appealing.

Understanding Graphic File Formats

When you add graphics to a Web page, it's important to choose the appropriate graphic file format. The three primary graphic file formats used in Web pages are GIF (Graphics Interchange Format), JPEG (Joint Photographic Experts Group), and PNG (Portable Network Graphics). GIF files download very quickly, making them ideal to use on Web pages. Though limited in the number of colors they can represent, GIF files have the ability to show transparent areas. JPEG files can display many colors. Because they often contain many shades of the same color, photographs are often saved in JPEG format. Files saved with the PNG format share advantages of both GIFs and JPEGs, but are not universally recognized by older browsers.

QUICKTIP

The status bar displays the download time for the page. Each time you add a new graphic to the page, you can see how much additional time is added to the total download time.

Understanding the Assets Panel

When you add a graphic to a Web site, it is added automatically to the Assets panel. The **Assets panel**, located in the Files panel group, displays all the assets in a Web site. The Assets panel contains nine category buttons that you use to view your assets by category. These include Images, Colors, URLs, Flash, Shockwave, Movies, Scripts, Templates, and Library. To view a particular type of asset, click the appropriate category button. The Assets panel is split into two panes. When you click the Images button, as shown in Figure C-20, the lower pane displays a list of all the images in your site and contains four columns. The top pane displays a thumbnail of the selected image in the list. You can view assets in each category in two ways. You can use the Site option button to view all the assets in a Web site, or you can use the Favorites option button to view those assets that you have designated as **favorites**, or assets that you expect to use repeatedly while you work on the site.

You might need to resize the Assets panel to see all four columns. To resize the Assets panel, undock the Files panel group and drag the window borders as needed.

Aligning Images

When you insert an image on a Web page, you need to position it in relation to other elements on the page. Positioning an image is referred to as aligning an image. By default, when you insert an image in a paragraph, its bottom edge aligns with the baseline of the first line of text or any other element in the same paragraph. When you select an image, the Align text box in the Property inspector displays the alignment setting for the image. You can change the alignment setting using the options on the Align list in the Property inspector.

The Align list options function differently than the Align buttons in the Property inspector. You use the Align buttons to center, left-align, or right-align an element without regard to how the element is aligned in relation to other elements.

FIGURE C-20
Assets panel

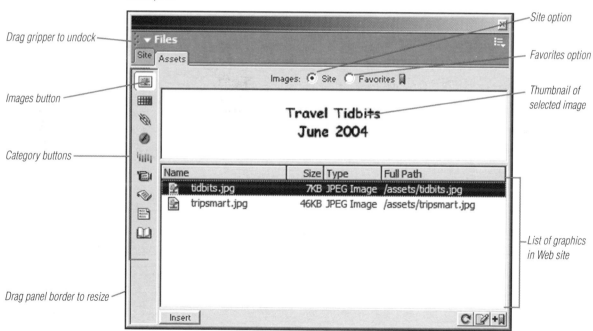

Drag gripper to undock

Images button

Category buttons

Drag panel border to resize

Site option

Favorites option

Thumbnail of selected image

List of graphics in Web site

Insert a graphic

1. Open dwc_1.htm from the unit_c folder where your data files are stored, then save it as **tours.htm** in the tripsmart root folder, overwriting the existing tours.htm file.

2. Set the path for the TripSmart banner as assets/tripsmart.jpg.

3. Position the insertion point in front of Our in the first paragraph, click the Image button on the Insert bar to open the Select Image Source dialog box, navigate to the unit_c assets folder, double-click zebra_mothers.jpg to insert this image on the page, then verify that the file was copied to your assets folder in the tripsmart root folder.

   Compare your screen to Figure C-21.

4. Click the Assets panel tab in the Files panel group (Win), or click the expander arrow next to the Files panel group (Mac), click the Images button on the Assets panel (if necessary), then click the Refresh Site List button at the bottom of the Assets panel to update the list of images in the TripSmart Web site.

   The Assets panel displays a list of all the images in the TripSmart Web site, as shown in Figure C-22. A thumbnail of the zebra image appears above the list.

   (continued)

FIGURE C-21
TripSmart tours page with inserted image

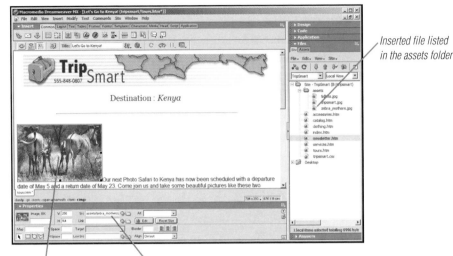

Inserted file listed in the assets folder

zebra_mothers.jpg file inserted

Path should begin with the word "assets"

FIGURE C-22
Image files for TripSmart Web site listed in Assets panel

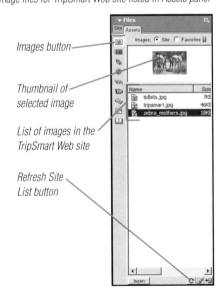

Images button

Thumbnail of selected image

List of images in the TripSmart Web site

Refresh Site List button

Working with Text and Graphics

FIGURE C-23

Assets panel with five images

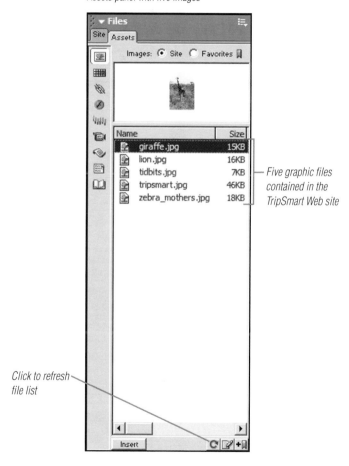

Click to refresh file list

Five graphic files contained in the TripSmart Web site

5. Insert the data file lion.jpg to the left of This at the beginning of the second paragraph, then refresh the Assets panel to verify that the lion.jpg file was copied to the assets folder of the TripSmart Web site.

> TIP The file lion.jpg is located in the assets folder in the unit_c folder where your data files are stored.

6. Insert the data file giraffe.jpg to the left of All safari vehicles at the beginning of the third paragraph, refresh the Assets panel to verify that the file was copied to the Web site, then save your work.

Your Assets panel should resemble Figure C-23.

You inserted the data file three images on the tours page and copied each image to the assets folder of the TripSmart Web site.

Align a graphic

1. Scroll to the top of the page, click the zebra image to select it, then expand the Property inspector (if necessary).

   Because an image is selected, the Property inspector displays tools you can use to set the properties of an image.

2. Click the Align list arrow in the Property inspector, then click Left.

   The zebra photo is now left-aligned and the paragraph text flows around its right edge as shown in Figure C-24. You might see a blue or yellow alignment icon next to the zebra image indicating that the image has been aligned.

   > TIP To show or hide alignment icons click View on the menu bar, point to Visual Aids, then click Invisible Elements.

   (continued)

FIGURE C-24
Left-aligned zebra image

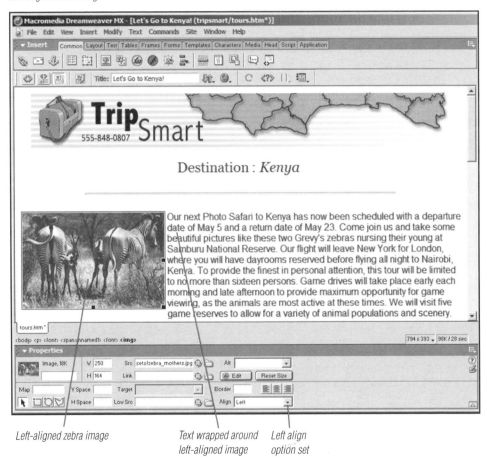

Left-aligned zebra image

Text wrapped around left-aligned image

Left align option set

FIGURE C-25

Aligned images on the tours page

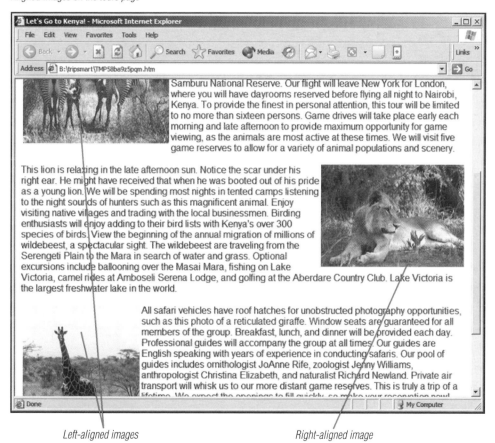

Left-aligned images   Right-aligned image

3. Select the the lion image, click the Align list arrow in the Property inspector, then click Right.

4. Align the giraffe image, using the Left Align option.

5. Save your work.

6. Preview the Web page in your browser, compare your screen to Figure C-25, then close your browser.

You used the Property inspector to set the alignment for the zebra, giraffe, and lion images. You then previewed the page in your browser.

ENHANCE AN IMAGE AND USE ALTERNATE TEXT

What You'll Do

 In this lesson, you will add borders around the images on the tours page, adjust the horizontal space around the images to set them apart from the text, and then add alternate text to describe each image on the page.

Enhancing an Image

After you place an image on a Web page, you have several options for enhancing it, or improving its appearance. To make changes to the image itself, such as removing scratches from it, or making it lighter or darker, you need to use an image editor such as Macromedia Fireworks or Adobe Photoshop. However, you can use Dreamweaver to enhance certain aspects of how images appear on a page. For example, you can add borders around an image or add horizontal and vertical space. **Borders** are frames that surround an image. Horizontal and vertical space is blank space above, below, and on the sides of an image that separates the image from text or other elements on the page. Adding horizontal or vertical space, which is the same as adding white space, helps images

Resizing graphics using an external editor

Each image on a Web page takes a specific number of seconds to download, depending on the size of the file. Larger files (in kilobytes, not width and height) take longer to download than smaller files. It's important to figure out the smallest acceptable size for an image on your Web page. Then, if you need to resize an image to reduce the file size, use an external image editor to do so, *instead* of resizing it in Dreamweaver. Although you can adjust the width and height settings of an image in the Property inspector to change the size of the image as it appears on your screen, these settings do not affect the file size. Decreasing the size of an image using the H Size (height) and W Size (width) settings in the Property inspector does *not* reduce the time it will take the file to download. Ideally you should use graphics that have the smallest file size and the highest quality possible, so that each page downloads in eight seconds or less.

stand out on a page. In the Web page shown in Figure C-26, the horizontal and vertical space around the small images in the center column helps make these images more prominent. Adding horizontal or vertical space does not affect the width or height of the image.

QUICK**TIP**

Because some linked images are displayed with borders, viewers might mistake an image that contains a border with a hyperlink. For this reason, you should use borders sparingly.

Using Alternate Text

One of the easiest ways to make your Web page viewer-friendly and handicapped-accessible is to use alternate text. **Alternate text** is descriptive text that appears in place of an image while the image is downloading or when the mouse pointer is placed over it. You can program some browsers to display only alternate text and to download images manually. Alternate text can be "read" by a **screen reader**, a device used by the visually impaired to convert written text on a computer monitor to spoken

words. Screen readers and alternate text make it possible for visually impaired viewers to have an image described to them in detail. You can also set up Dreamweaver to prompt you to enter alternate text whenever you insert an image on a page.

FIGURE C-26
Museum of Fine Arts Web site

Add a border

1. Select the zebra image, then expand the Property inspector (if necessary).

2. Type **2** in the Border text box, as shown in Figure C-27, then press [Tab] to apply the border to the zebra image.

3. Repeat Step 2 to add borders to the lion and giraffe images.

4. Save your work.

You added a 2-pixel border to each image on the tours page.

Add horizontal space

1. Select the zebra image, type **10** in the H Space text box in the Property inspector, press [Tab], then compare your screen to Figure C-28.

   The text is more evenly wrapped around the image and is easier to read, since it is not so close to the edge of the image.

2. Repeat Step 1 to set the H Space to 10 for the lion and giraffe images.

   The spacing under each picture differs because of the difference in the lengths of the paragraphs.

3. Save your work.

You added horizontal spacing around each image on the tours page.

FIGURE C-27
Using the Property inspector to add a border

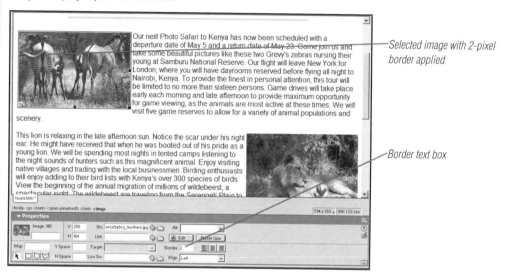

Selected image with 2-pixel border applied

Border text box

FIGURE C-28
Using the Property inspector to add horizontal space

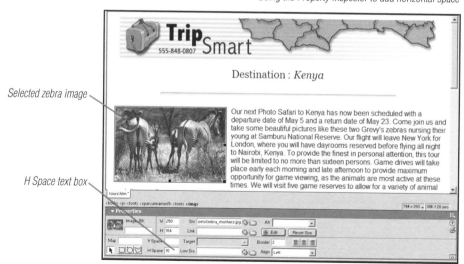

Selected zebra image

H Space text box

FIGURE C-29

Property inspector showing altered width and height settings of giraffe image

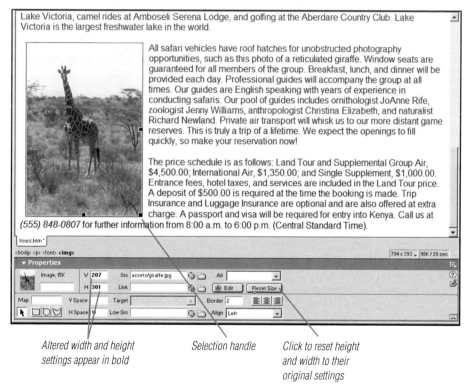

Altered width and height
settings appear in bold

Selection handle

Click to reset height
and width to their
original settings

1. Select the giraffe image, press and hold [Shift], then slowly drag the bottom-right corner selection handle of the giraffe image down and to the right about an eighth of an inch to increase the image size slightly, as shown in Figure C-29.

   Holding [Shift] while you drag a corner selection handle keeps the image in proportion.

   TIP   To increase or decrease an image size significantly, resize the graphic using an image editor.

2. Resize the lion and giraffe images (if necessary).

   TIP   To return a resized graphic to its original size, click the Reset Size button in the Property inspector.

3. Save your work.

You adjusted the size of the giraffe image to improve the appearance of text around it.

Use alternate text

1. Select the zebra image, type **Two zebra mothers with their babies** in the Alt text box in the Property inspector, as shown in Figure C-30, then press [Enter] (Win) or [return] (Mac).

2. Preview the page in your browser, then point to the zebra image until the alternate text appears, as shown in Figure C-31.

3. Close your browser.

4. Select the lion image, type **Lion relaxing in the Kenyan sun** in the Alt text box in the Property inspector, then press [Enter] (Win) or [return] (Mac).

5. Select the giraffe image, type **Reticulated giraffe posed among acacia trees and brush** in the Alt text box in the Property inspector, then press [Enter] (Win) or [return] (Mac).

6. Save your work.

7. Preview the page in your browser, view the alternate text for each image, then close your browser.

You added alternate text to each of the four images on the page, then you viewed the alternate text in your browser.

FIGURE C-30
Alternate text setting in the Property inspector

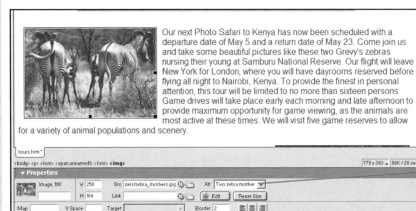

Alt text box

FIGURE C-31
Alternate text displayed in browser

Alternate text displayed on top of image

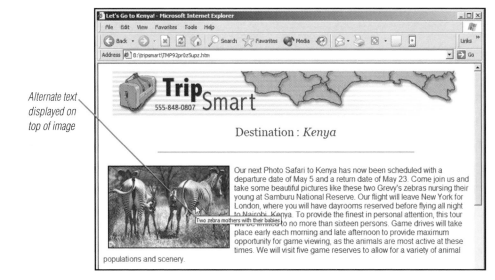

Working with Text and Graphics

FIGURE C-32

Preferences dialog box with Accessibility category selected

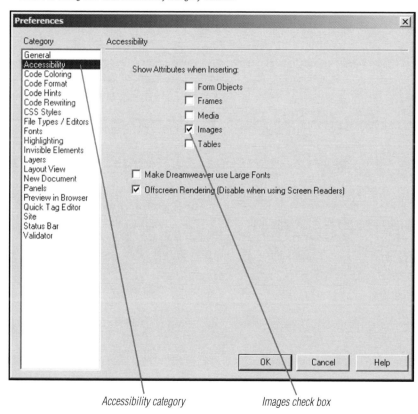

Accessibility category   Images check box

Set the alternate text accessibility option

1. Click Edit on the menu bar, click Preferences to open the Preferences dialog box, then click the Accessibility category.

2. Click the Images check box as shown in Figure C-32, then click OK.

   TIP   Once you set the Accessibility preferences, they will be in effect for all Web sites that you develop, not just the one that's open when you set them.

You set the Accessibility preferences to prompt you to enter alternate text each time you insert a graphic on a Web page.

INSERT A BACKGROUND IMAGE AND PERFORM SITE MAINTENANCE

What You'll Do

 In this lesson, you will insert a tiled image and then a seamless image. You will then use the Assets panel to delete them both from the Web site. You will also check for non-Web-safe colors in the Assets panel and delete one that you locate on the home page.

Inserting a Background Image

You can insert a background image on a Web page to provide depth and visual interest to the page, or to communicate a message or mood. **Background images** are graphic files used in place of background colors. Although you can use background images to create a dramatic effect, you should avoid inserting them on Web pages that have lots of text and other elements. Even though they might seem too plain, standard white backgrounds are usually the best choice for Web pages. If you choose to use a background image on a Web page, it should be small in file size, and preferably in GIF format. You can insert either a tiled image or a seamless image as a background. A **tiled image** is a small graphic that repeats across and down a Web page, appearing as individual squares or rectangles. A **seamless image** is a tiled image that is blurred at the edges so it appears to be one image. When you create a Web page, you should use either a background color or a background image, but not both, unless you have a need for

the background color to be displayed while the background image finishes downloading. The background in the Web page shown in Figure C-33 contains several images arranged in a table format.

Managing Graphics

As you work on a Web site, you might find that you accumulate files in your assets folder that are not used in the site. To avoid accumulating unnecessary files, it's a good idea to look at a graphic on a page first, before you copy it to the assets folder. If you inadvertently copy an unwanted file to the assets folder, you should delete it or move it to another location. This is a good Web-site management practice that will prevent the assets folder from filling up with unwanted graphics.

Removing a graphic from a Web page does not remove it from the assets folder in the local root folder of the Web site. To remove an asset from a Web site, you can first locate the file you want to remove in the Assets panel. You then use the Locate in

Site command to open the Site panel with the unwanted file selected. You then use the Delete command to remove the file from the site.

QUICKTIP

You cannot use the Assets panel to delete a file. You must use the Site panel to delete files and perform all file-management tasks.

Removing Colors from a Web Site

You can use the Assets panel to locate non-Web-safe colors in a Web site. **Non-Web-safe** colors are colors that may not be displayed uniformly across platforms. After you remove colors from a Web site, you should use the Refresh Site List button on the Assets panel to verify that these colors have been removed. Sometimes it's necessary to press [Ctrl] (Win) or [Command] (Mac)

while you click the Refresh Site List button. If refreshing the Assets panel does not work, try re-creating the site cache, then refreshing the Assets panel again

QUICKTIP

To re-create the site cache, open the Site panel, click Site on the Site panel menu bar, then click Recreate Site Cache (Win), or choose Site from the Document menu, then choose Recreate Site Cache (Mac).

FIGURE C-33
Mansion on Turtle Creek

Insert a background image

1. Click Modify on the menu bar, then click Page Properties to open the Page Properties dialog box.

2. Click the Browse button next to the Background Image text box, navigate to the unit_c assets folder, then double-click tile_bak.gif.

   The tile_bak.gif file is automatically copied to the TripSmart assets folder.

3. Click OK to close the Page Properties dialog box, then click the Refresh button to refresh the file list in the Assets panel.

   A blue tiled background made up of individual squares replaces the white background. See Figure C-34.

4. Repeat Steps 1 and 2 to replace the tile_bak.gif background image with the data file seamless_bak.gif, located in the unit_c assets folder.

   See Figure C-35. The seamless background makes it hard to tell where one square stops and the other begins.

5. Save your work.

You applied a tiled background for the tours page. Then you replaced the tiled background with a seamless background.

FIGURE C-34

Tours page with a tiled background

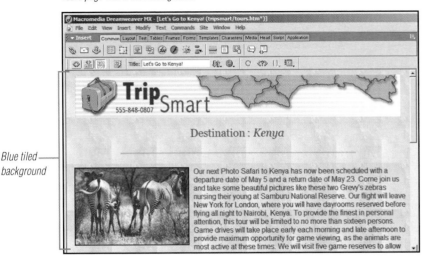

Blue tiled background

FIGURE C-35

Tours page with a seamless background

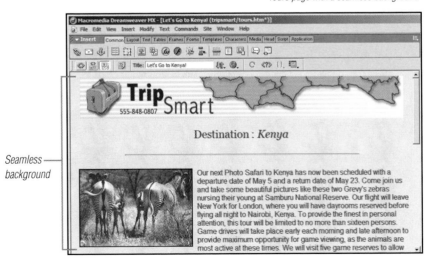

Seamless background

Working with Text and Graphics

1. Click Modify on the menu bar, then click
   Page Properties.

2. Select the text in the Background Image text
   box as shown in Figure C-36, press [Delete],
   then click OK.

   The background of the tours page is
   white again.

3. Save your work.

*You deleted the link to the background image file to
change the tours page background back to white.*

FIGURE C-36
Removing a background image

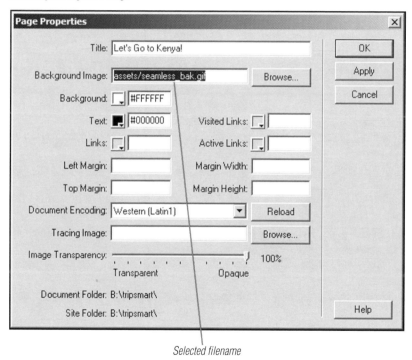

Selected filename

Delete files from a Web site

1. Click the Assets panel tab (Win), or expand the Files panel group (Mac) (if necessary).

2. Right-click (Win) or [control] click (Mac) seamless_bak.gif in the Assets panel, click Locate in Site to open the Site panel, select seamless_bak.gif in the Site panel (if necessary), press [Delete], then click OK in the dialog box that appears.

3. Repeat Step 2 to remove tile_bak.gif from the Web site, open the Assets panel, then refresh the Assets panel.

   Your Assets panel should resemble Figure C-37.

   You removed two image files from the TripSmart Web site, then refreshed the Assets panel.

FIGURE C-37
Images listed in Assets panel

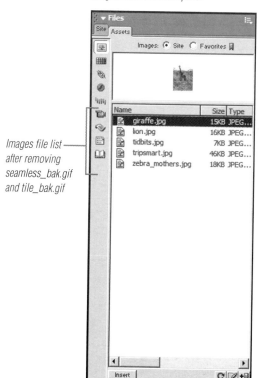

Images file list after removing seamless_bak.gif and tile_bak.gif

Managing graphic files

It is a good idea to store copies of your original Web site graphic files in a separate folder, outside the assets folder of your Web site. If you edit the original files, save them again using different names. Doing this ensures that you will be able to find a file in its original, unaltered state. You might have no need for certain files now, but you might need them later. Storing currently unused files also helps to keep your assets folder free of clutter. Storing copies of original Web site graphic files in a separate location also ensures that you have back-up copies in the event that you accidentally delete a file from the Web site that you need later.

FIGURE C-38
Colors listed in Assets panel

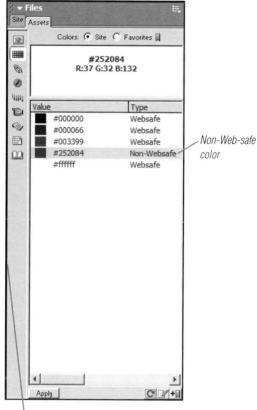

Non-Web-safe color

Drag this border to the left to expand panel width

FIGURE C-39
Non-Web-safe color removed from Assets panel

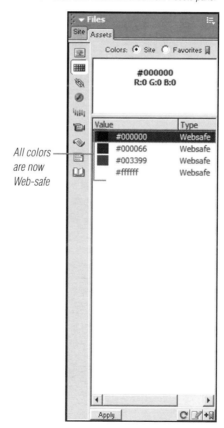

All colors are now Web-safe

Remove non-Web-safe colors from a Web site

1. Click the Colors button in the Assets panel to display the colors used in the Web site, then drag the left border of the Assets panel (if necessary) to expand it to the second column. ▥

   The Assets panel shows that color 252084 is non-Web-safe, as shown in Figure C-38. This color appears in a heading on the home page.

2. Click the Site panel tab (Win), or click Site on the menu bar, place your pointer on Open Site, then click TripSmart (Mac).

3. Double-click index.htm to open the home page.

4. Select The smart way to go!, click the Text Color button in the Property inspector to open the color picker, click the Strikethough button, type #003399 in the Color text box, press [Tab] to apply the new color, then click anywhere to deselect the text. ☐ ☑

   The heading text is now a different shade of blue with the Web-safe color #003399 applied.

5. Click the Assets panel tab, press and hold [Ctrl] (Win) or [Command] (Mac), click the Refresh Site List button then compare your screen to Figure C-39. ⟳

6. Save your work, preview the page in your browser, close your browser, then close all open files.

You removed one non-Web-safe color from the Web site, then refreshed the Assets panel.

Create unordered and ordered lists.

1. Open the Blooms & Bulbs Web site. (If you did not create this Web site in Units A and B, contact your instructor for assistance.)

2. Open the file dwc_2.htm from the unit_c data files folder, then save the file as **tips.htm** in the Blooms & Bulbs Web site, overwriting the existing tips.htm file.

3. Reset the path for the planting_tips.jpg graphic to the assets folder of the Blooms & Bulbs Web site.

4. Reset the path for the Blooms banner to the assets folder of the Blooms & Bulbs Web site.

5. Import the gardening_tips.htm file from the unit_c data files folder using the Import Word HTML command.

6. Copy the imported text, then close the gardening_tips.htm file without saving it.

7. Paste the copied text onto the tips page below the planting tips text graphic, then format the imported text as Arial, Helvetica, sans-serif, size 3.

8. Select the four lines of text below the Seasonal Gardening Checklist heading and format them as an unordered list.

9. Select the lines of text below the Basic Gardening tips heading and format them as an ordered list.

10. Save your work.

Create, apply, and edit Cascading Style Sheets.

1. Create a new CSS Style named **.seasons**, making sure the Make Custom Style (class) and the New Style Sheet File option buttons are both selected in the New CSS Style dialog box.

2. Name the style sheet file **blooms** in the Save Style Sheet File As dialog box.

3. Choose the following settings for the seasons style: Font = Arial, Helvetica, sans-serif, Size = 12 pixels, Style = normal, Weight = bold, and Color = #006633.

4. Change the Font setting to Default Font and the Size setting to None for the following text in the Seasonal Gardening Checklist: Fall:, Winter:, Spring:, and Summer:. (Be sure to include the colons.) Then, apply the seasons style to Fall:, Winter:, Spring:, and Summer:.

5. Edit the seasons style by changing the font size to 16 pixels.

6. Add an additional style called **headings** and define this style choosing the following type settings: Font = Arial, Helvetica, sans-serif, Size = 18 pixels, Style = normal, Weight = bold, and Color = #006633.

7. Apply the heading style to the two subheadings on the page: Seasonal Gardening Checklist and Basic Gardening Tips. (Make sure you remove any manual formatting before applying the style.)

8. Save your work and view the page in the browser.

9. Close the browser and the tips page.

Insert and align graphics.

1. Open the file dwc_3.htm from the unit_c data files folder, then save it as **plants.htm** in the Blooms & Bulbs Web site, overwriting the existing plants.htm file.

2. Verify that the path of the Blooms & Bulbs banner is set correctly to the assets folder in the blooms root folder.

3. Insert the iris.jpg file from the assets folder located in the unit_c data files folder to the left of the words Beautiful spring iris and add **Purple iris** as alternate text if prompted to do so.

4. Insert the tulips.jpg file from the unit_c assets folder file in front of the words Dramatic masses and add **Red and yellow tulips** as alternate text if prompted to do so.

5. Insert the pansies.jpg file from the unit_c assets folder in front of the words Pretty pansies and add **Deep violet pansies** as alternate text if prompted to do so.

6. Refresh the Site panel to verify that all three images were copied to the assets folder.

7. Left-align the iris image.

8. Left-align the tulips image.

9. Left-align the pansies image.

10. Save your work.

Enhance an image and use alternate text.

1. Apply a 2-pixel border and horizontal spacing of 5 pixels around the iris image.
2. Apply a 2-pixel border and horizontal spacing of 5 pixels around the tulips image.
3. Apply a 2-pixel border and horizontal spacing of 5 pixels around the pansies image.
4. Add the text **Purple iris** as alternate text for the iris image (if necessary).
5. Add the text **Red and yellow tulips** as alternate text for the tulips image (if necessary).
6. Add the text **Deep violet pansies** as alternate text for the pansies image (if necessary).
7. Add the text **Blooms & Bulbs banner** as alternate text for the banner.
8. Edit the Accessibility Preferences to prompt you for alternate text when inserting images (if necessary).
9. Add appropriate alternate text to the banner on the index and tips pages.
10. Save your work and close the index and tips pages.

Insert a background image and manage graphics.

1. Make sure the plants page is open, then insert the daisies.gif file from the unit_c assets folder as a background image.
2. Save your work.
3. Preview the Web page in your browser, then close your browser.
4. Remove the daisies.gif file from the background.

5. Open the Assets panel, then refresh the Site list.
6. Use the Site panel to delete the daisies.gif file from the list of images.

FIGURES C-40 AND C-41
Completed Skills Review

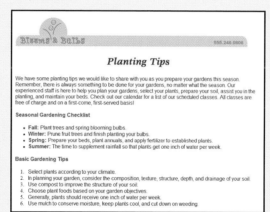

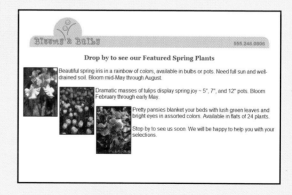

7. Refresh the Assets panel and verify that the daisies.gif file has been removed from the Web site.
8. View the colors used in the site in the Assets panel and verify that all are Websafe.
9. Save your work, then close the tips.htm page.

Use Figure C-42 as a guide to continue your work on the Rapids Transit Web site that you began in Project Builder 1 in Unit A. You are now ready to begin work on the guides page that explains the role of the guides in accompanying clients on float trips. You want to include a picture of one of the guides on the river and attractively format the text on the page. If you did not create this Web site in Unit A, contact your instructor for assistance.

1. Open the Rapids Transit Web site.
2. Open the file dwc_4.htm from the unit_c data files folder and save it in the rapids root folder as **guides.htm**, overwriting the existing guides.htm file.
3. Verify that the path for the banner is correctly set to the assets folder of the Rapids Transit Web site.
4. Insert the file buster_tricks.jpg from the assets folder located in the unit_c data files folder in an appropriate place on the page and copy the file to the assets folder.
5. Create alternate text for the buster_tricks image, add a border to the image, then choose an alignment setting for the image.
6. Add horizontal spacing of 5 to the buster_tricks image.

7. Create a new CSS Style called **.bodytext**, making sure that the Make Custom Style (class) and New Style Sheet File option buttons are checked in the New Style dialog box.
8. Save the style sheet file as **rapids** in the Rapids Transit Web site root folder.
9. Choose a font, size, style, color, and weight of your choice for the bodytext style.
10. Apply the bodytext style to the body text on the guides page.

11. Verify that the Accessibility Preference option is turned on, then add alternate text for any images in the Web site that do not yet have alternate text.
12. Save your work, then preview the page in your browser.
13. Close your browser, then close all open pages.

FIGURE C-42
Completed Project Builder 1

In this exercise you continue your work on the Jacob's Web site that you started in Project Builder 2 in Unit A. You are now ready to add two new pages to the Web site. One page will display one of the restaurant's most popular recipes and another page will show three pictures of Jacob's special desserts. Figures C-43 and C-44 show possible solutions for this exercise. Your finished pages will look different if you choose different formatting options.

1. Open the Jacob's Web site (If you did not create this Web site in Units A and B, contact your instructor for assistance).

2. Open the file rolls.htm in the unit_c data files folder and save it to the jacobs root folder as **recipes.htm**, overwriting the existing recipes.htm file.

3. Format the list of ingredients as an unordered list.

4. Create a CSS style named **.ingredients** and save the style sheet file as **jacobs** in the Jacob's Web site root folder, using any formatting options that you like.

5. Apply the ingredients style to the ingredients in the unordered list.

6. Add a style called .bodytext to the jacobs style sheet file using any formatting options that you like, and apply it to the body text on the recipes page.

7. Create a style called **.subheadings** using appropriate formatting options and apply it to the words ingredients and directions.

8. Create a style called **.headings** using appropriate formatting options and apply it to the words Grandmother's Rolls, then save your work.

9. Open the file dwc_5.htm from the unit_c data files folder and save it in the Jacob's Web site as **after_theatre.htm**.

10. Set the path for the Jacob's banner to the assets folder of the Jacob's Web site.

11. Edit the accessibility preferences to prompt you for alternate text when inserting images (if necessary).

12. Add the poached_pear.jpg, oranges.jpg, and cheesecake.jpg images from the assets folder in the unit_c data files folder, adding appropriate alternate text to each image.

FIGURE C-43
Completed Project Builder 2

13. Add alternate text to the Jacob's banner.

14. Format the images with borders, spacing, and alignment that make the page look attractive.

15. Attach the jacobs style sheet to the after_theatre page, then apply the bodytext style to the body text on the page. (To attach the style sheet, click the Attach Style Sheet button at the bottom of the CSS Styles panel, click Browse to open the Link External Style Sheet dialog box, double-click the jacobs.css file, then click OK.)

16. Save your work, then preview both pages in your browser.

17. Close your browser, then close both pages.

FIGURE C-44
Completed Project Builder 2

Dr. Chappell is a government historian who is conducting research on the separation of church and state. He has gone to the Library of Congress Web site to look for information he can use.

1. Open your browser, connect to the Internet, go to *www.course.com*, navigate to the page for this book, click the Student Online Companion link, then click Link 1 for this unit. The Library of Congress Web site is shown in Figure C-45.
2. Which fonts are used for the main content on the home page? Are the same fonts used consistently on the other pages in the Web site?
3. Do you see ordered or unordered lists on any pages in the Web site? If so, how were they used?
4. Use the Source command on the View menu to view the source code to see if a set of fonts was used. If so, which one?
5. Do you see the use of Cascading Style Sheets noted in the source code?
6. Go to the Google Web site at *www.google.com* or the Alta Vista Web site at *www.altavista.com* to find another informational Web site of interest. Compare the use of text on that site with the use of text on the Library of Congress Web site.

FIGURE C-45
Design Project

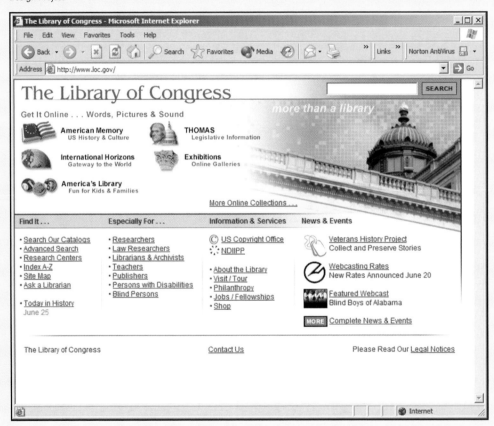

In this assignment, you continue to work on the group Web site that you started in Unit A. Depending on the size of your group, you can assign individual elements of the project to group members, or work collectively to create the finished product. There will be no data files supplied. You are building this Web site from unit to unit, so you must do each Group Project assignment in each unit to complete your Web site.

You will continue building your Web site by designing and completing a page that contains a list, headings, body text, graphics, and a background. During this process, you will develop a style sheet and add several styles to it. You will insert appropriate graphics on your page and enhance them for maximum effect. You will also check for non-Web-safe colors and remove any that you find.

1. Consult your storyboard and brainstorm as a group to decide which page to create and develop for this unit.

2. As a team, plan the page content for the page and make a sketch of the layout. You might want to create your sketch on a large piece of paper taped to the wall. Your sketch should include at least one ordered or unordered list, appropriate headings, body text, several graphics, and a background. Your sketch should also show where the body text and headings should be placed on the page and what styles should be used for each type of text. You should plan on creating at least two styles.

3. Assign a team member the task of creating this page and adding the text content to it.

4. Assign a team member the task of creating a Cascading Style Sheet for the Web site and adding to it the styles you decided to use. Assign the same team member the task of applying the styles to the appropriate content.

5. Access the graphics you gathered in Unit A and assign a team member the task of placing the graphics on the page so that the page matches the sketch you created in Step 2. This team member should also add a background image and appropriate alternate text for each graphic.

6. Assign a team member the task of checking for and removing any non-Web-safe colors.

7. Assign a team member the task of identifying any files in the Assets panel that are currently not used in the Web site. Decide as a group which of these assets should be removed, then assign a team member to delete these files.

8. As a team, preview the new page in a browser, then check for page layout problems and broken links. Make any necessary fixes in Dreamweaver, then preview the page again in a browser. Repeat this process until the group is satisfied with the way the page looks in the browser.

9. Use Figure C-46 to check all the pages of your site.

10. Close the browser, save your changes to the page, then close the page.

FIGURE C-46
Group Project check list

Web Site Check List
1. Does each page have a page title?
2. Does the home page have a description and keywords?
3. Does the home page contain contact information?
4. Does every page in the Web site have consistent navigation links?
5. Does the home page have a last updated statement that will
6. automatically update when the page is saved?
7. Do all paths for links and images work correctly?
8. Do all images have alternate text?
9. Are all colors Web-safe?
10. Are there any unnecessary files you can delete from the assets folder?
11. Is there a style sheet with at least two styles?
12. Did you apply the styles to page content?
13. Do all pages view well using at least two different browser settings?

UNIT D

WORKING WITH LINKS

1. Create external and internal links.

2. Create internal links to named anchors.

3. Insert Flash text.

4. Create, modify, and copy a navigation bar.

5. Manage Web site links.

Introduction

What makes Web sites so powerful are the links that connect one page to another within a Web site or to any page on the Web. Though you can add graphics, animations, movies, and other enhancements to a Web site to make it visually attractive, the links you include are often the most essential components of a Web site. Links that connect the pages within a Web site are always very important because they help viewers navigate between the pages of the site. However, if one of your goals is to keep viewers from leaving your Web site, you might want to avoid including links to other Web sites. For example, most e-commerce sites include only links to other pages in the site to discourage shoppers from leaving the site. In this unit you will create links to other pages in the TripSmart Web site and to other sites on the Web. You will also insert a navigation bar that contains graphics instead of text, and check the links in the TripSmart Web site to make sure they all work.

Understanding Internal and External Links

Web pages contain two types of links: internal links and external links. **Internal links** are links to Web pages in the same Web site, and **external links** are links to Web pages in other Web sites or to e-mail addresses. Both internal and external links have two important parts that work together. The first part of a link is the element that viewers see and click on a Web page, for example, text, a graphic, or a button. The second part of a link is the **path**, or the name and location of the Web page or file that will open when the element is clicked. Setting and maintaining the correct paths for all your links is essential to avoid having broken links in your site.

Tools You'll Use

Named Anchor button

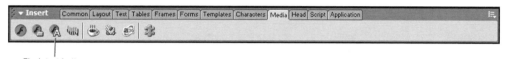

Flash text button

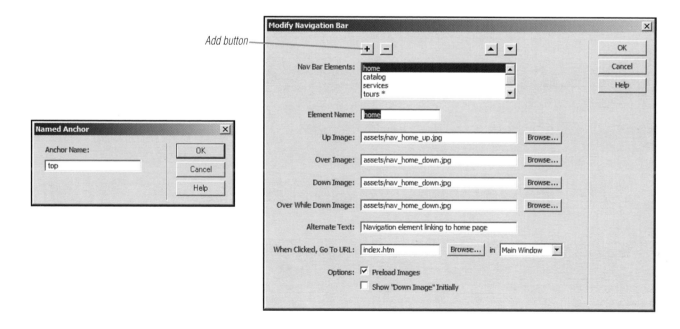

CREATE EXTERNAL AND INTERNAL LINKS

What You'll Do

 In this lesson, you will create external links on the TripSmart services page that link to several Web sites related to travel. You will also create internal links to other pages within the TripSmart Web site.

Creating External Links

A good Web page usually includes a variety of external links to other related Web sites so that viewers can get more information on a particular topic. To create an external link, you first select the text or object that you want to serve as a link, then you type the absolute path to the destination Web page in the Links text box in the Property inspector. An **absolute path** is a path used for external links that includes the complete address for the destination page, including the protocol (such as http://) and the complete **URL** (Uniform Resource Locator), or address, of the destination page. When necessary, the Web page filename and folder hierarchy are also part of an absolute path. Figure D-1 shows an example of an absolute path showing the protocol, URL, and filename. After you enter external links on a Web page, you can view them in the site map.

FIGURE D-1

An example of an absolute path

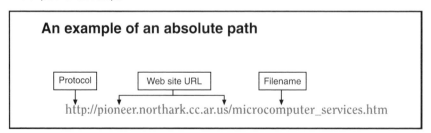

An example of an absolute path

| Protocol | Web site URL | Filename |

http://pioneer.northark.cc.ar.us/microcomputer_services.htm

Creating Internal Links

Each page in a Web site usually focuses on an individual category or topic. You should make sure that the home page provides links to each page in the site, and that all pages in the site contain numerous internal links so that viewers can move easily from page to page. To create an internal link, you first select the text element or graphic object that you want to make a link, then you use the Browse for File icon next to the Link text box in the Property inspector to specify the relative path to the destination page. A **relative path** is a type of path used to reference Web pages and graphic files within the same Web site. Relative paths include the filename and folder location of a file. Figure D-2 shows an example of a relative path. Table D-1 describes absolute paths and relative paths. Relative paths can either be site root relative or document relative.

You should take great care in managing your internal links to make sure they work correctly and are timely and relevant to the page content. You should design the navigation structure of your Web site so that viewers are never more than three or four clicks away from the page they are seeking.

FIGURE D-2
An example of a relative path

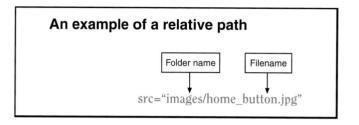

TABLE D-1: Description of absolute and relative paths

type of path	description	examples
Absolute path	Used for external links and specifies protocol, URL, and filename of destination page	http://www.yahoo.com/recreation
Relative path	Used for internal links and specifies location of file relative to the current page	services.htm or assets/tripsmart.gif
Root-relative path	Used for internal links when publishing to a server that contains many Web sites or where the Web site is so large it requires more than one server	/tripsmart/services.htm
Document-relative path	Used in most cases for internal links and specifies the location of file relative to current page	services.htm or assets/tripsmart.gif

Create an external link

1. Open the TripSmart Web site that you completed in Unit C, open dwd_1.htm from the unit_d folder where your data files are stored, then save it as **services.htm** to the tripsmart root folder, overwriting the existing services page.

2. Set the path for the TripSmart banner to the assets folder of the Web site.

3. Scroll down, then select CNN Travel Channel under the heading Travel Information Sites.

4. Click in the Link text box in the Property inspector, type **http://www.cnn.com/travel**, press [Enter] (Win) or [return] (Mac), then compare your screen to Figure D-3.

5. Repeat Steps 3 and 4 to create links for the following Web sites listed on the services page:

   US Department of State:
   http://travel.state.gov

   Yahoo!: **http://www.yahoo.com/**
   Recreation/Travel

   MapQuest: **http://www.mapquest.com**

   Rand McNally: **http://www.randmcnally.com**

   AccuWeather: **http://www.accuweather.com**

   The Weather Channel:
   http://www.weather.com

6. Save your work, preview the page in your browser, test all the links to make sure they work, then close your browser.

   TIP   You must have an active Internet connection to test the links. If clicking a link does not open a page, make sure you typed the URL correctly in the Link text box.

You opened the TripSmart Web site, replaced the existing services page, then added seven external links to other travel Web sites on the page. You also tested each link in your browser.

MACROMEDIA DREAMWEAVER D-6

Creating an external link to the CNN Travel Channel Web site

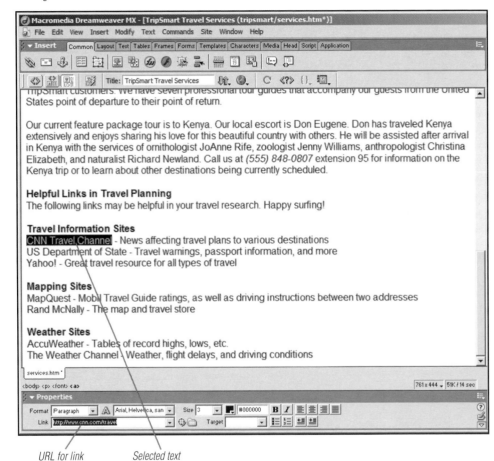

URL for link   Selected text

FIGURE D-4

Site map displaying external links on the services page

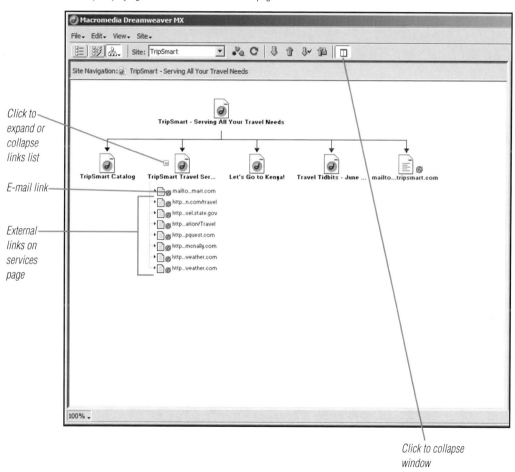

Click to expand or collapse links list

E-mail link

External links on services page

Click to collapse window

1. Mac users only: Click Site on the menu bar, point to Open Site, then click TripSmart to open the Site panel.

2. Click the View list arrow on the Site panel, click Map View (Win) or click the Site Map button (Mac), then click the Expand/Collapse button on the Site panel toolbar (Win). 🔲

   > TIP If you want to view or hide page titles in the site map, click View on the menu bar, then click Show Page Titles (Win) or click Site on the menu bar, point to Site Map View, then click Show Page Titles (Mac).

3. Click the plus sign to the left of the services page icon in the site map (if necessary) to view a list of the seven external links you created, as shown in Figure D-4.

   The TripSmart e-mail link also appears in the list.

4. Click the minus sign to the left of the services page icon in the site map to collapse the list of links.

5. Click the Expand/Collapse button on the toolbar, click the View list arrow on the Site panel, then click Local View (Win), or click the Site Files button on the Site panel to change to Local View (Mac). 🔲

You viewed the TripSmart site map and expanded the view of the services page to display the seven external links you added.

Create an internal link

1. Select on-line catalog in the paragraph under the Travel Outfitters heading.

2. Click the Browse for File icon in the Property inspector, then double-click catalog.htm in the Select File dialog box to set the relative path to the catalog page.

   Notice that catalog.htm appears in the Link text box in the Property inspector, as shown in Figure D-5.

   > TIP Using the Browse for File icon to set the relative path for an internal link is easier than typing the filename in the Link text box.

3. Scroll down as necessary, then select Kenya in the second paragraph under the Escorted Tours heading.

4. Click the Browse for File icon next to the Links text box in the Property inspector, then double-click tours.htm in the Select File dialog box to specify the relative path to the tours page.

   The word Kenya is now a link to the tours page.

5. Save your work, preview the page in your browser to verify that the internal links work correctly, then close your browser.

You created two internal links on the services page, and then tested the links in your browser.

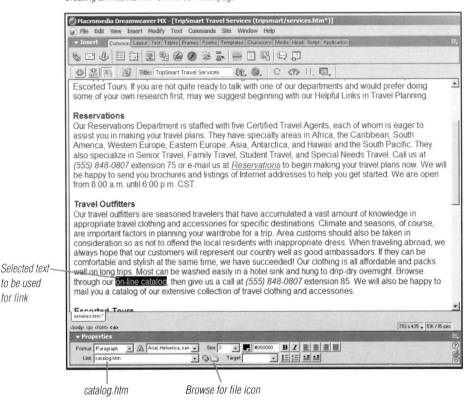

Selected text to be used for link

catalog.htm   Browse for file icon

Typing URLs

Typing URLs in the Link text box in the Property inspector can be very tedious. When you need to type a long and complex URL, it is easy to make mistakes and create a broken link. You can avoid such mistakes by copying and pasting the URL from the Address text box (Internet Explorer) or Location text box (Netscape Navigator and Communicator) to the Link text box in the Property inspector. Copying and pasting a URL ensures that the URL is entered correctly.

FIGURE D-6

Site map displaying external and internal links on the services page

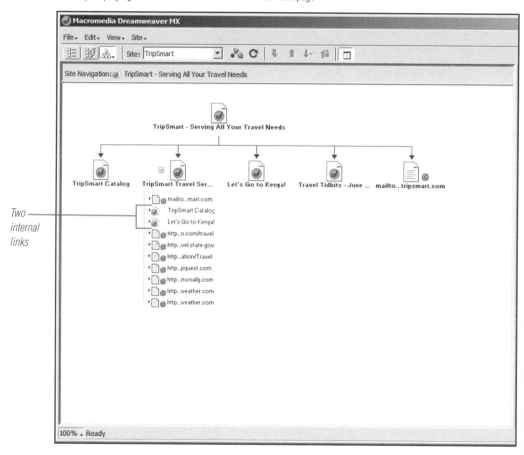

Two internal links

1. Click the View list arrow on the Site panel, click Map View, then click the Expand/Collapse button (Win) or click Site on the menu bar, point to Open Site, click TripSmart to open the Site panel, then click the Site Map button (Mac). ▢

2. Click the plus sign to the left of the services page icon.

   A list of 10 links appears below the services page icon as shown in Figure D-6. One is an e-mail link, seven are external links, and two are internal links.

   > TIP If your links do not display correctly, re-create the site cache. To re-create the site cache, click Site on the Site panel menu bar, then click Recreate Site Cache.

3. Click the Expand/Collapse button, click the View list arrow on the Site panel, then click Local View (Win), or click the Site Files button on the Site panel to change to Local view. ▢

You viewed the links on the services page in the site map.

CREATE INTERNAL LINKS TO NAMED ANCHORS

What You'll Do

In this lesson, you will insert five named anchors on the services page: one for the top of the page and four for each heading. You will then create internal links to each named anchor.

Inserting Named Anchors

Some Web pages have so much content that viewers must scroll repeatedly to get to the bottom of the page and then back up to the top of the page. To make it easier for viewers to navigate to specific areas of a page without scrolling, you can use a combination of internal links and named anchors. A **named anchor** is a specific location on a Web page that has a descriptive name. Named anchors act as targets for internal links and make it easy for viewers to jump to a particular place on the same page quickly. A **target** is the location on a Web page that a browser displays when an internal link is clicked. For example, you can insert a named anchor called "top" at the top of a Web page, then create a link to it at the bottom of the page. You can also insert named anchors in strategic places on a Web page, such as at the beginning of paragraph headings.

You insert a named anchor using the Insert Named Anchor button on the Common tab of the Insert bar, as shown in Figure D-7. You then enter the name of the Anchor in the Insert Named Anchor dialog box. You should choose short names that describe the named anchor location on the page. Named anchors are represented by yellow anchor icons on a Web page. You can show or hide named anchor icons by clicking View on the menu bar, pointing to Visual Aids, then clicking Invisible Elements.

Working with Links

Creating Internal Links to Named Anchors

Once you create a named anchor, you can create an internal link to it using one of two methods. You can select the text or graphic on the page that you want to make a link, then drag the Point to File icon from the Property inspector to the named anchor icon on the page. Or, you can select the text or graphic to which you want to make a link, then type the character # followed by the named anchor name (such as #top) in the Link text box in the Property inspector.

QUICKTIP

To avoid possible errors, you should create a named anchor before you create a link to it.

FIGURE D-7
Named Anchor button on the Insert bar

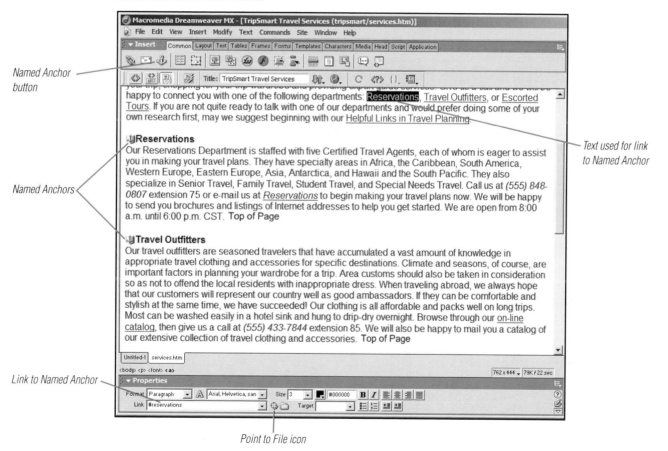

Named Anchor button

Named Anchors

Link to Named Anchor

Text used for link to Named Anchor

Point to File icon

Insert a named anchor

1. Click the TripSmart banner to select it, then press the Left Arrow key [←] to place the insertion point to the left of the banner.

2. Click View on the menu bar, point to Visual Aids, then verify that Invisible Elements is checked.

   TIP If there is no check mark next to Invisible Elements, then this feature is turned off. Click Invisible Elements to turn this feature on.

3. Click the Common tab on the Insert bar (if necessary).

4. Click the Named Anchor button on the Insert bar to open the Named Anchor dialog box, type **top** in the Anchor Name text box, compare your screen with Figure D-8, then click OK. ⚓

   An anchor icon now appears before the TripSmart banner.

   TIP Use lowercase letters, no spaces, and no special characters in named anchor names. You should also avoid using a number as the first character in a named anchor name.

(continued)

FIGURE D-8
Named Anchor dialog box

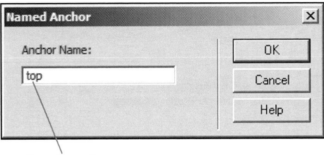

Name of new anchor

FIGURE D-9
Named anchors on services page

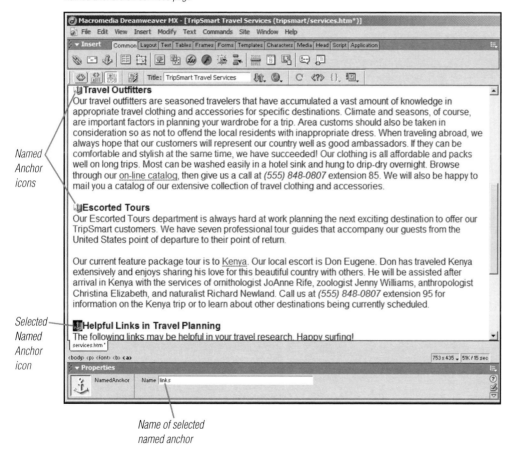

Named Anchor icons

Selected Named Anchor icon

Name of selected named anchor

5. Click to the left of the Reservations heading, then insert a named anchor called **reservations**.

6. Insert named anchors to the left of the Travel Outfitters, Escorted Tours, and Helpful Links in Travel Planning headings using the following names: **outfitters**, **tours**, and **links**.

   Your screen should resemble Figure D-9.

7. Save your work.

You created five named anchors on the services page; one at top of the page, and four that will help viewers quickly access the department headings on the page.

Create an internal link to a named anchor

1. Select the word Reservations in the second sentence of the first paragraph, then drag the Point to File icon from the Property inspector to the reservations named anchor as shown in Figure D-10. ⟐

   The word Reservations is now linked to the reservations named anchor. When viewers click the word Reservations, the browser will display the Reservations paragraph at the top of the browser window.

   > TIP The name of a named anchor is always preceded by a pound (#) sign in the Link text box in the Property inspector.

2. Create internal links for Travel Outfitters, Escorted Tours, and Helpful Links in Travel Planning in the first paragraph by first selecting each of these phrases, then dragging the Point to File icon to the appropriate named anchor icon. ⟐

   The phrases Travel Outfitters, Escorted Tours, and Helpful Links in Travel Planning are now links that connect to the Travel Outfitters, Escorted Tours, and Helpful Links in Travel Planning headings.

   > TIP Once you select the text you want to link, you might need to scroll down to view the named anchor on the screen. Once you see the named anchor on your screen, you can drag the Point to File icon on top of it.

   (continued)

FIGURE D-10

Dragging the Point to File icon to a named anchor

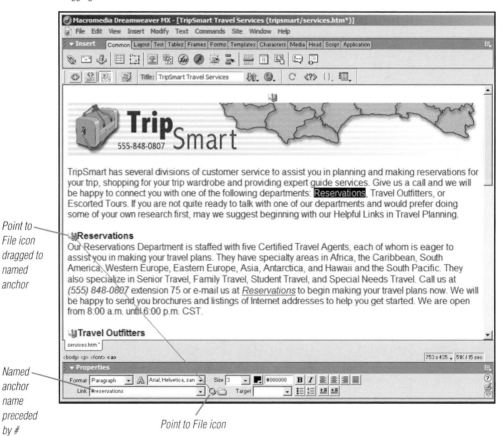

Point to File icon dragged to named anchor

Named anchor name preceded by #

Point to File icon

Services page in Internet Explorer with three internal links to named anchors

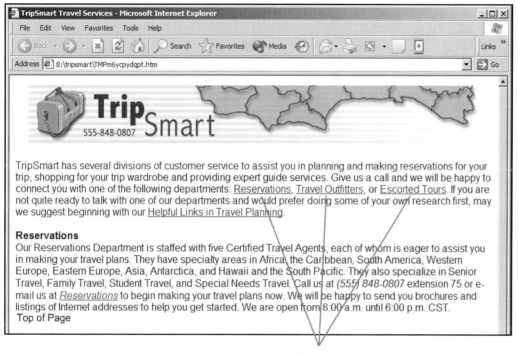

Internal links to named anchors

3. Save your work, preview the page in your browser as shown in Figure D-11, then test the links to each named anchor.

   Notice that when you click the Escorted Tours and Helpful Links in Travel Planning in the browser, their associated named anchors appear in the middle of the page instead of at the top. This happens because the services page is not long enough to position these named anchors at the top of the page.

4. Close your browser.

You created internal links to the named anchors next to the department headings on the services page. You then previewed the page in your browser and tested each link.

INSERT FLASH TEXT

What You'll Do

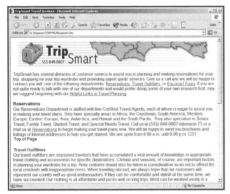

In this lesson, you will use the Insert Flash Text dialog box to create a button that links to the top named anchor on the services page. You will copy this button to several locations on the services page, and then change the alignment of each button.

Understanding Flash Text

Flash is a Macromedia software program that you can use to create vector-based graphics and animations. **Vector-based graphics** are graphics that are based on mathematical formulas, as opposed to other types of graphic files such as JPG and BMP, which are based on pixels. Vector-based graphics have a smoother look and are smaller in file size than pixel-based graphics. Because they download quickly, vector-based graphics are ideal for Web sites. **Flash text** is a vector-based graphic file that contains text. You can insert Flash text to add visual interest to an otherwise dull Web page or to help deliver or reinforce a message. You can use Flash text to create internal or external links. Flash text files are saved with the .swf filename extension.

QUICKTIP

In order to view Flash animations, you must have the Flash player installed on your computer. The Flash player is free software that lets you view movies created with Macromedia software.

Inserting Flash Text on a Web Page

You can create Flash text in Dreamweaver without opening the Flash program. To insert Flash text on a Web page, you use the Flash Text button on the Media tab of the Insert bar, as shown in Figure D-12. Clicking this button opens the Insert Flash Text dialog box, which you use to specify the settings for the Flash text. You first need to specify the text you want to create as Flash text by typing it in the Text text box. You can then specify the font, size, and color of the Flash text, apply bold or italic styles to it, and align it using left, center, or right alignment options. You can also specify a **rollover color**, or the color in which the text will appear when the mouse pointer is placed on it. You also need to enter the path for the destination link in the Link text box. The destination link can be an internal link to another page in the site or to a named anchor on the same page, or an external link to a page on another Web site.

You then use the Target list in the Property inspector to specify how to open the destination page. The four options on the Target list arrow are described in Table D-2.

QUICKTIP

Notice that the _parent option in the table specifies to display the page in the parent frameset. A **frameset** is a group of Web pages displayed using more than one **frame** or window.

Before you close the Insert Flash Text dialog box, you need to type a descriptive name for your Flash text file in the Save As text box. Flash text files must be saved in the same folder as the page that contains the Flash text. For this reason, you should save your Flash text files in the root folder of the Web site.

FIGURE D-12
Insert bar Media tab

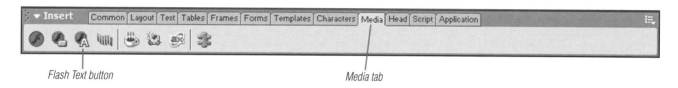

Flash Text button   Media tab

TABLE D-2: Options on the Target List	
target	**result**
_blank	Displays the destination page in a separate browser window
_parent	Displays the destination page in the parent frameset (replaces the frameset)
_self	Displays the destination page in the same frame or window
_top	Displays the destination page in the whole browser window

Create Flash text

1. Click after the last word on the services page, then insert a hard return.

2. Click the Media tab on the Insert bar, then click the Flash Text button to open the Insert Flash Text dialog box, as shown in Figure D-13.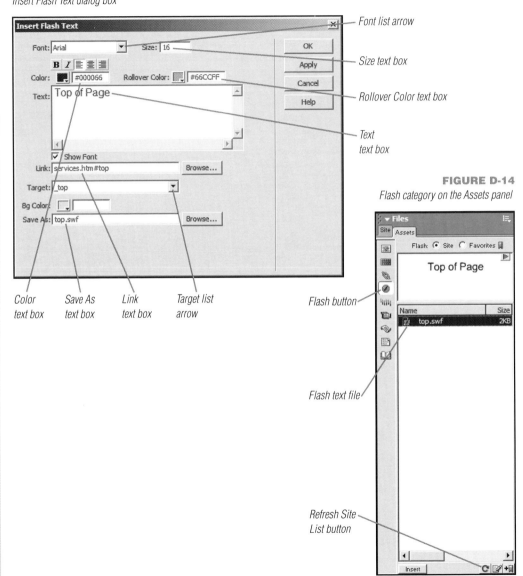

3. Type **Top of Page** in the Text text box, set the Font to Arial, set the Size to 16, set the Color to #000066, set the Rollover Color to #66CCFF, type services.htm#top in the Link text box, use the Target list arrow to set the Target at _top, type **top.swf** in the Save As text box, then click OK.

   The Top of Page Flash text now appears as a button at the bottom of the page. When a viewer clicks this button, the browser will display the top of the page.

4. Click the Assets tab in the Files panel group to open the Assets panel (Win), click the Flash button on the Assets panel (Win), or on Files panel group (Mac), as shown in Figure D-14, then click the Refresh Site List button.

5. Drag top.swf from the Assets panel to the end of the Reservations, Travel Outfitters, and Escorted Tours paragraphs to insert three more links to the top of the page.

6. Click the Site panel tab to open the Site panel (Win), then save your work.

(continued)

FIGURE D-13
Insert Flash Text dialog box

Font list arrow
Size text box
Rollover Color text box
Text text box

Color text box
Save As text box
Link text box
Target list arrow

FIGURE D-14
Flash category on the Assets panel

Flash button
Flash text file
Refresh Site List button

Working with Links

> TIP If the top of the page is already displayed, the window will not move when you click the Flash text.

You used the Insert Flash Text dialog box to create a Top of Page button that links to the top named anchor on the services page. You also inserted the Top of Page button at the end of each department paragraph, so viewers will be able to go quickly to the top of the page without scrolling.

FIGURE D-15
Flash text aligned to top

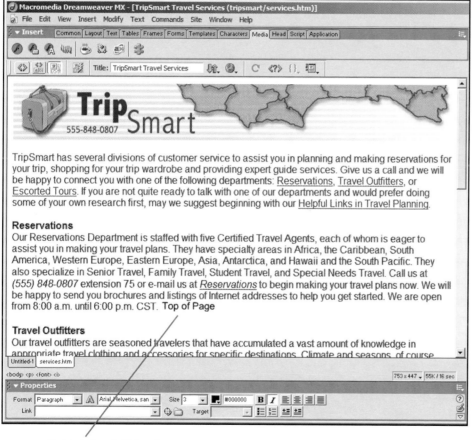

Change the alignment of Flash text

1. Click the Top of Page button at the end of the Reservations paragraph, expand the Property inspector, click the Align list arrow in the Property inspector, then click Top.

   The Top of Page button is now aligned with the top of the line of text, as shown in Figure D-15.

2. Apply the Top alignment setting to the Top of Page button located at the end of the Travel Outfitters and Escorted Tours paragraphs.

3. Collapse the Property inspector, turn off Invisible Elements, then save your work.

4. Preview the services page in your browser, test each Top of Page button, then close your browser.

You aligned the Flash text to improve its appearance on the page.

Flash text aligned with top of paragraph text line

CREATE AND MODIFY A NAVIGATION BAR

What You'll Do

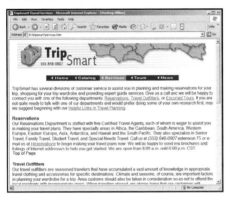

In this lesson, you will create a navigation bar that can be used to link to each major page in the Web site. The navigation bar will have five elements: home, catalog, services, tours, and newsletter. You will also copy the new navigation bar to the index, newsletter, and tours pages. On each page you will modify the appropriate element state to reflect the current page.

Creating a Navigation Bar Using Images

To make your Web site more visually appealing, you can create a navigation bar with graphics rather than text. Any graphics you use in a navigation bar must be created in a graphics software program, such as Macromedia Fireworks or Adobe Illustrator. In order for a browser to display a navigation bar correctly, all graphic links in the navigation bar must be exactly the same size. You insert a navigation bar using the Navigation Bar button on the Insert bar or the Navigation Bar command on the Insert menu to open the Insert Navigation Bar dialog box. You use this dialog box to specify the appearance of each graphic link, called an **element**, in each of four possible states. A **state** is the condition of the element in relation to the mouse pointer. The four states are as follows: **Up Image** (the state when the mouse pointer is not on top of the element), **Over Image** (the state when the mouse pointer is positioned on top of

the element), **Down Image** (the state when you click the element), and **Over While Down Image** (the state when you click the element and continue pressing and holding the left mouse button). You can create a rollover effect by using different colors or images to represent each element state. You can add many special effects to navigation bars or to links on a Web page. For instance, the Web site shown in Figure D-16 contains a navigation bar that uses rollovers and also contains images that link to featured items in the Web site.

QUICKTIP

You can place only one navigation bar on a Web page using the Insert Navigation Bar dialog box.

Copying and Modifying a Navigation Bar

After you create a navigation bar, you can copy and paste it to the other main pages in your site to save time. Make sure you place the navigation bar in the same position on each page. This practice ensures that the navigation bar will look the same on each page, making it much easier for viewers to navigate to all the pages in a Web site.

You can then use the Modify Navigation Bar dialog box to customize the appearance of the copied navigation bar on each page. For example, you can change the appearance of the services navigation bar element on the services page so that it appears in a different color. Highlighting the navigation element for the current page provides a visual reminder so that viewers can quickly tell which page they are viewing. This process ensures that the navigation bar will look consistent across all pages, but will be customized for each page.

FIGURE D-16
Universal Studios Web site

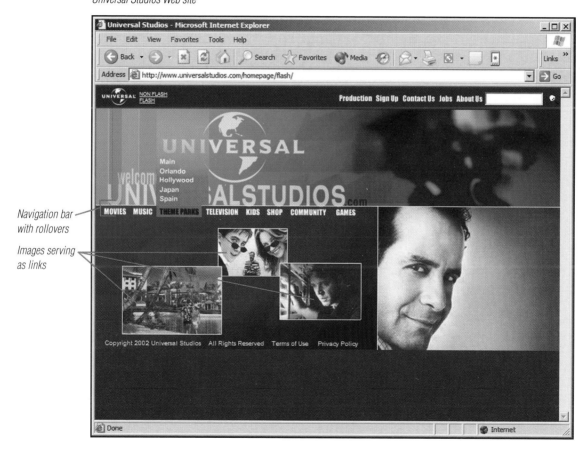

Navigation bar
with rollovers

Images serving
as links

Create a navigation bar using images

1. Position the insertion point to the right of the TripSmart banner on the services page, then press [Enter] (Win) or [return] (Mac).

   The insertion point is now positioned between the TripSmart banner and the first paragraph of text.

2. Click the Common tab on the Insert bar, then click the Navigation Bar button on the Insert bar to open the Insert Navigation Bar dialog box.

3. Type **home** in the Element Name text box, click the Insert list arrow at the bottom of the dialog box, then click Horizontally (if necessary), to specify that the navigation bar be placed horizontally on the page.

4. Click the Browse button next to the Up Image text box, navigate to the drive and folder where your data files are stored, double-click the unit_d folder, double-click the assets folder, then double-click nav_home_up.jpg.

   The path to the file nav_home_up.jpg appears in the Up Image text box, as shown in Figure D-17.

5. Use the Browse button next to the Over Image text box to specify a path to the file nav_home_down.jpg located in the unit_d assets folder.

(continued)

FIGURE D-17
Insert Navigation Bar dialog box

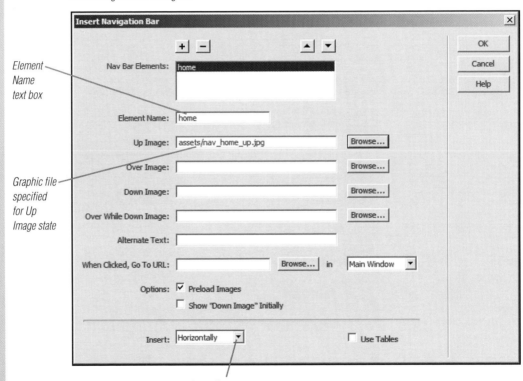

Element Name text box

Graphic file specified for Up Image state

Insert list arrow

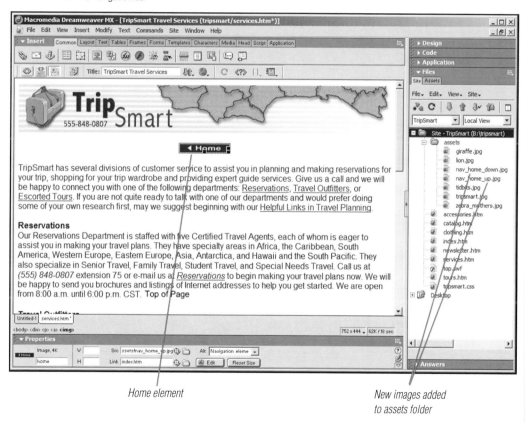

Home element   New images added
to assets folder

6. Use the Browse button next to the Down Image text box to specify a path to the file nav_home_down.jpg located in the unit_d assets folder, overwriting the existing file.

> TIP Instead of using the Browse button in Steps 6 and 7, you could copy the path of the nav_home_down.jpg file in the Over Image text box and paste it to the Down Image and Over While Down Image text boxes. You could also reference the nav_home_down.jpg file in the TripSmart assets folder once it is copied there in Step 5.

7. Use the Browse button next to the Over While Down Image text box to specify a path to the file nav_home_down.jpg located in the unit_d assets folder, overwriting the existing file.

   By specifying one graphic for the Up Image state, and another graphic for the Over Image, Down Image, and Over While Down Image states, you will create a rollover effect.

8. Type **Navigation bar element linking to home page** in the Alternate text box, click the Browse button next to the When Clicked, Go To URL text box, then double-click index.htm in the tripsmart root folder.

9. Click OK, refresh the Site panel to view the new images you added to the TripSmart assets folder, compare your screen to Figure D-18, then save your work.

You used the Insert Navigation Bar dialog box to create a navigation bar for the services page and added the home element to it. You used two images for each state, one for the up image state and one for the other three states.

Add elements to a navigation bar

1. Click Modify on the menu bar, then click Navigation Bar.

2. Click the Add button at the top of the Modify Navigation Bar dialog box, type **catalog** in the Element Name text box, then compare your screen with Figure D-19. ➕

   > TIP You use the Add button to add a new navigation element to the navigation bar, and the Delete button to delete a navigation element from the navigation bar. ➕ ➖

3. Click the Browse button next to the Up Image text box, navigate to the unit_d assets folder, click nav_catalog_up.jpg, then click OK (Win) or Choose (Mac).

   > TIP If a dialog box appears asking if you would like to copy the file to the root folder, click Yes, then click Save (Mac).

4. Use the Browse button next to the Over Image text box to specify a path to the file nav_catalog_down.jpg located in the unit_d assets folder.

5. Use the Browse button next to the Down Image text box to specify a path to the file nav_catalog_down.jpg located in the unit_d assets folder, overwriting the existing file.

6. Use the Browse button next to the Over While Down Image text box to specify a path to the file nav_catalog_down.jpg located in the unit_d assets folder, overwriting the existing file.

(continued)

FIGURE D-19

Adding navigation bar elements

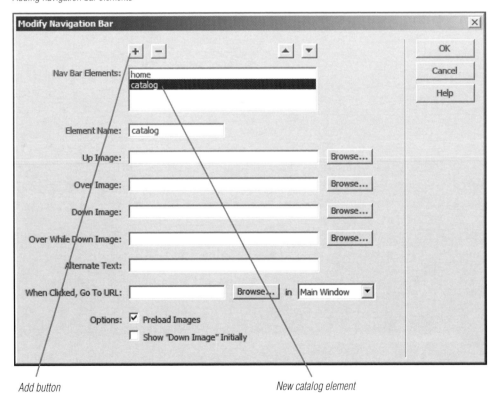

Add button

New catalog element

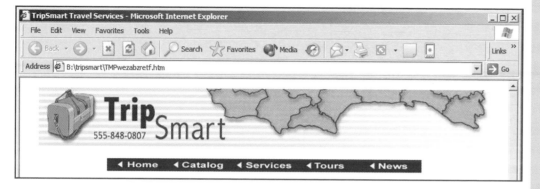

7. Type **Navigation bar element linking to catalog page** in the Alternate text box, click the Browse button next to the When Clicked, Go To URL text box, then double-click catalog.htm.

8. Using the information provided in Table D-3, add three more navigation bar elements in the Modify Navigation Bar dialog box called **services**, **tours**, and **newsletter**.

   > TIP   All files listed in the table are located in the assets folder of the unit_d folder where your data files are stored.

9. Click OK to close the Modify Navigation Bar dialog box, then compare your screen to Figure D-20.

10. Save your work, preview the page in your browser, check each link to verify that each element works correctly, then close your browser.

You completed the TripSmart navigation bar by adding four more elements to it, each of which contain links to the other four pages in the site. All images added to the navigation bar are now stored in the assets folder of the TripSmart Web site.

TABLE D-3: Settings to use in the Modify Navigation Bar dialog box for each new element

dialog box item	services element	tours element	newsletter element
Up Image file	nav_services_up.jpg	nav_tours_up.jpg	nav_news_up.jpg
Over Image file	nav_services_down.jpg	nav_tours_down.jpg	nav_news_down.jpg
Down Image file	nav_services_down.jpg	nav_tours_down.jpg	nav_news_down.jpg
Over While Down Image file	nav_services_down.jpg	nav_tours_down.jpg	nav_news_down.jpg
Alternate text	Navigation bar element linking to services page	Navigation bar element linking to tours page	Navigation bar element linking to newsletter page
When Clicked Go To URL	services.htm	tours.htm	newsletter.htm

Copy and paste a navigation bar

1. Place the insertion point to the left of the navigation bar, hold down the [Shift] key, then click to the right of the navigation bar.

2. Click Edit on the menu bar, then click Copy.

3. Double-click newsletter.htm in the Site panel to open the newsletter page.

4. Click to the right of the TripSmart banner, then press [Enter] (Win) or [Return] (Mac).

5. Click Edit on the menu bar, click Paste, then compare your screen to Figure D-21.

6. Save your work.

You copied the navigation bar from the services page and pasted it on the newsletter page.

Customize a navigation bar

1. Click Modify on the menu bar, then click Navigation Bar to open the Modify Navigation Bar dialog box.

2. Click newsletter in the Nav Bar Elements text box, then click the Show "Down Image" Initially check box, as shown in Figure D-22.

An asterisk appears next to newsletter in the Nav Bar Elements text box, indicating that this element will be displayed in the Down Image state initially. The light blue newsletter navigation element normally used for the Down Image state of the newsletter navigation bar element will remind viewers that they are on the tours page.

(continued)

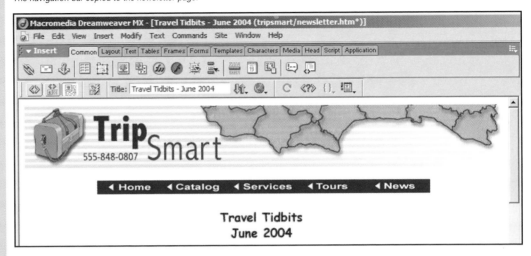

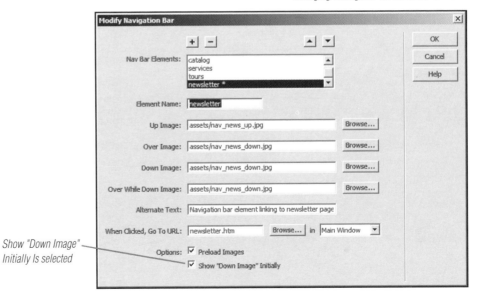

Show "Down Image" Initially Is selected

Working with Links

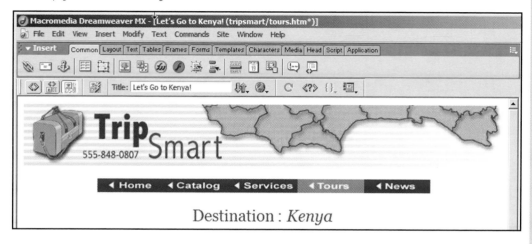

Creating an image map

Another way to create navigation links for Web pages is to create an image map. An image map is a graphic that has one or more hotspots placed on top of it. A **hotspot** is an area on a graphic that, when clicked, links to a different location on the page or to another Web page. For example, a map of the United States could have a hotspot placed on each state so that viewers could click a state to link to information about that state. To create a hotspot on an image, select the image on which you want to place the hotspot, then create the hotspot using one of the hotspot tools in the Property inspector.

3. Click OK to save the new settings and close the Modify Navigation Bar dialog box, then save and close the newsletter page.

4. Repeat Steps 1 through 3 to modify the navigation bar on the services page to show the Down Image initially for the services element, then save and close the services page.

5. Open the home page, paste the navigation bar under the TripSmart banner, then modify the navigation bar to show the Down Image Initially for the home element.

6. Delete the original navigation bar and the horizontal line on the home page, then save and close the home page.

7. Open the Tours page, paste the navigation bar under the TripSmart banner, then use the Modify Navigation Bar dialog box to specify that the Down Image be displayed initially for the tours element.

8. Delete the horizontal line on the page, then compare your screen to Figure D-23.

9. Save your work, preview the current page in your browser, test the navigation bar on the home, newsletter, services, and tours pages, then close your browser.

> TIP If you see some yellow HTML code on your page in Design View when you attempt to save your file, select both the beginning and ending tags, then press [Delete] to correct the error.

You modified the navigation bar on the newsletter page to show the newsletter element in the Down state initially. You then copied the navigation bar to two additional pages in the TripSmart Web site, modifying the navigation bar elements each time to show the down image state initially.

MANAGE WEB SITE LINKS

What You'll Do

 In this lesson, you will use some of Dreamweaver's reporting features to check the TripSmart Web site for broken links and orphaned files.

Managing Web Site Links

Because the World Wide Web changes constantly, Web sites may be up one day and down the next. To avoid having broken links on your Web site, you need to check external links frequently. If a Web site changes server locations or goes down due to technical difficulties or a power failure, the links to it become broken. An external link can also become broken when an Internet connection fails to work properly. Broken links, like misspelled words on a Web page, indicate that a Web site is not being maintained diligently.

Checking links to make sure they work is an ongoing and crucial task you need to

perform on a regular basis. You must check external links manually by reviewing your Web site in a browser and clicking each link to make sure it works correctly. The Check Links Sitewide feature is a helpful tool for managing your internal links. You can use it to check your entire Web site for the total number of links and the number of links that are OK, external, or broken, and then view the results of the link check in the Link Checker panel. The Link Checker panel also provides a list of all of the files used in a Web site, including those that are **orphaned files**, or files that are not linked to any pages in the Web site.

Considering navigation design issues

As you work on the navigation structure for a Web site, you should try to limit the number of links on each page to no more than is necessary. Too many links may confuse visitors to your Web site. You should also design links so that viewers can reach the information they want within three or four clicks. If finding information takes more than three or four clicks, the viewer may become discouraged or lost in the site. It's a good idea to provide visual clues on each page to let viewers know where they are, much like a "You are here" marker on a store directory at the mall.

FIGURE D-24
Link Checker panel displaying external links

External links
displayed

Show list arrow

FIGURE D-25
Link Checker panel displaying orphaned files

Show list arrow

Orphaned files

FIGURE D-26
Assets panel displaying links

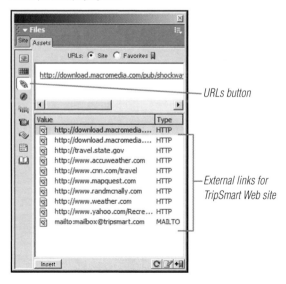

URLs button

External links for
TripSmart Web site

1. Click Site on the Site panel menu bar, then click Check Links Sitewide (Win), or click Site on the menu bar, then click Check Links Sitewide (Mac).

   The Results panel group opens with the Link Checker panel displayed. By default the Link Checker panel initially displays any broken internal links found in the Web site. The TripSmart Web site has no broken links.

2. Click the Show list arrow in the Link Checker panel, click External Links, then compare your screen to Figure D-24.

   Some external links are listed more than once because the Link Checker displays each instance of an external link.

3. Click the Show list arrow, then click Orphaned Files to view the orphaned files in the Link Checker panel, as shown in Figure D-25.

4. Click the Options button in the Results panel group title bar, then click Close Panel Group.

5. Open the Assets panel (if necessary), then click the URLs button in the Assets panel to display the list of links in the Web site.

   The Assets panel displays the external links used in the Web site. See Figure D-26.

6. Save your work, then close all open pages.

You used the Link Checker panel to check for broken links, external links, and orphaned files in the TripSmart Web site.

Create external and internal links.

1. Open the Blooms & Bulbs Web site. (If you did not create this Web site in Units A through C, contact your instructor for assistance.)
2. Open dwd_2.htm from the unit_d data files folder, then save it as **master_gardener.htm** in the Blooms & Bulbs Web site.
3. Verify that the banner path is set correctly to the assets folder in the Web site, and correct it if it is not.
4. Scroll to the bottom of the page, then link the National Gardening Association text to *http://www.garden.org.*
5. Link the Better Homes and Gardens Gardening Home Page text to *http://bhg.com/gardening.*
6. Link the Southern Living text to *http://www.southernliving.com.*
7. Save the file, then preview the page in your browser, verifying that each link works correctly.
8. Close your browser, then return to the master_gardener page in Dreamweaver.
9. Scroll to the paragraph about gardening issues, select the gardening tips text in the last sentence, then link the selected text to the tips.htm file in the blooms root folder.
10. Save the file, test the links in your browser, then close your browser.

Create internal links to named anchors.

1. Show Invisible Elements (if necessary).
2. Click the Common tab on the Insert bar (if necessary).
3. Insert a named anchor in front of the Grass heading named **grass**.
4. Insert a named anchor in front of the Trees heading named **trees**.
5. Insert a named anchor in front of the Plants heading named **plants**.
6. Insert a named anchor at the top of the page named **top**.
7. Use the Point to File icon in the Property Inspector to create a link from the word grass in the Gardening Issues paragraph to the grass named anchor.
8. Create a link from the word trees in the Gardening Issues paragraph to the trees named anchor.
9. Create a link from the word plants in the Gardening Issues paragraph to the plants named anchor.
10. Save your work, view the page in your browser, test all the links to make sure they work, then close your browser.

Insert Flash text.

1. Insert Flash text at the bottom of the page that will take you to the top of the page. Use the following settings: Type: Arial, Size: 16, Color: #006600, Rollover Color: #009933, Link: master_gardener.htm#top, Target: _top.
2. Save the Flash text file as **top.swf**.
3. Save the file, view the page in your browser, test the Flash text link, then close your browser.

Create, modify, and copy a navigation bar.

1. Using the Common tab of the Insert bar, insert a horizontal navigation bar at the top of the master_gardener page below the banner.
2. Type **home** as the first element name, then use the blooms_home_up.gif file for the Up Image state. This file is in the assets folder of the unit_d data files folder.
3. Specify the file blooms_home_down.gif file for the three remaining states. This file is in the assets folder of the unit_d data files folder.
4. Enter **Navigation element linking to the home page** as the alternate text, then set the index.htm file as the link for the home element.
5. Create a new element named **plants**, and use the blooms_plants_up.gif file for the Up Image state and the blooms_plants_down.gif file for the remaining three states. These files are located in the assets folder of the unit_d data files folder.
6. Enter **Navigation element linking to the plants page** as the alternate text, then set the plants.htm file as the link for the plants element.
7. Create a new element named **workshops**, and use the blooms_workshops_up.gif file for the Up Image state and the blooms_workshops_down.gif file for the remaining three states. These files are located in the assets folder of the unit_d data files folder.

8. Enter **Navigation element linking to the workshops page** as the alternate text, then set the workshops.htm file as the link for the workshops element.

9. Create a new element named **tips**, and use the blooms_tips_up.gif file for the Up Image state and the blooms_tips_down.gif file for the remaining three states. These files are in the assets folder of the unit_d data files folder.

10. Enter **Navigation element linking to the tips page** as the alternate text, then set the tips.htm file as the link for the tips element.

11. Create a new element named **ask**, then use the blooms_ask_up.gif file for the Up Image state and the blooms_ask_down.gif file for the remaining three states. These files are in the assets folder of the unit_d data files folder.

12. Enter the alternate text **Navigation element linking to the master gardener page**, then set the master_gardener.htm file as the link for the ask element.

13. Center the navigation bar (if necessary), then save the page and test the links in your browser.

14. Select and copy the navigation bar, then open the home page.

15. Delete the current navigation bar on the home page, then paste the new navigation bar in its place.

16. Modify the home element on the navigation bar to show the Down Image state initially.

17. Save the page, test the links in your browser, then close the browser and the page.

18. Modify the navigation bar on the master_gardener page so the Down Image is shown initially for the ask element, then save and close the master_gardener page.

19. Paste the navigation bar to the plants.htm page and the tips.htm page, making the necessary modifications so that the Down Image is shown initially for each element.

20. Save your work, preview all the pages in your browser, test all the links, then close your browser.

FIGURE D-27
Completed Skills Review

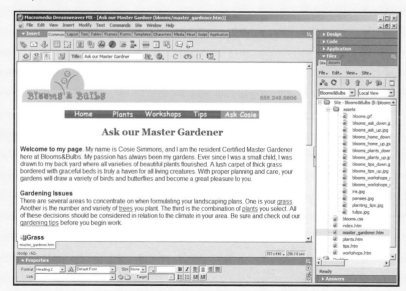

Manage Web site links.

1. Use the Link Checker panel to view broken links, external links, and orphaned files in the Blooms & Bulbs Web site.

2. If you see broken links or orphaned files, refresh the Site list in the Site panel to remove them. If this does not remove the broken links, re-create the site cache. If you still see broken links, check for typing errors in the Link text box for any broken links to correct them.

3. View the external links in the Assets panel.

4. Save your work, then close all open pages.

Use Figure D-28 as a guide to continue your work on the Rapids Transit Web site that you began in Project Builder 1 in Unit A. If you did not create this Web site in Unit A, contact your instructor for assistance. Mike Andrew, the owner, has asked you to create a new page for the Web site that lists helpful links for his customers. Also, because he no longer wants Equipment Rentals as an element in the navigation bar, he asked you to replace the existing navigation bar with a new one that contains the following elements: Home, Before You Go, Our Guides, and Country Store.

1. Open the Rapids Transit Web site. (If you did not create this Web site in Units A through C, contact your instructor for assistance.)
2. Open dwd_3.htm from the unit_d data files folder, then save it as **before.htm** in the Rapids Transit Web site root folder.
3. Save the buffalo_fall.gif file on the page in the assets folder of the Rapids Transit Web site, then set the path for the banner to the assets folder.
4. Create the following links:
Buffalo National River in the Arkansas Ozarks: **http://www.ozarkmtns.com/buffalo**
Map of the Buffalo National River: **http://www.ozarkmtns.com/buffalo/buffmap.html**

Arkansas, the Natural State: **http://www.arkansas.com**
Buffalo River Floater's Guide: **http://www.ozarkmtns.com/buffalo/bfg.html**
5. Design a navigation bar using either text or graphics, then place it on each page of the Web site. If you decide to use graphics for the navigation bar, you will have to create your own graphic files using a graphics program. There are no data files for you to use. (*Hint*: if you create your own graphic files, be sure to create two graphic files for each element: one for the Up Image state and one for the Down Image state.) To design a navigation bar using text, you simply type the

text for each navigation bar element, format the text appropriately, and insert links to each text element as you did in Unit B. The navigation bar should contain the following elements: Home, Before You Go, Our Guides, and Country Store.

6. Save each page, then check for broken links and orphaned files. You should see one orphaned file, rentals.htm, which has no links to other pages yet. You will link this page to the country store page later.

7. Test all links in your browser, close your browser, then close all open pages.

FIGURE D-28
Completed Project Builder 1

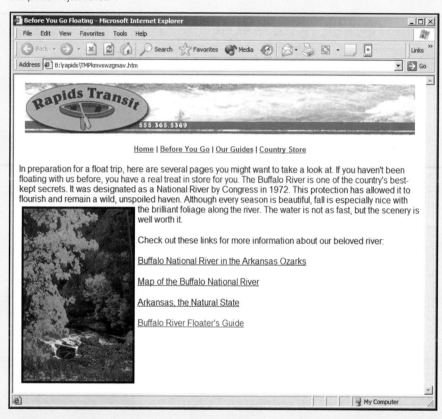

Use Figure D-29 as a guide to continue your work on the Jacob's Web site that you started in Project Builder 2 in Unit A. Chef Jacob has sent you a copy of this month's featured pre-theatre dinner menu to place on the Web site. He has also included some links to London theatre reviews. He has asked you to add this information to the Web site. He has also asked you to insert a new navigation bar on each page of the Web site to help viewers navigate through the site easily.

1. Open the Jacob's Web site. (If you did not create this Web site in Units A through C, contact your instructor for assistance.)
2. Open dwd_4.htm from the unit_d folder, then save it as **menus.htm** in the root folder of the Jacob's Web site, overwriting the existing file.
3. Change the path of the Jacob's banner so that it is set to the jacobs.jpg file in the assets folder of the Web site.
4. Select the text post-theatre dessert specials in the first paragraph, then link it to the after_theatre.htm page.

5. Select The London Theatre Guide - Online text, and link it to **http://www.londontheatre.co.uk/**.
6. Select the London Theatre Guide from the Society of London Theatre text, and link it to **http://www.officiallondontheatre.co.uk/**.
7. Select the London Theatre Tickets text, and link it to **http://www.londontheatrebookings.com/**.
8. Design a new navigation bar using either text or graphics, then place it at the top of the menus page. The navigation bar should contain the following elements: Home, Menus, Recipes, and Directions and Hours.

9. Copy the navigation bar, then paste it to the after_theatre.htm, index.htm, and directions.htm pages of the site. Delete the old navigation bar on any of the pages where it appears.
10. Insert a named anchor at the top of the menus page, then create Flash text at the bottom of the page to link to it.
11. Save all the pages, then check for broken links and orphaned files.
12. Preview all the pages in your browser, check to make sure the links work correctly, close your browser, then close all open pages.

FIGURE D-29
Completed Project Builder 2

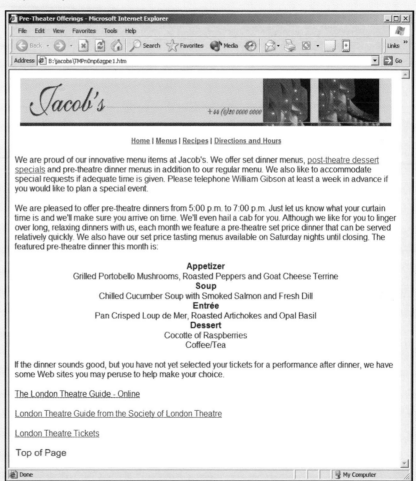

Grace Keiko is a talented young water-color artist who specializes in botanical works. She wants to develop a Web site to advertise her work, but isn't sure what she would like to include in a Web site, or how to tie the pages together. She decides to spend several hours looking at other artists' Web sites to help her get started.

1. Connect to the Internet, go to *www.google.com* or your favorite search engine, then type in keywords that will help you locate artist Web sites, such as the one shown in Figure D-30.

2. Spend some time looking at several of the artist Web sites that you find to familiarize yourself with the types of content that each contains.

3. What categories of page content would you include on your Web site if you were Grace?

4. What external links would you consider including?

5. Describe how you would place external links on the pages, and list examples of ones you would use.

6. Would you use text or graphics for your navigation bar?

7. Would you include rollover effects on the navigation bar elements? If so, describe how they might look.

8. How could you incorporate named anchors on any of the pages?

9. Sketch a Web site plan for Grace, including the pages that you would use as links from the home page.

10. Refer to your Web site sketch, then create a home page for Grace that includes a navigation bar, a short introductory paragraph about her art, and a few external links.

FIGURE D-30
Source for Design Project

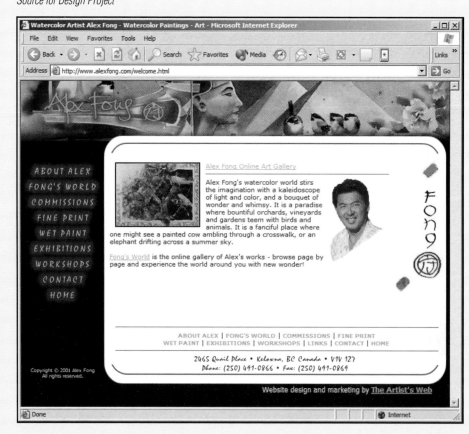

In this assignment, you will continue to work on the group Web site that you started in Unit A and developed in Units B and C. Depending on the size of your group, you can assign individual elements of the project to group members, or work collectively to create the finished product.

You will continue building your Web site by designing and completing a page with a navigation bar. After creating the navigation bar, you will copy it to each completed page in the Web site. In addition to the navigation bar, you will add several external links and several internal links to other pages as well as to named anchors. You will also link Flash text to a named anchor. After you complete this work, you will check for broken links and orphaned files.

1. Consult your storyboard and brainstorm as a team to decide which page or pages you would like to develop in this unit. Decide how to design and where to place the navigation bar, named anchors, Flash text, and any additional page elements you decide to use. Decide which reports should be run on the Web site to check for accuracy.
2. Assign everyone on the team the task of researching Web sites that could be included on one or more of your pages as external links of interest to your viewers.

Reconvene as a group to discuss your findings, then create a list of the external links you want to use. Using your storyboard as a guide, decide as a group where each external link should be placed in the site.
3. Assign a team member the task of adding external links to existing pages or creating any additional pages that contain external links.
4. Assign a team member the task of creating named anchors for key locations on the page, such as the top of the page, then linking appropriate text on the page to them.
5. Insert at least one Flash text object that links to either a named anchor or an internal link.

6. Brainstorm as a team to decide on a design for a navigation bar that will be used on all pages of the Web site.
7. Assign a team member the task of creating the navigation bar and copying it to all finished pages on the Web site. If you decided to use graphics for the navigation bar, assign a team member the task of creating the graphics that will be used.
8. Assign a team member the task of using the Link Checker panel to check for broken links and orphaned files.
9. Use the check list in Figure D-31 to make sure your Web site is complete, save your work, then close all open pages.

FIGURE D-31
Check list for Group Project

> **Web Site Check List**
> 1. Do all pages have a page title?
> 2. Does the home page have a description and keywords?
> 3. Does the home page contain contact information?
> 4. Does every page in the Web site have consistent navigation links?
> 5. Does the home page have a last updated statement that will automatically update when the page is saved?
> 6. Do all paths for links and images work correctly?
> 7. Do all images have alternate text?
> 8. Do all pages have page titles?
> 9. Are all colors Web-safe?
> 10. Are there any unnecessary files that you can delete from the assets folder?
> 11. Is there a style sheet with at least two styles?
> 12. Did you apply the style sheet to page content?
> 13. Does at least one page contain links to one or more named anchors?
> 14. Does at least one page contain Flash text that links to either a named anchor or an internal link?
> 15. Do all pages view well using at least two different browser settings?

UNIT E

WORKING WITH TABLES

1. Create a table.

2. Resize, split, and merge cells.

3. Insert and align graphics in table cells.

4. Insert text and format cell content.

5. Perform Web site maintenance.

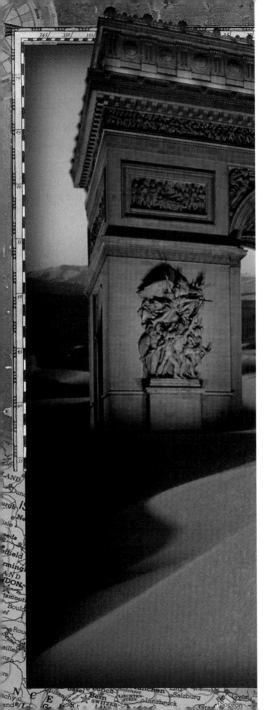

Introduction

You have learned how to place and align elements on a page and enhance them using various formatting options. However, page layout options are fairly limited without the use of tables. Tables offer another solution for organizing text and graphics on a page. **Tables** are placeholders made up of small boxes called **cells**, into which you can insert text and graphics. Cells in a table are arranged horizontally in **rows**, and vertically in **columns**. Using tables on a Web page gives you total control over the placement of each object on the page. In this unit, you will learn how to create and format tables, work with table rows and columns, and format the contents of table cells. You will also learn how to select and format table cells using table tags on the tag selector. Clicking a table tag on the tag selector selects the table element associated with that tag.

Inserting Graphics and Text in Tables

Once you insert a table on a Web page, it becomes very easy to place text and graphics exactly where you want them on the page. You can use a table to control both the placement of elements in relation to each other and the amount of space between each page element. Before you insert a table, however, you should always plan how your table will look with all the text and graphics in it. Even a rough sketch before you begin will save you time as you add content to the page.

Maintaining a Web Site

You already know how to check for broken links and non-Web-safe colors in your Web site. Dreamweaver also provides many other management tools to help you identify other problems. For instance, you can run a report to check for pages that have no page titles, or to search for images that contain no alternate text. It's a good idea to set up a schedule to run these and other reports on a regular basis.

Tools You'll Use

Table properties

Row properties

Cell properties

CREATE A TABLE

What You'll Do

In this lesson, you will create a table for the accessories page in the TripSmart Web site to showcase several items in the TripSmart online catalog. This page, along with the clothing page, will be linked from the catalog page in the Web site.

Understanding Table Views

There are two ways to create a table in Dreamweaver. You can use the Insert Table button on the Common tab of the Insert bar, or you can draw a table using tools on the Layout tab of the Insert bar. Each method for creating a table requires a specific view. You use **Standard View** when you want to use the Insert Table button to insert a table. You use **Layout View** when you want to draw a table using the tools on the Insert bar. You can choose the view you want by clicking the Standard View button or the Layout View button on the Layout tab of the Insert bar.

Creating a Table in Standard View

Creating a table in Standard View is useful when you want to create a table with a specific number of columns and rows. To create a table in Standard View, you use the Insert Table button on the Common tab of the Insert bar to open the Insert Table dialog box, which you use to enter values for the number of rows and columns, the border size, table width, cell padding, and cell spacing. The **border** is the outline or frame around the table and the individual cells and is measured in pixels. The width, which can be specified in pixels or as a percentage, refers to the width of the table. When the table width is specified as a percentage, the table width will adjust to the width of the browser window. When the table width is specified in pixels, the table width stays the same, regardless of the size of the browser window. **Cell padding** is the distance between the cell content and the **cell walls**, the lines inside the cell borders. **Cell spacing** is the distance between cells.

Setting Table Accessibility Preferences for Tables

You can make a table more accessible to visually handicapped viewers by adding a table caption and a table summary that can be read by screen readers. The table caption appears on the screen. The table summary does not. You can use the Preferences dialog box to prompt you to enter a caption and summary every time you insert a table. These features are especially useful for tables that are used for tabular data.

Drawing a Table in Layout View

You use Layout view when you want to draw your own table. Drawing a table is a good idea for those situations where you want to place page elements on a Web page, and have no need for a specific number of rows and columns. You can use the Draw Layout Cell button or the Draw Layout Table button on the Layout tab of the Insert bar to draw a cell or a table. After you draw the first cell, Dreamweaver plots a table for you automatically.

Planning a Table

Before you create a table, you should sketch a plan for it that shows its location on the Web page and the placement of text and graphics in its cells. You should also decide whether to include borders around the tables and cells. Setting the border value to zero causes the table to appear invisible, so that viewers will never know you used a table for the page layout unless they looked at the code. Figure E-1 shows a sketch of the table you will create on the TripSmart accessories page to organize graphics and text.

FIGURE E-1

Sketch of table on the accessories page

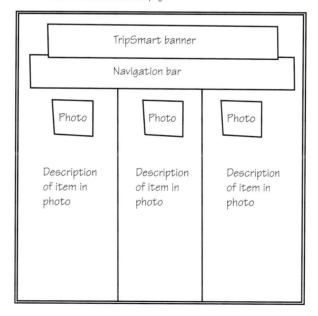

Set table accessibility preferences

1. Open the TripSmart Web site that you completed in Unit D, click Edit on the menu bar, then click Preferences to open the Preferences dialog box.

2. Click Accessibility in the Category list (if necessary).

3. Click the Show Attributes when Inserting Tables check box to place a checkmark in the option box, as shown in Figure E-2.

4. Click OK.

You set the Web site preferences to prompt you to enter accessibility properties when creating tables.

Create a table

1. Double-click accessories.htm in the Site panel to open the accessories page in Design view.

   The accessories page is blank.

2. Select the text Untitled Document in the Title text box on the Document toolbar, type **Featured Accessories**, then press [Enter] (Win) or [return] (Mac) to enter a title for the table.

3. Click the Common tab on the Insert bar (if necessary), then click the Insert Table button.

   (continued)

FIGURE E-2

Setting accessibility preferences for tables

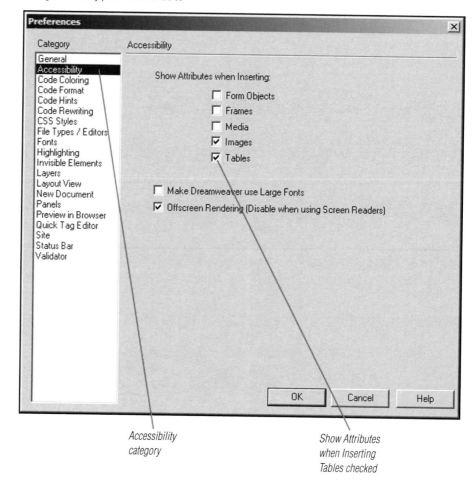

Accessibility category

Show Attributes when Inserting Tables checked

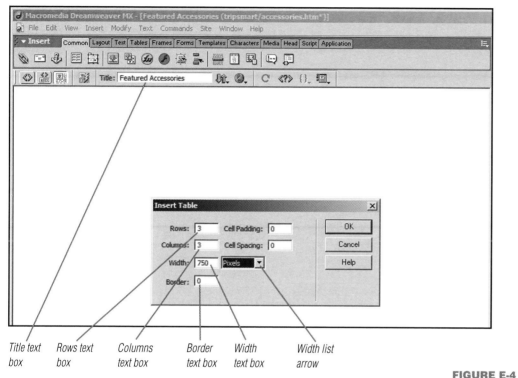

Title text box Rows text box Columns text box Border text box Width text box Width list arrow

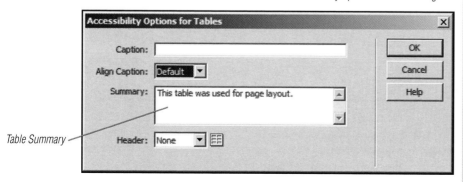

Table Summary

4. Type **3** in the Rows text box, type **3** in the Columns text box, type **750** in the Width text box, click the Width list arrow, click Pixels (if necessary), type **0** in the Border text box, as shown in Figure E-3, then click OK.

   The Accessibility Options for Tables dialog box opens.

5. Click in the Summary text box, type **This table was used for page layout.**, then compare your screen to Figure E-4.

6. Click OK to close the Accessibility Options for Tables dialog box.

   The table appears on the page, but the table summary is not visible. The summary will not appear in the browser, but will be read by screen readers.

   TIP   To edit accessibility preferences for a table, you must view the page in Code view or use the Code Inspector to edit the code directly.

7. Save your work.

You opened the accessories page in the TripSmart Web site and added a page title. You then created a table containing three rows and three columns and set the width at 750 pixels so it will appear in the same size regardless of the browser window size. Finally, you entered a table summary that will be read by screen readers.

Set table properties

1. Move the pointer slowly to the edge of the table until you see the pointer change to a four-sided arrow (Win), or 2-sided arrow (Mac), then click the table border to select the table, if necessary. ⟷

   TIP You can also select a table by (1) clicking the insertion point in the table, then clicking Modify, Table, Select Table; (2) selecting a cell in the table, then clicking Edit, Select All; or (3) clicking the table tag <table> on the tag selector.

2. Expand the Property inspector (if necessary) to display the current properties of the new table.

   TIP The Property inspector will only display information about the table if the table is selected.

3. Click the Align list arrow in the Property inspector, then click Center to center the table on the page, as shown in Figure E-5.

   The center alignment formatting ensures that the table will be centered in all browser windows, regardless of the screen size.

4. Save your work.

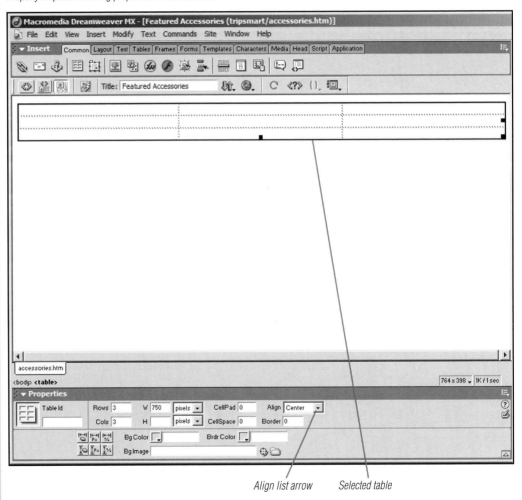

FIGURE E-5
Property inspector showing properties of selected table

Align list arrow *Selected table*

FIGURE E-6

Table in Layout View

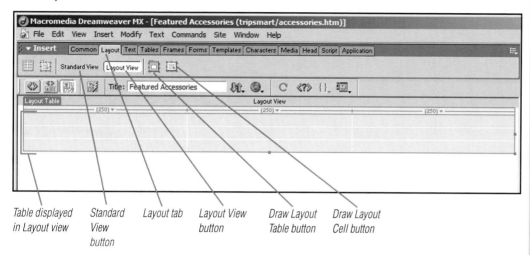

Table displayed
in Layout view

Standard
View
button

Layout tab

Layout View
button

Draw Layout
Table button

Draw Layout
Cell button

1. Click the Layout tab on the Insert bar, then click the Layout View button. [Layout View]

   The Getting Started in Layout View window might open, providing instructions on creating and editing a table in Layout View.

2. Click OK (if necessary) to close the Getting Started in Layout View window.

   The table appears in Layout View, as shown in Figure E-6.

3. Click the Standard View button on the Insert bar to return to Standard view. [Standard View]

4. Click the Common tab on the Insert bar.

You viewed the table in Layout view, then switched back to Standard view.

Setting table and cell widths

If you use a table to place all the text and graphics contained on a Web page, it is wise to set the width of the table in pixels. This ensures that the table will not resize itself proportionally if the browser window size is changed. If you set the width of a table using pixels, the table will remain one size, regardless of the browser window size. For instance, if the width of a table is set to slightly less than 800, the table will stretch across the whole width of a browser window set at a resolution of 800 × 600. The same table would be the same size on a screen set at 1024 × 768 and therefore would not stretch across the entire screen. Most designers design to a resolution of 800 × 600. Be aware, however, that if you set the width of your table at 800 pixels, your table will be too wide to print the entire width of the page, and part of the right side of the page will be cut off. If you are designing a table layout for a page that is likely to be printed by the viewer, you should make your table narrower to fit on a printed page. If you set a table width as a percentage, however, the table would resize itself proportionally in any browser window, regardless of the resolution. You can also set each cell width as either a percentage of the table or as fixed pixels.

RESIZE, SPLIT, AND MERGE CELLS

What You'll Do

 In this lesson, you will set the width of the table cells to be split evenly across the table. You will then split each of the three cells and place images in those cells. You will also merge some cells to provide space for the banner.

Resizing Table Elements

You can resize the rows or columns of a table manually. To resize a table, row, or column, you must first select the table, then drag one of the table's three selection handles. To change all the columns in a table so that they are the same size, drag the middle-right selection handle. To resize the height of all rows simultaneously, drag the middle-bottom selection handle. To resize the entire table, drag the right-corner selection handle.

To resize a row or column individually, drag the interior cell borders up, down, to the left, or to the right. You can also resize selected columns, rows, or individual cells by entering specific measurements in the W and H text boxes in the Property inspector specified either in pixels or as a percentage. Cells whose width or height is specified as a percentage will maintain that percentage in relation to the width or height of the entire table if the table is resized.

Resetting table widths and heights

After resizing columns and rows in a table, you might want to change the sizes of the columns and rows back to their previous sizes. To reset columns and rows to their previous widths and heights, click Modify on the menu bar, point to Table, then click Clear Cell Heights or Clear Cell Widths. Using the Clear Cell Heights command also forces the cell border to snap to the bottom of any inserted graphics, so you can also use this command to tighten up extra white space in a cell.

Splitting and Merging Cells

Using the Insert Table command creates a new table with evenly spaced columns and rows. Sometimes you might want to adjust the cells in a table by splitting or merging them. To **split** a cell means to divide it into multiple rows or columns. To **merge** cells means to combine multiple cells into one cell. Using split and merged cells gives you more flexibility and control in placing page elements on a page and can help you create a more visually exciting layout. When you merge cells, the HTML tag used to describe the merged cell changes from a width size tag to a column span or row span tag. For example, <td colspan="2"> is the code for two cells that have been merged into one cell that spans two columns.

QUICK TIP
You can split merged cells and merge split cells.

Using nested tables

You can insert a nested table in a table. A nested table is a table inside a table. To create a nested table, you place the insertion point in the cell where you want to insert the nested table, then click the Insert Table button on the Insert bar. The nested table is a separate table that can be formatted differently from the table in which it is placed. Nested tables are useful when you want part of your table data to have visible borders and part to have invisible borders. For example, you can nest a table with red borders inside a table with invisible borders. You need to plan carefully when you insert nested tables. It is easy to get carried away and insert too many nested tables, which makes it more difficult to apply formatting and rearrange table elements. Before you insert a nested table, consider whether you could achieve the same result by adding rows and columns or by splitting cells.

Resize columns

1. Click inside the first cell in the bottom row, then click the cell tag on the tag selector, as shown in Figure E-7. **<td>**

   Clicking the cell tag (the HTML tag for that cell) selects the corresponding cell in the table. The cell now has a dark border surrounding it, indicating it is selected.

   > TIP To select the entire table, click the table tag on the tag selector.

2. Type **33%** in the W text box in the Property inspector to change the width of the cell to 33 percent of the table width.

   > TIP You need to type the % sign next to the number you type in the W text box. Otherwise, the width will be expressed in pixels.

3. Repeat Steps 1 and 2 for the next two cells in the last row, using **33%** for the middle cell and **34%** for the last cell.

   The combined widths of the three cells now add up to 100 percent. As you add content to the table, the first two columns will remain 33 percent of the width of the table, and the third column will remain 34%.

4. Save your changes.

   You set the width of each of the three cells in the bottom row to ensure that the width of all three cells is equal.

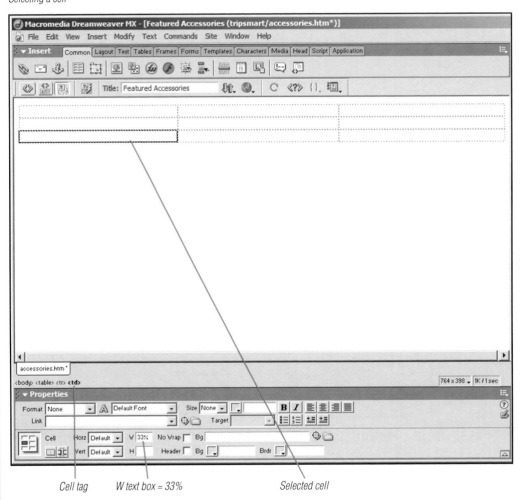

Cell tag   W text box = 33%   Selected cell

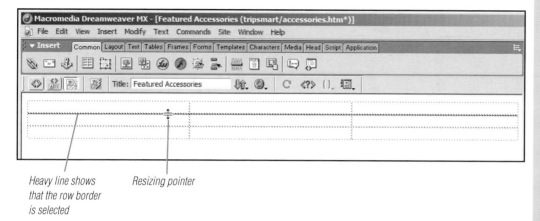

Heavy line shows
that the row border
is selected

Resizing pointer

Resize rows

1. Place the pointer over the bottom border of the first row until it changes to a two-sided arrow as shown in Figure E-8, then click and drag down about ¼ of an inch to increase the height of the row. ⬍

    The border turns darker when you select and drag it.

2. Click Window on the menu bar, point to Others, click History, then drag the slider in the History panel up one line to return the row to its original height.

3. Close the History panel group.

You changed the height of the top row, then used the History panel to change it back it to its original height.

HTML table tags

When formatting a table, it is important to understand the basic HTML table tags. The tags used for creating a table are <table> </table>. The tags used to create table rows are <tr></tr>. The tags used to create table cells are <td></td>. Dreamweaver places the   code into each empty table cell at the time it is created. The   code represents a **non-breaking space**, or a space that a browser will display on the page. Some browsers will collapse an empty cell, which can ruin the look of a table. The non-breaking space will hold the cell until content is placed in it, at which time it will be automatically removed.

Split cells

1. Click inside the first cell in the bottom row, then click the cell tag in the tag selector. **<td>**

2. Click the Splits Cells into Rows or Columns button in the Property inspector. ⬛

3. Click the Split Cells Into Rows option button (if necessary), type **2** in the Number of Rows text box (if necessary) as shown in Figure E-9, then click OK.

4. Repeat Steps 1 through 3 to split the other two cells in the bottom row to two rows each.

   > TIP   To create a new row identical to the one above it, place the insertion point in the last cell of a table, then press [Tab].

5. Save your work.

You split the three cells in the bottom row into two rows, creating a new row of cells.

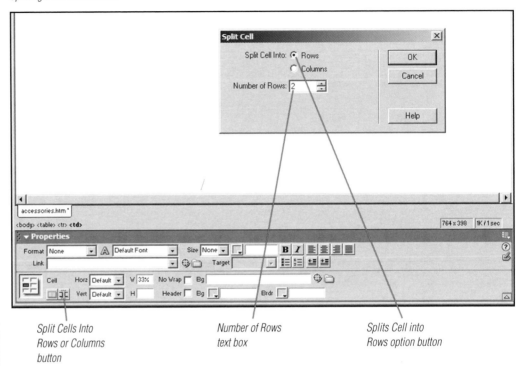

Split Cells Into
Rows or Columns
button

Number of Rows
text box

Splits Cell into
Rows option button

Adding or deleting a row

As you add new content to your table, you might find that you have too many or too few rows or columns. You can add or delete one row or column at a time or several at once. You use commands on the Modify menu to add and delete table rows and columns. When you add a new column or row, you must first select the existing column or row to which the new column or row will be adjacent. The Insert Row or Column dialog box lets you choose how many rows or columns you want to insert or delete, and where you want them placed in relationship to the selected row or column. The new column or row will have the same formatting and number of cells as the selected column or row.

FIGURE E-10
Merging selected cells into one cell

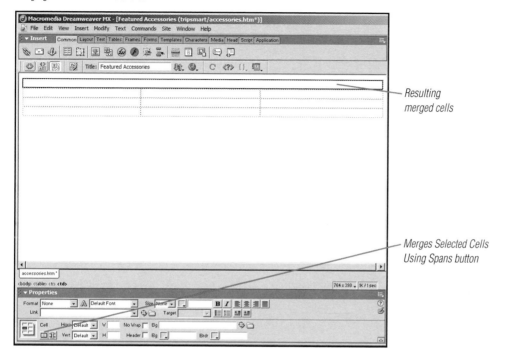

Resulting
merged cells

Merges Selected Cells
Using Spans button

FIGURE E-11
Code View for merged cells

```
7
8  <body>
9  <table width="750" border="0" align="center" cellpadding="0" cellspacing="0" summary="This table was
   used for page layout.">
10   <tr>
11     <td colspan="3"> </td>
12   </tr>
13   <tr>
14     <td> </td>
15     <td> </td>
16     <td> </td>
17   </tr>
18   <tr>
19     <td width="33%"> </td>
20     <td width="33%"> </td>
```

colspan
tag

Lesson 2   Resize, Split, and Merge Cells

Merge cells

1. Click in the first cell in the top row of the table to place the insertion point, then click and drag the pointer to the right to select the second and third cells in the top row.

2. Click the Merges Selected Cells Using Spans button in the Property inspector. ⬚

    The three cells are merged into one cell, as shown in Figure E-10. Merged cells are good placeholders for banners or page headings.

    | **TIP**   You can only merge cells that are adjacent to each other.

3. Click the Show Code View button, then view the code for the split and merged cells, as shown in Figure E-11. ◇

    Notice the table tags denoting the column span (td colspan="3") and the non-breaking spaces ( ) inserted in the empty cells.

4. Click the Show Design View button then save your work. 📱

You merged three cells in the first row to make room for the TripSmart banner.

INSERT AND ALIGN
GRAPHICS IN TABLE CELLS

What You'll Do

 In this lesson, you will insert the TripSmart banner in the top row of the table. You will then insert three graphics showing three TripSmart catalog items. After placing the three graphics, you will center them within their cells.

Inserting Graphics in Table Cells

You can insert graphics in the cells of a table using the Image button on the Insert bar or the Image command on the Insert menu. If you already have graphics saved in your Web site that you would like to insert in a table, you can drag them from the Assets panel into the table cells. When you add a large graphic to a cell, the cell expands to accommodate the inserted graphic. If you set the Preferences dialog box to prompt you for alternate text when inserting graphics, the Image Tag Accessibility Attributes dialog box will open after you insert a graphic, prompting you to enter alternate text. Figure E-12 shows the John Deere Web site, which uses a table for page layout and contains several images in its table cells. Notice that some images appear in cells by themselves, and some appear in cells containing text or other graphics.

Aligning Graphics in Table Cells

You can align graphics both horizontally and vertically within a cell. You can align a graphic horizontally using the Align Left, Align Right, and Align Center buttons or the Horz list arrow in the Property inspector. You can also align a graphic vertically by the top, middle, bottom, or baseline of a cell. To align a graphic vertically within a cell, use the Vert list arrow in the Property inspector, then choose an alignment option, as shown in Figure E-13.

FIGURE E-12
John Deere Web site

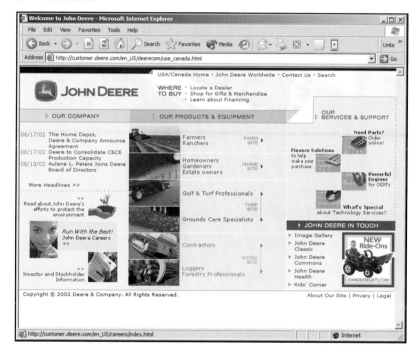

FIGURE E-13
Vertically aligning cell contents

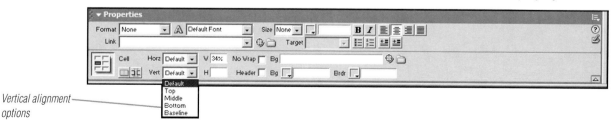

Vertical alignment options

Insert graphics in table cells

1. Open the Assets panel (if necessary), click the Images button on the Assets panel (if necessary), then drag the tripsmart.jpg graphic from the Assets panel to the top row of the table.

   The Image Tag Accessibility Attributes dialog box opens.

2. Type **TripSmart banner** in the Alternate Text text box, then click OK.

3. Click in the first cell in the third row to place the insertion point, insert packing_cube.jpg from the unit_e assets folder, then enter **Packing Cube** for the alternate text.

4. Repeat Step 3 to insert passport_holder.jpg and headphones.jpg in the next two cells, using **Passport Holder** and **Headphones** for the alternate text, then compare your screen to Figure E-14.

   > TIP Press [Tab] to move your insertion point to the next cell in a row. Press [Shift][Tab] to move your insertion point to the previous cell.

5. Refresh the Assets panel to verify that the three new graphics were copied to the TripSmart Web site assets folder.

6. Save your work.

7. Preview the page in your browser.

   Notice that the page would look better if each graphic were evenly distributed across the page.

8. Close your browser.

You inserted images into four cells of the table on the accessories page.

Graphics inserted into table cells

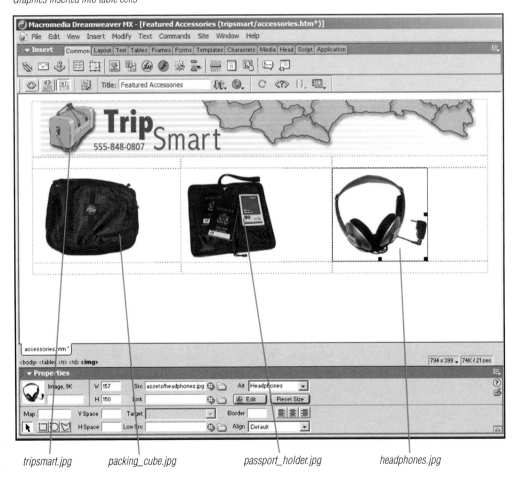

tripsmart.jpg   packing_cube.jpg   passport_holder.jpg   headphones.jpg

FIGURE E-15
Centering images in cells

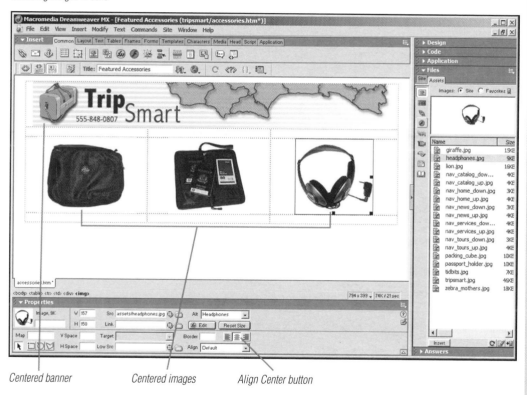

Centered banner   Centered images   Align Center button

1. Click the TripSmart banner, then click the Align Center button in the Property inspector.

2. Center-align the packing cube, passport holder, and headphones images, as shown in Figure E-15.

3. Save your work.

4. Preview the page in your browser, view the centered images, then close your browser.

You center-aligned the TripSmart banner and the three graphics within their respective cells.

INSERT TEXT AND FORMAT CELL CONTENT

What You'll Do

 In this lesson, you will type a heading for the accessories page and copy and paste descriptive text for each item on the page. You will then format the text to enhance its appearance on the page. Last, you will add descriptive names for each item and then format the text you added.

Inserting Text in a Table

You can enter text in a table either by typing it in a cell, copying it from another source and pasting it into a cell, or importing it from another program. Once you place text in a table cell, you can format it to make it more readable and more visually appealing on the page.

Formatting Cell Content

Making modifications and formatting changes to a table and its contents is easier to do in Standard view than in Layout view. To format the contents of a cell in Standard view, you select the contents in the cell, and then apply formatting to it. If a cell contains multiple objects of the same type, such as text, you can either format each item individually or select the entire cell and apply formatting that will be applied identically to all items. You can tell whether you have selected the cell contents or the cell by looking to see what options are showing in the Property inspector. Figure E-16 shows a selected graphic in a cell. Notice that the Property inspector displays options for formatting the object, rather than options for formatting the cell.

Formatting cells

Formatting cells is different than formatting cell contents. Formatting a cell can include setting properties that visually enhance the cell appearance, such as setting a cell width, assigning a background color, or setting global alignment properties for the cell content. To format a cell, you need to either select the cell or place the insertion point inside the cell you want to format, then choose the cell formatting options you want in the Property inspector. For example, to choose a fill color for a selected cell, you click the Background Color button in the Property inspector, then choose a color from the color picker.

In order to format a cell, you must expand the Property inspector to display the cell formatting options. In Figure E-17, notice that the insertion point is positioned in the passport holder cell, but the passport holder graphic is not selected. The Property inspector displays the formatting options for cells.

FIGURE E-16

Property inspector showing options for formatting cell contents

FIGURE E-17

Property inspector showing options for formatting a cell

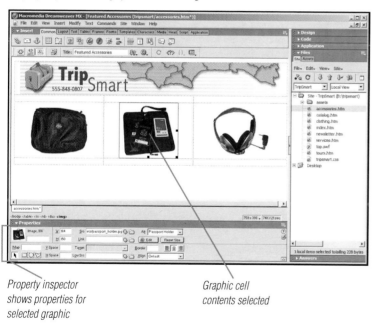

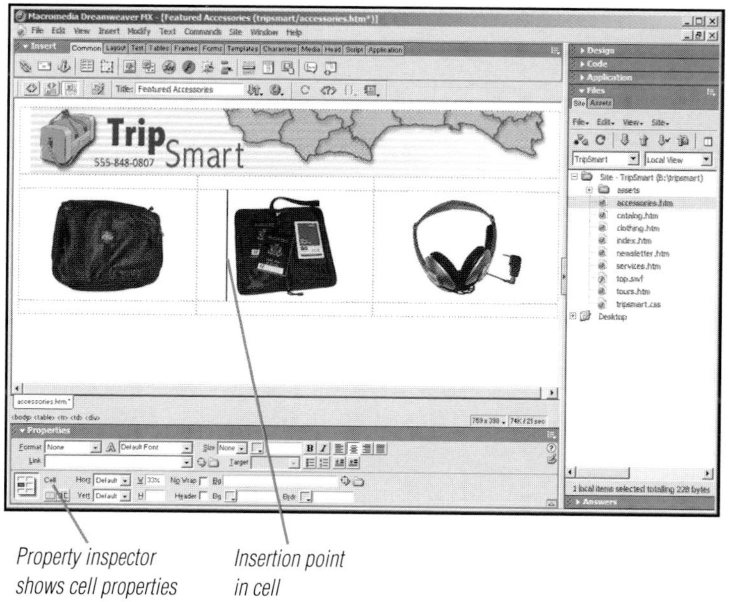

*Property inspector
shows properties for
selected graphic*

*Graphic cell
contents selected*

*Property inspector
shows cell properties*

*Insertion point
in cell*

Insert text

1. Click to the right of the TripSmart banner to place the insertion point, press [Enter] (Win) or [return] (Mac), then type **Featured Catalog Accessories**.

2. Open packing_cube.htm from the unit_e data files folder, click Edit on the menu bar, click Select All, click Edit on the menu bar, click Copy, then close packing_cube.htm.

3. Click in the cell under the packing cube image to place the insertion point, click Edit on the menu bar, then click Paste.

4. Repeat Steps 2 and 3 to paste all the text contained in the data files passport_holder.htm and headphones.htm in the cells below their respective images.

5. Click in the cell above the packing cube image to place the insertion point, type **Packing Cubes**, press [Tab], type **Passport Holder**, press [Tab], then type **Headphones**, as shown in Figure E-18.

6. Save your work.

You typed headings into four cells and copied and pasted descriptive text in the three cells under the three images.

Copying and pasting text into cells

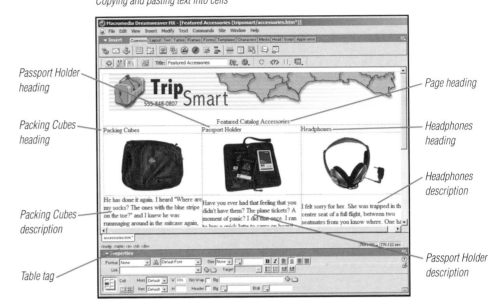

Passport Holder heading

Packing Cubes heading

Packing Cubes description

Table tag

Page heading

Headphones heading

Headphones description

Passport Holder description

Importing and exporting data from tables

You can import and export tabular data into and out of Dreamweaver. Tabular data is data that is arranged in columns and rows and separated by a **delimiter**: a comma, tab, colon, semicolon, or similar character. **Importing** means to bring data created in another software program into Dreamweaver, and **exporting** means to save data created in Dreamweaver in a special file format that can be inserted into other programs. Files that are imported into Dreamweaver must be saved as delimited files. **Delimited files** are database or spreadsheet files that have been saved as text files with delimiters such as tabs or commas separating the data. Programs such as Microsoft Access and Microsoft Excel offer many file formats for saving files. To import a delimited file, you click File on the menu bar, point to Import, then click Tabular Data. The Import Tabular Data dialog box opens, offering you formatting options for the imported table. To export a table that you created in Dreamweaver, you click File on the menu bar, point to Export, then click Table. The Export Table dialog box opens, letting you choose the type of delimiter you want for the delimited file.

FIGURE E-19

Formatting text using the Property inspector and Assets panel

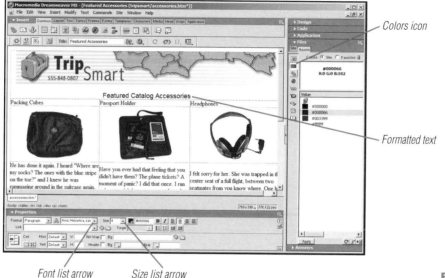

Colors icon

Formatted text

Font list arrow   Size list arrow

FIGURE E-20

Formatting catalog item descriptions

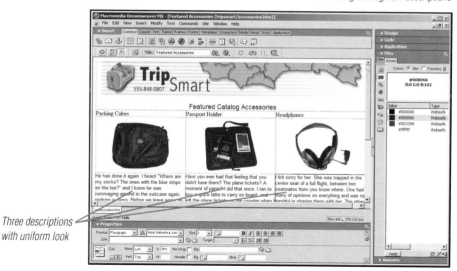

Three descriptions
with uniform look

1. Select the Featured Catalog Accessories text, click the Font list arrow in the Property inspector, click Arial, Helvetica, sans-serif, click the Size list arrow, then click 4.

2. Make sure that Featured Catalog Accessories is still selected, click the Colors button on the Assets panel, click and drag one of the shades of blue from the list of colors onto the selected text, then deselect the text.

   Compare your screen to Figure E-19.

3. Click in the cell below the packing cube image, then use the Property inspector to set the horizontal alignment to Left and the vertical alignment to Top.

4. Make sure the description text is still selected, then change the font to Arial, Helvetica, sans serif, size 2.

5. Repeat Steps 3 and 4 to format the description text in the cells below the passport holder and headphones graphics, using the same formatting applied to the packing cubes description text.

   Your screen should resemble Figure E-20.

You formatted text in table cells.

Format cells

1. Click the table tag on the tag selector to select the entire table.

2. Type **12** in the CellSpace text box in the Property inspector, then press [Enter](Win) or [return](Mac) to add 12 pixels of space between the cells, as shown in Figure E-21.

   The descriptions are easier to read now because you inserted a little white space between the columns.

3. Click in the cell with the Packing Cubes heading to place the insertion point.

4. Click the Background Color button in the Property inspector, then click the second color in the fourth row (#003399). ⬛

5. Repeat Step 4 to apply the background color #003399 to the next two cells containing the text Passport Holder and Headphones, then compare your screen to Figure E-22.

   The headings are no longer visible against the blue background.

6. Save your work.

You formatted table cells by adding cell spacing. You set the background color for three cells to blue.

FIGURE E-21
Changing the CellSpace amount

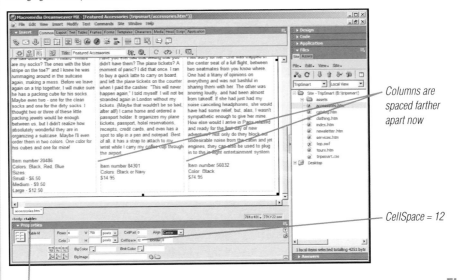

Columns are spaced farther apart now

CellSpace = 12

Table tag

FIGURE E-22
Formatted cell backgrounds

Cell backgrounds with color #003399 applied

FIGURE E-23

Formatted text labels

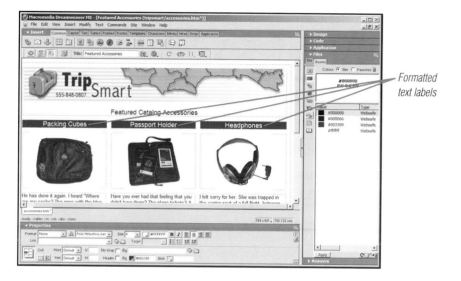

Formatted text labels

Modify cell content

1. Select the Packing Cubes text label in the cell above the packing cube image, use the Property inspector to format the text as Arial, Helvetica, sans-serif, Size 4, center-aligned, white (#FFFFFF) then deselect the text.

   Compare your screen with Figure E-23.

2. Repeat Step 1 to format the Passport Holder and Headphones text labels.

3. Scroll to the bottom of the page, select Item number 20486, then click the Bold button in the Property inspector. **B**

4. Apply bold formatting to the item numbers in the next two cells, as shown in Figure E-24.

5. Save your work, preview the accessories page in your browser, then close your browser.

6. Close the accessories page.

You formatted the text headings and the item numbers on the accessories page.

FIGURE E-24

Formatted item numbers

Item numbers with bold formatting applied

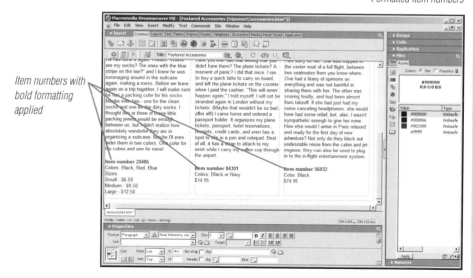

Lesson 4 Insert Text and Format Cell Content

PERFORM WEB SITE MAINTENANCE

What You'll Do

 In this lesson, you will use some of Dreamweaver's site maintenance tools to check for broken links, orphaned files, and missing alternate text. You will also verify that all colors are Web-safe. You will then correct any problems that you find.

Maintaining a Web Site

As you add pages, links, and content to a Web site, it can quickly become difficult to manage. It's important to perform maintenance tasks frequently to make sure your Web site operates smoothly. To keep a Web site "clean," you should use Dreamweaver site maintenance tools frequently. You have already learned about some of the tools described in the paragraphs below. While it is important to use them as you create and modify your pages, it is also important to run them at periodic intervals after publishing your Web site to make sure your Web site is always error-free.

Checking Links Sitewide

Before and after you publish your Web site, you should use the Link Checker panel to make sure all internal links are working. If the Link Checker panel displays any broken links, you should repair them. If the Link Checker panel displays any orphaned files, you should evaluate whether to delete them or link them to existing pages.

Using the Assets Panel

You should also use the Assets panel to check the list of images and colors used in your Web site. If you see images listed that are not being used, you should move them to a storage folder outside the Web site until you need them. You should also check the Colors list to make sure that all colors in the site are Web-safe. If there are non-Web-safe colors in the list, locate the elements to which these colors are applied and apply Web-safe colors to them.

Using Site Reports

You can use the Reports command on the Site menu to generate six different reports that can help you maintain your Web site. You choose the type of report you want to run in the Reports dialog box, shown in Figure E-25. You can specify whether to generate the report for the entire current local site, selected files in the site, or a selected folder. You can also generate a Workflow report to see files that have been checked out by others or to view the Design Notes attached to files.

Using the Site Map

You can use the site map to check your navigation structure. Does the navigation structure shown in the site map reflect a logically organized flowchart? Is each page three or four clicks from the home page? If the answer is no to either of these questions, you can make adjustments to improve the navigation structure.

Testing Pages

Finally, you should test your Web site using many different types and versions of browsers, platforms, and screen resolutions. You should test all links to make sure they connect to valid, active Web sites. Pages that download slowly should be trimmed in size to improve performance. You should analyze all feedback on the Web site objectively, saving both positive and negative comments for future reference to help you make improvements to the site.

FIGURE E-25
Reports dialog box

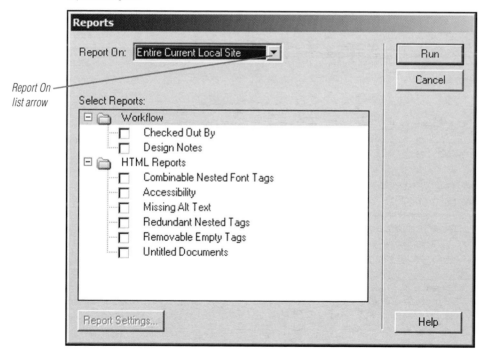

Report On list arrow

Check for broken links

1. Open the Site panel (if necessary).
2. Click Site on the Site panel menu bar, then click Recreate Site to Cache (Win) or click Site on the menu bar, then click Recreate Site Cache (Mac).
3. Click Site on the Site panel menu bar, point to Check Links Sitewide, click the Show list arrow in the Link Checker panel, then click Broken Links (if necessary).

   No broken links are listed in the Link Checker, as shown in Figure E-26.

You verified that there are no broken links in the Web site.

FIGURE E-26
Link Checker displaying no broken links

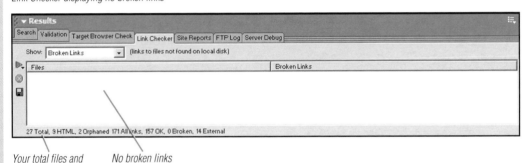

*Your total files and
total links may differ*　　*No broken links*

Check for orphaned files

1. Click the Show list arrow, then click Orphaned Files.

   As Figure E-27 shows, the accessories page and the clothing page appear as orphaned files. You will link the catalog page to these pages later.

   TIP If you have more than two orphaned files, click Site on the Site panel menu bar, click Recreate Site Cache, then check for orphaned files again.

2. Close the Results panel group.

You used the Link Checker to find two orphaned files in the Web site.

FIGURE E-27
Link Checker displaying orphaned files

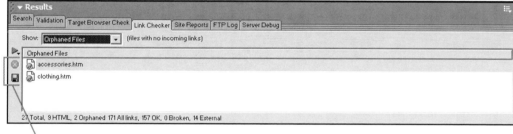

Two orphaned files listed

Remove orphaned files

1. Open dwe_1.htm from the unit_e data files folder and save it in the Web site as **clothing.htm**, overwriting the existing file.

2. Copy the hat.jpg, vest.jpg, and pants.jpg files on the clothing page to the assets folder in the Web site.

3. Change the path of the TripSmart banner path to the tripsmart.jpg image in the assets folder in the TripSmart Web site, then save and close the clothing page.

4. Open dwe_2.htm from the unit_e data files folder, then save it in the TripSmart Web site as **catalog.htm**, overwriting the existing file.

5. Copy the hats_on_the_amazon.jpg file to the assets folder in the Web site.

6. Check all internal links and images to verify that all paths are set correctly, then save and close the catalog page.

   TIP   Use the Modify Navigation Bar dialog box to change the paths of the navigation bar images and links to appropriate files in the TripSmart Web site.

7. Open the accessories page.

8. Place the insertion point in the last cell in the table, press [Tab] to insert a new row, then type **Back to catalog page**.

9. Format the Back to Catalog page text as Arial, Helvetica, sans serif, size 3, then link the Back to Catalog page text to catalog.htm.

   Compare your screen to Figure E-28.

   (continued)

FIGURE E-28

Link to catalog page on accessories page

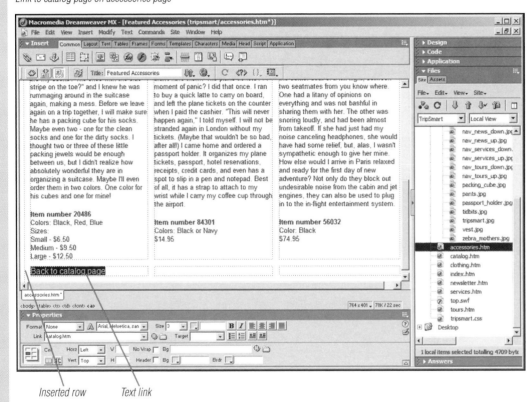

Inserted row   Text link

FIGURE E-29

Link to catalog page on clothing page

As we rounded the bend in the river, a gust of east wind whipped hats off heads and into the murky Amazon river that piranhas call home. Others peered sadly over the rail. I grinned like a caiman. My hat was tied securely and snug in place. Thank you, Safari Hat! My fellow explorers ended the day with red faces in more ways than one.

Item number 50501
Colors: Khaki, White
Sizes: Small, Medium, Large
$29.00

"Can you hold these for a few minutes, dear?" I've heard that before. She handed me her binoculars while she bartered with the natives. I slipped them into my pocket with my extra film and batteries. I was glad I had on my photographer's vest today. It held all our necessities: bottled water, guidebook, compass, and snacks; in addition to the camera, lenses, and flash attachment. What a worker!

Item number 52301
Colors: Khaki, Moss
Sizes: Small, Medium, Large
$54.95

Weather changes quickly in Kenya. As I sipped my English tea before we headed out to our early morning game viewing, I decided to wear my Kenya Convertible Pants. As the weather warmed, I unzipped the legs to cool off a bit. After the safari, we arrived for lunch at the Mount Kenya Safari Club. I zipped them back on and felt more presentable at such an elegant establishment. Propriety and comfort at one low price.

Item number 62495
Color: Khaki
Sizes: Small, Medium, Large, Extra-large
$39.50

Back to Catalog page

Link to catalog page

10. Save and close the accessories page, then open the clothing page.

11. Click the table tag to select it, then click Modify on the menu bar, point to Table, then click Clear Cell Heights to clear the cell heights for the new row.

12. Repeat Steps 8 and 9 to create a Back to Catalog page text link at the bottom of the clothing page, compare your screen with Figure E-29, then save and close the clothing page.

13. Re-create the Site Cache, click the Refresh button on the Site Panel, then run the Check Links Sitewide report again to verify that there are no orphaned files.

> TIP If the Link Checker panel shows orphaned files, re-create the Site Cache. If orphaned files still appear in the report, locate them in the Web site, then correct the paths that contain errors.

You corrected the two orphaned files by linking the accessories and clothing pages from the catalog page.

Verify that all colors are Web-safe

1. Click the Colors button on the Assets panel to view the Web site colors, as shown in Figure E-30.

   The Assets panel shows that all colors used in the Web site are Web-safe.

You verified that the Web site contains all Web-safe colors.

Check for untitled documents

1. Click Site on the menu bar, then click Reports to open the Reports dialog box.

2. Click the Untitled Documents check box, click the Report On list arrow, click Entire Current Local Site, as shown in Figure E-31, then click Run.

   The Site Reports panel opens and shows no files, indicating that all documents in the Web site contain titles.

3. Close the Results panel group.

You verified that the Web site contains no untitled documents.

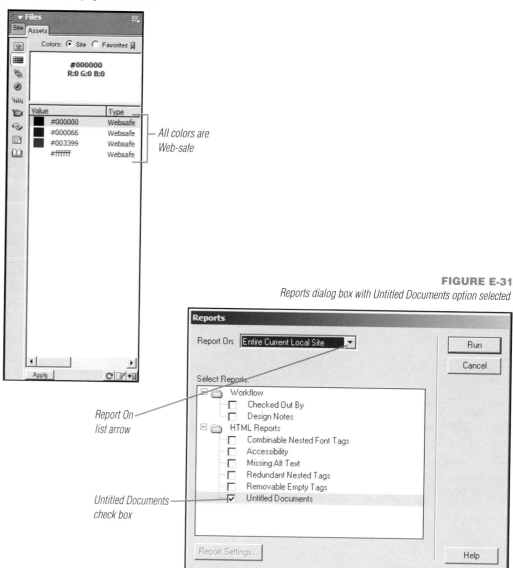

FIGURE E-30
Assets panel displaying Web-safe colors

All colors are
Web-safe

FIGURE E-31
Reports dialog box with Untitled Documents option selected

Report On
list arrow

Untitled Documents
check box

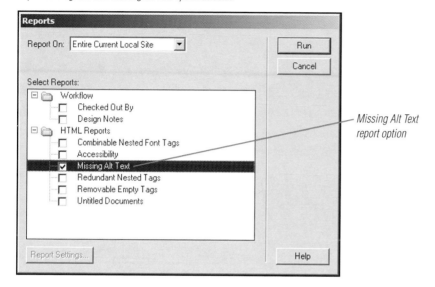

FIGURE E-32
Reports dialog box with Missing Alt Text option selected

Missing Alt Text report option

Check for missing alternate text

1. Using Figure E-32 as a guide, run another report that checks the entire current local site for missing alternate text.

Two pages contain images that are missing alternate text, as shown in Figure E-33.

2. Open the catalog page, then find the image that contains no alternate text.

3. Add appropriate alternate text to the image.

4. Repeat Steps 2 and 3 to locate the image on the home page that contains no alternate text, then add alternate text to it.

5. Save your work, then run the report again to check the entire site for missing alternate text.

No files should appear in the Site Reports panel.

6. Close the Results panel group, then close all open pages.

You ran a report to check for missing alternate text in the entire site. You then added alternate text to two images.

FIGURE E-33
Missing Alt Text Results dialog box

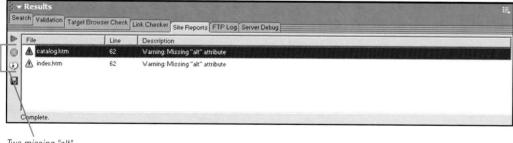

Two missing "alt" tags found

Create a table.

1. Open the Blooms & Bulbs Web site. (If you did not create this Web site in Units A through D, contact your instructor for assistance.)
2. Open workshops.htm from the Web site.
3. Insert a table on the page with the following settings: Rows: 5, Columns: 3, Width: 750 pixels, Border: 0.
4. Enter the text **This table was used for page layout.** in the Summary text box of the Accessibility Options for Table dialog box.
5. Center the table on the page, then use Figure E-34 as a guide for completing this exercise.
6. Save your work.

Resize, split, and merge cells.

1. Select the first cell in the first row, then set the cell width to **35%**.
2. Select the second cell in the first row, then set the cell width to **35%**.
3. Select the third cell in the first row, then set the cell width to **30%**.
4. Merge the third cell in the third row with the third cell in the fourth row.
5. Split the first cell in the third row into two rows.
6. Split the second cell in the third row into two rows.
7. Merge the three cells in the first row.
8. Merge the three cells in the second row.
9. Save your work.

Insert and align graphics in table cells.

1. Use the Assets panel to insert the Blooms & Bulbs banner in the first row and enter appropriate alternate text when prompted.
2. Center the banner.
3. Copy the navigation bar from the home page, paste it in the second row of the table, then center the navigation bar using the Horz list arrow in the Property inspector.
4. Modify the navigation bar to show the workshops element in the down image state and the home element in the up image state.
5. Use the Insert bar to insert the texas_rose.jpg file in the third cell of the third row (the merged cell) directly below the navigation bar. You can find the texas_rose.jpg file in the in the unit_e assets folder where your data files are stored. Add the alternate text **Texas Rose Festival logo** to the texas_rose.jpg when prompted, then center the image in the cell.
6. Use the tag selector to select the cell containing the texas_rose.jpg image, then set the vertical alignment to Top.
7. Use the Insert bar to insert the yellow_rose.jpg file from the unit_e assets folder in the second cell in the fifth row. Add the alternate text **Yellow roses** to the yellow_rose.jpg when prompted.
8. Use the Align list arrow to set the alignment of the yellow_rose.jpg to Left.

9. Select the cell containing the yellow_rose.jpg, then set the vertical alignment of the selected cell to Top.
10. Insert the tearoom.jpg file from the unit_e assets folder in the second cell of the last row, adding the alternate text **Rose arrangement in antique pitcher** when prompted.
11. Center the tearoom.jpg image.
12. Set the vertical alignment of the cell containing the tearoom.jpg image to Top.
13. Save your work.

Insert text and format cell content.

1. Type **Texas Rose Festival** in the second cell in the fourth row, insert a soft return, then type **Tyler, Texas**.
2. Type **Agenda** in the first cell in the fourth row.
3. Open the file agenda.htm from the unit_e data files folder, copy all the text in this file, close agenda.htm, then paste the text into the first cell in the fifth row.
4. Open the file nursery.htm from the unit_e data files folder, copy all the text from this file, paste it into the cell containing the yellow_rose.jpg image to the right of the image, then close the file.
5. Open the file tearoom.htm from the unit_e data files folder, copy all the text from this file, close the tearoom.htm file, then paste the text in the first cell in the last row.
6. Open the file exhibition.htm from the unit_e data files folder, copy all the text from this file, close the exhibition.htm file, then paste the text in the last cell in the last row.

7. Click to place the insertion point to the right of the texas_rose.jpg image, then insert a hard return.

8. Type **Price: $60**, create a soft return, type **includes:**, insert a soft return, type **Admissions, lunch,** insert a soft return, then type **snacks, and tea**. (*Hint*: if your table expands too much, select the table tag on the tag selector and it will revert back to its original size.)

9. Select the Texas Rose Festival text, then format it using the following settings: Font: Arial, Helvetica, sans-serif; Size: 5; Style: Bold; Alignment: Right; Color: #336633.

10. Select the Tyler, Texas text and format it using the following settings: Font: Arial, Helvetica, sans-serif; Size: 4; Color: #336633.

11. Select the cell containing Texas Rose Festival, Tyler, Texas, then set the vertical alignment to Top.

12. Select each of the paragraphs of text and format them using the following settings: Font: Arial, Helvetica, sans-serif; Size: 3; Vertical Alignment: Top.

13. Select the text under the texas_rose.jpg and format it using the following settings: Font: Arial, Helvetica, sans-serif; Size: 2; Style: Bold; Alignment: Center.

14. Select the cell with the word Agenda in it, then change the cell background color to #336633.

15. Format the word Agenda using the following settings: Font: Arial, Helvetica, sans-serif;

Size: 4; Style: Bold; Alignment: Center; Color: #FFFFFF.

16. Select the table, then change the cell spacing to 5.

17. Save your work, preview the page in your browser, then close your browser.

Perform Web site maintenance.

1. Use the Link Checker panel to check for broken links, then fix any broken links that appear.

2. Use the Link Checker panel to check for orphaned files. If any orphaned files appear in the report, take steps to link them to appropriate pages or remove them.

FIGURE E-34
Completed Skills Review

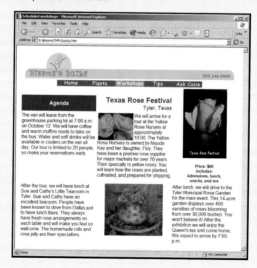

3. Use the Assets panel to check for non-Web-safe colors.

4. Run an Untitled Documents report for the entire local site. If the report lists any pages that have no titles, add page titles to the untitled pages. Run the report again to verify that all pages have page titles.

5. Run a report to look for missing alternate text. Add alternate text to any graphics that need it, then run the report again to verify that all images contain alternate text.

6. Save your work, then close all open pages.

In this exercise you will continue your work on the Rapids Transit Web site that you began in Project Builder 1 in Unit A and developed in Units B through D. Mike Andrew, the owner, has asked you to work on the page for his equipment rentals. He wants you to use a table for page layout.

1. Open the Rapids Transit Web site. If you did not create this Web site in Unit A, contact your instructor for assistance.
2. Open rentals.htm from the Web site.
3. Insert a table with the following settings: Rows: four, Columns: two, Width: 750 pixels, Border: 0. Enter an appropriate table summary when prompted. Center the table.
4. Merge the cells in the top row, then place the Rapids Transit banner into the resulting merged cell. Add the following alternate text to the image: **Rapids Transit banner,** then center the banner.
5. Merge the cells in the second row, copy the navigation bar from another page, then paste it into the merged cell.
6. Center the navigation bar.
7. Split the first cell in the third row into two rows, type **Equipment Rentals** in the first of these two rows, then format the Equipment Rentals text using the following settings: Font: Arial, Helvetica, sans serif; Color: #000099; Size: 4, Alignment: centered.
8. Format the E and R in Equipment Rentals one size larger than the rest of the text.
9. Place the kayak.jpg file from the unit_e assets folder in the first cell in the fourth row, add the following alternate text to the image, **Kayaking on the river**, then center the kayak.jpg image.
10. Use the tag selector to select the cell with the kayak.jpg image, then change the cell width to 30%.
11. Open the file rental_info.htm, paste the contents into the cell to the right of the image, then close the rental_info.htm file.
12. Format the paragraph as Arial, Helvetica, sans-serif, size 3, then set the vertical alignment to Top.
13. Merge the cells in the bottom row, then insert a new (nested) table with 3 rows, 4 columns, 100% width, and a border of 1. Set the cell padding and cell spacing for the nested table to 0. Enter **Rental prices** for the table summary.

14. Format the nested table border to color #000066, then set each cell width in any row to 25%.

15. Enter the equipment data below into your table then format the text as Arial, Helvetica, sans-serif, size 3.

Canoe	**$8.00**	**Life Jacket**	**$2.00**
Kayak	**$9.00**	**Helmet**	**$2.00**
Two-Man Rubber Raft	**$7.00**	**Dry Packs**	**$1.00**

16. Save your work, view the page in your browser, then compare your screen with Figure E-35.

17. Close the browser, open store.htm from the unit_e data files folder, then save it in the Web site, overwriting the existing store.htm file.

18. Save the fruit_basket.jpg file in the Web site assets folder, then set the banner path to the rapids.jpg file in the Rapids Transit Web site assets folder.

19. Run reports for broken links, orphaned files, missing alternate text, and untitled documents. Make corrections as necessary.

20. Save your work, then close all open pages.

FIGURE E-35
Completed Project Builder 1

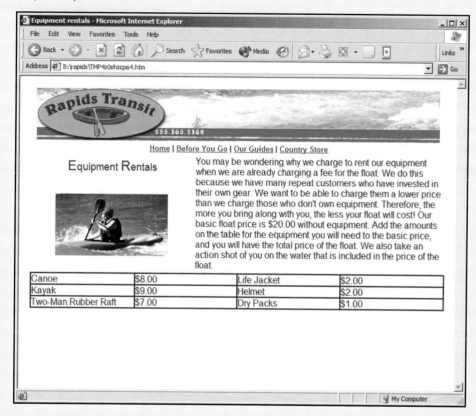

Use Figure E-36 as a guide to continue your work on the Jacob's Web site that you started in Project Builder 2 in Unit A and developed in Units B through D. Chef Jacob would like you to develop a short page listing his hours and directions to the restaurant. You decide to use a table to lay out the page.

1. If you did not create this Web site in Units A through D, contact your instructor for assistance.

2. Open the Jacob's Web site, then open directions.htm.

3. Type **Hours and Directions to Jacob's** for the page title, replacing the original title.

4. Create a table on the page with the following settings: Rows: seven, Columns: two, Width: 750 pixels, Border: 0, adding an appropriate table summary when prompted.

5. Center the table and set the two cells in the bottom row to 50% widths.

6. Merge the cells in the first row, then insert the Jacob's banner. Center-align the banner, then enter appropriate alternate text for it.

7. Merge the cells in the second row, copy the navigation bar from another page, then paste the navigation bar in the resulting merged cell. Center-align the navigation bar.

8. Merge the cells in the fourth row and enter **Our hours are:**, then format it as Arial, Helvetica, sans-serif, size 3, centered, and bold.

9. In the first cell in the fifth row, type **Sunday through Thursday**, enter a soft return, then type **11:00 a.m. to 10:00 p.m.** Format the text as Arial, Helvetica, sans-serif, size 2, centered.

10. In the second cell in the fifth row, type **Fridays and Saturdays**, enter a soft return, then type **11:00 a.m. to 12:00 a.m.** Format the text as Arial, Helvetica, sans-serif, size 2, centered.

11. Merge the cells in the sixth row, then type **We have three private rooms that are available for private parties with advance reservations.** Insert a soft return in front of the text. Format the text as Arial, Helvetica, sans-serif, size 3, centered.

12. Insert the file signature_dish.jpg from the unit_e assets folder in the first cell in the last row, enter appropriate alternate text when prompted, then center the image.

13. Open the file directions_paragraph.htm, copy and paste the text in the second cell in the last row then format the paragraph as Arial, Helvetica, sans-serif, size 3. Then set the vertical alignment to Middle.

14. Place the insertion point to the right of the signature_dish image, create a soft return, type **Set-price dinners**, create a soft return, then type **are served on Saturday evenings**.

15. Format the text as Arial, Helvetica, sans-serif, size 2, centered.

16. Save your work, then preview the page in your browser.

17. Run reports for broken links, orphaned files, missing alternate text, and untitled documents. Make corrections as necessary, then close all open pages.

FIGURE E-36
Completed Project Builder 2

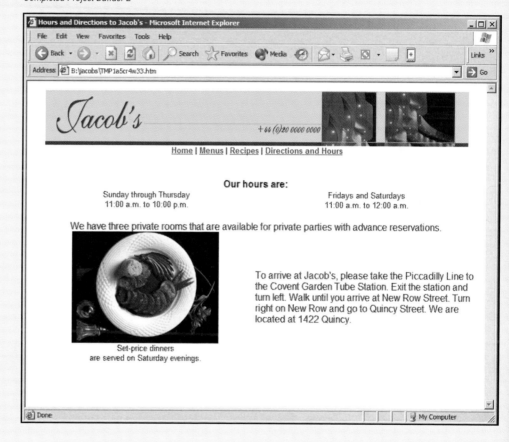

Vesta Everitt has opened a new shop called Needles and Thread that carries needlepoint, cross-stitching, and smocking supplies. She is considering creating a Web site to promote her services and products and would like to gather some ideas before she hires a Web designer. She decides to visit the L.L. Bean and Neiman Marcus Web sites to look for design ideas, as shown in Figures E-37 and E-38.

1. Connect to the Internet, go to *www.course.com*, navigate to the page for this book, click the Student Online Companion link, then click the first link for this unit.

2. Click View on your browser's menu bar, then click Source Command to view the source code for the Neiman Marcus home page.

3. Search the code for table tags. Note the number that you find.

4. Go to *www.course.com*, navigate to the page for this book, click the Student Online Companion link, then click the second link for this unit.

5. Repeat Steps 2 and 3 for the L.L. Bean home page.

6. Using a word processor or scrap paper, list five design ideas that you like from either of these pages. Be sure to specify which page was the source of each idea.

FIGURE E-37
Source for Design Project

FIGURE E-38
Source for Design Project

In this assignment, you will continue to work on the group Web site that you started in Unit A and developed in Units B through D. Depending on the size of your group, you can assign individual elements of the project to group members, or work collectively to create the finished product. There will be no data files supplied. You are building this Web site from unit to unit, so you must do each Group Project assignment in each unit to complete your Web site.

You will continue building your Web site by designing and completing a page that contains a table used for page layout. After completing your page, you will run several reports to test the Web site.

1. If you did not create this Web site in Units A through D, contact your instructor for assistance.

2. Meet as a group to review and evaluate your storyboard. Choose a page or pages to develop in which you will use a table for page layout.

3. Plan the content for the new page (or pages) by making a sketch of the table that shows where the content will be placed in the table cells. Split and merge cells and align each element as necessary to create a visually attractive layout.

4. Assign one or more team members the task of creating the table and placing the content in the cells using the sketch for guidance.

5. After you complete the pages, assign a team member to run a report that checks for broken links in the Web site. The team member should also correct any broken links that appear in the report.

6. Assign a team member the task of running a report on the Web site for orphaned files and correct any if found.

7. Assign a team member the task of running a report on pages that are missing alternate text. The team member should also add alternate text to elements that need it.

8. Assign a team member the task of running a report on any pages that do not have page titles and add titles to any pages, as needed.

9. Assign a team member the task of checking for any non-Web-safe colors in the Web site. If any are found, the team member should replace them with Web-safe colors.

10. As a group, preview all the pages in your browser and test all links. Evaluate the pages for both content and layout, then use the checklist in Figure E-39 to make sure your Web site is completed.

11. Assign team members the task of making any modifications necessary to improve the pages.

FIGURE E-39
Group Project check list

Web Site Checklist
1. Title any pages that have no page titles.
2. Check to see that all pages have consitent navigation links.
3. Check to see that all links work correctly.
4. Check to see that all images have alternate text.
5. Remove any non-Web-safe colors.
6. Delete any unnecessary files.
7. Remove any orphaned files.
8. Use tables for layout when possible.
9. View all pages using at least two different browser settings.
10. Verify that the home page has keywords, a description, and a point of contact.

UNIT F

COLLECTING DATA WITH FORMS

1. Plan and create a form.

2. Format a form.

3. Work with form objects.

4. Create a jump menu.

Introduction

If you want to collect information from viewers who visit your Web site, you can add forms. Forms on a Web page are no different from forms in everyday life. Your checks are simple forms that ask for six pieces of information every time you fill them out: the date, the amount in digits, the amount written out, the name of the check's recipient, a comment/memo about the check, and your signature. A form on a Web page consists of **form objects** such as text boxes or radio buttons into which viewers type information or from which they make selections.

In this unit you will begin working with a new Web site for Northwest Warehouse, a leading retailer of portable computer devices that also offers technical training and consulting services. You will add a form to a page on this Web site that asks viewers to provide information about themselves and their interests.

Using Forms to Collect Information

Forms are just one of the many different tools that Web developers use to collect information from viewers. They can range from the simple to the complex. A simple form can contain a single button that submits information to the Web server. More complex forms can collect contact information, or even allow students to take exams online and receive grades after a short wait. You can use forms to insert information into databases, or to find a specific record in a database. The range of uses for forms is limited only by your imagination.

All forms need to be connected to an application that will process the information that the form collects. This application can store the form data in a database, or simply send it to you in an e-mail message. You need to specify how you want the information used, stored, and processed.

Tools You'll Use

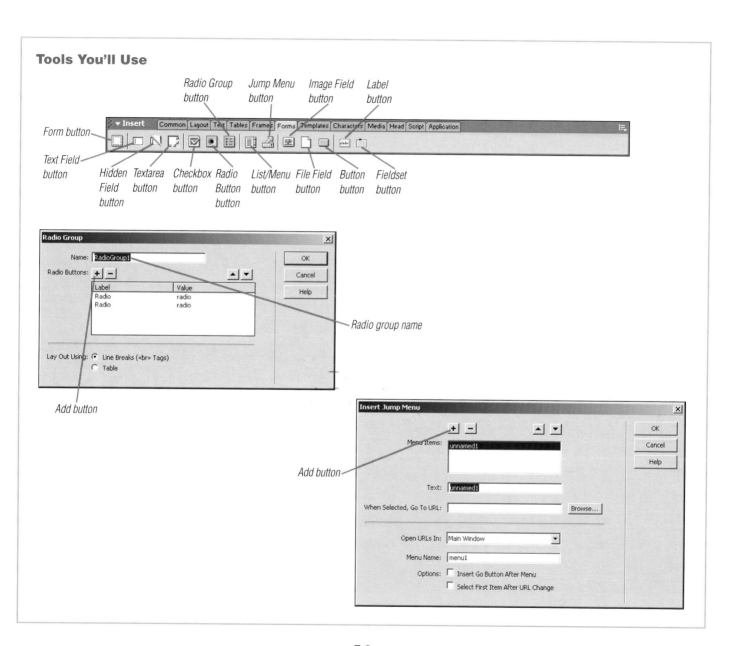

PLAN AND CREATE A FORM

What You'll Do

In this lesson, you will add a new form to the survey.htm page in the Northwest Warehouse Web site.

Planning a Form

Before you use Dreamweaver to create a form, it's a good idea to write down the information you want to collect and the order in which you want to collect it. It's also a good idea to make a sketch of the form. Planning your form content at the beginning saves you from worrying about the organization of the information when you create the form in Dreamweaver. The survey page of the Northwest Warehouse Web site will contain a form that asks viewers to fill in their contact information and sign up for a quarterly newsletter. Figure F-1 shows a sketch of the form that you will create in this unit.

When planning your form content, you should organize the information in a logical order that will make sense to viewers. For instance, no one will expect to fill in their address before their name, simply because it isn't typically done that way. Almost all forms, from your birth certificate to your IRS tax forms, request your name before your address, so you should

follow this standard. Placing information in an unusual order will only confuse and irritate your viewers.

QUICKTIP

People on the Internet are notoriously hurried and will often provide only information that is required or that is located on the top half of the form. Therefore, it's a good idea to put the most important information at the top of your form.

Creating Forms

Once you have finished planning your form content, you are ready to create the form in Dreamweaver. To create a form on a Web page, you use the Insert Form button on the Forms tab of the Insert bar. Clicking the Insert Form button will insert a dashed red outline around the area of the form tags. In order to make your form function correctly, you then need to configure the form so that it "talks" to the scripts or e-mail server, and processes the information submitted by the viewer. By itself, a form can do nothing. It has to have some type of script or program running behind it that will process the information to be used in a certain way.

There are two primary types of programs that can process the information your form collects: server-side applications and scripts on the Web page itself. **Server-side applications** are programs that reside on the Web server and interact with the information collected in the form. The most common types of server-side applications are **Common Gateway Interface (CGI)** scripts, **Cold Fusion** programs, and **Active**

Server Pages (ASP) applications. The most common types of scripts stored on a Web page are created with a scripting language called **JavaScript**, or **Jscript** if you are using a Microsoft Web browser. Both server-side applications and scripts collect the information from the form, process the information, and react to the information the form contains.

You can process form information in a variety of ways. The easiest and most common way is to collect the information from the form and e-mail it to the owner of the Web site. You can also specify that form data be

stored in a database for the Web site owner to use at a later date. You can even specify that the application do both: collect the form data in a database, as well as send it in an e-mail message. You can also specify that the form data be processed instead of stored. For instance, you can create a form that totals the various prices and provides a total price to the site viewer on the order page, without recording any subtotals in a database or e-mail message. In this example, only the final total of the order would be stored in the database or sent in an e-mail message.

FIGURE F-1

Sketch of Web form you will add to survey page

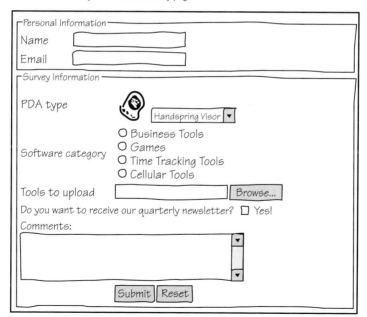

You can also create forms that make changes to your Web page based on information entered by viewers. For example, you could create a form that asks viewers to select a background color for a Web page. In this type of form, the information could be collected and sent to the processor. The processor could then compare the selected background color to the current background color, and change the color if it is different from the viewer's selection.

Setting Form Properties

After you insert a form, you need to use the Property inspector to specify the application that will process the form information, and to specify how the information will be sent to the processing application. The **Action property** in the Property inspector specifies the application or script that will process the form data. Most of the time the Action property is the name and location of a CGI script, such as

/cgi-bin/myscript.cgi; a Cold Fusion page, such as mypage.cfm; or an Active Server Page, such as mypage.asp. Figure F-2 shows the properties of a selected form with the Action property set to a CGI script.

FIGURE F-2

Form controls in Dreamweaver

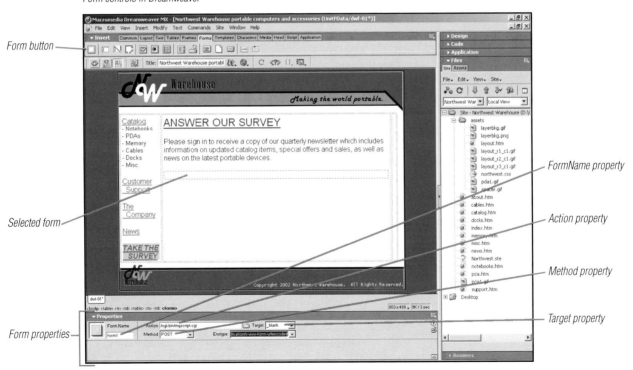

Form button

Selected form

Form properties

FormName property

Action property

Method property

Target property

The **Method property** specifies the HyperText Transfer Protocol (HTTP) method used to send the form data to the Web server. The **GET method** specifies that ASCII data collected in the form will be sent to the server appended to the URL or file included in the Action property. For instance, if the Action property is set to /cgi-bin/myscript.cgi, then the data will be sent as a string of characters after the address, as follows: /cgi-bin/myscript.cgi?a+collection+of+data+collected+by+the+form. Data sent with the GET method is usually limited to 8K or less, depending on the Web browser. The **POST method** specifies that the form data be sent to the processing script as a binary or encrypted file, allowing you to send data securely. When you specify the POST method, there is no limit to the amount of information that can be collected in the form, and the information is secure.

The **FormName property** specifies a unique name for the form. The name can be a string of any alphanumeric characters and cannot include spaces. The **Target property** lets you specify the window in which you want the form data to be processed.

Understanding CGI Scripts

CGI is one of the most popular tools used to collect form data. CGI allows a Web browser to work directly with the programs that are running on the server and also makes it possible for a Web site to change in response to user input. CGI programs can be written in Perl or in C, depending on the type of server that is hosting your Web site. When a CGI script collects data from a Web form, it passes the data to a program running on a Web server, which in turn passes the data back to your Web browser, which then makes changes to the Web site in response to the form data. The resulting data is then stored in a database or sent to an e-mail server, which then sends the information in an e-mail message to a designated recipient. Figure F-3 illustrates how a CGI script processes information collected by a form.

FIGURE F-3
Illustration of CGI process on Web server

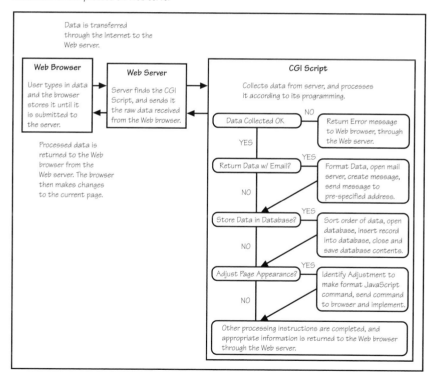

Create the Northwest Warehouse Web site (Win)

1. Open Windows Explorer and navigate to the unit_f data files folder, so that the contents of the unit_f data files folder appear in the right pane.

2. Press and hold [Ctrl], then drag the northwest folder from the unit_f folder in the right pane to the drive and folder in the left pane where you want to store the Northwest Warehouse Web site, as shown in Figure F-4.

3. Close Windows Explorer, start Dreamweaver, click Site on the Site panel menu bar, then click Import.

   The Import Site dialog box opens.

4. Use the Select list arrow to navigate to the northwest folder located in the unit_f data files folder, click Northwest.ste as shown in Figure F-5, then click Open.

   The Choose Local Root Folder for Site Northwest Warehouse opens.

5. Click the Select list arrow, navigate to the northwest folder that you dragged in Step 2, then click Select.

   The dialog box closes and the Northwest Warehouse Web site should now be visible in the Site panel. Because you used the Import command to import the Northwest Warehouse site, all the links that were created in this site are preserved in the northwest folder that you copied.

   (continued)

FIGURE F-4

Dragging the northwest folder to another folder (Win)

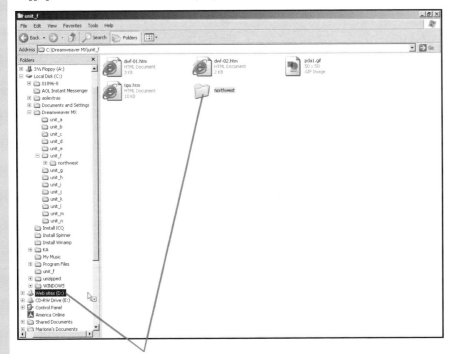

Drag the northwest folder from the right pane to the folder in the left pane where you want to store the Web site files

FIGURE F-5

Import Site dialog box (Win)

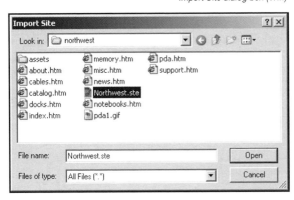

Collecting Data with Forms

FIGURE F-6

Site Definition for Northwest Warehouse dialog box (Win)

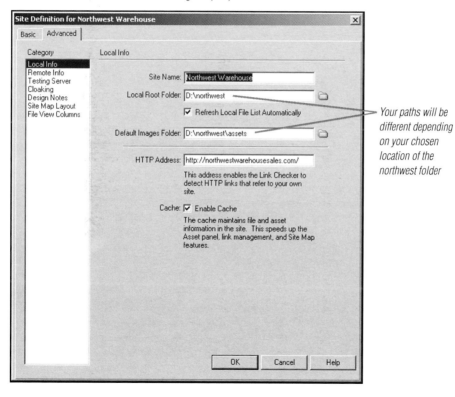

6. Click Site on the Site panel menu bar, click Edit Sites, select the Northwest Warehouse site, then click Edit.

7. Click the Advanced tab (if necessary), click the Local Info category (if necessary), then verify that the Local Root folder is set to the northwest folder you dragged in Step 2.

8. Change the Default Images Folder path to the assets folder located in the northwest folder that you dragged in Step 2.

9. Compare your screen with Figure F-6, click OK, then click Done.

You copied the northwest folder from the unit_f data files folder to a different folder on your computer or external drive. You then imported the Northwest Warehouse site and verified that the root folder was set to the northwest folder that you copied. You also set the default images folder to the assets folder of the northwest folder.

Create the Northwest Warehouse Web site (Mac)

1. Open Finder, then navigate to the folder on your computer or external drive where you want to store the Northwest Warehouse Web site.

2. Click File on the menu bar, then click New Finder Window to open another version of Finder, then open to the unit_f data files folder.

3. Open the unit_f data files folder in one pane, then drag the northwest folder from the unit_f folder to the drive and folder where you want to store the Northwest Warehouse Web site as shown in Figure F-7.

4. Close the Finder windows, start Dreamweaver (if necessary), click Site on the menu bar, then click Import.

   The Import Site dialog box opens.

5. Click Northwest.ste in the northwest folder that you moved in Step 3, then click Open.

   The Choose Local Root Folder for Site Northwest Warehouse opens.

   (continued)

FIGURE F-7

Dragging the northwest folder to a new location (Mac)

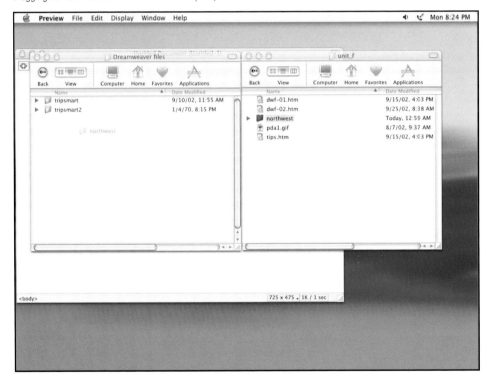

FIGURE F-8

Site Definition for Northwest Warehouse dialog box (Mac)

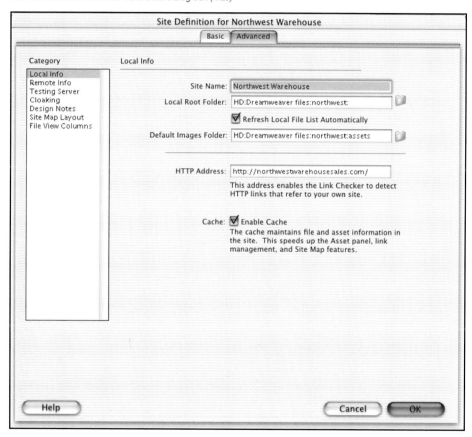

Site Definition for Northwest Warehouse

Basic | Advanced

Category

Local Info
Remote Info
Testing Server
Cloaking
Design Notes
Site Map Layout
File View Columns

Local Info

Site Name: Northwest Warehouse

Local Root Folder: HD:Dreamweaver files:northwest:

☑ Refresh Local File List Automatically

Default Images Folder: HD:Dreamweaver files:northwest:assets

HTTP Address: http://northwestwarehousesales.com/

This address enables the Link Checker to detect
HTTP links that refer to your own site.

Cache: ☑ Enable Cache

The cache maintains file and asset information in
the site. This speeds up the Asset panel, link
management, and Site Map features.

Help   Cancel   OK

6. Click the Select list arrow, navigate to the northwest folder that you moved in Step 3, then click Choose.

The Choose Images Folder for Site Northwest Warehouse dialog box opens.

7. Click the assets folder in the northwest folder, then click Choose.

This sets the Default Images Folder path to the assets folder located in the northwest folder.

The dialog box closes and the Northwest Warehouse Web site should now be visible in the Site panel.

8. Click Site on the menu bar, click Edit Sites, select the Northwest Warehouse site, then click Edit.

9. Click the Advanced tab (if necessary), then click the Local Info category (if necessary).

10. Compare your screen with Figure F-8, click OK, then click Done.

You copied the northwest folder from the unit_f data files folder to a different folder on your computer or external drive. You then imported the Northwest Warehouse site and set the default images folder to the assets folder of the northwest folder.

Insert a form

1. Open the Northwest Warehouse Web site (if necessary).

2. Open the file dwf-01.htm from the unit_f folder where your data files are stored, then save it as **survey.htm** to the northwest folder of the Northwest Warehouse Web site.

3. Change the path of the banner graphic at the top of the page to the file layout_r1_c1.gif located in the assets folder of the Web site.

4. Change the path of the graphic at the bottom of the page to the file layout_r3_c1.gif located in the assets folder of the Web site.

5. Select the text ***Insert Form Here*** in the middle of the page, then press [Delete].

6. Click the Forms tab on the Insert bar, then click the Form button to insert a new form on the page. 🔲

   A dashed red rectangular outline appears on the page, as shown in Figure F-9.

   > TIP   You will only be able to see the form if Invisible Elements are turned on. To turn on Invisible Elements, click View on the menu bar, point to Visual Aids, then click Invisible Elements.

7. Save your work.

You inserted a new form on the survey page of the Northwest Web site.

Form button

Form outline

FIGURE F-10

Property inspector showing properties of selected form

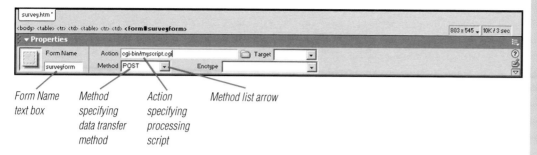

Form Name text box | Method specifying data transfer method | Action specifying processing script | Method list arrow

1. Click the Form tag **<form>** in the tag selector located on the status bar to select the form and display the form properties in the Property inspector.

2. Select form1 in the Form Name text box in the Property inspector, then type **surveyform**.

3. Click the Method list arrow in the Property inspector, then click POST (if necessary).

4. Type **cgi-bin/myscript.cgi** in the Action text box in the Property inspector, then compare your screen to Figure F-10.

   This is the name of the CGI script that will process the form information.

5. Save your work.

You configured the form on the survey page.

Using CGI scripts

You can use CGI scripts to start and stop external programs or to specify that a page update automatically based on viewer input. You can use CGI scripts to create surveys, site search tools, and games. You can even use CGI to do basic tasks such as record entries to a guest book or count the number of people who have accessed a specific page of your site. CGI also lets you create dynamic Web documents "on the fly" so that pages can be generated in response to preferences specified by the viewer.

Unless you have a specific application that you want your script applied to, you can probably find a low-priced script at one of the sites listed in the Student Online Companion for this book. Go to *www.course.com*, navigate to the page for this book, click the Student Online Companion link, then click the CGI Script Resources links for this unit.

FORMAT A FORM

What You'll Do

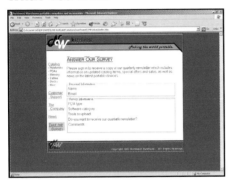

In this lesson, you will insert a table to create a basic structure for the form on the survey page. You will also organize the form into two categories of information by inserting two fieldsets. Finally, you will add and format form labels.

Using Tables to Lay Out a Form

Just as you can use a table to help place page elements on a Web page, you can also use tables to help lay out a form. To make sure that your labels and form objects appear in the exact positions you want on a Web page, you can place them in table cells. When you use a table to lay out a form, you usually place labels in the first column and place form objects in the second column, as shown in Figure F-11. Although there are different ways to lay out form elements, this two-column approach is probably the cleanest and simplest.

Using Fieldsets to Group Form Objects

If you are creating a long form on a Web page, you might want to organize your form elements in sections to make it easier for viewers to fill out the form. You can use fieldsets to group similar form elements together. A **fieldset** is an HTML tag used to group related form elements together. You can have as many fieldsets on a page as you want. In Figure F-12, several form elements are grouped in a box with the heading Personal Information. This box was created using a fieldset. To create a fieldset, you use the Fieldset button on the Forms tab of the Insert bar.

QUICKTIP
You can use fieldsets around table cells, or include whole tables within fieldsets.

Adding Labels to Form Objects

When you create a form, you need to include form field labels so that viewers know what information you want them to enter in each field of the form. Because labels play such an important part in identifying the information that the form collects, you need to make sure to use labels that make sense to your viewers. For example, First Name and Last Name are good form field labels, because viewers understand clearly what information they should enter. However, a label such as Top 6 Directory Names might confuse viewers and cause them to leave it blank or enter incorrect information. When you create a form field label, you should use a simple name that makes it obvious what information viewers should enter in the form field. If creating a simple and obvious label is not possible, then include a short paragraph that describes the information that should be entered into the form field.

You can add labels to a form using one of two methods. You can simply type a label in the appropriate table cell of your form, or use the Label button on the Forms tab of the Insert bar to link the label to the form object.

FIGURE F-11

Web site that uses a table to lay out a form

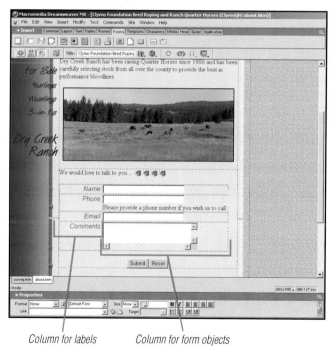

Column for labels   Column for form objects

FIGURE F-12

Web site that uses fieldsets to organize related form elements

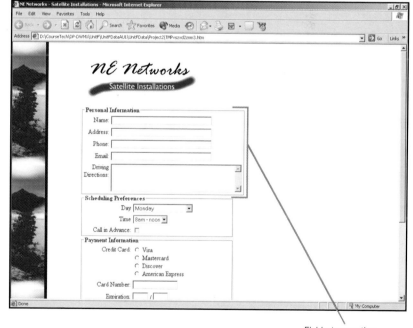

Fieldset separating Personal Information from Scheduling Preferences

Create fieldsets

1. Place the insertion point inside the dashed red outline of the form (if necessary).

2. Click the Fieldset button on the Forms tab of the Insert bar to open the Fieldset dialog box. 🗔

   Notice that the view changes to Code and Design view, and the insertion point is now positioned in the Code view pane.

3. Type **Personal Information** in the Label text box.

4. Compare your screen to Figure F-13, then click OK.

5. Click to the right of the closing </fieldset> tag in the Code view pane, press [Enter] (Win) or [return] (Mac), then click Refresh in the Property inspector. 🔄 Refresh

   The fieldset label Personal Information now appears in the form outline in the Design view pane, and new code appears in the Code view pane, as shown in Figure F-14.

6. Click the Fieldset button on the Insert bar to open the Fieldset dialog box, type **Survey Information**, click OK, then click anywhere in the Design view pane. 🗔

   The Survey Information fieldset appears below the Personal Information fieldset in the Design view pane.

7. Save your work.

You created two fieldsets with the labels Personal Information and Survey Information that will organize form elements into two separate areas on the form.

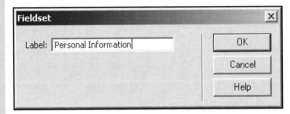

Fieldset button

Fieldset code

Visible fieldset label

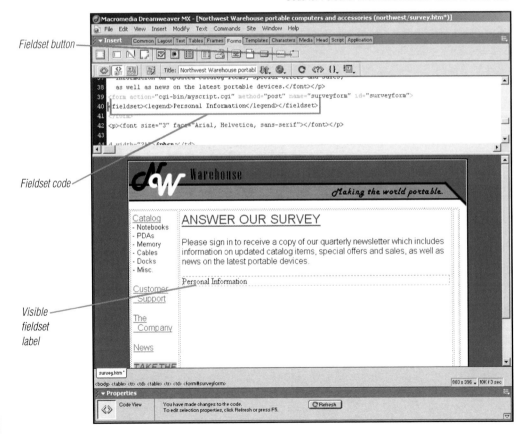

FIGURE F-15
Adding a table within a fieldset

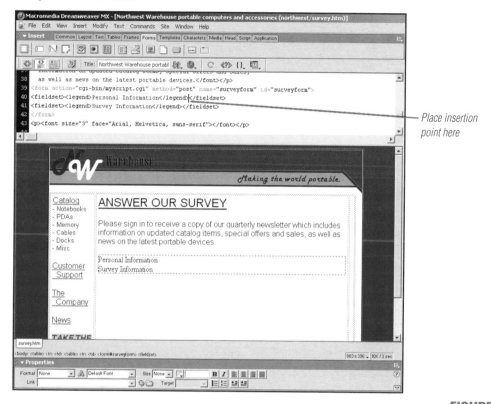

Place insertion point here

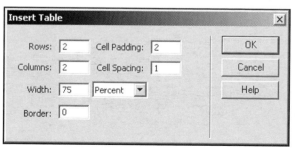

FIGURE F-16
Insert Table dialog box

1. Click to place the insertion point between the </legend> and </fieldset> tags for the Personal Information fieldset in the Code view pane as shown in Figure F-15.

2. Click the Tables tab on the Insert bar, then click the Insert Table button on the Insert bar.

3. In the Insert Table dialog box, set Rows to **2**, Columns to **2**, Cell Padding to **2**, Cell Spacing to **1**, Width to **75 percent**, and Border to **0**.

4. Compare your screen to Figure F-16, then click OK.

   The Accessibility Options for Tables dialog box opens.

5. Click in the Summary text box, type **Table used for form layout purposes**, then click OK.

   You might have to scroll up in the Code view pane to see the table inserted between the Personal Information and Survey Information fieldset tags.

6. Place the insertion point between the </legend> and </fieldset> tags for the Survey Information fieldset in the Code view pane.

   TIP   If you have trouble finding these tags, select the Survey Information fieldset in the Design view pane.

7. Click the Insert Table button on the Insert bar.

   (continued)

8. In the Insert Table dialog box, set Rows to **6**, Columns to **2**, Cell Padding to **2**, CellSpacing to **1**, Width to **75 percent**, and Border to **0**, click OK, then add appropriate text to the Summary text box in the Accessibility Options for Tables dialog box.

9. Click the Show Design View button on the Document toolbar to view the entire form with the two tables added, as shown in Figure F-17, then save your work . ▣

You added two tables to each fieldset of the form on the survey page.

Add form labels to table cells

1. Click in the top left cell of the Personal Information table to set the insertion point.

2. Type **Name**.

3. Click in the bottom left cell of the Personal Information table to set the insertion point.

4. Type **Email**.

5. Click in the top left cell of the Survey Information table to set the insertion point.

6. Type **PDA type**, press [↓], type **Software category**, press [↓], type **Tools to upload**.

7. Format each label you typed in Steps 2 through 6 in Arial, Helvetica, sans-serif, then compare your screen to Figure F-18.

8. Save your work.

You added five form labels to table cells in the form and formatted them in Arial, Helvetica, sans-serif.

FIGURE F-17
Tables inserted in fieldsets in Design view

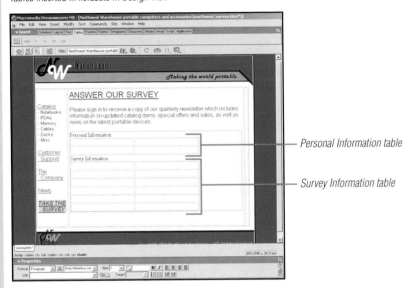

Personal Information table

Survey Information table

FIGURE F-18
Typing labels in table cells

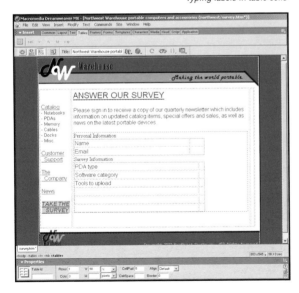

FIGURE F-19
Adding a label to a form using the Label button

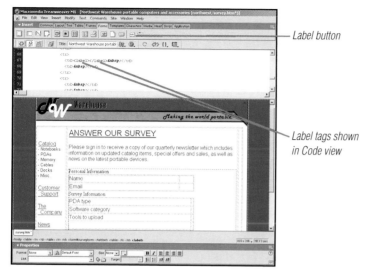

Label button

Label tags shown in Code view

FIGURE F-20
New labels added using Label button in Code and Design view

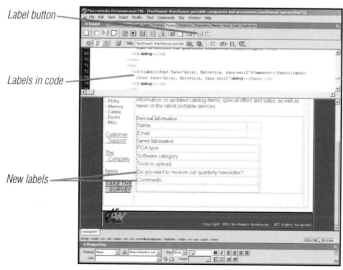

Label button

Labels in code

New labels

1. Click in the cell below the Tools to upload label.

2. Click the Forms tab on the Insert bar, then click the Label button on the Insert bar.

   The view changes to Code and Design view. The insertion point is positioned in the Code view pane between the tags <label> and </label> which were automatically added when you clicked the Label button. See Figure F-19.

3. Type **Do you want to receive our quarterly newsletter?**, then click anywhere in the Design view pane.

   The label appears in the table cell in the Design view pane.

4. Click in the cell below Do you want to receive our quarterly newsletter?.

5. Click the Label button on the Insert bar, then type **Comments:**.

6. Click Refresh in the Property inspector to refresh the page in Design view. [C Refresh]

   TIP You can also press [F5] to refresh the page in Design view.

7. Apply the Arial, Helvetica, sans-serif font combination to the new labels then compare your screen to Figure F-20. [C Refresh]

8. Click the Show Design View button, then save your work.

You added two new labels to the form on the survey page using the Label button.

WORK WITH FORM OBJECTS

What You'll Do

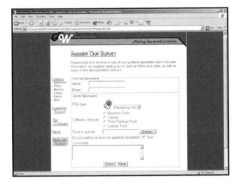

In this lesson, you will add form objects to the form on the survey page.

Understanding Form Objects

A form provides a structure in which you can place form objects. Form objects—which are also called **form elements, form controls,** or **fields**—are the components of a form such as checkboxes, text boxes, and radio buttons that allow viewers to provide information and interact with the Web site. You can use form objects in any combination to collect the information you require. Figure F-21 shows a form that contains a wide range of form objects.

Text fields are the most common type of form object and are used for collecting a string of characters, such as a name, address, password, or e-mail address. For some text fields, such as those collecting dollar amounts, you might want to set an initial value of 0. Use the Text Field button on the Insert bar to insert a text field.

A **text area field** is a text field that can store several lines of text. You can use text area fields to collect descriptions of problems, answers to long questions, comments, or even a résumé. Use the Textarea button on the Insert bar to insert a text area.

You can use **checkboxes** to create a list of options from which a viewer can make multiple selections. For instance, you could add a series of checkboxes listing hobbies and ask the viewer to select the ones that interest him/her. You could also use a checkbox to answer a yes or no question.

You can use **radio buttons** to provide a list of options from which only one selection can be made. A group of radio buttons is called a **radio group.** Each radio group you create allows only one selection from within that group. You could use radio groups to ask viewers to select their annual salary range, their age group, or the t-shirt color they want to order. Use

Collecting Data with Forms

the Radio Group button on the Insert bar to insert a radio group.

You can insert a **menu** or **list** on a form using the List/Menu button on the Insert bar. You use menus when you want a viewer to select a single option from a list of choices. You use lists when you want a viewer to select one or more options from a list of choices. Menus are often used to provide navigation on a Web site, while lists are commonly used in order forms to let viewers choose from a list of possibilities.

Menus must be opened to see all of the options they contain, whereas lists display some of their options all of the time. When you create a list, you need to specify the number of lines that will be visible on the screen by setting a value for the Height property in the Property inspector.

Using **hidden fields** makes it possible to provide information to the Web server and form processing script without the viewer knowing that the information is being sent. For instance, you could add a hidden field

that tells the server who should receive an e-mail message and what the subject of the message should be. You can also use hidden fields to collect information from a viewer without his/her knowledge. For instance you can use a hidden field to send you the viewer's browser type or their IP address.

You can insert an **image field** into a form using the Image Field button on the Insert bar. You can use the Image Field button to create buttons that contain custom graphics.

FIGURE F-21

Web site displaying all possible form objects

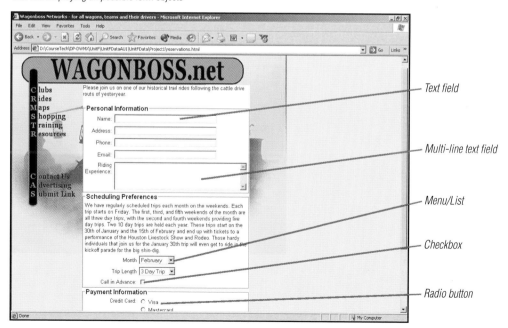

If you want your viewers to upload files to your Web server, you can insert a **file field**. You could insert a file field to let your viewers upload sample files to your Web site, or to post photos to your Web site's photo gallery.

All forms must include a Submit button, which a viewer clicks to transfer their form data to the Web server. You can also insert a Reset button, which lets viewers clear data from a form and reset it to its default values. You can also insert a plain button to trigger an action on the page that you specify. You can insert a Submit, Reset, or plain button using the Button button on the Insert bar.

Jump menus are navigational menus that let viewers go quickly to different pages in your site or to different sites on the Internet. You can create jump menus quickly and easily by using the Jump Menu button on the Forms tab of the Insert bar.

Figure F-22 shows the Forms tab of the Insert bar with all of the form object buttons labeled. When you insert a form object in a form, you need to use the Property inspector to specify a unique name for it.

You can also use the Property inspector to set other appropriate properties for the object, such as the number of lines or characters you wish the object to display.

QUICKTIP

To obtain form controls designed for creating specific types of forms, such as online tests and surveys, you can visit the Macromedia Dreamweaver Exchange and search available extensions (http://www.macromedia.com/exchange/dreamweaver).

FIGURE F-22
Forms tab of Insert bar showing form object buttons

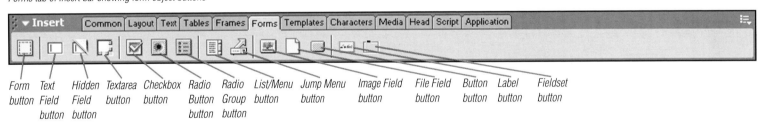

Form button | Text Field button | Hidden Field button | Textarea button | Checkbox button | Radio Button button | Radio Group button | List/Menu button | Jump Menu button | Image Field button | File Field button | Button button | Label button | Fieldset button

FIGURE F-23
Property inspector showing properties of selected text field

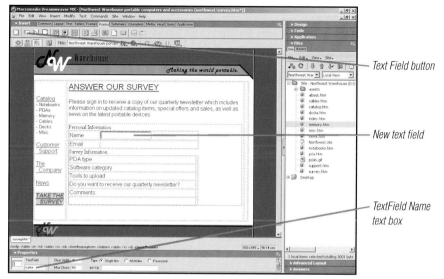

Text Field button

New text field

TextField Name
text box

FIGURE F-24
Form with single text fields added

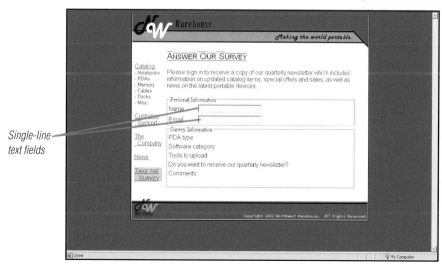

Single-line
text fields

1. Place the insertion point in the table cell to the right of the Name label in the form.

2. Click the Text Field button on the Forms tab of the Insert bar. ☐

3. Select textfield in the TextField Name text box in the Property inspector, then type **name** as shown in Figure F-23.

4. Click the Single line option button in the Property inspector (if necessary).

5. Type **25** in the Char Width text box in the Property inspector.

   This specifies that 25 characters will be visible inside this text field when displayed in a browser.

6. Type **100** in the Max Chars text box in the Property inspector.

   This specifies that a user can type no more than 100 characters in this field.

7. Repeat Steps 2 through 6 to create another single-line text field to the right of the Email label, using **email** for the TextField name, and specifying **25** for Char Width and **100** for Max Chars.

8. Save your work, preview the page in your browser, compare your screen to Figure F-24, then close your browser.

You added two single-line text fields to the form and previewed the page in your browser.

Insert a multiple-line text field

1. Click to the right of the Comments: label, then press [Shift] [Enter] (Win) or [Shift] [return] (Mac) to insert a line break.

   Be sure to click in the same cell as the Comments: label (and not in the cell to the right of it).

2. Click the Textarea button on the Forms tab of the Insert bar.

3. Select textarea in the TextField Name text box in the Property inspector, then type **comments** as shown in Figure F-25.

4. Click the Multi line option button in the Property inspector (if necessary).

5. Type **40** in the Char Width text box in the Property inspector.

   This specifies that 40 characters will be visible inside this text field when the page is displayed in a browser.

6. Type **4** in the Num Lines text box in the Property inspector.

   This specifies that the text box will display four lines of text.

7. Save your work.

You added a multiple-line text field to the form.

Insert a checkbox

1. Place the insertion point in the table cell to the right of Do you wish to receive our quarterly newsletter?

   (continued)

FIGURE F-25

Property inspector with properties of selected text area displayed

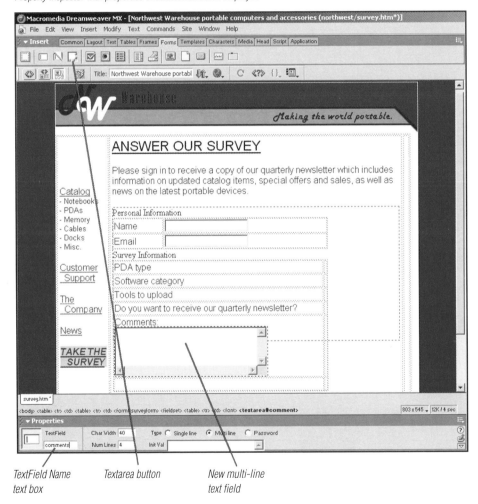

TextField Name text box

Textarea button

New multi-line text field

Property inspector with checkbox properties displayed

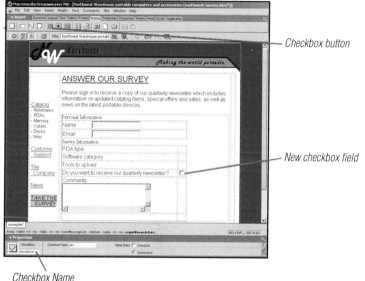

Checkbox button

New checkbox field

Checkbox Name
text box

Survey page in Internet Explorer with checkbox added to the form

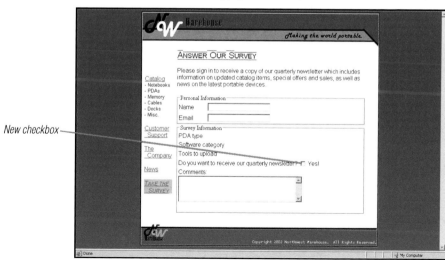

New checkbox

2. Click the CheckBox button on the Insert bar to insert a checkbox in the form. ☑

3. Type **newsletter** in the Checkbox Name text box in the Property inspector.

4. Type **Yes** in the Checked Value text box in the Property inspector.

   This is the value that will be sent to your script or program when the form is processed.

5. Click the Initial State Unchecked option button in the Property inspector (if necessary), as shown in Figure F-26.

   Selecting the Checked option would make a check mark appear in the checkbox by default.

6. Click to the right of the checkbox, type **Yes!**, then format the Yes! text in Arial, Helvetica, sans-serif.

   TIP If the Yes! label appears on the line below the checkbox, make the table wider by dragging the right table border so that the label appears to the right of the checkbox.

7. Merge the cell that contains Do you want to receive our quarterly newsletter? with the cell next to it that contains the checkbox.

8. Merge the Comments cell with the cell next to it, preview the page in your Web browser, compare your screen to Figure F-27, then close your browser.

9. Save your work.

You added a checkbox to the form that will let viewers subscribe to the Northwest Warehouse newsletter.

Add radio groups to a form

1. Click in the table cell to the right of Software category.

2. Click the Radio Group button on the Forms tab of the Insert bar to open the Radio Group dialog box. 🗔

3. Type **Category** in the Name text box.

4. Click the first instance of Radio in the Radio Buttons list to select it, then type **Business Tools**.

5. Click the first instance of radio in the Value column of the Radio Buttons list to select it, then type **business**.

   You specified that the first radio button will be named Business Tools and set business as the value that will be sent to your script or program when the form is processed.

6. Verify that the Layout Using Line Breaks option button is selected.

   TIP If Layout Using Table is selected, then the radio buttons will appear in a separate table within the currently selected table.

7. Repeat Steps 2 through 6 to add three more radio buttons named **Games**, **Time Tracking Tools**, and **Cellular Tools**, using the values **games**, **time tools**, and **cellular**.

   TIP To add a new radio button, click the Add button. ✚

8. Compare your screen with Figure F-28, then click OK to close the Radio Group dialog box.

   TIP If the radio buttons appear on more than 4 lines, make the table wider.

   (continued)

FIGURE F-28
Radio Group dialog box

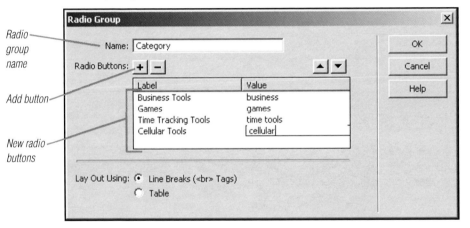

FIGURE F-29
Survey page in Internet Explorer showing new radio group

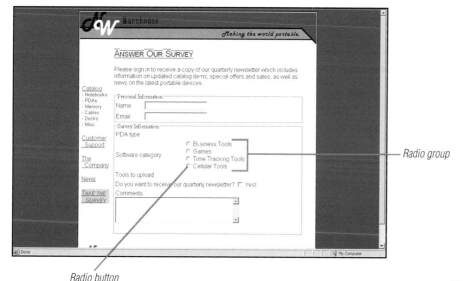

Radio group

Radio button

FIGURE F-30
Image added to the form

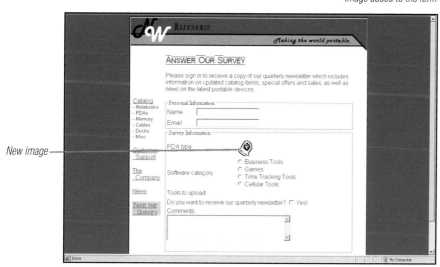

New image

9. Format the radio button labels in Arial, Helvetica, sans-serif.

10. Save your work, preview the page in your browser, compare your screen to Figure F-29, then close your browser.

> TIP To create radio buttons that are not part of a radio button group, click the Radio Button button on the Insert bar.

You added a radio button group that will let viewers choose the category of items about which they want to receive information.

Add an image field

1. Click in the empty table cell to the right of PDA type.

2. Click the Image Field button on the Insert bar to open the Select Image Source dialog box.

3. Navigate to the unit_f data files folder.

4. Click pda1.gif from the list, then click OK (Win) or Choose (Mac).

   The pda1.gif file is automatically copied to your assets folder, because you set the assets folder as the default images folder for the Web site.

5. Click the Refresh button on the Site panel toolbar.

   The pda1.gif image now appears in the Site panel.

6. Save your work, preview the page in your browser, compare your screen with Figure F-30, then close your browser.

You added an image to the form.

Add a menu

1. Click to the right of the pda1.gif image to place the insertion point.

2. Click the List/Menu button on the Forms tab of the Insert bar. 🖽

3. Type **type** in the List/Menu Name text box.

4. Verify that the Type Menu option button is selected in the Property inspector as shown in Figure F-31, then click the List Values button to open the List Values dialog box.

5. Click below the Item Label column heading (if necessary), then type **Handspring Visor**.

6. Click below the Value column heading, then type **visor**.

   This value will be sent to the processing program when a viewer chooses this menu option.

7. Click the Add button, then add **Palm Pilot** as a new Item label with the value **palm**. ✚

8. Add the following three item labels: **HP Jornada**, **Sony Clie**, and **Compaq iPAQ**, setting the values as **jornada**, **clie**, and **ipaq**.

9. Compare your screen to Figure F-32, then click OK.

10. Save your work, preview the page in your browser, click the List arrow to view the menu, compare your screen to Figure F-33, then close your browser.

You added a menu to the form on the survey page.

FIGURE F-31
Property inspector showing properties of selected list/menu

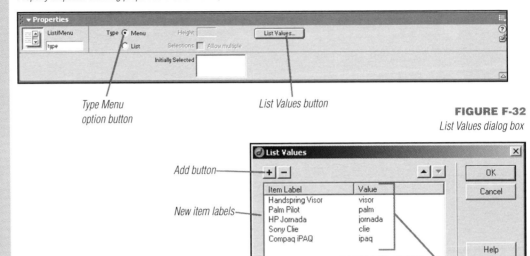

Type Menu option button

List Values button

FIGURE F-32
List Values dialog box

Add button

New item labels

Values of new items

FIGURE F-33
Survey page in Internet Explorer with menu open

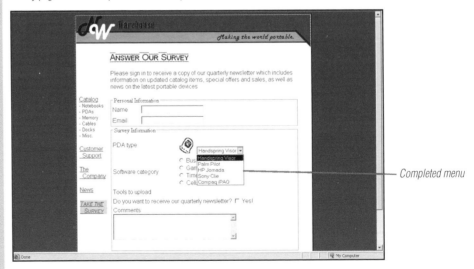

Completed menu

FIGURE F-34
File field properties

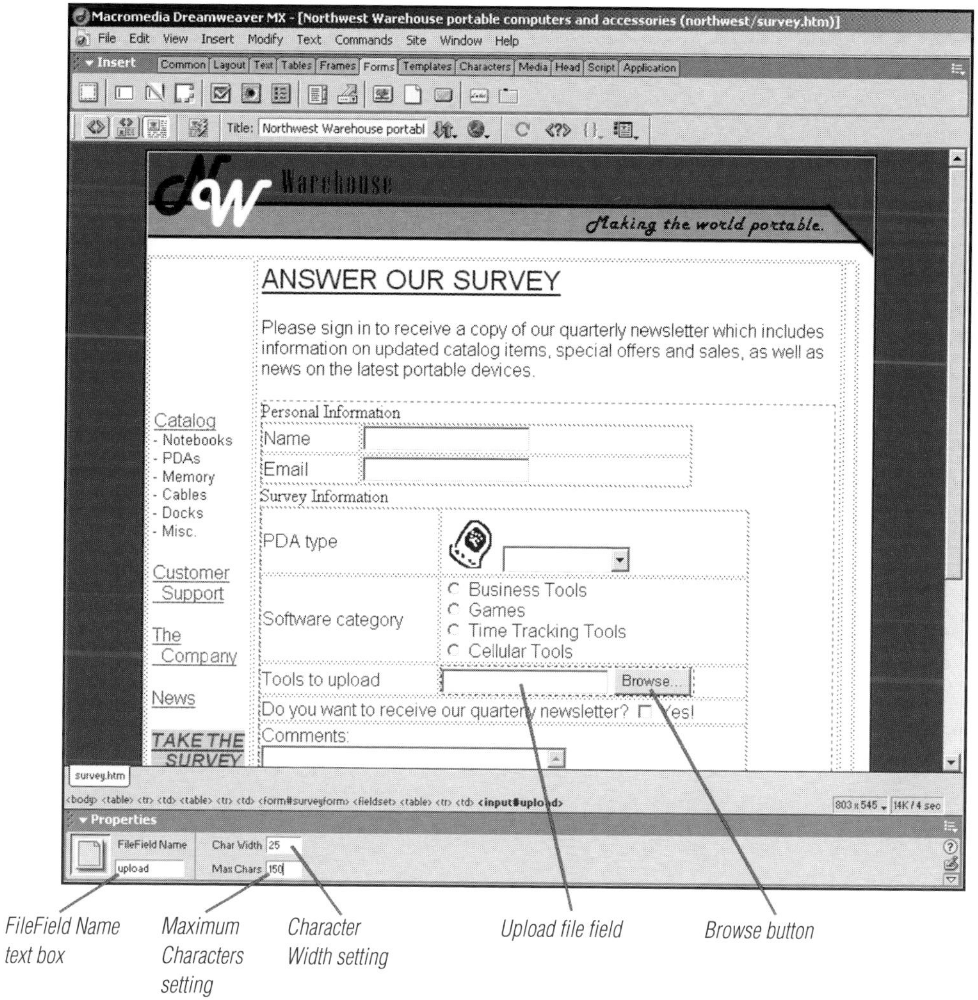

FileField Name
text box

Maximum
Characters
setting

Character
Width setting

Upload file field

Browse button

1. Click in the table cell to the right of Tools to upload.

2. Click the File Field button on the Insert bar. 🗋

   A text field and a Browse button are added to the form. Viewers will use these items to select a file from their computer and upload it to the Web server.

3. Type **upload** in the FileField Name text box in the Property inspector.

4. Type **25** in the Char Width text box in the Property inspector.

5. Type **150** in the Max Chars text box in the Property inspector, then compare your screen to Figure F-34.

   Setting the MaxChars to 150 will let users look for files that contain long file names. You could increase this value even more to allow users to look deep within a folder structure to locate a file.

6. Save your work.

You added a file field that will let viewers upload files to another computer on the Web.

Insert hidden fields

1. Click to the left of Personal Information at the top of the form.

2. Click the Hidden Field button on the Insert bar.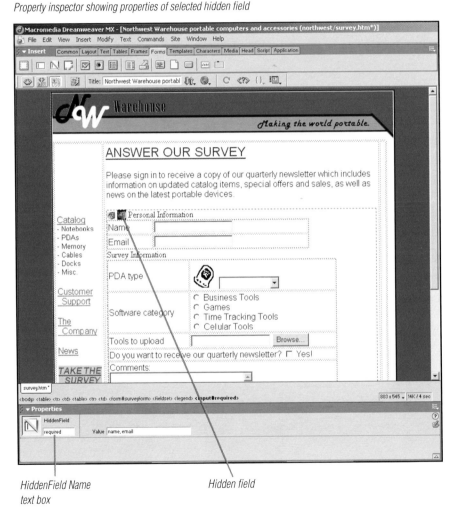

   A Hidden Field icon appears at the insertion point.

   > TIP If you see no Hidden Field icon, click View on the menu bar, point to Visual Aids, then click Invisible Elements.

3. Type **recipient** in the HiddenField Name text box in the Property inspector.

4. Type **heather@northwestwarehouse.com** in the Value text box in the Property inspector.

   You just added a hidden field used by a CGI script to mail the contents of the form to the e-mail address *heather@northwestwarehouse.com*.

5. Click to the right of the recipient hidden field icon, then click the Hidden Field button on the Insert bar.

6. Type **required** in the HiddenField Name text box, then type **name, email** in the Value text box in the Property inspector, as shown in Figure F-35.

   Typing name, email in the Value text box specifies that viewers must enter text in both the Name and Email fields before the script can process the form. These names must match the names of other fields in your form exactly.

7. Save your work.

You added two hidden fields to the form.

FIGURE F-35

Property inspector showing properties of selected hidden field

HiddenField Name
text box

Hidden field

FIGURE F-36

New Submit and Reset buttons added to form

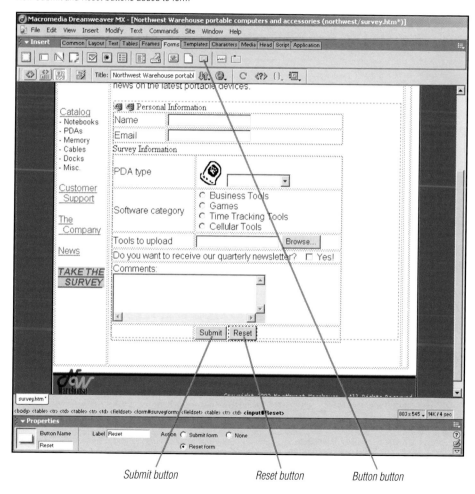

Submit button   Reset button   Button button

1. Click in the second cell of the last row of the Survey Information table.

2. Click the Button button on the Forms tab of the Insert bar. ⬜

   TIP   If a dialog box appears asking you to insert the form tag, click No. This is an error that is sometimes generated by Dreamweaver.

3. Verify that the Submit form option button is selected in the Property inspector.

   When a viewer clicks this Submit button, the information in the form will be sent to the processing script.

4. Verify that Submit is entered in the ButtonName text box and the Label text box in the Property inspector.

   The name Submit is automatically set when you select the Submit form option in the Property inspector.

5. Click the Button button on the Forms tab of the Insert bar, click the Reset form option button in the Property inspector, name the new button Reset, set the Label property to **Reset**, then compare your screen to Figure F-36. ⬜

   When a viewer clicks this Reset button, the form will remove any information typed by the viewer.

6. Save your work.

You added a Submit button and a Reset button to the form.

CREATE A JUMP MENU

What You'll Do

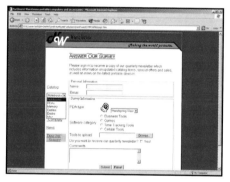

In this lesson you will add a jump menu to the survey page of the Northwest Warehouse Web site.

Understanding Jump Menus

If your Web site contains a large number of pages, you can add a jump menu to make it easier for viewers to navigate through the site. Jump menus are menus that let viewers go directly from the current Web page to another page in the site with a single click. You can also use jump menus to provide links to other Web sites. You can create jump menus using the Jump Menu button on the Forms tab of the Insert bar to open the Insert Jump Menu dialog box. Figure F-37 shows an example of a jump menu on the Wallowa County Chamber of Commerce Web site.

Creating a jump menu is faster and easier than creating a navigation bar. When you create a navigation bar that contains images, you need to spend significant time creating two or three images for each link, each of which takes up a certain amount of precious space on the page. Jump menus are more compact and can fit on a single line. Jump menus only take up additional space when you open the menu. Even then, a jump menu won't disrupt the layout of your pages, because the menu opens on top of your existing page layout.

Adding a Go button to a jump menu

If you want, you can add a Go button to a jump menu that viewers must click in order to jump to the selected page on the menu. Adding a Go button is optional. Many designers choose not to use Go buttons because they require viewers to make one more click to navigate to the page they want, and the goal of the jump menu is to minimize the number of clicks. To add a Go button to a jump menu, check the Insert Go Button After Menu checkbox in the Insert Jump Menu dialog box.

Before you insert a jump menu, it's a good idea to write down a list of all the pages in your Web site that you want to include in the jump menu.

Updating Jump Menus

As you add pages to your Web site, you will probably want to add additional links to your jump menu. Fortunately, updating and modifying a jump menu is easy in Dreamweaver. To add or remove links to a jump menu, select the jump menu, then click List Values in the Property inspector to open the List Values dialog box. You can use this dialog box to add or delete a jump menu item.

Testing Jump Menus

Clicking broken links in a Web site can frustrate and irritate viewers. To prevent them from experiencing this frustration you must test, test, test, and test again until you are sure that there are no misplaced or broken links in your jump menu. The easiest way to test your jump menu is to preview the page in your browser and click each link. When an option in your menu is selected, the page it represents will automatically open, unless the menu contains a Go button. If there is a Go button, you must click Go in order to open the selected page.

FIGURE F-37
Jump menu on Wallowa County Chamber of Commerce Web site

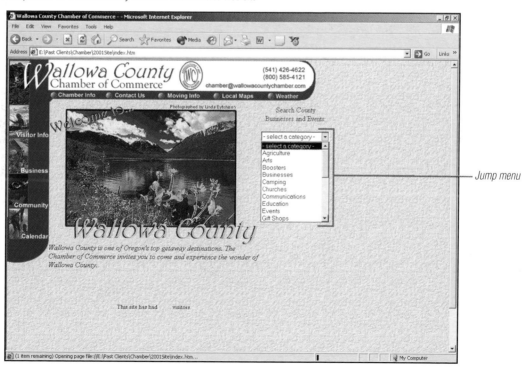

Jump menu

Insert a jump menu

1. Select the items below the Catalog link on the left side of the survey page, then press [Delete].

2. Click the Jump Menu button on the Insert bar to open the Insert Jump Menu dialog box.

3. Type **Notebooks** in the Text text box.

4. Type **notebooks.htm** in the When Selected Go To URL text box.

5. Click the Add button, type **PDAs** in the Text text box, then type **pda.htm** in the When Selected Go To URL field. **+**

6. Repeat Step 5 to add the following menu items and corresponding URLs:

   Memory / memory.htm, Cables / cables.htm, and **Docks / docks.htm**.

7. Click the Open URLS In list arrow, then click Main Window (if necessary).

8. Type **Main Menu** in the Menu Name text box, then compare your screen to Figure F-38.

9. Click OK, save your work, preview the page in your browser, test the menu links, compare your screen to Figure F-39, then close your browser.

   TIP If possible, you should add all the menu options at one time. Changing and adding options afterward is a more difficult task.

You inserted a jump menu on the survey page.

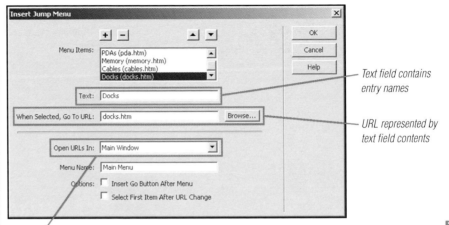

Text field contains entry names

URL represented by text field contents

Target where Menu Items will open

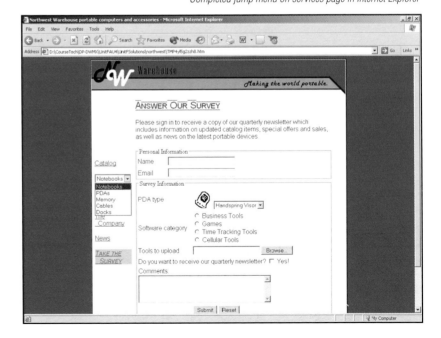

Collecting Data with Forms

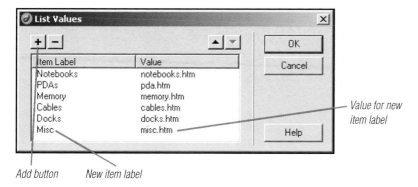

Value for new
item label

Add button   New item label

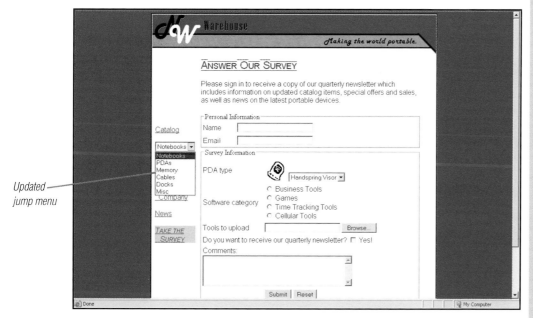

Updated
jump menu

Modify a jump menu

1. Click the jump menu to select it.
2. Click the List Values button in the Property inspector to open the List Values dialog box.
3. Click the Add button, type **Misc** in the Item Label column, press [Tab], type **misc.htm** in the Value column, then compare your screen to Figure F-40. **+**
4. Click OK, then save your work.
5. Preview the page in your browser, compare your screen to Figure F-41, close your browser, then close the survey page.

You added a new item to the jump menu on the survey page.

Plan and create a form.

1. Open the Blooms & Bulbs Web site that you completed in Units A through E. (If you did not create this Web site, contact your instructor for assistance.)
2. Open the tips page.
3. Scroll to the bottom of the page, then insert a form below the last line of text.
4. Set the Form Action to **cgi-bin/myscript.cgi**.
5. Set the Form Method to **POST**.
6. Name the form **SubmitTips**.
7. Set the Form target to **_self**.
8. Save your work.

Format a form.

1. Insert a fieldset in the form with the label **Submit Your Favorite Gardening Tip**.
2. Insert a table within this fieldset that contains 8 rows and 2 columns. Set the border to **0**, the Cell Padding to **2**, the Cell Spacing to **1**, the width to **75 percent** and include an appropriate table summary.
3. Type **Email** in the first cell in the first row.
4. Type **Category** in the first cell in the second row.
5. Type **Subject** in the first cell in the third row.
6. Type **Description** in the first cell in the fourth row.

7. Merge both cells in the fifth row of the table, then type the label **Upload image showing results** in the resulting merged cell.
8. Merge both cells in the sixth row of the table, then insert the label **How long have you been gardening?** in the resulting merged cell.
9. Merge both cells in the seventh row of the table, then insert the label **Receive notification when new tips are submitted?** in the resulting merged cell.
10. Save your work.

Work with form objects.

1. Click in the second cell of the first row, then insert a text field with the name **email**. Set the Char Width property to **30** and the Max Chars property to **150**.
2. Select the second cell of the third row, then insert a text field with the name **subject**. Set Char Width to **30** and Max Chars to **150**.
3. Select the second cell of the fourth row, then insert a textarea with the name **description**. Set Char Width to **40**, and Num Lines to **5**.
4. Insert a checkbox to the right of the Receive notification when new tips are submitted label. Set the name of the checkbox to **receivetips** and specify a Checked Value of **yes**.

5. Insert a radio group named **DurationGardener** to the right of How long have you been gardening? that contains the following labels: **1 - 5 years**, **5 - 10 years**, **over 10 years**. Use the following corresponding values for each label: **1-5**, **5-10**, and **10+**.
6. Insert a list/menu named **category** in the cell to the right of Category. Set the type to **List** and the height to **3**. Use the List Values dialog box to add the following item labels: **Weed control**, **General growth**, and **Pest control**, and set the corresponding values for each to **weeds**, **growth**, and **pests**.
7. Insert a file field named **results** to the right of the label Upload image showing results.
8. Insert a hidden field named **recipient** in the first cell of the eighth row that has the value **webmaster@bloomsandbulbs.com**.
9. Insert a Submit button named **Submit** in the second cell of the eighth row.
10. With your insertion point to the right of the Submit button, insert a Reset button named and labeled **Reset**.
11. Save your work.

Create a jump menu.

1. Set the insertion point at the bottom of the tips page below the new form.
2. Type **Visit these sites for more home and garden improvement tips:** then format this text in bold.
3. Insert a jump menu.
4. Create a menu item named **Home and Garden Television** linked to the URL *http://www.hgtv.com.*
5. Create a menu item named **Master Gardener** linked to the URL *http://www.themastergardenershow.com.*
6. Create a menu item named **Mother Nature's Tips** linked to the URL *http://www.mothernature.com.*
7. Specify to open the URLs in the **Main Window**.
8. Name the jump menu **Tips**.
9. Add a Go button after the menu. (*Hint*: In the Insert Jump Menu dialog box, click the Insert Go button after menu checkbox.)
10. Save your work.
11. Preview the page in your browser and test all links.
12. Close your browser, then close all open pages.

FIGURE F-42

Completed Skills Review

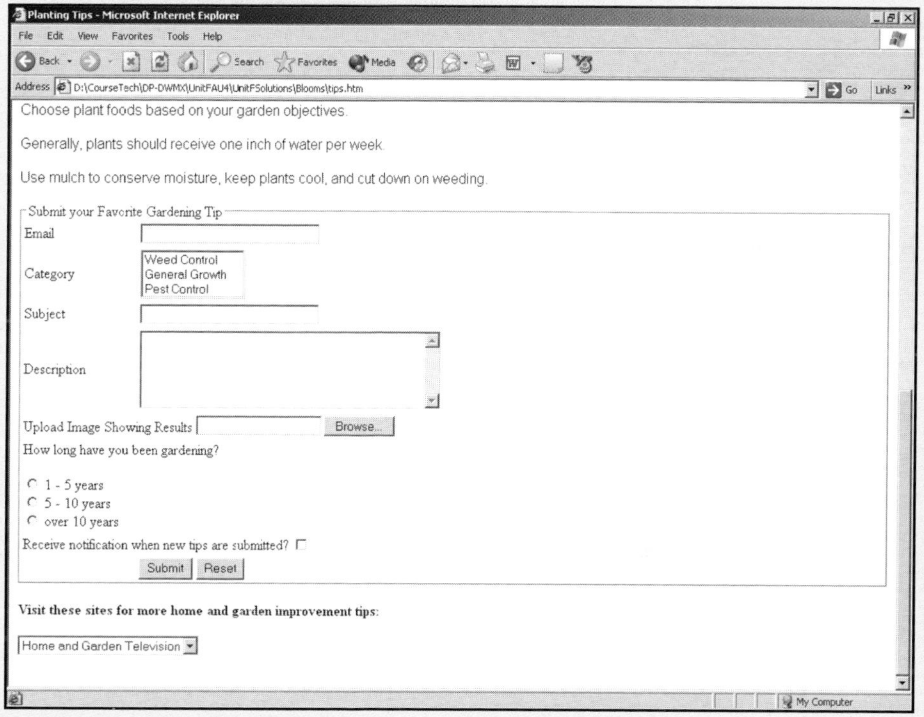

In this exercise you will continue your work on the Rapids Transit Web site you created in Units A through E. Your boss, Mike Andrew, wants you to create a form to collect reservation and payment information from viewers who are interested in signing up for one of your prescheduled 3- or 5-day river trips.

1. Open the Rapids Transit Web site. (If you did not create this Web site in Units A through E, contact your instructor for assistance.)

2. Open the file dwf_02.htm from the unit_f data files folder, save it to the rapids root folder as **reservations.htm**, then set the source of the banner graphic to rapids.jpg in the assets folder of the Web site.

3. Insert a form named **reservations** below the text Rapids Transit Reservations. Specify the action for the form as **/cgi-bin/myscript.cgi** and the method as **POST**.

4. Create a fieldset in the form with the label **Personal Information**.

5. Insert a table in the Personal Information fieldset that contains 5 rows, 2 columns, and a border set to 0. Specify an appropriate table summary.

6. Type the following labels in the cells in the first column: **Name**, **Address**, **Phone**, **Email**, and **Rafting experience**, then right-align them.

7. Insert single-line text fields in the first four cells in the second column that have the following names: **name**, **address**, **phone**, and **email**. Set the Char Width to **30** and the Max Chars to **100** for each of these text fields.

8. In the second cell of the fifth row insert a text area named **experience** that has Char Width set to **40** and Num Lines set at **4**.

9. Click below the Personal Information table in the form and insert a fieldset labeled **Scheduling Preferences**.

10. Insert a table in this fieldset that contains 4 rows, 2 columns, and a border set to 0. Specify an appropriate table summary.

11. Merge the two cells in the first row of the table, then type the following text into this merged cell:
We offer regularly scheduled trips every weekend. Each trip starts on Friday. We offer three-day trips on the first, third, and fifth weekends of the month, and five-day trips on the second and fourth weekends of the month. Two ten-day trips are held each year over Memorial Day and Labor Day.

12. Type the following labels in the remaining cells in the first column: **Month**, **Trip length**, and **Call in advance?**, then right-align them.

13. Insert a checkbox with the name **callme** in the cell to the right of Call in advance? and specify a Checked Value of **yes**.

14. Select the second cell of the second row and insert a list/menu named **month**. Set the type to **menu**. Add the following item labels: **May**, **June**, **July**, **August**, and **September**, and set the corresponding values to **may**, **june**, **july**, **august**, and **september**.

15. Insert a list/menu named **triplength** in the cell to the right of Trip length. Set the type to **menu**. Add the following item labels: **3-day trip**, **5-day trip**, and **10-day trip**, then set the corresponding values **3**, **5**, and **10**.

16. Click below the Scheduling Preferences table (make sure to place the insertion point inside the form), then insert a fieldset

labeled **Payment Information - Credit Cards Collected by Phone**.

17. Insert a table in the Payment Information fieldset that contains 2 rows, 2 columns, and has a border set to 0.

18. Type **Payment Type** in the first column, first row, of this new table.

19. Insert a radio group named **paytype** in the cell to the right of Payment Type that contains the item labels **Visa**, **Mastercard**, **Discover**, **American Express**, **Pay Pal**, and **Mailed Check**. Set the corresponding values to **visa**, **mc**, **disc**, **amexp**, **paypal**, **mailcheck**. Right-align these labels.

20. Insert a hidden field named **recipient** in the first cell of the second row that has the value **mailbox@rapidstransit.com**.

21. Insert a Submit button and a Reset button in the second cell of the fourth row.

22. Save your work, preview the page in your browser, test all the menus and links, compare your screen to Figure F-43, close your browser, then close the reservations page.

FIGURE F-43

Completed Project Builder 1

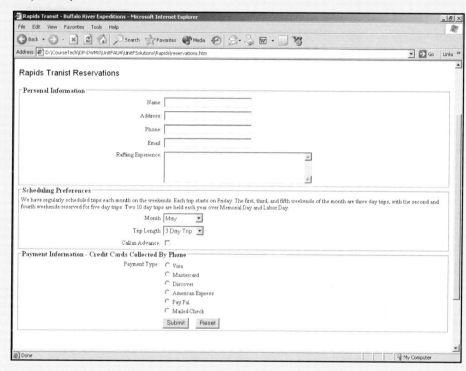

Use Figure F-44 and Figure F-45 as a guide to continue your work on the Jacob's Web site you created in Project Builder 2 in Units A through E. Chef Jacob wants you to create a form that allows people to submit their favorite family recipes for his recipe contest.

1. Open the Jacob's Web site that you completed in Unit E. (If you did not create this Web site in Units A through E, contact your instructor for assistance.)
2. Open recipes.htm.
3. Click to the left of the Grandmother's Rolls heading, type **Chef Jacob's Family Recipe Contest**, then insert a hard return.
4. Use the CSS Styles panel to apply the headings style to this new text, if necessary.
5. Insert a line break below the Chef Jacob's Family Recipe Contest heading, then type the following text:
   Chef Jacob wants to pay you for your best family recipe! Submit your favorite family recipe between August 1 and October 31. If Chef Jacob chooses your entry as the best in its category, you will win $500!

6. Apply the bodytext style to the text you just typed.
7. Insert a hard return after this introductory text, then insert a form named **recipecontest**, with the action **/cgi-bin/myscript.cgi** and the method **POST**.
8. Insert a table in the form that contains 8 rows, 2 columns, and a border set to 0. Specify an appropriate table summary.
9. In the first column of cells, type the following labels: **Name**, **Address**, **Phone**, **Email**, **Category**, **Recipe**, and **Preparation time**.
10. In the second cell of the first, second, third, and fourth rows, insert text fields with the following names: **name**, **address**, **phone**, and **e-mail**. Set the Char Width to **30** and the Max Chars to **100** for each of these text fields.
11. Insert a text area in the second cell of the sixth row named **recipe** that has Char Width set to **40** and Num Lines set to **8**.
12. Insert a list/menu in the second cell of the fifth row named **category**. Set the type to **Menu**, insert the label items **Dessert**, **Entree**, **Side dish**, and **Appetizer**, and set the corresponding item label values to **dessert**, **entree**, **side dish**, and **appetizer**.

13. Insert a radio group in the second cell of the seventh row named **preptime**, with the item labels **Under 15 minutes**, **15 - 45 minutes**, and **Over 45 minutes**. Set the corresponding values to **-15**, **15-45**, and **45+**.
14. Insert a hidden field in the first cell of the eighth row named **recipient** with the value **mailbox@jacobs.com**.
15. Insert a Submit button and a Reset button in the second cell of the eighth row.
16. Scroll to the bottom of the page and insert a jump menu below the Directions paragraph with the following four menu items: **Home**, **Menus**, **Recipes**, **Directions and Hours**. Set the corresponding values to **index.htm**, **menus.htm**, **recipes.htm**, and **directions.htm** as appropriate.
17. Name your jump menu **Site map**.
18. Save your work, preview the page in a browser, test the links in the jump menu, close your browser, then close the recipes page.

FIGURE F-44

Completed Project Builder 2 – top of page

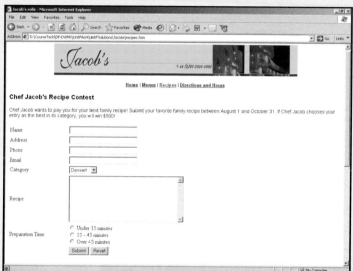

FIGURE F-45

Completed Project Builder 2 – bottom of page

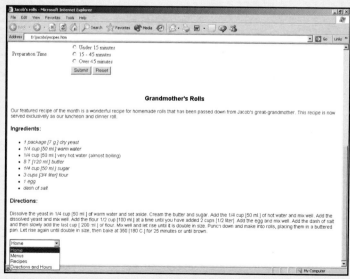

Figure F-46 shows the Girls and Boys Town site, a past selection for the Macromedia Site of the Day. To visit the current Girls and Boys Town Web site, connect to the Internet, go to *www.course.com*, navigate to the page for this book, click the Student Online Companion link, then click the link for this unit. The current page may vary from the figure, since dynamic Web sites are frequently updated to reflect constantly changing information.

This site uses many form objects to collect donations from viewers. This form is well organized, and requests information that most people are comfortable giving over the Internet, such as name, address, and phone number. The form also contains text fields where viewers can specify a donation amount and pay using a credit card. Because the form is secure, viewers should feel comfortable providing their credit card numbers.

Explore this site, print it out, then answer the following questions:

1. Does this site use forms to collect information? If so, identify each of the form objects used to create the form.
2. Is the form organized logically? Explain why or why not.

3. What CGI script is being used to process the form? And where is that script located? Remember the name of the processing CGI script is included in the Action attribute of your form tag. (*Hint*: To view the code of a page in a browser, click View on the menu bar of your browser, then click Source.)
4. What types of hidden information are being sent to the CGI script?
5. Is this form secure?

6. Could the information in this form be collected with different types of form objects? If so, which form objects would you use?
7. Does the form use tables for page layout?
8. Does the form use fieldsets? If so, identify the fieldset labels used.
9. Does the form use labels for its fields? If so, were the labels created using the <label> element or with text labels in table cells?

FIGURE F-46
Design Project

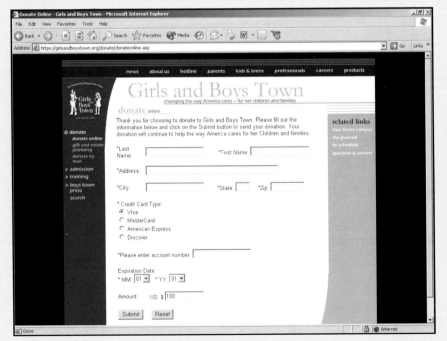

In this project, you will continue to work on the group project that you have been developing since Unit A. Depending on the size of your group, you can assign individual elements of the project to group members, or work collectively to create the finished product.

You will continue building your Web site by designing and completing a page that contains a form to collect visitor information as it relates to the topic of your site.

1. If you did not create this Web site in Units A through E, contact your instructor for assistance.

2. Meet as a group to review your storyboard. Choose a page to develop that will use a form to collect information. Choose another page that you already developed, on which you will place a jump menu.

3. Plan the content for the new page by making a list of the information that you will collect and the types of form objects you will use to collect that information. Plan to include at least one of every type of form object you learned about in the unit. Be sure to specify whether you will organize the form into fieldsets and how you will use a table to structure the form.

4. Assign team members the task of creating the form, its labels, and its contents.

5. Assign another group of members the task of creating the jump menu.

6. After the assigned members complete the page containing the form and the page containing the jump menu, assign another team member the task of running a report that checks for broken links in the Web site. The team member should also correct any broken links that appear in the report.

7. Assign a team member the task of testing the form by previewing it in a browser, entering information into it, and submitting it. The team member should then check to make sure the information gets to its specified location, whether that is a database or an e-mail address.

8. As a group, preview all the pages in a browser, then test all menus and links. Evaluate the pages for both content and layout.

9. Review the Web site checklist shown in Figure F-47. Assign team members the task of making any modifications necessary to improve the form, the jump menu, or the page containing the form.

10. Close all open pages.

FIGURE F-47
Web Site Check List

Web Site Check List

1. Do all navigation links work?
2. Do all images appear?
3. Are all colors Web safe?
4. Do all form objects align correctly with their labels?
5. Do any extra items appear on the form that need to be removed?
6. Does the order of form fields make sense?
7. Does the most important information appear at the top of the form?
8. Did you test the pages in at least two different browsers?
9. Do your pages look good in at least two different screen resolutions?

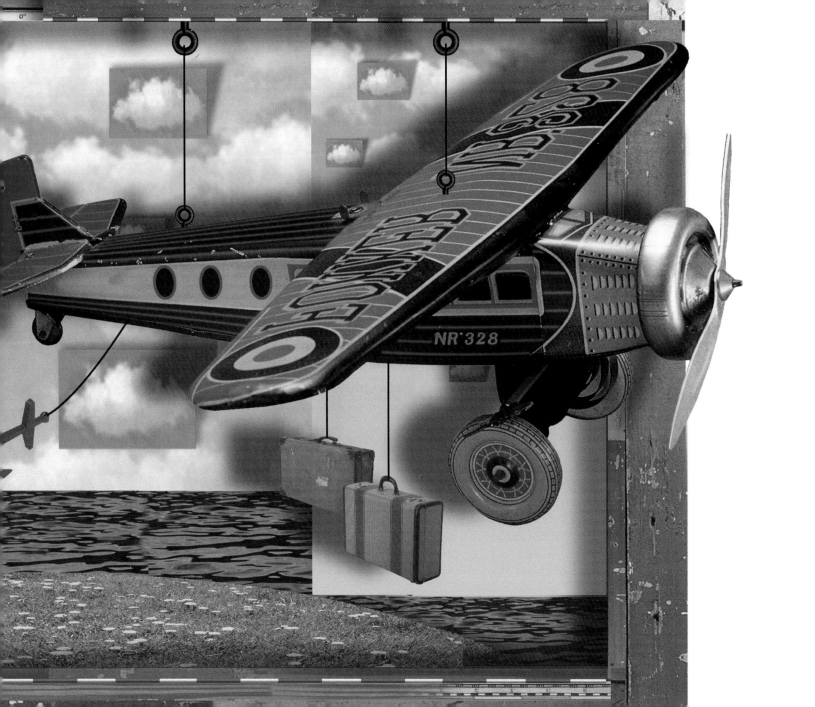

UNIT G

POSITIONING OBJECTS WITH LAYERS

1. Create a layer.

2. Set the position and size of a layer.

3. Use the Layers panel.

4. Configure layer preferences.

5. Convert layers to tables and tables to layers.

Introduction

If you want to control with precision the position of text and graphic elements on your Web pages, then you need to use layers. **Layers** are containers in which you can place text and graphics and which you can use to position elements on a Web page according to specific pixel coordinates. Using layers, you can position elements next to each other as well as on top of each other in a stack. In this unit you will use layers to place text and graphics on a page.

Using Layers versus Tables for Page Layout

Like tables, layers let you control the appearance of your Web page. But unlike tables, layers allow you to stack your information in a vertical pile, allowing for just one piece of information to be visible at a time. Tables are also static, which makes it difficult to change them on the fly. Layers, on the other hand, are treated as their own documents, so that you can easily change their contents. Dreamweaver even includes the JavaScript behavior to do so. **Behaviors** in Dreamweaver are simple action scripts that allow you to perform common tasks quickly, either on a Web page while it is being viewed in a browser, or to a Web page while you are creating it in Dreamweaver.

The biggest factor you should consider when deciding between layers or tables for page layout, is the browsers that will be used to view the pages. If you think a high percentage of Netscape Navigator 4.0 users will view your site, then you should use tables for laying out your pages. Netscape Navigator 4.0 and earlier versions do not support all of the formatting and options available with layers in Dreamweaver. All versions of Internet Explorer 4 and later support Dreamweaver's layers fully.

Tools You'll Use

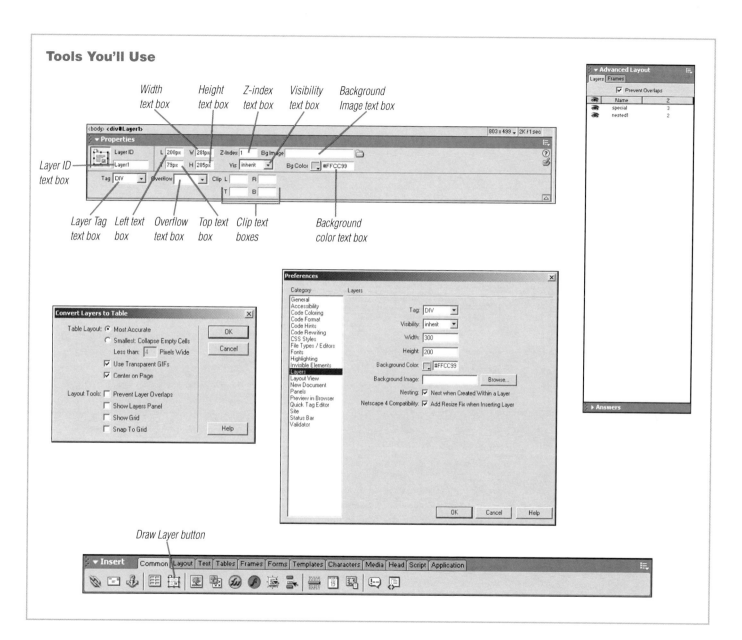

Width text box
Height text box
Z-index text box
Visibility text box
Background Image text box

Layer ID text box

Layer Tag text box
Left text box
Overflow text box
Top text box
Clip text boxes
Background color text box

Draw Layer button

CREATE A LAYER

What You'll Do

 In this lesson, you will draw a layer on the Northwest Warehouse home page and set its properties using the Property inspector. You will also insert a background image in the layer and set its background color. You will also add text to the layer and format it. Finally, you will add an image to the layer.

Understanding Layers

Layers are one of the newer developments in the world of Web page layout and design. Using layers, you can stack elements on top of each other and specify that only certain elements be visible at certain times or in specified conditions. Layers can be used to create special effects on a Web page. For instance, you can use layers to build a whole image from individual pieces. You can also use them to create a jigsaw puzzle that allows you to slide the pieces into their positions one at a time. You can also use layers to create dynamic pages that contain moving parts or objects that become visible or invisible based on a selection made by the Web site viewer.

Using layers to lay out a Web page is like working with a stack of transparency sheets that you can stack on top of each other. Figure G-1 illustrates how to use layers to stack graphical elements on top of each other to create the single image of a flower.

To insert a layer, you can use the Draw Layer button on the Common tab of the Insert bar and drag a rectangular shaped layer anywhere on your page, as shown in Figure G-2. You can also insert a layer using the Insert Layer command. Specify the exact dimensions, color, and other specifications of a new layer by changing the layer settings in the Preferences dialog box.

Using HTML Tags to Create Layers

You can create layers in Dreamweaver using one of two HTML tags: <div> or <span>. Both tags support all types of images, backgrounds, and advanced formatting options for layers. The default tag in Dreamweaver is the <div> tag because it is supported by all browsers, including the early versions of Netscape Navigator. Netscape Navigator browsers prior to version 4.5 do not support the <span> tag.

Understanding Layer Content

A layer is like a separate document within a Web page. It can contain the same types of elements that a page can, such as background colors, images, links, tables, and text. You can also make the contents of a layer work directly with a specified Dreamweaver behavior to make the page interact with a viewer in a certain way.

Using Advanced Layer Formatting

You should be careful not to add too much content to a layer. If a layer contains more information than it can readily display, you will need to use the advanced layer formatting controls to format the content so that it appears the way you want it to. You can control the appearance of a selected layer by making changes to the Clip, Visibility, and Overflow properties in the Property inspector.

The **Clip property** identifies the portion of a layer's content that is visible when displayed in a Web browser. By default, the clipping region matches the outside borders of the layer, but you can change the amount that is visible by clipping one or all sides of the layer. For instance, if you set the Left Clip property at 10 pixels, then everything from the eleventh pixel to the right will be displayed in the browser. If you clip off 10 pixels from the right side, you will need to subtract 10 from the total width of the layer and then type this value in the Clip R text box in the Property inspector. The clip setting can only be applied to layers that have an Overflow attribute set to a value other than visible.

The **Visible property** lets you control whether the selected layer is visible. You can set the Visible property to visible, hidden, or **inherit**, which means that the visibility of the layer is automatically inherited from its parent layer or page.

The **Overflow property** specifies how to treat excess content that does not fit inside a layer. You can choose to make the content visible, specify that scroll bars appear on the layer, hide the content, or let the current layer automatically deal with the extra content in the same manner as its parent layer or page.

FIGURE G-1

Using layers to create a single image

FIGURE G-2

Inserting a layer with the Draw Layer button

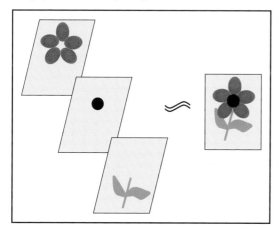

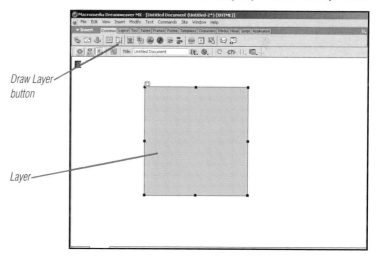

Draw Layer button

Layer

Draw a layer

1. Open the home page of the Northwest Warehouse Web site that you imported and developed in Unit F. (If you did not import and develop this Web site in Unit F, contact your instructor for assistance.)

2. Click the Common tab of the Insert bar (if necessary), then click the Draw Layer button. ▣

3. Drag a rectangle in the upper-right corner of the home page that is approximately 4 inches wide and 2 inches tall, then compare your screen to Figure G-3.

   A new layer appears on the page, but is not selected. A Layer icon also appears in the upper-left corner of the layer.

   | TIP   You can also insert a layer by clicking Insert on the menu bar, then clicking Layer.

4. Click the Layer icon in the upper-left corner of the page to select the layer you just drew.

   | TIP   You can also select a layer by clicking one of its borders.

5. Save your work.

You used the Draw Layer button to draw a layer on the home page.

FIGURE G-3
New layer added to the homepage

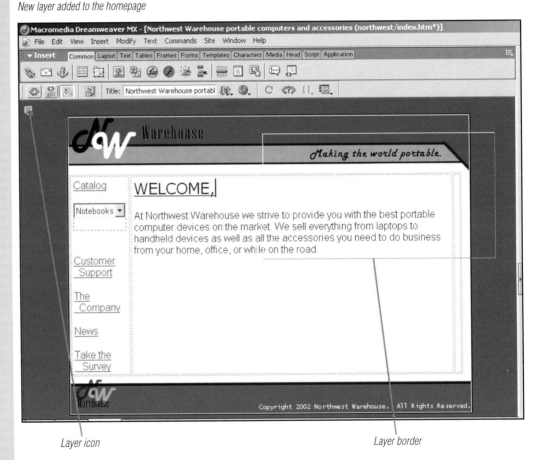

Layer icon   Layer border

FIGURE G-4

Property inspector showing properties of selected layer

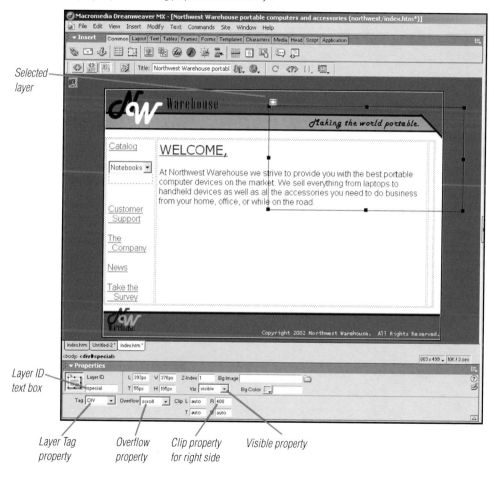

Selected layer

Layer ID text box

Layer Tag property

Overflow property

Clip property for right side

Visible property

1. With the layer selected, select Layer1 in the Layer ID text box in the Property inspector, then type **special**.

2. Verify that DIV is selected in the Tag text box of the Property inspector.

    TIP   The <span> tag is not supported as a means of creating a layer in Netscape Navigator, so you should use the <div> tag for maximum compatibility.

3. Set Overflow to **scroll** in the Property inspector.

4. Set Vis to **visible** in the Property inspector.

5. Type **400** in the Clip R text box in the Property inspector, then press [Enter] (Win) or [return] (Mac).

    When you specify the clip measurement of one side, measurements for the other three clip fields fill in automatically.

6. Save your work, then compare your screen to Figure G-4.

    The L, T, W, and H settings in the Property inspector specify the position and size of the layer. Your settings will probably differ from those shown in the figure because you probably drew your layer with slightly different measurements.

You specified a name and other HTML properties for the selected layer.

Set a background image

1. Click the Browse for File icon next to the Bg Image text box in the Property inspector to open the Select Image Source dialog box.

2. Navigate to the unit_g assets folder, then select the file layerbg.gif as shown in Figure G-5.

3. Click OK (Win) or Choose (Mac), then compare your screen to Figure G-6.

   TIP   If a dialog box opens asking if you want to copy this file to your site, click Yes to open the Copy File As dialog box, navigate to the assets folder of the Northwest Warehouse Web site, then Click Save.

   Your screen might look different than the figure, depending on the size of the layer that you drew.

4. Save your work.

You added a background image to the special layer.

FIGURE G-5
Select Image Source dialog box

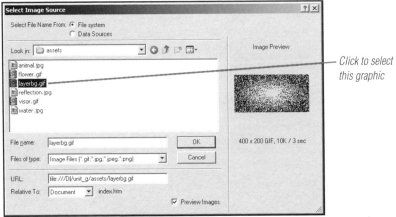

Click to select this graphic

FIGURE G-6
Layer containing a background image

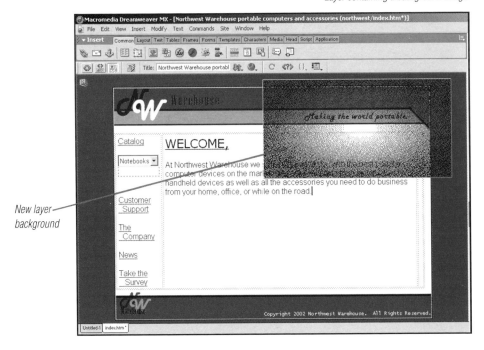

New layer background

FIGURE G-7
Color picker with new background color selected

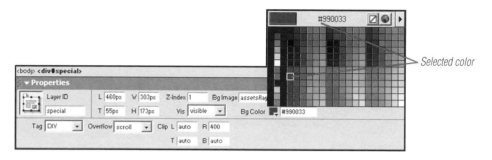

Selected color

1. With the layer selected, click the Bg Color button in the Property inspector to open the color picker.

2. Select the dark maroon color in the first column that has the hex value #990033, as shown in Figure G-7.

   The transparent area of the image is now filled with the maroon background color you selected, as shown in Figure G-8.

3. Save your work.

You added a background color to the layer.

FIGURE G-8
Layer background image with maroon color applied

Background color
shows through
transparent areas
of image

Add text to a layer

1. Click inside the layer to set the insertion point.

2. Type **Special Sale**.

3. Format Special Sale in white Arial, Helvetica, sans-serif, size 4, center-aligned.

4. Click to the right of Special Sale, press and hold [Shift], then press [Enter] (Win) or [return] (Mac) to insert a line break.

5. Type **TODAY ONLY!!**

   The same formatting you applied to the first line of text is automatically applied to this new line of text.

6. Press [Enter] (Win) or [return] (Mac), type **Handspring Visor Deluxe only $129.00 + shipping**, then format this text in white Arial, Helvetica, sans-serif, size 3.

7. Save your work, preview the page in your Web browser, compare your screen with Figure G-9, then close your browser.

You added text to the layer and formatted it.

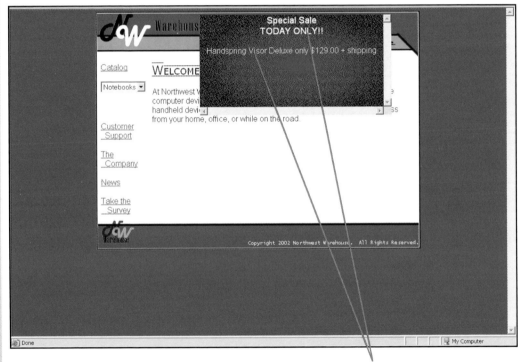

Text added to layer

FIGURE G-10

Select Image Source dialog box

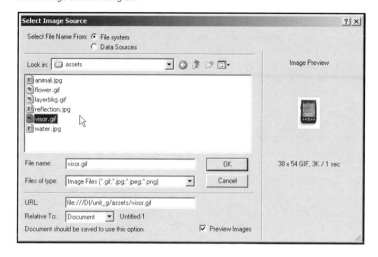

FIGURE G-11

Image added to layer

New image

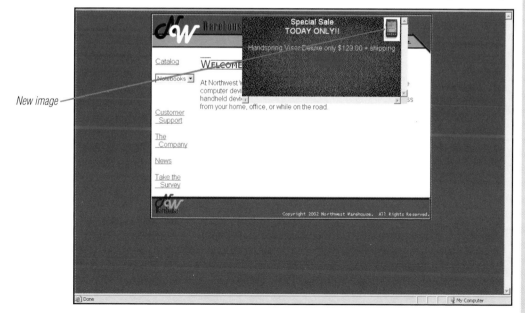

1. Click to the left of the text Special Sale to set the insertion point.

2. Click the Image button on the Common tab of the Insert bar to open the Select Image Source dialog box.

3. Navigate to the unit_g assets folder, then click visor.gif as shown in Figure G-10.

4. Click OK (Win) or Choose (Mac), type appropriate alternate text in the Image Tag Accessibility Attributes dialog box, then click OK.

   TIP   If the Image Tag Accessibility Attributes dialog box does not appear, type appropriate alternate text in the Alt text box in the Property inspector.

5. Use the Align list arrow in the Property inspector to set the image alignment to **Right**.

6. Save your work, preview the page in your Web browser, then compare your screen to Figure G-11.

You added an image to the layer.

SET THE POSITION AND SIZE OF A LAYER

What You'll Do

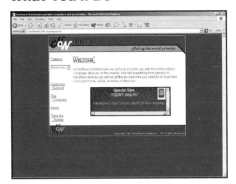

In this lesson, you will use the Property inspector to position and size layers on the home page of the Northwest Warehouse Web site.

Understanding Absolute Positioning

One of the greatest benefits of using layers to lay out a page is that you can position them precisely using a practice called **absolute positioning**. A layer is positioned absolutely by specifying the distance between the upper-left corner of the layer and the upper-left corner of the page or layer in which it is contained. Figure G-12 illustrates how an absolutely positioned layer keeps its relative position on a page when the page is scrolled. Because Dreamweaver treats layers as if they are separate documents contained within a page, layers do not interrupt the flow of content on the page or layer in which they are contained. This means that layers placed on top of a page will hide the contents of the page.

Absolutely positioned layers have no impact on the location of other layers. In other words, if you position a layer using absolute positioning, the remaining page elements that follow it within the code will continue along with the flow of the page, ignoring the presence of the absolutely

positioned layer. This means you can create overlapping layers. You can create dynamic effects with overlapping layers on a Web page by using JavaScript or CGI programs to change the attributes associated with each layer in response to actions by the viewer. For instance, a layer could move or change its size when a viewer clicks or moves the mouse over a link on the page or in the layer.

Setting Positioning Attributes

You can control the absolute positioning of layers by setting five primary attributes, four of which are available in the Property inspector. These attributes work together to create a layer that will hold its position on a page.

The **Position property** plays the most important role in turning a standard <div> or <span> tag into your positioned layer. Use this property to define how an object is positioned on the page. Standard HTML allows for fixed, absolute, relative, static, or floating positioned objects, but Dreamweaver only uses the absolute value.

When configuring your layers in Dreamweaver, you do not need to set this property. It is automatically set to absolute when you create a layer.

The **Left property** in the Property inspector specifies the distance between the left edge of your layer and the left edge of the page or layer that contains it. The **Top property** in the Property inspector specifies the distance between the top edge of your layer and the top edge of the page or layer that contains it.

The **Width** and **Height properties** specify the dimensions of the layer, most often in pixels, although it can be specified as a percentage of your screen dimension. For instance, you can specify that your layer be 250 pixels by 250 pixels, or you can set it to 25% by 25%, which will create a layer that is roughly 200 by 150 on a fully expanded Web browser in an 800×600 resolution monitor.

Use the **Z-index property** in the Property inspector to specify the vertical stacking order of layers on a page. If you think of the page itself as layer 0, then any number higher than that will appear on top of the page. For instance, if you have three layers with the z-index values of 1, 2, and 3, then 1 will appear below 2 and 3, while 3 will always appear above 1 and 2. You can create a dynamic Web site by adjusting the z-index settings on the fly using Dreamweaver's built-in JavaScript behaviors within the Web page you are creating.

QUICKTIP
You cannot set z-index values below zero.

FIGURE G-12

Scrolling a page containing an absolutely positioned layer

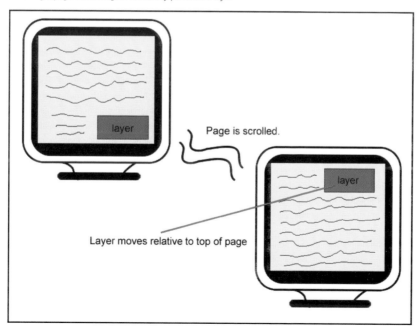

Page is scrolled.

layer

layer

Layer moves relative to top of page

Set the left and top position of a layer

1. Click the layer border to select the layer.

2. Type **375px** in the Left (L) text box, then press [Enter] (Win) or [return] Mac.

   The layer moves automatically to the position you specified.

3. Type **250px** in the Top (T) text box, then press [Enter] (Win) or [return] Mac.

4. Save your work, preview the page in your browser, compare your screen to Figure G-13, then close your browser.

You adjusted the top left corner position of the layer.

Set layer height and width

1. Click the border to select the layer (if necessary).

2. Set Width (W) to **375px** in the Property inspector.

   The layer automatically adjusts its width to the dimension you specified.

3. Set Height (H) to **125px**.

   The layer automatically adjusts to the height you specified. Notice that the top left corner stays in the same position.

4. Save your changes, preview the page in your Web browser, compare your screen with Figure G-14, then close your browser.

You adjusted the height and width of the layer.

FIGURE G-13

Layer moved down and to the left on the page

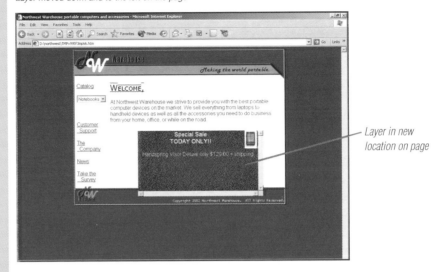

Layer in new location on page

FIGURE G-14

Home page in Internet Explorer showing layer with height and width adjusted

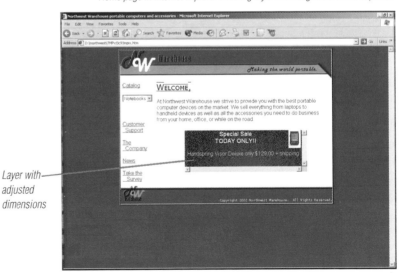

Layer with adjusted dimensions

FIGURE G-15
New layer obscuring special layer

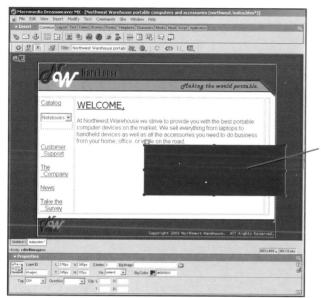

*Images layer on
top of special layer*

FIGURE G-16
Special layer moved on top of images layer

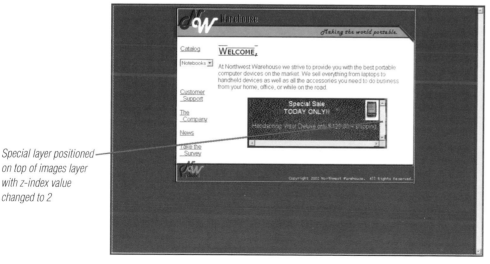

*Special layer positioned
on top of images layer
with z-index value
changed to 2*

Set a layer's z-index value

1. Create another layer anywhere on the page, select it, then name it **images**.

   A second layer icon appears in the upper-left corner of the document window.

2. Select the images layer (if necessary), then adjust its size and position by setting the following properties in the Property inspector: Left=**370px**, Top = **245px**, Width= **385px**, and Height = **135px**.

   The new layer is now positioned on top of the special layer.

3. Change the background color of the images layer to black, then compare your screen with Figure G-15.

4. Change the z-index value of the images layer to **1** in the Property inspector.

5. Click the layer icon for the special layer to select it.

6. Change the z-index value of the special layer to **2** in the Property inspector.

   The special layer is now positioned on top of the images layer because you set its z-index value to 2.

7. Save your work, preview the page in your browser, compare your screen to Figure G-16, then close your browser.

You added a new layer named images to the home page, and specified its dimensions and position on the page using the Property inspector. You also changed the background color of the images layer to black. You then adjusted the vertical stacking order of the two layers by setting the z-index values for each in the Property inspector.

USE THE LAYERS PANEL

What You'll Do

In this lesson, you will use the Layers panel to change the name of a layer, view and hide a layer, and work with nested layers.

Controlling Layers

You can use the **Layers panel** to control the visibility, name, and z-index order of all the layers on a Web page. You can also use the Layers panel to see how a layer is nested within the page structure, and to change the nesting status of a layer. **Nested layers** are layers whose HTML code is included within another layer's code. A nested layer does not affect the way a layer appears to the page viewer; it only affects the location of the code itself. To change the nesting status of a layer, drag the nested layer to a new location in the Layers panel. Figure G-17 shows the Layers panel with a nested layer.

You can open the Layers panel by opening the Window menu, pointing to Others, then clicking Layers. This makes the Layers panel difficult to find, but it is generally unnecessary to have it available all of the time. You can access the same information that is available in the Layers panel by selecting the layer and viewing its settings in the Property inspector.

Using the Layers panel is the easiest way to change a series of layer names, control layer visibility while testing a site, and control the visible stacking order of layers. The Layers panel also keeps track of all the layers on a page, making it easy to review the settings for each.

Layers panel

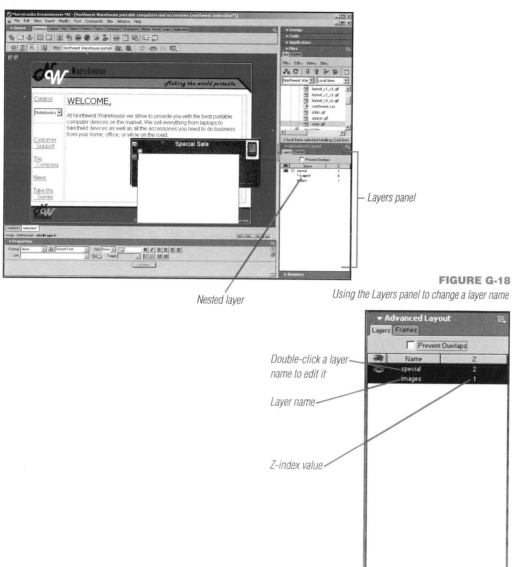

Nested layer

FIGURE G-18

Using the Layers panel to change a layer name

Double-click a layer name to edit it

Layer name

Z-index value

Change the name of a layer

1. Click Window on the menu bar, point to Others, then click Layers.

   The Advanced Formatting panel group opens with the Layers panel displayed, as shown in Figure G-18.

2. Click special in the Layers panel (if necessary) to select the special layer.

3. Double-click the name special to select it and open it for editing.

4. Type **salesad**, then press [Enter] (Win) or [return] (Mac).

   The name of the layer is now salesad.

5. Save your work.

You used the Layers panel to change the name of one of the layers on the home page.

Controlling layer visibility

1. Click in the eye-icon column for the images layer in the Layers panel, then compare your screen with Figure G-19.

   The eye icon appears closed in the Layers panel for the images layer, and the images layer no longer appears in the document window.

2. Click in the eye-icon column for the images layer again.

   Clicking the eye icon a second time makes the layer visible, as shown in Figure G-20. The eye icon now appears open in the Layers panel.

3. Click in the eye-icon column for the images layer again.

   Clicking the eye icon a third time makes the layer inherit the visibility status of its parent objects. In this case, the parent object of the images layer is the home page. Because the home page is visible, the images layer is visible too.

4. Save your work.

You used the Layers panel to change the visibility status of the images layer.

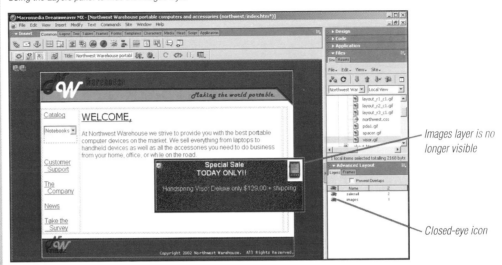

Images layer is no longer visible

Closed-eye icon

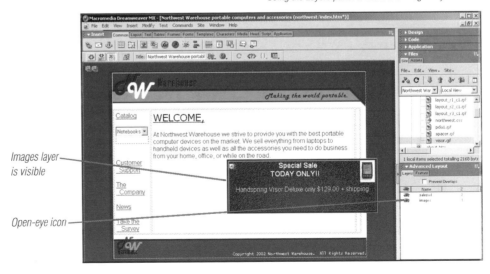

Images layer is visible

Open-eye icon

FIGURE G-21

Formatted nested layer

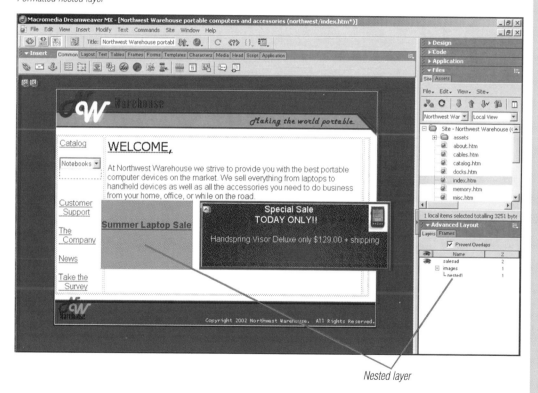

Nested layer

1. Click the images layer in the Layers panel, then click in the images layer in the document window to place the insertion point.

2. Click Insert on the menu bar, then click Layer.

   A new layer is inserted as a nested layer of the images layer.

3. Use the Layers panel to select this new nested layer, then name this new layer **nested1**.

4. Set the Top dimension to **0px** and the Left dimension to **-200px**.

5. Set the Width dimension to **185px** and the Height dimension to **135px**.

   These dimensions specify the position and size of the nested layer in relation to the top left corner of the images layer.

6. Set the background color to **#CC9999**.

7. Click in the nested1 layer to place the insertion point, press [Enter] (Win) or [return] (Mac), type **Summer Laptop Sale**, format this text in Arial, Helvetica, sans-serif, size 4, bold, center-aligned, and then set the text color to **#990033**.

8. Insert a link from this text to the notebooks.htm page, then compare your screen to Figure G-21.

9. Save your work.

You created a nested layer within the images layer.

CONFIGURE LAYER PREFERENCES

What You'll Do

 In this lesson, you will configure the default preferences for layers.

Setting Layer Preferences

If you know that you want all new layers to have a consistent appearance, you can save time by using the Preferences dialog box to set default specifications for new layers. Once you set layer preferences, you can then use the Insert Layer command to insert a layer that has the size and color settings you specified. When you draw a new layer using the Draw Layer button, the background color and image options specified in the Preferences dialog box are applied to the new layer. Figure G-22 shows an example of a page that contains four different layers. One of the layers was inserted based on settings in the Preferences dialog box. The other three were customized with different colors and dimensions.

Fixing the Netscape Resize Problem

Netscape Navigator 4 was one of the first browsers that had support for layers, but it had a problem. It did not adjust the position of layers based on changes in the screen size. As you can imagine, this created oddly formatted pages after the screen size was altered, or whenever adjustments were made to the page appearance during the processing of any scripts contained on the page.

To fix this problem, you can use the Preferences dialog box to specify that a special JavaScript function automatically be added to the code of any page that contains layers. This code is shown in Figure G-23.

QUICKTIP

If you convert tables to layers on a Web page, the code for the Netscape Resize Fix is not automatically added to the code for your page. To add the code, you need to add one additional layer to the page, which can be removed after adding the code. Before you remove the layer, however, open Code view and make sure that the code has been added.

FIGURE G-22

Page containing default layer and customized layers

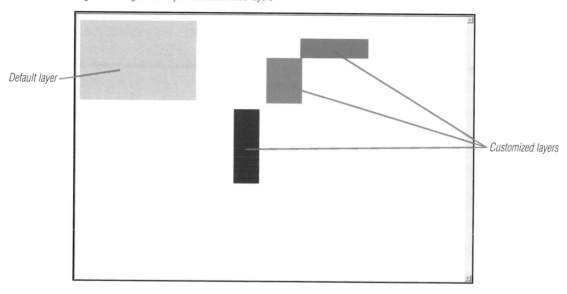

Default layer

Customized layers

FIGURE G-23

JavaScript function added to page containing layers in Code view

New code that
addresses Netscape 4
resize problem

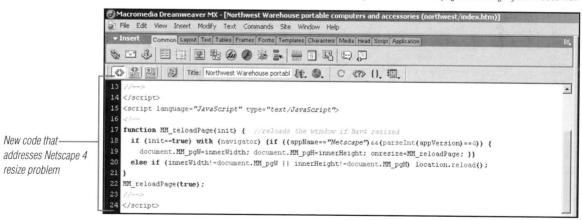

Control the appearance of a layer

1. Click Edit on the menu bar, then click Preferences to open the Preferences dialog box.

2. Click Layers in the Category list.

3. Click the Tag list arrow, then click DIV (if necessary).

4. Click the Visibility list arrow then click visible.

5. Type **300** in the Width text box, then type **200** in the Height text box.

6. Set the Background color to **#CCCCCC**.

   TIP If you want all layers to have a default background image, you could also specify an image file in the Background Image text box.

7. Compare your settings to Figure G-24, then click OK.

8. Click Insert on the menu bar, click Layer, then compare your screen with Figure G-25.

   A new layer appears on the page that has a gray background and is 300px wide by 200px high, as you specified in your preferences.

9. Click Edit on the menu bar, then click Undo Insert to remove this layer.

10. Save your work.

You used the Preferences dialog box to adjust the default appearance of new layers.

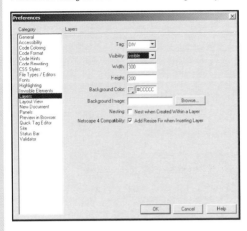

FIGURE G-25
New layer with new default layer settings applied

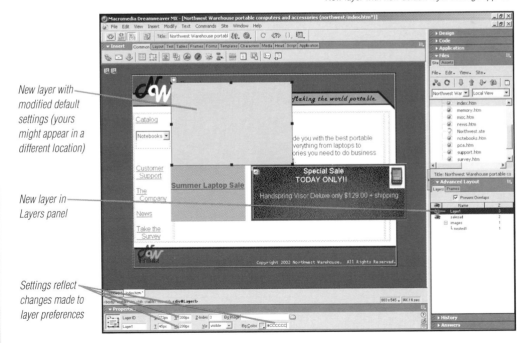

New layer with modified default settings (yours might appear in a different location)

New layer in Layers panel

Settings reflect changes made to layer preferences

FIGURE G-26

Reload Page function for the Netscape Resize Fix error

```
 8  <!--
 9  function MM_jumpMenu(targ,selObj,restore){ //v3.0
10    eval(targ+".location='"+selObj.options[selObj.selectedIndex].value+"'");
11    if (restore) selObj.selectedIndex=0;
12  }
13  //-->
14  </script>
15  <script language="JavaScript" type="text/JavaScript">
16  <!--
17  function MM_reloadPage(init) {  //reloads the window if Nav4 resized
18    if (init==true) with (navigator) {if ((appName=="Netscape")&&(parseInt(appVersion)==4)) {
19      document.MM_pgW=innerWidth; document.MM_pgH=innerHeight; onresize=MM_reloadPage; }}
20    else if (innerWidth!=document.MM_pgW || innerHeight!=document.MM_pgH) location.reload();
21  }
22  MM_reloadPage(true);
23  //-->
24  </script>
25  </head>
26  <body bgcolor="#990033" text="#000000" link="#990033" vlink="#0000FF" alink="#990066" leftmargin="5" topmarg
27  <div id="salesad" style="position:absolute; visibility:visible; left:375px; top:250px; width:375px; height:1
28    <p align="center"><font color="#FFFFFF" size="3" face="Arial, Helvetica, sans-serif"><img src="assets/viso
29      Sale<br>
30      TODAY ONLY!!</font></p>
31    <p align="center"><font color="#FFFFFF" size="3" face="Arial, Helvetica, sans-serif">Handspring
32      Visor Deluxe only $129.00 + shipping<br>
33      </font></p>
34  </div>
```

New code added to deal with Netscape resize problem

Adjust for Netscape resize problems

1. Click Edit on the menu bar, then click Preferences.

2. Click Layers in the Category list (if necessary).

3. Verify that the Netscape 4 Compatibility checkbox is checked, then click OK.

4. Click the Show Code View button on the Document toolbar.

5. Scroll to the top of the page.

6. Verify that the MM_reloadPage function has been added to the code for the page, as shown in Figure G-26.

7. Click the Show Design View button on the Document toolbar.

8. Save your work.

You set up Dreamweaver to deal with the Netscape layer resize problem.

CONVERT LAYERS TO TABLES AND TABLES TO LAYERS

What You'll Do

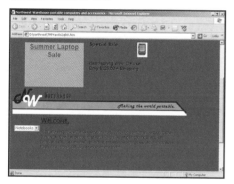

 In this lesson, you'll convert layers to tables and tables to layers on the Northwest Warehouse home page.

Using Layers and Tables for Page Layout

Layers and tables are the two most common formats that Web designers use to lay out Web pages. The ability to convert easily between these two different layout styles is one of Dreamweaver's most powerful features.

Of course, like anything else, there are good and bad aspects to using each type of layout. The primary reason to use tables over layers is that all versions of Web browsers prior to Internet Explorer 4.0 and Netscape Navigator 4.5 are unable to read layers. All versions of browsers, however, are able to read tables.

Converting Layers to Tables

When you convert layers to tables, you need to keep a few important rules in mind. First, you cannot convert overlapping layers. Therefore, you must adjust the positioning of overlapping layers prior to converting them to a table. This sometimes forces you to make changes to the layout of your page. Second, you cannot convert nested layers into tables, which means that you need to remove any code relating to nested layers. This might require you to change the nesting of your layers in the layers pane by dragging your layer to a new location. You can convert the layers on a page to a table by clicking Modify on the menu bar, pointing to Convert, then clicking Layers to Tables.

Converting Tables to Layers

To convert tables on a Web page to layers, click Modify on the menu bar, point to Convert, then click Tables to Layers. Unlike converting layers to tables, nested tables do not create a problem for the conversion program. Any nested tables contained on a page will be properly converted into layers, but you will probably lose the formatting information contained in the table cell holding the nested table. Also, because tables cannot overlap, you don't need to worry about changing your page layout before converting to layers.

FIGURE G-27
Web page that uses layers for page layout

FIGURE G-28
Web page that uses tables for page layout

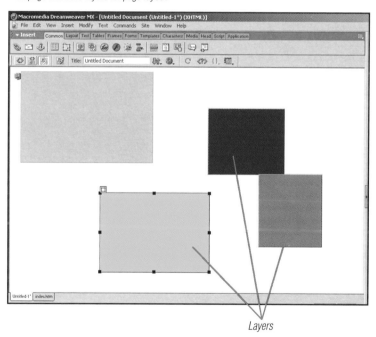

Layers

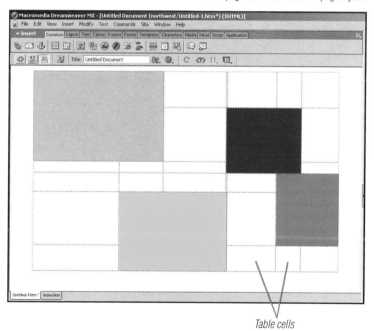

Table cells

Convert layers to a table

1. Open the Layers panel (if necessary), then drag the nested1 layer between the salesad and images layers in the Layers panel.

   This layer moves out of the visible range of the page because it is now located –200 pixels to the left of the top left corner of the page.

   > TIP If you have nested layers, you will be warned that your files won't be compatible with 3.0 browsers, and the conversion won't complete.

2. Select the nested1 layer in the layers panel, then set Left to **175px** and Top to **250px**.

3. Click the images layer in the Layers panel, then press [Delete].

   Overlapping layers can't be converted to tables.

4. Click Modify on the menu bar, point to Convert, then click Layers to Table.

   This opens the Convert Layers to Table dialog box shown in Figure G-29.

5. Verify that Most Accurate is selected, verify that Use Transparent GIFs is selected, then click Center on Page to select it.

6. Click OK.

   The layers are automatically converted to tables, as shown in Figure G-30. The remaining content contained in the layers now appears above the other content on the page.

7. Do not save your work, as you do not want to save this change.

You converted layers into a table on the home page.

FIGURE G-29

Convert Layers to Table dialog box

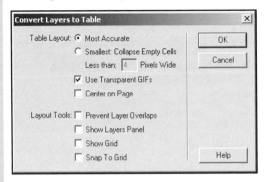

FIGURE G-30

Layers converted into table on the home page

Content from layers now contained in table cells

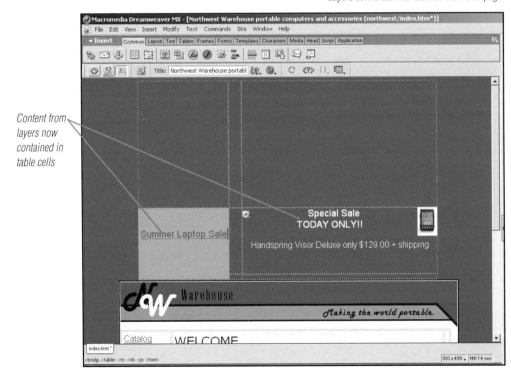

Convert Tables to Layers	☒
Layout Tools: ☑ Prevent Layer Overlaps	OK
☐ Show Layers Panel	Cancel
☐ Show Grid	Help
☑ Snap To Grid	

Convert a table to layers

1. Click Modify on the menu bar, point to Convert, then click Tables to Layers to open the Convert Tables to Layers dialog box, as shown in Figure G-31.

2. Verify that Prevent Layer Overlaps is selected, verify that Show Layers Panel is checked, verify that Show Grid is not selected, then verify that Snap to Grid is not selected.

3. Click OK.

   The page now contains layers, which now appear in the same location of the table cells you converted. Notice that the conversion did not return the page to the original layout you created with layers, because the conversion was based on the layout of the table.

4. Save your work, preview the page in your browser, compare your screen to Figure G-32, then close your browser.

5. Click Edit on the menu bar, then click Undo Convert to Layers.

6. Click Edit on the menu bar, then click Undo Convert to Table.

   The home page reverts back to the layout you created in the last lesson with the salesad layer and the nested1 layer in their previous positions.

7. Save your work, then close the home page.

You converted a table into layers, then used the Undo command to restore the layers you created in the last lesson.

FIGURE G-32

Table converted into layers on the home page

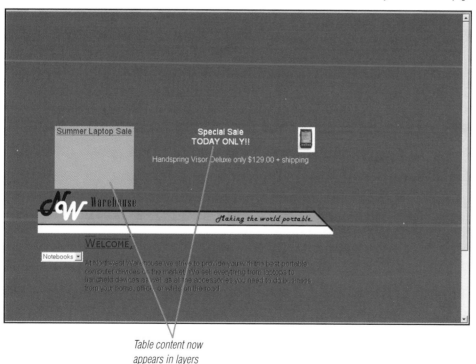

Table content now
appears in layers

Create a layer.

1. Open the Blooms & Bulbs Web site that you created in Units A through F, then open the home page. (If you did not complete this Web site in Units A through F, contact your instructor for assistance.)

2. Use the Draw Layer button to draw a long thin rectangle, about 1.5 inches tall by 3 inches wide on the bottom half of your page. Name this layer **sale**.

3. Select the sale layer, then change the background color to **#CCFF99**.

4. Set the Vis property to **default**.

5. Set the Overflow property to **visible**.

6. Place the insertion point in the sale layer, insert a hard return, then type **SPECIAL SPRING SALE!**.

7. Insert a line break, then type **All bulbs and shrubs are 30% off!!**.

8. Center the text, then format it in Arial, Helvetica, sans-serif, size 4, bold.

9. Click to the left of SPECIAL to set the insertion point, then insert the image flower.gif located in the unit_g assets folder. Set the Align attribute of this image to Absolute Middle.

10. Save your work.

Set the position and size of a layer.

1. Select the sale layer, then set the Left property to **235px**.

2. Set the Top property to **275px**.

3. Set the Width property to **425px**.

4. Set the Height property to **150px**.

5. Set the Z-index property to **2**.

6. Save your work.

Use the Layers panel.

1. Open the Layers panel (if necessary).

2. Change the sale layer's name to **springsale**.

3. Set the Vis property to **visible**.

4. Save your work.

Configure layer preferences.

1. Use the Preferences dialog box to change the settings for default layers using the following settings: Bg Color- **#CCFF99**, Visibility- **visible**, Width- **400px**, Height- **150px**.

2. Insert a new layer using the appropriate menu command, then name this layer **announcements**.

3. Select the announcements layer, then change the background color to **#006633**.

4. Set the Vis property to **default** and the Overflow property to **visible**.

5. Place the insertion point in the layer, insert a line break, then type **NEW SUMMER BULBS AVAILABLE!**.

6. Center the text, then format it in white Arial, Helvetica, sans-serif, size 3, bold.

7. Select the announcements layer, then set the Left property to **450px**.

8. Set the Top property to **15px**.

9. Set the Width property to **320px**.

10. Set the Height property to **55px**.

11. Set the Z-index property to **3** (if necessary).

12. Save your work.

Convert layers to tables and tables to layers.

1. Select the springsale layer.

2. Use the Convert Layers to Table dialog box to convert the layer to a table. (Hint: Make sure the Most Accurate, Use Transparent GIFs, and Center on Page options are all selected in the dialog box.)

3. Use the Convert Tables to Layers dialog box to convert the table back to layers. (*Hint*: Make sure that Prevent Layer Overlaps and Snap to Grid are both selected in the dialog box.)

4. Use the History panel to undo your last two steps, so that the original springsale and announcements layers appear on the page. (*Hint*: If grid lines appear on the page, click View, point to Grid, then click Show Grid to remove them.)

5. Save your work, preview the page in your browser, compare your screen to Figure G-33, close your browser, then close the home page.

FIGURE G-33
Completed Skills Review

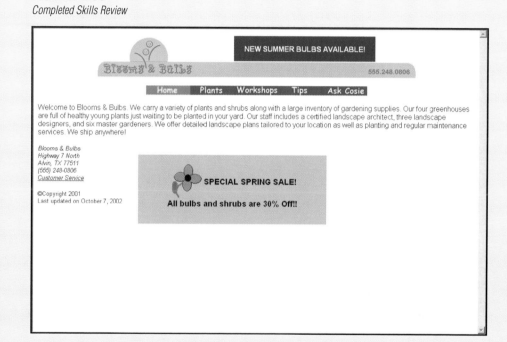

In this exercise you will continue your work on the Rapids Transit Web site you created in Project Builder 1 in Units A through F. Your boss, Mike Andrew, wants you to create a layer on the home page that shows an image of some of the sights people might see on a typical rafting trip.

1. Open the Rapids Transit Web site that you completed in Unit F, then open the home page. (If you did not complete this Web site in Units A through F, contact your instructor for assistance.)

2. Draw a layer that is roughly 1 inch tall and 1.5 inches wide on the upper-right corner of the page. Draw the layer so it covers part of the logo and part of the white space on the page. Name the layer **water**.

3. Set the background color of the layer to **transparent** by selecting the Strike-through button on the color picker toolbar.

4. Insert a background image using the file water. jpg from the unit_g assets folder.

5. Use the layer resize handles to adjust the size of the layer to show only the waterfall.

6. Set the Top property to **80px**.

7. Set the Left property to **80%**.

8. Add the following text to the layer above the image of the water: **View Our Falls!**.

9. Format View Our Falls! in white Arial, Helvetica, sans-serif, size 2, bold, right-aligned.

10. Set the Overflow property to **hidden**.

11. Select the water layer, then copy it.

12. Use the Paste command to paste a copy of the water layer on the page. (Notice that a copy of the water layer appears in the Layers panel.)

13. Use the Layers panel to select this copied layer, then name it **reflection**.

14. Drag the reflection layer down to the blank area on the page, just to the right of the Rapids Transit address information.

15. Change the background image in the reflection layer to the file reflection.jpg located in the unit_g assets folder.

16. Replace the View Our Falls! text with the text **Fishing** in the reflection layer.

17. Paste a second copy of the water layer on the page. Use the Layers panel to select this copied layer, then name it **animals**.

18. Drag the animals layer down to the blank area of your page, just to the right of the reflection layer.

19. Change the background image in the animals layer to the file animal.jpg located in the unit_g assets folder. Copy this image file to the assets folder of the Web site.

20. Replace the View Our Falls! text with the text **Wildlife**.

21. Save your work, preview the page in a browser, compare your screen to Figure G-34, close your browser, then close the home page.

FIGURE G-34

Completed Project Builder 1

Use Figure G-35 as a guide to continue your work on the Jacob's Web site you created in Project Builder 2 in Units A through F. Chef Jacob wants you to configure Dreamweaver to set up the preferences for layers created on his Web site. He also wants you to add two layers that announce the recipe contest countdown.

1. Open the Jacob's Web site that you completed in Unit F, then open the home page. (If you did not create the Jacob's Web site in Units A through F, contact your instructor for assistance.)
2. Use the Preferences dialog box to specify the following settings for new layers: Tag-**DIV**, Visibility- **inherit**, Width- **300px**, Height- **200px**, Background Color- **#FFCC99**. Also, make sure that Nested when Created within a Layer is selected and that Add Resize Fix when Inserting Layer is selected.
3. Use the Insert Layer command to insert a new layer on the page, then adjust its location so that the Top property is set at **320px** and the Left property is set at **160px**.
4. Name the layer **contest**.
5. Place the insertion point in the layer, then type **Chef Jacob's**. Insert a line break, then type **Recipe Contest Countdown**.
6. Format the text in Arial, Helvetica, sans-serif, size 6, centered, and set the color to **#660033**.

7. Resize the layer so that the Height property is set to **125px**.
8. Draw a new layer that is approximately 1 inch tall by 3 inches wide, to the right of the contest layer. Name this layer **daysleft**.
9. Position the daysleft layer so that the Top property is set to **415px** and the Left property is set to **400px**.

10. Change the background color to **#660033**.
11. Place the insertion point in the daysleft layer, insert a line break, then type **Only 15 Days Left!!!**. Format this text in Arial, Helvetica, sans-serif, size 5, centered, and set the color to **#FFCC99**.
12. Save your work, preview the page in your browser, close your browser, then close the home page.

FIGURE G-35
Completed Project Builder 2

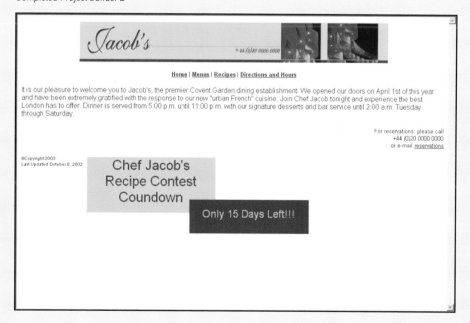

George Phillips has decided to create a Web site about his band, which plays mostly Country music with noticeable blues overtones. George needs to develop a Web site that will advertise his band's work and let people listen to samples of their songs. Because he has never developed a Web site before, George decides to look at other band sites for ideas and inspiration. George has decided to use layers instead of tables to lay out his Web site, because he read that layers give you greater control over the placement of elements.

1. Open your browser, connect to the Internet, go to *www.course.com*, navigate to the page for this book, click the Student Online Companion link, then click Link 1 for this unit. The site shown in Figure G-36 appears. This is the site for Sony Music USA.
2. How are layers used in this site?
3. How are layers used to prevent an overload of information in one area of the screen?
4. How are layers used to add more color to the Web site?
5. Layers can be changed on the fly by incorporating JavaScript into the page code. What property of the layers on this site would need to be adjusted to make each layer appear all the time, and not just when the mouse is placed over them?

6. Can George use layers to stack photos together and make them rotate in a slide show as done on this site? If so, what properties should he use to manipulate their stacking order?
7. If George wanted his layers moved to a new location on his page, what two properties would JavaScript need to change when viewers look at the page?

8. Search the Internet looking for other music related Web sites that use layers. How does their implementation compare to the use of layers on the Sony site?
9. What other ways could Sony have used layers in this site? What ways could George use layers in his site? Make a list and discuss it with your team members or class.

FIGURE G-36
Design Project

For this assignment, you will continue to work on the group project that you have been developing since Unit A. Depending on the size of your group, you can assign individual elements of the project to group members or work collectively to create the finished product. There will be no data files supplied. You are building this Web site from unit to unit, so you must do each Group Project assignment in each unit to complete your Web site.

You will continue building your Web site by designing and completing a page that uses layers rather than tables to control the layout of information.

1. Consult your storyboard and brainstorm as a group to decide which page to create and develop for this unit. Draw a sketch of the page to show how you will use layers to lay out the content.
2. Assign team members the tasks of creating the new page for the site and setting the default preferences for layers. These team members should also add the appropriate number of layers to the new page and configure them appropriately, making sure to name them and set the properties for each.
3. Assign other team members the task of adding text, background images, and background colors to the layers.

4. Assign a team member the task of creating the navigation links that will allow you to add this page to your site.
5. Assign a member of your team the task of updating the other pages of your site so that each page includes a link to this new page.
6. Assign team members the task of adding images in the layers (where appropriate), making sure to align them with text so they look good.

FIGURE G-37
Web Site Check List

7. Assign a member the task of checking to ensure that all layers are properly stacked using their Z-index property.
8. Save your work, preview the page in your browser, make any necessary modifications to make the page look good, close your browser, then close all open pages.

Web Site Check List

1. Are all pages properly stacked with z-index values assigned correctly?
2. Do all pages have titles?
3. Do all navigation links still work?
4. Are all colors in your layers Web-safe?
5. Does the use of layers in your Web site improve the site navigation?
6. Do any extra layers appear that need to be removed?
7. Do your pages look acceptable in at least the two major browsers?
8. Do layers hide any information on your pages?
9. Do all images in your layers appear correctly?

USING FRAMES FOR PAGE LAYOUT

1. Insert a frame.

2. Configure frames.

3. Add content to frames.

4. Create NoFrames content.

Introduction

One of the biggest debates among Web developers is whether or not to use frames to lay out Web pages. A **frame** is a fixed region in a browser that can display a Web page and act independently from other pages displayed in other frames within the browser. Frames are best used to contain information that will not change as a visitor interacts with your site, such as a copyright notice or a navigation bar that appears at the top or left of every page in your site.

There are many points of view on this topic, but overall, frames are a useful tool that, when used properly, can improve the navigation of a Web site and can also decrease the loading time of each page in your site. In this unit, you will use frames to lay out the content for a new page in the Northwest Warehouse Web site.

Using Frames for Page Layout

As with any debate, Web designers who prefer using layers or tables for page layout support their preferred methods vehemently, and are sometimes critical of using frames. Many viewers do not like sites that use frames because they make it difficult to know where you are in a site. Frames can also make navigating a site more difficult for viewers who have disabilities.

On the positive side, frames are often a better choice than layers for page layout because they can be viewed by older browsers and can reduce page download time. Tables can actually increase page download time because of the vast number of tags used to create a table. Layers add little additional download time, because they use only a few extra tags and only a small amount of style sheet positioning code to control the layout.

Fortunately, you can use any or all of these three methods for laying out your Web pages. None of these practices is mutually exclusive, and you can design a dynamic site that loads quickly and is easy to navigate, using any one of these three methods.

Tools You'll Use

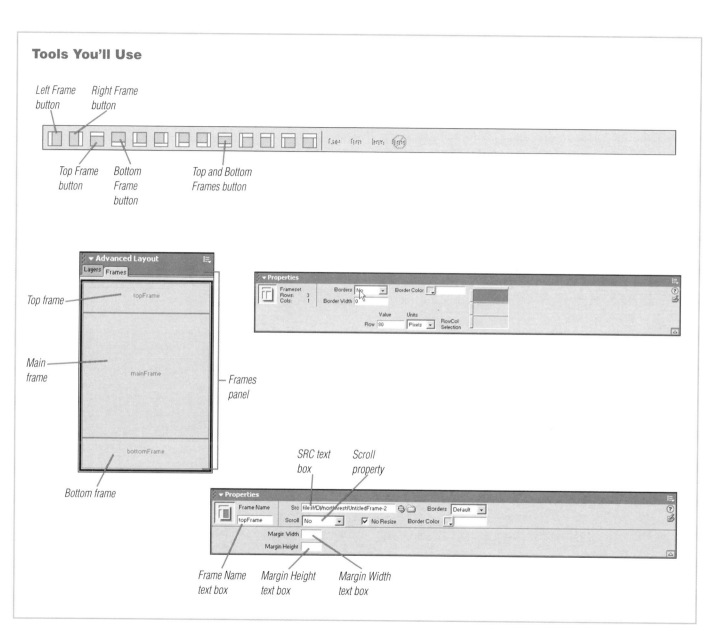

Left Frame button

Right Frame button

Top Frame button

Bottom Frame button

Top and Bottom Frames button

Top frame

Main frame

Bottom frame

Frames panel

SRC text box

Scroll property

Frame Name text box

Margin Height text box

Margin Width text box

INSERT A FRAME

What You'll Do

 In this lesson, you will open a new untitled page in the Northwest Warehouse Web site, then apply a predefined frameset to it. You will then save the page as a frameset.

Understanding Frames and Framesets

When you lay out a Web page using frames, you first need to create a frameset. A **frameset** is a document that contains the instructions that tell a browser how to lay out a set of frames showing individual documents on a page, including the size and position of the frames. Once you create a frameset, which is most commonly the home page if the entire site is based on frames, you then need to specify the Web pages that you want to display in each frame. Figure H-1 shows a frameset containing three frames that display three different Web pages.

Choosing a Predefined Frameset

Dreamweaver comes with thirteen different predefined framesets. To choose a predefined frameset for a page, you click one of the buttons on the Frames tab of the Insert bar shown in Figure H-2. The blue area on each button represents the frame that will display the current page.

Designing pages using frames

When you plan the content of a Web site using frames, you need to take into account that you will have a smaller area of the screen to display your information. When you lay out the content of each page, make sure it fits in the dimensions of the frames. If the information is too wide or too tall, viewers will need to scroll to see it all. This is especially important when you are working with graphics, because unlike text, graphics cannot adjust their size by wrapping down to the next line.

You can also choose a predefined frameset by clicking Insert on the menu bar, pointing to Frames, then clicking the name of the layout you wish to use.

Adding Content to Frames

Once you choose the layout of your frameset, you then need to create new pages or choose existing pages to place in the frames in the frameset. In most cases, a top frame will display a page that contains a logo or a series of navigational images or buttons. Most left-hand frames display a page containing a list of links or navigational images. Bottom frames are most commonly used for displaying a series of text links and copyright statements that protect the rights of the site owner. Though right-hand frames are rare, they can be used to display secondary information to accentuate the contents of the frame that contains the primary body information.

Saving a Frameset and Frames

When you create a frames-based page, you need to ensure that you save both the frameset and all of the individual pages that are stored in each frame. The first document you must save is the frameset. To

FIGURE H-1
Frameset layout

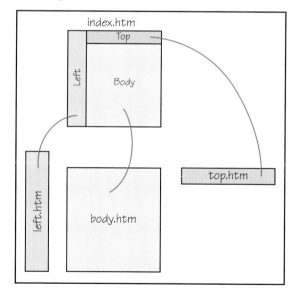

FIGURE H-2
Predefined frameset layout buttons on Frames tab of Insert bar

save a frameset, use the Save Frameset command on the File menu, as shown in Figure H-3. You can save each individual frame by selecting a frame and clicking Save Frame from the File menu, or you can select Save All from the File menu to save all the frames in the frameset.

QUICKTIP

Using the Save All option makes it difficult to tell which page you are saving at a given time, since Dreamweaver provides only the default names of UntitledFrameset and UntitledFrame as the default page names.

When you lay out a Web page using frames, you will always be working with one more page than is visible in the frameset. For instance, imagine that you created a frameset that contains three frames. One frame displays a navigation bar at the top of every page, another frame displays a copyright statement at the bottom of every page, and a third frame displays text. In this example you would need to have a minimum of four documents. The first would be the frameset file that contains the information for laying out the frames themselves. The second would be the page containing the navigation bar. The third would be the page containing the copyright statement. The fourth would be the page that will appear in the middle frame of the frameset. Any additional documents that you want to load using the links in the frames would typically appear in the middle frame.

FIGURE H-3
Save options for frames and framesets

Click to save frameset

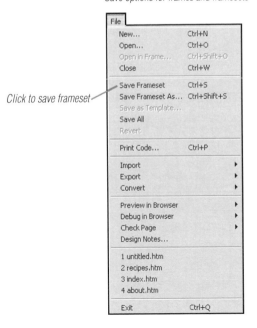

New page with Top and Bottom frameset layout applied

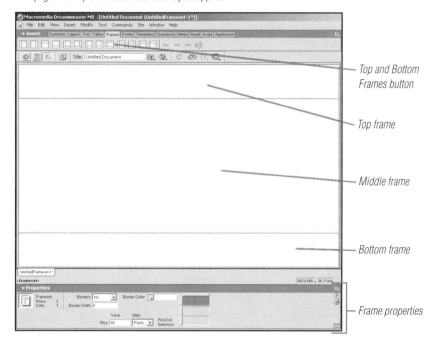

— Top and Bottom
Frames button

— Top frame

— Middle frame

— Bottom frame

— Frame properties

FIGURE H-5

Save As dialog box

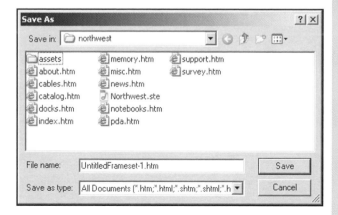

Create a frameset

1. Open the Northwest Warehouse Web site that you imported and developed in Units F and G. (If you did not import and develop this Web site in Units F and G, contact your instructor for assistance.)

2. Add a new page to the northwest root folder, then open this new untitled page.

   TIP To create a new page, click File on the Site panel menu bar, then click New File.

3. Click the Frames tab on the Insert bar.

4. Click the Top and Bottom Frames button on the Insert bar.

   Three frames appear in the document window, as shown in Figure H-4.

   TIP You can also apply the Top and Bottom Frames layout by clicking Insert on the menu bar, pointing to Frames, then clicking Top and Bottom.

You opened a new blank page and applied a predefined frameset to it.

Save a frameset

1. Click File on the menu bar, then click Save Frameset to open the Save As dialog box, as shown in Figure H-5.

   The contents of the northwest folder appear in the dialog box.

2. Type **mybrandlaptops.htm** in the File name text box, then click Save.

You saved the new page as a frameset.

CONFIGURE FRAMES

What You'll Do

In this lesson, you will name the three frames contained in the mybrandlaptops frameset. You will also adjust the size of one frame in the frameset and set the Border and Scroll properties for each frame. Finally, you will set the margin height and width for each frame.

Understanding Frames Configuration

After you create a frameset, you will need to configure each of the frames it contains. Configuring frames is relatively simple and consists of three tasks. First, you need to name each frame. Second, you need to specify frame sizes. Finally, you need to set the border and scroll bar properties for each frame.

Selecting Frames

In order to configure a frame, you first must select it using the Frames panel. The Frames panel is a panel that shows a visual representation of the frameset. To select a frame, click the frame you want in the Frames panel. To open the Frames panel click Window on the menu bar, point to Others, then click Frames.

Naming Frames

Simply put, all frames must have a name. The name is used to control the destination of links within pages contained in the frame and the frameset. The name of the frame will go into the target property of any link that you want to open in a location other than the frame in which the link itself is located.

For instance, if you create a frame named body, the name body must be referenced in the target property of every link (within other frames) that you wish to open inside the body frame. Figure H-6 illustrates how this works.

Frame names are also used to automate the loading of pages into a Web browser using JavaScript. Using JavaScript, you can write a program that will alter the contents of the frame by loading content with a script, or by using the script to load a new page. A script will also allow you to change images and other objects on the page by simply referencing the name of the object within the named frame.

Setting Frame Size

If you choose a predefined frameset, the size of each frame is automatically set. However, you can make frames larger or smaller by dragging the frame borders. You can also adjust the size of a frame by manipulating its dimensions in the <frameset> tags on the frameset page.

You can format frames using a specific set of dimensions, such as 100 pixels or 1 inch. You can also specify frame size as a percentage of the screen size. For instance, you can size a frame so that it takes up just a few more pixels of space than an image in the frame, or you can size a frame so that a specific percentage of screen space is taken up no matter how large the screen is. Figure H-7 shows frames formatted with percentage dimensions that change based on the screen size (resolution), as well as frames formatted with exact dimensions whose size stays the same no matter what the screen size.

Unlike tables, frames will not resize themselves to adjust to larger and smaller amounts of information. This means that when you set the size of your frames, you need to know the dimensions of any images that will be displayed within that frame. For instance, if you want to display the banner for your company in the top frame, make sure the top frame is as large as the banner. If the frame is only 50 pixels tall, and the banner is 75 pixels tall, then the bottom 25 pixels of the banner will not be visible, and viewers will need to scroll to see it.

Controlling Frame Borders and Scroll Bars

You can specify the use of scroll bars and borders in the frames in your Web site. You can control the presence of scroll bars for a selected frame by adjusting the Scroll property in the Property inspector. You can use different scroll settings for each frame in a frameset. For instance, you can specify the use of scroll bars on the body frame, but not on the top and bottom frames. You can also specify whether to show borders around a frame by setting the Borders property in the Property inspector. You can also use the Property inspector to specify a border color. Adding borders around frames can help separate them in a browser, and improve the appearance of your site. Setting the Scroll property to Yes also creates visible borders around a frame.

FIGURE H-6
Understanding frames and links

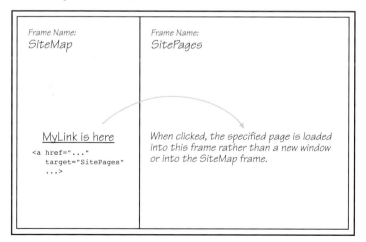

FIGURE H-7
Setting frame sizes in different resolutions using pixels and percentages

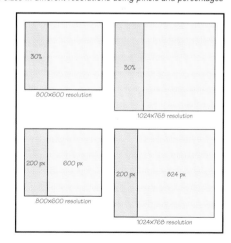

Set frame names

1. Click Window on the menu bar, point to Others, then click Frames to open the Frames panel.

2. Click the top frame in the Frames panel to select it.

3. Type **logoframe** in the Frame Name text box in the Property inspector, press [Enter] (Win) or [return] (Mac), then compare your screen to Figure H-8.

4. Click the middle frame in the Frames panel to select it.

5. Type **infoframe** in the Frame Name text box in the Property inspector, then press [Enter] (Win) or [return] (Mac).

6. Click the bottom frame in the Frames panel to select it.

7. Type **copyrightframe** in the Frame Name text box in the Property inspector, then press [Enter] (Win) or [return] (Mac).

8. Click File on the menu bar, then click Save Frameset.

You named the three frames in the mybrandlaptops frameset.

FIGURE H-8
Selected frame in document window

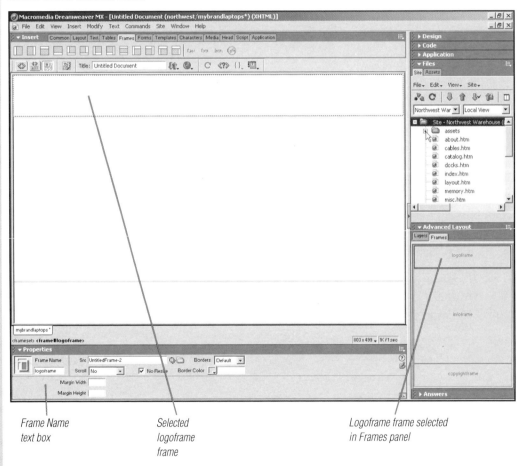

Frame Name
text box

Selected
logoframe
frame

Logoframe frame selected
in Frames panel

Using Frames for Page Layout

FIGURE H-9
Adjusting frame sizes

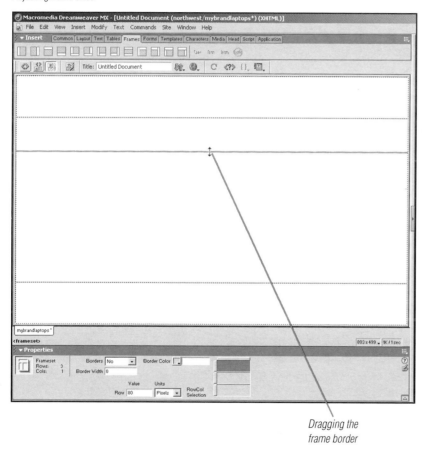

Dragging the
frame border

1. Position the mouse pointer on the bottom border of the top frame until the pointer changes to a ↕.

2. Drag the border down about half an inch, as shown in Figure H-9.

3. Click the logoframe frame in the Frames panel to select it (if necessary).

4. Verify that No Resize is checked in the Property inspector.

   This prevents viewers from resizing the frame to ensure that it will keep the same dimensions.

5. Click the copyrightframe frame in the Frames panel.

6. Verify that No Resize is checked in the Property inspector.

7. Save the frameset.

You changed the size of the top frame in the frameset and specified that the top and bottom frames not resize.

Set frame borders and border colors

1. Select the logoframe frame.

2. Click the Borders list arrow in the Property inspector, then click No.

3. Select the copyrightframe frame.

4. Click the Borders list arrow in the Property inspector, then click Yes.

5. Change the border color to **#000000**, then compare your screen to Figure H-10.

   Because you set the border color to black, a black line appears across the bottom of the page.

6. Save the frameset.

You specified that the border not appear for the top frame and that the border appear for the bottom frame. You also set the border color to black for the bottom frame.

FIGURE H-10
Configured frame borders

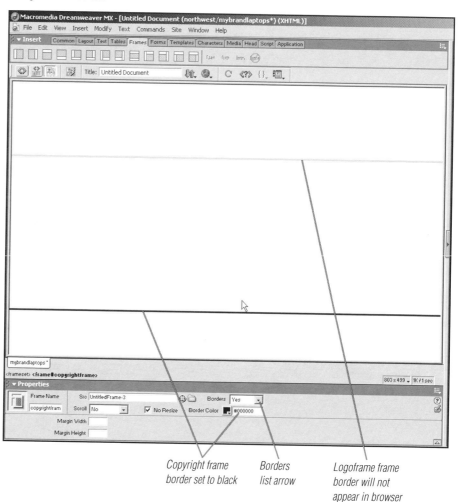

Copyright frame
border set to black

Borders
list arrow

Logoframe frame
border will not
appear in browser

Scroll bars added to the infoframe frame

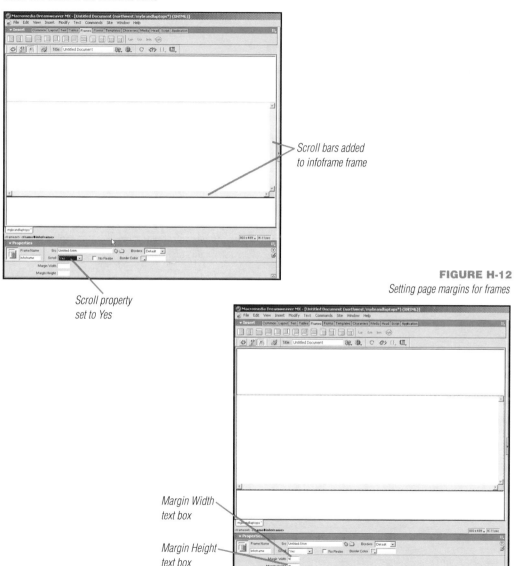

Scroll bars added
to infoframe frame

Scroll property
set to Yes

FIGURE H-12
Setting page margins for frames

Margin Width
text box

Margin Height
text box

Configure frame scrollbars

1. Select the logoframe frame.
2. Click the Scroll list arrow in the Property inspector, then click No (if necessary).
3. Select the infoframe frame, click the Scroll list arrow in the Property inspector, click Yes, then compare your screen to Figure H-11.
4. Verify that Scroll property is set to No for the copyrightframe frame.
5. Save the frameset.

You set the Scroll property to No for the top and bottom frames and Yes for the middle frame.

Control page margins

1. Select the logoframe frame.
2. Type **0** in the Margin Width text box in the Property inspector, then press [Enter] (Win) or [return] (Mac).
3. Type **0** in the Margin Height text box in the Property inspector, then press [Enter] (Win) or [return] (Mac).
4. Select the infoframe frame, set Margin Width to **10** and Margin Height to **10**, then compare your screen to Figure H-12.
5. Select the copyrightframe frame, set Margin Width to **0**, then set Margin Height to **0**.
6. Save the frameset.

You set the page margins for the three frames in the mybrandlaptops frameset.

ADD CONTENT TO FRAMES

What You'll Do

 In this lesson, you will add content to frames in the mybrandlaptops frameset. First, you will specify source files to appear in the logoframe frame and the copyrightframe frame. Then you will add a table, text, and graphics to the bodyframe frame.

Understanding How to Add Content to a Frame

After you create a frameset, you need to add content to the frames it contains. There are two ways you can do this. You can either load existing documents into each frame, or you can create new pages from scratch in each frame. The frameset shown in Figure H-13 contains three frames, two of which contain loaded documents. The middle frame contains no content.

Loading Existing Pages in a Frame

The easiest way to add content to a frame is to load an existing page or file into the

frame. This works well when you want to convert a site from a non-frames layout to a frames layout, because you already have existing pages that were created in the previous version of the site. To do this, select the frame, then specify the name of the file you want to load in the SRC text box in the Property inspector.

When you load an existing page into a frame, you can then make modifications to the page, just as you would if it were not in the frame. By loading documents into the frames of a frameset, you are simply specifying that multiple Web pages appear in a Web browser at the same time.

Creating Content from Scratch

If you want to create a completely new page that will be displayed in a frame, you can do so from within the frame itself. Creating a new page in a frame is just as simple as creating a page outside of a frame. You simply place the insertion point in the frame and start typing. You can then apply fonts or formatting attributes to the text, or add images or tables, just as if you were creating a new page from scratch outside of a frame.

FIGURE H-13

Mybrandlaptops frameset showing two frames with loaded documents and one empty frame

Top frame with loaded document

Middle frame with no content

Bottom frame with loaded document

Specify a source file to display in a frame

1. Open the file dwh_01.htm from the unit_h data files folder, then save it as **top.htm** to the Northwest Warehouse Web site.

2. Copy the topbanner.png graphic at the top of the page to the Northwest Web site's assets folder.

3. Open the file dwh_02.htm from the unit_h data files folder, then save it as **bottom.htm** to the Northwest Warehouse Web site.

4. Copy the bottombanner.png graphic to the Northwest Web site's assets folder.

5. Open the mybrandlaptops.htm frameset, then select the logoframe frame.

6. Click the Browse for File icon next to the SRC text box in the Property inspector to open the Select HTML File dialog box, as shown in Figure H-14.

7. Select top.htm from the file list, then click OK (Win) or Choose (Mac).

8. Select the copyrightframe frame, then click Browse for File next to the SRC text box in the Property inspector to open the Select HTML File dialog box.

9. Select bottom.htm from the file list, click OK (Win) or Choose (Mac), then compare your screen to Figure H-15.

You set the source for the logoframe frame to the file top.htm. You also set the source for the copyrightframe frame to the file bottom.htm.

FIGURE H-14
Select HTML dialog box

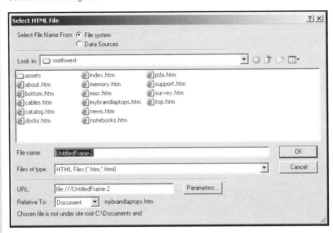

FIGURE H-15
Frameset with top and bottom frames loaded with existing files

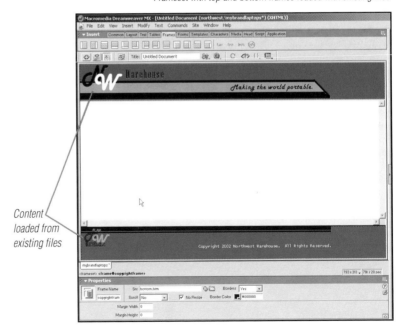

Content loaded from existing files

Using Frames for Page Layout

FIGURE H-16
Table added to infoframe frame

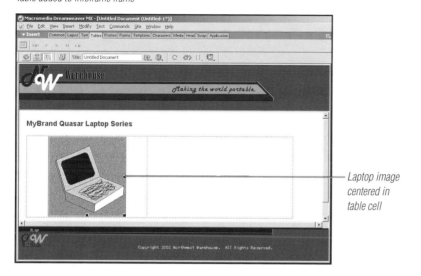

Laptop image
centered in
table cell

FIGURE H-17
Infoframe frame with all content added

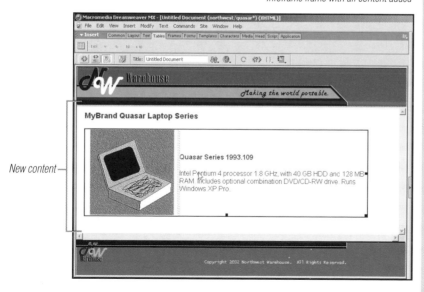

New content

1. Click in the infoframe frame, then type **MyBrand Quasar Laptop Series**.

2. Format the text in Arial, Helvetica, sans-serif, size 4, bold, with the color set to **#0000FF**.

3. Press [Enter] (Win) or [return] (Mac), then insert a table that has 2 columns and 1 row, and is 90% of the width of the page, and has no borders.

4. Click in the left cell of the table, then insert the image file laptop.gif from the unit_h assets folder.

5. Center the image in the table cell, then compare your screen to Figure H-16.

6. Click in the right cell of the table, then type **Quasar Series 1993.109**.

7. Format this text in black Arial, Helvetica, sans-serif, size 3, bold, then insert a hard return.

8. Type **Intel Pentium 4 processor 1.8 GHz, with 40 GB HDD and 128 MB RAM. Includes optional combination DVD/CD-RW drive. Runs Windows XP Pro.**, format this text in Arial, Helvetica, sans-serif, size 3, then compare your screen to Figure H-17.

9. Click File on the menu bar, click Save Frame As to open the Save As dialog box, type **quasar.htm** in the File name text box, then click Save.

   The frame is saved as a separate file called quasar.htm to the northwest root folder.

You added a table to the bodyframe frame and then added content to the table cells.

CREATE NOFRAMES CONTENT

What You'll Do

In this lesson, you will add NoFrames content to the Northwest Warehouse Web site.

Understanding NoFrames Content

For different reasons, some viewers might not be able to view content that is contained in frames. For instance, some viewers turn off support for frames in their browser, and others might be using an older version of a browser that does not support frames. However, all viewers will still be able to view your site's content if you provide NoFrames content for every frameset in your site. **NoFrames content** is alternate content that can be viewed without frames. NoFrames content is added only to the frameset page. It is not added to any of the other pages that are viewed within one of the frames, so you only have

to create one set of NoFrames content for each frameset in your site.

Adding NoFrames Content

NoFrames content provides viewers with a way to view a frames-based site without using frames. They view a special set of data provided at the end of the main frameset page which appears like any other Web page.

To add NoFrames content to a frameset document, click Modify on the menu bar, point to Frameset, then click Edit NoFrames Content to open a new page in the document window. You use this new page, which is part of the frameset document file, to lay out the NoFrames content. To do this, copy the images and text from all of the pages displayed in each frame and lay them out just as you would on a standard non-frames page. When you finish laying out the NoFrames content, you then need to change the links so that they point to other non-frames-based pages with the same content. It doesn't do any good to load NoFrames content on one page, only to reload the frames again on the next page. Providing full NoFrames content essentially means that you are creating a copy of your Web site that doesn't use frames at all. This can be the same as creating two full versions of your Web site, unless you only provide links to your documents which would appear in the main informational frame in your frameset. Figure H-18 shows the NoFrames content of the mybrandlaptops frameset. Figure H-19 shows the same content in the frameset.

FIGURE H-18

NoFrames content of mybrandlaptops frameset

FIGURE H-19

Mybrandlaptops frameset with content loaded in frames

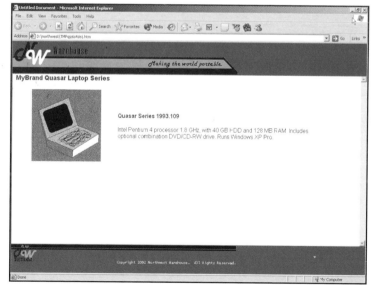

Add NoFrames content to a Web page

1. Click in the infoframe frame to set the insertion point, click Edit on the menu bar, then click Select All.

   All the content in the infoframe is selected.

2. Click Edit on the menu bar, then click Copy.

3. Click Modify on the menu bar, point to Frameset, then click Edit NoFrames Content.

   The NoFrames Content window appears. You will use this to create the content for the non-frames version of the Web page.

4. Click in the upper-left corner of the document window to set the insertion point.

5. Click Edit on the menu bar, then click Paste.

   The content from the infoframes frame is pasted in the NoFrames Content window, as shown in Figure H-20.

   (continued)

FIGURE H-20

NoFrames Content window containing pasted content from infoframe frame

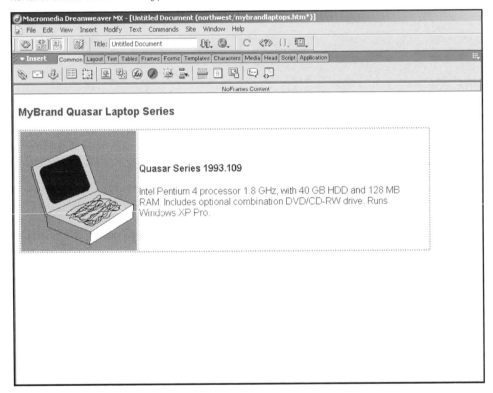

FIGURE H-21
NoFrames Content window

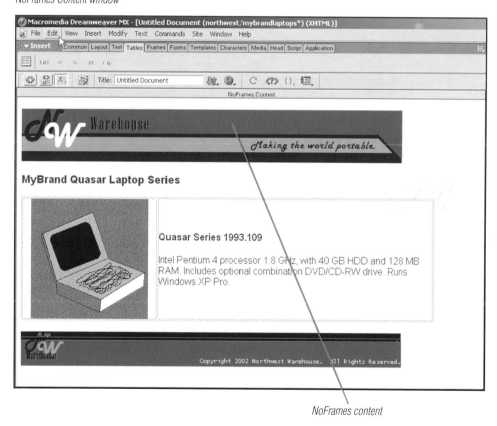

NoFrames content

6. Click to the left of MyBrand to set the insertion point, press [Enter] (Win) or [return] (Mac), press [↑] to position the insertion point on the first line, click Insert on the menu bar, then click Image to open the Select Image Source dialog box.

7. Navigate to the assets folder of the Northwest Warehouse Web site (if necessary), select the topbanner.png image from the file list, then click OK (Win) or Choose (Mac).

8. Insert the bottombanner.png image from the assets folder of the Web site below the table, then compare your screen to Figure H-21.

9. Click File on the menu bar, click Save All, then close all open pages.

You added NoFrames content to the Northwest Warehouse Web site.

Insert a frame.

1. Open the Blooms & Bulbs Web site that you created in Units A through G. (If you did not create this Web site in Units A through G, contact your instructor for assistance.)
2. Add a new page to the Web site, then open this new untitled page.
3. Apply the Left Frame predefined frameset to the page.
4. Drag the right border of the left frame about a half inch to the right to increase its size, then save the frameset as **home.htm**.

Configure a frame.

1. Use the Frames panel to select the left frame in the frameset.
2. Name the left frame **navigation**.
3. Name the right frame **information**.

4. Use the Property inspector to specify that the navigation frame not resize.
5. Set the Borders property of the navigation frame to Yes.
6. Change the Border Color of the navigation frame to **#009900**.
7. Set the Scroll property of the navigation frame to No.
8. Set Margin Width of the navigation frame to **7**.
9. Set Margin Height of the navigation frame to **7**.
10. Save the frameset.

Add content to frames.

1. Select the information frame.

2. Set the SRC property for the information frame to the index.htm page in the Web site.
3. Type **Blooms and Bulbs** in the navigation frame, then format it in black Arial, Helvetica, sans-serif, size 4, centered.
4. Insert a hard return after this text.
5. Type **Home**, insert a hard return, type **Plants**, insert a hard return, type **Workshops**, insert a hard return, type **Tips**, insert a hard return, then type **Ask Cosie**. Format this text in Arial, Helvetica, sans-serif, size 3, centered.
6. Set the page background color for the navigation frame to **#66CC33**. (*Hint*: To set the page background for a page within a frame, select the frame then use the Page Properties dialog box to change the background color.)

7. Save the navigation frame as **toc.htm**, then save the frameset.

Create NoFrames content.

1. Select the contents of the home page contained in the information frame and copy it.
2. Open the Edit NoFrames Content window.
3. Paste the home page contents in the Edit NoFrames Content window.
4. Save your work, then close the Edit NoFrames Content window.
5. Preview the page in a browser, compare your screen with Figure H-22, close your browser, then close all open pages.

FIGURE H-22

Completed Skills Review

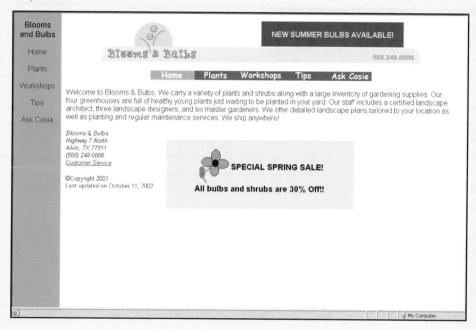

In this exercise you will continue your work on the Rapids Transit Web site that you began in Project Builder 1 in Unit A. If you did not create this Web site in Units A through G, contact your instructor for assistance. Mike Andrew has asked you to create a site map for the Rapids Transit site using frames that will allow visitors to view the individual pages of the site in one frame while still being able to view the site map in another frame.

1. Open the Rapids Transit Web site. (If you did not create this site in Units A through G, contact your instructor for assistance.)
2. Open a new untitled page.
3. Apply the Right Frame predefined frameset to this page, then save this frameset as **sitemap.htm**.
4. Name the right frame **sitemap**, then name the left frame **sitepages**.
5. Specify that the sitepages frame not resize.
6. Set the Borders property for the sitepages frame to No.
7. Set the Scroll property for the sitepages frame to Auto.
8. Set Margin Width to **5** and Margin Height to **5** for the sitepages frame.
9. Set the SRC property for the sitepages frame to the index.htm page of the Web site.
10. Save the sitemap frame as **sitelist.htm**.

11. Using Figure H-23 as a guide, add the following text to the sitemap frame: **Site Map**, **Home**, **Before You Go**, **Our Guides**, **Country Store**, **Reservations**. Format the text as shown in the figure, and resize the frame as necessary.
12. Link each of the headings you typed in the sitemap frame to their appropriate pages.

(*Hint*: For each link, set the target to the sitepages frame.)
13. Set the page background color for the sitemap frame to **#66FFCC**.
14. Preview the frameset in a browser, test all links, then close your browser.

FIGURE H-23
Completed Project Builder 1

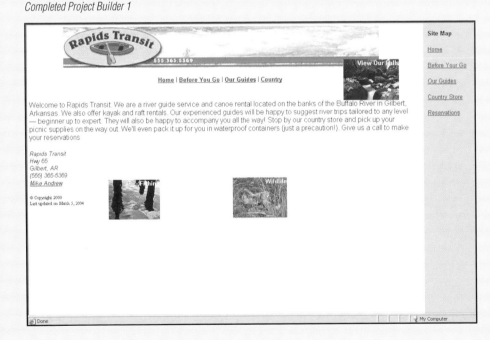

Use Figure H-24 as a guide to continue your work on the Jacob's Web site that you started in Project Builder 2 in Unit A. Chef Jacob needs you to develop a page that will allow you to view all of his recipes. You decide that frames would be the best solution.

1. Open the Jacob's Web site that you completed in Unit G. (If you did not create this site in Units A through G contact your instructor for assistance.)
2. Open a new untitled page.
3. Apply the Left and Nested Bottom Frames predefined frameset to this page, then save the frameset as **recipepages.htm**.
4. Name the right frame **recipepages**, then name the left frame **recipemap** and the bottom frame **logoframe**.
5. Specify that the recipemap frame not resize, and set the Borders property to No.
6. Set the page background color for the recipemap frame to **#FFCC99**.
7. Use Figure H-23 as a guide to enter the following text items in the recipemap frame: **Recipe List**, **Desserts**, **Appetizers**, **Breads**, **Main Dishes**, **Meat Dishes**, **Salads**. Format the text items as shown in the figure.
8. Save the recipemap frame as **recipelist.htm**.
9. Load the recipes.htm document into the recipepages frame.

10. Insert the jacobs.jpg image into the logoframe frame, then set the page background color to **#FFCC99**.
11. Save the logoframe page as **logopage.htm**.
12. Delete the logo from the recipe page shown in the recipepages frame.
13. Save your changes to the recipe page.

14. Create NoFrames content for the text in the frameset.
15. Save your work, preview the frameset in a browser, then close the browser and close all open pages.

FIGURE H-24
Completed Project Builder 2

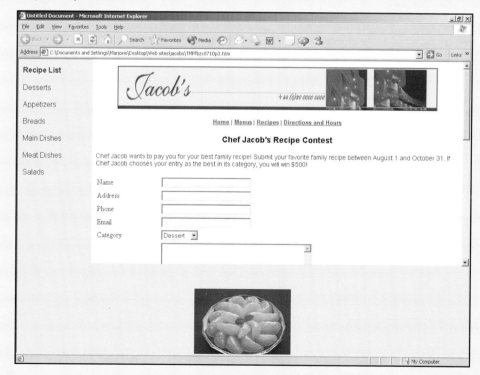

George Le Peleffe has decided to build a Web site to showcase his mechanic-related tools and hardware sales business. He knows that few Web sites on the Internet use frames, but he wants to use them in his site. With less than 20% of sites on the Internet currently using frames, he has to really look for them online. In order to get ideas for his site, he visits the *snapon.com* Web site, as shown in Figure H-25, and the *matcotools.com* Web site.

1. Connect to the Internet, go to *www.course.com*, navigate to the page for this book, click the Student Online Companion link, and then click the links for this unit.
2. Do these sites use frames for page layout? Can you tell by the appearance of the pages, or do you need to scroll through their contents to find out?
3. How could the page layout of these sites be improved by using frames? Or could they?
4. Draw a map showing how you would convert the *snapon.com* site to frames.
5. Draw a map showing how you would convert the *matcotools.com* site to frames.
6. Browse through the sites. Do any of the pages in either site use frames? If so, describe how they are used.

7. Take some notes on what you would do with this site. Think of at least five design ideas that you like from this page, and note how using frames could improve on that idea.

8. Search the Internet for five other sites that use frames. Make a list of the sites you find, and write a summary for each that discusses how the design of each has been improved by the use of frames.

FIGURE H-25
Design Project

In this assignment you will continue to work on the group Web site that you started in Unit A. Depending on the size of your group, you can assign individual elements of the project to group members, or work collectively to create the finished product. There will be no data files supplied. You are building this Web site from unit to unit, so you must do each Group Project assignment in each unit to complete your Web site.

You will continue building your Web site by designing and completing a page that contains frames. After completing your Web site, be sure to run appropriate reports to test the site.

1. If you did not create this Web site in Units A through G, contact your instructor for assistance.
2. Meet as a group to review and evaluate your storyboard. Choose a page or series of pages to develop for which you will use a frameset.
3. Plan the content for your new frameset so that the layout works well with both the new and the old pages in your site. Sketch a plan for the frameset you will create, showing which content will be placed in each frame. The content can be new pages that you create and load into the frames, existing pages that you load into the frames, or new content that you create in the frames.

4. Assign one or more team members to create the frameset document, choosing an appropriate predefined format that matches your sketch.
5. If necessary, assign one or more team members to create any new pages that will be loaded into the frames.
6. Assign other team members to load any existing pages that you've chosen into the frames.
7. Assign one or more team members to ensure that all links open in the correct frame.
8. Assign a team member to run a report to ensure that all of the links connecting to the frames work correctly.
9. As a group, preview all of the pages in your Web browser and test all of the links.
10. Evaluate your pages for content and layout. Use the check list in Figure H-26 to make sure your Web site is complete.
11. Assign team members to make any modifications that are necessary to improve your pages.

FIGURE H-26
Web Site Check Lists

Web Site Check List
1. Do all pages have titles?
2. Do all navigation links work?
3. Do all images appear?
4. Are all colors Web-safe?
5. Did you test the pages in at least two different browsers?
6. Do your pages look good in at least two different screen resolutions?
7. Does your contact information appear on every page?
8. Do all frames have names?
9. Do all pages link to the new frames pages?
10. Have you saved all frames and frameset documents?

ADDING MULTIMEDIA ELEMENTS

1. Add Macromedia Flash objects.

2. Add rollover images.

3. Add sounds and popup messages.

UNIT I
ADDING MULTIMEDIA ELEMENTS

Introduction

You can use Dreamweaver to add multimedia files created in other programs to the pages of your Web site. Some of the external multimedia file types that Dreamweaver allows you to insert include Macromedia Fireworks graphics and behaviors; Macromedia Flash movies, text, and buttons; Macromedia Director and Shockwave movies and presentations; Java applets; ActiveX controls; server-side controls; and a variety of plug-ins. This means you can create complex, interactive Web sites with multimedia effects that can be viewed within the pages themselves, rather than loading an external document player such as Windows Media Player or RealPlayer by Real Networks. In this unit, you will use Dreamweaver to add Flash objects and various multimedia effects to the Northwest Warehouse Web site.

Understanding Multimedia

The term "multimedia" has different meanings, depending on who you are talking to, and the industry in which they work. For our purposes, **multimedia** is the combination of visual and audio effects with text to create a fully engaging experience with a Web site. Although this might be an open-ended definition, it is the experience you are striving for when you add video and audio elements to a Web page. Think about the experience of watching a movie. You are engaged not just by the actors, but also by the sounds and special effects you experience. You want to create this same type of experience for your Web site viewers by adding multimedia elements to your pages.

You can use Dreamweaver to insert a wide variety of multimedia effects on your Web pages, including Flash buttons, movies, and text; Shockwave movies; and a series of built-in JavaScript behaviors such as sounds, rollover images, and popup messages and menus.

Tools You'll Use

Flash button

Flash Button button

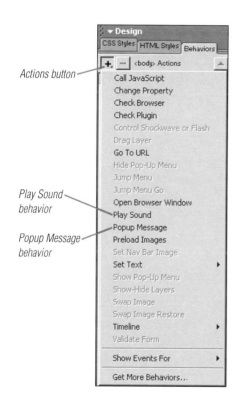

Actions button

Play Sound behavior

Popup Message behavior

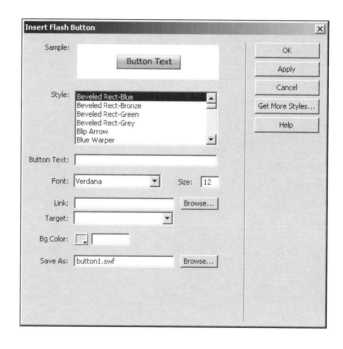

ADD MACROMEDIA FLASH OBJECTS

What You'll Do

In this lesson, you will insert two Flash buttons on the about page of the Northwest Warehouse Web site. You will also insert a Flash movie on the support page and then play the movie both in Dreamweaver and in a browser.

Understanding Macromedia Flash

Macromedia Flash is a software program that allows you to create low-bandwidth animations and interactive elements that can be placed on your Web pages. These animations use a series of vector-based graphics that load quickly and merge with other graphics and sounds to create short movies. Figure I-1 shows a Web page that contains several Flash objects. Figure I-2 shows the Macromedia Flash program used to create Flash objects.

Once these short movies are created, you can place them directly on your Web pages.

In order to view Flash movies, you need the Macromedia Flash Player, a software program that is embedded in the latest versions of both Internet Explorer and Netscape Navigator. If you are using an older browser that does not support the version of Flash used to create your movie, you can download the latest Flash player from the Macromedia Web site, located at *http://www.macromedia.com*. At this point, roughly 96% of Web viewers can view Flash 3, 4, and 5 movies, and about 70% of viewers are able to view Flash 6 files.

Collecting Flash objects

Macromedia and their devoted product users provide you with a variety of download-able Flash buttons which are available on the Macromedia Exchange Web site, located at *http://www.macromedia.com/exchange/*. At this site you can find collections of different buttons, such as space and planet theme sets, and just about anything else you might want. If you can't find a movie or button that tantalizes you, you can download a demo version of Macromedia Flash to create your own Flash objects.

Because Flash buttons and Flash text created in Dreamweaver are based on Flash 5 technology, nearly all viewers will be able to see them no matter what browser they are using.

Inserting Flash Buttons and Movies

A **Flash button** is a button made from a small, pre-defined Flash movie that can be inserted on a Web page to provide navigation on your Web site. Like all Flash objects, Flash buttons are saved with the .swf file extension. Using Dreamweaver, you can insert customized Flash buttons on your Web pages without having

Macromedia Flash installed. To do this, use the Flash Button button on the Media tab of the Insert bar to open the Insert Flash Button dialog box, where you can choose from more than 17 different styles of buttons. You also use this dialog box to specify the button text, formatting, an internal or external page to which to link the button, a background color, and a filename for the button.

QUICKTIP

If the button styles provided in the Insert Flash Button dialog box do not fit your needs, you can download additional styles, use Flash to create your own buttons, or have someone else create custom-made buttons for you.

Using Macromedia Flash, you can create Flash movies that include a variety of multimedia elements, such as audio files (both music and voice-overs), animated objects, scripted objects, clickable links, and just about any other animated or clickable object imaginable. Flash movies can be used to add presentations to your existing Web site or to create an entire Web site. To add a Flash movie to a Web page, click the Flash button on the Media tab of the Insert bar to open the Select File dialog box, then choose the Flash movie you want to insert.

FIGURE I-1
Web site containing Flash objects

FIGURE I-2
Macromedia Flash MX program window

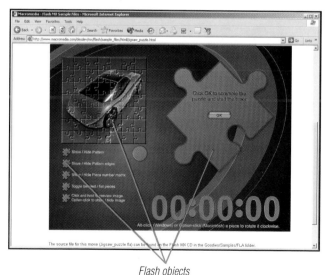

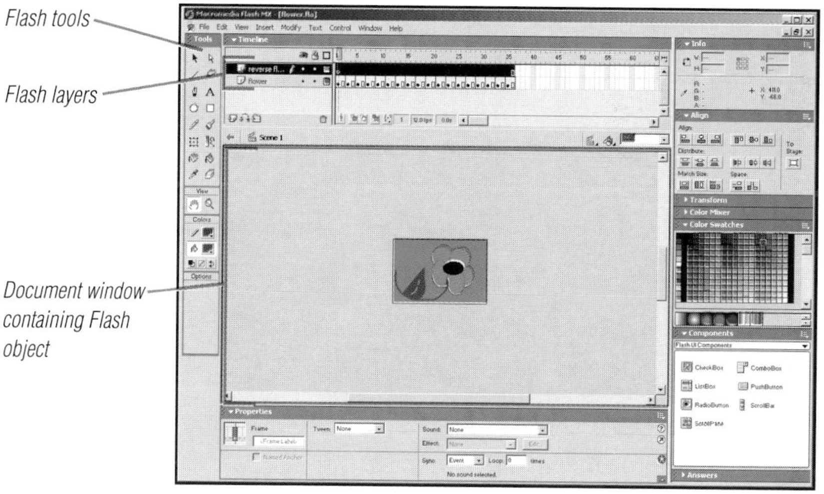

Flash objects

Flash tools

Flash layers

Document window
containing Flash
object

Insert Flash buttons

1. Open the Northwest Warehouse Web site that you completed in Unit H, then open the about page. (If you did not complete this Web site in Units F through H, contact your instructor for assistance.)

2. Click at the end of the paragraph on the about page to set the insertion point, then press [Enter] (Win) or [return] (Mac).

3. Click the Align Center button in the Property inspector. ≣

4. Click the Media tab of the Insert bar, then click the Flash Button button on the Insert bar to open the Insert Flash Button dialog box, as shown in Figure I-3. 🖼

5. Select Soft-Raspberry from the Style list.

6. Type **Company News** in the Button Text text box.

7. Click the Font list arrow, click Impact, then type **14** in the Size text box.

(continued)

FIGURE I-3
Insert Flash Button dialog box

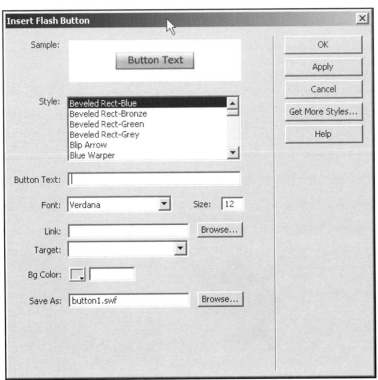

FIGURE I-4

Flash buttons added to the about page

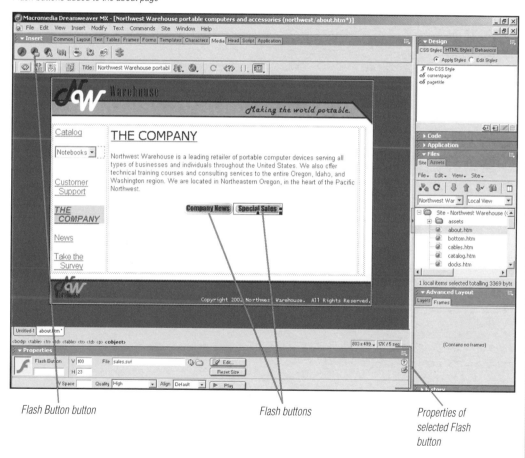

Flash Button button

Flash buttons

Properties of
selected Flash
button

8. Click the Browse button to the right of the Link text box to open the Select File text box, select news.htm in the file list, then click OK (Win) or Choose (Mac).

9. Click the Bg Color button to open the color picker, then click the white square.

10. Type **news.swf** in the Save As text box, then click OK.

11. Add another Flash button to the right of the Company News button that has the button text **Special Sales**, apply the same formatting settings used for the Company News button, link the Special Sales button to the misc page in the Northwest Warehouse Web site, then save this button as **sales.swf**.

12. Save your changes, then compare your screen to Figure I-4.

> TIP If you preview this page in your browser, you might discover that the Flash buttons do not work. Sometimes a Web site must be published on a Web server in order for Flash buttons to work in a browser.

13. Close the about page.

You added two Flash buttons to the about page of the Northwest Warehouse Web site.

Insert Flash movies

1. Open the support page of the Northwest Warehouse Web site.

2. Click to the right of the CUSTOMER SUPPORT heading to place the insertion point, then press [Enter] (Win) or [return] (Mac).

3. Click the Flash button on the Media tab of the Insert bar to open the Select File dialog box.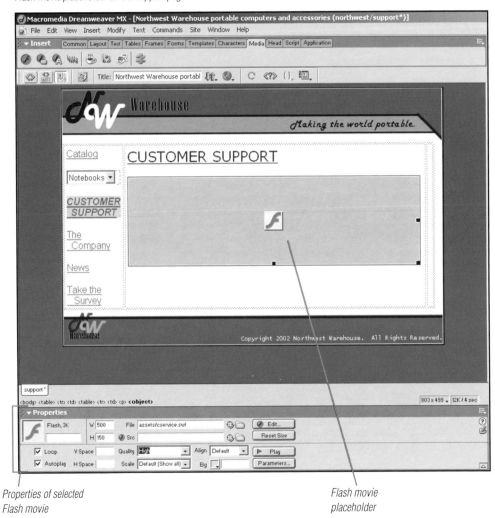

4. Navigate to the unit_i assets folder, select the file cservice.swf, then click OK (Win) or Choose (Mac).

   A Flash movie placeholder appears on the page, as shown in Figure I-5.

   TIP   If a dialog box opens asking if you want to copy the Flash movie to the Web site, click Yes, navigate to the root folder of the Web site, then click Save.

5. Save your changes.

You inserted a Flash movie on the support page of the Northwest Warehouse Web site.

FIGURE I-5

Flash movie placeholder on the support page

*Properties of selected
Flash movie*

*Flash movie
placeholder*

FIGURE I-6
Flash movie playing in Dreamweaver

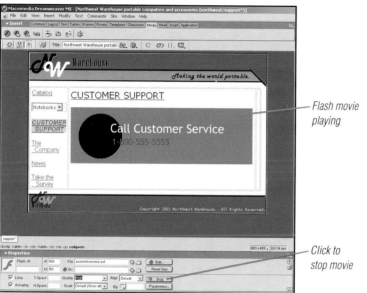

Flash movie
playing

Click to
stop movie

FIGURE I-7
Flash movie playing in Internet Explorer

Play a Flash movie in Dreamweaver and in a browser

1. Click the Play button in the Property inspector to view the cservice.swf movie you inserted, as shown in Figure I-6.

2. Save your work, preview the page in your browser, compare your screen to Figure I-7, then close your browser.

   TIP To play Flash movies in Dreamweaver and in your browser, you must have Shockwave Player installed on your computer. If Shockwave Player is not installed, you can download it at the Macromedia Web site (*www.macromedia.com*). Ask your instructor for assistance.

3. Close the support page.

You played a Flash movie on the support page in the Northwest Warehouse Web site in Dreamweaver and in your browser.

Lesson 1 Add Macromedia Flash Objects

ADD ROLLOVER IMAGES

What You'll Do

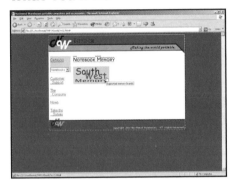

 In this lesson, you will add a rollover image to the memory page of the Northwest Warehouse Web site.

Understanding Rollover Images

A rollover image is an image that changes its appearance when the mouse pointer is placed over it in a browser. A rollover image actually consists of two images. The first image is the one that appears when the mouse pointer is not positioned over it, and the second image is the one that appears when the mouse pointer is positioned over it. Rollover images are often used to help create a feeling of action and excitement on a Web page. For instance, suppose you are creating a Web site that promotes a series of dance classes. You could create a rollover image using two images of a dancer in two different poses. When a viewer places the mouse pointer over the image of the dancer in the first pose, the image would change to show the dancer in a different pose, creating a feeling of movement and action.

QUICKTIP

You can also add a link to a rollover image, so that the image will change only when the image is clicked.

Adding Shockwave movies

Macromedia Shockwave is part of the Macromedia Director Shockwave Studio, a software suite used to create full-blown interactive, multimedia presentations that combine text, graphics, video, animations, and sound. Adding Shockwave files to your Web pages can add excitement, sizzle, and interactivity to engage your users. To add a Shockwave movie to a Web page in Dreamweaver, click the Shockwave button on the Media tab of the Insert bar to open the Select File dialog box, select the file you want, then click OK. Shockwave files have a .dcr file extension.

Adding Rollover Images

You add rollover images to a Web page using the Rollover Image button on the Common tab of the Insert bar shown in Figure I-8. Doing this opens the Insert Rollover Image dialog box, which you use to specify both the original image and the rollover image that will be swapped in when the mouse is positioned over the original image.

QUICKTIP

It's a good idea to click the Preload rollover image checkbox in the Insert Rollover Image dialog box to ensure that the rollover image appears without a delay.

Rollover images can also be used to display an image associated with a text link. For instance, suppose you are creating a Web site for an upcoming election. You could create a Web page that contains a list of candidates for the election, and add a rollover image for each candidate's name that would cause a photograph of the candidate to appear when the mouse is placed over his or her name. You can also use this effect to make appropriate images appear when you point to different menu options. For instance, Figure I-9 shows the Nurses Anytime Web site, which uses rollover images to highlight each menu option on its home page.

FIGURE I-8
Common tab of the Insert bar

Rollover Image button

FIGURE I-9
Nurses Anytime Web site with rollover images

Rollover image changes when mouse pointer is positioned over new menu item

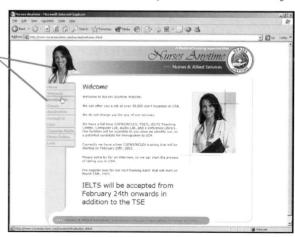

Add a rollover image

1. Open the memory page of the Northwest Warehouse Web site.

2. Click to the right of the NOTEBOOK MEMORY heading to set the insertion point, then press [Enter] (Win) or [return] (Mac).

3. Click the Common tab of the Insert bar, then click the Rollover Image button on the Insert bar to open the Insert Rollover Image dialog box. 🖻

4. Type **Memory** in the Image Name text box, then compare your screen to Figure I-10.

5. Click the Browse button next to the Original Image text box, navigate to the unit_i assets folder, select the file nwmemory.png from the file list, then click OK.

(continued)

FIGURE I-10
Insert Rollover Image dialog box

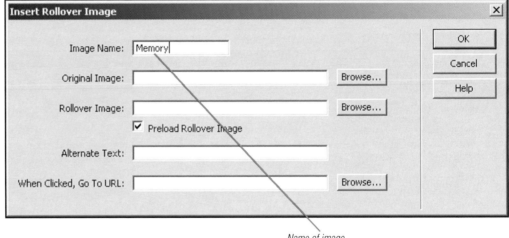

Name of image

Adding Multimedia Elements

FIGURE I-11
Memory page with rollover image in Internet Explorer

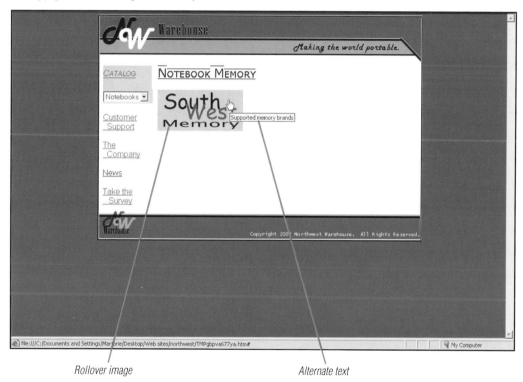

Rollover image   Alternate text

6. Click the Browse button next to the Rollover Image text box, navigate to the unit_i assets folder, select the file swmemory.png from the file list, then click OK.

7. Check the Preload Rollover Image checkbox.

8. Type **Supported memory brands** in the Alternate Text text box, then click OK.

9. Save your work, preview the page in your browser, place the mouse pointer over the image to see the rollover effect, compare your screen to Figure I-11, then close your browser.

You added a rollover image to the memory page of the Northwest Warehouse Web site.

ADD SOUNDS AND POPUP MESSAGES

What You'll Do

In this lesson, you will add a sound effect and a popup message to the memory page of the Northwest Warehouse Web site.

Adding Interactive Elements

You can make your Web pages come alive by adding interactive elements such as sounds to them. For instance, if you are creating a Web page about your favorite animals, you could attach the sound of a dog barking to a photograph of your dog so that the barking sound would play when the viewer clicked the photograph. You can add sound and other multimedia actions to elements by attaching behaviors to them. **Behaviors** are sets of instructions that you can attach to page elements that tell the page element to respond in a specific way when an event occurs, such as when the mouse pointer is positioned over the element. When you attach a behavior to an element, JavaScript code for the behavior is automatically generated and inserted into the code for your page.

Using the Behaviors Panel

You can use the Behaviors panel located in the Design panel group to insert a variety of JavaScript-based behaviors on a page. For instance, using the Behaviors panel you can automate tasks, respond to visitor selections and mouse movements, add sounds, create games, or add automatic dynamic effects to a Web page. To insert a behavior, click the Actions button on the Behaviors panel to open the Actions menu, as shown in Figure I-12, then click a behavior from the menu.

Inserting Sound Effects

Sound effects can add a new dimension to any Web site. You can use sounds to enhance the effect of positioning the mouse on a rollover image, clicking a link, or even loading or closing a page. By adding sounds, you can make your pages cheep, chirp, click, squawk, or even belch if you so desire.

To apply a sound effect, select the link or object to which you want the sound effect added, and then select the Play Sound behavior located on the Actions menu of the Behaviors panel.

Inserting Popup Messages and Alert Boxes

Popup messages and **alert boxes** are messages that open in a browser to either clarify information, alert viewers of an action that is being taken, or even say "goodbye and thank you for visiting the Web site." You can add popup messages using the Behaviors panel.

Popup messages can be quite annoying to Web site viewers, so be judicious when adding them to your pages. Typically, you should only use them when it is imperative to confirm an action or provide viewers with more information about the site they are visiting or leaving, or about the information they are submitting in a form.

FIGURE I-12

Behaviors panel with Actions menu open

Actions button

Actions menu

Add sound effects

1. Select the rollover image you added to the memory page, click Window on the menu bar, then click Behaviors to open the Behaviors panel.

2. Click the Actions button on the Behaviors panel toolbar to open the Actions menu, then click Play Sound to open the Play Sound dialog box as shown in Figure I-13. ➕

3. Click the Browse button, navigate to the unit_i assets folder, select chord.wav from the file list, then click OK (Win) or Choose (Mac).

   TIP If a dialog box opens asking if you want to copy the chord.wav file to the Web site, click Yes, navigate to the root folder of the Web site, then click Save.

4. Click OK to close the Play Sound dialog box.

   Notice that (on MouseOver) is listed as an Event and Play Sound is listed as an Action in the Behaviors panel. This means that the Play Sound behavior will be triggered when the mouse pointer is positioned over the specified object.

5. Save your work, preview the page in your browser, test the sound effect, then close your browser.

You added a sound effect to an image on the memory page of the Northwest Warehouse Web site.

FIGURE I-13
Play Sound dialog box

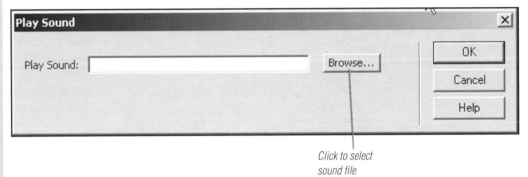

Click to select
sound file

FIGURE I-14

Popup Message dialog box

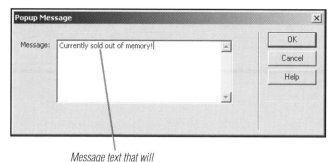

Add a popup message

1. Click the NorthWest Memory image on the memory page to select it, then open the Behaviors panel (if necessary).

2. Click the Actions button on the Behaviors panel toolbar, then click Popup Message to open the Popup Message dialog box.

3. Type **Currently sold out of memory!** in the Message text box, as shown in Figure I-14.

4. Click OK.

5. Save your changes, preview the page in your browser, then move the pointer over the NorthWest Memory image.

   The image changes to SouthWest Memory, the chord.wav file plays, and the popup message opens, as shown in Figure I-15.

6. Click OK, close your browser, close the memory page, then close all other open pages.

You added a popup message to an image on the memory page of the Northwest Warehouse Web site.

FIGURE I-15

Popup message on memory page in Internet Explorer

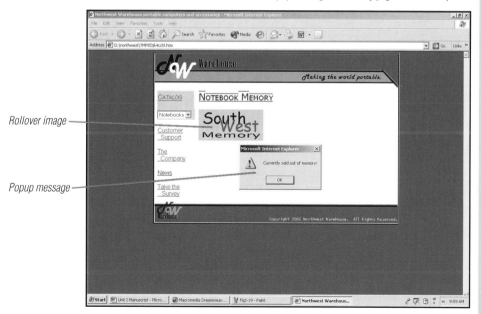

Rollover image

Popup message

Add Flash objects.

1. Open the Blooms & Bulbs Web site that you created in Units A through H, then open the home.htm page that you created in Unit H. (If you did not create this Web site in Units A through H, contact your instructor for assistance.)

2. Delete the Blooms and Bulbs heading in the left frame.

3. Replace the Home text in the left frame with a Flash button that has the following settings: Button Text=**Home**, Font=**Verdana**, Size=**12**, Background color=**#66CC33**, Button style=**Beveled Rect-Green**, Link=**index.htm**, Target=**information**, Save As=**home.swf**.

4. Replace the Plants, Workshops, Tips, and Ask Cosie text items in the left frame with Flash buttons that have the same formatting settings as the Home Flash button you

created. Link each button to the appropriate page in the site, and save the buttons using the following file names, as appropriate: **plants.swf**, **workshops.swf**, **tips.swf**, and **cosie.swf**. (*Hint*: If the buttons are too wide to fit in the left frame, resize the frames by selecting the frameset in the tag selector, then setting the Column property in the Property inspector to 150 pixels.)

5. Insert the flower.swf Flash movie located in the unit_i assets folder directly below the Ask Cosie Flash button.

6. Play the flower.swf movie in Dreamweaver, save your work, preview the page in your browser, then close your browser.

7. Save your work.

Add rollover images.

1. Delete the flower picture in the springsale layer.

2. Insert a rollover image named **flowers** in the springsale layer. Set the Original image to **flower.gif** located in the assets folder of the Blooms & Bulbs Web site. Set the Rollover image to **flowerreverse.jpg** located in the unit_i assets folder. Specify appropriate alternate text.

Add sounds and popup messages.

1. Select the Tips link at the top of the index page in the information frame.

2. Use the Behaviors panel to add a Popup Message behavior to the selected button that contains the following message text: **Any tips given from this site are solely the opinion of the site owner and other visitors and should be used with discretion.**

3. Select the Home link at the top of the index.htm page in the information frame, and attach the Play Sound behavior using the file chord.wav located in the unit_i assets folder. Then attach this same Play Sound behavior to the other navigation links at the top of this page.

4. Save your work, compare your screen to Figure I-16, then preview the page in your browser.

5. Close the home.htm frameset.

FIGURE I-16
Completed Skills Review

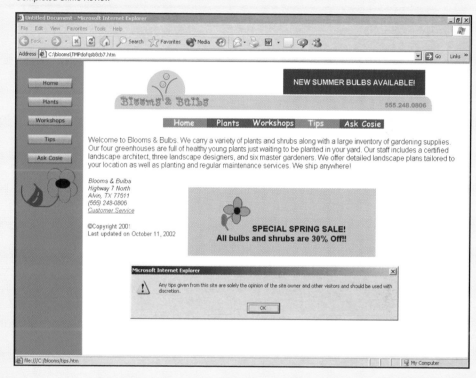

In this exercise you will continue your work on the Rapids Transit Web site that you began in Project Builder 1 in Unit A. Mike Andrew, the site owner, would like you to replace all the links at the top of the Web site with Flash buttons. He also wants you to add an informational popup message to the banner on the home page.

1. Open the Rapids Transit Web site that you created in Units A through H, then open the home page. (If you did not create this site in Units A through H contact your instructor for assistance.)

2. Select the Home link in the navigation bar, then replace it with a Flash button that has the Glass-Turquoise style.

3. Set the Button Text to **Home**, the formatting to **Lucida Console**, then size to **12**, and the background color to white (**#FFFFFF**).

4. Link the button to index.htm.

5. Save the button as **home.swf**.

6. Replace each of the other links in the navigation bar with Flash buttons that use the same formatting as the Home Flash button you created. Save each button with the following names, as appropriate: **before.swf**, **guides.swf**, **store.swf**, and **sitemap.swf**. Link each button to its appropriate page in the site.

7. Copy the new navigation bar, then paste it to the top of all the other pages in the Web site. Delete the old navigation bars on each page. Do not paste the navigation bar to the sitelist.htm page.

8. Add a Popup Message behavior to the Rapids Transit banner on the home page that has the following text: **Wonderful views of the fauna and flora of Arkansas**.

9. Save your work, preview all the pages in your browser, test all links, test the popup message, then compare your screen to Figure I-17.

10. Close all open pages.

FIGURE I-17
Completed Project Builder 1

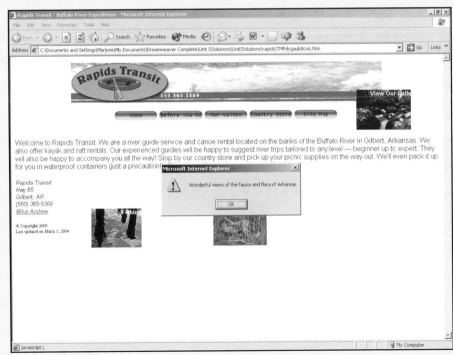

Use Figure I-18 as a guide to continue your work on the Jacob's Web site that you started in Project Builder 2 in Unit A. Chef Jacob has decided that he wants to replace the text links on the directions page with Flash buttons and add a Flash movie to the site.

1. Open the Jacob's Web site. (If you did not create this site in Units A through H, contact your instructor for assistance.)

2. Open the directions page.

3. Replace the Home link at the top of the page with a Flash button. Choose a style, background color and font that will work well with the existing color scheme and design of the Jacob's Web site.

4. Link the button to index.htm, and save it as **home.swf**.

5. Replace each of the other links in the navigation bar with Flash buttons, using the same formatting and fonts that you used for the Home button. Save the files using the filenames **menus.swf**, **recipes.swf**, and **directions.swf**, as appropriate.

6. Align each button to the top of the current line.

7. Click to the right of the paragraph of directions, then insert a hard return.

8. Insert the Flash movie file map.swf from the unit_i assets folder.

9. Close all open pages except for the directions page.

10. Add the Play Sound behavior to the photo of the dinner on the directions page, using the chord.wav file located in the unit_i assets folder.

11. Save your work, then preview the page in your browser, test the Play Sound behavior, compare your screen to Figure I-18, then close your browser.

12. Close the directions page.

FIGURE I-18
Completed Project Builder 2

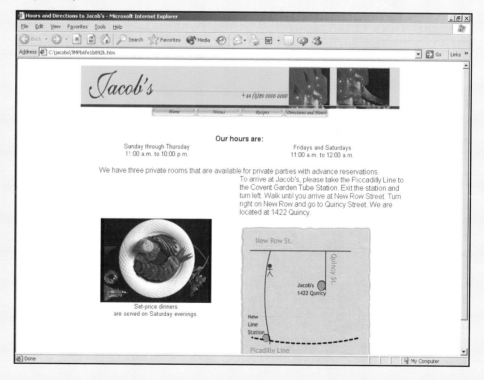

Jorden Lies wants to create a Web site devoted to his baseball memorabilia sales business. He believes that emulation is the best form of flattery, so he decides to create it in the same fashion as the official Major League Baseball site, shown in Figure I-19. Jorden wants to include baseball photos, game schedules, player profiles, and even a store to order memorabilia. He does not have the capability to create his own Flash objects, so he decides to use the Flash capabilities that are built into Dreamweaver to add his own Flash buttons and Flash text to his site. He also plans to add rollover images and a few sounds on some of the pages for effect.

1. Connect to the Internet, go to *www.course.com*, navigate to the page for this book, click the Student Online Companion link, and then click the link for this unit.
2. Which elements in the site are Flash objects?
3. Which objects in the site are made with rollover images?
4. How has adding the Flash effects improved the appearance of this site?

5. Go through the site and locate any popup message boxes. Make a list of all the popup message boxes you find.
6. Make a list of sounds that would be appropriate to add to this site, and where you would place them.

7. Create a sketch of Jorden's site that contains at least 5 pages. Indicate in your sketch what multimedia elements you plan to insert in the site, including where you would add Flash objects, rollover images, and sounds.

FIGURE I-19
Design Project

In this assignment you will continue to work on the group Web site that you started in Unit A. Depending on the size of your group, you can assign individual elements of the project to group members or work collectively to create the finished product. There will be no data files supplied. You are building this Web site from unit to unit, so you must do each Group Project assignment in each unit to complete your Web site.

You will continue building your Web site by designing and completing a page that contains multimedia content or by adding multimedia content to existing pages. After completing your Web site, be sure to run appropriate reports to test the site.

1. If you did not create this Web site in Units A through H, contact your instructor for assistance.

2. Meet as a group to review and evaluate your storyboard. Choose a page, or series of pages, to develop in which you will include Flash objects as well as other multimedia content, such as rollover images, sounds, and popup messages.

3. Plan the content for your new page so that the layout works well with both the new and old pages in your site. Sketch a plan for the multimedia content you wish to add, showing which multimedia elements you will use and where you will place them.

4. Assign one or more team members the task of creating the Flash buttons and Flash text you identified in your sketch, choosing appropriate formatting.

5. Assign one or more team members the task of adding rollover images to the page.

6. Assign other team members the task of adding the popup messages and sounds to the page.

7. Assign one or more team members to ensure that the Flash objects are linked to the correct pages and frames.

8. Assign a team member to run a report on your new page(s) to ensure that all links work correctly.

9. As a group, preview the new page (or pages) in your browser and test all links. Evaluate your pages for content and layout. Use the check list in Figure I-20 to make sure your Web site is complete.

10. Assign team members to make any modifications that are necessary to improve the page.

FIGURE I-20
Web Site Check List

> ### Web Site Check List
> 1. Do all Flash buttons load correctly?
> 2. Do all Flash text objects roll over and change color correctly?
> 3. Do all Flash movies play properly in your browser?
> 4. Do all links work?
> 5. Do all sounds play correctly?
> 6. Are there any missing images or links on the pages?
> 7. Do all pages have a title?
> 8. Do all rollover images display properly?

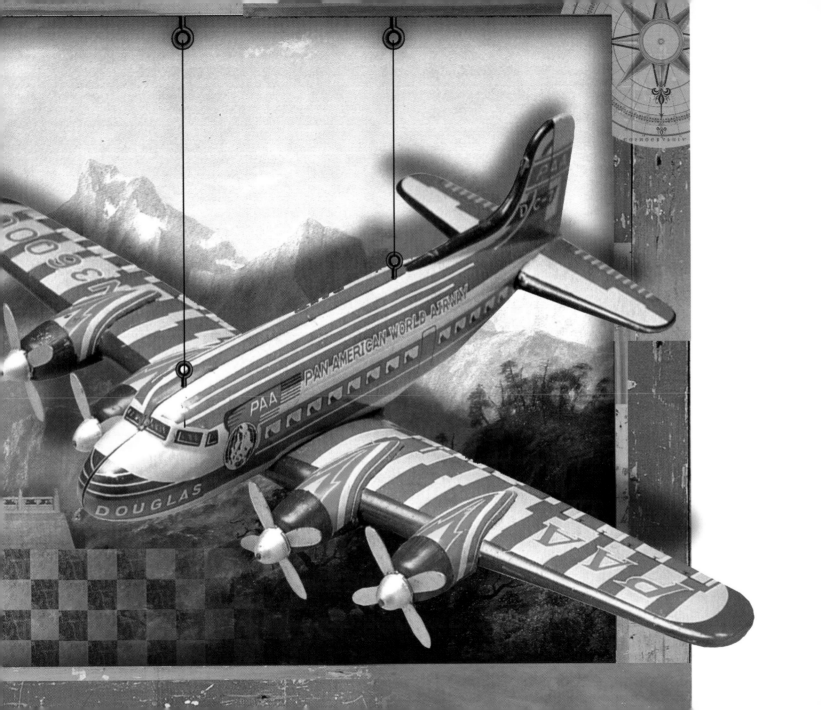

UNIT J

CREATING INTERACTIONS

USING BEHAVIORS AND TIMELINES

1. Animate layers using timelines.

2. Change text using behaviors.

3. Swap images and create pop-up windows and menus.

UNIT J
CREATING INTERACTIONS USING BEHAVIORS AND TIMELINES

Introduction

Dreamweaver MX makes it possible to create visually dynamic Web pages that contain interactive elements without writing a line of code. For instance, you can create animations that grab the attention of your viewers by using layers and the **Timelines panel**, a set of tools that allow you to control the movement of an animated layer. You can also create many interactive elements on your Web pages using behaviors.

In this unit, you will import a new Web site that promotes and sells a line of insecticide products. You will then create an animation of a layer on one of the pages using the Timelines panel and attaching the Play Timeline and Stop Timeline behaviors. You will also use behaviors to make text appear in a layer, a text field, and the status bar when the mouse pointer is positioned over a link or image. Finally, you will use behaviors to create pop-up windows and menus, and to **swap** an image, which is similar to creating a rollover effect.

Using Animations and Interactive Elements Effectively

Because Dreamweaver makes it easy to create animations and interactive elements, you might be tempted to create lots of them. However, be aware that too many animations and special effects could distract and annoy your viewers and cause them to leave your site. Make sure that you have a good reason before you add sounds, pop-up elements, or animations to a page. Also, make sure that the graphics you choose for your animations and interactive elements are appropriate for the content and design of the site. If your site is promoting a serious topic such as world hunger, or is marketing a buttoned-down organization such as a law firm, you should avoid adding frivolous graphics that could detract from the message of the site.

QUICKTIP

Behaviors and animations created with timelines use JavaScript and DHTML. Therefore, viewers must be using a browser that is version 4 or later to view them.

Tools You'll Use

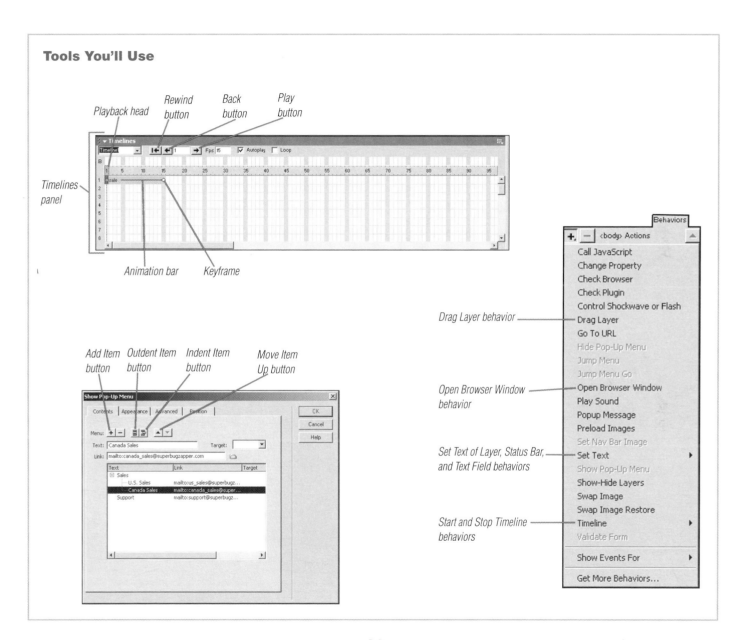

Playback head

Rewind button

Back button

Play button

Timelines panel

Animation bar

Keyframe

Add Item button

Outdent Item button

Indent Item button

Move Item Up button

Drag Layer behavior

Open Browser Window behavior

Set Text of Layer, Status Bar, and Text Field behaviors

Start and Stop Timeline behaviors

ANIMATE LAYERS USING TIMELINES

What You'll Do

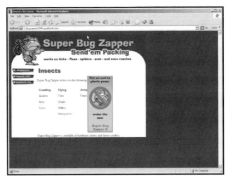

In this lesson, you will first create the Super Bug Zapper Web site, a site that will promote and sell a line of insecticide products. You will then create an animation on the insects page by adding a layer to a timeline and setting an animation path for it. You will view the animation both in Dreamweaver and in your browser, and will then add a behavior to make the layer draggable.

Animating Layers

In addition to their use in positioning text and graphics on a Web page, layers can also be animated to help make your pages come to life. For instance, you could create an ad for a new product in a layer, then animate the layer so that it circles around the home page to attract a viewer's attention.

Using the Timelines Panel

To animate a layer, you need to add it to the Timelines panel, as shown in Figure J-1. The Timelines panel contains tools and a time-line that allow you to control the motion of an animated layer over a specified period of time. When you add a layer to a timeline, it is represented by a blue **animation bar** in one of the rows, or **animation channels**, of the timeline. Animation channels are composed of **frames**, each of which represents the position of a layer at a particular moment in the animation. A timeline can have up to thirty-two animation channels, making it possible to animate several layers at the same time. An animation bar shows the length of the layer's animation. The small circles at each end of an animation bar represent **keyframes**, which are the start and end points of an animation.

> **QUICKTIP**
> You can stretch the duration of an animation by dragging the last keyframe to the right to increase the length of the animation bar. The animation path will be the same, but the animation will occur over a longer period of time.

To open the Timelines panel, click Window on the menu bar, point to Others, then click Timelines. To add a layer to a time-line, select the layer, click Modify on the menu bar, point to Timeline, then click Add Object to Timeline.

> **QUICKTIP**
> You can also open the Timelines panel by pressing [Alt][F9].

Using Behaviors to Animate a Layer

Once you add a layer to a timeline, you then need to set the start and stop positions of the animated layer. To do this, move the layer to the position you want it at the start of the animation, click the first frame in the timeline, click a blank area on the page so that only the body tag appears in the tag selector, and then choose the Play Timeline behavior on the Actions menu of the Behavior panel. Once this starting position is set, you can then drag the layer to a different location on the page to set the path of the animation. When you drag the layer, a line appears that represents the layer's path of motion, as shown in Figure J-2. Once you have positioned the layer where you want it, click the ending keyframe in the Behaviors channel of the Timelines panel, then use the Stop Timeline behavior to set the end point of the animation. The Behaviors channel is located above the animation channels, and is used to trigger a behavior at a specific frame in an animation.

QUICKTIP

In order to use the Play Timeline and Stop Timeline behaviors, you must make sure that only the body tag appears in the tag selector.

Adding Keyframes

An animated layer always moves in a straight line between two keyframes. To change the motion path of a layer from a straight path to a curved one, add one or more keyframes between the starting and ending keyframes, then drag the intermediary keyframe to the location you want the path to curve.

Previewing Animations Using the Timelines Panel

Once you create an animation, you can preview it in Dreamweaver by clicking the Play button in the Timelines panel toolbar or

---

FIGURE J-1
Timelines panel

Behaviors channel
Frame numbers
Animation channel numbers
Animation bar
Keyframe

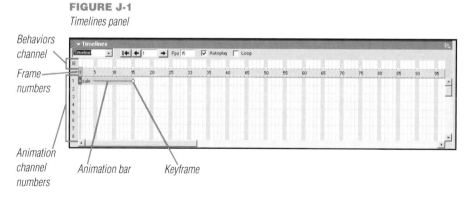

FIGURE J-2
Animated layer

Starting position of animated layer
Ending position of animated layer
Path of animation
Behaviors channel

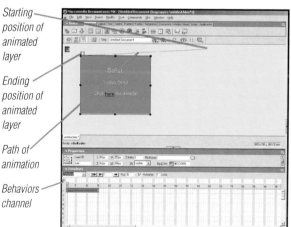

---

dragging the red **playback head** from the first keyframe to the end keyframe. You can use the other buttons in the Timelines panel toolbar to preview an animation, as shown in Figure J-3. Use the Rewind button to move the layer to the first frame in the animation. Use the Back button to move the layer one frame to the left. You can also view the position of a layer at any point in the animation by clicking a frame anywhere in the animation bar. The coordinates of the layer's position at that frame will appear in the Property inspector and the layer will move to the appropriate position in the document window.

QUICKTIP

When you design an animation, Dreamweaver automatically generates the JavaScript code, making it possible to view animations in a browser without any plugins. Because JavaScript code and layers are used to create animations, only browsers later than 4.0 will be able to display them.

Creating Draggable Layers

If you want to give your viewers the control to position layers on a page, you can add the Drag Layer behavior, which allows viewers to move layers around the screen as they wish. The Drag Layer dialog box is used to specify the amount of dragging control you want viewers to have. For instance, you can specify that the dragging area be restricted to a particular area of the page. You can also specify a **drop target**, or a set position on the page where you want the layer to be placed, and then specify that the layer snap into the drop target position if dragged within a certain range.

QUICKTIP

You can have Dreamweaver automatically record an animation path for you. To do this, select the layer you want to animate, click Modify on the menu bar, point to Timeline, click Record Path of Layer, then drag the layer around the screen to create the desired path.

FIGURE J-3
Viewing the Timelines panel toolbar buttons

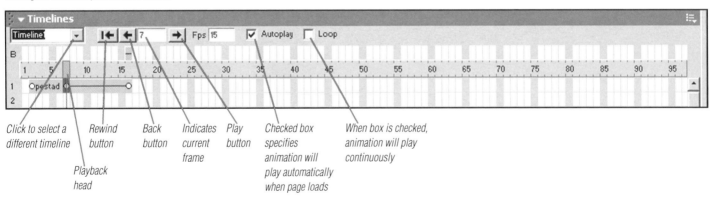

Click to select a different timeline
Playback head
Rewind button
Back button
Indicates current frame
Play button
Checked box specifies animation will play automatically when page loads
When box is checked, animation will play continuously

FIGURE J-4

Viewing the bugzapper folder in Windows Explorer (Win)

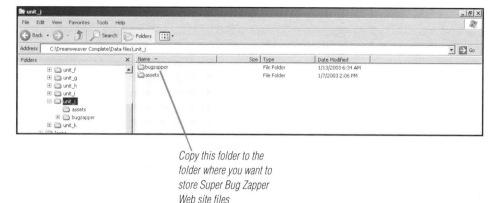

Copy this folder to the folder where you want to store Super Bug Zapper Web site files

FIGURE J-5

Site Definition dialog box with settings for Super Bug Zapper Web site (Win)

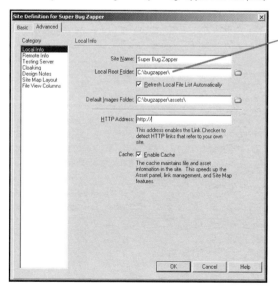

Specify folder where you want to store Super Bug Zapper Web site (your folder may be different)

Create the Super Bug Zapper Web site (Win)

1. Open Windows Explorer, then navigate to the unit_j data files folder so that the contents appear in the right pane, as shown in Figure J-4.

2. Copy the bugzapper folder in the unit_j data files folder, then paste it to the drive and folder in the left pane where you want to store the Super Bug Zapper Web site.

3. Close Windows Explorer, start Dreamweaver, click Site on the Site panel menu bar, then click New Site to open the Site Definition for Unnamed Site 1 dialog box.

4. Click the Advanced tab (if necessary), type **Super Bug Zapper** in the Site Name text box, then set the Local Root Folder to the bugzapper folder that you pasted in Step 2.

5. Set the Default Images Folder to the assets folder located in the bugzapper folder that you pasted in Step 2, compare your screen to Figure J-5, then click OK.

   The files for the Super Bug Zapper Web site are now displayed in the Site panel.

6. Open the index page, the contact_us page, the products page, and the insects page, then read each page to familiarize yourself with the site.

7. Close all open pages.

You copied the bugzapper folder from the unit_j data files folder to the drive and folder where you want to store the Web site files. You also used the Site Definition dialog box to name the site, set the location of the root folder, and specify the folder for storing images.

Create the Super Bug Zapper Web site (Mac)

1. Open Finder, then navigate to the folder on your computer where you want to store the Super Bug Zapper Web site.

2. Open another version of Finder, then open the unit_j data files folder.

3. Drag the bugzapper folder from the unit_j folder to the drive and folder where you want to store the Super Bug Zapper Web site, as shown in Figure J-6.

4. Close the Finder windows, start Dreamweaver, click Site on the menu bar, then click New Site to open the Site Definition for Unnamed Site1 dialog box.

5. Type **Super Bug Zapper** in the Site Name text box, then set the Local Root Folder to the bugzapper folder that you dragged in Step 3.

6. Set the Default Images folder to the assets folder located in the bugzapper folder that you dragged in Step 3, compare your screen to Figure J-7, then click OK.

7. Open the index page, the contact_us page, the products page, and the insects page of the Super Bug Zapper Web site, read each page to familiarize yourself with the site, then close all open pages.

You copied the bugzapper folder to a different drive and folder. You then named the site and set the root and default images folders.

FIGURE J-6
Copying the bugzapper folder using Finder (Mac)

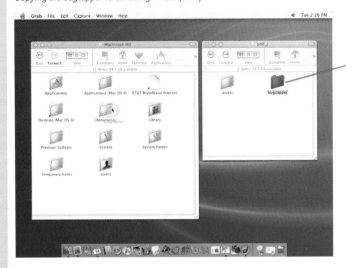

Copy this folder to the folder where you want to store Super Bug Zapper Web site files

FIGURE J-7
Site Definition dialog box with settings for Super Bug Zapper Web site (Mac)

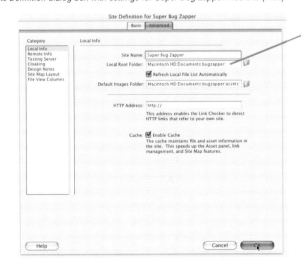

Specify folder where you want to store Super Bug Zapper Web site (your folder may be different)

Creating Interactions Using Behaviors and Timelines

FIGURE J-8

Pestad layer added to timeline

Pestad layer —

Timelines panel —

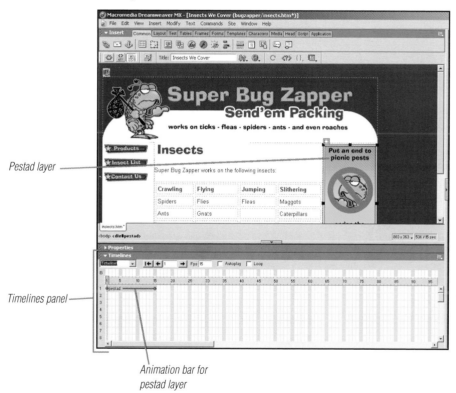

Animation bar for
pestad layer

1. Open the insects page of the Super Bug Zapper Web site.

2. Click Window on the menu bar, point to Others, then click Timelines to open the Timelines panel.

3. Minimize the Property inspector (if necessary).

   Minimizing the Property inspector will allow you to see more of the page in the document window.

4. Open the Layers panel, then select the pestad layer in the document window.

   The orange layer containing the text Put an end to picnic pests is selected.

5. Click Modify on the menu bar, point to Timeline, then click Add Object to Timeline.

   A dialog box opens, explaining that the timeline can animate certain aspects of the layer.

   > TIP You can also add a layer to a timeline by dragging the layer to the timeline.

6. Click OK, then compare your screen to Figure J-8.

   A blue animation bar that represents the pestad layer appears in the timeline.

You added the pestad layer to the timeline on the insects page.

Add start and stop frames to a timeline

1. Click in the black area to the right of the Super Bug Zapper banner so that only the body tag appears in the tag selector.

2. Click frame 1 in the Behaviors channel in the Timelines panel as shown in Figure J-9.

3. Open the Behaviors panel, then click the Actions button to open the Actions pop-up menu.

4. Point to Timeline, then click Play Timeline to open the Play Timeline dialog box, as shown in Figure J-10.

5. Click OK to accept Timeline1 as the specified timeline.

   The Behaviors panel now lists onLoad under the Event column and Play Timeline in the Actions column.

6. Click frame 15 in the Behaviors channel in the Timelines panel.

7. Click the Actions button in the Behaviors panel toolbar to open the Actions pop-up menu, point to Timeline, then click Stop Timeline.

   The Stop Timeline dialog box opens.

8. Click the Stop Timeline list arrow, click Timeline1, click OK, then save your changes.

You used the Behaviors panel to specify that the animation start when the page loads. You also specified that the animation stop at frame 15.

FIGURE J-9

Setting the Play Timeline frame in the Behaviors channel of the Timelines panel

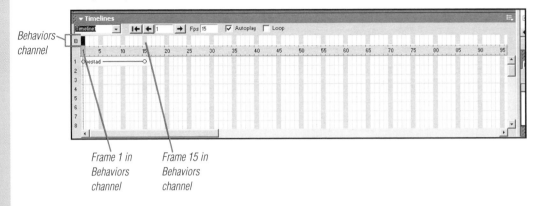

Behaviors channel

Frame 1 in Behaviors channel

Frame 15 in Behaviors channel

FIGURE J-10

Play Timeline dialog box

FIGURE J-11

Dragging a layer to set an animation path

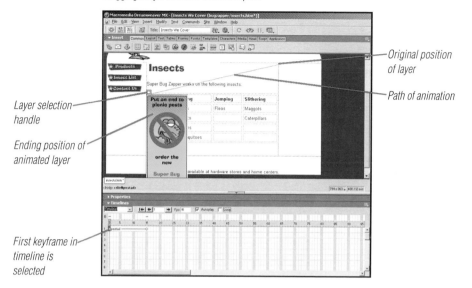

Original position of layer

Path of animation

Layer selection handle

Ending position of animated layer

First keyframe in timeline is selected

FIGURE J-12

Using a keyframe to create a curve in an animation path

Curved animation path after dragging middle keyframe

Drag layer to this position to create curve in animation path

New keyframe added to frame 5

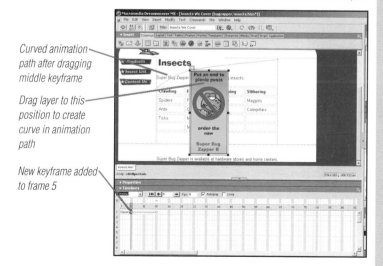

1. Click the first keyframe in the timeline, then select the pestad layer (if necessary).

2. Click the pestad layer selection handle so that the pointer changes to a double-headed arrow (Win) or a hand (Mac), then drag the layer down and to the left about an inch below the Insects heading, as shown in Figure J-11. ⬦

   A line appears from the layer's old position to its new position. This line represents the path of motion that the layer will take in the animation.

3. Click frame 5 in the timeline, right-click (Win) or press and hold [control] then click (Mac) to open the pop-up menu, then click Add Keyframe.

4. Make sure that the frame 5 keyframe is selected in the timeline, then drag the pestad layer selection handle up about ½ inch, as shown in Figure J-12.

   The line that shows the path of motion for the layer is now curved, because you moved the keyframe.

5. Save your work.

You added a keyframe to the pestad animation bar in the timeline and then dragged the layer to create a curve in the animation path.

Preview an animation in Dreamweaver and your browser

1. Drag the red playback head in the Timelines panel from frame 1 to frame 15 to preview the animation in the document window, as shown in Figure J-13.

   | TIP   Use the Back button on the Timelines panel toolbar to move the layer back one frame in the animation.

2. Click the Rewind button on the Timelines panel toolbar to move the layer back to the first frame of the animation. ![rewind]

3. Make sure the Autoplay checkbox is checked on the Timelines panel toolbar.

4. Preview the page in your browser.

   The insects page appears in your browser, and the layer moves across the page according to the path you specified.

   | TIP   If you want to view the animation again, click the Refresh button on your browser's toolbar.

5. Compare your screen to Figure J-14, then close your browser.

You previewed the insects page in Dreamweaver and in your browser and saw the animation you created.

FIGURE J-13
Previewing the animation in Dreamweaver

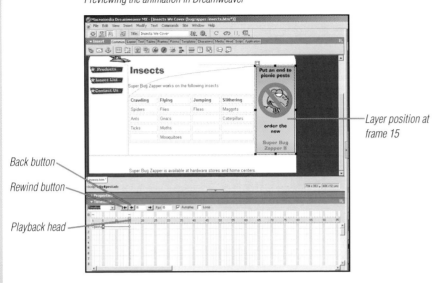

Layer position at frame 15

Back button

Rewind button

Playback head

FIGURE J-14
Previewing the animation in Internet Explorer

Layer position midway through animation

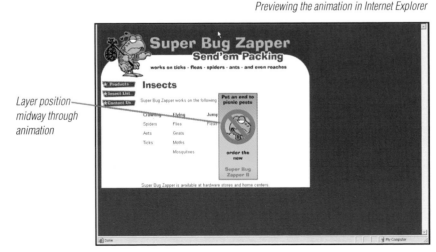

Creating Interactions Using Behaviors and Timelines

FIGURE J-15

Drag Layer dialog box

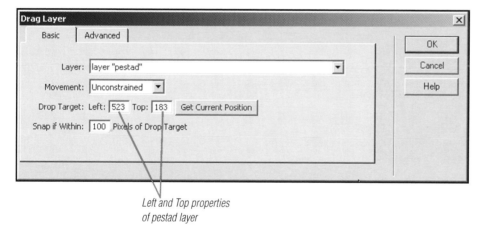

Left and Top properties
of pestad layer

1. Click and hold the Play button on the Timelines panel toolbar to move the pestad layer to frame 15. ➡

   The pestad layer should now be positioned at the right edge of the page.

2. Click in the black area above the banner so that only the body tag is showing in the tag selector.

3. Click the Actions button on the Behaviors panel toolbar to open the Actions menu, then click Drag Layer to open the Drag Layer dialog box. +,

4. Set Layer to layer "pestad" (if necessary), set Movement to Unconstrained (if necessary), click Get Current Position to specify the Left and Top settings, type **100** in the Snap if Within text box, compare your screen to Figure J-15, then click OK.

5. Save your changes, then preview the page in your browser.

6. Drag the layer around in your browser window, then test whether it snaps into place when you drag it close to its position at the end of the animation.

7. Close your browser, then close the insects page.

You attached the Drag Layer behavior to the pestad layer and specified that the layer snap into its drop target position when placed within a range of 100 pixels of the drop target.

CHANGE TEXT USING BEHAVIORS

What You'll Do

In this lesson, you will create and name an empty layer and then use the Set Text of Layer behavior to make specified text appear in the layer when the mouse pointer is positioned over a certain link. You will also use the Set Text of Status Bar behavior to make customized text appear in the status bar. Finally, you will use the Set Text of Text Field behavior to make text appear in a text field.

Using Behaviors to Change Text

There are several behaviors that can be attached to links or objects that will cause text to appear in various ways on a page. Using behaviors, you can set the text of a layer, change the text in the status bar, and display text in a form field.

Changing Text in a Layer

Sometimes you might want certain text to appear on a page only after a viewer has positioned the mouse pointer over a particular link or object. Making text appear in this way can help keep your page clear of unnecessary text, and can also draw attention to information related to a specific link. To do this, you first need to create and name an empty layer on the page where you want the text to appear. Next, select the link that you want to act as the trigger for displaying the text. Finally,

choose the Set Text of Layer behavior and use the Set Text of Layer dialog box to specify the text that you want to appear in the layer.

Changing the Text of the Status Bar

By default, the status bar in a browser contains information about the current state of what is displayed on screen. For instance, if you position the mouse pointer over a link, the status bar will display the URL for that link. You can customize the text that appears in the status bar so that when a viewer selects an object or positions the mouse pointer over an object or link, the status bar will display text that is related to that object. For instance, rather than the status bar displaying the URL for a link, you could specify that it display a description of the link.

Displaying Text in a Form Field

You can also attach a behavior to a link to make specified text appear in a form field when the mouse pointer is positioned over a particular object or link. The process is similar to that of changing text in a layer, except that you use the Set Text of Text Field behavior. First, create a new text field using the Text Field button on the Forms tab of the Insert bar. Next, select the object or link that you want to serve as the trigger for the text, then choose the Set Text for Text Field behavior to open a dialog box where you will specify the text that you want to appear. Figure J-16 shows an example of a page on which customized text appears in a layer, on the status bar, and in a text field when the mouse pointer is positioned over a link.

FIGURE J-16
Text displayed in a layer, text field, and the status bar triggered by positioning the mouse pointer on a link

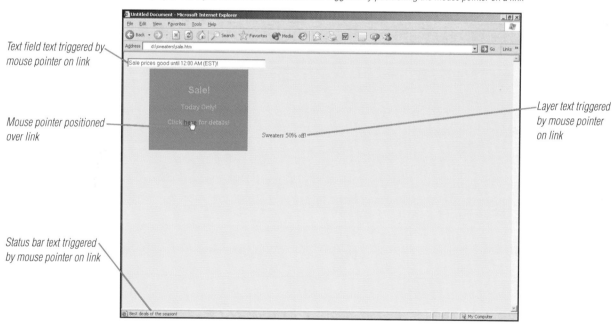

Text field text triggered by mouse pointer on link

Mouse pointer positioned over link

Layer text triggered by mouse pointer on link

Status bar text triggered by mouse pointer on link

Change text in a layer

1. Open the contact_us page in the Super Bug Zapper Web site.

2. Use the Draw Layer button on the Common tab of the Insert bar to insert a new layer that is approximately 2½ inches wide and 1½ inches high to the right of the Contact Us heading.

3. Select the layer, open the Property inspector (if necessary), name the new layer **support**, set the background color of the layer to white (if necessary), then compare your screen to Figure J-17.

4. Select the link info@superbugzapper.com, click the Actions button on the Behaviors panel toolbar to open the Actions menu, point to Set Text, then click Set Text of Layer to open the Set Text of Layer dialog box. ➕

5. Type **Support is open Monday through Friday, 5:00 AM to 5:00 PM (PST).** in the New HTML text box, then click OK.

6. Save your changes, preview the page in your browser, position your mouse pointer over the info@superbugzapper.com link, compare your screen to Figure J-18, close your browser, then close the contact_us page.

You created and named a new layer on the contact_us page. You then added a behavior to display text in the support layer when the mouse pointer is positioned over the information link.

FIGURE J-17
New, empty layer on contact_us page

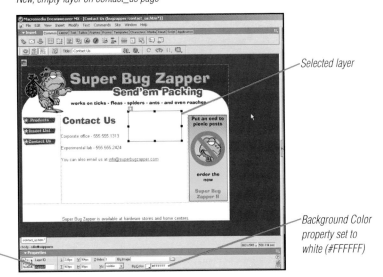

Selected layer

Background Color property set to white (#FFFFFF)

Layer ID property set to support

FIGURE J-18
Viewing layer text on the contact_us page in Internet Explorer

Layer text triggered by position of mouse pointer over link

Mouse pointer positioned over link

Creating Interactions Using Behaviors and Timelines

FIGURE J-19
Set Text of Status Bar dialog box

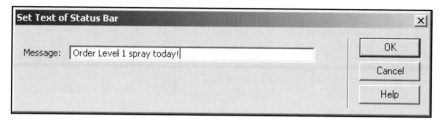

Set Text of Status Bar   ☒

Message: Order Level 1 spray today!   OK

                                              Cancel

                                              Help

FIGURE J-20
Testing the status bar messages in Internet Explorer

Status bar text
triggered by
position of
mouse pointer
over yellow can

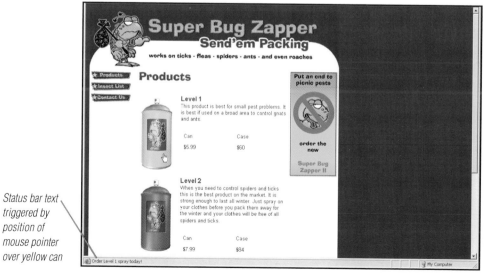

Lesson 2   Change Text Using Behaviors

Add text to the status bar

1. Open the products page in the Super Bug Zapper Web site.

2. Select the yellow can image on the page, click the Actions button on the Behaviors panel toolbar to open the Actions menu, point to Set Text, then click Set Text of Status Bar.

    The Set Text of Status Bar dialog box opens.

3. Type **Order Level 1 spray today!** in the Message text box, compare your screen to Figure J-19, then click OK.

4. Using the same method as in Steps 2 and 3, set the text of the status bar for the blue can image to **Order Level 2 spray today!**

5. Set the text of the status bar for the red can image to **Order the ultimate in pest control!**

6. Save your changes, preview the page in your browser, position the pointer over the yellow can, then compare your screen to Figure J-20.

7. Position the pointer over the blue and red cans to test the status bar message, close your browser, then close the products page.

You attached the Set Text of Status Bar behavior to the images on the products page so that a marketing message will appear in the status bar when the mouse pointer is positioned over each image.

Change the text of a text field in a form

1. Open the index page in the Super Bug Zapper Web site.

2. Click to the right of the Welcome heading to set the insertion point, then click the Text Field button on the Forms tab of the Insert bar.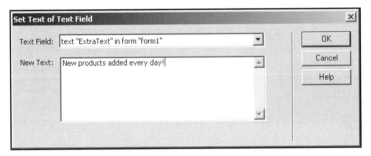

   An alert box opens, asking whether you want to add a form tag.

3. Click Yes.

4. Select the text field, use the Property inspector to name the text field **ExtraText**, then set Char Width to **55**.

5. Select the products page link in the second paragraph, open the Actions menu in the Behaviors panel, point to Set Text, then click Set Text of Text Field.

   The Set Text of Text Field dialog box opens.

6. Type **New products added every day!** in the New Text text box as shown in Figure J-21, then click OK.

   (continued)

FIGURE J-21
Set Text of Text Field dialog box

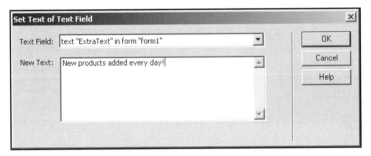

Creating Interactions Using Behaviors and Timelines

7. Save your changes, preview the page in your browser, position the mouse pointer over the products page link, compare your screen to Figure J-22, close your browser, then close the index page.

You added a text field to the home page. You then attached the Set Text of Text Field behavior to the products page link to specify that a marketing message appear in the text field when the mouse pointer is positioned over it.

FIGURE J-22

Viewing the form text in Internet Explorer

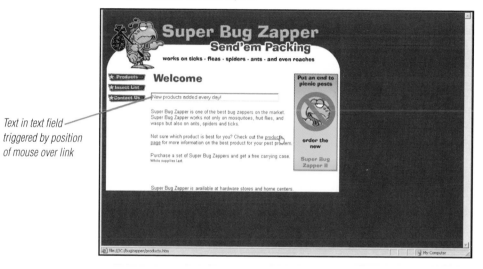

Text in text field triggered by position of mouse over link

SWAP IMAGES AND CREATE POP-UP WINDOWS AND MENUS

What You'll Do

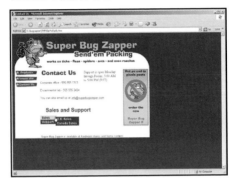

▶ In this lesson, you will use the Swap Images behavior to add a rollover image to the products page. You will also add a pop-up window to the home page that contains an ad for a product. Finally, you will add a pop-up menu to the contact_us page that allows viewers to choose from a list of e-mail contacts.

Creating Interactive Elements Using Behaviors

You can use behaviors to create many interesting and dynamic effects that keep your viewers engaged in your Web site. You can create rollover effects using the Swap Images behavior. You can also use behaviors to create pop-up windows and menus.

Swapping Images

You have already learned how to create rollover images using the Rollover Image button on the Common tab of the Insert bar. You can achieve similar rollover effects using the Swap Image behavior. By attaching this behavior to an object, you can specify that a new object appear when the mouse pointer is positioned over the original object. The Swap Image dialog box is used to specify the name and location of the image you want to swap.

QUICKTIP

Make sure that you swap in an image that has the same height and width as the original image. If not, the image you swap in will appear condensed or stretched out to match the dimensions of the original image.

Creating Pop-Up Windows

Sometimes you might want to allow a viewer to click a link on a page that will open another window showing a larger view of the link. You may have encountered this while shopping on the Web. For instance, if you've ever ordered clothes from a Web site, you might have clicked a small image of a shirt to view the same shirt up close in a larger window. What's handy about this is that you can make the pop-up window the exact size as the image. To create a pop-up window, select the link you want to serve as the trigger, then choose the Open Browser Window behavior from the Actions menu of the Behaviors panel. This opens the Open Browser Window dialog box, which is used to name the pop-up window, specify the URL that you want to display in it, and set the window's dimensions and other attributes, such as whether to include scroll bars and a status bar.

QUICKTIP

You can use a single pop-up window to show several different images. To do this, specify the same pop-up window name in the Open Browser Window dialog box for each trigger to which you attach the Open Browser Window behavior.

Creating Pop-Up Menus

If you want to let your viewers choose an item from a long list that links to a URL, you might want to add a pop-up menu to your Web page using the Show Pop-Up Menu behavior. This behavior lets you create, edit, and format a Fireworks pop-up menu in Dreamweaver. Fireworks MX is a powerful graphics program that is part of Macromedia Studio MX. In order to use the Show Pop-Up Menu behavior, you must have Fireworks MX installed on your system. Using this behavior, you can create beautiful pop-up menus without writing any program code. Figure J-23 shows an example of a pop-up menu featured on the Macromedia support Web site.

To use the Show Pop-Up Menu behavior, you must first select an image. This behavior can only be attached to images. Next, use the Actions menu of the Behaviors panel to choose the Show Pop-Up Menu

behavior, which opens the Show Pop-Up Menu dialog box. Use the four tabs of this dialog box to specify the contents, appearance, position, and other attributes of the menu. The Contents tab lets you specify the names of each menu item. You can indent menu items under other menu items to create a hierarchical structure. The Appearance tab is used to specify either a vertical or horizontal menu layout, and to set the fonts, colors, and formatting of the menu items in both the **up state** (the state when the mouse pointer is not positioned over an item) and **over state** (the state when the mouse pointer is positioned over an item). Use the Advanced tab to set cell padding and spacing and to specify border properties. Use the Position tab to specify the position of the trigger image from which you want the menu to open.

FIGURE J-23
Pop-up menu example featured on the Macromedia Support Web site

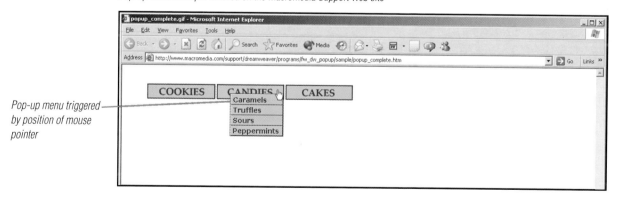

Pop-up menu triggered by position of mouse pointer

Swap images

1. Open the products page, then click the yellow can image to select it.

2. Open the Actions menu on the Behaviors panel, then click Swap Image to open the Swap Image dialog box.

3. Click the Browse button next to the Set Source To text box to open the Select Image Source dialog box, navigate to the assets folder of the Super Bug Zapper Web site, click can_yellow_over.gif as shown in Figure J-24, then click OK (Win) or Choose (Mac) to return to the Swap Image dialog box.

4. Click the Preload Images checkbox, click the Restore Images on MouseOut checkbox, then click OK.

   > TIP Checking the Preload image check-box ensures that the rollover effect happens quickly, with no delay.

5. Save your changes, preview the page in your browser, position the mouse pointer over the yellow can, compare your screen to Figure J-25, close your browser, then close the products page.

You used the Swap Images behavior to create a rollover effect for one of the products shown on the products page.

FIGURE J-24

Preview of swapped-in image in Select Image Source dialog box

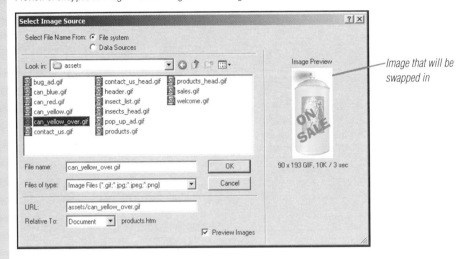

Image that will be swapped in

FIGURE J-25

Swapped-in image on the products page shown in Internet Explorer

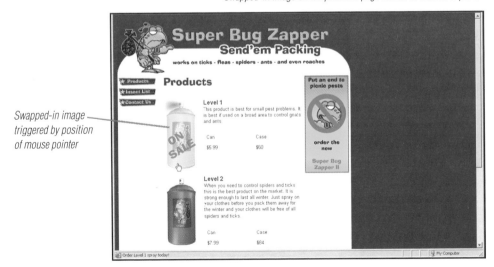

Swapped-in image triggered by position of mouse pointer

Creating Interactions Using Behaviors and Timelines

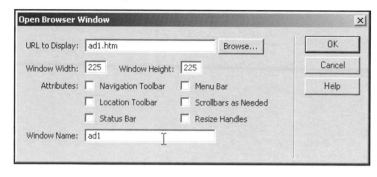

Create a pop-up window

1. Open the index page of the Super Bug Zapper Web site.

2. Click above the banner at the top of the page so that only the body tag appears in the tag selector, open the Actions menu in the Behaviors panel, then click Open Browser Window.

   The Open Browser Window dialog box opens.

3. Click the Browse button next to the URL to Display text box, click the ad1.htm file located in the bugzapper root folder, then click OK (Win) or Choose (Mac).

4. Type **225** in the Window Width text box, type **225** in the Window Height text box, make sure none of the Attributes checkboxes are selected, type **ad1** in the Window Name text box, compare your screen to Figure J-26, then click OK.

5. Save your changes, preview the page in your browser, compare your screen to Figure J-27, close your browser, close the window containing the ad1 page, then close the index page.

You attached the Open Browser Window behavior to trigger the opening of the ad1 page when the home page is opened in a browser.

FIGURE J-27
Pop-up window containing ad1 page in Internet Explorer

Pop-up window ———

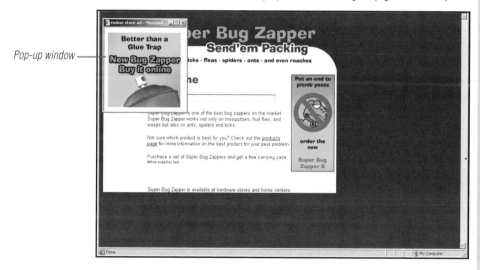

Lesson 3   Swap Images and Create Pop-Up Windows and Menus

Create a pop-up menu

1. Open the contact_us page.

2. Click to the right of the link info@superbugzapper.com in the last line of text to set the insertion point, press [Enter] (Win) or [return] (Mac), then insert the image sales.gif from the assets folder of the Web site.

3. Open the Actions menu in the Behaviors panel, then click Show Pop-Up Menu to open the Show Pop-Up Menu dialog box.

4. Type **Sales** in the Text text box, then click the Add Item button. ➕

5. Type **U.S. Sales** in the Text text box, click the Indent Item button, type **mailto:us_sales@superbugzapper.com** in the Link text box, then click the Add Item button. ➕

6. Type **Canada Sales** in the Text text box, type **mailto:canada_sales@superbugzapper.com**, then click the Add Item button. ➕

7. Type **Support** in the Text text box, click the Outdent Item button, type **mailto: support@superbugzapper.com** in the Link text box, compare your screen to Figure J-28, then click OK.

8. Save your changes, preview the page in your browser, position the mouse pointer over the Sales and Support link to view the pop-up menu, point to Sales, compare your screen to Figure J-29, then close your browser.

You added a pop-up menu to the contact_us page that contains four menu items.

FIGURE J-28

Contents tab of Show Pop-Up Menu dialog box

Outdent Item button

Add Item button

Indent Item button

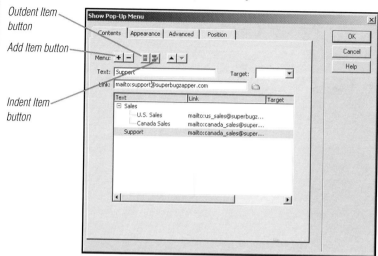

FIGURE J-29

Testing the pop-up menu in Internet Explorer

Pop-up menu

FIGURE J-30

Appearance tab of the Show Pop-Up Menu dialog box

Up State Text color
set to #FFFF33

Up State Cell color
set to #660000

Over State Text color
set to #660000

Over State Cell color
set to #FFFF33

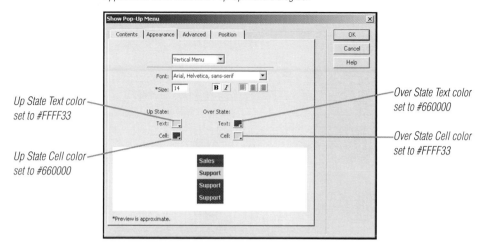

FIGURE J-31

Viewing the formatted pop-up menu in Internet Explorer

Pop-up menu with
formatting settings
applied

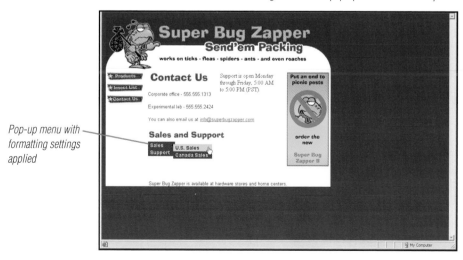

Format a pop-up menu

1. Click the Sales and Support graphic on the contact_us page to select it (if necessary), then double-click the OnMouseOver behavior in the Behaviors panel to open the Show Pop-Up Menu dialog box.

2. Click the Appearance tab, verify that Vertical Menu is selected, set Font to Arial, Helvetica, sans-serif, set Size to **14**, then click the Bold button. **B**

3. Set the Up State Text color to **#FFFF33** (yellow), set the Up State Cell color to **#660000** (maroon), set the Over State Text color to **#660000**, set the Over State Cell color to **#FFFF33**, then compare your screen to Figure J-30.

4. Click the Advanced tab, set Cell Padding to **5**, then make sure the Pop-up Borders checkbox is not checked.

5. Click the Position tab, click the Below and at Left Edge of Trigger button, then click OK.

6. Save your changes, preview the page in your browser, position the mouse pointer over the Sales and Support link to view the pop-up menu, point to Sales, point to U.S. Sales, compare your screen to Figure J-31, close your browser, then close the contact_us page.

You changed the fonts and colors of the text on the pop-up menu. You also added cell padding, specified that no borders appear around the cells, and changed the position of the open menu in relation to the trigger.

Animate layers using timelines.

1. Open the Blooms & Bulbs Web site that you created and developed in Units A through I, then open the index page.

2. Select the springsale layer, then add it to the timeline in the Timelines panel.

3. Drag the springsale animation bar so that the end keyframe is positioned at frame 30 in the timeline, and the beginning keyframe is positioned at frame 15.

4. Click frame 15 in the timeline, then drag the springsale layer up so that the top is positioned in the middle of the page, just below the Blooms & Bulbs banner. This will be the springsale layer's position at the beginning of the animation.

5. Attach the Play Timeline behavior to frame 15 of the springsale animation.(*Hint*: When you attach the behavior, make sure that you select a blank area of the page, so that only the <body> tag appears in the tag selector.)

6. Attach the Stop Timeline behavior to frame 30 of the Behaviors channel in the timeline.

7. Add a keyframe to the animation at frame 20, then drag the springsale layer about an inch to the right to create a curve in the animation path.

8. Attach the Drag Layer behavior to the springsale layer. Set Movement to Unconstrained, specify the Drop Target as the end position of the animation, then specify that the layer snap if within 75 pixels of the drop target.

9. Preview the animation in the document window and in your browser to make sure the animation works and that the layer is draggable and snaps into the drop target position.

10. Close your browser and the index page.

Changze text using behaviors.

1. Open the plants page.

2. Insert a new, empty layer that is approximately 3½ inches wide and 1½ inches high just below the Drop by to see our Featured Spring Plants heading. Drag the layer so that it appears centered under the heading, and insert line spaces as necessary to fit the layer between the heading and the paragraphs below.

3. Name the layer **text**, and set the background color of the layer to white.

4. Attach the Set Text of Layer behavior to the top photograph, specifying the text as **Blooms mid-May through August**.

FIGURE J-32
Completed Skills Review: plants page

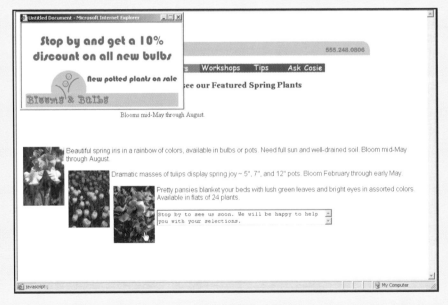

Creating Interactions Using Behaviors and Timelines

5. Attach the Set Text of Layer behavior to the middle photograph, specifying the text as **Blooms February through early May**.

6. Attach the Set Text of Layer behavior to the bottom photograph, specifying the text as **Blooms mid-May through August**.

7. Use the Set Text of Status Bar behavior to each of the navigation bar buttons on the plants page, using the following text for each button, as appropriate: Home—**Go to Home page**; Plants—**Go to Plants page**; Workshops—**Go to Workshops page**; Tips—**Go to Tips page**; Ask Cosie—**Go to Ask Cosie page**.

8. Cut the last paragraph of text on the page.

9. Insert a text field below the third paragraph.

10. Name the text field **message**, set the Char Width property to **50**, and set the Type property to Multiline.

11. Attach the Set Text of Text Field to the bottom photograph, then paste the paragraph text that you cut in Step 8 in the Set Text of Text Field dialog box.

12. Save your work.

Swap images and create pop-up windows and menus.

1. Open the master_gardener page, then insert a hard return after the Ask Our Master Gardener heading.

2. Insert the iris.jpg image file from the assets folder of the Web site in the new line you inserted below Ask our Master Gardener.

3. Attach the Swap Image behavior to the iris.jpg image file, and set the source to the tulips.jpg image file located in the assets folder of the Web site.

4. Open a new, untitled page, then save the file as **popup.htm** in the root folder of the Blooms & Bulbs Web site.

5. Insert the blooms_bulbs_popup_ad.gif image file from the unit_j assets folder, click Yes to copy the file to the assets folder of the Web site, then save and close the popup page.

6. Open the plants page (if necessary), then click another place on the page so that only the <body> tag is showing in the tag selector.

7. Attach the Open Browser Window behavior, specifying popup.htm as the URL to Display. Set Window Width to **390**, Window Height to **200**, and Window Name to **popup**.

8. Save your changes, preview the page in your browser, make sure the popup.htm page opens, test to make sure the layer, status bar, and text field text appear, compare your screen to Figure J-32, then close your browser.

9. Open the master_gardener page.

10. Insert the experts.jpg image file from the unit_j assets folder directly below the iris.jpg image that you inserted in Step 2. Click Yes to copy the file to the assets folder.

11. Attach the Show Pop-Up Menu behavior to the experts.jpg image. In the Show Pop-Up Menu dialog box, add the following menu items with associated links: **Vegetable Gardening** (link: **mailto:vegetables@blooms.com**), **Weed Control** (link: **mailto:weeds@blooms.com**), **Flowers** (assign no link to this menu item).

12. Add the following three menu items and links indented below the Flowers menu item: **Annuals** (link: **mailto:annuals@blooms.com**), **Perennials** (link: **mailto:perennials@blooms.com**), **Bulbs** (link: **mailto:bulbs@blooms.com**).

13. Format the menu items using the following settings: Vertical Menu; Font: Arial, Helvetica, sans-serif, size 14, bold; Up State Text: white; Up State Cell: #006633 (green); Over State Text: #006633; Over State Cell: white.

14. Set Cell Padding at **5**, and specify that no border appear.

15. Set the position of the menu to Below and at Left Edge of Trigger.

16. Save your changes, preview the page in your browser, test the menu to make sure all items appear as specified, test to make sure the images swap in and out, then close your browser and all open pages.

In this Project Builder, you will continue your work on the Rapids Transit Web site that you began in Project Builder 1 in Unit A. Mike Andrew, the owner, has asked you to create an animation that will draw viewers' attention to the week's rental special. You decide to create a new, brightly-colored animated layer that will invite viewers to position their mouse pointers over the image of the kayak to see the weekly special. You will then attach the Set Text of Layer behavior to the kayak image, so that information about the weekly special will appear in the animated layer when the mouse pointer is positioned over it. You will also use the Set Text of Status Bar behavior to add customized text to the status bar.

1. Open the Rapids Transit Web site that you created in Units A through I, then open the rentals page. (If you did not create this Web site in Unit A, contact your instructor for assistance.)
2. Draw a layer below the table that is approximately 3½ inches wide and 1½ inches high. Center the layer as best you can under the table. Name the layer **special**.
3. Set the background color of the special layer to yellow (**#FFFF00**).
4. Type the following text in the layer: **Place your mouse pointer over the kayak to see this week's special!**. Format the text in Arial, Helvetica, sans-serif, size 3, bold.
5. Add the special layer to the timeline.

6. Increase the length of the special animation bar so that it ends at frame 30. (*Hint*: Drag the right edge of the animation bar to increase its length.)
7. Use the Play Timeline and Stop Timeline behaviors to animate the special layer so that the animation begins at frame 1 in the upper-right corner of the page, and ends at frame 30 in a centered position just below the table.
8. Add two keyframes to the animation and use them to create two curves in the path of motion between frames 1 and 30.
9. Attach the Drag Layer behavior to the special layer. Set the drop target as its ending position in the animation, then specify that the layer snap if within 100 pixels of the drop target.

10. Save your work, then preview the animation in the document window and in your browser.
11. Attach the Set Text of Layer behavior to the image of the kayak using the text **Get $2.00 off any rental!**
12. Attach the Set Text of Status Bar behavior to the image of the kayak using the text **We have all your rental needs.**
13. Save your work, preview the page in your browser, make sure that the animation works correctly and that you can drag the layer, position your mouse pointer over the kayak image, then compare your screen to Figure J-33.
14. Close your browser, then close the rentals page.

FIGURE J-33
Completed Project Builder 1

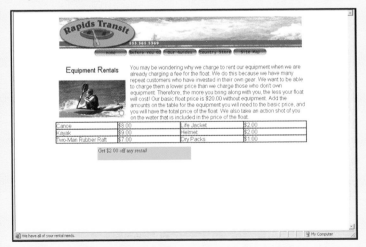

In this Project Builder, you will continue your work on the Jacob's Web site that you started in Project Builder 2 in Unit A. Chef Jacob would like to draw viewers' attention to his dessert specials. You decide to create a pop-up window that will display two different ads for desserts. You also decide to use the Set Layer Text behavior to show descriptions of the desserts when the mouse pointer is placed over them.

1. Open the Jacob's Web site. (If you did not create this site in Units A through I, contact your instructor for assistance.)
2. Open a new, untitled page in the root folder of the Web site, then name this page **popup1.htm**.
3. Insert the image file jacobs_popup1.gif from the unit_j assets folder on the popup1.htm page.
4. Title the page **Friday special**, then save and close the popup1.htm page.
5. Open a second, untitled page in the root folder of the Web site, then name this page **popup2.htm**.
6. Insert the image file jacobs_popup2.gif from the unit_j assets folder on the popup2.htm page.
7. Change the background color of the page to black, title the page **Free dessert**, then save and close the popup2.htm page.
8. Open the after_theatre.htm page, then attach the Open Browser Window behavior

to the photograph of orange slices, specify the URL to Display setting as popup2.htm, set Window Width to **390** and Window Height to **200**. Name the window **popup**.
9. Attach the Open Browser Window behavior to the photograph of the cake slice. Specify the URL to Display setting as popup1.htm, set Window Width to **390** and Window Height to **200**. Name the window **popup**.
10. Draw a new, empty layer next to the cheesecake photograph that is approximately 2½ inches wide and 1½ inches high, then name

the layer **text**. Attach the Set Text of Layer behavior to each of the three dessert photos on the page, using appropriate descriptive text for each photograph.
11. Save your changes, then preview the page in your browser. Position the mouse pointer over each of the three photographs to make sure that the appropriate text appears in the layer and that the popup window opens and displays the correct page. Compare your screen to Figure J-34.
12. Close your browser, then close all open pages.

FIGURE J-34
Completed Project Builder 2

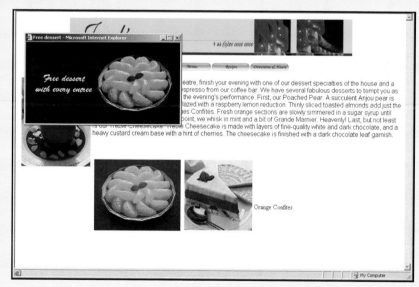

Figure J-35 shows the home page of ISITE Design's Web site, a site that was created using Macromedia Dreamweaver, and was named Macromedia site of the day. This site showcases the work of the ISITE design firm, and also provides information about the company.

1. Connect to the Internet, then go to *www.course.com*. Navigate to the page for this book, click the Student Online Companion, then click the link for this unit.

2. Spend some time exploring the site so that you are familiar with it.

3. What animations do you see, and how are they used to enhance the viewer's experience?

4. Do you see any rollover images? If so, describe them and comment on their effectiveness.

5. Do you see any examples of the Set Text of Layer behavior? If so, where do you see it implemented, and how effective is it?

6. Do you see any examples of the Set Text of Navigation Bar behavior? If so, where? If not, where would you recommend this behavior be implemented?

7. Based on the content and design of this site, what kind of corporate culture does this company have?

8. Go to *www.google.com* or another search engine. Do a search on "Web development and design" to locate other Web design sites.

9. Write down the names of three Web design companies whose sites contain examples of animations, pop-up menus, pop-up windows, and other behaviors that you learned about in this unit.

10. Write a short paragraph about each site on your list, describing how the site incorporates each of the elements and commenting on their effectiveness.

FIGURE J-35
Design Project

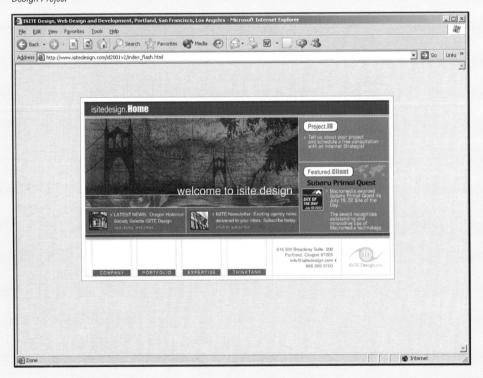

In this assignment, you will continue to work on the group Web site that you created in Units A through I. Depending on the size of your group, you can assign individual elements of the project to group members, or work collectively to create the finished product.

You will continue to enhance your Web site and make it more interactive by adding animated layers, pop-up windows and menus, and by attaching the Set Text behaviors to images to make specified text appear in layers, the status bar, and text fields.

1. Consult your storyboard and brainstorm as a team to decide the page or pages to which you would like to add the following elements: animated layers, pop-up windows, pop-up menus, and rollover images. Also, decide as a group how and where to use the Set Text behaviors to draw viewers' attention to important information. As you discuss where and how to implement these various elements, you can choose to work with existing pages or create new ones.

2. Discuss as a group whether you will need additional graphics for any of the animations that you plan. If so, assign a team member the task of obtaining appropriate graphics.

3. Assign a team member (or several team members) the task of creating the animations on the page or pages you chose.

4. Assign a team member the task of using the Set Text behaviors to add customized text to layers, text fields, and the status bar, according to the group decisions made in Step 1.

5. Assign a team member the task of creating at least two pop-up windows.

6. Assign a team member the task of creating a pop-up menu. The pop-up menu items can be linked to other pages in the site, other pages outside of the site, or e-mail addresses. The pop-up menu should be formatted to match the color, fonts, and design of the site.

7. Assign a team member the task of using the Swap Images behavior to create rollover effects.

8. Assign a team member the task of using the Link Checker panel to check for broken links and orphaned files.

9. Meet as a group to preview all the pages and offer constructive suggestions for improvements. Use the Web Site Check List in Figure J-36 to make sure you completed everything according to the assignment.

10. Assign a team member the task of making any necessary changes.

11. Save your work, then close all open pages.

FIGURE J-36
Web Site Check List

Web Site Check List
1. Does your site include at least one animation and one pop-up menu?
2. Does your site include two pop-up windows?
3. Does your site include rollover images?
4. Do all animations work correctly?
5. Does all text that you set using the Set Text behaviors appear correctly?
6. Do all images have appropriate alternate text?
7. Do all links work correctly?
8. Are there any unnecessary files you can delete?
9. Are all colors Web-safe?
10. Do all pages view well using at least two different browser settings?

UNIT K

CREATING AND USING TEMPLATES

1. Create templates with editable and optional regions.

2. Enhance and nest templates.

3. Use templates to create pages.

4. Use templates to update a site.

Introduction

When you create a Web site, it's important to make sure that each page has a unified look so that viewers know they are in your site no matter what page they are viewing. For instance, you should make sure that common elements such as the navigation bar and company banner appear in the same place on every page and that every page has the same background color. One way to make sure that every page in your site has a consistent appearance is through the use of templates. A **template** is a special kind of page that contains both **locked regions**, which are areas on the page that cannot be modified by users of the template, as well as other types of regions that users can change or edit. For instance, an **optional region** is an area in the template that users can choose to show or hide, and an **editable region** is an area where users can add or change content.

Using templates not only ensures a consistent appearance throughout a Web site, but also saves considerable development time.

Templates are especially helpful if different people will be creating pages in your site. In this unit, you will create a template from an existing page in the Super Bug Zapper Web site, and define editable and optional regions in it. You will also create a nested template, add a repeating table to a template, and create editable attributes for various elements in a template.

Understanding How to Use Templates

The ideal process for using templates is for one person (the template author) to create a template that has a locked region containing the design elements common to every page in the site, as well as regions where content can be added or changed. Once the template is fully developed, other team members can use it to create each page of the site, adding appropriate content to the editable regions of each page. If the template author makes changes to the template, all pages to which the template is attached can be automatically updated to reflect those changes.

Tools You'll Use

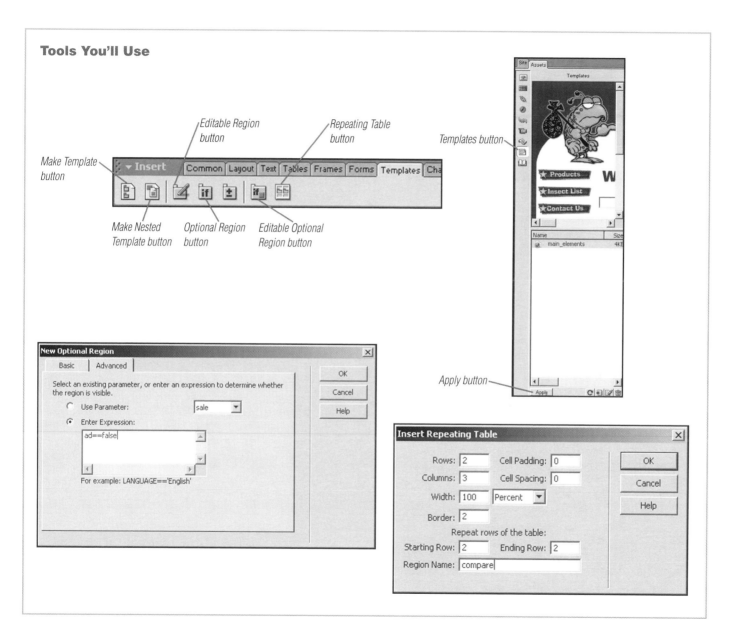

Make Template button

Editable Region button

Repeating Table button

Templates button

Make Nested Template button

Optional Region button

Editable Optional Region button

Apply button

New Optional Region

Basic | Advanced

Select an existing parameter, or enter an expression to determine whether the region is visible.

○ Use Parameter: `sale`

◉ Enter Expression:

`ad==false`

For example: LANGUAGE=='English'

OK | Cancel | Help

Insert Repeating Table

Rows: `2` Cell Padding: `0`

Columns: `3` Cell Spacing: `0`

Width: `100` `Percent`

Border: `2`

Repeat rows of the table:

Starting Row: `2` Ending Row: `2`

Region Name: `compare`

OK | Cancel | Help

CREATE TEMPLATES WITH EDITABLE AND OPTIONAL REGIONS

What You'll Do

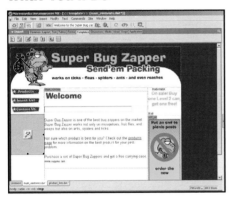

 In this lesson, you will create a template based on the index page of the Super Bug Zapper Web site. You will then define editable regions, optional regions, and editable optional regions in the template.

Creating a Template from an Existing Page

If you have already created and designed a page that you think looks great, and you want to use the layout and design for other pages in your site, you can save the page as a template using the Save As Template command. Templates are saved with a .dwt extension, and are stored in the Templates folder in the root folder of your Web site. If your site does not have a Templates folder, one will automatically be created for you the first time you save a template. To view a list of templates in your site, open the Templates folder in the Site panel. To preview a template before opening it, open the Assets panel, click the Templates button on the Assets panel toolbar, then click a template in the list. The template appears in the preview window above the templates list, as shown in Figure K-1.

Defining Editable Regions

By default, when you save a template, all content on the page will be locked, which means that no one else will be able to add content or modify any part of the template to create new pages. If your template is going to be used effectively, you need to have at least one editable region in it so that other users can add content. To specify a page element as an editable region, use the Editable Region button on the Templates tab of the Insert bar to open the New Editable Region dialog box, which you use to specify a name for the region. Editable regions are outlined in blue on the template page, and the names of the editable regions appear in blue shaded boxes, as shown in Figure K-2.

Defining Optional Regions

In addition to editable regions, you can also add optional regions to a template. An **optional region** is an area in a template that users can choose to either show or hide. For instance, you could make a graphic an optional region, so that users of the template can decide whether or not to show it on the page they are creating.

An optional region's visibility is controlled by the conditional statement if. To specify a page element as an optional region, select the element, then use the Optional Region button on the Templates tab of the Insert bar to open the New Optional Region dialog box, where you can name the region and specify whether to show or hide it by default.

Defining Editable Optional Regions

If you want to give users the ability to show or hide a page element, as well as make modifications to it, then you can define the element as an **editable optional region**. For instance, you might want to make an advertisement an editable optional region so that users of the template could change its text and specify whether to show or hide it. To define an element as an editable optional region, select the element, then use the Editable Optional Region button on the Templates tab of the Insert bar to open the New Optional Region dialog box, where you can name the region and specify whether to show or hide it by default.

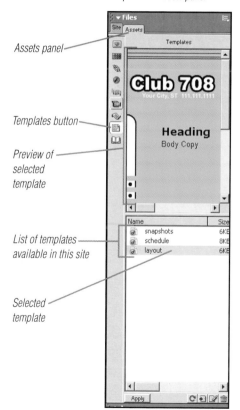

FIGURE K-1

Templates in Assets panel

Assets panel

Templates button

Preview of selected template

List of templates available in this site

Selected template

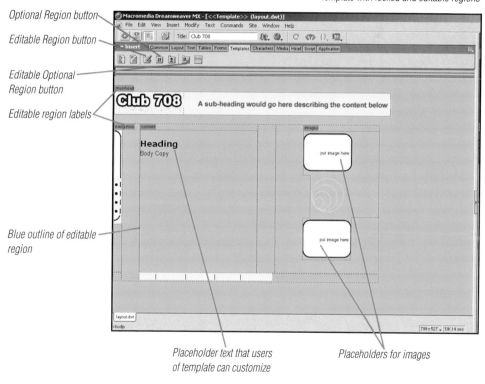

FIGURE K-2

Template with locked and editable regions

Optional Region button

Editable Region button

Editable Optional Region button

Editable region labels

Blue outline of editable region

Placeholder text that users of template can customize

Placeholders for images

Create a template from an existing page

1. Open the Super Bug Zapper Web site, then open the index page.

2. Click File on the menu bar, then click Save as Template to open the Save As Template dialog box.

3. Type **main_elements** in the Save As text box, compare your screen to Figure K-3, click Save, then click the Refresh button on the Site panel toolbar. C

   Notice that the Templates folder, which contains the main_elements template, now appears in the Site panel.

4. Open the Assets panel, click the Templates button to view the list of templates in the site, click the main_elements template in the list (if necessary), then compare your screen to Figure K-4. ▤

   > TIP To create a template from scratch, click File on the menu bar, click New to open the New Document dialog box, click the General tab, click Basic page in the Category list, click HTML Template in the Basic page list, then click Create.

You created a template from the home page of the Super Bug Zapper Web site.

Save As Template dialog box

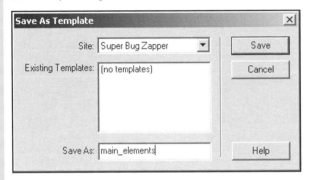

Assets panel showing saved templates in the Super Bug Zapper Web site

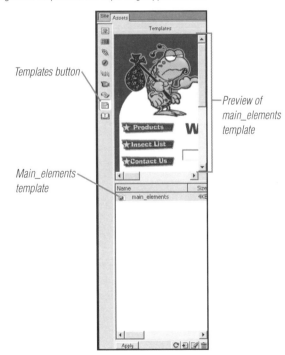

Templates button

Main_elements template

Preview of main_elements template

Creating and Using Templates

FIGURE K-5

Main_elements template with editable region added

Editable Region button

Editable region label

Editable region marked by blue outline

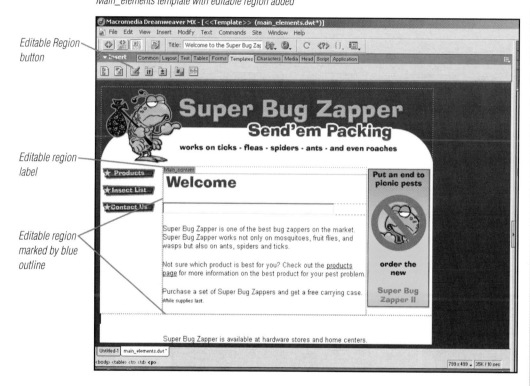

1. Click the Welcome heading in the document window to select it, press and hold [Shift], then click to the right of While supplies last at the bottom of the cell to select all of the content in that cell.

2. Click the Editable Region button on the Templates tab of the Insert bar to open the New Editable Region dialog box.

    TIP You can also press [Ctrl][Alt][V] (Win) or [command][alt][V] (Mac) to open the New Editable Region dialog box.

3. Type **Main_content** in the Name text box, click OK, click anywhere to deselect the text, then compare your screen to Figure K-5.

    The text Main_content appears in a blue shaded box above the Welcome heading.

4. Save your changes.

    TIP To remove an editable region from a template, select the editable region in the document window, click Modify on the menu bar, point to Templates, then click Remove Template Markup.

You created an editable region in the main_elements template.

Create an optional region

1. Select the orange rectangle that contains the bug image, press [←] to place the insertion point to the left of the orange rectangle, then press [Enter] (Win) or [return] (Mac).

   There is now space above the graphic where you can type text for an ad.

2. Press [↑] to move the insertion point to the blank line at the top of the cell, then type **On sale! Buy one Level 2 can, get one free!**.

3. Format the text in Arial, Helvetica, sans-serif, size 3, centered, bold, orange (#FF9900).

4. Select the text you typed in Step 2 (if necessary), then click the Optional Region button on the Templates tab of the Insert bar to open the New Optional Region dialog box.

5. Make sure the Basic tab is displayed, type **sale** in the Name text box, verify that Show by Default is checked, compare your screen to Figure K-6, then click OK.

   A blue shaded box containing the If sale text now appears above the ad text, as shown in Figure K-7.

6. Save your changes.

You added and formatted text to create an ad in the main_elements template. You then defined this ad as a new optional region named sale, so that users of the template can choose whether to show or hide this element.

FIGURE K-6
New Optional Region dialog box with settings for sale optional region

Name of new optional region

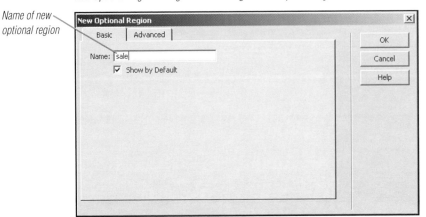

FIGURE K-7
Main_elements template with new optional region added

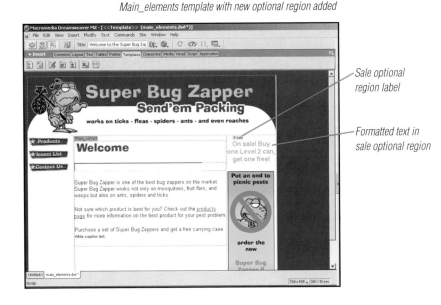

Sale optional region label

Formatted text in sale optional region

FIGURE K-8

Main_elements template with new editable optional region added

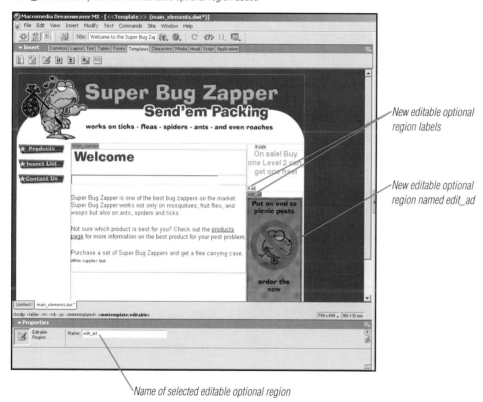

New editable optional region labels

New editable optional region named edit_ad

Name of selected editable optional region

1. Select the orange rectangle that contains the bug graphic.

2. Click the Editable Optional Region button on the Templates tab of the Insert bar to open the New Optional Region dialog box.

3. Type **ad** in the Name text box, then click OK.

   Two blue shaded boxes with the text If ad and EditRegion4 appear above the orange rectangle.

   > TIP If the blue shaded labels are not positioned above the orange rectangle, but are located either beside or below it, then the orange rectangle is probably positioned outside the editable region. If so, drag the orange rectangle into the blue outline of the editable region.

4. Click the blue shaded box containing the text EditRegion4, use the Property inspector to change its name to **edit_ad,** press [Enter](Win) or [return] (Mac), then compare your screen to Figure K-8.

5. Save your work.

You specified that the orange rectangle be an editable optional region in the main_elements template.

ENHANCE AND NEST TEMPLATES

What You'll Do

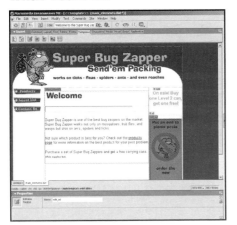

In this lesson, you will specify that the sale optional region appear when the ad region is not showing. You will then create another template that is nested in the main_elements template, and insert a repeating table in it. You will define the cell background color in the table as an editable attribute. Finally, you will insert an image in the template and specify that its Source property be editable.

Setting Parameters for Optional Regions

If your template will be used by many people, it might be a good idea to include several optional regions in it so that users of the template can pick and choose from a wide range of content elements. You might also want to set parameters for optional regions, specifying that they are displayed or hidden based on specific conditions. For instance, let's say you have two optional regions named red and blue, respectively. You could set the blue optional region parameter to red so that the blue optional region would appear only when the red optional region is showing, and would be hidden only when the red optional region is hidden. Use the Advanced Settings tab of the New Optional Region dialog box to set the parameters of an optional region. You can also use the Advanced Settings tab to write a conditional expression based on JavaScript. For instance, you could write the expression *red == false* to specify that the blue optional region appear only when the red

optional region is hidden, as shown in Figure K-9.

Nesting Templates

If you are working on a complex Web site that has many different pages used by different people or departments, you might need to create **nested templates**, which are templates that are based on another template. Nested templates are helpful when you want to define a page or parts of a page in greater detail. An advantage of using nested templates is that any changes made to the original template can be automatically updated in the nested template.

To create a nested template, create a new page based on the original template, then use the Save As Template command to save the page as a nested template. You can then make changes to the nested template by adding or deleting content and defining new editable regions. Note that editable regions in the original template are passed on as editable regions to the nested template. However, if you add a new editable or optional region to an editable region that was passed on from the original template, the original editable region changes to a locked region in the nested template.

Creating Repeating Regions and Repeating Tables

Many Web sites contain elements whose format is repeated over and over again. For instance, a site that sells products uses the same format to list catalog items. In a template, you can define these areas as **repeating regions**, and you can define the areas within these regions as either locked or editable. You can also insert repeating tables in a template. A **repeating table** is a table in a template that has a pre-defined structure, making it very easy for template users to add content. To add a repeating table, set the insertion point where you want the table to be placed, then use the Repeating Table button on the Templates tab of the Insert bar, as shown in Figure K-10. This opens the Insert Repeating Table dialog box, which allows you to set the number of rows and columns, and other properties for the table, and also specify the number of editable rows the table will have. When a user creates a page based on a template containing a repeating table, the top row will be locked, and the rows below will be editable.

FIGURE K-9
Advanced tab of New Optional Region dialog box

FIGURE K-10
Templates tab of the Insert bar

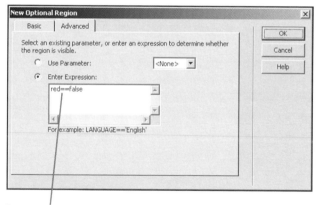

Expression specifies to show current optional region when red optional region is not showing

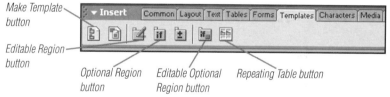

Make Template button

Editable Region button

Optional Region button

Editable Optional Region button

Repeating Table button

Creating Editable Attributes

There might be times when you want users of your template to be able to change certain attributes of an element in a locked region. For instance, perhaps you want to give users the ability to change the cell background color of the top row in a repeating table, or change the source file for an image in a locked area of the template. You can use the Editable Tag Attributes dialog box, shown in Figure K-11, to specify that certain attributes of locked regions be editable. To do this, choose an attribute of a selected element, specify to make it editable, assign it a label, and specify its type and its default setting. When you define editable attributes of elements in locked regions, template users can make changes to the element's attributes using the Template Properties dialog box.

FIGURE K-11
Editable Tag Attributes dialog box

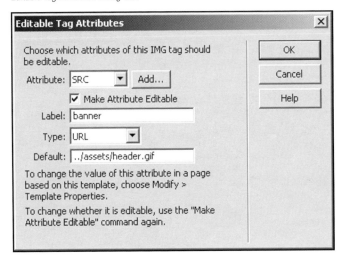

Advanced tab of the New Optional Region dialog box with expression entered

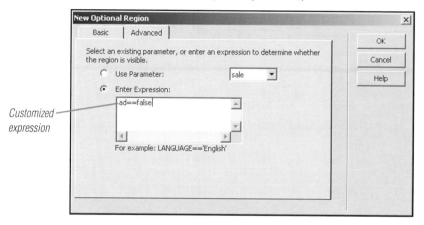

Customized
expression

Adjust advanced settings

1. Click the If sale optional region label above the text On sale! Buy one Level 2 can, get one free!

   Clicking the label selects the sale optional region.

2. Click Edit in the Property inspector to open the New Optional Region dialog box, then click the Advanced tab.

3. Click the Enter Expression radio button, select sale in the Enter Expression text box, then press [Delete].

4. Type **ad==false** in the Enter Expression text box, then compare your screen to Figure K-12.

   This expression specifies that the sale optional region will be shown only if the ad optional region (the orange rectangle) is not showing.

5. Click OK, then compare your screen to Figure K-13.

   The expression that you wrote now appears above the sale optional region.

6. Save your changes.

You used the Advanced tab of the New Optional Region dialog box to write an expression that specifies the sale optional region be shown if the ad region is not showing.

FIGURE K-13

Main_elements template with expression added to optional region

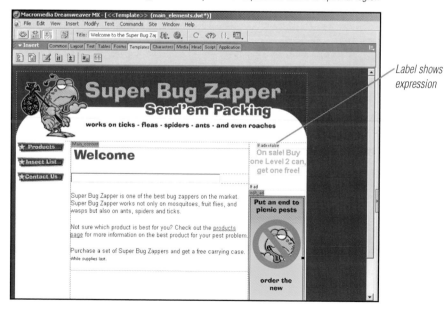

Label shows
expression

Nest a template in another template

1. Click File on the menu bar, then click New to open the New Document dialog box.

2. Click the Templates tab, click Site "Super Bug Zapper" in the Templates For column, click main_elements in the middle column, compare your screen to Figure K-14, then click Create.

3. Click File on the menu bar, then click Save as Template to open the Save As Template dialog box.

   A dialog box might open, warning that users of this template will not be able to create new paragraphs in this region.

4. Click OK (if necessary) to close the dialog box and open the Save As Template dialog box, type **product_info** in the Save As text box, then click Save.

   The product_info file now appears in the Assets panel.

   You created a new page based on the main_elements template, then saved it as a template named product_info.

Insert a repeating table

1. Click below the last line of paragraph text in the Main_content editable region, then click the Repeating Table button on the Templates tab of the Insert bar.

   The Insert Repeating Table dialog box opens.

   (continued)

Creating and Using Templates

FIGURE K-14
New from Template dialog box

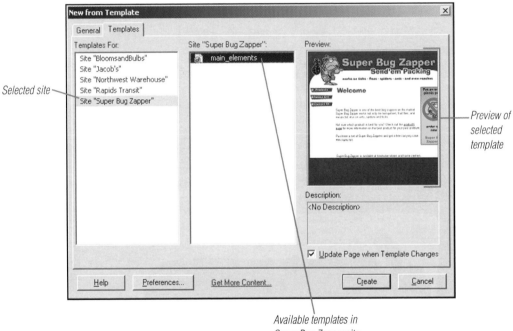

Selected site

Preview of selected template

Available templates in Super Bug Zapper site

FIGURE K-15
Insert Repeating Table dialog box

Insert Repeating Table ×

Rows: `2`	Cell Padding: `0`
Columns: `3`	Cell Spacing: `0`
Width: `100` `Percent ▼`	
Border: `2`	

Repeat rows of the table:

Starting Row: `2`	Ending Row: `2`

Region Name: `compare`

OK
Cancel
Help

FIGURE K-16
Repeating table object with formatted text added

Repeating Table button

Repeating table

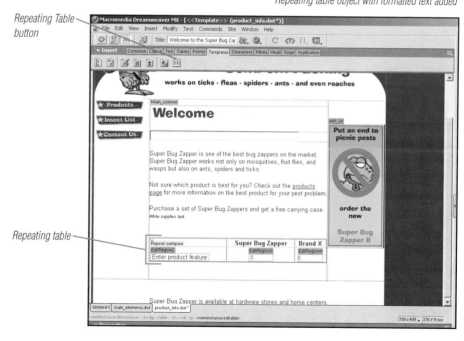

2. Type **2** in the Rows text box, type **3** in the Columns text box, set Width at **100 Percent**, set Border to **2**, type **2** in the Starting Row text box, type **2** in the Ending Row text box, type **compare** in the Region Name text box, compare your screen to Figure K-15, then click OK.

   The table is added below the paragraph text. Notice that the Main_content editable region label is now yellow, indicating that this region is now locked.

3. Type **Feature** in the first cell in the first row, type **Super Bug Zapper** in the second cell of the first row, type **Brand X** in the third cell in the third row.

   > TIP You won't be able to see the word "Feature" as you type it in the first cell because the Repeat: compare blue shaded box obscures it.

4. Click in the EditRegion2 box, type **Enter product feature**, click in the EditRegion3 box, type **X**, click in the EditRegion4 box, then type **X**.

5. Format all text in the table in Arial, Helvetica, sans-serif, size 2.

   > TIP To format text in an editable region, you must select the table cell.

6. Apply bold formatting to the text in the top row of the table, center-align the text in the second and third columns, then compare your screen to Figure K-16.

You inserted a repeating table in the Main_content editable region in the product_info template. You then entered column headings and placeholder text in the table and formatted the text.

Modify a template

1. Select the Welcome heading, the text field, form field, and paragraph text in the cell that contains the repeating table, then press [Delete].

2. Select the repeating table, press [←] to set the insertion point to the left of the table, then insert a new editable region named **product_content**.

   A new editable region appears.

3. Delete the text "product content" that appears in the new editable region, click Insert on the menu bar, then click Table to open the Insert Table dialog box.

4. Set Rows to **1**, Columns to **2**, Border to **0**, Cell Padding to **0**, Width to **100 Percent**, then click OK.

5. Insert the file can_yellow.gif from the assets folder of the Web site in the first cell in the table, then center-align it.

6. Type **Insert product text** in the second cell of the table, then format the text in Arial, Helvetica, sans-serif, size 3, left-aligned.

7. Drag the middle border of the table so that the two cells are the same size, then compare your screen to Figure K-17.

8. Save your changes.

   TIP   If a dialog box opens telling you that you have inserted a repeating region inside a <P> tag, click OK to close the dialog box.

You deleted content from the product_info template, then added a new editable region to it. You then inserted a table in the editable region, and added placeholder content in the table.

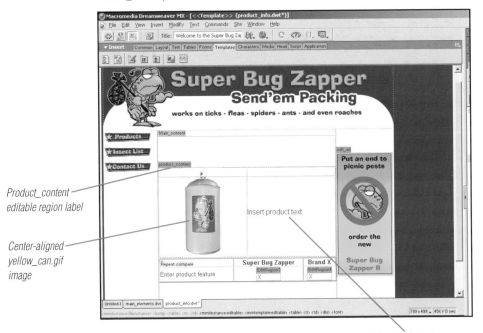

Product_content
editable region label

Center-aligned
yellow_can.gif
image

Placeholder text

FIGURE K-18

Editable Tag Attributes dialog box with settings for Color attribute

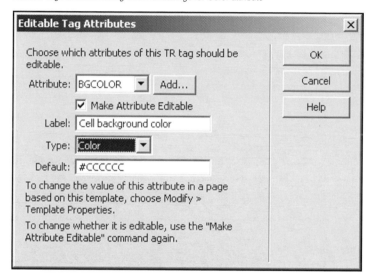

Create editable attributes for color

1. Select the three cells in the top row of the repeating table.

2. Click the Background Color button in the Property inspector to open the color picker, then click the light gray color box (#CCCCCC).

3. Click Modify on the menu bar, point to Templates, then click Make Attribute Editable to open the Editable Tag Attributes dialog box.

4. Verify that BGCOLOR is selected in the Attribute list box, then click the Make Attribute Editable checkbox.

5. Type **Cell background color** in the Label text box, click the Type list arrow, then click Color.

   The Default color is automatically set to #CCCCCC, the color that is currently applied.

6. Compare your screen to Figure K-18, then click OK.

   Notice that the top row of the table is now white, instead of gray. It changed to white because the color of these cells is now an editable attribute.

7. Save your changes, then close the product_info template.

   TIP If a dialog box opens telling you that you have inserted a repeating region inside a <P> tag, click OK to close the dialog box.

You specified that the color attribute of the top row of the repeating table be editable, so that users of the template can change the color.

Create editable attributes for a URL

1. Open the main_elements template (if necessary).

2. Click just below the Contact Us navigation button on the left side of the page to set the insertion point, then insert the image side_ad_1.gif from the unit_k assets folder.

   TIP If a dialog box opens, informing you that the image file is outside the root folder, be sure to specify to save the file to the assets folder of the Web site.

3. Select the side_ad_1.gif graphic (if necessary), click Modify on the menu bar, point to Templates, then click Make Attribute Editable to open the Editable Tag Attributes dialog box.

   SRC appears in the Attribute text box.

4. Click the Make Attribute Editable checkbox to make SRC an editable attribute, type **left side ads** in the Label text box, click the Type list arrow, click URL, compare your screen to Figure K-19, then click OK.

   The side_ad_1.gif image is now replaced with a gray box placeholder, as shown in Figure K-20. This happens because you made the source file an editable attribute.

5. Do not save your changes.

You inserted an image in a locked region of the main_elements template. You then made the image's SRC attribute editable, so that template users will be able to specify that a different image file appear.

FIGURE K-19
Editable Tag Attributes dialog box with settings for URL attribute

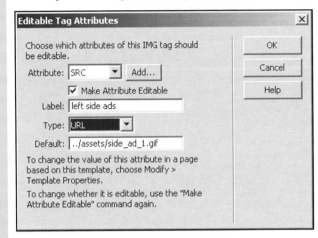

FIGURE K-20
Main_elements template after making URL attribute editable

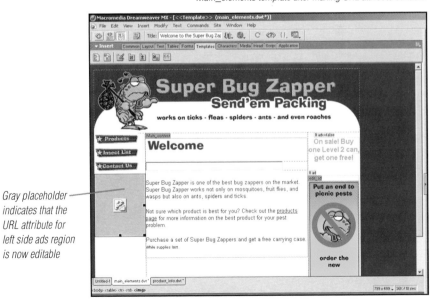

Gray placeholder indicates that the URL attribute for left side ads region is now editable

Creating and Using Templates

FIGURE K-21

Update Template Files dialog box

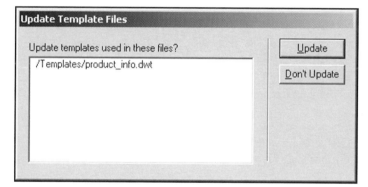

1. Click File on the menu bar, then click Save to open the Update Template Files dialog box, as shown in Figure K-21.

2. Click Update to open the Update Pages dialog box.

   The Status area indicates that one file was examined and one file was updated.

3. Click Close to close the Update Pages dialog box.

   You don't need to update any pages because at this point, no pages in the site are based on the main_elements template.

4. Open the product_info template.

   Notice that the sale_ad_1.gif image now appears below the Contact Us button, indicating that the changes you made to the main_elements template were updated in this template.

You saved the main_elements template and then updated the product_info template to incorporate the saved changes.

USE TEMPLATES TO CREATE PAGES

What You'll Do

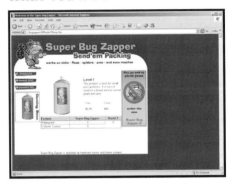

 In this lesson, you will use the product_info template to create a new page in the Super Bug Zapper Web site. You will add content to the editable regions on your new page and use the Template properties dialog box to make changes to selected objects. You will add content to a repeated table and change the cell background color of the top row in the table. You will also insert a link on the page. Finally, you will apply the main_ elements template to the contact_us page.

Creating Pages with Templates

There are huge advantages to using a template to create a page. First, it saves a lot of time, because part of the content and format of your page is already set. Second, it ensures that the page you create matches the look and format of other pages in the site. You can create a page based on a template using many different methods. One way is to click File on the menu bar, click New to open the New Document dialog box, click the Templates tab, select the template you want to use, then click Create.

> **QUICKTIP**
>
> You can also create a new page based on a template by right-clicking (Win) or control-clicking (Mac) a template in the Assets panel, then clicking New from Template.

Modifying Editable Regions

When you create a new page that is based on a template, certain areas of the new page will be locked. You can tell which areas are locked by the appearance of the mouse pointer. When positioned over a locked region, the mouse pointer will appear in the shape of a circle with a line cutting through it, as shown in Figure K-22. Editable regions are outlined in blue and marked with a blue shaded label.

Editing, deleting, or adding content in editable regions of a template-based page works just like it does on any other page. Simply select the element you want to modify and make your changes, or click in the editable region and insert the new content.

Modifying Object Attributes

Sometimes a template author might apply editable attributes for some elements in locked regions to allow template users to make certain modifications to them. If you want to make changes to editable attributes, you need to use the Template Properties dialog box. Figure K-23 shows the Template Properties dialog box with all the editable attributes for the page listed and the banner property selected. The banner's source attribute is editable. To change the source file of the banner to a different file, you would type the URL for the graphic you want in the banner text box.

Using Repeating Tables

Making changes to a repeating table in a template-based document is easier than creating a table from scratch, because a repeating table contains an already-defined structure. To add content to the table, simply click in the blue outlined areas of a table cell, then type text or insert graphics.

QUICKTIP

Use the buttons in the top row of a repeating table to add or delete rows, or to move a row up or down in the table.

Creating Links in Template-Based Pages

When you add a link to a page that is based on a template, it is important to use document relative links. If you use links that are not document relative, they will not work.

FIGURE K-22
Working with a template-based page

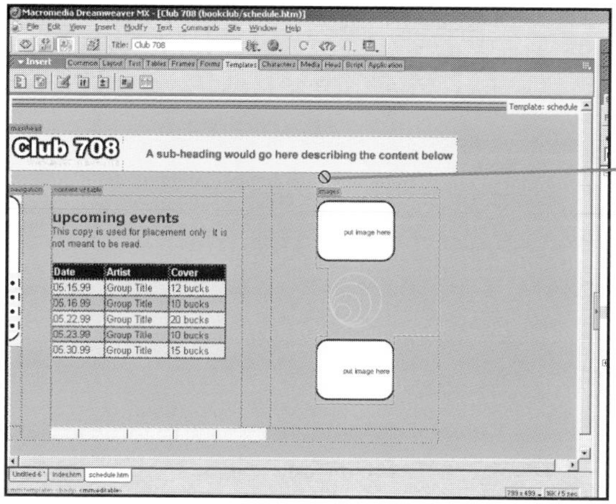

FIGURE K-23
Template Properties dialog box

Selected property

Mouse pointer positioned over a locked region

Type a different URL here to change the source file of the banner property

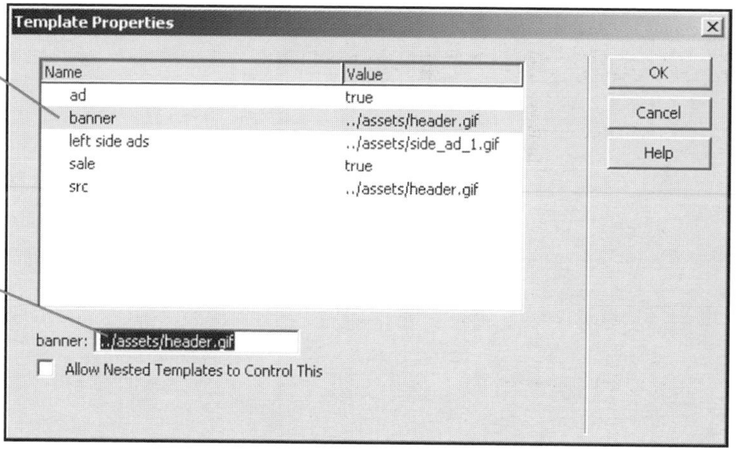

The path to a link actually goes from the template file (not from the template-based page) to the linked page. To ensure that all of your links are document relative, select the page element to which you want to add a link, then drag the Point to File icon from the Property inspector to the page you want to link to in the Site panel, as shown in Figure K-24.

Attaching a Template to an Existing Page

Sometimes you might need to apply a template to a page that you have already created. For example, suppose you create a page for your department in your company's Web site, then your manager tells you that it must be based on the template created by the marketing department. Before you attach a template to an existing page, you should delete any elements from your page that also appear in the template. For instance, if both your page and the template have a company logo, you should delete the logo on your page. If you don't delete it, the logo will appear twice. Once you delete all the duplicate content on your page, attach the template by opening your page, selecting the template in the Assets panel, and clicking Apply in the Assets panel. When you do this, the Inconsistent Region Names dialog box opens, allowing you to specify in which regions of the template to place the document head and body content from your page.

QUICKTIP

You can also attach a template to an open page by dragging the template from the Assets panel to the document window.

FIGURE K-24

Using the Point to File icon to specify a document-relative link

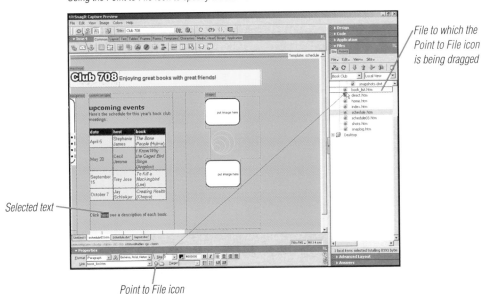

File to which the Point to File icon is being dragged

Selected text

Point to File icon

FIGURE K-25

New from Template dialog box

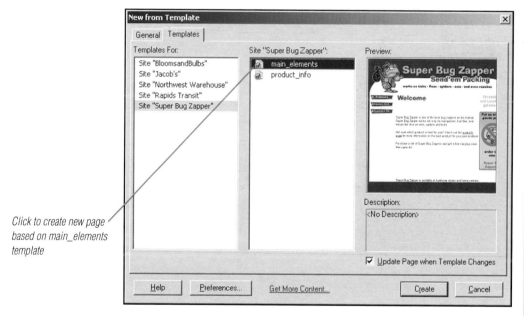

Click to create new page based on main_elements template

1. Click File on the menu bar, click New, then click the Templates tab (if necessary) to open the New from Template dialog box.

2. Click Site "Super Bug Zapper" in the Templates For list box, click main_elements in the Site "Super Bug Zapper" list box (if necessary), compare your screen to Figure K-25, then click Create.

   A new untitled page opens with the main_elements template applied to it.

3. Click File on the menu bar, click Save As to open the Save As dialog box, type **index.htm** in the File Name text box, then click Save.

   A dialog box opens, asking if you want to overwrite the existing index.htm file.

4. Click Yes (Win) or Replace (Mac).

   The index page contains the exact content of the old index page, but it is now based on the main_elements template.

   > TIP   Another way to create a new page based on a template is to open a new untitled page, click the Make Template button on the Templates tab of the Insert bar to open the Save As Template dialog box, select a template from the list, then click OK.

5. Close the index page.

You created a new page in the Super Bug Zapper Web site that has the main_elements template applied to it. You then saved this page as index.htm, overwriting the existing index page.

Modify editable regions in a template

1. Open a new, untitled page that is based on the main_elements template.

2. Delete the text field and form field and all the paragraph text below the Welcome heading.

   TIP To delete the text field and form field, right-click (Win) or control-click (Mac) each item, then click Remove Tag.

3. Open the insects page, select the sentence Super Bug Zapper works on the following insects: and the four-column table below it, use the Copy command to copy the selection, then close the insects page.

   TIP Do not select the orange layer that is positioned on top of the table.

4. Return to the untitled page, click below the Welcome heading to set the insertion point, then paste the content you copied from the insects page.

5. Save the file as insects.htm, replacing the original insects page.

6. Select the Welcome heading, then change the SRC property in the Property inspector to the insects_head.gif file in the assets folder of the Web site.

7. Save your changes, then compare your screen to Figure K-26.

You deleted content from the editable region of an untitled page based on the main_elements template. You then pasted content from the insects page to the editable region of the untitled page, and saved the untitled page as insects.htm.

FIGURE K-26

New insects page with main_elements template applied

Editable region labels indicate page is based on a template

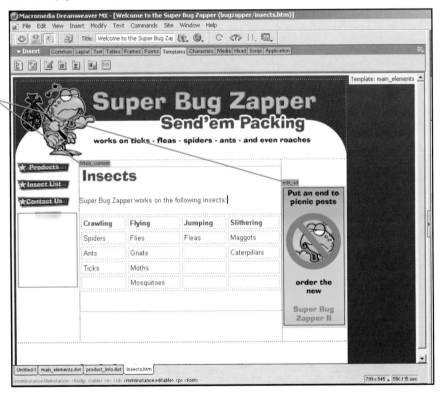

Template Properties dialog box with ad value set to false

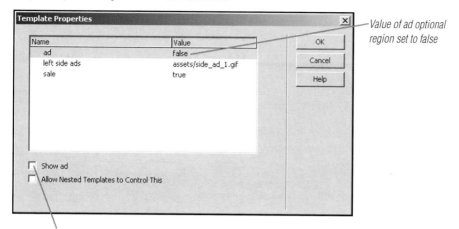

Value of ad optional
region set to false

Check mark removed to
change value of ad
optional region to false

Modify object attributes

1. Click Modify on the menu bar, then click Template Properties to open the Template Properties dialog box.

2. Click ad in the Name list, click the Show ad checkbox to remove the check mark, then compare your screen to Figure K-27.

   The value of the ad property changes to false.

3. Click OK, then compare your screen to Figure K-28.

   The orange ad no longer appears on the page, and the text contained in the sale optional region now appears.

4. Save your changes, then close the insects page.

You used the Template Properties dialog box to change the ad property to a value of false so that the ad is now hidden and the sale optional region appears.

FIGURE K-28
Insects page with value of ad optional region set to false

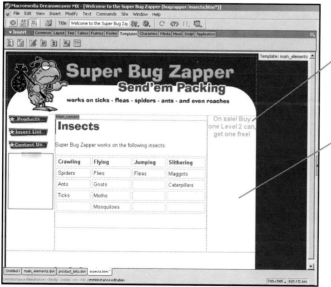

Sale optional region
appears because
expression specifies
to show it when ad
value is set to false

Ad optional region
does not appear
because ad value
is set to false

Add links to template-based pages

1. Create a new page based on the product_info template, then save the page as product_level_1.htm.

2. Open the products page, then use the Copy command to copy all the content in the cell to the right of the yellow can image.

3. Click in the cell below $5.99, type **Click here for more information.**, select the text you just typed, then drag the Point to File icon next to the Link text box in the Property inspector to the product_level_1.htm file in the Site panel.

4. Switch to the product_level_1.htm page, select the text Insert product text in the cell next to the yellow can, paste the content you copied from the products page, then drag the right border of the cell containing the yellow spray can (if necessary) so that both columns are roughly the same width.

5. Select the orange rectangle containing the ad for Super Bug Zapper II, then drag the Point to File icon next to the Link text box in the Property inspector to the contact_us.htm page in the Site panel, as shown in Figure K-29.

6. Save your changes, preview both pages in your browser, test both links you added, then close your browser.

You created a new page called product_level_1.htm based on the product_info template. You then made changes to the editable region of the product_level_1.htm page by pasting content in it from the products page. Finally, you added a link from the orange Super Bug Zapper II ad to the contact_us page using the Point to File icon.

FIGURE K-29

Dragging the Point to File icon to the contact_us page in the Site panel

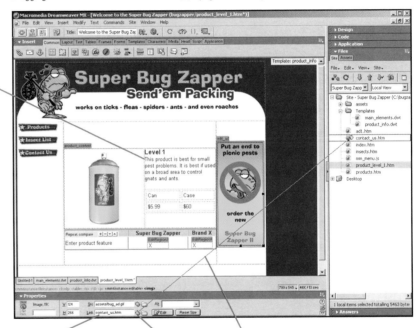

Pasted text from products page

Link text box containing link to contact_us page   *Point to File icon*   *Path of dragged Point to File icon*

FIGURE K-30

Template Properties dialog box with changes made to Cell background color

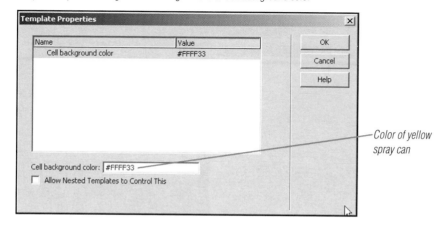

— *Color of yellow spray can*

FIGURE K-31

Product_level_1.htm page with changes made to table

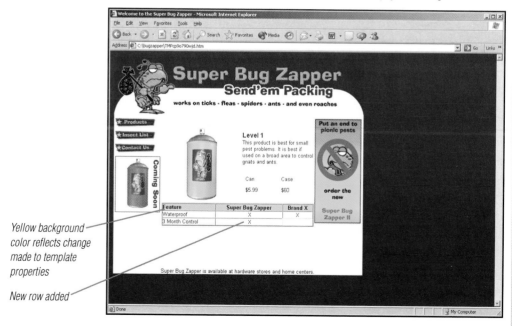

Yellow background color reflects change made to template properties

New row added

1. Return to the product_level_1 page (if necessary), select Enter product feature in the first cell of the second row of the repeating table at the bottom of the page, then type **Waterproof**.

2. Click the Plus button in the top row of the table to add a new row, type **3 Month Control** in the first cell in the third row, then delete the X in the third cell of the third row. ⊞

3. Click Modify on the menu bar, then click Template Properties to open the Template Properties dialog box.

4. Click Cell background color in the list, change the Cell background color to **#FFFF33**, compare your screen to Figure K-30, then click OK.

   The cells in the top row of the table now have a yellow background.

5. Save your changes, preview the page in your browser, compare your screen to Figure K-31, close your browser, then close the product_level_1 page.

You added text and a new row to the repeating table. You also used the Template Properties dialog box to change the cell background color of the top row of the table to yellow.

Attach a template to an existing page

1. Open the contact_us page.

2. Delete the banner at the top of the page, delete the Products, Insect List, and Contact Us navigation buttons, then delete the orange rectangle containing the ad for the Super Bug Zapper II.

   All the content that is also contained in the main_elements template is removed. Doing this ensures that these elements will not appear twice when you apply the template.

3. Delete the top and bottom rows of the table, merge the three remaining table cells together, then set the width of the table to **392** pixels.

   > TIP   To delete a row in a table, click in the row you want to delete, click Modify on the menu bar, point to Table, then click Delete Row.

4. Delete any line spaces above the Contact Us heading (if necessary), then compare your screen to Figure K-32.

5. Open the Assets panel, click the Templates button, select main_elements, then click Apply to open the Inconsistent Region Names dialog box, as shown in Figure K-33.

   > TIP   You can also apply a template to a page by dragging the template from the Assets panel to the page in the document window.

   This dialog box shows a list of items on the contact_us page that have no corresponding regions in the main_elements template. You need to specify in which editable region of the template to place each item.

   (continued)

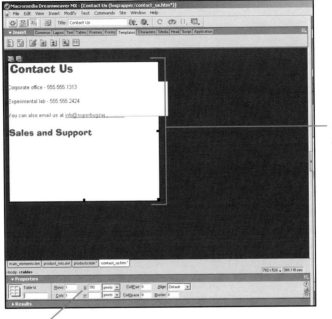

Remaining page elements after removing shared template elements

Table width set to 392 pixels

FIGURE K-33
Inconsistent Region Names dialog box

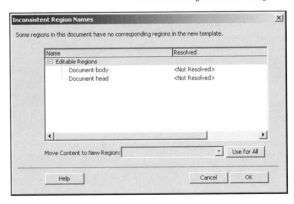

FIGURE K-34

Contact_us page with main_elements template applied

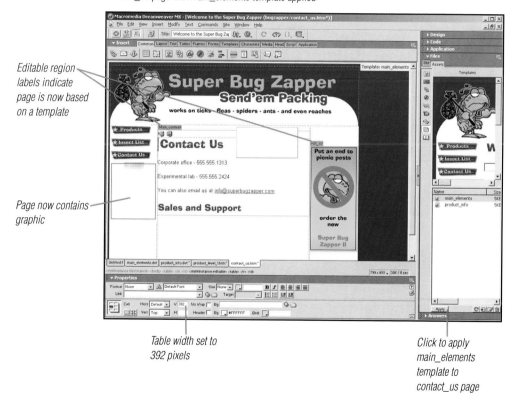

Editable region labels indicate page is now based on a template

Page now contains graphic

Table width set to 392 pixels

Click to apply main_elements template to contact_us page

6. Select Document body, click the Move Content to New Region list arrow, then click Main_content.

7. Click Document head, click the Move Content to New Region list arrow, then click Nowhere.

   Because you clicked Nowhere for the Document head content, Dreamweaver will delete this content.

8. Click OK, compare your screen to Figure K-34, then save your changes.

9. Following the same process you used in Steps 1 through 8, attach the main_elements template to the products.htm page, save your changes, then close the contact_us page and the products page.

You opened the contact_us page and deleted page elements that are shared by the main_elements template. You then applied the main_elements template to the contact_us page, and used the Inconsistent Region Names dialog box to specify to place the document body in the Main_content editable region of the template. You then used the same process to apply the main_elements template to the products page.

USE TEMPLATES TO UPDATE A SITE

What You'll Do

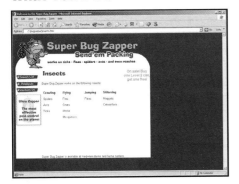

In this lesson, you will make a change to the main_elements template, then update the site so that all pages and linked templates reflect the change.

Making Changes to a Template

If you create a successful site that draws large numbers of faithful viewers, your site will probably enjoy a long life. However, like everything else, Web sites need to change with the times. Your company might decide to make new products or offer new services. It might get purchased in a leveraged buy-out by a multi-million dollar conglomerate. When changes occur in your company, on a large or small scale, you will need to make changes to your Web site's appearance and functionality. If your Web site pages are based on a template or group of templates, you will have a much easier time making those changes.

You use the same skills to make changes to a template as you would when creating a template. Start by opening the template from the Site panel or Assets panel, then

Using Macromedia templates

If you are a licensed Dreamweaver user, you can take advantage of the large collection of beautiful templates that Macromedia creates for the exclusive use of its customers. The wide-ranging templates are a great starting point for many different types of Web sites—from weddings, to clubs, to professions, and even special events. To preview and download the templates, go to *www.macromedia.com/software/ dreamweaver/download/templates/*.

Creating and Using Templates

add, delete, or edit content as you would on any non-template-based page. You can turn locked regions into editable regions using the New Editable Region command. To change an editable region back into a locked region, select the region, right-click, then click Remove Tag <mmtemplate:editable>.

Updating All Pages Based on a Template

One of the greatest benefits of working with templates is that any change you make to a template can be made automatically to all nested templates and pages that are based on the template. When you save a template that you have made modifications to, the Update Template Files dialog box opens, asking if you want to update all the files in your site that are based on that template, as shown in Figure K-35. When you click Update, the Update Pages dialog box opens and provides a summary of all the files that were updated.

FIGURE K-35
Update Template Files dialog box

Files based on the main_elements template

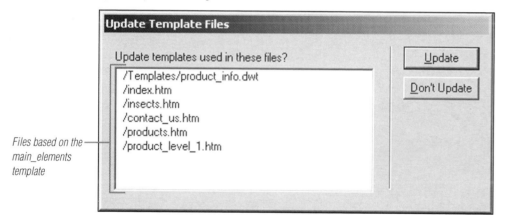

Make changes to a template

1. Switch to the main_elements template.

2. Drag the Products navigation button on the left side of the page so that it is positioned between the Insect List button and the Contact Us button, as shown in Figure K-36.

3. Open the insects page.

   The Products navigation button is located in its original position, above the other two buttons. The change you made to the template was not made on this page because you have not yet saved the template or updated the site.

4. Close the insects page.

You opened the main_elements template and moved the Products navigation button to a new location.

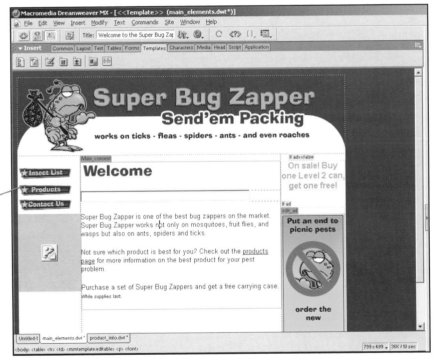

Products navigation button moved between other two buttons

FIGURE K-37

Update Pages dialog box listing files that were updated in Super Bug Zapper Web site

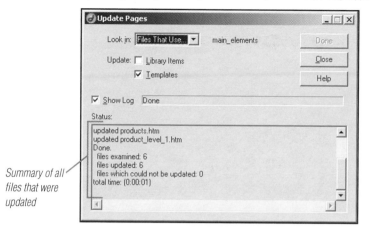

Summary of all files that were updated

FIGURE K-38

Insects page with template changes incorporated

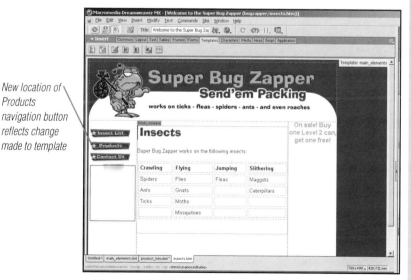

New location of Products navigation button reflects change made to template

1. Return to the main_elements template (if necessary), Click File on the menu bar, then click Save.

   The Update Template Files dialog box opens.

2. Click Update to open the Update Pages dialog box, shown in Figure K-37.

   The Status area shows that six files were examined and six files were updated.

3. Click Close.

4. Open the insects page, then compare your screen to Figure K-38.

   The Products navigation button is positioned between the other two navigation buttons, reflecting the change in the template.

5. Close the insects page, the main_elements template, and all other open pages.

You saved the main_elements template and used the Update Template Files dialog box and the Update Pages dialog box to specify that all pages in the site be updated to reflect the template modifications.

Create templates with editable and optional regions.

1. Open the Blooms & Bulbs Web site that you created and developed in Units A through J, then open the master_gardener page. (If you did not create this Web site in Units A through J, contact your instructor for assistance.)

2. Save the master_gardener page as a template called **master_gardener.dwt**.

3. Select the heading Ask our Master Gardener and all the content below it, down to and including Southern Living (do not select the Flash text), then define this selected area as an editable region named **master_content**.

4. Click to the left of the "Top of Page" Flash text to set the insertion point, then insert a table that has one row and two columns, no borders, no cell padding, and a Width set to **100 Percent**.

5. Insert an optional region in the first cell of the table named **master_tip**. Delete the text master_tip from the table cell.

6. Insert the graphic file master_gardening_tip.gif from the unit_k assets folder in the master_tip optional region, then drag the right border of the first table cell over to the right edge of the graphic.

Enhance and nest templates.

1. Insert an editable optional region in the second cell of the table named **tips**. Use the

Advanced tab of the New Optional Region dialog box to use the master_tip parameter.

2. Use the Property inspector to change the name of the new editable region to **edit_tip**.

3. Type **It is best not to water in the evening.** in the edit_tip editable region, then format this text in Arial, Helvetica, sans-serif, size 3.

4. Save your changes.

5. Create a new page based on the master_gardener template, then save the new untitled page as a template named **product_listing.dwt**.

6. Select the heading Ask our Master Gardener, then type **Available Products**.

7. Delete all of the content below the Available Products heading in the master_content editable region.

8. Insert a repeating table named **product_list** below the Available Products heading that has two rows and two columns, Border set to **1**, Width set to **100 Percent**, Cell Padding and Cell Spacing set to **0**, and Starting Row and Ending Row set to **2**.

9. Center-align the table, type **Product Name** in the first cell of the first row, type **Price** in the second cell of the first row, type **Enter product name here** in the first cell of the second row, then type **Enter price here** in the second cell of the second row.

10. Format all of the text in the table in Arial, Helvetica, sans-serif, size 3, center-aligned. Apply bold formatting to the text in the top row.

11. Set the background color for the top row of the table to **#CCFF99**, then make the cell background color for the top row of the table an editable attribute. Specify the label as **Cell background color**, and set Type to **Color**.

12. Insert a new optional region below the Available Products heading named **image**. Delete the text image from the image optional region. Insert the flower.gif image from the assets folder of the Web site in the image optional region, then center-align it.

13. Make the SRC attribute for flower.gif an editable attribute. Specify the label as **Flower picture** and set Type to **URL**.

14. Save your changes.

Use templates to create pages.

1. Create a new page in the Blooms & Bulbs Web site that is based on the master_gardener template.

2. Delete the Ask Our Master Gardener heading and the photograph below it in the master_content editable region.

3. Open the tips page, use the Copy command to copy all content below the Planting Tips heading, then close the tips page.

4. Open the untitled page, select all of the content below the Ask Our Experts heading, then paste the content you copied from the tips page.

5. Save the page as **tips.htm**, overwriting the existing tips page.

6. Change the SRC property of the Ask Our Experts heading to the planting_tips.jpg file in the assets folder of the Web site, remove any blank lines above the Planting Tips heading (if necessary), then save your changes.

7. Create a new page based on the product_listing template, then save the page as **product_list.htm**.

8. Use the Template Properties dialog box to change the SRC attribute of the flower picture in the image optional region to **/assets/yellow_rose.jpg**.

9. Insert a link from the tip text It is best not to water in the evening. to the tips page.

10. Replace the placeholder text in the second row of the table with **Leather Work Gloves**

in the Product Name column and **$24.99** in the Price column, then add a new row that contains **Shovel** in the Product Name column and **$19.99** in the Price column.

11. Change the background cell color of the top row of the table to **#66CC33**, save your changes, preview the page in your browser, compare your screen to Figure K-39, then close the product_list page.

12. Open the plants page, delete the Blooms & Bulbs banner and the navigation buttons, then apply the master_gardener template to the page. Specify to move the Document body content to the master_content editable region, and the Document head content to Nowhere. Delete any extra blank lines and

rearrange layers as needed to make the page look attractive. Save your changes, preview the page in your browser, then compare your screen to Figure K-40.

Use templates to update a site.

1. Open the master_gardener template, then select the table at the bottom of the page in the master_tip editable region.

2. Change the Cell Padding property to **10**, save the template, then update all files and templates in the site.

3. Save your changes, preview all pages in your browser, close the browser, then close all open pages.

FIGURE K-39
Completed Skills Review: product_list page

FIGURE K-40
Completed Skills Review: plants page

In this Project Builder, you will use templates to enhance the Rapids Transit Web site that you began in Project Builder 1 in Unit A.

1. Open the Rapids Transit Web site that you created in Units A through J, open the home page, then save it as a template named **rapids_info.dwt**.
2. Delete the fishing, wildlife, and falls layers.
3. Insert a table above the paragraph text that has two rows, two columns, no borders, Cell Padding set to **5**, Cell Spacing set to **0**, and Width set to **100 Percent**.
4. Merge the two cells in the second column.
5. Set the vertical alignment of the first cell in the first row to Top.
6. Insert an editable region in the first cell of the table named **title**, then type **Welcome** into this editable region. Format the Welcome text using a font, size, and color that is appropriate for the design of the page.
7. Insert an editable region in the cell below the title editable region named **side_image**, then insert the buffalo_fall.gif file from the assets folder of the Web site in this new editable region. Drag the right border of the cell containing the photo to the right edge of the photo.
8. Set the vertical alignment to **Top** for the cell on the right side of the table, then insert an editable region named main_content into it.

9. Move the paragraph text at the bottom of the page into the main_content editable region.
10. Select the Rapids Transit address, phone number, and e-mail link, then define this selected content as an optional region named **contact_info**.
11. Save your changes, preview the template in a browser, compare your screen to Figure K-41, then close your browser.
12. Open a new page based on the rapids_info template, then save it as **index.htm**, over-writing the existing page.
13. Open the store page, delete all elements on this page that are common to the rapids_info template, delete the photo of the fruit basket, then merge all of the cells of the table together and remove any extra line spacing.

14. Apply the rapids_info template to the store page. Specify to move the Document body content to the main_content editable region.
15. Change the SRC property of the side_image to fruit_basket.jpg located in the assets folder of the Web site, then replace the Welcome heading with **Country Store**. Use the Template Properties dialog box to hide the contact_info optional region.
16. Using Steps 13–15 as a guide, apply the rapids_info template to the guides page. Make any adjustments so that the graphics are appropriate and the page is attractive.
17. Save your changes, then close the rapids_info template and all other open pages.

FIGURE K-41

Completed Project Builder 1: rapids_info template

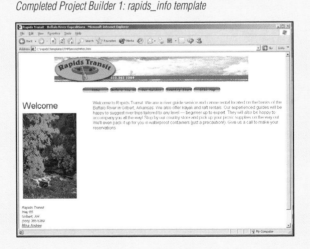

In this Project Builder, you will continue your work on the Jacob's Web site that you started in Project Builder 2 in Unit A. Chef Jacob would like to make sure that the pages of the Web site have a consistent appearance. He has asked you to create a template based on the menus page that contains editable and optional regions.

1. Open the Jacob's Web site. (If you did not create this site in Units A through J, contact your instructor for assistance.)

2. Open the menus page, then save it as a template called **menus.dwt**.

3. Insert a table above the paragraph text that has three rows and one column, no borders, Cell Padding and Cell Spacing set to **0**, and Width set to **100 Percent**.

4. Insert an editable region in the top row of the table named **intro**, then move the first two paragraphs of text into the intro editable region.

5. Insert a new table in the second row of the table that has one row, two columns, no borders, and Width set to **100 Percent**. Insert an optional region in the left-hand cell of this table named **special**.

6. Insert the graphic file specials_logo.gif from the unit_k assets folder in the special optional region, then drag the right border of the table cell to the right edge of the specials_logo image. Copy the file

specials_logo.gif to the assets folder of the Web site.

7. Insert a new optional region named **special_text** in the table cell next to the specials_logo image. Use the Advanced tab of the New Optional Region dialog box to specify to use the special parameter.

8. Move the Menu text below the table into the special_text optional region, then center-align the text (if necessary).

9. Insert a new editable region called after_dinner_text in the cell below the specials_logo image, then move the remaining text below the table into this editable

region. Set the background color of this table cell to **#FFCC99**.

10. Make any necessary formatting adjustments such as changing cell alignment, adding cell padding or spacing, or moving objects to make the page look attractive and professional.

11. Create a new page based on the menus template, make no changes to the editable regions, then save the page as menus.htm, overwriting the existing menus page. Preview the menus page in a browser, then compare your screen to Figure K-42.

12. Close your browser, then close all open pages.

FIGURE K-42
Completed Project Builder 2

Macromedia offers registered users of Dreamweaver the benefit of downloading and using professionally designed templates from their Web site. There are a wide range of templates that are appropriate for different kinds of organizations and events. Figure K-43 shows an example of a template that would be suitable for a site about an inn.

1. Connect to the Internet, then go to *www.course.com*. Navigate to the page for this book, click the Student Online Companion, then click the link for this unit.

2. Spend some time exploring the templates on this site by previewing each one and opening each page.

3. Think of an idea for a new site that you would like to create. The site can be for a club, organization, event, or any topic or person that interests you. Draw an outline and a sketch of the site, including the content that will be on each page.

4. After you have completed your sketch, look through the Macromedia templates available at the Student Online Companion, then choose an appropriate template for your site. (Note: Skip to Step 9 if downloading files is not permitted.)

5. If permitted by your instructor, download the template and copy the folder that contains the template files to a folder on your computer or external drive.

6. Use Dreamweaver to define a new site with an appropriate name that uses the site folder you downloaded as the root directory. Specify the Images folder as the default folder for images.

7. Open the site, then modify the pages of the sample site to match your site sketch. Replace any placeholder graphics, text, and other elements with content that is appropriate for your site's subject.

8. Save all pages in your site, preview them in a browser, print out each page, then close your browser and close all open pages.

9. If downloading files is not permitted, choose an appropriate template from the site and print out each page. Mark up each printed page, indicating how you would modify the template elements or replace particular elements with content appropriate for your site.

FIGURE K-43
Source for Design Project

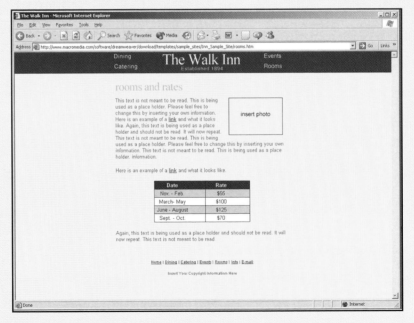

In this assignment, you will continue to work on the group Web site that you created in Units A through J. Depending on the size of your group, you can assign individual elements of the project to group members, or work collectively to create the finished product.

You will continue to enhance your Web site by using templates. You will first create a template from one of your existing pages and define editable and optional regions in it. You will also insert a repeating table and set editable attributes for specific elements. You will then apply the template to a page and add content to the editable regions.

1. Consult your storyboard and brainstorm as a team to decide which page you would like to save as a template. You will use the template to create at least one other page in your site.

2. Work as a group to create a sketch of the template page you will create. Mark the page elements that will be in locked regions. Identify and mark at least one area that will be an editable region, one area that will be an optional region, and one area that will be an editable optional region. Your sketch (and your template) should also include a repeating table.

3. Assign a team member (or several team members) the task of saving the selected page as a template, then defining the editable regions in it.

4. Assign a team member the task of adding the optional regions and editable optional regions that you planned in your sketch.

5. Assign a team member the task of creating a repeating table that has one editable attribute.

6. Assign a team member the task of making any necessary formatting adjustments to the table to make sure it looks attractive, and then saving the template. This person should then create a new page based on the template, using the same name of the page on which the template is based, so that the earlier version of the page is overwritten.

7. Assign a team member the task of applying the template to another existing page of the site, making sure to delete all repeating elements contained in the template.

8. Meet as a group to review the template(s) and the template-based pages, and offer constructive suggestions for improvements. Use the check list in Figure K-44 to make sure you completed everything according to the assignment.

9. Assign a team member the task of making any necessary changes.

10. Save your work, then close all open pages.

FIGURE K-44
Web Site Check List

Web Site Check List

1. Does your template include at least one editable region?
2. Does your template include at least one optional region?
3. Does your template include at least one editable optional region?
4. Does your template include a repeating table?
5. Are all links on template-based pages document-relative?
6. Do all editable regions have appropriate names?
7. Do all links work correctly?
8. Does the repeating table have an editable attribute?
9. Are all colors Web-safe?
10. Do all pages view well using at least two different browser settings?

USING STYLES AND STYLE SHEETS

1. Create and use HTML styles.

2. Create and use inline styles.

3. Work with external CSS style sheets.

Introduction

In Unit C, you learned how to create, apply, and edit Cascading Style Sheets (CSS). Using CSS is the best and most powerful way to ensure that all elements in a Web site are formatted consistently. The advantage of using CSS is that all of your formatting rules are kept in a separate or **external** style sheet file, so that you can change the appearance of every page to which the style sheet is attached by modifying the style sheet file. For instance, suppose your external style sheet contains a style called headings that is applied to all top-level headings in your Web site. If you decide that you want the headings to be red to make them more prominent, you could simply change the color attribute to red in the style sheet file, and all headings in the Web site would change instantly to red. You would not need to alter the content of the Web site at all.

You can also create **inline** CSS styles, which are styles whose code is located within the HTML code of a Web page. The advantage of inline styles is that you can use them to override an external style. For instance, if all headings in your Web site are red because the external style applied to them specifies red as the color attribute, you could change the color of one of those headings to blue by creating and applying an inline style that specifies blue as the color attribute. However, in general, you should avoid using inline styles to format all the pages of a Web site; it is a better practice to keep formatting rules in a separate file from the content.

If you think a large segment of your viewers will be using older browsers (earlier than 4.0), then you should not use CSS to format your Web site. However, you can still save time and ensure formatting consistency in your site by using HTML styles. An **HTML style** is a named set of formatting attributes that can be applied to text to ensure formatting consistency for common text elements across all pages of a Web site. HTML styles consist of font attributes and can only be applied to text.

In this unit, you will create and apply HTML styles, inline styles, and work with external CSS Style Sheets to format the Super Bug Zapper Web site.

Tools You'll Use

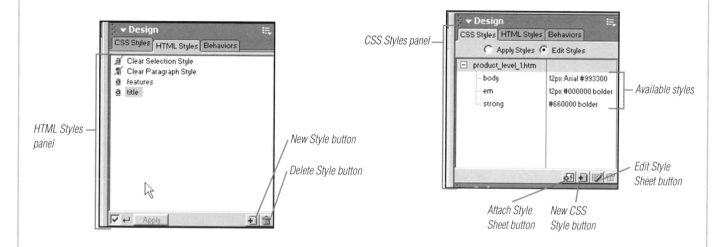

HTML Styles panel

New Style button

Delete Style button

CSS Styles panel

Available styles

Edit Style Sheet button

Attach Style Sheet button

New CSS Style button

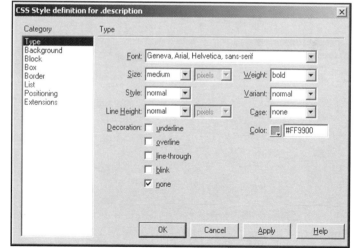

CREATE AND USE HTML STYLES

What You'll Do

In this lesson, you will create two HTML styles and then apply them to selected text. You will also edit an HTML style.

Understanding HTML Styles

It's a good idea to use a consistent set of formatting attributes for repeating text elements in a Web site. For instance, if your Web site contains a long list of product names and descriptions, you might choose to format the product names in large red Arial, and the descriptions in small black italic Arial. You could use the Property inspector to apply these formatting attributes to each text element manually; however, creating HTML styles for each type of text element and then applying those styles with a single mouse click saves considerable time and effort.

Using the HTML Styles Panel

You use the HTML Styles panel, shown in Figure L-1, to view and apply HTML styles. Each style listed is preceded by one of two symbols. The ¶ symbol indicates a **paragraph style**, which is a style that is applied to an entire paragraph. To apply a paragraph style, place the insertion point in the paragraph you want to format, then click the desired paragraph style in the HTML Styles panel.

The **a** symbol indicates a **selection style**, which is a style that is applied to selected text. To apply a selection style, select the text you want to format, then click the desired selection style in the HTML Styles panel.

QUICKTIP

To clear a paragraph style, place the insertion point in the paragraph, then click Clear Paragraph Style in the HTML Styles panel. To clear a selection style, select the text, then click Clear Selection Style in the HTML Styles panel.

Creating and Editing HTML Styles

To create an HTML style, use the New Style button in the HTML Styles panel to open the Define HTML Style dialog box, shown in Figure L-2. This dialog box is used to name the style, to specify whether to apply the style to selected text or a paragraph, and to set font attributes such as type, color, and size.

If you have already formatted a particular type of text element, you can save time creating an HTML style by selecting the formatted text, then clicking the New Style button. The Define HTML Style dialog box will open and will show the formatting attributes for the selected text. To save the style, specify a name and click OK.

To make changes to an existing style, double-click the style in the HTML Styles panel to open the Define HTML Style dialog box, then change the settings as you wish.

Understanding Benefits and Disadvantages of HTML Styles

HTML styles can save significant time in formatting the text in your Web site. However, they are not as powerful as CSS styles. For one thing, if you make changes to an HTML style, the changes are not reflected in the text elements to which the style is applied. In order to change the formatting of the text, you need to reapply the style. So, why use HTML styles over CSS styles? The main reason is that HTML styles are guaranteed to be recognized by all browsers. CSS styles work only in browsers later than 3.0.

FIGURE L-1
HTML Styles panel

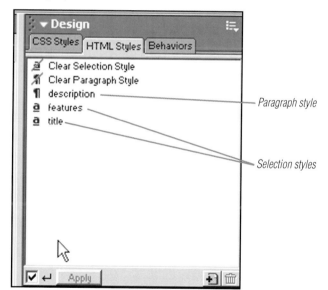

Paragraph style

Selection styles

FIGURE L-2
Define HTML Style dialog box

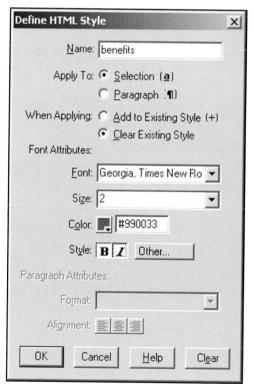

Create an HTML style

1. Open the product_level_1 page in the Super Bug Zapper Web site, open the Design panel group, then click the HTML Styles tab.

2. Click the New Style button in the HTML Styles panel to open the Define HTML Style dialog box.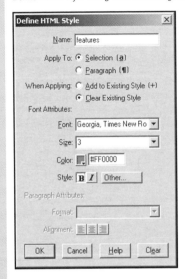

3. Type **features** in the Name text box; verify that the Selection radio button is selected; verify that the Clear Existing Style radio button is selected; set Font to **Georgia, Times New Roman, serif**; set Size to **3**; set Color to red (**#FF0000**); click the Bold button, and then compare your screen to Figure L-3 .

4. Click OK.

5. Select the Level 1 heading in the cell to the right of the yellow spray can, then click the New Style button in the HTML Styles panel to open the Define HTML Style dialog box.

   The current settings reflect the formatting of the selected text.

6. Type **title** in the Name text box, then click OK.

   Your HTML Styles panel should resemble Figure L-4.

   You added two HTML styles to the product_ level_1 page.

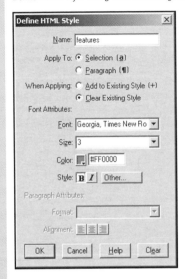

FIGURE L-4
Features and title styles added to HTML Styles panel

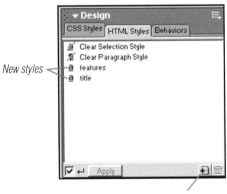

New styles

New Style button

FIGURE L-5

Product_level_1 page with features and title styles applied to text

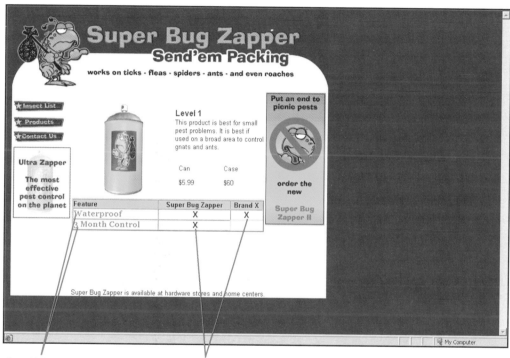

Text with features
style applied

Text with title style applied

1. Select Waterproof in the second row of the repeating table, then click features in the HTML Styles panel.

   The features style is applied to the word Waterproof.

2. Apply the features style to 3 Month Control in the third row of the repeating table.

3. Apply the title style to the Xs in the second and third rows of the repeating table.

4. Save your changes, preview the page in a browser, compare your screen to Figure L-5, then close your browser.

You applied the features and title styles to selected text on the product_level_1 page.

Clear an HTML style

1. Apply the title style to the words Can and Case in the cell to the right of the yellow spray can.

   The words Can and Case are now formatted in maroon, size 3, bold, reflecting the formatting of the title style.

   > TIP To apply a style to all of the text in a table cell, select the table cell, then click the desired style in the HTML Styles panel.

2. Select the table cells containing the words Can and Case (if necessary), click Clear Selection Style in the HTML Styles panel, then compare your screen to Figure L-6.

   The title style is removed from the selected words, which are now formatted in the default font and no longer match the style of the paragraph text in the table cell.

3. Format the words Can and Case in **Arial**, **Helvetica**, **sans-serif**, size 2, then click anywhere to deselect the table cells (if necessary).

You applied the title style to two words on the product_level_1 page. You then cleared the style and used the Property inspector to restore the original formatting to the words.

FIGURE L-6

Selected table cells after clearing selection style

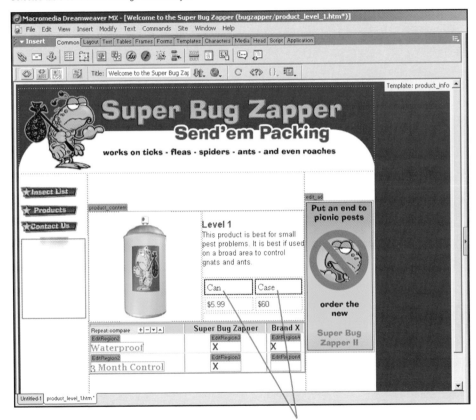

Text with title style removed

FIGURE L-7

Modifying a style using the Define HTML Style dialog box

1. Double-click the features style in the HTML Styles panel to open the Define HTML Style dialog box.

2. Change the font to **Arial, Helvetica, sans-serif**. Change the color to **#CC0033** and the size to **2**, then compare your screen to Figure L-7.

3. Click OK.

   Notice that the formatting of the text Waterproof and 3 Month Control remained the same and did not change to reflect the modifications you made to the features style. You need to apply the style again.

4. Apply the features style to the text Waterproof and 3 Month Control in the repeating table.

5. Save your changes, preview the page in your browser, compare your screen to Figure L-8, close your browser, then close the products_level_1 page.

You changed the font, color, and size settings of the features style, then applied the modified style to selected text.

FIGURE L-8

Product_level_1 page with modified features style applied to text

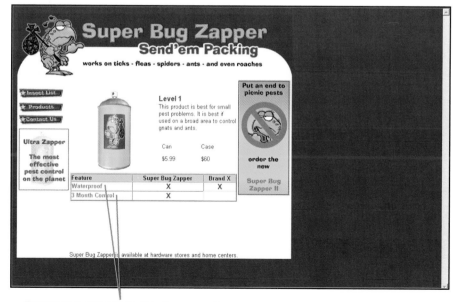

Text appears in bold red Arial, Helvetica, sans-serif after applying modified features style

CREATE AND USE INLINE STYLES

What You'll Do

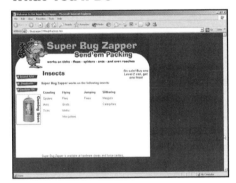

In this lesson, you will create, apply, and modify an inline style on the insects page. You will also redefine the strong HTML tag, so that all instances of bold formatting will appear in red. You will then edit the strong style and see those edits automatically applied to all text to which the strong tag is attached. Finally, you will delete a style.

Understanding Inline Styles

In Unit C you learned how to create and use an external CSS style sheet to apply consistent formatting to the elements of a Web site. An external style sheet is a separate file with a .css extension that contains a collection of rules for formatting elements of a Web site. External style sheets can be applied to multiple pages, and are therefore great tools to help ensure formatting consistency across all pages of a Web site. Sometimes, however, you might want to create a style that is used only on a single page of your Web site. You can do this using **inline styles**, or styles whose code is embedded in the code of a particular page. Inline styles are handy when you want a particular page in your Web site to contain formatting that is different from the rules specified in an external style sheet. If both an external style and internal style are applied to a single element, the inline style overrides the external style.

Creating, Applying, and Modifying a Custom Style

To create an inline style, you use the New CSS Style button in the CSS Styles panel to open the New CSS Style dialog box, shown in Figure L-9. You use this dialog box to create both inline styles as well as styles that are added to external style sheets. To specify the new style as an inline style, click the This Document Only radio button in the Define In section. If you click the New Style Sheet File radio button, you will need to name and save a new CSS style sheet using the Save Style Sheet File As dialog box.

You use the New CSS Style dialog box to create a **Custom style** (also known as a **class style**), which contains a combination of formatting attributes that can be applied to a block of text or other page elements. When you name a custom style, you must begin the name with a period (.).

After you name the style and click OK, the CSS Style definition dialog box will open with settings for the Type category displayed, as shown in Figure L-10. This dialog box contains eight different categories whose settings can be defined. To specify the settings for a category, click the category, then enter the settings. When you finish specifying settings for all of the desired categories, click OK.

Once you create a custom style, it appears in the CSS Styles panel. To apply a custom style to an element on a Web page, select the element, then click the style in the CSS Styles panel.

To edit a custom style, click the style you want to edit, click the Edit Style Sheet button in the CSS Styles panel, then use the CSS Style definition dialog box to change the settings as you wish. Any changes that you make to the style are automatically reflected on the page; all elements to which the style is attached will update to reflect the change.

Redefining HTML Tags

When you use the Property inspector to format a Web page element, a pre-defined HTML tag is added to that element. Sometimes, you might want to change

FIGURE L-9
New CSS Style dialog box

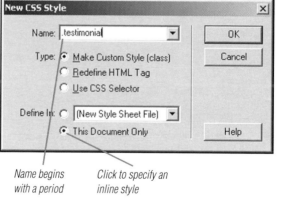

Name begins with a period

Click to specify an inline style

FIGURE L-10
CSS Style definition dialog box

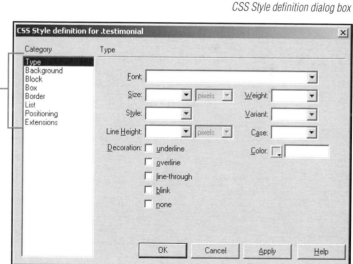

Choose any category to open dialog box for that category

the definition of an HTML tag to add more "pizzazz" to elements that have that tag. For instance, perhaps you want all text that has the <em> tag, which is the tag used for italic formatting, to appear in purple bold. To change the definition of an HTML tag, click the Redefine HTML Definition button in the New CSS Style dialog box, click the Tag list arrow to view all available HTML tags, click the tag you want to redefine,

then click OK to open the CSS Style definition dialog box, where you specify the desired formatting settings. Once you save the style and apply that tag, selected text will be formatted according to the altered settings you specified. To edit the settings, click the Edit Styles radio button in the CSS Styles panel, as shown in Figure L-11, to display the list of customized HTML tags. Select the HTML tag you want to

change, then click the Edit Style Sheet button to open the CSS Style definition dialog box where you can make any changes you want.

QUICKTIP

To delete an inline style, click the style you wish to delete, then click the Delete CSS Style button in the CSS Styles panel.

FIGURE L-11
CSS Styles panel with Edit Styles radio button selected

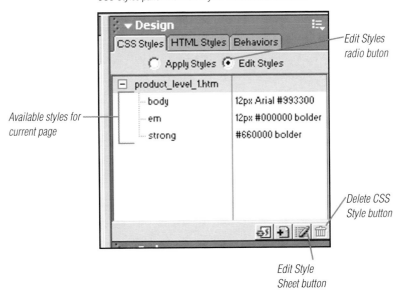

Edit Styles radio buton

Available styles for current page

Delete CSS Style button

Edit Style Sheet button

FIGURE L-12

New CSS Style dialog box with settings for .description style

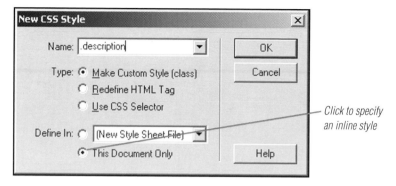

Click to specify
an inline style

FIGURE L-13

CSS Style definition for .description dialog box with type settings specified

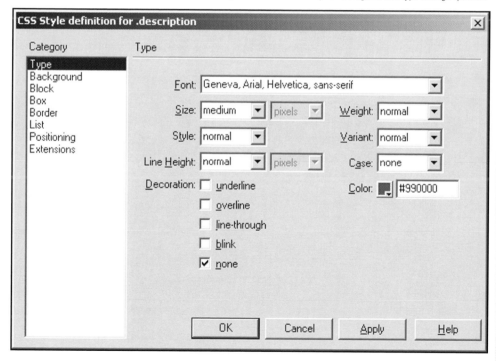

1. Open the insects page, then click the CSS Styles tab in the Design panel group to open the CSS Styles panel.

2. Click the Apply Styles radio button in the CSS Styles panel (if necessary), then click the New CSS Style button in the CSS Styles panel to open the New CSS Style dialog box.

3. Type **.description** in the Name text box, verify that the Make Custom Style (class) radio button is selected, click the This Document Only radio button, then compare your screen to Figure L-12.

4. Click OK to open the CSS Style definition for .description dialog box, which has the Type category selected.

5. Set Font to **Geneva**, **Arial**, **Helvetica**, **sans-serif**; set Size to **medium**; set Style to **normal**; set Line Height to **normal**; set Decoration to **none**; set Weight to **normal**; set Variant to **normal**; set Case to **none**; set Color to **#990000**, then compare your screen to Figure L-13.

6. Click OK.

The description style now appears in the CSS Styles panel.

You created a new inline style named .description and defined the type settings for it.

Apply a custom style

1. Click the Options button in the Property inspector title bar to open the Options menu, then click CSS Mode (Win), or click the Toggle CSS/HTML Mode button in the Property inspector (Mac).

   The Font attribute options in the Property inspector are replaced with options for choosing CSS styles.

2. Select the text Super Bug Zapper works on the following insects:.

3. Click the CSS Style list arrow in the Property inspector, click description as shown in Figure L-14, then click away from the selection to deselect the text.

   The selected text now appears in maroon and has the description style applied to it.

4. Select the text Super Bug Zapper works on the following insects:, click the CSS Style list arrow in the Property inspector, click No CSS Style in the CSS Styles panel to remove the description style from the selected text, then click anywhere to deselect the text.

5. Select the text Super Bug Zapper works on the following insects:, click description in the CSS Styles panel, click anywhere to deselect the text, then compare your screen to Figure L-15.

   (continued)

FIGURE L-14
Applying the description style using the Property inspector

Selected text

CSS Style list arrow

Click to apply description style to selected text

Options button

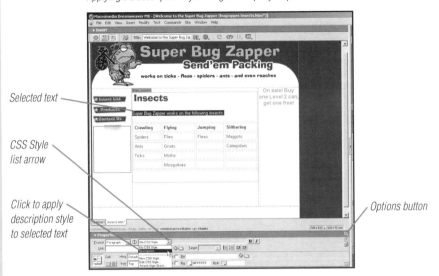

FIGURE L-15
Selected text with description style applied

Text with description style applied

Description style

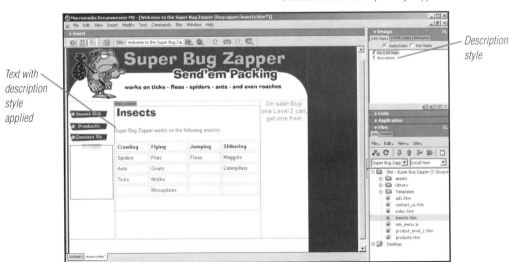

Using Styles and Style Sheets

FIGURE L-16
CSS Style definition for .description dialog box with modified type settings

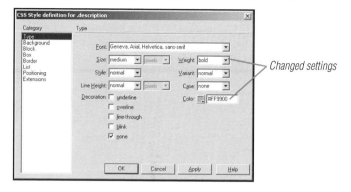

Changed settings

FIGURE L-17
Insects page after changes made to description style

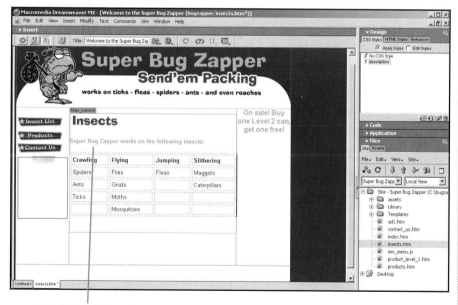

*Text with description style
now appears in bold orange*

6. Click the Options button in the title bar of the Property inspector, then click HTML mode (Win) or click the Toggle CSS/HTML Mode button in the Property inspector (Mac) to restore the font options to the Property inspector.

You changed the Property inspector to CSS mode, and then used it to apply the description style to selected text. You then used the Property inspector to remove the description style, and then reapplied the style using the CSS Styles panel.

Modify a custom style

1. Click the description style in the CSS Styles panel, then click the Edit Style Sheet button in the CSS Styles panel.

   The CSS Style definition for .description dialog box opens.

2. Change the color to **#FF9900**, change Weight to **bold**, then compare your screen to Figure L-16.

3. Click OK, then compare your screen to Figure L-17.

   The text with the description style applied to it automatically changed to orange bold, reflecting the changes that you made to the style.

You made formatting changes to the Type category of the description style. You then saw these formatting changes reflected in text with the description style applied to it.

Redefine an HTML tag

1. Click the New CSS Style button in the CSS Styles panel to open the New CSS Style dialog box.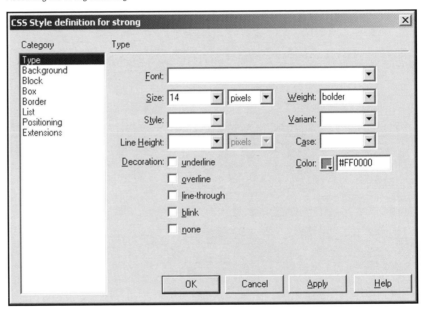

2. Click the Redefine HTML Tag radio button, click the Tag list arrow, scroll down (if necessary), then click strong.

   The strong tag is the tag that controls bold formatting.

   TIP   To scroll quickly to the tags that begin with the letter s, type s after you click the Tag list arrow.

3. Click OK to open the CSS Style definition for strong dialog box, set Size to **14 pixels**, set Weight to **bolder**, set Color to red (**#FF0000**), compare your screen to Figure L-18, then click OK.

4. Select Super Bug Zapper in the sentence above the insects table, then click the Bold button in the Property inspector, then deselect the text.

   The selected text now appears in red bold, reflecting the changes you made to the strong tag. Notice that the ad text on the page also changed to red because it is formatted in bold and contains the strong tag.

5. Using Steps 1-3 as a guide, create a new CSS style that redefines the h2 HTML tag, setting Size to **12 pixels**, Style to **normal**, Weight to **bold**, and Color to **#FF9900**.

(continued)

FIGURE L-18

Redefining the strong HTML tag

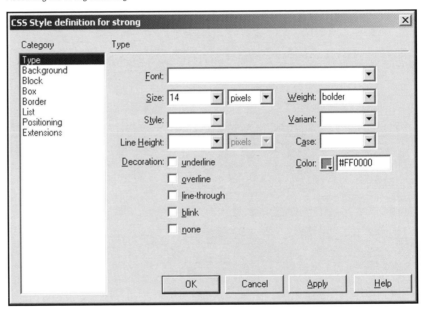

Using Styles and Style Sheets

FIGURE L-19

Insects page with h2 style and strong style applied to selected text

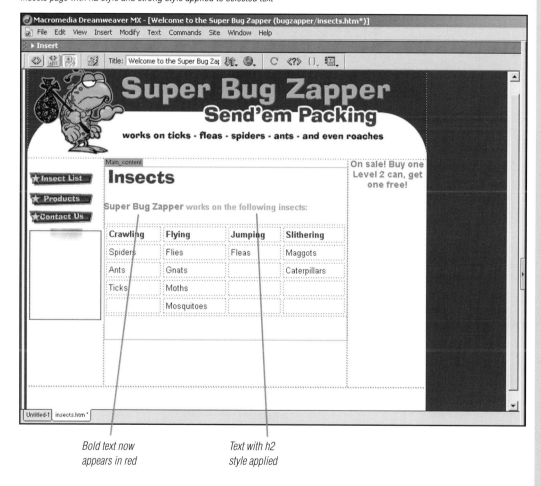

Bold text now
appears in red

Text with h2
style applied

6. Select the text Super Bug Zapper works on the following insects:, then click No CSS Style in the CSS Style panel to remove the description style from the selected text.

   You must remove a style from text before applying another style; otherwise the new style will not be applied.

7. Click the Format list arrow in the Property inspector, click Heading 2, deselect the text, then compare your screen to Figure L-19.

   The h2 style is applied to the selected text. Notice that Super Bug Zapper still appears in red bold, because the strong tag takes precedence over the h2 tag.

   > TIP You can tell which tag takes precedence by its position in the tag selector. Tags with greater precedence are positioned to the right of other tags in the tag selector.

You used the New CSS Style dialog box to redefine the strong and h2 HTML tags. You also applied the styles to selected text.

Edit an inline style

1. Click the Edit Styles radio button in the CSS Styles panel to view the styles for the insects page, then compare your screen to Figure L-20.

2. Double-click the strong style in the CSS Styles panel to open the CSS Style definition for strong dialog box, change the color to **#990000**, then click OK.

   The words Super Bug Zapper change to maroon, reflecting the change you made to the style. The ad text also changes to maroon because it contains the strong tag.

3. Edit the h2 style to change the color to maroon (#990000), then compare your screen to Figure L-21.

You used the CSS Styles panel to change the color settings for the strong and h2 inline styles.

FIGURE L-20
CSS Styles panel with Edit Styles radio button selected

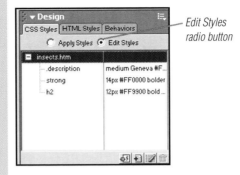

Edit Styles radio button

FIGURE L-21
Insects page after modifying strong and h2 styles

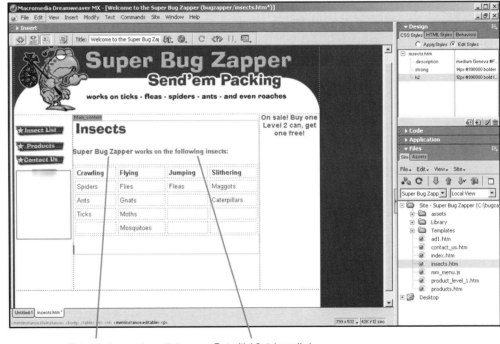

Text with strong style applied now appears in maroon

Text with h2 style applied now appears in maroon

Using Styles and Style Sheets

Delete an inline style

1. Click the description style in the CSS Styles panel to select it.

2. Click the Delete CSS Style button, then compare your screen to Figure L-22.

   The description style is removed from the CSS Styles panel. If any text on this page had the description style applied to it, the style formatting would be removed from the text.

   > TIP You can also delete an inline style by right-clicking (Win) or control-clicking (Mac) the style in the CSS Styles panel, then clicking Delete.

3. Save your changes, then close the insects page.

You used the CSS Styles panel to delete the description style.

FIGURE L-22
CSS Styles panel after deleting description style

Description style
no longer appears

Delete CSS Style button

WORK WITH EXTERNAL CSS STYLE SHEETS

What You'll Do

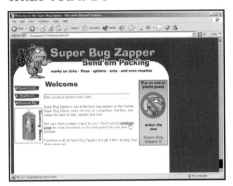

In this lesson, you will attach the external CSS style sheet super_bug_zapper.css to a page in the Super Bug Zapper Web site. You will then make a formatting change in the style sheet and see that change reflected on the page. You will also add hyperlink styles and custom code to the super_bug_zapper style sheet. You will then attach the super_bug_zapper style sheet to a template. Finally, you will delete a style from the super_bug_zapper style sheet.

Using External CSS Style Sheets

If you want to ensure consistent formatting across all elements of a Web site, it's a good idea to use external CSS style sheets instead of HTML styles or inline styles. Most Web developers prefer to use external CSS style sheets so they can make changes to the appearance of a Web site without changing any content. Using inline styles requires you to make changes to the styles on each page, which takes more time and leaves room for error and inconsistency.

Attaching an External CSS Style Sheet to a Page or Template

One of the big advantages of using external CSS style sheets is that you can attach them to pages that you've already created. When you do this, all of the rules specified in the style sheet are applied to the HTML tags on the page. So for instance, if your external style sheet specifies that all first-level headings are

formatted in Arial 14-point red bold, then all text in your Web page that has the <h1> tag will change to reflect these settings when you attach the style sheet to the page. To attach an external style sheet to a page, open the page, then use the Attach Style Sheet button in the CSS Styles panel to open the Link External Style Sheet dialog box, shown in Figure L-23. Use this dialog box to browse for the external style sheet file you want to attach, and to specify whether to link or import the file. In most cases, you should choose to link the file so that the content of the page is kept separate from the style sheet file.

If all the pages in your site are based on a template, you can save an enormous amount of time and development effort by attaching an external style sheet to the template. Doing this saves you from having to attach the style sheet to every page in the site; you only have to attach it to the template file. Then, when you make changes to the style sheet, those changes will be reflected in the template and will be updated in every page to which the template is attached when you save the template.

Adding Hyperlink Styles to a CSS Style Sheet

You can use an external style sheet to create styles for all links in a Web site. To do this, open the style sheet so it appears in the document window, then click the New CSS Style button to open the New CSS

Style dialog box. Click the Use CSS Selector radio button, then choose one of the selectors from the list, as shown and described in Figure L-24. After you choose a selector and click OK, the CSS Style definition dialog box opens, which you can use to specify the formatting of the selected link.

Adding Custom Code to a CSS Style Sheet

You can make changes to a style sheet by changing its code or adding code directly

into the style sheet file. To do this, open the style sheet file so that it appears in the document window, click where you want to add code, then type the code you want. For instance, you can add code to the body tag of the style sheet that changes the colors of a viewer's scroll bar to match the colors of your Web site.

FIGURE L-23
Link External Style Sheet dialog box

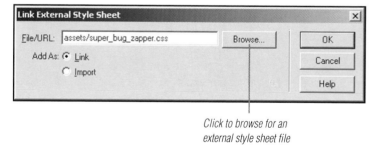

Click to browse for an
external style sheet file

FIGURE L-24
New CSS Style dialog box with Selector list open

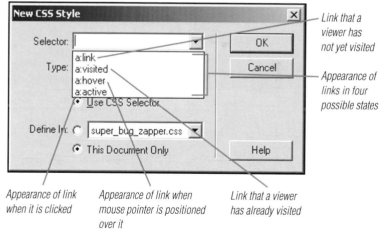

Link that a
viewer has
not yet visited

Appearance of
links in four
possible states

Appearance of link
when it is clicked

Appearance of link when
mouse pointer is positioned
over it

Link that a viewer
has already visited

Attach a style sheet to an existing page

1. Open the index page.

2. Click the Attach Style Sheet button in the CSS Styles panel to open the Link External Style Sheet dialog box, then click the Link radio button (if necessary). ⊡

3. Click Browse to open the Select Style Sheet File dialog box, navigate to the unit_l data files folder, click the super_bug_zapper.css file, compare your screen to Figure L-25, then click OK (Win) or Choose (Mac).

   A dialog box opens, asking if you would like to copy the super_bug_zapper.css file to the root folder of the Web site.

4. Click Yes to open the Copy File As dialog box, then click Save to copy the file to the root folder and return to the Link External Style Sheet dialog box.

5. Compare your screen to Figure L-26, then click OK.

6. Click the Edit Styles radio button (if necessary) in the CSS Styles panel.

   The super_bug_zapper.css file appears in the CSS Styles panel, with the body style indented below it.

You attached the external style sheet file super_bug_zapper.css to the index page. You also copied the super_bug_zapper.css file to the assets folder of the Web site.

FIGURE L-25
Select Style Sheet File dialog box

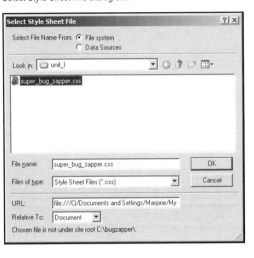

FIGURE L-26
Link External Style Sheet dialog box

Using Styles and Style Sheets

FIGURE L-27

Modifying the a:link style

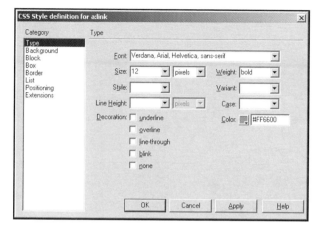

FIGURE L-28

Index page after modifying a:link style

Link appears
in bold
orange

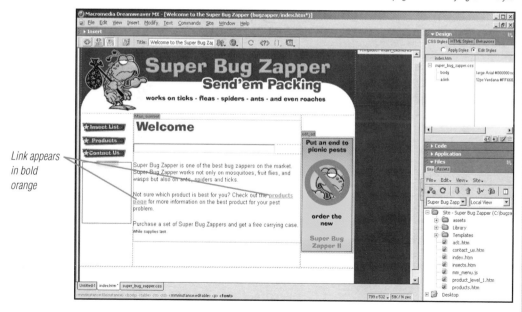

Modify an external CSS style sheet

1. Click the Refresh button on the Site panel toolbar. ⟳

2. Double-click the super_bug_zapper.css file in the root folder in the Site panel.

   The super_bug_zapper.css file opens in the document window.

3. Click the New CSS Style button in the CSS Styles panel to open the New CSS Style dialog box. ⊞

4. Click the Use CSS Selector radio button.

5. Click the Selector list arrow, click a:link, then click OK to open the CSS Style definition for a:link dialog box.

6. Set Font to **Verdana**, **Arial**, **Helvetica**, **sans-serif**; set Size to **12 pixels**; set Weight to **bold**; set Color to **#FF6600**; compare your screen to Figure L-27, and then click OK.

   The super_bug_zapper.css page now contains new code that reflects the type settings you specified for the a:link style.

7. Save your changes, switch to the index page, then compare your screen to Figure L-28.

   The products page link in the paragraph text now appears in bold orange, reflecting the formatting changes that you made to the a:link style.

You opened the super_bug_zapper.css file and made modifications to the a:link style using the CSS Style definition dialog box.

Add hyperlink styles

1. Open the super_bug_zapper.css file (if necessary).

2. Click the New CSS Style button in the CSS Styles panel to open the New CSS Style dialog box.

3. Click the Use CSS Selector radio button (if necessary).

4. Click the Selector list arrow, click a:hover, then click OK to open the CSS Style definition for a:hover dialog box.

5. Set Font to **Verdana**, **Arial**, **Helvetica**, **sans-serif**; set Size to **12 pixels**; set Weight to **bolder**; set Color to **#990033**, and then click OK.

   The super_bug_zapper.css page now contains new code that reflects the font specifications you set for the a:hover style.

6. Save your changes, switch to the index page, preview the page in your browser, position the mouse pointer over the products page link, then compare your screen to Figure L-29.

   The products page link in the paragraph text now appears in bold maroon, reflecting the formatting changes that you made to the a:hover style.

7. Close your browser.

You opened the super_bug_zapper.css file and then made modifications to the a:hover style using the CSS Style definition dialog box.

FIGURE L-29
Index page after modifying a:hover style

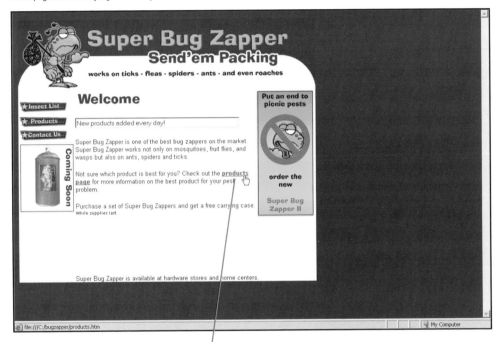

Link appears in bold maroon after changing a:hover style

Using Styles and Style Sheets

FIGURE L-30

Adding custom code to the super_bug_zapper.css file

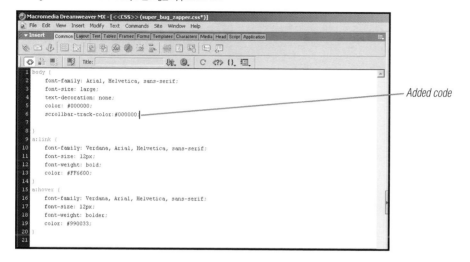

Added code

FIGURE L-31

Index page in Internet Explorer after adding custom code to the super_bug_zapper.css file

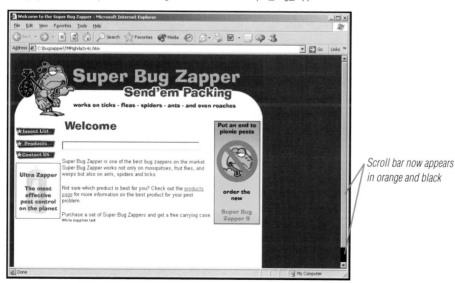

Scroll bar now appears in orange and black

Add custom code to a style sheet

1. Open the super_bug_zapper.css file (if necessary).

2. Locate the body tag on the page, then click to the right of the semicolon in line 5 to set the insertion point.

3. Press [Enter] (Win) or [return] (Mac) to move the insertion point to line 6.

4. Type **scrollbar-track-color:#000000;** then compare your screen to Figure L-30.

   Make sure to type the semicolon (;) at the end of the line of code.

5. Press [Enter] (Win) or [return] (Mac) to position the insertion point on line 7, then type **scrollbar-face-color:#F7ab4b;**.

6. Save your changes, open the index page, preview the page in your browser, then compare your screen to Figure L-31.

   Your scroll bar now appears in black and orange, reflecting the custom code you added to the super_bug_ zapper.css file.

7. Close your browser, then save and close the index page.

You opened the super_bug_zapper.css file and added custom code to specify that the face of the scroll bar and the scroll bar track appear in orange and black to match the colors of the Super Bug Zapper Web site.

Use a style sheet with a template

1. Open the main_elements template, then click the Attach Style Sheet button on the CSS Styles panel to open the Link External Style Sheet dialog box.

2. Click the Link radio button, click Browse to open the Select Style Sheet File dialog box, navigate to the root folder of the Web site, click the super_bug_ zapper.css file, click OK, then click OK (Win) or Choose (Mac).

3. Save your changes, then update all other files in the Web site.

4. Open the super_bug_zapper.css file, click the Edit Styles radio button in the CSS Styles panel (if necessary), then double-click the body style in the CSS Styles panel to open the CSS Style definition for body dialog box.

5. Change the color to **#660000**, click OK, then click anywhere to deselect the text, then compare your screen to Figure L-32.

6. Save your changes, open the main_elements template and view the change to the body text color, then compare your screen to Figure L-33.

7. Switch to the super_bug_zapper.css file, select #660000 in line 5 of the code, type **#000000**, then save your changes.

You attached the super_bug_zapper.css style sheet to the main_elements template. You then changed the body text color in the super_bug_zapper.css style sheet and viewed the change in the main_elements template. You then changed the body text color back to black.

FIGURE L-32

Super_bug_zapper.css file after making change to body style color

New color reflects changes made in CSS Style definition dialog box

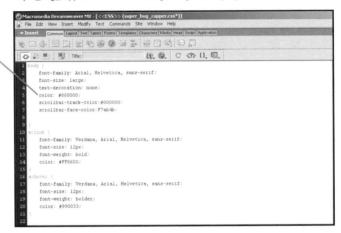

FIGURE L-33

Main_elements template after changing color of body style

Text with body style applied to it now appears in maroon

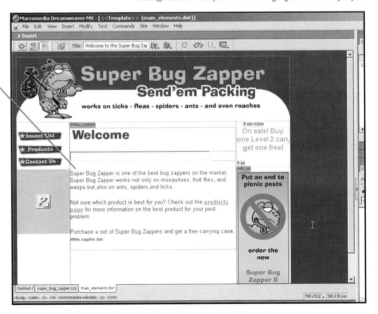

FIGURE L-34
Selected a:link code in super_bug_zapper.css file

Selected
a:link code

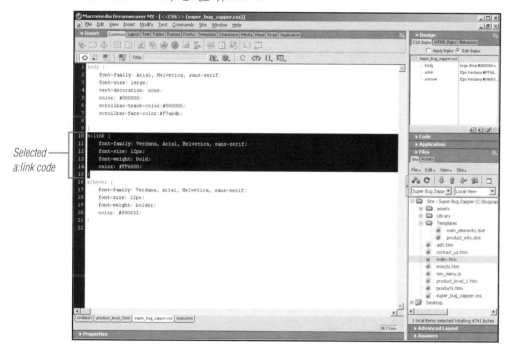

1. Open the super_bug_zapper.css file (if necessary).

2. Select the a:link tag and the five lines of code below it (including color:#FF6600 and the bracket on line 15), then compare your screen to Figure L-34.

3. Press [Delete] (Win) or [del] (Mac), then save your changes.

   Notice that the a:link style no longer appears in the CSS Styles panel.

4. Open the index page.

   Notice that the products page text link no longer appears in maroon, indicating that the a:link style has been deleted from the style sheet.

   > TIP   You can detach a style sheet from a template or Web page by clicking the style sheet file in the CSS Styles panel, then clicking the Delete CSS Style button. When you do this, the file is no longer linked to the Web page, but it is not actually deleted; it remains in its original location on your hard drive.

5. Close all open pages.

You deleted the a:link style from the super_bug_zapper.css file and then saved your changes.

Create and use HTML styles.

1. Open the Blooms & Bulbs Web site that you created and developed in Units A through K, then open the plants page. (If you did not create this Web site in Units A through K, contact your instructor for assistance.)

2. Create a new HTML style named **bloom_ body_text**. Specify the style to apply to paragraphs and to clear any existing style. Set the font to **Arial, Helvetica, sans-serif**, size **2**, dark green (**#003300**).

3. Apply the bloom_body_text style to the three paragraphs of text on the plants page.

4. Edit the bloom_body_text style to change the size to **3** and the color to **#006633**.

5. Reapply the bloom_body_text style to the three paragraphs of text on the plants page.

6. Save your changes, then preview the page in your browser.

Create and use inline styles.

1. Delete the layer named text that is located just below the Drop by to see our Featured Spring Plants heading on the plants page.

2. Delete any blank lines between the heading and the paragraph text, as necessary, to improve the appearance of the page.

3. Select the text Available in flats of 24 plants in the third paragraph, then type **Bloom mid-May through August.**

4. Create a new custom inline style named **.bloomtimes** on the plants page that has the following type settings: Font= **Arial, Helvetica, sans-serif**, Size= **14 pixels**, Style= **italic**, Weight= **bold**, and Color= **#FF0000**.

5. Apply the bloomtimes style to the sentence Bloom mid-May through August. in the first paragraph.

6. Apply the bloomtimes style to the sentence Bloom February through early May. in the second paragraph.

7. Apply the bloomtimes style to the sentence Bloom mid-May through August. in the third paragraph.

8. Modify the bloomtimes style to change the color to dark green (**#006633**) and the weight to **normal**.

9. Create a new custom style named **.tiptext** that has the following settings: Font= **Arial, Helvetica, sans-serif**, Size= **12 pixels**, Style= **italic**, Weight= **normal**, Color= **#FF0000**.

10. Apply the tiptext style to the sentence It is best not to water in the evening.

11. Redefine the strong HTML tag on the plants page using the following settings: Font= **Arial, Helvetica, sans-serif**, Size= **14 pixels**, style= **normal**, Weight= **bold**, Color= **#66CC66**.

12. Apply bold formatting to the text Beautiful spring iris in the first paragraph, Dramatic masses of tulips in the second paragraph, and Pretty pansies in the third paragraph.

13. Edit the strong style to change the size to 16 pixels and the weight to bolder.

14. Delete the tiptext style, save your changes, preview the plants page in your browser, then compare your screen to Figure L-35.

Work with external CSS style sheets.

1. Open the master_gardener page, then attach the blooms.css style sheet that you created in Unit C to this page.

2. Open the blooms.css file, then use the CSS Selector to add the a:link style to the blooms.css file. Set Font to **Arial, Helvetica, sans-serif**; set Size to **14 pixels**; set Weight to **normal**, and set Color to dark green (**#006633**).

3. Save your changes, switch to the master_ gardener page and make sure that the text links on the page now appear in green.

4. Switch to the blooms.css file, then use the CSS Selector to add the a:hover style to the blooms.css file. Set Font to **Arial, Helvetica, sans-serif**; set Size to **14 pixels**; set Weight to **bold**, and set Color to light green (**#66CC33**).

5. Save your changes, then preview the master_gardener page in your browser and make sure that the links appear according to the settings you specified.

6. Redefine the body tag in the blooms.css file. Set Font to **Arial**, **Helvetica**, **sans-serif**, Style to **normal**, and Color to black (**#000000**).

7. Type **scrollbar-track-color:#006633;** in the line below color:#000000; in the body tag.

8. Press [Enter] (Win) or [return] (Mac) to insert a new line, then type **scrollbar-face-color:#CCFF99;**.

9. Save your changes, switch to the master_ gardener.htm page, preview the page in your browser, then close your browser.

10. Attach the blooms.css style sheet to the master_gardener.dwt template.

11. Save the master_gardener template, then update all files in the site.

12. Preview the master_gardener template in your browser, position the mouse pointer over the gardening tips link, compare your screen to Figure L-36, then close your browser.

13. Save and close all open files.

FIGURE L-35

Completed Skills Review: plants page

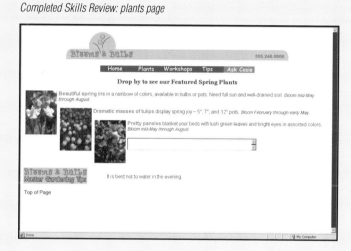

FIGURE L-36

Completed Skills Review: master_gardener template

In this Project Builder you will continue your work on the Rapids Transit Web site that you began in Project Builder 1 in Unit A. Mike Andrew, the owner, has decided that he wants to use styles and style sheets to ensure the consistent format of elements in the Rapids Transit Web site. You will start by adding an HTML style for formatting the company name consistently. You will then attach the rapids.css style sheet to the rapids_info template and add new styles to it.

1. Open the Rapids Transit Web site that you created in Units A through K.

2. Open the rapids_info template, then create a new HTML selection style called **rapids_transit** that has the following settings: Font= **Arial**, **Helvetica**, **sans-serif**; Size= **3**, Color= **#0099FF**, Style= **bold**.

3. Apply the rapids_transit style to the text Rapids Transit in the first line of paragraph text.

4. Create a new custom style in the rapids_info template named **.ad**. Set Font to **Arial**, **Helvetica**, **sans-serif**; set Size to **12 pixels**; and set Color to **#003366**.

5. Apply the ad custom style to the Rapids Transit contact information located below the paragraph text.

6. Edit the ad style to change the weight to bold and the style to italic.

7. Attach the rapids.css style sheet to the rapids_info template, save the template, then update all files in the site.

8. Apply the bodytext style to the paragraph text in the rapids_info template.

9. Edit the bodytext style to change the size to **16 pixels**.

10. Use the CSS Selector to modify the a:link and a:hover styles in the rapids.css file. Use any fonts, styles, decorations, and colors you think are appropriate with the colors and design of the site.

11. Save the rapids.css file, then open the store page.

12. Use the Template Properties dialog box to specify to show the contact_info optional region on the store page.

13. Save your changes, preview the store page in your browser, place the mouse pointer over the text link on the page, then compare your screen to Figure L-37. Your screen might look different depending on the choices you made in Step 10.

14. Switch to the rapids_info template, preview the page in your browser, compare your screen to Figure L-38, then close the rapids_info template and all open pages.

FIGURE L-37
Completed Project Builder 1: store page

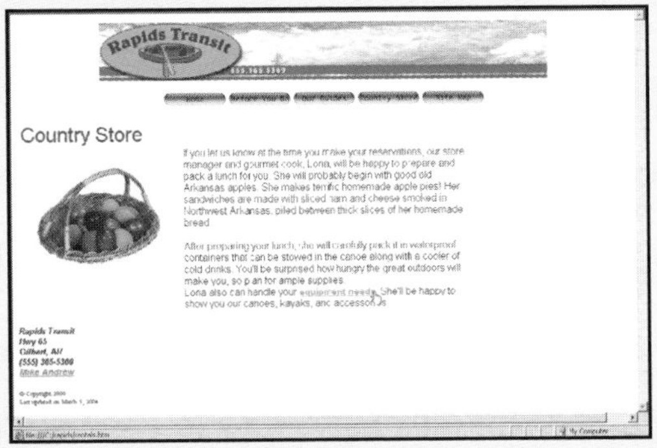

FIGURE L-38
Completed Project Builder 1: rapids_info template

In this Project Builder, you will continue your work on the Jacob's Web site that you started in Project Builder 2 in Unit A. Chef Jacob wants to ensure that certain text elements and text links in the Web site are formatted consistently. He has provided you with instructions for how he would like the links to be formatted. He has also asked you to add code to the style sheet that will make the scrollbar appear in colors that match the Web site when viewed in a browser.

1. Open the Jacob's Web site that you created in Units A through K. (If you did not create this site in Units A through K, contact your instructor for assistance.)
2. Open the menus template, then attach the jacobs.css style sheet that you created in Unit C to this file.
3. Add a new CSS style to the jacobs.css style sheet. Use the CSS Selector to choose a:link, then set Font to **Arial**, **Helvetica**, **sans-serif**; Size to **14 pixels**; Weight to **bolder**, and Color to dark purple (**#660033**).
4. Add another new CSS style to the jacobs.css style sheet. Use the CSS Selector to choose a:hover, then set Font to **Arial**, **Helvetica**, **sans-serif**; Size to **14 pixels**; Weight to **bolder**, and Color to dark blue (**#000099**).

5. Add a new style to the jacobs.css style sheet that redefines the body tag. Set Font to **Arial**, **Helvetica**, **sans-serif**; Size to **16 pixels**; Style to **normal**, and Color to black (**#000000**).
6. Add the following line of code to the end of the body tag in the jacobs.css style sheet file: **scrollbar-track-color:#660033;**.
7. Add the following line of code below the code you just typed: **scrollbar-face-color:#FFCC99;** .

8. Save your changes, then close the jacobs.css style sheet.
9. Preview the menus template in a browser, position the mouse pointer over one of the text links, then compare your screen to Figure L-39.
10. Close your browser, save the menus template, update all pages in the site, then close the menus template.

FIGURE L-39
Completed Project Builder 2

Many of today's leading Web sites use CSS style sheets to ensure consistent formatting and positioning of text and other elements. For instance, CNET.com, a premier source of technical news on the Internet, uses CSS. Figure L-40 shows the CNET.com home page.

1. Connect to the Internet, then go to *www.course.com*. Navigate to the page for this book, click the Student Online Companion, then click the link for this unit.

2. Spend some time exploring the many pages of this site.

3. When you finish exploring all of the different pages, return to the home page. Click View on your browser's menu bar, then click Source to view the code for the page.

4. Look in the head content area for code relating to the CSS style sheet used. Note whether any styles are defined for a:link or a:hover and write down the specified formatting for those styles. Write down any other code you see that relates to styles.

5. Close the Source window, then look at the home page. Make a list of all the different text elements that you see on the page and that you think should have CSS styles applied to them.

6. Spend time looking at other Web sites that you frequently use. Use the Source command on the View menu of your browser window to determine whether the site uses CSS.

7. Write down the name of another site you find that uses CSS, then print out its home page and the source code that contains CSS Styles.

FIGURE L-40
Source for Design Project

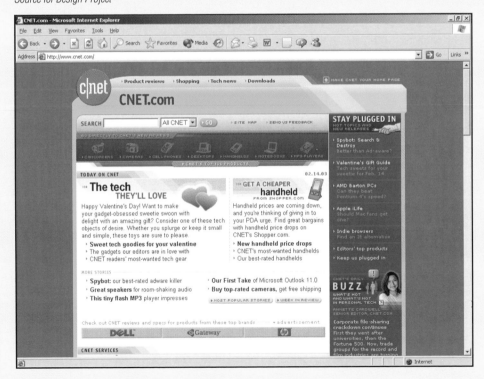

In this assignment, you will continue to work on the group Web site that you created in Units A through K. Depending on the size of your group, you can assign individual elements of the project to group members, or work collectively to create the finished product.

You will continue refining your Web site by using CSS style sheets, inline styles, and HTML styles to format the text in your Web site consistently. You will start by attaching the style sheet you created in Unit C.

1. Meet as a group to view the pages of your Web site and write a plan in which you define styles for all of the text elements in your site. Your plan should include how you will use an external style sheet, as well as inline styles and HTML styles. You can use either the external style sheet you created in Unit C, or create a new one. Your plan should include at least one custom style, one style that redefines an HTML tag, and one style that uses the CSS Selector.

2. Decide as a group whether you will attach your style sheet to individual pages in the site, or whether you will attach it to the template you created in Unit K.

3. Based on the decision you arrived at in Step 2, assign a team member (or members) the task of attaching the external style sheet to the template you created in Unit K or to the individual pages of the site. Be sure to save the template after attaching the style sheet, and update all pages in the site.

4. Assign a team member the task of defining and applying the HTML styles you identified in your plan.

5. Assign a team member the task of creating and applying the inline styles you identified in your plan.

6. Assign a team member the task of creating and applying the styles that will be added to the external style sheet.

7. Assign a team member the task of adding custom code to the body tag of your external style sheet to change the colors of the scroll bar to match the colors of your site.

8. Meet as a group to review the pages and make sure that all text elements appear as they should and look appropriate. Use the Web Site Check List in Figure L-41 to make sure you have completed everything according to the assignment.

9. Assign a team member the task of making any necessary changes.

10. Save your work, then close all open pages.

FIGURE L-41
Web Site Check List

Web Site Check List

1. Do all text elements in the site have a style applied to them?
2. Does your site have at least one HTML style?
3. Does your site have at least one inline style?
4. Is an external style sheet attached to each page in the site or to a template to which each page is attached?
5. Did you define and apply at least one custom style, one style that redefines an HTML tag, and one style that defines links?
6. Did you add custom code to the body tag of the style sheet to change the colors of the scroll bar in a browser to match the colors of the site?
7. Do all links work and appear according to the formatting you specified?

UNIT

M

WORKING WITH LIBRARY ITEMS AND SNIPPETS

1. Create and modify library items.

2. Add library items to pages.

3. Add and modify snippets.

Introduction

When creating a Web site, chances are good that you will want certain graphics or text blocks to appear in more than one place in the site. For instance, you might want the company tag line in several different places, or a footer containing links to the main pages of the site at the bottom of every page. Library items and snippets can help you work with these repeating elements more efficiently.

Understanding Library Items

If you want an element to appear repeatedly, then it's a good idea to save it as a library item. A **library item** is content that can contain text or graphics and is saved in a separate file in the Library folder of your Web site. The advantage of using library items is that when you make a change to the library item and then update the site, all instances of that item will be updated to reflect the change.

Understanding Snippets

Another way to use the same content repeatedly throughout a site is to insert code snippets. **Code snippets** are reusable pieces of code that can be inserted on a page. Dreamweaver provides a wide variety of ready-made code snippets you can use to create footers, drop-down menus, headers, and other elements.

In this unit, you will work with library items and code snippets to enhance the Super Bug Zapper Web site.

Tools You'll Use

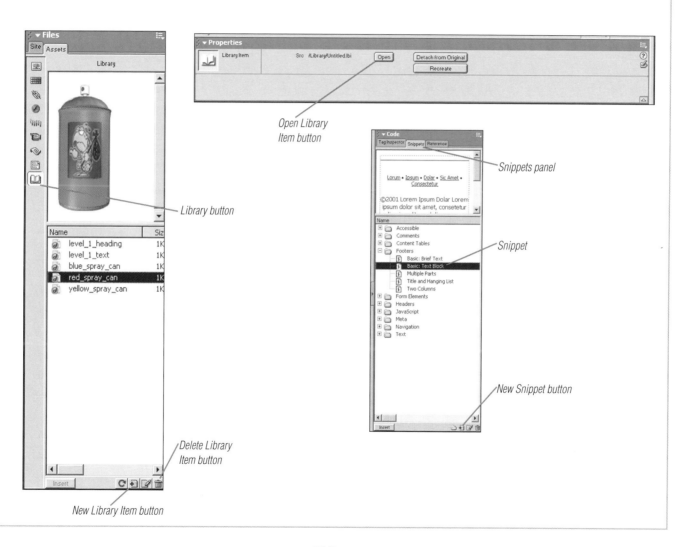

CREATE AND MODIFY LIBRARY ITEMS

What You'll Do

In this lesson, you will create two text-based library items containing content from the products page. You will also create a library item that contains the navigation bar images in the main_elements template. You will then add an image for a home navigation bar button to the navigation_bar library item and update the site so that every page contains the Home button. You will also edit one of the text-based library items and update the site to reflect those edits.

Understanding the Benefits of Library Items

Using library items for repetitive elements—especially those that need to be updated frequently—can save you considerable time. For instance, suppose you want to feature a customer-of-the-month photograph on every page in your site. You could create a library item named customer_photo, and add it to every page. Then, when you need to update the site to show a new customer photo, you could simply replace the photo contained in the library item and the photo would be updated throughout the site. Library items can contain a wide range of content, including text, images, tables, and sounds.

Viewing and Creating Library Items

To view library items, open the Assets panel, then click the Library button. The library items appear in a list, and a preview of the selected library item appears above the list, as shown in Figure M-1. To save text or an image as a library item, select the item in the document window, then drag it to the Assets panel. The item that you dragged will appear in the preview window in the Assets panel and in the library item list with the temporary name Untitled assigned to it. Type a new name, then press [Enter] (Win) or [return] (Mac) to give the library item a permanent name. Library items on a Web page appear in shaded yellow in the document window. When you click a library item in the document window, the entire item is selected and the Property inspector changes to display three buttons that you can use to work with the library item, as shown in Figure M-2.

QUICKTIP

You can also view a list of available library items by expanding the Library folder in the Site panel.

Modifying Library Items

You cannot edit library items on the Web page in which they appear. In order to make changes to a library item, you need to open it. To open a library item, select the item in the document window, then click Open in the Property inspector. The library item will appear in the document window, where you can make edits or add content to it. When you are satisfied with your edits, save the library item using the Save command on the File menu. When you do this, the Update Library Item dialog box will appear, asking if you want to update all instances of the library item throughout the site.

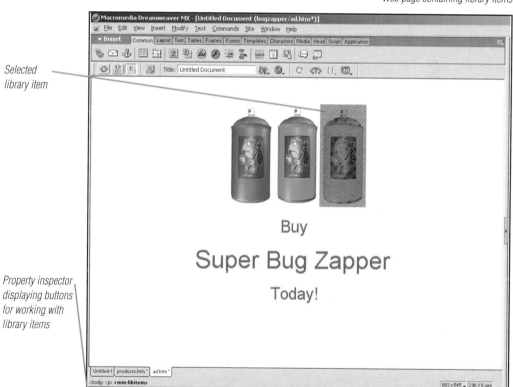

Preview of selected library item

Library button

Library items

Selected library item

Selected library item

Property inspector displaying buttons for working with library items

Create a text-based library item

1. Open the Super Bug Zapper Web site, then open the products page.

2. Open the Assets panel, then click the Library button.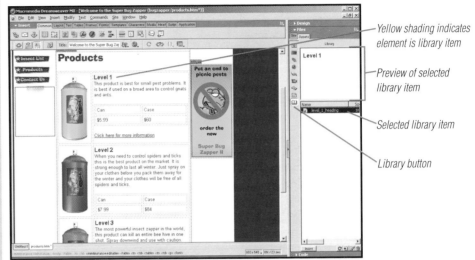

3. Select the Level 1 heading in the cell to the right of the yellow spray can image, then drag it to the Assets panel.

   The Level 1 heading that you dragged is now an unnamed library item in the Assets panel.

4. Type **level_1_heading**, press [Enter] (Win) or [return] (Mac) to name the library item, click away from the library item to deselect it, then compare your screen to Figure M-3.

   Notice that the Level 1 heading now has a shaded yellow background, indicating it is a library item.

5. Select the paragraph text below the Level 1 heading in the cell to the right of the yellow spray can image, then drag the selection to the Assets panel.

   The paragraph text that you dragged is now an unnamed library item in the Assets panel.

6. Type **level_1_text**, press [Enter] (Win) or [return] (Mac) to name the library item, click in the document window to deselect the library item, then compare your screen to Figure M-4.

You created two text-based library items from text on the products page.

FIGURE M-3

Assets panel showing new level_1_heading library item

Yellow shading indicates element is library item

Preview of selected library item

Selected library item

Library button

FIGURE M-4

Assets panel showing two new library items

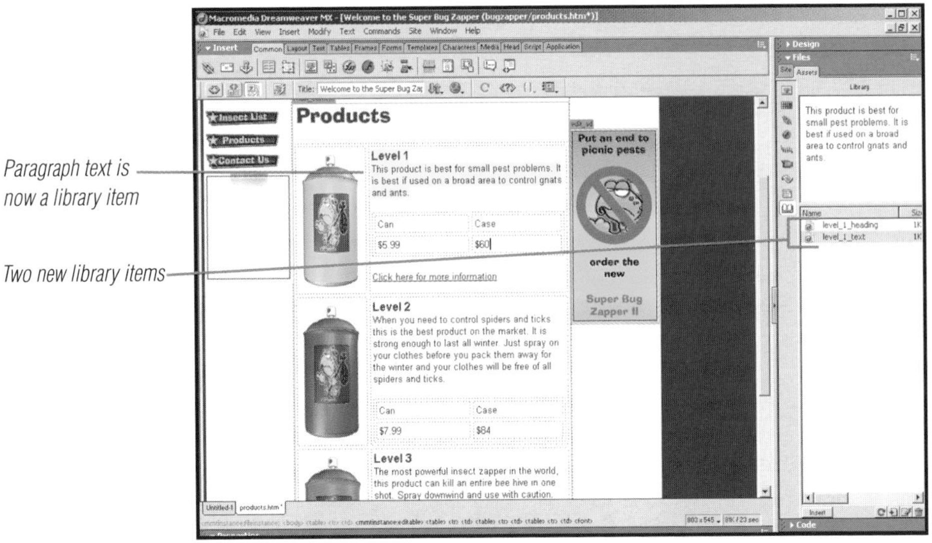

Paragraph text is now a library item

Two new library items

FIGURE M-5
Assets panel after naming navigation_bar library item

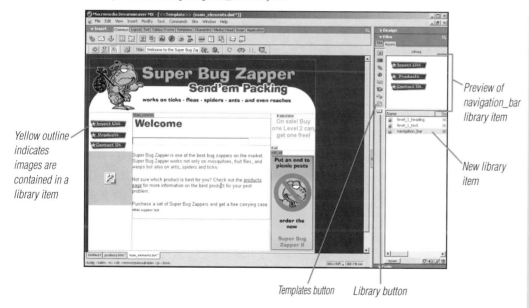

Yellow outline indicates images are contained in a library item

Preview of navigation_bar library item

New library item

Templates button   *Library button*

1. Click the Templates button on the Assets panel, then double-click the main_elements template to open it. 🖹

2. Click the Library button on the Assets panel to display the library items in the Web site. 📖

3. Click the Insect List navigation button on the left side of the main_elements template, press and hold [Shift], click the Contact Us button to select all three navigation buttons, then release the [Shift] key.

4. Drag the selected buttons to the Assets panel.

   The three navigation bar buttons appear in the preview window at the top of the Assets panel, and a new untitled library item appears selected in the library item list.

   TIP If a dialog box opens informing you that the buttons might appear differently on other pages because the style sheet information is not copied, click OK.

5. Type **navigation_bar**, press [Enter] (Win) or [return] (Mac) to name the library item in the Assets panel, click away from the library item to deselect it, then compare your screen to Figure M-5.

6. Save your changes, then update all templates and pages in the site.

You created a library item named navigation_bar that contains the three navigation bar images in the main_elements template. You then saved the template and updated all templates and pages in the site.

Edit an image-based library item

1. Click the Insect List navigation button on the left side of the main_elements template.

   Clicking the Insect List button selected all of the buttons in the navigation_bar library item. The Property inspector now displays buttons you can use to work with library items.

2. Click Open in the Property inspector to open the navigation_bar library item.

   The three navigation buttons in the navigation_bar library item appear in the document window.

   | TIP You can also open a library item by double-clicking it in the Assets panel.

3. Click the Insect List button in the document window to select it, press [←], then press [Enter] (Win) or [return] (Mac).

   You inserted a hard return above the Insect List button.

4. Press [↑] to move the insertion point to the top line, then compare your screen to Figure M-6.

   (continued)

FIGURE M-6

Preparing to add the Home button to the navigation_bar library item

Blank line added here

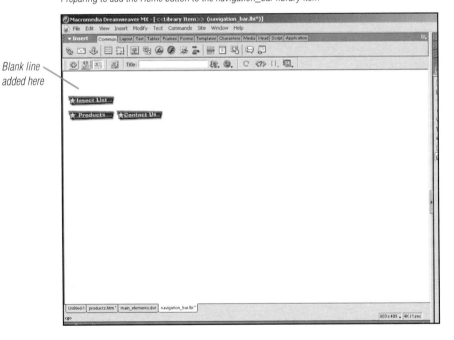

FIGURE M-7

Navigation_bar library item in document window after adding Home button

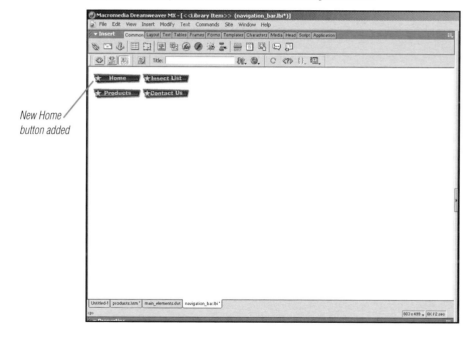

New Home
button added

5. Insert the home.gif image file located in the unit_m assets folder, then save the home.gif image to the assets folder of the Web site.

6. Click the Insect List button, press [←], then press [Backspace] (Win) or [del] (Mac) to move the Insect List button to the right of the Home button.

7. Click the Home button to select it, click the Browse for File icon next to the Link property in the Property inspector to open the Select File dialog box, navigate to the root folder of the Web site, click index.htm, then click OK (Win) or Choose (Mac).

   Notice that the tag selector shows the tags <p> (the paragraph tag), <a> (the link tag), and <img> (the image tag).

8. Click anywhere to deselect the Home button, then compare your screen to Figure M-7.

You added the Home button to the navigation_bar library item.

Update library items

1. Click File on the menu bar, then click Save to open the Update Library Items dialog box.

   The dialog box asks if you want to update the library item on the pages shown.

2. Click Update to open the Update Pages dialog box.

   This is the same dialog box that appears when you save a template. The only difference is that the Library Items checkbox is checked.

3. Click the Look in list arrow, click Entire Site, click Start, then compare your screen to Figure M-8.

4. Click Close, open the main_elements template, then compare your screen to Figure M-9.

   Notice that the Home navigation button now appears on this page, reflecting the change you made to the navigation_bar library item.

5. Save the main_elements template, then update all pages in the site.

You saved the navigation_bar library item and updated all pages in the site to incorporate the changes you made.

FIGURE M-8

Update Pages dialog box with Library Items checked

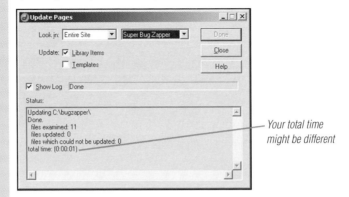

Your total time might be different

FIGURE M-9

Main_elements template showing updated navigation_bar library item

Home button added to library item

FIGURE M-10

Level_1_text library item after editing

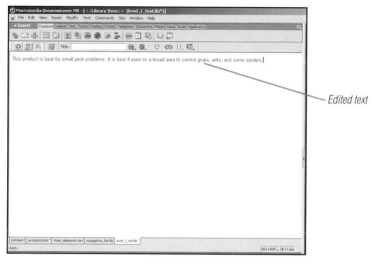

Edited text

1. Open the products page, then click the paragraph text below the Level 1 heading to select the level_1_text library item.

2. Click Open in the Property inspector to open the level_1_text library item.

3. Select the text gnats and ants. at the end of the second sentence, type **gnats, ants, and some spiders.**, then compare your screen to Figure M-10.

4. Save your changes, update all pages in the site, then close the level_1_text library item.

5. Open the products page, then compare your screen to Figure M-11.

   The paragraph text under the Level 1 heading reflects the edits you made to the level_1_text library item.

You edited the text in the level_1_text library item, then saved the changes and updated the site.

FIGURE M-11

Products page after edits made to level_1_text library item

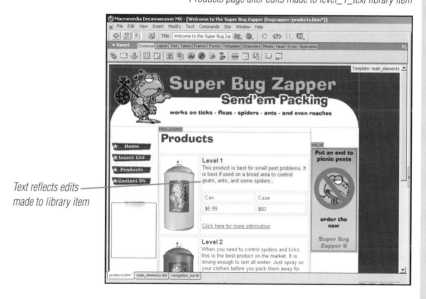

Text reflects edits made to library item

ADD LIBRARY ITEMS TO PAGES

What You'll Do

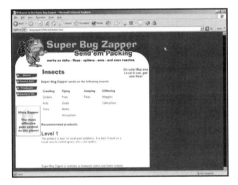

 In this lesson, you will add the two text-based library items you created to the insects page. You will then delete one of the library items and restore the deleted item using the Recreate command.

Adding Library Items to a Page

Once you create a library item, it's easy to add it to any page in a Web site. All you need to do is drag the library item from the Assets panel to the desired location on the page. When you insert a library item, the actual content and a reference to the library item are copied into the code. The inserted library item is shaded in yellow in the document window, and will be automatically updated to reflect any changes you make to the library item.

QUICKTIP

You can also insert a library item on a page by selecting the item in the Assets panel, then clicking Insert.

There may be times when you don't want content to be updated when you update the library item. For instance, suppose you want one of your pages to include photos of all past customers-of-the-month. You would insert content from the current library item, but you do not want the photo to change when the library item is updated to reflect next month's customer photo. To achieve this, you would insert the content of a library item on a page without inserting the reference to the library item. To do this, press and hold [Ctrl] (Win) or [command] (Mac) as you drag the library item from the Assets panel to the document window. The content from the library item will be inserted on the page, but it will not be linked to the library item.

Making Library Items Editable on a Page

There may be times when you would like to make changes to a particular instance of a library item on one page, without making those changes to other instances of the library item in the site. You can make a library item editable on a page by breaking its link to the library item. To do this, select the library item, then click Detach from Original in the Property inspector. Once you have detached the library item, you can edit the content like you would any other element on the page. Keep in mind, though, that this edited content will not be updated when you make changes to the library item.

Deleting and Recreating Library Items

If you know that you will never need to update a library item again, you might want to delete it. To delete a library item, select it in the Assets panel, then click the Delete button. Deleting a library item only removes it from the Library folder; it does not change the contents of the pages that contain that library item. All instances of the deleted library item will still appear in shaded yellow in the site. Be aware that you cannot use the Undo command to bring back a library item. However, you can undelete a library item by selecting any instance of the item in the site and clicking Recreate in the Property inspector. After you recreate a library item, it reappears in the Assets panel and you can make changes to it and update all pages in the site again. Figure M-12 shows the Library Item Property inspector.

FIGURE M-12
Library Item Property inspector

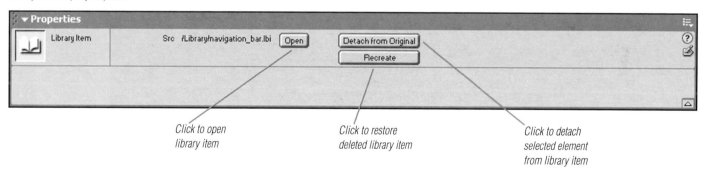

Click to open
library item

Click to restore
deleted library item

Click to detach
selected element
from library item

Add a library item to a page

1. Open the insects page.

2. Click below the insects table in the Main_content editable region to set the insertion point, type **Recommended products:**, then press [Enter] (Win) or [return] (Mac).

3. Format the Recommended products: text in **Arial, Helvetica, sans-serif**, size **2**, bold, maroon (**#990000**).

4. Open the Assets panel (if necessary), then drag the level_1_heading library item from the Assets panel to below the Recommended products: text you just typed, then click anywhere to deselect the heading.

   The Level 1 heading now appears where you dragged it. Notice that it is shaded in yellow, indicating it is a library item.

5. Click to the right of the Level 1 heading, press and hold [Shift], then press [Enter] (Win) or [return] (Mac) to place the insertion point on the line below the Level 1 heading.

6. Drag the level_1_text library item from the Assets panel to the line below the Level 1 heading on the insects page, deselect the text, then compare your screen to Figure M-13.

7. Save your changes.

You added the level_1_heading and level_1_text library items to the insects page.

FIGURE M-13
Insects page with library items added

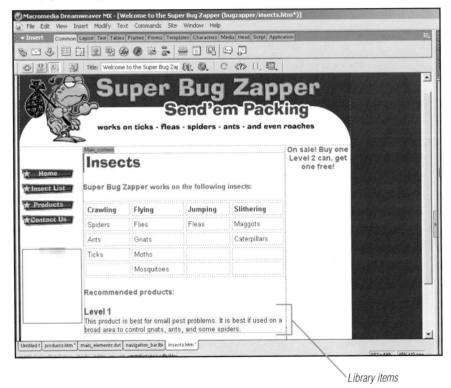

Library items

FIGURE M-14

Insects page after detaching library items

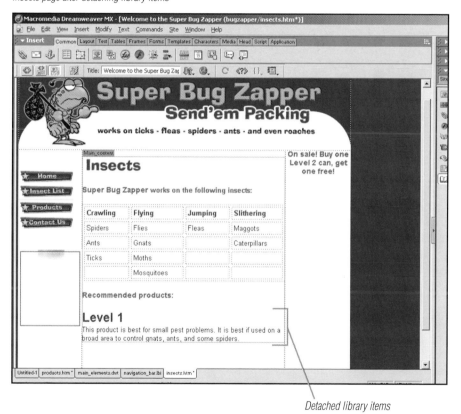

Detached library items

1. Click the Level 1 heading on the insects page.

   Clicking the heading selects it because it is a library item. The Property inspector now displays three buttons relating to library items.

2. Click Detach from Original in the Property inspector.

   A dialog box opens, warning you that the item will no longer be automatically updated when the original library item changes.

3. Click OK.

   Notice that the heading no longer appears in shaded yellow, indicating it is no longer a library item.

4. Select the paragraph text below the Level 1 heading, then detach this text from the level_1_text library item.

5. Change the size of the Level 1 heading to 5, deselect the text, then compare your screen to Figure M-14.

   The size of the heading is now larger. The level_1_heading library item remains unchanged.

6. Save your changes.

You detached the Level 1 heading from the level_1_heading library item and the paragraph text from the level_1_text library item to make both of these text elements editable on the insects page. You then increased the size of the Level 1 heading on the insects page.

Delete a library item

1. Select the level_1_text library item in the Assets panel.

2. Click the Delete button in the Assets panel.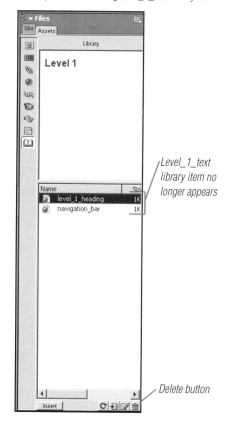

   A dialog box opens, asking if you are sure you want to delete the library item.

3. Click Yes, then compare your screen to Figure M-15.

   The level_1_text library item no longer appears in the Assets panel.

You deleted the level_1_text library item in the Assets panel.

FIGURE M-15

Assets panel after deleting level_1_text library item

Level_1_text library item no longer appears

Delete button

FIGURE M-16

Assets panel after recreating level_1_text library item

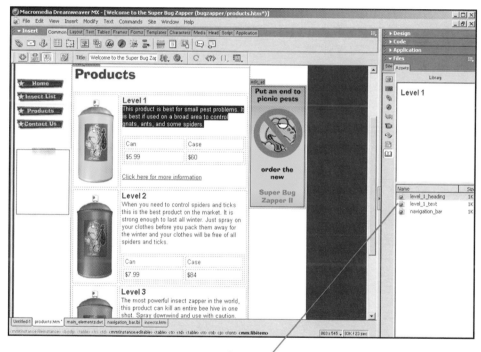

Recreated
level_1_text
library item

1. Open the products page.

   The paragraph text under the Level 1 heading still appears in shaded yellow, indicating it is still a library item, even though you deleted the library item to which it is attached.

2. Click the paragraph text under the Level 1 heading to select it.

3. Click Recreate in the Property inspector, then compare your screen to Figure M-16.

   The level_1_text library item is added to the Assets panel.

4. Save your changes.

You recreated the level_1_text library item that you deleted in the previous set of steps.

ADD AND MODIFY SNIPPETS

What You'll Do

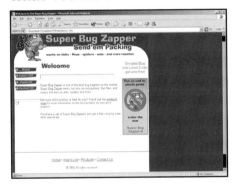

 In this lesson, you will add a predefined snippet from the Snippets panel to create a new footer in the main_elements template. You will then replace the placeholder text and links in the snippet with appropriate text and links. Finally, you will save the modified snippet as a new snippet, so that you can add it to other pages.

Using the Snippets Panel

Creating a Web site is a huge task, so it's nice to know that you can save time by using ready-made code snippets to create various elements of your site. The Snippets panel, located in the Code panel group, contains a large collection of reusable code snippets organized in folders named by element type. The Snippets panel contains two panes, as shown in Figure M-17. The lower pane contains folders that can be expanded to view the snippets. The upper pane displays a preview of the selected snippet. Use the buttons at the bottom of the Snippets panel to insert a snippet, create a new folder in the Snippets panel, create a new snippet, edit a snippet, or remove a snippet.

Inserting and Modifying Snippets

Adding a snippet to a page is an easy task; simply drag the snippet from the Snippets panel to the desired location on the page. Once you position a snippet, you will need to replace the placeholder text, links, and images with appropriate content.

> **QUICKTIP**
>
> You can also add a snippet to a page by selecting the snippet in the Snippets panel, then clicking Insert.

Creating New Snippets

Once you've modified a snippet so that it contains text and graphics appropriate for your site, you might want to save it with a new name. Doing this will save time when using this snippet on other pages. To save a modified snippet as a new snippet, select the snippet content in the document window, then click the New Snippet button in the Snippets panel to open the Snippet dialog box. Use this dialog box to name the snippet and give it a description. Because the Snippet dialog box displays the snippet code, you can make edits to the code here if you wish. Any new snippets you create will appear in the Snippets panel.

FIGURE M-17
Snippets panel

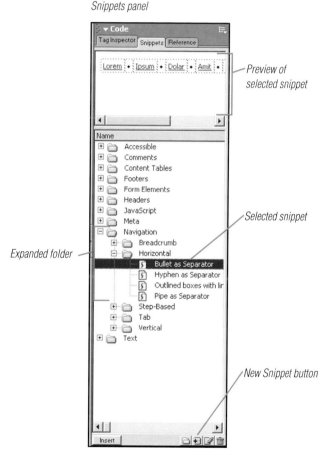

Add a predefined snippet to a page

1. Open the main_elements template.

2. Scroll to the bottom of the page, select the sentence Super Bug Zapper is available at hardware stores and home centers., then press [Delete] (Win) or [del] (Mac).

3. Open the Code panel group, then click the Snippets tab to open the Snippets panel.

4. Click the plus sign (+) (Win) or the triangle (Mac) next to the Footers folder in the Snippets panel to display the contents of the Footers folder.

5. Drag the Basic: Text Block in the Footers folder to the bottom row of the table in the main_elements template, as shown in Figure M-18.

6. Save your changes, then update all templates and pages in the site.

You deleted the footer in the main_elements template, then added a predefined footer from the Snippets panel.

FIGURE M-18
Main_elements template after adding snippet

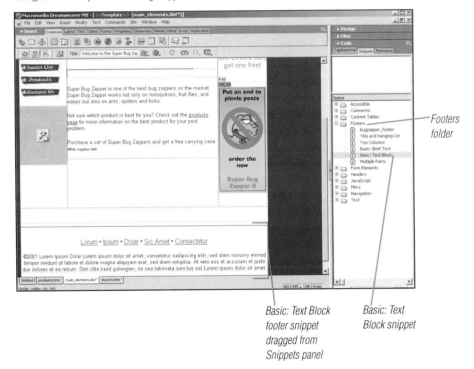

Footers folder

Basic: Text Block footer snippet dragged from Snippets panel

Basic: Text Block snippet

FIGURE M-19

Main_elements template after editing snippet placeholder text

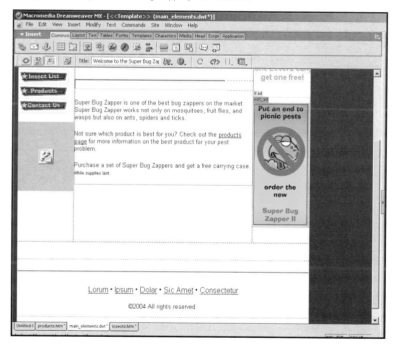

Modify snippet text

1. Click between the copyright symbol (©) and 2001 in the paragraph text below the placeholder links in the footer, press and hold [Shift], then click to the right of the period at the end of the paragraph.

   The entire paragraph, except for the © at the beginning of the paragraph should be selected.

2. Type **2004 All rights reserved.**, then compare your screen to Figure M-19.

3. Save your changes, then update all templates and pages in the site.

You edited the placeholder text contained in the footer snippet in the main_elements template.

Modify snippet links

1. Select the Lorum placeholder link in the bottom row of the table in the main_elements template, then type **Home**.

2. Replace the Ipsum placeholder link with **Insect List**, replace the Dolar placeholder link with **Products**, then replace the Sic Amet placeholder link with **Contact Us**.

3. Delete the Consectetur placeholder link, then delete the black dot to the right of the Contact Us link.

4. Open the Site panel, select the Home link in the footer in the main_elements template, then use the Point to File icon in the Property inspector to set the Link property to the index page, as shown in Figure M-20.

5. Use the Point to File icon to set the Link property for the Products, Insect List, and Contact Us links.

6. Save your changes, then update all other templates and pages in the site.

7. Preview the main_elements template in your browser, test all the links in the footer, then close your browser.

You changed the names of the placeholder links and used the Point to File icon to create links to the four main pages in the Super Bug Zapper Web site.

FIGURE M-20

Using the Point to File icon to create document-relative links in the footer

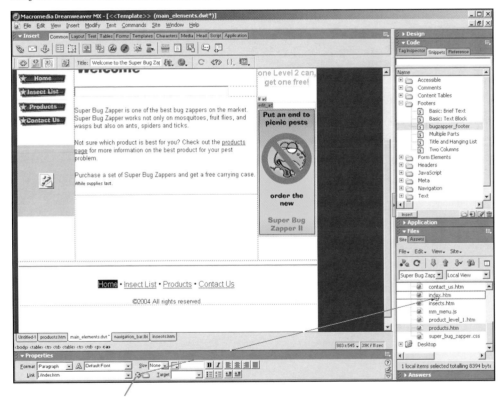

Point to File icon

FIGURE M-21

Snippet dialog box

Name text box

Description
text box

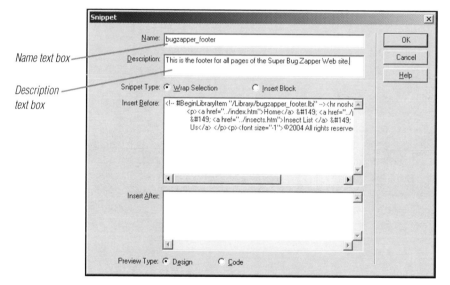

1. Select the footer in the main_elements template.

2. Click the New Snippet button in the Snippets panel to open the Snippet dialog box.

3. Type **bugzapper_footer** in the Name text box.

4. Type **This is the footer for all pages of the Super Bug Zapper Web site.** in the Description text box, then compare your screen to Figure M-21.

5. Click OK.

   The bugzapper_footer snippet now appears in the Snippets panel. You can insert it on any page by dragging it to the desired location in the document window.

6. Close all open pages and templates, then close Dreamweaver.

You copied the footer from the main_elements template and saved it as a snippet called bugzapper_footer.

Create and modify library items.

1. Open the Blooms & Bulbs Web site that you created and developed in Units A through L, then open the master_gardener template. (If you did not create this Web site in Units A through L, contact your instructor for assistance.)

2. Scroll down the page until the Further Research heading and paragraph text is visible on your screen, select the text *cosie@blooms&bulbs.com*, then convert this selected text into a library item named **contact_e-mail**.

3. Select the phone number *(555)248-0806* in the paragraph below the Further Research heading, then convert this selection into a library item named **contact_number**.

4. Edit the contact_number library item so that the last four digits in the phone number are **0807**.

5. Save and update the contact_number library item, then check to make sure the phone number in the paragraph text changed to reflect your edit.

6. Open the tips page, then insert the flower.gif image from the assets folder of the Web site under the Planting Tips heading.

7. Convert the flower.gif image to a library item named **flowers**.

8. Open the flowers library item, select the flower.gif image, copy the image, then use the Paste command twice so that the flowers library item contains three flower images.

9. Save and update the flowers library item, close the flowers library item, then save the tips page.

Add library items to pages.

1. Place the insertion point at the end of the first paragraph on the tips page. Type **And remember, if you have questions, call or e-mail our experts at**.

2. Insert the contact_e-mail library item to the right of the text you just typed.

3. Type **or** to the right of the contact_e-mail library item you inserted.

4. Insert the contact_number library item to the right of the word or that you just typed, then type a period (.) after the contact_number library item.

5. Make the contact_e-mail library item editable on the page, select cosie in the address, then type **tips**, so that the e-mail address is changed to *tips@blooms&bulbs.com*.

6. Delete the flowers library item.

7. Recreate the flowers library item.

8. Save your changes, preview the tips page in your browser, compare your screen to Figure M-22, close your browser, then close the tips page.

Add and modify snippets.

1. Open the master_gardener template.

2. Scroll to the bottom of the page so that the Top of Page Flash button is visible.

3. Insert the Basic: Text Block snippet, located in the Footers folder of the Snippets panel, at the bottom of the page, below the Top of Page Flash button.

4. Replace the paragraph text below the placeholder links with the following text: **Copyright 2004. Thank you for your business!**
5. Replace the placeholder links in the footer with links to the home, plants, workshops, tips, and master_gardener pages.
6. Create a new snippet from the footer you just inserted. Name the snippet **blooms_footer**, and give it an appropriate description.
7. Save your changes, update all pages in the site, preview the master_gardener template in your browser, then compare your screen to Figure M-23.
8. Test the links in the footer to make sure they work, close your browser, then close the master_gardener template.

FIGURE M-22

Completed Skills Review: tips page

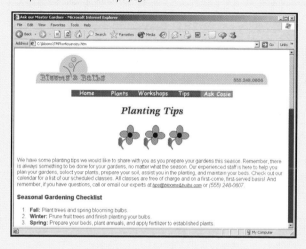

FIGURE M-23

Completed Skills Review: master_gardener template

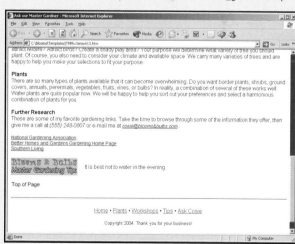

In this Project Builder you will continue your work on the Rapids Transit Web site that you began in Project Builder 1 in Unit A. Mike Andrew, the owner, has asked you to add the Rapids Transit address and phone number to every page of the Web site. He also asked you to create a new footer for every page that provides links to the main pages of the site and gives copyright information. You decide to use library items and snippets to incorporate these items.

1. Open the Rapids Transit Web site that you created in Units A through L, then open the rapids_info template. (If you did not create this Web site in Units A through L, contact your instructor for assistance.)
2. Convert the Rapids Transit address information at the bottom of the page into a library item named **rapids_address**.
3. Convert the Rapids Transit phone number into a library item named **rapids_phone**.
4. Add the rapids_address and rapids_phone library items to the bottom of the before and rentals pages.
5. Open the reservations page and replace the contact information at the bottom of the page with the rapids_address and rapids_phone library items.
6. Open the rapids_address library item and add the zip code **72636**. Save and update the rapids_address library item, then open

the rapids_info template and make sure the zip code appears in the address to reflect your edits.
7. Replace the copyright notice and last updated notice at the bottom of the rapids_info template with a footer using any snippet you want from the Footers folder of the Snippets panel.
8. Replace the placeholder links in the footer with links to the main pages of the Web site.
9. Use the Point to File icon to set the Link property for each link. Replace the placeholder paragraph text in the footer with the text **Copyright 2004. All rights reserved.**

10. Create a new snippet named **rapids_footer** that is based on the footer you created. Specify an appropriate description.
11. Save the rapids_info template, then update all pages in the site.
12. Add the rapids_footer snippet to the bottom of the before and rentals pages. Replace the copyright notice on the reservations page with the rapids_footer snippet. Center the links and text in the footer (if necessary).
13. Save your changes, preview the rapids_info template in your browser, compare your screen to Figure M-24, then test all links in the footer to make sure they work.
14. Close all open pages.

FIGURE M-24
Completed Project Builder 1

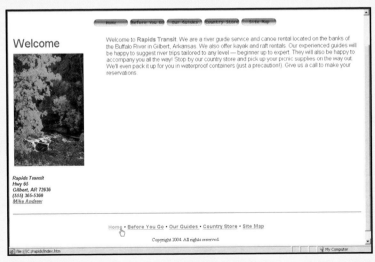

In this Project Builder, you will continue your work on the Jacob's Web site that you started in Project Builder 2 in Unit A. Chef Jacob has asked you to convert the Jacob's logo on the menus template into a library item. He has also asked you to add a footer to every page in the site that contains a copyright notice and links to all of the pages.

1. Open the Jacob's Web site. (If you did not create this site in Units A through L, contact your instructor for assistance.)

2. Open the menus template, then convert the blue Jacob's logo below the paragraph text into a library item named **jacobs_blue_logo**.

3. Open the jacobs_blue_logo library item, then type the text **Be sure to check this week's specials!** on the line below the image. Select the text you just typed, then set the Link property for the selected text to the menus page. Save, update, and close the library item.

4. Detach the jacobs_blue_logo library item from the menus template, then delete the text Be sure to check this week's specials!. Save your changes, then update all pages in the site.

5. Open the recipes page. Insert the jacobs_blue_logo library item in the table cell to the left of the Submit and Reset buttons.

6. Delete the form element at the bottom of the recipes page and the drop-down menu it

contains. (*Hint*: To delete the form element, select it, right-click (Win) or [control] Click (Mac), then click Remove Tag).

7. Insert a footer below the Directions paragraph using a snippet of your choice from the Footers folder of the Snippets panel.

8. Replace the placeholder paragraph text in the footer with an appropriate copyright notice and message.

9. Replace the placeholder links with links to the four main pages of the site. Set the Link property for each link to the appropriate page in the site. Center align all content in the footer.

10. Create a new snippet from the footer you

created named **jacobs_footer**. Give it an appropriate description.

11. Convert the footer you created into a library item named **footer**.

12. Insert the footer library item at the bottom of the other pages in the Web site. Delete the previous copyright notice on the index page. Detach the footer library item from the original on each page, then center-align the footers.

13. Save your changes, preview the recipes page in your browser, compare your screen to Figure M-25, test all the links in the footer, then close your browser.

14. Close all open pages.

FIGURE M-25
Completed Project Builder 2

Library items and snippets are commonly used in Web sites to ensure that repetitive information is updated quickly and accurately. Figure M-26 shows a Web site that was recently featured as a Macromedia Site of the Day.

1. Connect to the Internet, then go to *www.course.com*. Navigate to the page for this book, click the Student Online Companion, then click the link for this unit.

2. Spend some time exploring the pages of this site to become familiar with its elements. Do you see many repeating elements?

3. If you were developing this site, which images or text would you convert into library items? Print out two pages from this Web site and write a list of all the text and visual elements from these pages that you would make into library items.

4. Go to your favorite search engine, such as Google (*www.google.com*) or AltaVista (*www.altavista.com*), and type in search words relating to one of your favorite hobbies or interests.

5. Locate a site that interests you, then print out two pages from the site.

6. Write a list of all the elements shown on the printed pages that you think should be made into library items.

FIGURE M-26
Source for Design Project

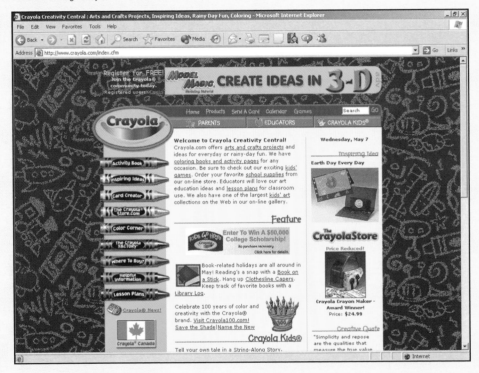

In this assignment, you will continue to work on the group Web site that you created in Units A through L. Depending on the size of your group, you can assign individual elements of the project to group members, or work collectively to create the finished product.

You will continue to enhance your Web site by using library items and snippets.

1. Consult your storyboard and brainstorm as a team to decide which text and graphic elements in the site should be converted into library items. Write a list of these items.

2. Discuss what content to include in a footer that you will add to each page of the site using a snippet.

3. Assign a team member the task of converting all the text elements you identified in your list into library items.

4. Assign a team member the task of inserting the library items that were created in Step 3 in appropriate places in the Web site.

5. Assign a team member the task of converting all the graphic elements you identified in Step 1 into library items.

6. Assign a team member the task of inserting the graphic library items that were created in Step 5 in appropriate places in the Web site.

7. Assign a team member the task of editing two of the library items that were created, then saving and updating all instances of the library item in the site.

8. Assign a team member the task of adding a footer to the Web site using one of the snippets in the Footers folder of the Snippets panel. This team member should replace all placeholder links with appropriate links to each major page in the site and should also replace placeholder text with text that is suitable for your site.

9. Assign a team member the task of creating a new snippet from the footer that was created in Step 8. This teammate should also insert this snippet on the other pages of the site.

10. Save your work, preview all pages in a browser, and test all the links. Use the Web Site Check List in Figure M-27 to make sure your Web site is complete.

11. Assign a team member the task of making any necessary changes, then saving and closing all open pages.

FIGURE M-27
Web Site Check List

Web Site Check List

1.   Have you converted all repeating text elements into library items?
2.   Have you converted all repeating graphic elements, such as logos, into library items?
3.   Did you save and update the library items after making edits to them?
4.   Do all links work?
5.   Did you add the footer to all pages in the Web site?
6.   Does your copyright notice appear below the links in the footer?

MANAGING A WEB
SERVER AND FILES

1. Publish a Web site and transfer files.

2. Check files out and in.

3. Cloak files.

4. Import and export a site definition.

MANAGING A WEB SERVER AND FILES

Introduction

Once you have created all the pages of your Web site, finalized all the content, and performed site maintenance to ensure that all links work, all colors are Web-safe, and all orphaned pages are eliminated, you are ready to publish your site to a remote server so the rest of the world can access it. In this unit, you will start by defining the remote site for the Super Bug Zapper Web site. You will then transfer files to the remote site and learn how to keep them up to date. You will also check out a file so that it is not available to other teammates while you are editing it, and learn how to cloak files. When a file is **cloaked** it is excluded from certain processes, such as being transferred to the remote site. Finally, you will export the site definition file from the Super Bug Zapper Web site so that other users can import the site.

Preparing to Publish a Site

Before you publish a site to a remote server so that it is available to the rest of the world, it is extremely important that you test it to make sure the content is accurate and up to date, and that everything is functioning properly. If you use the Web at all, you have probably felt frustrated when you click a link that doesn't work, or have to wait for pages that load slowly because of large graphics and animations. Remember that a typical Web viewer has a short attention span and limited patience. Before you publish your site, make sure to use the Link Checker panel to check for broken links and orphaned files. Make sure that all image paths are correct and that all images load quickly and have alternate text. Verify that all pages have titles, and remove all non-Web-safe colors. View the pages in at least two different browsers to ensure that everything works correctly. The more you test, the better the chances that your viewers will have a positive experience and stay at your site.

Tools You'll Use

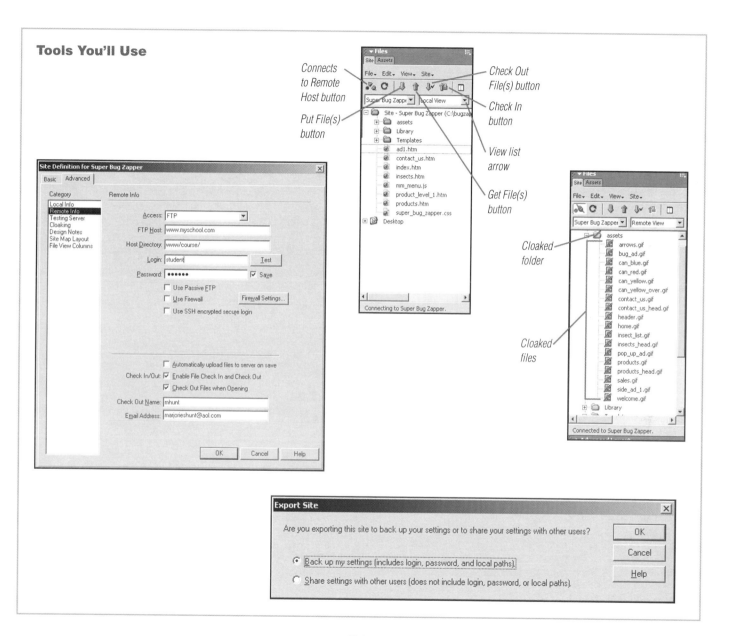

Connects to Remote Host button

Put File(s) button

Check Out File(s) button

Check In button

View list arrow

Get File(s) button

Cloaked folder

Cloaked files

Site Definition for Super Bug Zapper

Basic | Advanced

Category | Remote Info

Local Info
Remote Info
Testing Server
Cloaking
Design Notes
Site Map Layout
File View Columns

Access: FTP

FTP Host: www.myschool.com

Host Directory: www/course/

Login: student

Password: ●●●●●●   ☑ Save   Test

☐ Use Passive FTP
☐ Use Firewall   Firewall Settings...
☐ Use SSH encrypted secure login

☐ Automatically upload files to server on save

Check In/Out: ☑ Enable File Check In and Check Out
☑ Check Out Files when Opening

Check Out Name: mhunt

Email Address: marjorieshunt@aol.com

OK | Cancel | Help

Export Site

Are you exporting this site to back up your settings or to share your settings with other users?

OK
Cancel
Help

◉ Back up my settings (includes login, password, and local paths).

○ Share settings with other users (does not include login, password, or local paths).

PUBLISH A WEB SITE
AND TRANSFER FILES

What You'll Do

In this lesson, you will set up remote access to either an FTP folder or a local/network folder for the Super Bug Zapper Web site. You will also view a Web site on a remote server, upload files to it, and synchronize the files.

Defining a Remote Site

As you learned in Unit A, publishing a site means transferring all files for a site to a Web server. A **Web server** is a computer that is connected to the Internet with an IP (Internet Protocol) address so that it is available on the Internet. Before you can publish a site to a Web server, you must first define the remote site by specifying the Remote Info settings in the Advanced tab of the Site Definition dialog box. You can specify remote settings when you first create a new site and define the root folder (as you did in Unit A when you defined the remote access settings for the TripSmart Web site), or you can do it after you have completed all of your pages and are confident that it is ready for public viewing. To specify the remote settings for a site, you must first choose an Access setting, which specifies the type of server you will use. The most common Access setting is FTP (File Transfer Protocol). If you specify FTP, you will need to specify an address for the server and the name of the folder on the

FTP site in which your root folder will be stored. You will also need to enter login and password information. Figure N-1 shows an example of FTP settings in the Remote Info category of the Site Definition dialog box.

QUICKTIP

If you do not have access to an FTP site, you can publish a site to a local/network folder. Use the alternate steps provided in this lesson to publish your site to a local/network folder.

Viewing a Remote Site

Once you have defined a site to a remote location, you can then view the remote folder in the Site panel by choosing Remote View from the View list. If your remote site is located on an FTP server, you will need to connect to it first by clicking the Connects to Remote Host button on the Site panel toolbar. If you defined your site on a local/network folder, then you don't need to use the Connect to Remote Host button; the root folder and any files and folders it contains will appear in the Site panel when you switch to Remote view.

Transferring Files to and from a Remote Site

After you define a remote site, you will need to transfer or **upload** your files from the local version of your site to the remote host. To do this, view the site in Local view, select the files you want to upload, then click the Put File(s) button on the Site panel toolbar, shown in Figure N-2. Once you click this button, the files will be transferred to the remote site. To view the uploaded files, switch to Remote view.

If a file you select for uploading requires other files, such as graphics, a dialog box will open after you click the Put File(s) button asking if you want those files (known as **dependent files**) to be uploaded. By clicking Yes, all dependent files in the selected page will be uploaded to the appropriate folder in the remote site. If a file that you wish to upload is located in a folder in the local site, the entire folder will be automatically transferred to the remote site.

QUICK**TIP**

To upload an entire site to a remote host, select the root folder, and then click the Put File(s) button. Before doing this, consult with your instructor to find out if you can transfer files directly from the local root folder. Sometimes you will need to move the files you want to upload in an intermediary folder before transferring them to the remote site.

If you are developing or maintaining a Web site in a group environment, there might be times when you want to transfer or **download** files that other teammates have

FIGURE N-1

FTP settings in the Remote Info category of the Site Definition dialog box

FIGURE N-2

Site panel with Remote View selected

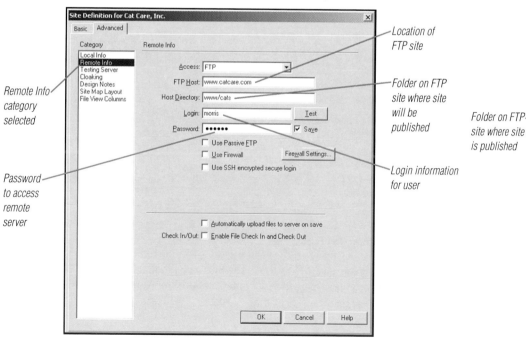

Remote Info category selected

Password to access remote server

Location of FTP site

Folder on FTP site where site will be published

Login information for user

Put File(s) button

Folder on FTP site where site is published

Remote View selected

created from the remote site to your local site. To do this, change to Remote view, select the files you want to download, then click the Get File(s) button on the Site panel toolbar.

Synchronizing Files

In order to keep a Web site up to date—especially one that contains several pages and involves several team members—you will need to update and replace files. Team members might make changes to pages on the local version of the site, or make additions to the remote site. If many people are involved in maintaining a site, or if you are constantly making changes to the pages, ensuring that both the local and remote sites have the most up-to-date files could get confusing. Thankfully, you can use the Synchronize command to keep things straight. The Synchronize command instructs Dreamweaver to compare the dates of the saved files in both versions of the site, then transfers only the files that have changed. To synchronize files, use the Synchronize Files dialog box, shown in Figure N-3. You can synchronize an entire site or just selected files. You can also specify whether to upload newer files to the remote site, download newer files from the remote site, or both.

FIGURE N-3
Synchronize Files dialog box

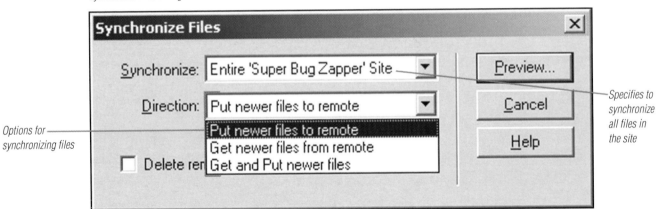

Options for synchronizing files

Specifies to synchronize all files in the site

FIGURE N-4

Site Definition for Super Bug Zapper Web site with FTP settings specified

Remote Info category selected

Type username here

Type password here

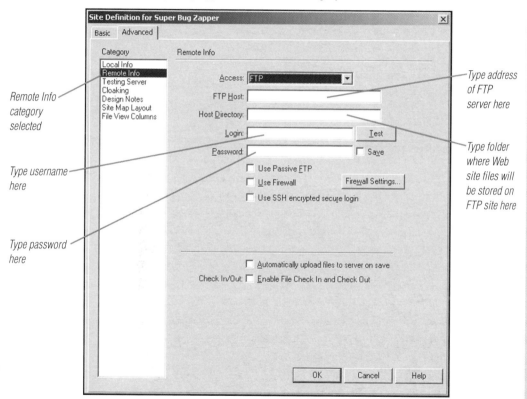

Type address of FTP server here

Type folder where Web site files will be stored on FTP site here

NOTE: Complete these steps only if you know you can store the Super Bug Zapper files on an FTP site, and you know the login and password information.

1. Open the Super Bug Zapper Web site, click Site on the Site panel menu bar (Win) or on the main menu bar (Mac), then click Edit Sites.

2. Click Super Bug Zapper in the Edit Sites dialog box (if necessary), then click Edit.

3. Click the Advanced tab (if necessary), click Remote Info in the Category list, click the Access list arrow, click FTP, then compare your screen to Figure N-4.

4. Enter the FTP Host, Host Directory, Login, and Password information in the dialog box.

   Your instructor will provide you with this information. If you do not have access to an FTP site, complete the exercise called Set up Web server access on a local or network folder on the next page.

   TIP Ask your instructor about setting file and folder permissions, if necessary.

5. Click OK, then click Done to close the Edit Sites dialog box.

You set up remote access information for the Super Bug Zapper Web site using an FTP site folder.

Set up Web server access on a local or network folder

NOTE: Complete these steps if you do not have the ability to post files to an FTP site and could not complete the previous exercise.

1. Using Windows Explorer (Win) or Mac Finder (Mac), create a new folder on your hard drive or on a shared drive named **bugzapper**_yourlastname. (For instance, if your last name is Jones, name the folder **bugzapper_jones**.)

2. Switch back to Dreamweaver, open the Super Bug Zapper Web site (if necessary), click Site on the Site panel menu bar (Win) or on the main menu bar (Mac), then click Edit Sites to open the Edit Sites dialog box.

3. Click Super Bug Zapper, click Edit to open the Site Definition for Super Bug Zapper dialog box, click the Advanced tab, then click Remote Info in the Category list.

4. Click the Access list arrow, then click Local/Network.

5. Click the Browse for File icon next to the Remote Folder text box to open the Choose Remote Root Folder for Site Super Bug Zapper dialog box, navigate to the folder you created in Step 1, select the folder, then click Select (Win) or Choose (Mac).

6. Make sure the Refresh Remote File List Automatically checkbox is checked, compare your screen to Figure N-5, click OK, then click Done.

You created a new folder and specified it as the remote location for the Super Bug Zapper Web site.

FIGURE N-5

Site Definition for Super Bug Zapper dialog box with Local/Network settings specified

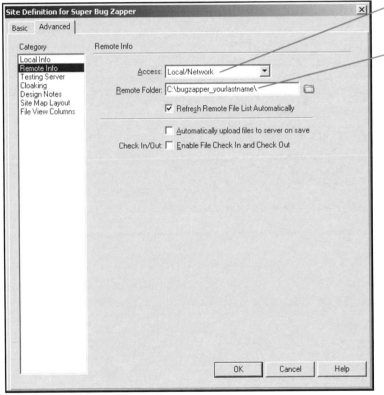

Local/Network setting selected

Local or network drive and folder where remote site will be published (your drive may differ and the folder name should end with your last name)

FIGURE N-6

Connecting to the remote site

Connects to Remote Host button

Remote View selected

Folder on FTP site where Super Bug Zapper site is stored (yours will differ)

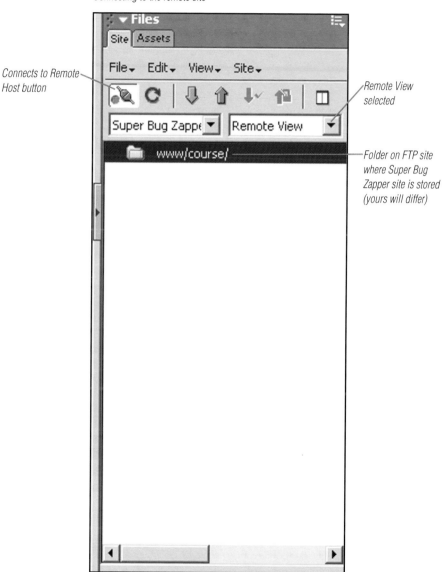

View a Web site on a remote server

1. Click the View list arrow in the Site panel, then click Remote View (Win), or click Site on the menu bar, point to Open Site, then click Super Bug Zapper to open the Site panel with Local and Remote views displayed (Mac).

   If you specified your remote access to a local or network folder, then the bugzapper_ yourlastname folder will appear in the Site panel now. If your remote access is set to an FTP site, you will need to complete Step 2 to see the remote access folder.

2. Click the Connects to Remote Host button in the Site panel (if necessary), then compare your screen to Figure N-6.

   The Site panel changes to show the contents of the remote server that you specified as your remote host. The folder you specified should be empty, because you have not yet uploaded any files to it.

   > TIP Mac users can see both Local and Remote views at once. Windows users must use the View list in the Site panel to choose either Local or Remote view.

You used the Site panel to set the view for the Super Bug Zapper site to Remote view. You then connected to the remote server to view the contents of the remote folder you specified.

Upload files to a remote server

1. Click the View list arrow in the Site panel, then click Local View (Win).

   The Site panel now displays the contents of the local version of the Super Bug Zapper Web site.

2. Click the products page to select it, then click the Put File(s) button on the Site panel toolbar.

   The Dependent Files dialog box opens, asking if you want to include dependent files.

3. Click Yes.

   The products page, along with all the other image files, library items, and templates used in the products page are copied to the remote server. The Status dialog box appears and flashes the names of each file as they are uploaded.

4. Change to Remote view (Win), expand the assets folder (if necessary), expand the Library folder, then compare your screen to Figure N-7.

   The remote site now contains the products page as well as several images, three library items, and the super_bug_zapper external style sheet file, all of which are needed by the products page.

   TIP You might need to expand the bugzapper_yourlastname folder in order to view the assets folder.

You used the Put File(s) button to upload the products page, and all files that are dependent on the products page.

FIGURE N-7

Remote view of the Super Bug Zapper Web site after uploading products page

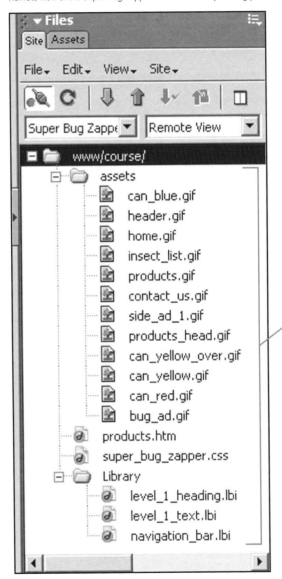

Products page and its dependent files in remote site

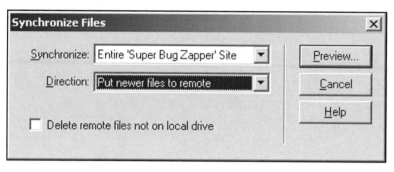

Synchronize files

1. Switch to Local view (if necessary), click Site on the Site panel menu bar (Win) or on the main menu bar (Mac), then click Synchronize to open the Synchronize Files dialog box.

2. Click the Synchronize list arrow, then click Entire 'Super Bug Zapper' Site.

3. Click the Direction list arrow, then click Put newer files to remote (if necessary), then compare your screen to Figure N-8.

4. Click Preview.

    The Status dialog box might appear and flash the names of all the files from the local version of the site that need to be uploaded to the remote site. Then the dialog box shown in Figure N-9 opens and lists all the files that need to be uploaded to the remote site.

5. Click OK.

    All the files from the local Super Bug Zapper Web site are now contained in the remote version of the site. The dialog box changes to show all the files that were uploaded.

6. Click Close to close the dialog box.

    TIP If you want to keep a record of your synchronizations, you could click Save Log, specify a location and name for the synchronization log, then click Save.

You synchronized the Super Bug Zapper Web site files to copy all remaining files from the local root folder to the remote root folder.

FIGURE N-9
Files that need to be uploaded to remote site

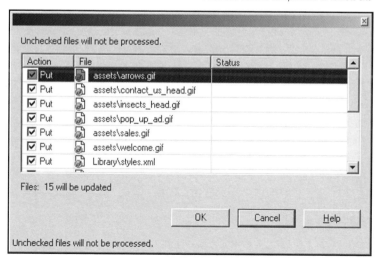

CHECK FILES OUT AND IN

What You'll Do

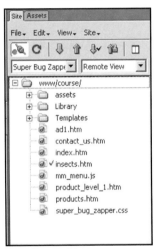

 In this lesson, you will use the Site Definition dialog box to enable the Check In/Check Out feature. You will then check out the insects page, make a change to it, then check it back in.

Managing a Web Site with a Team

When you work on a large Web site, chances are that many people will be involved in keeping the site up to date. Different individuals will need to make changes or additions to different pages of the site by adding or deleting content, changing graphics, updating information, and so on. If everyone had access to all of the pages at all times, big problems could arise. For instance, what if you and your teammate both made edits to the same page at the same time? If you post your edited version of the file to the site after your teammate posts his edited version of the same file, the file that you upload will overwrite your teammate's version and none of his changes will be incorporated. Not good! Fortunately, you can avoid this scenario by using Dreamweaver's collaboration tools.

Checking Out and Checking In Files

Using Dreamweaver's Check In/Check Out feature will ensure that team members do not overwrite each other's pages. When this feature is enabled, only one person can work on a file at a time. To check out a file, click the file you want to work on in the Site panel, then click the Check Out File(s) button on the Site panel toolbar. Files that you have checked out are marked with green check marks in the Site panel. Files that your teammates have checked out are marked with red check marks.

After you finish editing a checked-out file, you will need to save and close the file, then click the Check In button to check the file back in and make it available to other users.

When you check in a file after editing it, a lock icon appears next to it, indicating that the file is checked in and that you cannot make edits to it unless you check it out again. Figure N-10 shows the Check Out File(s) and Check In buttons on the Site panel toolbar, as well as files that have been checked out and checked back in.

Enabling the Check In/Check Out Feature

In order to use the Check In /Check Out feature with a team of people, you must first enable it. To turn on this feature, check the Enable File Check In and Check Out checkbox in the Remote Access settings of the Site Definition dialog box.

FIGURE N-10

Check Out File(s) and Check In buttons on the Site Panel toolbar

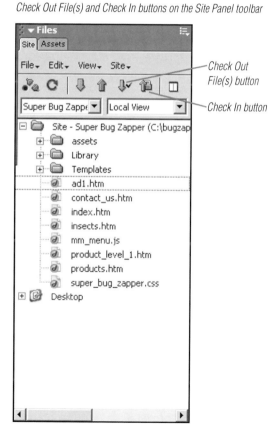

Enable the Check In/Check Out feature

1. Click Site on the Site panel menu bar (Win) or on the main menu bar (Mac), click Edit Sites to open the Edit Sites dialog box, click Super Bug Zapper in the list (if necessary), then click Edit to open the Site Definition for Super Bug Zapper dialog box.

2. Click Remote Info in the Category list, then click the Enable File Check In and Check Out checkbox.

   Notice that some additional options appear below the checkbox.

3. Check the Check Out Files when Opening checkbox (if necessary).

4. Type your name using lowercase letters and no spaces in the Check Out Name text box.

5. Type your e-mail address in the Email Address text box.

6. Compare your screen to Figure N-11, click OK to close the Site Definition for Super Bug Zapper dialog box, then click Done to close the Edit Sites dialog box.

You used the Edit Sites Definition for Super Bug Zapper dialog box to enable the Check In/Check Out feature and let site collaborators know when you are working with a file in the site.

Check out a file

1. Switch to Local view (if necessary), make sure that you are connected to the remote site, then click the insects page in the Site panel to select it.

(continued)

MACROMEDIA DREAMWEAVER N-14

FIGURE N-11
Enabling the Check In/Check Out feature

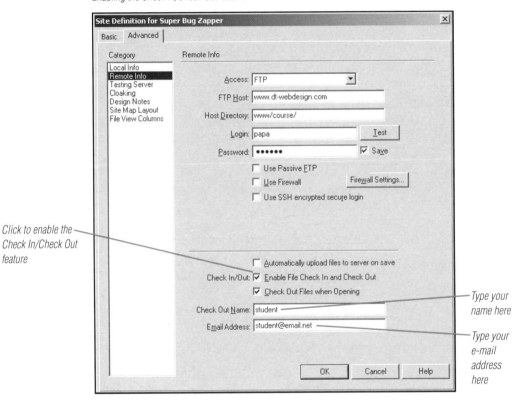

Click to enable the Check In/Check Out feature

Type your name here

Type your e-mail address here

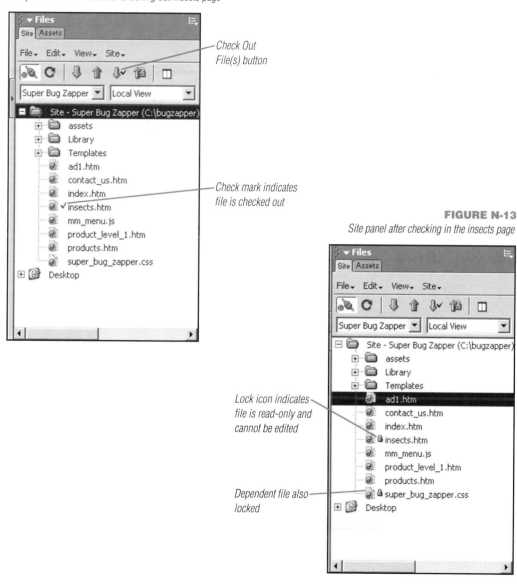

Check Out
File(s) button

Check mark indicates
file is checked out

FIGURE N-13

Site panel after checking in the insects page

Lock icon indicates
file is read-only and
cannot be edited

Dependent file also
locked

2. Click the Check Out File(s) button on the Site panel toolbar.

   The Dependent Files dialog box appears, asking if you want to check out all files that are needed for the insects page.

3. Click Yes, click another file in the Site panel to deselect the insects page, then compare your screen to Figure N-12.

   The insects file now has a check mark next to it, indicating you have checked it out.

You checked out the insects page so that no one else can use it.

Check in a file

1. Open the insects page, type **Cockroaches** in the table cell below Ticks on the insects page, then save your changes.

2. Close the insects page, then click the insects page in the Site panel to select it (if necessary).

3. Click the Check In button on the Site panel toolbar.

   The Dependent Files dialog box opens, asking if you want to check in dependent files too.

4. Click Yes, click another file in the Site panel to deselect the insects page, then compare your screen to Figure N-13.

   A check mark no longer appears next to the insects page in the Site panel.

You made a content change on the insects page, then checked in the insects page, making it possible for others to open and modify the page.

CLOAK FILES

What You'll Do

 In this lesson, you will cloak the assets folder so that it is excluded from various operations, such as the Put, Get, Check In, and Check Out commands. You will also use the Site Definition dialog box to cloak all .gif files in the site.

Understanding Cloaking Files

There may be times when you want to exclude a particular file or files from being uploaded to a server. For instance, suppose you have a page that is not quite finished and needs more work before it is ready to be viewed by the rest of the world. You can exclude such files by **cloaking** them, which marks them for exclusion from several commands, including Put, Get, Synchronize, Check In, and Check Out. Cloaked files are also excluded from site-wide operations, such as checking for links or updating a template or library item. You can cloak a folder or specify a type of file to cloak throughout the site.

QUICKTIP

By default, the cloaking feature is enabled. However, if for some reason it is not turned on, open the Site Definition dialog box, click the Advanced tab, click the Cloaking category, then click the Enable Cloaking checkbox.

Cloaking a Folder

There may be times when you want to cloak an entire folder. For instance, if you are not concerned with replacing outdated image files, you might want to cloak the assets folder of a Web site to save time when synchronizing files. To cloak a folder, select the folder, click Site on the Site panel menu bar, point to Cloaking, then click Cloak. The folder you cloaked and all the files it contains will appear with red slashes across them, as shown in Figure N-14. To uncloak a folder, click Site on the Site panel menu bar (Win) or on the main menu bar (Mac), point to Cloaking, then click Uncloak.

QUICKTIP

To uncloak all files in a site, click Site on the Site panel menu bar (Win) or on the main menu bar (Mac), point to Cloaking, then click Uncloak All.

Cloaking Selected File Types

There may be times when you want to cloak a particular type of file, such as a .swf file. To cloak a particular file type, open the Site Definition dialog box, click the Cloaking category, click the Cloak Files Ending With checkbox, then type a file name in the text box below the checkbox. All files throughout the site that have the specified file extension will be cloaked.

FIGURE N-14
Cloaked assets folder in the Site panel

Red slash indicates folder is cloaked

Cloaked files

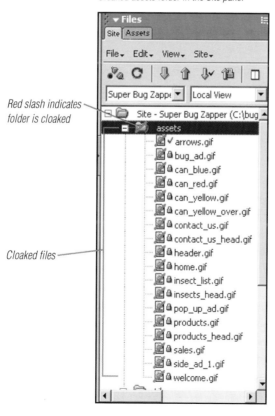

Cloak and uncloak a folder

1. Verify that Local view is displayed in the Site panel, click Site on the Site panel menu bar (Win) or on the main menu bar (Mac), then click Edit Sites to open the Edit Sites dialog box.

2. Click Edit to open the Site Definition for Super Bug Zapper dialog box, click Cloaking in the Category list, verify that the Enable Cloaking checkbox is checked, click OK, then click Done.

3. Click the assets folder in the Site panel, click Site on the Site panel menu bar (Win) or on the main menu bar (Mac), point to Cloaking, click Cloak, expand the assets folder (if necessary), then compare your screen to Figure N-15.

   A red slash now appears on top of the assets folder in the Site panel, indicating that all files in the assets folder are cloaked and will be excluded from putting, getting, checking in, checking out, and many other operations.

   > TIP You can also cloak a folder by right-clicking (Win) or control-clicking (Mac) the folder, pointing to Cloaking, then clicking Cloak.

4. Right-click (Win) or control-click (Mac) the assets folder, point to Cloaking, then click Uncloak.

   The assets folder and all the files it contains no longer appear with red slashes across them, indicating they are no longer cloaked.

You cloaked the assets folder so that this folder and all the files it contains will be excluded from many operations, including uploading and downloading files. You then uncloaked the assets folder.

FIGURE N-15
Assets folder after cloaking

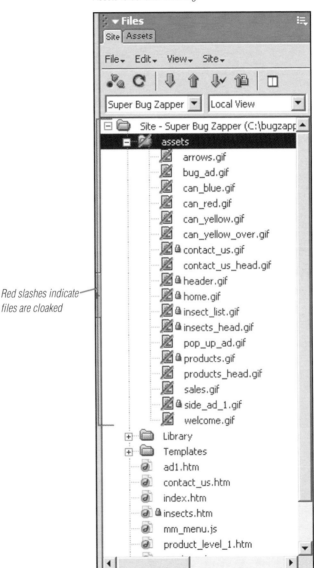

Red slashes indicate
files are cloaked

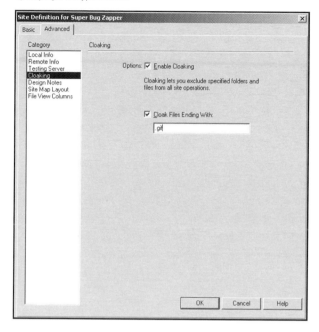

Cloak selected file types

1. Right-click (Win) or control-click (Mac) the assets folder in the Site panel, point to Cloaking, then click Settings to open the Site Definition for Super Bug Zapper dialog box with the Cloaking category selected.

2. Click the Cloak Files Ending With checkbox, select the text in the text box that appears, type **.gif** in the text box, then compare your screen to Figure N-16.

3. Click OK.

   A dialog box opens, indicating that the site cache will be recreated.

FIGURE N-17

Assets folder in Site panel after cloaking .gif files

4. Click OK, open the assets folder (if necessary), then compare your screen to Figure N-17.

   All of the .gif files in the assets folder appear with red slashes across them, indicating that they are cloaked. Notice that the assets folder is not cloaked.

You cloaked all the .gif files in the Super Bug Zapper Web site.

Assets folder
not cloaked

All .gif files
cloaked

IMPORT AND EXPORT A SITE DEFINITION

What You'll Do

 In this lesson, you will export the site definition file for the Super Bug Zapper Web site. You will then import the Super Bug Zapper Web site.

Exporting a Site Definition

If you work on a Web site for a long time, it's likely that at some point you will want to move it to another machine or share it with other collaborators or teammates who will help you maintain it. The site definition for a Web site contains important information about the site, including its URL, preferences that you've specified, and other secure information such as the login and password information. You can use the Export command to export the site definition file to another location. To do this, simply click Site on the Site panel menu bar (Win) or on the main menu bar (Mac), then click Export to open the Export Site dialog box, shown in Figure N-18. This dialog box offers two options for how to export the .ste file. The back up option includes all settings, including the login, password, and local path information. This is a good option to use if you want a backup of the site. The share settings option allows other users to work on a

different version of the site that is stored in a different folder from the original site. With the share settings option, users can enter their own login information.

If you are concerned with security, you might want to choose the back up option so that you don't have to share password information with others who will import the site. After you choose one of these options and click OK, another Export Site dialog box will open, prompting you to specify a location to save the .ste file. Because the site definition file contains password information that you will want to keep secret from other site users, you should never save the site definition file to the Web site. Instead, save it to an external folder.

Importing a Site Definition

If you want to set up another user with a copy of your Web site, you can import the site definition file. To do this, use the

Import command on the Site menu to open the Import Site dialog box, navigate to the .ste file you want to import, then click Open. If you used the sharing option when you created the .ste file, you can specify a new local root folder for the site, where the original Web site files will be copied. This enables you to create a copy of the site located in a different root folder. If you specified the back up option in the Export Site dialog box, the new site will use the same root folder as the original site, making it possible for several team members to have access to the same root folder.

FIGURE N-18
Export Site dialog box

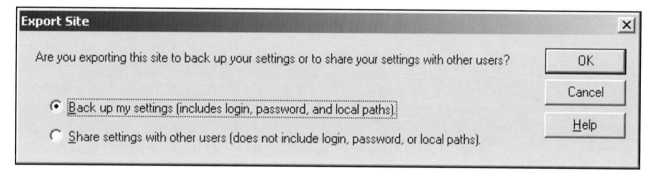

Export a site definition

1. Use Windows Explorer (Win) or Mac Finder (Mac) to create a new folder somewhere on your hard drive or external drive named **bugzapper_site_definition**.

2. Switch back to Dreamweaver, click Site on the Site panel menu bar (Win) or on the main menu bar (Mac), then click Export to open the Export Site dialog box.

   If the dialog box shown in Figure N-19 opens, complete Step 3. If this dialog box does not open, it means that your user preferences file automatically specified one of these settings. If you do not see this dialog box, skip to Step 4.

3. Verify that the Back up my settings radio button is selected, then click OK.

   A new Export Site dialog box opens.

4. Navigate to and select the bugzapper_site_definition folder that you created in Step 1, as shown in Figure N-20, then click Save.

You used the Export command to create the site definition file and saved it to the bugzapper_site_definition folder.

Import a site definition

1. Click Site on the Site Panel menu bar (Win) or on the main menu bar (Mac), then click New Site to open the Site Definition for Unnamed Site 1 dialog box.

   The settings show temporary names for the root folder and the default images folder, which are sufficient for this exercise.

   (continued)

FIGURE N-19
Specifying export settings

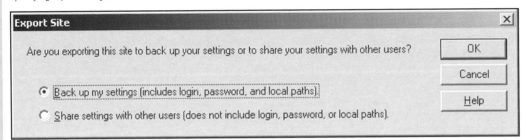

FIGURE N-20
Saving the bugzapper.ste file to the bugzapper_site_definition folder

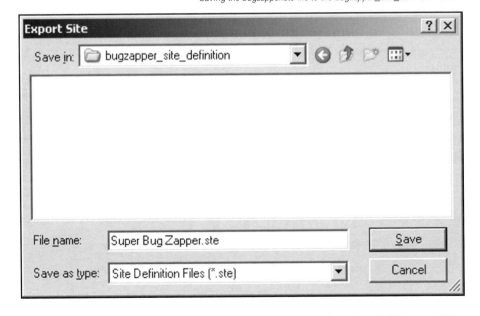

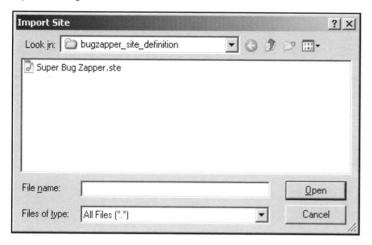

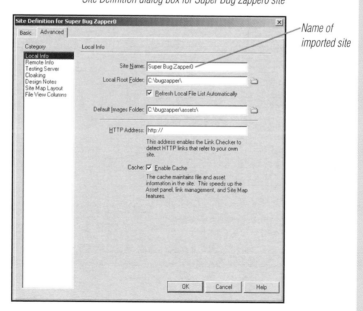

Name of
imported site

2. Click OK to accept the settings.

3. Click Site on the Site panel menu bar (Win)
   or on the main menu bar (Mac), then click
   Import to open the Import Site dialog box.

4. Navigate to the bugzapper_site_definition
   folder you created in the previous exercise,
   compare your screen to Figure N-21, select
   the file Super Bug Zapper.ste, then click Open.

   A dialog box opens and says that a site
   named Super Bug Zapper already exists. It
   will name the imported site Super Bug
   Zapper0 so that it has a unique name.

5. Click OK.

6. Click Site on the Site panel menu bar (Win) or
   on the main menu bar (Mac), click Edit Sites
   to open the Edit Sites dialog box, click Edit,
   then compare your screen to Figure N-22.

   The settings show that the Super Bug
   Zapper0 site has the same root folder and
   default images folder as the Super Bug
   Zapper site. Both of these settings are specified in the Super_Bug_Zapper.ste file that
   you imported. Importing a site in this way
   makes it possible for multiple users with different computers to work on the same site.

7. Click OK, click Done, close the Super Bug
   Zapper0 Web site, then save and close all
   open pages of the Super Bug Zapper Web site.

   TIP If a dialog box opens warning that
   the root folder chosen is the same as the
   folder for the site "Super Bug Zapper,"
   click OK.

You imported the Super Bug Zapper.ste file.

Publish a Web site and transfer files.

1. Open the Blooms & Bulbs Web site that you created and developed in Units A through M. (If you did not create this Web site in Units A through M, contact your instructor for assistance.)
2. Set up Web server access for the Blooms & Bulbs Web site on an FTP server or a local/network server (whichever is available to you) using appropriate settings. (Your instructor will provide you with this information.)
3. View the Blooms & Bulbs remote site in the Site panel.
4. Upload the iris.jpg file to the remote site, then view the remote site.

5. Upload the master_gardener template and all dependent files to the remote site, then view the remote site to make sure all files were transferred.
6. Synchronize all files in the Blooms & Bulbs Web site, so that all files from the local site are uploaded to the remote site.
7. Save your changes.

Check files out and in.

1. Enable the Check In/Check Out feature.
2. Check out the plants page and all dependent pages.
3. Open the plants page, change the heading Drop by to see our Featured Spring Plants to size **5**, then save your changes.
4. Check in the plants page.

Cloak files.

1. Verify that cloaking is enabled in the Blooms & Bulbs Web site.
2. Cloak the assets folder, then uncloak it.
3. Cloak all the .jpg files in the Blooms & Bulbs Web site.
4. Save your changes.

Import and export a site definition.

1. Create a new folder named blooms_definition on your hard drive or external drive.
2. Export the Blooms & Bulbs site definition to the blooms_definition folder. Choose the setting that lets you back up your settings, including the password, login, and local paths information.

3. Create a new, untitled site.
4. Import the Blooms & Bulbs site definition to create a new site called Blooms & Bulbs0.
5. Make sure that all files from the Blooms & Bulbs Web site appear in the Site panel for the imported site. Expand the assets folder, then compare your screen to Figure N-23.

FIGURE N-23
Completed Skills Review

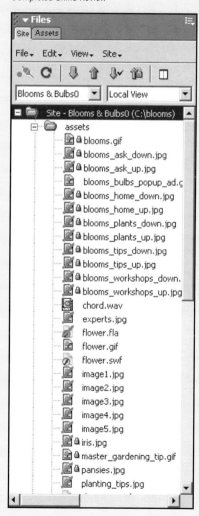

In this Project Builder you will publish the Rapids Transit Web site that you have developed throughout this book to a remote server or local/network folder. Mike Andrew has provided instructions for where to publish the site on a remote server so that the rest of the world will be able to access it on the Web. You will specify the remote settings for the site, upload files to the remote site, check files out and in, and cloak files. Finally, you will export and import the site definition.

1. Open the Rapids Transit Web site that you created in Units A through M. (If you did not create this Web site in Units A through M, contact your instructor for assistance.)

2. If you did not do so in Project Builder 1 in Unit A, use the Site Definition dialog box to set up Web server access for a remote site using either an FTP site or a local or network folder. (Ask your instructor to supply this information to you.)

3. Upload the index page and all dependent files to the remote site.

4. View the remote site to make sure that all files uploaded correctly.

5. Synchronize the files so that all other files on the local Rapids Transit site are uploaded to the remote site.

6. Enable the File Check In/Check Out feature.

7. Check out the rentals page and all dependent files.

8. Open the rentals page, change the price of the canoe rental to **$10.00**, save your changes, close the rentals page, then check in the rentals page and all dependent pages.

9. Cloak all .jpg files in the Web site.

10. Export the site definition to a new folder named **rapids_definition**.

11. Create a new, untitled site, then import the Rapids Transit.ste file to create a new site named Rapids Transit0.

12. Save your changes, expand the assets folder in the Site panel (if necessary), then compare your screen to Figure N-24.

FIGURE N-24
Completed Project Builder 1

In this Project Builder, you will finish your work on the Jacob's Web site that you started in Project Builder 2 in Unit A. Chef Jacob has asked you to publish the Jacob's Web site to a remote server and transfer all the files from the local site to the remote site. He has also asked you to enable the Check In/Check Out feature so that other staff members may collaborate on the site. He would also like you to cloak some of the files to exclude them from synchronization and other operations. Finally, he has asked you to export and import the site definition file.

1. Open the Jacob's Web site that you created in Units A through M. (If you did not create this site in Units A through M, contact your instructor for assistance.)
2. If you did not do so in Project Builder 2 in Unit A, use the Site Definition dialog box to set up Web server access for a remote site using either an FTP site or a local or network folder. (Ask your instructor to supply this information to you.)
3. Upload the after_theatre.htm page and all dependent files to the remote site.
4. View the remote site to make sure that all files uploaded correctly.
5. Synchronize the files so that all other files on the local Jacob's site are uploaded to the remote site.
6. Enable the File Check In/Check Out feature.

7. Check out the recipes page and all its dependent files.
8. Open the recipes page, apply bold formatting to the words Name, Address, Phone, E-mail, Category, Recipe, and Preparation Time in the left column of the table.
9. Save your changes, close the page, then check in the recipes page and all dependent pages.

FIGURE N-25
Completed Project Builder 2

10. Cloak all .gif files in the Web site.
11. Export the site definition to a new folder named **jacobs_definition**.
12. Create a new, untitled site, then import the Jacobs.ste file to create a new site named Jacobs0.
13. Expand the root folder and the assets folder in the Site panel (if necessary), then compare your screen to Figure N-25.

Throughout this book you have used Dreamweaver to create and develop several Web sites that contain different elements, many of which are found in popular commercial Web sites. For instance, Figure N-26 shows the National Park Service Web site, which contains photos and information on all the national parks in the United States. This Web site contains many types of interactive elements, such as pop-up windows, rollovers, and jump menus—all of which you learned to create in this book.

1. Connect to the Internet, then go to *www.course.com*. Navigate to the page for this book, click the Student Online Companion, then click the link for this unit.

2. Spend some time exploring the pages of this site to familiarize yourself with its elements.

3. Type a list of all the elements in this Web site that you have learned how to create in this book. After each item, write a short description of where and how the element is used in the site.

4. Visit one of your favorite Web sites. (If you don't have a favorite Web site, visit a search engine site such as *www.google.com*, type in keywords relating to a topic or hobby that interests you, then locate a site on that topic or hobby that contains interactive elements.)

5. Type a list of all the elements in your chosen site that you have learned how to create in this book, then write a short description of where and how the element is used in the site.

6. Print out the home page and one or two other pages that contain some of the elements you described and attach it to your list.

FIGURE N-26
Source for Design Project

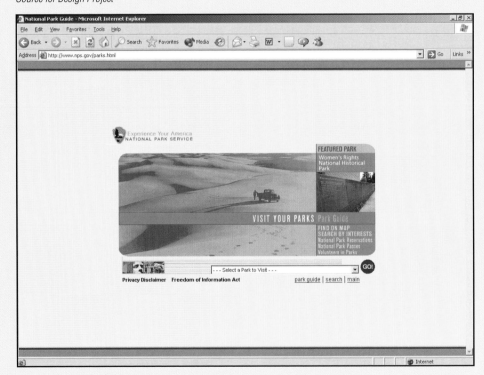

In this assignment, you will finish your work on the group Web site that you created and developed in Units A through M. Depending on the size of your group, you can assign individual parts of this assignment to group members, or work collectively.

You will publish your site to a remote server or local or network folder.

1. Before you begin the process of publishing your Web site to a remote server, meet as a group to review your Web site and make sure that it is ready for public viewing. Use Figure N-27 to assist you in making sure your Web site is complete. If you find problems, assign team members to make the necessary changes to finalize the site.

2. Assign a team member the task of asking your instructor where you should publish your site. The folder where you will publish your site can be either an FTP site or a local/network folder. If you are publishing to an FTP site, be sure to write down all the information you will need to publish to the site, including the URL of the FTP host, the directory on the FTP server where you will publish your site's root folder, and the login and password information.

3. Assign a team member the task of using the Site Definition dialog box to specify the remote settings for the site using the information that your instructor provided in Step 2.

4. Assign another team member the task of transferring one of the pages and its dependent files to the remote site, then viewing the remote site to make sure the appropriate files were transferred.

5. Assign a team member the task of synchronizing the files so that all the remaining local pages and dependent files are uploaded to the remote site.

6. Assign a team member the task of enabling the Check In/Check Out feature.

7. Assign a team member the task of checking out one of the pages. This team member should also open the checked-out page, make a change to it, save the change, close the page, then check the page back in.

8. Assign a team member the task of cloaking a particular file type of the group's choosing.

9. Assign a team member the task of exporting the site definition for the site to a new folder somewhere on your hard drive or on an external drive. Choose the option of backing up all settings.

10. Assign a team member the task of importing the site to create a new version of the site.

11. Close the imported site, save and close all open pages (if necessary), then exit Dreamweaver.

FIGURE N-27
Web Site Check List

Web Site Check List

1. Are you satisfied with the content and appearance of every page?
2. Are all paths for all links and images correct?
3. Does each page have a title?
4. Do all images appear?
5. Are all colors Web-safe?
6. Do all images have appropriate alternate text?
7. Have you eliminated any orphaned files?
8. Have you deleted any unnecessary files?
9. Have you viewed all pages using at least two different browser settings?
10. Does the home page have keywords and a description?

Read the following information carefully!!

Find out from your instructor the location of the Data Files you need and the location where you will store your files.

- To complete many of the units in this book, you need to use Data Files. Your instructor will either provide you with a copy of the Data Files or ask you to make your own copy.

- All the Data Files are organized in folders named after the unit in which they are used. For instance, all Unit A Data Files are stored in the unit_a folder. You should leave all the Data Files in these folders; do not move any Data File out of the folder in which it is originally stored.

- If you need to make a copy of the Data Files, you will need to copy a set of files from a file server, standalone computer, or the Web to the drive and location where you will be storing your Data Files.

- Your instructor will tell you which computer, drive letter, and folders contain the files you need, and where you will store your files.

- You can also download the files by going to *www.course.com*. See the inside back cover of the book for instructions to download your files.

Copy and organize your Data Files.

- Copy the folders that contain the Data Files to a Zip drive, network folder, hard drive, or other storage device.

- As you build each Web site, the exercises in this book will guide you to copy the Data Files you need from the appropriate Data Files folder to the folder where you are storing the Web site. Your Data Files should always remain intact because you are copying (and not moving) them to the Web site.

- Because you will be building a Web site from one unit to the next, sometimes you will need to use a Data File that is already contained in the Web site you are working on.

Find and keep track of your Data Files and completed files.

- Use the **Data File Supplied** column to make sure you have the files you need before starting the unit or exercise indicated in the **Unit** column.

- Sometimes the file listed in the **Data File Supplied** column is one that you created or used in a previous unit, and that is already part of the Web site you are working on. For instance, if the file jacobs/recipes.htm is listed in the **Data File Supplied** column, this means that you need to use the recipes.htm file in the Jacob's Web site that you already created.

- Use the **Student Creates File** column to find out the filename you use when saving your new file for the exercise.

Files used in this book

Macromedia Dreamweaver MX

Unit	Data File Supplied	Student Creates File	Used In
A	dwa_1.htm contact.swf newsletter.swf services.swf tours.swf assets/tripsmart.jpg assets/trps_log.gif		Lesson 2
	dwa_2.htm assets/tripsmart.jpg	accessories.htm catalog.htm clothing.htm newsletter.htm services.htm tours.htm	Lessons 4 and 5
	dwa_3.htm dwa_4.htm assets/bloom_log.gif assets/blooms.gif	plants.htm workshops.htm tips.htm	Skills Review
	dwa_5.htm assets/rapids.jpg	guides.htm rentals.htm store.htm	Project Builder 1
	dwa_6.htm assets/jacobs.jpg	directions.htm menus.htm recipes.htm	Project Builder 2
	none		Design Project
	none		Group Project
B	dwb_1.htm packing_essentials.htm assets/tidbits.jpg assets/tripsmart.jpg		Lesson 2
	dwb_2.htm gardening_tips.htm assets/blooms.gif assets/planting_tips.jpg		Skills Review

Unit	Data File Supplied	Student Creates File	Used In
	none		Project Builder 1
	none		Project Builder 2
	none		Design Project
	none		Group Project
C	how_to_pack.htm		Lesson 1
		tripsmart.css	Lesson 2
	dwc_1.htm assets/tripsmart.jpg assets/giraffe.jpg assets/lion.jpg assets/zebra_mothers.jpg		Lesson 3
	assets/seamless_bak.gif assets/tile_bak.gif		Lesson 5
	dwc_2.htm dwc_3.htm gardening_tips.htm assets/blooms.gif assets/daisies.gif assets/iris.jpg assets/pansies.jpg assets/planting_tips.jpg assets/tulips.jpg	blooms.css	Skills Review
	dwc_4.htm assets/buster_tricks.jpg assets/rapids.jpg	rapids.css	Project Builder 1
	dwc_5.htm rolls.htm assets/cheesecake.jpg assets/jacobs.jpg assets/oranges.jpg assets/poached_pear.jpg	jacobs.css	Project Builder 2
	none		Design Project
	none		Group Project

Unit	Data File Supplied	Student Creates File	Used In
D	dwd_1.htm assets/tripsmart.jpg		Lesson 1
		top.swf	Lesson 3
	assets/nav_catalog_down.jpg assets/nav_catalog_up.jpg assets/nav_home_down.jpg assets/nav_home_up.jpg assets/nav_news_down.jpg assets/nav_news_up.jpg assets/nav_services_down.jpg assets/nav_services_up.jpg assets/nav_tours_down.jpg assets/nav_tours_up.jpg		Lesson 4
	dwd_2.htm assets/blooms.gif assets/blooms_ask_down.jpg assets/blooms_ask_up.jpg assets/blooms_home_down.jpg assets/blooms_home_up.jpg assets/blooms_plants_down.jpg assets/blooms_plants_up.jpg assets/blooms_tips_down.jpg assets/blooms_tips_up.jpg assets/blooms_workshops_down.jpg assets/blooms_workshops_up.jpg	top.swf	Skills Review
	dwd_3.htm assets/buffalo_fall.gif assets/rapids.jpg		Project Builder 1
	dwd_4.htm assets/jacobs.jpg		Project Builder 2
	none		Design Project
	none		Group Project
E	assets/headphones.jpg assets/packing_cube.jpg assets/passport_holder.jpg assets/tripsmart.jpg		Lesson 3

Unit	Data File Supplied	Student Creates File	Used In
	headphones.htm packing_cube.htm passport_holder.htm		Lesson 4
	dwe_1.htm dwe_2.htm assets/hat.jpg assets/hats_on_the_amazon.jpg assets/nav_catalog_down.jpg assets/nav_catalog_up.jpg assets/nav_home_up.jpg assets/nav_home_down.jpg assets/nav_news_down.jpg assets/nav_news_up.jpg assets/nav_services_down.jpg assets/nav_services_up.jpg assets/nav_tours_down.jpg assets/nav_tours_up.jpg assets/pants.jpg assets/vest.jpg		Lesson 5
	assets/tearoom.jpg assets/texas_rose.jpg assets/yellow_rose.jpg agenda.htm exhibition.htm nursery.htm tearoom.htm		Skills Review
	rental_info.htm store.htm assets/fruit_basket.jpg assets/kayak.jpg		Project Builder 1
	directions_paragraph.htm assets/signature_dish.jpg		Project Builder 2
	none		Design Project
	none		Group Project

Unit	Data File Supplied	Student Creates File	Used In
F	**northwest folder containing these files:**		
	about.htm		Lesson 1
	cables.htm		Lessons 1 and 4
	catalog.htm		Lesson 1
	docks.htm		Lessons 1 and 4
	index.htm		Lesson 1
	memory.htm		Lessons 1 and 4
	misc.htm		Lessons 1 and 4
	news.htm		Lesson 1
	Northwest.ste		Lesson 1
	notebooks.htm		Lessons 1 and 4
	pda.htm		Lessons 1 and 4
	support.htm		Lesson 1
	northwest/assets folder containing these files:		
	layerbkg.gif		Lesson 1
	layout.htm		Lesson 1
	layout_r1_c1.gif		Lesson 1
	layout_r2_c1.gif		Lesson 1
	layout_r3_c1.gif		Lesson 1
	northwest.css		Lesson 1
	spacer.gif		Lesson 1
	other files:		Lesson 1
	dwf-01.htm		Lessons 1-4
	pda1.gif		Lesson 3
	blooms/tips		Skills Review
	dwf-02.htm		Project Builder 1
	jacobs/recipes.htm		Project Builder 2
G	northwest/index.htm		Lessons 1-5
	layerbg.gif		Lesson 1
	visor.gif		Lesson 1
	blooms/index.htm		Skills Review

Unit	Data File Supplied	Student Creates File	Used In
	flower.gif		Skills Review
	rapids/index.htm		Project Builder 1
	water.jpg		Project Builder 1
	animal.jpg		Project Builder 1
	reflection.jpg		Project Builder 1
	jacobs/index.htm		Project Builder 2
H		northwest/mybrandlaptops.htm	Lessons 1-4
	dwh_01.htm		Lesson 3
	dwh_02.htm		Lesson 3
	laptop.gif		Lesson 3
		northwest/quasar.htm	Lesson 3
	topbanner.png		Lesson 4
	bottombanner.png		Lesson 4
		blooms/home.htm	Skills Review
		blooms/toc.htm	Skills Review
		rapids/sitemap.htm	Project Builder 1
		rapids/sitelist.htm	Project Builder 1
		jacobs/recipepages.htm	Project Builder 2
		jacobs/recipelist.htm	Project Builder 2
	jacobs/jacobs.jpg		Project Builder 2
		jacobs/logopage.htm	Project Builder 2
I	northwest/about.htm		Lesson 1
		northwest/news.swf	Lesson 1
		northwest/sales.swf	Lesson 1
	cservice.swf		Lesson 1
	northwest/memory.htm		Lesson 2
	nwmemory.png		Lesson 2
	swmemory.png		Lesson 2
	chord.wav		Lesson 3
		blooms/home.swf	Skills Review
		blooms/plants.swf	Skills Review

Unit	Data File Supplied	Student Creates File	Used In
		blooms/workshops.swf	Skills Review
		blooms/tips.sws	Skills Review
	flower.swf		Skills Review
	flowerreverse.jpg		Skills Review
	blooms/assets/flower.gif		Skills Review
	chord.wav		Skills Review
	rapids/index.htm		Project Builder 1
		rapids/home.swf	Project Builder 1
		rapids/before.swf	Project Builder 1
		rapids/guides.swf	Project Builder 1
		rapids/store.swf	Project Builder 1
		rapids/sitemap.swf	Project Builder 1
	jacobs/directions.htm		Project Builder 2
		jacobs/home.swf	Project Builder 2
		jacobs/recipes.swf	Project Builder 2
		jacobs/directions.swf	Project Builder 2
	map.swf		Project Builder 2
	chord.wav		Project Builder 2
J	**bugzapper folder containing these files:**		Lesson 1
	ad1.htm		Lessons 1 and 3
	index.htm		Lessons 1-3
	insects.htm		Lesson 1
	contact_us.htm		Lessons 1-3
	products.htm		Lessons 1 and 2
	bugzapper/assets folder containing these files:		Lesson 1
	header.gif		Lesson 1
	products_head.gif		Lesson 1
	contact_us_head.gif		Lesson 1
	insect_head.gif		Lesson 1
	welcome.gif		Lesson 1

Unit	Data File Supplied	Student Creates File	Used In
	bug_ad.gif		Lesson 1
	can_blue.gif		Lesson 1
	can_red.gif		Lesson 1
	can_yellow.gif		Lesson 1
	can_yellow_over.gif		Lessons 1 and 3
	pop_up_ad.gif		Lesson 1
	sales.gif		Lesson 1
	contact_us.gif		Lesson 1
	insect_list.gif		Lesson 1
	products.gif		Lesson 1
	blooms/index.htm		Skills Review
	blooms/plants.htm		Skills Review
	blooms/master_gardener.htm		Skills Review
	blooms/assets/iris.jpg		Skills Review
	blooms/assets/tulips.jpg		Skills Review
	experts.jpg		Skills Review
		blooms/popup.htm	Skills Review
	blooms_bulbs_popup_ad.gif		Skills Review
	rapids/rentals.htm		Project Builder 1
		jacobs/popup1.htm	Project Builder 2
		jacobs/popup2.htm	Project Builder 2
	jacobs_popup1.gif		Project Builder 2
	jacobs_popup2.gif		Project Builder 2
	jacobs/after_theatre.htm		Project Builder 2
K		bugzapper/Templates/main_elements.dwt	Lessons 1, 2, and 4
		bugzapper/Templates/product_info.dwt	Lessons 2 and 3
	side_ad_1.gif		Lesson 2
		bugzapper/index.htm	Lesson 3
		bugzapper/insects.htm	Lesson 3 and 4
		product_level_1.htm	Lesson 3

Unit	Data File Supplied	Student Creates File	Used In
	bugzapper/contact_us.htm		Lesson 3
	blooms/master_gardener.htm	blooms/Templates/master_	Skills Review
	master_gardening_tip.gif		Skills Review
			Skills Review
	blooms/assets/flower.gif		Skills Review
		blooms/tips.htm	Skills Review
	blooms/assets/planting_tips.jpg	blooms/assets/planting_tips.jpg	Skills Review
		blooms/product_list.htm	Skills Review
	blooms/plants.htm		Skills Review
		rapids/rapids_info.dwt	Project Builder 1
		rapids/index.htm	Project Builder 1
	rapids/store.htm		Project Builder 1
	rapids/assets/buffalo_fall.gif		Project Builder 1
	rapids/guides.htm		Project Builder 1
	rapids/assets/fruit_basket.jpg	rapids/assets/fruit_basket.jpg	Project Builder 1
	rapids/assets/buster_tricks.jpg	rapids/assets/buster_tricks.jpg	Project Builder 1
		jacobs/Templates/menus.dwt	Project Builder 2
	specials_logo.gif		Project Builder 2
		jacobs/menus.htm	Project Builder 2
L	bugzapper/product_level_1.htm		Lesson 1
	bugzapper/insects.htm		Lesson 2
	bugzapper/index.htm		Lesson 3
	super_bug_zapper.css		Lesson 3
	bugzapper/main_elements.dwt		Lesson 3
	blooms/plants.htm		Skills Review
	blooms/master_gardener_page.htm		Skills Review
	blooms/blooms.css		Skills Review
	blooms/master_gardener.dwt		Skills Review

Unit	Data File Supplied	Student Creates File	Used In
	rapids/rapids_info.dwt		Project Builder 1
	rapids/rapids.css		Project Builder 1
	jacobs/menus.dwt		Project Builder 1
	jacobs/jacobs.css		Project Builder 1
M	bugzapper/products.htm		Lesson 1
	bugzapper/main_elements.dwt	bugzapper/main_elements.dwt	Lessons 1 and 3
		bugzapper/Library/level_1_heading.lbi	Lesson 1
		bugzapper/Library/level_1_text.lbi	Lesson 1
		bugzapper/Library/navigation_bar.lbi	Lesson 1
	bugzapper/insects.htm		Lesson 2
	blooms/master_gardener.dwt	blooms/master_gardener.dwt	Skills Review
		blooms/Library/contact_e-mail.lbi	Skills Review
		blooms/Library/contact_number.lbi	Skills Review
	blooms/assets/flower.gif		Skills Review
		blooms/Library/flowers.lbi	Skills Review
	rapids/rapids_info.dwt		Project Builder 1
		rapids/Library/rapids_address.lbi	Project Builder 1
		rapids/Library/rapids_phone.lbi	Project Builder 1
	rapids/before.htm		Project Builder 1
	rapids/rentals.htm		Project Builder 1
	rapids/reservations.htm		Project Builder 1
	jacobs/menus.dwt		Project Builder 2
		jacobs/Library/jacobs_blue_logo.lbi	Project Builder 2
	jacobs/recipes.htm		Project Builder 2

Unit	Data File Supplied	Student Creates File	Used In
N		bugzapper_studentlastname folder	Lesson 1
	bugzapper/assets/can_blue.gif		Lesson 1
	bugzapper/products.htm		Lesson 1
	bugzapper/insects.htm		Lesson 2
		bugazapper_site_definition folder	Lesson 4
		Super_Bug_Zapper.ste	Lesson 4
	blooms/assets/iris.jpg		Skills Review
		blooms_definition folder	Skills Review
		Blooms&Bulbs.ste	Skills Review
	rapids/rentals.htm		Project Builder 1
		rapids_definition folder	Project Builder 1
			Project Builder 1
	jacobs/recipes.htm		Project Builder 2
		jacobs_definition folder	Project Builder 2
		Jacobs.ste	Project Builder 2

Absolute path
A path containing an external link that references a link on a Web page outside of the current Web site, and includes the protocol "http" and the URL, or address, of the Web page.

Absolute positioning
The positioning of a layer according to the distance between the layer's upper-left corner and the upper-left corner of the page or layer in which it is contained.

Absolute URL
A fixed URL starting with http://, used when linking to a Web page outside of your Web site.

Action
A response to an event trigger that causes a change, such as text changing color.

Action property
Property that specifies the application or script that will process form data.

Alert box
See **popup message**.

Aligning an image
Positioning an image on a Web page in relation to other elements on the page.

Alternate text
Descriptive text that can be set to appear in place of an image while the image is downloading or when a user places the mouse pointer over the image.

Animation
Effect created by rapidly playing a series of still images in a sequence, which creates the illusion of movement.

Animation bar
Blue bar in the Timelines panel that represents the movement of an animated layer.

Animation channel
Row in the Timelines panel composed of frames, each of which represents the position of an animated layer at a particular moment in an animation.

Assets folder
A subfolder in a Web site in which you store most of the files that are not Web pages, such as images, audio files, and video clips.

Assets panel
A panel that contains nine categories of assets, such as images, used in a Web site. Clicking a category button will display a list of those assets.

Background color
A color that fills an entire Web page, frame, table, cell, or document.

Background image
A graphic file used in place of a background color.

Banner
Graphic that appears across the top of a Web page that can incorporate the company's logo, contact information, and navigation buttons.

Behavior
A preset piece of JavaScript code that can be attached to page elements. A behavior tells the page element to respond in a specific way when an event occurs, such as when the mouse pointer is positioned over the element.

Behaviors channel
The area at the top of the Timelines panel that is used to trigger a behavior at a specific frame in an animation.

BMP
Bitmapped file. A file format used for images that is based on pixels.

Body
The part of a Web page that is seen when the page is viewed in a browser window.

Border
An outline that surrounds a cell, table, or frame.

Broken links
Links that cannot find the intended destination file for the link.

Browser
Software used to display Web pages, such as Microsoft Internet Explorer or Netscape Navigator.

C

Cascading Style Sheet (CSS)
A file used to assign sets of common formatting characteristics to page elements such as text, objects, and tables.

Cell padding
The distance between the cell content and cell walls in a table.

Cell spacing
The distance between cells in a table.

Cell walls
The edges surrounding a cell.

Cells
Small boxes within a table that are used to hold text or graphics. Cells are arranged horizontally in rows and vertically in columns.

Checkbox
Form object that can be used on a Web page to let viewers choose from a range of possible options.

Child page
A page at a lower level in a Web hierarchy that links to a parent page.

Class style
See **custom style**.

Client-side scripting language
Computer code that runs within a Web browser.

Clip property
Property that determines the portion of a layer's content that will be visible when displayed in a Web browser.

Cloaked file
File that is marked to be excluded from certain processes, such as being transferred to the remote site.

Code and Design view
A Web page view that is a combination of Code view and Design view.

Code snippets
See **snippets**.

Code view
A Web page view that shows a full screen with the HTML code for the page. Use this view to read or edit the code.

Cold Fusion
Development tool that can be used to build data-driven Web applications.

Columns
Table cells arranged vertically.

Comments
Helpful text describing portions of the HTML code, such as a JavaScript function.

Common Gateway Interface (CGI)
Server-side application used for processing data in a form.

Contents
The Macromedia Help feature that lists topics by category.

Custom style
A style that can contain a combination of formatting attributes that can be applied to a block of text or other page elements. Custom style names begin with a period (.).

D

Debug
To find and correct coding errors.

Declaration
The property and value of a style in a Cascading Style Sheet.

Default base font
The font that is applied by default to any text that is entered on a page created in Dreamweaver.

Default font color
The color the browser uses to display text, links, and visited links if no other color is assigned.

Default link color
The color the browser uses to display links if no other color is assigned. The default link color is blue.

Definition lists
Lists composed of terms with indented descriptions or definitions.

Delimiter
A comma, tab, colon, semicolon, or similar character that separates tabular data.

Dependent file
File that another file needs in order to be complete, such as an image or navigation bar element.

Description
A short summary of Web site content that resides in the head section.

Design view

The view that shows a full-screen layout and is primarily used when designing and creating a Web page.

Document

A page created in Dreamweaver.

Document toolbar

A toolbar that contains buttons for changing the current Web page view, previewing and debugging Web pages, and managing files.

Document-relative path

A path referenced in relation to the Web page that is currently displayed.

Domain name

An IP address expressed in letters instead of numbers, usually reflecting the name of the business represented by the Web site.

Down image state

The state of a page element when the element has been clicked.

Download

Transfer a file or files from a remote server to a computer.

Download time

The time it takes to transfer a file to another computer.

Drop target

Position on a page where a layer will snap in position if dragged within a specified range of it.

DSL

Digital Subscriber Line. A type of high-speed Internet connection.

Editable optional region

An area in a template where users can add or change content, and that users can also choose to show or hide.

Editable region

An area in a template where users of the template can add or change content.

Enable cache

A setting to direct the computer system to use space on the hard drive as temporary memory or cache while you are working in Dreamweaver.

Event trigger

An event, such as a mouse click on an object, that causes a behavior to start.

Export data

To save data that was created in Dreamweaver in a special file format so that you can bring it into another software program.

External CSS style sheet

Collection of rules stored in a separate file that control the formatting of content in a Web page. External CSS style sheets have a .css file extension.

External links

Links that connect to Web pages in other Web sites.

Favorites

The Dreamweaver Help feature that allows you to add topics to the Favorites window so that you can view them later without having to search.

Field

See **form object**

Fieldset

HTML tag used to group related form elements together.

File field

Form object that allows viewers to upload files to a Web server.

Fill

The color category (such as solid, gradient, or pattern) applied to an object, as well as its type and amount of edge.

Flash button object

Button made from a small, predefined Flash movie that can be inserted on a Web page to provide navigation in a Web site.

Flash text

A vector-based graphic file that contains text.

Floating workspace

A way to work with Dreamweaver that allows each document and panel to be displayed in its own window.

Font combination

A set of three fonts that specifies which fonts a browser should use to display the text on a Web page.

Form control
See **form object**.

Form element
See **form object**.

Form object
An object on a Web page, such as a text box, radio button, or checkbox, that collects information from viewers. Also referred to as **form element**, **form control**, or **field**.

FormName property
Property that specifies a unique name for a form.

Frame
Fixed region in a browser that can display a Web page and act independently from other pages displayed in other frames within the browser window.

Frameset
A document that contains the instructions that tell a browser how to lay out a set of frames showing individual documents on a page, including the size and position of the frames.

Frames panel
Panel in the Advanced Layout panel group that shows a visual representation of the frameset and that is used for selecting frames.

FTP
File Transfer Protocol. The process of uploading and downloading files to and from a remote site.

GET method
Method property that specifies that ASCII data collected in a form will be sent to the server appended to the URL or file included in the Action property.

GIF
Graphics interchange format. Type of file format used for images placed on Web pages that can support both transparency and animation.

Head content
The part of a Web page that is not viewed in the browser window. It includes meta tags, which are HTML codes that include information about the page, such as keywords and descriptions.

Headings
Six different styles that can be applied to text: Heading 1 (the largest size) through Heading 6 (the smallest size).

Height property
Property that specifies the height of a layer either in pixels or as a percentage of the screen's height.

Hexadecimal value
A value that represents the amount of red, green, and blue in a color and is based on the Base 16 number system.

Hidden field
Form object that makes it possible to provide information to the Web server and

form processing script without the viewer knowing that the information is being sent.

History panel
A panel that lists the steps that have been performed in Dreamweaver while editing and formatting a document.

Home page
Usually the first Web page that appears when viewers visit a Web site.

HTML
Hypertext Markup Language. The language Web developers use to create Web pages.

HTML style
A named set of formatting attributes that can be applied to text to ensure consistency for common text elements across all pages of a Web site.

Hyperlink
Graphic or text element on a Web page that users click to display another location on the page, another Web page on the same Web site, or a Web page on a different Web site. Hyperlinks are also known as links.

Image field
Form object used to insert an image in a form.

Import data
To bring data created in another software program into an application.

Index

The Macromedia Help feature that displays topics in alphabetical order.

Inline CSS style

A CSS style whose code is contained within the HTML code of a Web page.

Insert bar

A toolbar that contains icons that allow you to insert objects such as images, tables, and horizontal rules.

Integrated workspace

The Dreamweaver interface where all windows and panels are integrated into one large window with the panels docked on the right side of the screen.

Interactivity

Allows visitors to your Web site to affect its content.

Internal links

Links to Web pages within the same Web site.

IP address

An assigned series of numbers, separated by periods, that designates an address on the Internet.

ISP

Internet Service Provider. A service to which you subscribe in order to be able to connect your computer to the Internet.

JavaScript

A Web-scripting language that interacts with HTML code to create interactive content.

JPEG file

Joint photographic experts group. Type of file format used for images that appear on Web pages, typically used for photographs.

Jump menu

Navigational menu that lets viewers go quickly to different pages in a site or to different sites on the Internet.

Keyframe

Frame in an animation bar that signifies a change in motion for an animated layer. Keyframes are represented by small circles on an animation bar.

Keywords

Words that relate to the content of a Web site and reside in the head content.

Layers

Containers used to divide and arrange the elements of a Web page in a logical front to back order. A layer can contain multiple objects, all of which are managed in the Layers panel.

Layers panel

Panel in the Advanced Layout panel group that is used to control the visibility, name, and z-index stacking order of layers on a Web page.

Layout view

A Dreamweaver view that is used for drawing tables.

Left property

Property that specifies the distance between the left edge of a layer and the left edge of the page or layer that contains it.

Library item

Content that can contain text or graphics and is saved in a separate file in the Library folder of a Web site.

List

Element on a Web page from which viewers can make a choice from several options. Lists are often used in order forms.

List form object

A form object that lets users choose one or more options from a list of choices.

Local root folder

A folder on your hard drive, Zip disk, or other external drive that will hold all the files and folders for a Web site.

Locked region

An area on a template that cannot be changed by users of the template.

Macromedia Flash Player

A program that needs to be installed on a computer to view Flash movies.

mailto: link
An e-mail address that is formatted as a
link that will open the default mail program
with a blank, addressed message.

Menu
Element on a Web page from which Web
viewers can make choices. Menus are often
used for navigation in a Web site.

Menu bar
A bar located under the title bar in a program window that lists the names of menus
from which you can select commands.

Menu form object
A form object, commonly used for navigation on a Web site, that lets viewers select a
single option from a list of choices.

Merge cells
To combine multiple cells in a table into
one cell.

Meta tags
HTML codes that include information about
the page, such as keywords and descriptions, and reside in the head content.

Method property
Property that specifies the HyperText
Transfer Protocol (HTTP) method used to
send form data to a Web server.

Motion path
The animation trail of an animated layer on
a page.

Multimedia
Content that combines text, graphics,
sound, animation, or interactivity to create
a fully engaging experience.

Named anchor
An invisible object on a Web page that
serves as a destination point for links on
other parts of the page

Navigation bar
A group of buttons that link to different
areas inside or outside a Web site.

Nested layer
Layer whose HTML code is included within
another layer's code.

Nested table
A table within a table.

Nested template
A template that is based on another
template.

NoFrames content
Alternate content of a Web site that can be
viewed without frames.

Objects
The individual elements in a document,
such as text or images.

Optional region
Region in a template that template users
can choose either to show or hide.

Ordered list
List of items that need to be placed in a
specific order, where each item is preceded
by a number or letter.

Orphaned files
Files that are not linked to any pages in a
Web site.

Overflow property
Property that specifies how to handle
excess content that does not fit inside
a layer.

Over image state
The state of a page element when the
mouse pointer is positioned over it.

Over While Down image state
The state of a page element when the
mouse pointer is clicked and held over it.

Panel
A window that contains related commands
and tools used to view, organize, and modify objects on a Web page.

Panel groups
Groups of panels, such as Design, Code
Application, and Files, that contain related
panels from which you can choose related
commands.

Paragraph style
HTML style that is applied to an entire paragraph.

Parent page
A page at a higher level in a Web hierarchy that links to other pages on a lower level.

Playback head
Red tool in the Timelines panel that shows which frame of an animation is currently displayed in the document window. You can drag the playback head to view an animation.

PNG
Portable network graphics. A type of file format for graphics.

Point of contact
A place on a Web page that provides viewers a means of contacting a company.

Pop-up menu
A menu that appears when you move the pointer over a trigger image in a browser.

Popup message
Message that opens in a browser to either clarify or provide information, or alert viewers of an action that is being taken.

Position property
Property used to define a layer's position on a page.

Post method
Method property that specifies that form data be sent to the processing script as a binary or encrypted file, so that data will be sent securely.

Property inspector
Panel where you modify selected objects and set tool properties and other options. Depending on the activity or action you are performing, information on the Property inspector changes.

Publish a Web site
To make a Web site available for viewing on the Internet or on an intranet.

Radio button
Form object that can be used to provide a list of options from which only one selection can be made.

Radio group
A group of radio buttons from which viewers can make only one selection.

Reference panel
A panel used to find answers to coding questions, covering topics such as HTML, JavaScript, and Accessibility.

Refresh Local File List Automatically option
A setting that directs Dreamweaver to automatically reflect changes made in your file listings.

Relative path
A path used with an internal link to reference a Web page or graphic file within the Web site.

Relative URL
A link based on its location as it relates to the current page in the Web site's folder; use to link to a page within your Web site.

Remote server
A Web server that hosts Web sites and is not directly connected to the computer housing the local site.

Repeating region
An area in a template whose format is repeated over and over again. Used for presenting information that repeats, such as product listings in a catalog.

Repeating table
A table in a template that has a predefined structure, making it very easy for template users to add content to it.

Resolution
The number of pixels per inch in an image; also refers to an image's clarity and fineness of detail.

Rollover image
An image on a Web page that changes its appearance when the mouse pointer is positioned over it.

Root relative path
A path referenced from a Web site's root folder.

Rows
Table cells arranged horizontally.

Sans-serif fonts
Block-style characters used frequently for headings, subheadings, and Web pages.

Screen reader
A device used by the visually impaired to convert written text on a computer monitor to spoken words.

Seamless image
A tiled image that is blurred at the edges so that it appears to be all one image.

Search
The Macromedia Help feature that allows you to enter a keyword to begin a search for a topic.

Selection style
HTML style that is applied to selected text.

Selector
The name assigned to a style in a Cascading Style Sheet.

Serif fonts
Ornate fonts with small extra strokes at the beginning and end of characters. Used frequently for paragraph text in printed materials.

Server-side application
An application that resides on a Web server and interacts with the information collected in a form.

Site panel
A window that is very similar to Windows Explorer (Windows) or Finder (Mac). Used to view and manage files and folders in a

Web site. The Site panel contains a list of all the folders and files in a Web site.

Snippet
A reusable piece of code that can be inserted on a page to create footers, headers, drop-down menus, and other items.

Split cells
To divide cells into multiple cells.

Standard view
A view that is used to insert a table using the Insert Table button.

States
The four appearances a button can assume in response to a mouse action. These include: Up, Over, Down, and Over While Down.

Status bar
A bar at the bottom of the document window that displays HTML tags being used at the insertion point location as well as other information, such as estimated download time for the current page.

Styles
Preset attributes, such as size, color, and texture, that you can apply to objects and text.

Table
Grid of rows and columns that can either be used to hold tabular data on a Web page or can be used as a basic design tool for page layout.

Tabular data
Data that is arranged in columns and rows and separated by a delimiter.

Tag selector
A location on the status bar that displays HTML tags for the various page elements, including tables and cells.

Tags
Determine how the text in HTML should be formatted when a browser displays it.

Target
The location on a Web page that the browser will display in full view when an internal link is clicked, or the frame that will open when a link is clicked.

Target property
Property that specifies the window in which you want form data to be processed.

Template
A special page that contains both locked regions, which are areas on the template page that cannot be modified by users of the template, as well as other types of regions that users can change or edit.

Text area field
A text field in a form that can store several lines of text.

Text field
Form object used for collecting a string of characters such as a name, address, or password.

TIFF
Tagged image file format.

Tiled image
A small graphic that repeats across and down a Web page, appearing as individual squares or rectangles.

Timelines panel
A set of tools used to control the movement of an animated layer.

Top property
Property that specifies the distance between the top edge of a layer and the top edge of the page or layer that contains it.

Unordered lists
Lists of items that do not need to be placed in a specific order and are usually preceded by bullets.

Unvisited links
Links that have not been clicked by the viewer.

Up image state
The state of a page element when the mouse pointer is not on the element.

Upload
Transfer files to a remote server.

URL
Uniform resource locator. An address that determines a route on the Internet or to a Web page.

Visible property
Property that lets you control whether the selected layer is visible or hidden.

Visited links
Links that have been previously clicked or visited. The default color for visited links is purple.

Web design program
A program for creating interactive Web pages containing text, images, hyperlinks, animation, sounds, and video.

Web-safe colors
Colors that are common to both Macintosh and Windows platforms.

Web server
A computer dedicated to hosting Web sites that is connected to the Internet and configured with software to handle requests from browsers.

Web site
Related Web pages, stored on a server, that users can download using a Web browser.

White space
An area on a Web page that is not filled with text or graphics.

Width property
Property that specifies the width of a layer either in pixels or as a percentage of the screen's width.

Workspace
The area in the Dreamweaver program window where you work with documents, movies, tools, and panels.

Z-index property
Property that specifies the vertical stacking order of layers on a page. A z-index value of 1 indicates that a layer's position is at the bottom of the stack. A z-index position of 3 indicates that the layer is positioned on top of two other layers.

Note: Page references of terms referring to Macintosh or Windows platforms that either are unique to one of the platforms or appear on separate pages are followed with (Mac) or (Win).

sign, D-14
¶ symbol, L-4

A

absolute paths
    defined, D-4, D-5
    examples, D-4, D-5, D-6
    URLs, D-4, D-5, D-6
absolute positioning, G-12
access, remote. *See* remote access
accessibility
    alternate text, C-23, C-26, C-27, E-33
    guidelines, B-5
    screen readers, C-23
    tables, E-5, E-6, E-7
    techniques, B-5
    testing, B-5
Action property (forms), F-6
Actions button, I-3, I-14, I-15, I-16, I-17, J-10
Active Server Pages (ASP) applications, F-5
ActiveX controls, I-2
Add buttons
    forms, F-3, F-26, F-28
    jump menus, F-3, F-34, F-35
    navigation bars, D-3, D-24
Add Item button, J-3, J-24
adding. *See* inserting
address. *See* IP address
Adobe Illustrator, D-20
Adobe Photoshop, C-22

alert boxes, I-15
Align buttons, C-17
Align list, C-3, C-17, C-20, C-21
aligning
    Flash text, D-19
    graphics, C-17, C-20–21, E-17, E-20
    layers, G-12–15
    table graphics, E-17, E-19
    text, B-16
Alt text box, C-3, C-26
alternate text
    accessibility option, C-27
    features, C-23
    inserting, C-26
    missing, checking for, E-33
anchors, named. *See* named anchors
animating layers, J-4–13
    adding layers, J-4
    behaviors for, J-5
    draggable layers, J-6, J-13
    keyframes, J-5, J-11
    start frames, J-5, J-10
    stop frames, J-5, J-10
animation bar, J-4, J-5, J-6, J-9, J-11
animation channels, J-4, J-5
animations. *See also* animating layers
    browser requirements, J-2
    effective use, J-2
    extending duration, J-4
    gathering, A-17
    previewing, J-5–6, J-12
    recording paths, J-6
Answers panel group, A-5
Application panel group, A-5, A-9
applications
    form-processing, F-2, F-4–5
    server-side, F-5

Apply Styles option, C-3
assets. *See also* Assets panel; graphics
    backing up, C-32
    deleting, C-28–29, C-32
assets folder. *See also* Assets panel; graphics
    copying graphics, A-27, C-18–19
    creating, A-16, A-22, A-24
    default images folder, A-25
    defined, A-16, A-22
    managing, C-28–29, C-32
    saving graphics, B-14, C-2
    subfolders, A-23
Assets panel. *See also* assets folder; graphics
    categories, C-16, C-17
    creating Flash text, D-18
    creating library items, M-4, M-6, M-7
    deleting graphics, C-28–29, C-32
    deleting library items, M-13, M-16
    deleting non-Web-safe colors, C-29, C-33
    displaying links, D-29
    features, C-16
    formatting cell content, E-21
    illustrated, C-17
    inserting graphics, C-18–19, E-16, E-18
    inserting library items, M-12, M-14
    location, C-16
    maintaining sites, E-26
    options, C-16
    recreating library items, M-13, M-17
    sizing, C-17
    undocking, C-17
    verifying colors, E-32
    viewing library items, M-4
Attach Style Sheet button, C-13, L-3, L-20, L-22, L-26
attributes. *See* properties

Back button, J-3, J-6, J-12
background color, B-5
  background images vs., C-28
  layers, G-9
  setting, B-9
background images
  background color vs., C-28
  defined, C-28
  deleting, C-31
  inserting, C-30
  layers, G-8
  preferred format, C-28
  seamless images, C-28, C-30
  tiled images, C-28, C-30
backups, C-32
banners
  defined, A-10
  illustrated, A-12
behaviors
  animating layers, J-5
  browser requirements, J-2
  changing text, J-14–19
  creating interactive elements, J-20
  defined, G-2
  features, J-2
  inserting, I-14, I-15
Behaviors channel, J-5, J-10
Behaviors panel
  animation start/stop, J-10
  creating pop-up menus, J-21, J-24
  creating pop-up windows, J-23
  formatting pop-up menus, J-25
  illustrated, I-15
  inserting popup messages, I-15, I-17
  inserting sound effects, I-16
  inserting text, J-17
  modifying text, J-16, J-18

  overview, I-14
  swapping images, J-22
Bindings, A-9
bitmapped files. *See* BMP (bitmapped) files
BMP (bitmapped) files, A-31
Bobby Web site, B-5
body, B-5
Bold button, C-9
Border text box, C-3, C-24
borders, C-24
  adding, C-24
  creating space, C-22–23
  defined, C-22
  frames, H-9, H-12
  limiting use, C-23
  tables, E-4
Bottom Frame button, H-3
broken links
  avoiding, B-18, D-2, D-8
  checking, D-29, E-26, E-28, N-2
  defined, B-18
  jump menus, F-33
  site map identifying, A-30
Browse for File icon, A-27, B-21
browsers
  affecting control options, G-2, G-24, H-2
  color settings, B-5
  defined, A-2
  Flash compatibility, I-4
  JavaScript requirements, J-2, J-6
  playing Flash movies, I-9
  reading layers, G-2, G-24
  status bar text, J-14, J-17
  supporting CSS, C-10, L-2, L-5
  supporting HTML styles, L-5
  testing pages, A-17, B-31, B-33, E-27
  varying, A-17, B-31

bulleted lists
  Cascading Style Sheet, C-12–14
  defined, C-4
  formatting, C-4
bullets, C-4
Button button, F-3, F-22, F-31
buttons. *See also specific button names*;
    radio buttons; Flash buttons
  forms, F-22, F-31
  gathering, A-17

cache
  defined, A-20
  enabling, A-20
  re-creating, C-29
capital letters. *See* uppercase letters
Cascading Style Sheets (CSS), C-2. *See
    also* external CSS style sheets; inline
    CSS styles
  adding styles, C-15
  advantages, C-10, L-2
  applying, C-13
  attaching to documents, C-13
  browsers supporting, C-10, L-2, L-5
  components, C-11
  creating, C-12
  custom styles, L-10–11
  declarations, C-11
  editing, C-14
  example, C-11
  features, C-10, L-2
  file extension, C-10
  font selection, C-12, C-13, C-14
  formatting, C-12, C-15
  selectors, C-11
  styles panel, L-3

case-sensitivity, B-14

CAST (Center for Applied Special Technology), B-5

Category buttons, C-17

cell padding, E-4

cell spacing, E-4

cells
aligning graphics, E-17, E-19
defined, E-2
form labels, F-14, F-18
formatting, E-21, E-24
formatting content, E-20, E-23
inserting graphics, E-2, E-16, E-18
inserting text, E-2, E-20, E-22
merging, E-11, E-15
modifying content, E-25
properties, E-3
sizing, E-10, E-12, E-13
splitting, E-11, E-14
tags, E-12
walls, E-4
widths, E-9

Center for Applied Special Technology (CAST), B-5

CGI scripts, F-5, F-7, F-13, G-12

Check In button, N-3, N-13, N-15

Check Links Sitewide feature, D-28, D-29

Check Out File(s) button, N-3, N-12, N-13, N-15

Checkbox button, F-3, F-22, F-25

checkboxes
features, F-20
illustrated, F-21
inserting, F-24–25

checked out pages, A-30

checking files in/out, N-12–15

checklist, planning, A-15

child pages
defined, A-16
illustrated, A-16

class styles. See custom styles

Clean Up Word HTML Results window, B-10, B-15

Clip property, G-5, G-7

cloaking files, N-16–19
defined, N-2, N-16
features, N-16
illustrated, N-3
selected file types, N-17, N-19

cloaking folders, N-16–17, N-18

Code and Design view, B-25
defined, A-5
opening, A-8

Code inspector
features, B-25
illustrated, B-25
using, B-27
view options, B-27
viewing code, B-25, B-27, B-28, B-29

Code panel group, A-5
displaying, A-9
illustrated, A-9
Reference panel, B-25, B-28

code snippets. See snippets

Code view, B-25
defined, A-5
example, B-8
illustrated, A-8
opening, A-8
options, B-25

Cold Fusion programs, F-5

collaboration tools. See team management

collapsing
panel groups, A-5, A-9

Property inspector, C-5, C-9

site maps, A-33, B-23

windows, D-7

Color Cubes palette, B-4

colors
background, B-5, B-9, C-28, G-9
deleting, C-29, C-33
editable attributes, K-17
font, B-16
frame borders, H-9, H-12
graphic file formats, C-16, C-28
hexadecimal values, B-9
links, B-5, B-33
non-Web-safe, C-29, C-33
palettes, B-4, B-5
pop-up menus, J-25
rollover, D-17, D-18
setting, B-9, B-16
text, B-16
unvisited links, B-5
visited links, B-5, B-33
Web-safe, B-4, B-5, E-26, E-32

Colors button, C-3

columns, E-2
deleting, E-14
inserting, E-14
sizing, E-10, E-12

comments, inserting, B-28

Common Gateway Interface (CGI) scripts, F-5, F-7, F-13

Connects to Remote Host button, N-3, N-4, N-9

contact links, B-18, B-22

Continuous Tones palette, B-4

Convert Layers to Table dialog box, G-26

Convert Tables to Layers dialog box, G-27

Copy command shortcut, B-10

copying
    graphics, A-27
    navigation bars, D-20–21, D-26
    shortcut, B-10
    URLs, D-8
CSS. *See* Cascading Style Sheets (CSS)
CSS Style definition dialog box, L-11, L-12,
    L-13, L-15, L-21, L-23
CSS Styles panel, C-10, C-12, C-13, C-14,
    C-15. *See also* Cascading Style
    Sheets (CSS)
.css extensions, C-10
custom styles, L-10–11
    applying, L-11, L-14–15
    creating, L-10–11, L-13
    external CSS style sheets, L-21, L-25
    modifying, L-11, L-15
    naming, L-10
customizing
    browser status bar text, J-14, J-17
    external CSS style sheets, L-21, L-25
    navigation bars, D-21, D-26–27
Cut command shortcut, B-10

data
    exporting, E-22
    importing, E-22
    loss prevention, B-13
date objects
    code, B-29
    inserting, B-29
.dcr extensions, I-10
debugging view, A-5
declarations, C-11
default base font, B-11
default font, B-5

default images folder, A-25
default link, B-5
Define HTML Style dialog box, L-4, L-5,
    L-6, L-9
defining
    editable optional regions, K-5, K-9
    editable regions, K-4, K-7
    layers, G-7
    optional regions, K-4–5, K-8
    remote sites, N-4
    Web sites, A-17, A-20
definition lists, C-5
Delete CSS Style button, L-3, L-12, L-19
Delete Library Item button, M-3,
    M-13, M-16
deleting
    assets, C-28–29, C-32
    background images, C-31
    colors, C-29, C-33
    columns, E-14
    external CSS style sheets, L-27
    graphics files, C-28–29, C-32
    inline CSS styles, L-12, L-19
    library items, M-13, M-16
    non-Web-safe colors, C-29, C-33
    pages, A-17
    rows, E-14
delimited files, E-22
delimiters, E-22
dependent files, N-5
Description button, B-7, B-8
Description dialog box, B-8
descriptions
    Code view, B-8
    defined, B-4
    entering, B-7, B-8
    example, B-8

Design panel group, A-5
Design view
    defined, A-5
    modifying, A-8–9
    opening, A-8
DHTML, J-2
displaying
    panel groups, A-4–5, A-9
    panels, A-4–5
    site maps, A-31
    toolbars, A-4
<div> tag, G-4, G-7, G-12
docking panel groups, A-5
document-relative paths, D-5
Document toolbar
    defined, A-4
    displaying, A-4
    hiding, A-4
    illustrated, A-5
document window
    defined, A-4
    illustrated, A-5
documents, untitled, E-32
domain name, A-14
double-spaced text, B-12
Down Image state, D-20, D-23, D-26
download times
    determining, A-4, C-16
    frames, H-2
    graphics, C-16, C-22, D-16
    layout options affecting, H-2
    status bar, C-16
    target length, C-22
    testing, E-27
downloading
    Flash button objects, I-4
    Flash player, I-4

remote files, N-5–6
templates, K-30
Drag Layer behavior, J-6, J-13
Drag Layer dialog box, J-6, J-13
draggable layers, J-6, J-13
Draw Layer button, G-3, G-4, G-5, G-6, G-20
drop targets, J-6

e-mail forms, F-2, F-5
e-mail links, B-18, B-22, B-23
Edit Sites dialog box, N-7, N-8, N-14, N-18
Edit Style Sheet button, L-3, L-11, L-12, L-15
Edit Styles option, C-3
editable attributes
    color, K-17
    creating, K-17, K-18
    features, K-12
    modifying, K-21, K-25
    templates, K-12, K-17, K-18, K-21, K-25
    URLs, K-18
Editable Optional Region button, K-3, K-5,
    K-9, K-11
editable optional regions
    creating, K-5, K-9
    defined, K-5
Editable Region button, K-3, K-4, K-5,
    K-7, K-11
editable regions
    colors, K-17
    creating, K-4, K-7
    defined, K-2
    identifying, K-20
    illustrated, K-7
    locking, K-31
    modifying, K-20, K-24, K-31

nesting templates, K-10–11
    unlocking, K-31
Editable Tag Attributes dialog box, K-12,
    K-17, K-18
editing. See modifying
editors, external, C-22
elements, D-20
    navigation bar, D-20–21, D-22–25
    states, D-20
<em> tags, L-12
Enable Cache option, A-20
enhancing images, C-22–23, C-24–25
entering
    descriptions, B-7, B-8
    keywords, B-7
    text, B-12
errors, finding. See testing pages
Expand/Collapse button, A-33, B-23,
    D-7, D-9
expander arrow, A-5, A-9
expanding
    panel groups, A-5, A-8–9
    Property inspector, C-4, C-5
    site maps, A-33
    Site panel, A-30, B-23
Export Site dialog box, N-20, N-21, N-22
exporting
    data, E-22
    defined, E-22
    delimiters, E-22
    site definitions, N-20, N-22
extensions, filename
    CSS, C-10
    Flash objects, D-16, I-5
    Shockwave files, I-10
    Site panel files, A-28, A-29
    Web page files, B-14

external CSS style sheets, L-20–27
    adding hyperlink styles, L-21, L-24
    attaching to existing page,
        L-20–21, L-22
    attaching to templates, L-20–21, L-26
    customizing, L-21, L-25
    deleting, L-27
    features, L-2, L-10, L-20
    modifying, L-23
external editors, C-22
external links
    components, D-2
    creating, D-4, D-6
    defined, D-2
    site map, D-7
    viewing, D-7
external style sheets. See external CSS
    style sheets

favorites, C-16
Favorites option button, C-16, C-17
fields, form. See form objects
Fieldset button, F-3, F-14, F-16, F-22
Fieldset dialog box, F-16
fieldsets
    adding tables to, F-17–18
    around cells, F-14
    creating, F-16
    defined, F-14
    example, F-15
    tables within, F-14
File Field button, F-3, F-22, F-29
file fields
    features, F-22
    inserting, F-29

file formats
  background images, C-28
  graphics, C-16
File Transfer Protocol (FTP)
  defined, A-17
  host information, A-21
  transferring files, N-2, N-5–6, N-10
  uploading files, N-5, N-10
  Web server access, A-21, N-7
filenames
  case-sensitivity, B-14
  choosing, B-14
  extensions. *See* extensions, filename
  home page, A-23, B-14
  naming conventions, A-28, A-29, B-14
files
  backing up, C-32
  checking in/out, N-12–15
  cloaking, N-2, N-3, N-16–19
  corrupt, B-13
  deleting, C-28–29, C-32
  delimited, E-22
  download times. *See* download times
  downloading, N-5–6
  graphic. *See* graphics
  graphic formats, C-16, C-28
  naming, A-28, A-29
  orphaned, D-28, D-29, E-29, E-30–31
  preventing loss, B-13
  saving, B-13
  sizes, C-22
  storing, A-16–17
  synchronizing, N-6, N-11, N-16
  transferring. *See* transferring files
  uploading, N-5, N-10
Files panel group, A-5
  displaying, A-9

Fireworks. *See* Macromedia Fireworks
Flash Button button, I-3, I-5, I-6, I-7
Flash button objects. *See also* Flash
  buttons
  defined, A-11
  illustrated, A-12, I-5
Flash buttons, I-3. *See also* Flash button
  objects
  defined, I-5
  downloading, I-4
  filename extensions, I-5
  illustrated, I-7
  inserting, I-5, I-6–7
  properties, I-7
  styles, I-5
Flash movies
  features, I-5
  illustrated, I-9
  inserting, I-5, I-8
  placeholders, I-8
  playing, I-9
  properties, I-8
  viewing, I-4
Flash objects. *See also specific objects*
  downloading, I-4
  illustrated, I-5
  inserting, I-4–9
  overview, I-4
Flash player
  defined, D-16
  downloading, I-4
Flash program, I-2
  features, D-16, I-4
  vector-based graphics, D-16, I-4
Flash text
  aligning, D-19
  defined, D-16

  filename extensions, D-16
  formatting, D-16–17, D-18–19
  inserting, D-16–19
  rollover colors, D-17, D-18
Flash text button, D-3, D-17
floating workspace, A-6
folders. *See also specific folder types*
  cloaking, N-16–17, N-18
  default images, A-25
  hierarchy, A-16–17
  inserting, A-22–23, A-24
  naming, A-16, A-24
  root. *See* root folders
font combination, B-11
fonts. *See also* formatting text; text
  base font, B-11
  choosing, B-17
  classifications, B-17
  colors, B-16
  in CSS. *See* Cascading Style
    Sheets (CSS)
  default, B-5, B-11
  modifying, B-11
  printing, B-17
  ransom note effect, B-17
  sans-serif, B-17
  serif, B-17
  setting, B-16–17
  sizes, B-11, B-13, B-17
  variations, B-11, B-17
Form button, F-3, F-4, F-6, F-12, F-22
form controls. *See* form objects; forms
form elements. *See* form objects; forms
form field. *See* form objects; forms
form objects, F-20–35. *See also* forms
  buttons (inserting), F-22, F-31
  buttons (program menu), F-22

changing behaviors, J-15, J-18–19
checkboxes, F-20, F-21, F-24–25
defined, F-20
file fields, F-22, F-29
hidden fields, F-21, F-30
illustrated, F-21
image fields, F-21, F-27
inserting buttons, F-22, F-31
jump menus, F-22, F-32–35
lists, F-21
menus, F-21, F-22, F-28
modifying text, J-15, J-18–19
radio buttons, F-20, F-21, F-26–27
radio groups, F-20–21, F-26–27
text area fields, F-20
text fields, F-20, F-21, F-23, F-24, J-15, J-18–19
types, F-20–22
Format list, B-11
formats, file. *See* file formats
formatting
    bulleted lists, C-4
    Cascading Style Sheets, C-12, C-15
    cell content, E-20, E-23
    cells, E-21, E-24
    Flash text, D-16–17, D-18–19
    forms, F-14–19
    horizontal rules, B-26
    layers, G-5, G-20–23
    mixing, B-11, B-17
    modifying, B-32
    navigation bars, B-20
    nested layers, G-19
    ordered lists, C-5, C-9
    paragraphs, B-11
    pop-up menus, J-25

radio buttons, F-26–27
text. *See* formatting text
unordered lists, C-4, C-7
formatting text, A-10, B-13
    behaviors changing, J-14–19
    Cascading Style Sheets, C-10–15
    colors, B-16
    Flash text, D-18–19
    line breaks, B-12
    Microsoft Word files, B-15
    ordered lists, C-4–5, C-8, C-9
    properties, B-16–17
    repeating tables, K-15
    table cells, E-20, E-23
    unordered lists, C-4, C-6, C-7
FormName property, F-6, F-7
forms, F-1–31. *See also* form objects
    Action property, F-6
    applications processing, F-2, F-4–5
    CGI scripts, F-5, F-7, F-13
    changing pages, F-6
    features, F-2
    field labels, F-15, F-18, F-19
    fieldsets, F-14, F-15, F-16, F-17–18
    formatting, F-14–19
    FormName property, F-6, F-7
    GET method, F-7
    inserting, F-4–6, F-12
    Method property, F-6, F-7
    planning, F-4
    POST method, F-7
    processing information, F-2, F-4–7
    properties, F-6–7, F-13
    specific, controls, F-22
    tables, F-14, F-15, F-17–18
    Target property, F-6, F-7

frames, D-17, H-1–21
    adding content, H-5, H-14–17
    borders, H-9, H-12
    colors, H-9, H-12
    configuring, H-8–13
    creating content, H-15
    defined, H-2
    download times, H-2
    features, H-2, H-4, H-6
    inserting, H-4–7
    JavaScript functions, H-8
    layers vs., H-2
    left-hand, H-5
    links relationship, H-8, H-9
    loading existing pages, H-14
    naming, H-8, H-10
    NoFrames content, H-18–21
    page margins, H-13
    right-hand, H-5
    saving, H-5–6
    scroll bars, H-9, H-13
    selecting, H-8
    sizing, H-8–9, H-11
    specifying source file, H-16
    tables vs., H-2
    working document visibility, H-6
frames (animation), J-4
    starting, J-10
    stopping, J-10
Frames panel, H-3, H-8, H-10, H-11
framesets
    creating, H-7
    defined, D-17, H-4
    layout, illustrated, H-5
    predefined, H-4–5
    saving, H-5–6, H-7
FTP. *See* File Transfer Protocol (FTP)

Get File(s) button, N-3, N-6
GET method, F-7
GIF files. *See* Graphics Interchange Format (GIF) files
Go buttons, F-32, F-33
goals, planning, A-14–15
graphics, A-10, A-11. *See also* assets
    aligning, C-17, C-20–21, E-17, E-20
    alternate text, C-23, C-26, C-27, E-33
    Assets panel. *See* Assets panel
    background images, C-28, C-30, C-31
    backing up, C-32
    borders, C-22, C-23, C-24
    choosing, A-17
    copying, A-27
    deleting, C-28–29, C-32
    download times, C-16, C-22, D-16
    downloading manually, A-10
    elements, D-20
    enhancing images, C-22–23, C-24–25
    external editors, C-22
    file formats, C-16, C-28
    gathering, A-17
    inserting, C-18–19, E-2, E-16, E-18, G-11
    layer, inserting, G-11
    managing, C-28–29, C-32
    optimizing sizes, C-22
    pasting, A-27
    paths, C-18
    saving, B-14, C-2
    seamless images, C-28, C-30
    sizing, C-22, C-25
    spacing, C-22–23
    storing, B-14, C-2
    tiled images, C-28, C-30
    using sparingly, A-10, C-2

    vector-based, D-16, I-4
    widths, C-22, C-25
Graphics Interchange Format (GIF) files
    background images, C-28
    features, C-16
grippers, A-5

H Size (height) settings. *See* heights
handicap access. *See* accessibility
Head category buttons, B-7
head content, B-2
    creating, B-4–5
    defined, B-4
    descriptions. *See* descriptions
    keywords. *See* keywords
    viewing, B-6
heading styles, B-11, B-16–17, B-20, C-15
Height property
    layers, G-13, G-14
    menu lists, F-21
heights
    graphics, C-22, C-25
    layers, G-13, G-14
    tables, E-10
Help system
    bookmarks, A-11
    illustrated, A-13
    keywords, A-13
    structure, A-11
    using, A-11, A-13
hexadecimal values, B-9
Hidden Field button, F-3, F-22, F-30
hidden fields
    defined, F-21

    features, F-21
    inserting, F-30
hiding toolbars, A-4
hierarchies
    folders, A-16
    Web pages, A-16
History panel
    default settings, B-24
    exiting, B-26
    features, B-24
    illustrated, B-25, B-26
    opening, B-26
    options, B-24, B-25
    settings, B-24, B-25
    undoing changes, B-24, B-26, E-13
    using, B-24, B-26
home page
    defined, A-2
    filename, A-23, B-14
    links, B-21
    parent pages and, A-16
    path, A-26, A-32
    setting, A-23, A-26, A-32
horizontal rules
    code, B-27
    defined, B-26
    formatting, B-26, B-32
    gathering, A-17
    modifying, B-32
    reference information, B-28
horizontal space
    advantages, C-22–23
    defined, C-22
    inserting, C-24
hotspots, D-27
.htm extensions, B-14

HTML (Hypertext Markup Language), A-2

HTML code
    inserting comments, B-28
    viewing, B-25, B-27, B-28, B-29

HTML styles
    advantages, L-5
    applying, L-7
    browsers supporting, L-5
    clearing, L-4, L-8
    creating, L-4–5, L-6
    defined, L-2
    disadvantages, L-5
    features, L-4, L-5
    modifying, L-5, L-9

HTML Styles panel, L-3, L-4, L-5, L-6,
    L-8, L-9

HTML tags
    cells, E-12
    creating layers, G-4
    redefining, L-11–12, L-16–17
    tables, E-1, E-11, E-12, E-13, E-15, E-22
    tag selector. *See* tag selector
    unordered lists, C-7

.html extensions, B-14

hyperlinks. *See* links

Hypertext Markup Language (HTML), A-2

image-based library items, M-7, M-8–9

Image Field button, F-3, F-21, F-22, F-27

image fields
    features, F-21
    inserting, F-27

image maps, D-27

images. *See* background images; graphics

Images button, C-3, C-16, C-17

images folder, default, A-25

Import Site dialog box, N-21, N-23

Import Tabular Data dialog box, E-22

Import Word HTML command, B-10

importing
    data, E-22
    defined, E-22
    delimited files, E-22
    Microsoft Word files, B-10, B-15
    site definitions, N-20–21, N-22–23
    text, B-10–11, B-15

Inconsistent Region Names dialog box,
    K-22, K-28, K-29

Indent item button, J-3, J-24

index.htm, A-23
    links, B-21
    setting home page, A-23, A-26, A-32

inline CSS styles, L-2, L-10–19
    applying, L-11, L-14–15
    creating, L-10–11, L-13
    deleting, L-12, L-19
    features, L-10, L-20
    modifying, L-11, L-15, L-18

Insert bar, A-4, A-5

Insert Date dialog box, B-29

Insert Flash Button dialog box, I-5, I-6

Insert Flash Text dialog box, D-18

Insert Form button, F-4

Insert Jump Menu dialog box, F-34

Insert Named Anchor dialog box, D-10, D-12

Insert Navigation Bar dialog box, D-20, D-22

Insert Repeating Table dialog box, K-11, K-15

Insert Rollover Image dialog box, I-11, I-12

Insert Table button, E-4, E-6, E-11, F-17–18

Insert Table dialog box, E-7, K-16

inserting
    alternate text, C-26
    background images, C-30

behaviors, I-14, I-15

borders, C-24

buttons, F-22, F-31

cell text, E-2, E-20, E-22

checkboxes, F-24–25

columns, E-14

comments, B-28

date objects, B-29

file fields, F-29

Flash buttons, I-5, I-6–7

Flash movies, I-5, I-8

Flash text, D-16–19

folders, A-22–23, A-24

forms, F-4–6, F-12

frames, H-4–7

graphics, C-18–19, E-2, E-16,
    E-18, G-11

hidden fields, F-30

horizontal space, C-24

hyperlink styles, L-21, L-24

image fields, F-27

jump menus, F-34

keyframes, J-5, J-11

labels, F-18, F-19

layers, G-4, G-6

layers (animation), J-9

library items, M-12, M-14

links, B-18, B-21, B-22

menus (forms), F-21, F-28

named anchors, D-10, D-12–13

NoFrames content, H-18–21

popup messages, I-15, I-17

radio buttons, F-26–27

radio groups, F-26–27

repeating tables, K-14–15

rollover images, I-11–13

rows, E-14

seamless images, C-30
Shockwave movies, I-10
snippets, M-18, M-20
sound effects, I-14–15, I-16
status bar text, J-17
tables into fieldsets, F-17–18
text, B-12, E-2, E-20, E-22, G-10, J-17
text fields (forms), F-23, F-24
tiled images, C-30
Web pages, A-17, A-23, A-28–29
white space, C-22–23
interactive elements, I-14. *See also specific
interactive elements*
creating, J-20
effective use, J-2
internal links
components, D-2
creating, D-5, D-8
defined, D-2
named anchor, D-11, D-14–15
relative paths, D-5
site map, D-9
viewing, B-23, D-9
Internet Explorer
changing status bar text, J-14, J-17
copying URLs, D-8
Flash compatibility, I-4
layers, G-2
playing Flash movies, I-9
testing pages, A-17
Internet Services Providers (ISPs),
A-17, A-21
Invisible Elements command, A-27, D-10,
D-12, D-19
IP address, A-14
Italic button, B-13

Java applets, I-2
JavaScript functions, F-5
behaviors, I-14, I-15
browser requirements, J-2, J-6
changing images, H-8
creating dynamic effects, B-25, G-12
defined, B-25
frames, H-8
loading content, H-8
multimedia features, I-2, I-14
navigation contingency, A-22
rollovers, B-25
sizing layers, G-20, G-21
Joint Photographic Experts Group (JPEG)
files, A-31, C-16
JPEG files. *See* Joint Photographic Experts
Group (JPEG) files
Jscript. *See* JavaScript functions
Jump Menu button, F-3, F-22, F-32, F-34
jump menus, F-32–35
defined, F-22
features, F-22, F-32
inserting, F-34
modifying, F-35
testing, F-33, F-34
updating, F-33

keyboard shortcuts, B-10
keyframes
defined, J-4
inserting, J-5, J-11
keywords
Code view, B-8
defined, B-4
entering, B-7
formulating, B-4–5, B-7

Help system, A-13
search engine parameters, B-7
title pages and, A-30
Keywords button, B-7

Label button, F-3, F-15, F-19, F-22
labels, F-15, F-18, F-19
layers, G-1–27. *See also* animating layers
absolute positioning, G-12
advanced formatting, G-5
aligning, G-12–15
animating. *See* animating layers
background color, G-9
background images, G-8
content, G-5
controlling, G-16–19
converting, to tables, G-24, G-26
defined, G-2
defining, G-7
download times, H-2
draggable, J-6, J-13
drawing, G-4, G-6
drop targets, J-6
features, G-2, G-4, G-12, G-24, H-2
formatting, G-20–23
frames vs., H-2
heights, G-13, G-14
HTML tags creating, G-4
illustrated, A-12
images, G-11
inserting, G-4, J-9
left position, G-13, G-14
modifying text, J-14, J-16
naming, G-16, G-17
nested, G-16, G-19

Netscape Navigator, G-2, G-4, G-20, G-21, G-23, G-24
positioning, G-12–15, G-20, G-21
preferences, G-20–23
properties, G-5, G-6, G-12–13
sizing, G-20, G-21, G-23
tables vs., G-2, G-24, H-2
text, G-10
top position, G-13, G-14
visibility, G-4, G-5, G-7, G-16, G-18, G-26
widths, G-13, G-14
z-index values, G-13, G-15, G-16, G-17
Layers panel, G-16–19. *See also* layers
controlling visibility, G-18
features, G-16
inserting layers, J-9
naming layers, G-16, G-17
nesting layers, G-16, G-19
layout, page. *See* page layout
Left Frame button, H-3
left-hand frames, H-5
Left property, G-13, G-14
Library button, M-3, M-5, M-6, M-7
library items
advantages, M-2, M-4
creating, M-4, M-6, M-7
defined, M-2
deleting, M-13, M-16
features, M-2, M-4
image-based, M-7, M-8–9
inserting, M-12, M-14
making editable, M-12–13, M-15
modifying, M-5, M-8–9, M-11
recreating, M-13, M-17
text-based, M-6, M-11
updating, M-10
viewing, M-4

line breaks, B-12
Link Checker panel, D-28, D-29, E-26, E-28, N-2
Link External Style Sheet dialog box, L-20, L-22, L-24, L-26
links. *See also* navigation bars; navigation structure
bordered images, C-23
broken. *See* broken links
colors, B-5
components, D-2
defined, A-10
e-mail, B-18, B-22, B-23
external, D-2, D-4, D-6, D-7
frames relationship, H-8, H-9
hotspots, D-27
illustrated, A-11, A-12
image maps, D-27
inserting, B-18, B-21, B-22
internal, D-2, D-5, D-8, D-9, D-11, D-14–15
managing, D-5, D-28–29
paths. *See* paths
point of contact, B-18
rollover images, I-10
snippet, modifying, M-22
styles, L-21, L-24
template-based, K-21–22, K-26
testing. *See* testing pages
types, D-2
unvisited, B-5
viewing, B-23, D-7, D-9
visited, B-5, B-33
List Item button, C-4, C-5
List/Menu button, F-3, F-21, F-22, F-28
List Properties dialog box, C-4, C-5, C-7

lists, C-2, C-4–9
definition lists, C-5
menus (forms), F-21
ordered lists, C-4–5, C-8, C-9
unordered lists, C-4, C-6, C-7, C-12–14
local folders, N-8
Local Root Folder text box, A-10
local sites, A-21
Local View command, D-7
Locate in Site command, C-28–29
locked regions
changes causing, K-11
converting editable regions, K-31
default state, K-4
defined, K-2
example, K-18
identifying, K-20, K-21
unlocking, K-31

Macromedia Director, I-2
Macromedia Director Shockwave Studio, I-10
Macromedia Fireworks, C-22, D-20
Macromedia Flash. *See* Flash program
Macromedia Flash Player. *See* Flash player
Macromedia Shockwave, I-2, I-10
maintaining sites, E-2, E-26–33. *See also* testing pages
alternate text, E-33
color verification, E-26, E-32
links, D-28–29, E-26, E-27, E-28
navigation structure, E-27
orphaned files, E-29, E-30–31
site reports, E-26, E-27
tools, E-26–27
untitled documents, E-32
updating templates, K-30–33

Make Nested Template button, K-3
Make Template button, K-3, K-11, K-23
managing
    files. *See* files; transferring files
    graphics, C-28–29, C-32
    links, D-5, D-28–29
    teams. *See* team management
    Web servers. *See* remote servers;
        remote sites; Web servers
Map View command, A-30
margins (page), H-13
menu bar
    choosing commands, A-4
    defined, A-4
    illustrated, A-5
menus (forms)
    features, F-21
    inserting, F-21, F-28
    jump menus, F-22, F-32–35
menus, pop-up, J-21, J-24, J-25
merge cells, E-11, E-15
Meta icon, B-6
meta tags, B-4
Method property, F-6, F-7
Microsoft Internet Explorer. *See* Internet
    Explorer
Microsoft Word files
    importing, B-10, B-15
    saving as HTML, B-15
mixing formatting, B-11, B-17
modem speeds, A-17
Modify Navigation Bar dialog box, D-21
modifying
    cell content, E-25
    custom styles, L-11, L-15
    external CSS style sheets, L-23

font, B-11
formats, B-32
horizontal rules, B-32
HTML styles, L-5, L-9
HTML tags, L-11–12, L-16–17
inline CSS styles, L-11, L-15, L-18
jump menus, F-35
library items, M-5, M-8–9, M-11
navigation bars, D-21, D-24–27
properties, A-4
repeating tables, K-21
screen resolution, B-32
snippets, M-18, M-21, M-22
templates. *See* modifying templates
views, A-5, A-8–9, A-12
Web pages, A-17, B-30, B-32
window sizes, B-32
modifying templates, K-2, K-16, K-30–33
    editable attributes, K-21, K-25
    editable regions, K-20, K-24, K-31
monitor sizes, B-31
mouse pointer states, D-20
movies. *See* Flash movies; Shockwave
    movies
multi-line text fields, F-21, F-24
multimedia, I-2–17
    alert boxes, I-15
    defined, I-2
    features, I-2
    Flash objects, I-4–9
    gathering files, A-17
    interactive elements, I-14, J-2, J-20
    limiting use, B-2
    popup messages, I-15, I-17
    rollover images, I-10–13
    sound effects, I-14–15, I-16

Name text box, C-12
Named Anchor button, D-3, D-10,
    D-11, D-12
named anchors. *See also* internal links
    defined, D-10
    error avoidance, D-11
    examples, D-10
    icons, D-13, D-14
    inserting, D-10, D-12–13
    naming, D-12
naming
    custom styles, L-10
    files. *See* filenames
    folders, A-16, A-24
    frames, H-8, H-10
    layers, G-16, G-17
    named anchors, D-12
    sites, A-20
Navigation Bar button, D-20
Navigation Bar command, D-20
navigation bars
    copying, D-20–21, D-26
    creating, B-20, D-20–23
    customizing, D-21, D-26–27
    defined, A-10, B-19
    elements, D-20–21, D-22–25
    features, B-19
    formatting, B-20, D-22–23
    images, D-22–23
    limitation, D-20
    links, B-19, B-21
    modifying, D-21, D-24–27
    pasting, D-26
    rollovers, D-20
navigation structure. *See also* links
    defined, A-2
    effective, A-22, B-2, D-28

illustrated, A-11
intuitive, B-2
maintaining, E-27
user-friendly, B-18, D-28
nested layers, G-16, G-19
nested tables, E-11
nested templates
creating, K-10–11, K-14
features, K-10
updating, K-19
Netscape Navigator
changing status bar text, J-14, J-17
copying URLs, D-8
Flash compatibility, I-4
layers, G-2, G-4, G-20, G-21, G-23, G-24
sizing, G-20, G-21, G-23
testing pages, A-17
network folders, N-8
New CSS Style button, C-3, C-15, L-3,
L-10, L-13, L-16
New CSS Style dialog box, L-10, L-11,
L-12, L-13, L-16, L-21
New Editable Region dialog box, K-4, K-7
New from Template dialog box, K-14, K-23
New Library Item button, M-3
New Optional Region dialog box, K-5, K-8,
K-9, K-11, K-13
New Snippet button, M-3, M-23
New Style button, L-3, L-5, L-6
NoFrames content, H-18–21
features, H-18
inserting, H-18–21
non-Web-safe colors
defined, C-29
deleting, C-29, C-33
Numbered List styles, C-5
numbered lists. See ordered lists

Open Browser Window dialog box,
J-21, J-23
Optional Region button, K-3, K-5, K-8, K-11
optional regions
advanced settings, K-13
creating, K-4–5, K-8
defined, K-2, K-4
parameters, K-10, K-13
Ordered List button, C-5, C-8
ordered lists
creating, C-4–5, C-8
defined, C-4
examples, C-5
features, C-5
formatting, C-5, C-9
orphaned files, D-28, D-29
identifying, E-29
removing, E-30–31
Outdent Item button, J-3, J-24
Over Image state, D-20, D-22
Over While Down Image state, D-20, D-23
Overflow property, G-5, G-7

page content
collecting, A-17
storing, A-16–17
page hierarchy, A-16
page layout
control options, G-2, G-24, H-2
frames. See frames
layers. See layers
margins, H-13
overview, B-2
planning, B-6
principles, B-2

tables. See tables
templates, B-6
white space, B-2
Page Properties dialog box, B-9
Page Titles option button, A-32
pages. See Web pages
panel groups. See also specific
panel groups
active, A-5
collapsing, A-5, A-9
default open, A-5
defined, A-4
displaying, A-9
docking, A-5
expanding, A-5, A-8–9
floating, A-9
illustrated, A-5, A-8, A-9
opening, A-9
undocking, A-5, A-9
panels
defined, A-4
displaying, A-4–5, A-9
illustrated, A-5
paragraph styles, L-4, L-8
paragraphs
formatting, B-11
heading styles, B-11, B-16–17, B-20
parent pages
defined, A-16
illustrated, A-16
Paste command shortcut, B-10
pasting
graphics, A-27
navigation bars, D-26
shortcut, B-10
URLs, D-8

paths
    absolute, D-4, D-5, D-6
    animation, recording, J-6
    defined, A-26
    document-relative, D-5
    graphics, C-18
    home page, A-26, A-32
    link, overview, D-2
    relative, D-5
    root-relative, D-5
PICT files, A-31
placeholders
    Flash movies, I-8
    text, K-5, K-15, K-18
planning sites, A-14–17
    checklist, A-15
    forms, F-4
    goals, A-14–15
    page layout, B-6
    questions list, A-14–15
    storyboards, A-15–16
    tables, E-2, E-5
Play button, J-3, J-5, J-6, J-13
Play Sound dialog box, I-16
Play Timeline behavior, J-2, J-5, J-10
Play Timeline dialog box, J-10
playback head, J-3, J-6, J-12
PNG files. *See* Portable Network Graphics
    (PNG) files
point of contact links, B-18, B-22
Point to File icon, K-22, K-26
pop-up menus
    creating, J-21, J-24
    example, J-21
    features, J-21
    formatting, J-25

Popup Message dialog box, I-17
popup messages
    defined, I-15
    inserting, I-15, I-17
pop-up windows
    creating, J-20–21, J-23
    features, J-20, J-21
Portable Network Graphics (PNG) files,
    A-31, C-16
Position property, G-12–13
positioning layer objects. *See* layers
POST method, F-7
pound (#) sign, D-14
power failure, B-13
preferences
    History panel, B-24, B-25
    layers, G-20–23
    table accessibility, E-5, E-6, E-7
preventing data loss, B-13
Preview/Debug in Browser button, B-33
previewing animations, J-5–6, J-12
printing
    fonts, B-17
    site maps, A-31
properties. *See also specific properties*
    modifying, A-4
    setting, B-5, B-9
Property inspector. *See also specific*
    properties
    collapsing, C-5, C-9
    defined, A-4
    editing page title, B-6
    expanding, C-4, C-5
    formatting text. *See* text, formatting
    illustrated, A-3, A-5, A-27, C-5
    location, A-4

publishing sites, A-21, N-4–11. *See also*
    remote servers; remote sites
    defined, A-17
    options, A-17
    overview, A-21
    preparation, N-2
Put File(s) button, N-3, N-5, N-10

Radio Button button, F-3, F-22, F-29
radio buttons
    features, F-20
    formatting, F-26–27
    illustrated, F-21
    inserting, F-26–27
Radio Group button, F-3, F-21, F-22, F-26
radio groups
    defined, F-20
    features, F-20–21
    inserting, F-26–27
ransom note effect, B-17
Recreate Site Cache command, C-29
Reference button, B-28
Reference panel, B-25, B-28
Refresh buttons, A-3
    Assets panel, C-30, C-33
    Property inspector, F-16, F-19
    Site panel, A-3, A-28, B-14
Refresh Local File List Automatically
    option, A-20
Refresh Remote File List Automatically
    option, N-8
Refresh Site List button, C-18, C-19,
    C-29, D-18
relative paths
    creating, D-8

defined, D-5

document-relative, D-5

examples, D-5

root-relative, D-5

remote access setup, A-21

Remote Info category, N-4, N-5, N-7, N-8, N-14

remote servers

access set-up, A-21, N-7

defined, A-21

publishing preparation, N-2

remote sites

connecting to, N-4–5, N-9

defined, A-21

defining, N-4

downloading files, N-5–6

synchronizing files, N-6, N-11, N-16

transferring files, N-5–6, N-10

uploading files, N-5, N-10

viewing, N-4–5, N-9

repeating regions, K-11

Repeating Table button, K-3, K-11, K-14, K-15

repeating tables, K-11, K-14–15, K-21, K-27

reports, E-26, E-27

missing alternate text, E-33

untitled documents, E-32

Reports command, E-26

Reports dialog box, E-26, E-27, E-32, E-33

Reset buttons (forms), F-22, F-31

Reset Size (graphics) button, C-25

resizing. *See* sizing

resolution. *See* screen resolution

Results panel group, D-29

Rewind button, J-3, J-6, J-12

Right Frame button, H-3

right-hand frames, H-5

Rollover Image button, I-11, I-12

rollover images

defined, I-10

features, I-10, I-11

illustrated, I-11, I-13

inserting, I-11–13

links, I-10

rollovers

colors, D-17, D-18

defined, B-25

example, D-21

swapping images, J-2, J-20, J-22

root folders

creating (Mac), A-19, A-24

creating (Win), A-18, A-24

defined, A-16

local site, A-21

root-relative paths, D-5

rows, E-2

deleting, E-14

inserting, E-14

properties, E-3

sizing, E-10, E-13

sans-serif fonts, B-17

Save As Template dialog box, K-6, K-14, K-23

Save Frameset command, H-6

Save Style Sheet File As dialog box, L-10

saving

changes, B-13

frames, H-5–6

framesets, H-5–6, H-7

graphics, B-14, C-2

Microsoft Word files, B-15

site maps, A-31

templates, K-6, K-19

screen readers, C-23

screen resolution

choosing, B-33

default window sizes, B-31, B-32

modifying, B-32

sizing frames, H-9

sizing layers, G-13

sizing tables/cells, E-9

testing pages, A-17, B-31, B-32, E-27

screen size. *See* screen resolution

scripts. *See* CGI scripts; JavaScript functions

scroll bars (frames), H-9, H-13

seamless images

defined, C-28

inserting, C-30

Select File dialog box, I-5, I-8, I-10

Select HTML dialog box, H-16

Select Image Source dialog box, G-8, J-22

Select Style Sheet File dialog box, L-22, L-26

selectors, C-11

serif fonts, B-17

server-side applications, F-5

server-side controls, I-2

servers. *See* Web servers

Set Text of Field dialog box, J-18

Set Text of Layer dialog box, J-14, J-15, J-16, J-17

Set Text of Status Bar dialog box, J-17

Set Text of Text Field dialog box, J-18

Shockwave movies, I-2

filename extensions, I-10

inserting, I-10

Shockwave Player, I-9
shortcuts, B-10
Show Code and Design Views button,
    A-3, A-8
Show Code View button, A-3, A-8, A-12
Show Design View button, A-3, A-8
Show Pop-Up Menu dialog box, J-21,
    J-24, J-25
simplicity, B-2
single-spaced text, B-12
Site Definition dialog box, A-20, A-21,
    N-4, N-5
    checking files in/out, N-13, N-14
    cloaking files, N-16, N-17, N-18
    creating Web sites, F-9, F-11, J-7, J-8
    specifying settings, N-8
Site Definition Remote Info dialog box, A-21
site definitions
    exporting, N-20, N-22
    importing, N-20–21, N-22–23
Site Map button (Mac), A-33, B-23, D-7, D-9
Site Map command, A-30
Site Map Layout option, A-32
Site Map View option, A-26, A-33, B-23, D-7
site maps
    checking navigation structure, E-27
    collapsing, A-33, B-23
    creating, A-30
    defined, A-2, A-23, A-30
    expanding, A-33
    external links, D-7
    features, A-30, E-27
    illustrated, A-31
    internal links, D-9
    layout options, A-32
    link views, B-23
    printing, A-31

saving, A-31
viewing, A-30–31, A-33, B-23, D-7, D-9
Web page use, A-31
Site option button, C-16, C-17
Site panel
    checking broken links, E-28
    checking files in/out, N-12–15
    cloaking files, N-16–19
    cloaking folders, N-16–17, N-18
    collapsing, B-23
    expanding, A-30, B-23
    functions of, A-2, A-17
    managing site links, D-29
    setting home page, A-23, A-26
    transferring files, N-5–6, N-10
    uploading files, N-5, N-10
    viewing links, D-7, D-9
    viewing remote sites, N-4–5, N-9
sites. See Web sites
sizing
    Assets panel, C-17
    cells, E-10, E-12, E-13
    columns, E-10, E-12
    frames, H-8–9, H-11
    graphics, C-22, C-25
    rows, E-10, E-13
    tables, E-9, E-10, E-12, E-13
Snippet dialog box, M-19, M-23
snippets
    creating, M-19, M-23
    defined, M-2
    inserting, M-18, M-20
    links, M-22
    modifying, M-18, M-21, M-22
    predefined, M-20
    text, M-21

Snippets panel, A-9, M-3, M-18, M-19,
    M-20, M-22
sound effects, I-14–15, I-16
source files, H-16
space
    adding, C-22–23
    advantages, C-22–23
    horizontal, C-22–23, C-24
    vertical, C-22–23
    white, C-22–23
spacing
    cells, E-4
    graphics, C-22–23
    text, B-12
<span> tag, G-4, G-7, G-12
split cells, E-11, E-14
Src text box, A-27, B-14
stacking elements. See layers
Standard toolbar
    defined, A-4
    displaying, A-4
    hiding, A-4
    illustrated, A-5
starting Dreamweaver
    Macintosh, A-7
    Windows, A-6
states, D-20
Status bar
    functions, A-4
    illustrated, A-5
    location, A-4
status bar (browsers), J-14, J-17
Stop Timeline behavior, J-2, J-3, J-5, J-10
storing
    graphics, C-2
    non-Web page files, A-16, A-22–23
    Web pages, A-16

storyboards, A-15–16
  advantages, A-15–16
  defined, A-15
  illustrated, A-16
  software, A-16
Strikethrough button, C-15
strong tag, L-16
style sheets. *See* Cascading Style Sheets
  (CSS); external CSS style sheets; HTML
  styles; inline CSS styles
Submit buttons (forms), F-22, F-31
Swap Image dialog box, J-20, J-22
Swap Images behavior, J-20, J-22
swapping images, J-2. *See also* rollover
  images; rollovers
  features, J-20
  procedure, J-22
.swf extensions, D-16, I-5
Synchronize Files dialog box, N-6,
  N-11, N-16
synchronizing files, N-6, N-11, N-16

tables, E-1–25. *See also* cells
  accessibility preferences, E-5, E-6, E-7
  aligning graphics, E-17, E-19
  borders, E-4
  columns, E-2, E-10, E-12, E-14
  converting, to layers, G-25, G-27
  creating, E-4–9
  defined, E-2
  download times, H-2
  exporting data, E-22
  features, G-2, G-24, H-2
  fieldsets containing, F-14, F-17–18
  form layouts, F-14, F-15, F-17–18
  frames vs., H-2

heights, E-10
illustrated, A-11, A-12
importing data, E-22
inserting graphics, E-2, E-16, E-18
inserting text, E-2, E-20, E-22
layers vs., G-2, G-24, H-2
Layout View, E-4, E-5, E-9
nested, E-11
planning, E-2, E-5
properties, E-3, E-8
repeating, K-11, K-14–15, K-21, K-27
rows, E-2, E-3, E-10, E-13, E-14
sizing, E-9, E-10, E-12, E-13
Standard View, E-4, E-9
tags, E-1, E-11, E-12, E-13, E-15, E-22
views, E-4
widths, E-9, E-10
Tabular Data, E-22
tag selector, E-1
  defined, A-4
  illustrated, A-5
Target list, D-17
Target property, F-6, F-7
targets, D-10
team management, N-12
  checking files in/out, N-12–15
  downloading files, N-5–6
  planning sites. *See* planning sites
  sharing templates, K-2
  synchronizing files, N-6, N-11, N-16
  tracking checked out files, A-30
Template properties dialog box, K-12, K-21,
  K-25, K-27
templates, K-2–33
  advantages, K-2, K-20
  attaching style sheets, L-20–21, L-26
  attaching to existing page, K-22, K-28–29

creating, K-4, K-6
creating new pages, K-20, K-23
default state, K-4
defined, B-6, K-2
downloading, K-30
editable attributes, K-12, K-17, K-18,
  K-21, K-25
editable optional regions, K-5, K-9
editable regions. *See* editable regions
features, K-2, K-20, K-22
Help information, A-13
links, K-21–22, K-26
locked regions. *See* locked regions
modifying, K-2, K-16, K-30–33
nesting, K-10–11, K-14, K-19
optional regions, K-2, K-4–5, K-8,
  K-10, K-13
regions, K-2
repeating regions, K-11
repeating tables, K-11, K-14–15,
  K-21, K-27
saving, K-6, K-19
updating, K-30–33
testing pages, A-17, B-30, E-27. *See also*
maintaining sites
  accessibility, B-5
  broken links, D-29, E-26, E-28, N-2
  browsers, A-17, B-31, B-33, E-27
  example, B-33
  frequency, B-30
  importance, A-17
  jump menus, F-33, F-34
  links, D-28–29, E-26, E-27, E-28
  modem speeds, A-17
  orphaned files, D-28, D-29
  publishing preparation, N-2
  varying browsers, A-17, B-31

window sizes, B-31, B-32
yellow HTML code, D-27
text
    aligning, B-16
    alternate text, C-23, C-26, C-27, E-33
    behaviors changing, J-14–19
    creating, B-10–11
    definition lists, C-5
    double-spaced, B-12
    effective, A-10
    Flash. *See* Flash text
    fonts. *See* fonts
    formatting. *See* formatting text
    forms. *See* form objects
    heading styles, B-11, B-16–17, B-20
    illustrated, A-12
    importing, B-10–11, B-15
    inserting, B-12, E-2, E-20, E-22,
        G-10, J-17
    keyboard shortcuts, B-10
    layers, G-10
    lists, C-2, C-4–9
    single-spaced, B-12
    spacing, B-12
text area fields, F-20
text-based library items, M-6, M-11
Text Color button, B-16, C-9, C-15, C-33
Text Field button, F-3, F-20, F-22, F-23
text fields
    features, F-20
    illustrated, F-21
    multi-line, F-21, F-24
    single-line, F-23
text files
    gathering, A-17
    storing, A-16–17
Textarea button, F-3, F-20, F-22, F-24

thumbnails, C-16, C-17, C-18
tiled images
    defined, C-28
    inserting, C-30
timelines. *See also* Timelines panel
    inserting keyframes, J-5, J-11
    inserting layers, J-9
    start frames, J-5, J-10
    stop frames, J-5, J-10
Timelines panel. *See also* timelines
    creating draggable layers, J-13
    features, J-2, J-4
    previewing animations, J-5–6, J-12
    toolbar buttons, J-6
title bar, A-5
Title icon, B-6
titles
    Code view, B-8
    editing, B-6
    keywords and, A-30
    search engine use, A-30
    text box, B-6
toolbars. *See also* specific toolbar names
    displaying, A-4
    hiding, A-4
Top and Bottom Frames button, H-3, H-7
Top Frame button, H-3
Top property, G-13, G-14
transferring files, A-21
    FTP capability. *See* File Transfer
        Protocol (FTP)
    remote sites, N-2, N-5–6, N-10
Tutorials command, A-11

"under construction" pages, B-30
undocking panel groups, A-5, A-9

undoing changes, B-24, B-26
Uniform Resource Locator (URL)
    absolute paths, D-4, D-5, D-6
    copying, D-8
    defined, D-4
    editable attributes, K-18
    error avoidance, D-8
    examples, D-4, D-5, D-6
    pasting, D-8
    typing, D-8
Unordered List button, C-4, C-5, C-6
unordered lists
    bulleted lists, C-4, C-12–14
    creating, C-4, C-6
    defined, C-4
    ending, C-6
    formatting, C-4, C-7
    HTML tags, C-7
untitled documents, E-32
unvisited links, B-5
Up Image state, D-20, D-22
Update Library Item dialog box, M-5, M-10
Update Pages dialog box, K-19, K-31,
    K-33, M-10
Update Template Files dialog box, K-19,
    K-31, K-33
updating
    jump menus, F-33
    library items, M-10
    nested templates, K-19
    pages, K-31, K-33
    templates, K-30–33
uploading files, N-5, N-10
uppercase letters, A-16, A-20
URL. *See* Uniform Resource Locator (URL)
Using Dreamweaver command, A-11

vector-based graphics, D-16, I-4
vertical space
    advantages, C-22–23
    defined, C-22
video files, A-17
viewing
    code, B-25, B-27, B-28, B-29
    external links, D-7
    Flash movies, I-4
    head content, B-6
    HTML code, B-25, B-27, B-28, B-29
    internal links, B-23, D-9
    library items, M-4
    links, B-23, D-7, D-9
    page elements, A-10–11, A-12
    remote sites, N-4–5, N-9
    site maps, A-30–31, A-33, B-23,
        D-7, D-9
views. See also specific views
    changing, A-5, A-8–9, A-12
    defined, A-5
Visible property, G-5, G-7
visited links, B-5, B-33
visually impaired tools. See accessibility

W Size (width) settings. See widths
Web pages, A-2
    adding, A-17, A-23, A-28–29
    body, B-5
    checked out, A-30
    creating, A-15, A-17, K-20, K-23
    deleting, A-17
    design, A-17
    elements, A-10–11, A-12

exiting, A-12
filenames. See filenames
forms changing, F-6
modifying, A-17, B-30, B-32
opening, A-10, A-12
properties, B-5
site maps. See site maps
targets, D-10
templates. See templates
testing. See testing pages
titles, A-30
"under construction", B-30
updating, K-31, K-33
viewing elements, A-10–11, A-12
window sizes, B-31, B-32
Web-safe colors
    palettes, B-5
    using, B-4
    verifying, E-26, E-32
Web servers
    access set-up, A-21, N-7, N-8
    defined, A-17, N-4
    local folders, N-8
    network folders, N-8
    remote. See remote servers
Web sites
    accessibility, B-5
    backing up, C-32
    creating (Mac), F-10–11, J-8
    creating (Win), F-8–9, J-7
    defined, A-2
    defining, A-17, A-20
    deleting assets, C-28–29, C-32
    deleting colors, C-29, C-33
    descriptions, B-4, B-7, B-8

keywords. See keywords
maintaining, E-2, E-26–33
naming, A-20
planning. See planning sites
simplicity, B-2
site definitions, N-20–23
updating, K-30–33
white space
    adding, C-22–23
    effective use, B-2
Width property, G-13, G-14
widths
    cells, E-9
    graphics, C-22, C-25
    layers, G-13, G-14
    tables, E-9, E-10
window sizes. See screen resolution
windows, pop-up. See pop-up windows
Word files. See Microsoft Word files
Workflow report, E-26
workspace, A-4–5
    components, A-4–5
    Dreamweaver 4 vs. MX, A-6
    illustrated, A-5
    layout options, A-6
    Macintosh user, A-6
Workspace Setup dialog box, A-6

yellow HTML code, D-27

Z-index property, G-13
z-index values, G-13, G-15, G-16, G-17

The Design Professional Series

**If there are Data Files to accompany your book, you choose how to get them.
Please refer to the Data Files List at the end of the book for instructions on
using and organizing the Data Files you need.**

Instructors

► Data Files are on the Instructor's Resource CD-ROM, which you can copy to your network for student use.
► Download the Data Files via the World Wide Web by following the instructions below.
► Contact us via e-mail at reply@course.com.
► Call Course Technology's Customer Service department for fast and efficient delivery.

Students

► Obtain your Data Files from your instructor, network, or lab center.
► Download the Data Files via the World Wide Web by following the instructions below.

Instructions for Downloading the Data Files from the World Wide Web*

1. Open your browser and enter the URL www.course.com.
2. When the course.com Web site appears, follow the link to find your Data Files (listed as student files, student downloads or data disk files).
3. Browse for your book by entering the ISBN of your book.
4. Click the link for student downloads.
5. Click the link for the data files you want to download.
6. If the File Download dialog box appears, make sure the Save this program to disk option is selected, and then click the OK button.
7. If the Save As dialog box appears, make sure the location listed in the Save in box is the location as chosen by your instructor.
8. The filename of the compressed file appears in the File name text box (e.g., 3500-8.exe).
9. Click either OK or Save, whichever choice your browser gives you.
10. If a dialog box indicates that the download is complete, click the OK button (or the Close button, depending on which operating system you are using). Close your browser.
11. Open Windows Explorer and display the contents of the folder to where you downloaded the file. Double-click the downloaded filename on the right side of the Windows Explorer window.
12. In the WinZip Self-Extractor window, specify the drive and folder name to unzip the files to. Click Unzip.
13. When the WinZip Self-Extractor displays the number of files unzipped, click the OK button. Click the Close button in the WinZip Self-Extractor dialog box.
14. You are now ready to access your Data Files.
15. Please refer to the Data Files List at the end of the book for information on using and organizing your Data Files.

*To download Macintosh Data files, please follow steps 1–3. When the textbook page displays, follow the online screen instructions for downloading Macintosh Data Files.

USER LEVEL

BASIC   INTERMEDIATE   ADVANCED

MACROMEDIA®
DREAMWEAVER® MX

Learn how to create professional-looking Web sites with the *Design Professional Series!*
This series recognizes the unique learning environment of graphic design and multimedia
students who want both step-by-step instructions for quick reference, and in-depth
explanations of how to apply the skills.

This book offers:

- Basic to intermediate coverage of Dreamweaver MX skills
- Creative projects with sophisticated Data Files
- Full-color pictures
- Mac and PC instructions
- Instructor's Resources to facilitate use in the classroom

Sherry Bishop is a computer information systems instructor at North Arkansas College
in Harrison, Arkansas. Her emphasis is in multimedia applications. She has authored
several college textbooks and presents at conferences and workshops around the country.
Marjorie Hunt has spent many years working in instructional design, specifically as it
relates to presenting high technology in the classroom. She is also a freelance writer and
editor who has authored five books for Course Technology. She lives in Kingston,
Massachusetts.
Piyush Patel is the Director of the Multi-Media & Digital Communications Program at
Northern Oklahoma College, where he has over 5 years of classroom experience, and the
founder of Digital-Tutors.com. This is his second book in the Design Professional Series.

Make sure you visit the Design Professional Series Web site at
http://www.course.com/designprofessional for all the latest product
information, interviews with authors, and software updates. And, sign
up to be a Design Professional reviewer—we'd love to hear from you.

Check out these other great titles
from the Design Professional Series:

MACROMEDIA® FLASH™ MX

11 units that cover
basic to advanced
Flash skills

MACROMEDIA® FIREWORKS® MX

8 units that cover
basic to intermediate
Fireworks skills

WEB COLLECTION

14 units that cover
basic to intermediate
Macromedia Flash MX,
Dreamweaver MX, and
Fireworks MX skills

COURSE
●**com**

9 780619 110994   90000>

ISBN 0-619-11099-6